THE SIRIUS MYSTERY

TO MY WIFE OLIVIA –

there is no greater mystery than the daily awe and wonder
of being together

The Sirius Mystery

New Scientific Evidence of
Alien Contact 5,000 Years Ago

———————————— ◆ ————————————

Robert Temple

Destiny Books
Rochester, Vermont

Destiny Books
One Park Street
Rochester, Vermont 05767
www.InnerTraditions.com

Destiny Books is a division of Inner Traditions International

First U.S. edition published by Destiny Books in 1998
Copyright © 1998 by Robert Temple

LIBRARY OF CONGRESS CATALOGING-IN-PUBLICATION DATA

Temple, Robert K. G.
    The Sirius mystery : new scientific evidence of alien contact 5,000 years ago/
Robert Temple.—1st U.S. ed.
        p.   cm.
    Includes bibliographical references and index.
    ISBN 0-89281-750-X (alk. paper)
    1. Civilization, Ancient—Extraterrestrial influences.   2. Dogon (African people)
3. Sirius.   I. Title.
CB156.T45   1998
930—dc21   98-7783
                                                                    CIP

Printed and bound in Canada

10 9 8 7

Acknowledgements

For this new edition I especially wish to thank Mark Booth of Century in London. His excellent editing and his vision for these subjects is most inspiring. I do not know which is more pleasant – his company or his conversation. Or can they be separated?

My literary agent Bill Hamilton of A. M. Heath is humorous, enthusiastic, capable, helpful, stimulating ... does he have any faults? Probably not.

My wife Olivia has been closely involved in every stage of the preparation of the new edition, and her advice is always the final word on turns of phrase.

I wish to thank Miss Jenny Zhu for her marvellous help assisting me in the British Library in gathering further material.

Roderick Brown, with his eye for detail and acute insight, has been a superb editor for the new edition and has made several excellent suggestions for improvements. Readers can thank him for being able to see what a pale fox and a dugong look like.

Liz Rowlinson of Century has done an excellent job of editing and organizing the vast quantities of material for this book.

The staff of the British Library, long-suffering because of my mountains of huge volumes and endless difficulties of finding books during the move to a new building, deserve thanks for their help and patience.

I wish to thank all of the people who have written to me over the years with interesting information, and I regret that I have not been able to deal with very much of it. But it is all appreciated, and I still hope to continue to consider it, as this will always be an ongoing subject.

I also wish to thank Robert Bauval for introducing me to Bill Hamilton and together with Jay Weidner persuading me to renew my interest in this subject, which had been in suspended animation for many years.

I also wish to thank the Dogon Tribe, on behalf of us all, for making this investigation possible in the first place.

Author's Note

Summaries follow each chapter in Part Two. The sheer amount of the material dealt with makes it advisable for the reader to put it into a smooth perspective by reading over these summaries which have been prepared so that the reader may refresh his memory if he wishes. The author can offer no apology for the complexity of the material, but he can present these slight aids for its comprehension.

Every effort has been made to trace the ownership of all illustrative material reproduced in this book. Should any error or omission in acknowledgement have been made the author offers his apologies and will make the necessary correction in future editions.

Contents

APPENDICES

THE SIRIUS MYSTERY

Chapter 1

The Sirius Mystery Today

How could the ancient and secret traditions of an African tribe contain highly precise astrophysical information about invisible stars in the Sirius star system? Some of it has only been discovered very recently by modern scientists, half a century after it was recorded by anthropologists studying the tribe.

The situation regarding *The Sirius Mystery* has changed completely since the initial edition of the book was published in 1976.[1] At that time the Dogon tribal tradition insisted upon the existence of a third star in the system of Sirius which modern astronomers could not confirm. Some critics said this proved the hypothesis of the book to be false. If the Earth had been visited by intelligent beings from the system of the star Sirius in the distant past, and they had left behind all this precise information about their star system, the fact that they described the existence of a third star, a Sirius C, whose existence could not be confirmed by modern astronomy rendered the whole account untrustworthy. However, the existence of Sirius C has now been confirmed after all.

The basis of science is that you put forward a hypothesis containing a prediction, and you then seek to verify or refute that prediction. If the prediction is confirmed, the hypothesis is considered to be verified. The hypothesis of *The Sirius Mystery* has now been verified in a dramatic fashion. In 1976 and in the years immediately following I predicted on numerous occasions that the existence of a small red dwarf star would be verified in the Sirius system, to be called Sirius C according to the standard naming schemes of astronomy (there already being an A and a B). This has now happened. In 1995 the French astronomers Daniel Benest and J. L. Duvent published the results of years of study in the journal *Astronomy and Astrophysics* stating that a small red dwarf star, Sirius C, seems to exist in the system of the star Sirius.[2] They have detected a perturbation which cannot be explained by any other means.

This verification is a highly specific astrophysical prediction which has now been confirmed. It is not as if I had predicted that, say, a comet would approach Earth during 1997. There are many comets, and one might approach Earth at any time. But when one predicts that a star will be discovered in a specific star system and that it will be a particular type of star, and when this indeed happens twenty years later, that is rewarding.

What is the hypothesis, then, which has been so startlingly confirmed in the best traditions of science?

It is that our planet has at some time in the past been visited by intelligent beings from the system of the star Sirius. This suggestion is no longer considered as astounding as it was in 1976. After all, *The Sirius Mystery* generated enormous discussion around the world, and has done so continuously since its appearance. Many years have passed and public opinion has undergone a sea change. This book seems to have founded a genre of books, and there are several bearing the names of Sirius or Orion in their titles. In the 1970s it was the 'New Agers' who were the first to adopt the sentiments of *The Sirius Mystery*, and my phrase 'cosmic trigger' even became the title of one of several books discussing such issues at great length. (See Bibliography for Robert Anton Wilson.) I was recently surprised to learn that the Internet has many web sites discussing *The Sirius Mystery*, and there seems to be a whole Sirius Industry out there in cyberspace somewhere. A friend recently asked me: 'Don't you ever use a search engine to look up "Sirius", "Dogon", etc.?' I have to admit I don't. Although I do use the Internet, I don't have time to consult websites discussing my own work – I leave that to others – but I'm glad to learn that the interest is so large, and I just hope that they've got all the information correct.

Many of my pleas in 1976 have been answered: for instance, a young man read the appendix about Proclus and decided to do his PhD about him, and has now published a very extensive book on the subject of Proclus (see Postscript to my Appendix II). Another man read my book in 1977 while travelling in Egypt and decided to undertake his own researches relating to the subject: his name is Robert Bauval, and his articles and his book *The Orion Mystery* have explored some fascinating possibilities about the Sirius cult and the Egyptian pyramids. He contacted me several times and when we finally met, he urged me strongly to revise and reprint this book. I took his suggestion seriously, as you can see.

Since the original publication of *The Sirius Mystery* was a whole generation ago, few will recall the amazing excitement generated by its appearance. No book quite like that had ever been published before. But I had to apologize constantly for talking about little green men, and some close friends dropped me entirely and never spoke to me again because extraterrestrials at that time were not deemed socially acceptable, nor any discussion of them. For instance, an older woman with whom I had had what I thought was a close friendship for years, turned her back on me completely after publication of *The Sirius Mystery*, and mutual friends said it was because I had published something about spacemen, which she thought was simply an appalling thing to do. A number of British scholars whom I knew used to ridicule the fact that I had discussed something as lowbrow as spacemen, and I was therefore clearly not a respectable person.

But the critical reception of *The Sirius Mystery* in the British press in its first year was universally ecstatic. It got favourable lead reviews on the day of publication in *The Times* and the *Telegraph*, and then a seemingly endless mass of reviews in nearly every newspaper and magazine in Britain – all favourable. No one was more surprised than my publisher, who had dragged his feet for about three years after delivery of the manuscript before the book came out. (My advance for the book was £500, if you want to know, and no royalties were due for three or four years after delivery because of publication delays.) But the book then went on to become a worldwide bestseller, even in such unexpected places as the former Yugoslavia. The country where it was most appreciated was Germany, where it was on the bestseller list for more than six months. Soon after initial publication, the book was favourably reviewed in a lead review by a professor of astronomy for *Nature* Magazine. Later it was reviewed in *Time* Magazine. It was featured on a *Horizon* programme on BBC Television (also a *Nova* programme on PBS in the USA). The British astronomical community, which is not an arrogant community, seemed relatively unshocked by my book. This was possibly because a number of leading astronomers knew me, and I had 'done the right thing' by first airing the subject matter in *The Observatory*, published by the Royal Greenwich Observatory.[3] This had gained the personal support and backing of Professor William McCrea, who as a President of the Royal Astronomical Society, Gold Medal winner, and one of the nicest people in England, commanded universal respect and affection amongst his colleagues, So much was I accepted as part of the background radiation, albeit a rather aberrant part of it, that some good-humoured joking about me appeared in *The Observatory*. I was thrilled when a spoof appeared in their joke issue of October, 1977,[4] as I enjoy anything of that kind. In Germany some cartoons about the Sirius Mystery appeared in newspapers, and that delighted me too. A newspaper cartoonist in America spoofed the Sirius Mystery, and Faith Hubley, an Oscar-winning film animator, did some charmingly fey animated films inspired by it (only generally inspired, so no income alas). I remember going to see her in New York and holding her three Oscars all at once – how many people have *three* Oscars on view in their sitting rooms? I certainly met a lot of interesting characters through the Sirius Mystery. But others I avoided. For instance, the late Timothy Leary was very keen for me to join him in California for some joint grooving on the subject of Sirius, after he got out of prison, but the idea of such a thing was so repellant to me that it still makes me shudder. There is nothing I hate quite so much as drugs and the drug-culture.

The Sirius Mystery had many strange and unexpected consequences in the world of the arts, of all things! The German composer Karlheinz Stockhausen was inspired to write a symphonic poem entitled *Sirius* and announced to the world that he had visited Sirius and that he used compositional techniques learned there. Music from the Sirius system was different – he said it was like *his*! The novelist Doris Lessing was, according to a mutual friend, originally inspired by it to write her series of five science fiction novels, the first of which was entitled *Shikasta* and is the diary of an alien with a mission to Earth. In her introduction to the novel, written in 1978, she mentions the Dogon tribe and the *Epic of Gilgamesh*.[5] Another of the volumes was *The Sirian Experiments*,[6] which I went out of my way to solicit an opportunity to review in a London magazine at the time, to attempt to counteract a dismissive review of *Shikasta* published earlier by Tim Heald, whom I knew in days of yore and who had slammed Doris Lessing for writing science fiction. (She later wrote and thanked me for 'being a good friend'.) I found her foray into this genre extremely interesting. She has been so much influenced by Idries Shah's Sufi movement that she has developed many profound philosophical notions, and it is a great credit to her that these include an awareness of the importance of Earth's relationship to other worlds. The fact that such a major novelist was prepared to write five serious novels about extraterrestrial intelligence is important, but unfortunately a great many people amongst the literati resented it and were contemptuous.

My own personal experiences in the aftermath of the publication of *The Sirius Mystery* have been in many ways lamentable. What did please me was that so many people wrote to me with such interesting ideas and suggestions – far too many for me to consider thoroughly. I wish that one day I would be able to find time to go through these letters and make a proper study of some of the ideas in them. I had to give up replying to people, as there were too many of them. And of course there is the strange phenomenon of 'nut mail' – but you never know for sure and it is often a good idea to keep it. One man who was obsessed with the Bermuda Triangle and claimed to have sailed through the area extensively making strange discoveries wrote to me telling me that people were trying to kill him. I thought he was indulging in paranoid fantasies. But he was later really murdered, and his limbless body was washed up at Canvey Island in Essex. I was able to give his letters to the police as part of a murder investigation, although at first the police tried to brush me off and only accepted the evidence after the *Daily Telegraph* threatened to run a story about their negligence in a homicide. A somewhat disturbed American girl who was a millionaire followed me round the world asking me to father her 'starchild' and was a terrible nuisance until her family had her committed and took her money away from her: then she wasn't able to pay for the air tickets anymore and I was left in peace. I often think of the £25,000 in cash which she said she had buried beside a runway at Birmingham Airport as a 'hedge against inflation'. Not only has it declined in value by now, but it must be very soggy. The other people she was obsessed by were the Moody Blues, a pop group who must have become as sick of hearing her babble on about me as I became of hearing her raving about them.

But the sad part of the aftermath of *The Sirius Mystery* was the extreme and virulent hostility towards me by certain security agencies, most notably the American ones. Since I am myself an American by origin, I found this insulting and distressing. On several occasions I was targeted in ways so extreme that they seemed to me hysterical beyond all belief. I am certain that false information was entered into my security files to blacken my reputation. I was blackballed even in some organizations which seem to me so harmless that I still cannot understand it. To give an example, I was co-editing a magazine at one time and decided to join the Foreign Press Association in London so that I could have lunch there and get a press pass. I was told I needed two members to recommend me, and was given names of two American journalists in London who should be happy to do so. So I asked Bonnie Angelo of Time-Life, and she was delighted. (I later wrote for her London bureau for several years and did British science reporting for *Discover* Magazine.) I then went to another man who was equally friendly and he said he would, and signed my form. That particular man, whom I do not wish to identify, had certain connections in Washington, if you take my meaning. A few hours later, Catherine Postlethwaite, the Secretary of the FPA, told me she had had a hysterical phone call from the man insisting that he wanted to use his blackball against me and stop me joining the FPA. She was completely astonished and said to him he had just signed my form and now on the same day he was trying to blackball me, and how could he possibly explain that? He refused to explain, but was relentlessly insistent. She and the Council took the view in the end that the man was acting unreasonably, for whatever motives, and they overruled his blackball. But I recognized a pattern of behaviour which has assailed me on many occasions. There was another time, for instance, when I had commenced what was meant to be a profitable association with a man I knew to make several series of corporate videos, with me as writer and co-producer and his company providing the finance and facilities. We made one video and suddenly everything stopped mysteriously. After some time he told me: 'I really wanted to do these projects with you, but I can't, and even though I am not supposed to tell you, I felt that I owed you an explanation. The fact is that I have had the CIA from America on the phone to me practically every day for the past three weeks harassing me and telling me I must not work with you, and as much as I like you, my life isn't worth living with this kind of continual pressure and interruption of my work every day by hysterical American officials. So that is the reason, and the only reason, why I am withdrawing from our projects together.' I thanked him for being so honest with me.

Several other people were as well. Indeed, one old fellow I was friendly with, retired Brigadier Shelford Bidwell, actually told me that he had been asked to read *The Sirius Mystery* and write a thorough report on it for the British security services. He had found it rather difficult because it was not his kind of subject! He hadn't meant to tell me this, but he slipped up when chatting over tea and said by way of being pleasant how interesting *The Sirius Mystery* was. When I expressed astonishment that he had read something so far from all his other interests, he first said that he had read every word meticulously, as if that explained everything. When I protested that this was really quite unbelievable, he had to explain why he had done so. He was so sheepish and embarrassed that I spared him further questioning so that he wouldn't have to spend the rest of his life with a security breach on his conscience. Another old friend, whom I had known when he was a policeman in a panda car and who is now a famous British police commissioner, said he had been approached by MI5 to do a security report on me. He had found it disturbing that there was such suspicion attached to me, and he couldn't explain it, since he wasn't given an explanation himself. He tried to tell them there was nothing at all suspicious about me and that he knew me well, and he wrote up everything he could find out about me trying to demonstrate that I was harmless. But they didn't seem to want to be told that and were obviously unsatisfied, which disturbed him even more.

This persecution went on for more than fifteen years. It cost me income, career opportunities, advancement, and friends. I often wonder about it, especially the frenzied aspects of it. Why were so many people in high places foaming at the mouth in such an uncontrollable manner? Just what was it that I had done? I have never known.

In my opinion, based on both instinct and information, it was the Soviet Union which was most active in suppressing serious study of both extraterrestrial intelligence and paranormal phenomena. It may seem ironical that although the American CIA persecuted me for so many years, I lay much of the blame for this with the Soviet Union, acting through their agents, the Aldrich Ames types.

I believe the CIA was both duped and manipulated by Soviet agents in its midst, not just with regard to myself but also many similar subjects. The Soviet Union was absolutely determined to have a monopoly on paranormal research, for instance, and would stop at nothing. I believe they actually 'took some people out', by administering drugs to them which damaged their brains, leaving them alive but in such a confused state that they would discredit themselves. I met at least two brilliant scientists involved in paranormal research who later underwent such drastic personality changes, substantially deprived of their rational powers, that they appeared to have become converted into mental zombies. Both lived in America, and must have been targeted by the KGB. Wise people involved in such subjects take extensive precautions: Uri Geller, who once contacted me and asked me to come and see him, I found living in isolation in a huge house in Britain surrounded by guard dogs and security devices. I'm sure he has his reasons. And it was chiefly about the threat he perceived from the KGB that he wished to talk to me. That was before the collapse of the Soviet Union. Naturally I was inclined to agree with his fears. (Uri did say, by the way, that he had never actually read *The Sirius Mystery*. He said that he only reads paperbacks which he can fit on to his exercise bicycle. He is very keen on keeping fit, and sometimes cycles frantically in his shorts while he talks to visitors. Whilst he was talking to me about the KGB he was engaged in this desperate exercise, fighting the war against fat.)

There were two employees of NASA who made attacks on me which I thought went far beyond mere critical disagreement. This was all the more distressing for me because I had been friends for some years with a delightful man, Captain Robert Freitag of the US Navy, who was Deputy Director of the Advanced Programs department of NASA's Office of Space Flight. Bob Freitag and I met through Arthur C. Clarke and when he came to London, Bob and I would often meet for dinner, as we were both very keen on good food and I would try to find something unusual, such as a Hungarian restaurant. On a visit to Washington I called in to see Bob Freitag and he said he had a very bright fellow who worked for him called Jesco von Puttkamer, whom he wanted me to meet. He called him in and I told them both about *The Sirius Mystery*.

This man was actually *Baron* Jesco von Puttkamer, and I believe he was one of the Germans who came to the United States with Werner von Braun. But I was shocked when later von Puttkamer maligned me in an astonishing manner on official NASA writing paper (in German) to my German publishers, a separate arm of which had apparently asked him to review my book for a journal. The letter said (11 July 1977) of me (my translation) that 'he acts like a UFO-follower and leaps directly to the most farfetched hypothesis, which requires an assumption of an assumption of an assumption, namely that of extraterrestrial astronauts, simply because he believes it. This is rather religious than scientific. . . . Temple's work . . . in the scientific sense is worthless; the evidences which he puts forward represent no proofs. The thesis which he put forward to my opinion presents not the slightest evidence, not to mention proof.' Von Puttkamer went on to say that he was available to give a lecture in Frankfurt if they wanted him to.

I wrote to Bob Freitag on September 3, 1977, and said: 'My German publishers, Umschau Verlag, have sent me a copy of a highly objectionable letter about me and my book *The Sirius Mystery* written to them by your friend Puttkamer on NASA stationery, signing it from the Advanced Programs Office. As this could be construed as an official expression of NASA sentiments, I must ask you to send both to me and to my German publishers a letter disassociating NASA from the sentiments expressed by Puttkamer . . . (he) says that I used his name in a television broadcast as supporting my hypothesis. This is entirely untrue. He says that I did this 'in a completely fabricated performance, which would obviously serve to

9

give the book status'. I am very disturbed at this outpouring of vituperation from your friend. . . . Puttkamer then goes on to attribute to me ideas which do not appear in my book (such as that the story of Gilgamesh records the visit of spacemen, which is I believe an idea of von Däniken's) based on things discussed in parts of the book, namely the second half, which he admits he has not even read.'

Bob Freitag was not pleased by von Puttkamer's behaviour, and Bob wrote to me on September 16, 1977, saying of von Puttkamer:

'I was unaware of the contents of his letter and the problem it has caused for you.

'First, I hasten to disassociate the Advanced Programs Office and NASA from the views expressed by Mr. von Puttkamer. These are certainly his private views . . . I have instructed him to get in touch with you and the firm to provide quickly the disclaimer that he was speaking privately and not expressing a NASA viewpoint. . . . I remain interested in your plans for a new book and would be pleased to be kept up to date on your plans and progress. I would like the opportunity of discussing this in London . . .'

Von Puttkamer followed with a letter dated October 7, 1977, saying of his views: 'It does not represent anything like an "official NASA position". The use of the stationery may have given you that impression (using it was a thoughtlessness which I regret) . . . I regret that this caused the appearance of an "official expression of NASA sentiment" to you.' He also said that he had not meant to attack me personally. Despite being a NASA scientist he had also put forward a very weird hypothesis, astronomically completely impossible, that Sirius B had once been visible to the naked eye. Such ignorance of astrophysics surprised me; his statement completely ignored the parallax which would prevent Sirius B, whatever kind of star it was earlier in its history, from being differentiated from Sirius A by the naked eye. So much for Jesco von Puttkamer, who never entered the fray again.

But it was much more difficult to deal with the behaviour of another NASA employee, who was not under Captain Freitag and whose actions could not be so easily rebuked. I do not propose to name this man, but his activities were revealed to me by Arthur Clarke who telephoned me from Sri Lanka telling me that the man, whom he did not previously know, had contacted him in order to criticize me very stridently. Arthur said he thought I ought to know this because he had the impression that the man was contacting quite a lot of other people in the same way, one of whom was Isaac Asimov (whom I knew only slightly). He believed there were half a dozen other people 'of equal importance and stature' to whom this man was maligning me.

In 1977 the BBC made a 90-minute television documentary special for their series *Horizon*, entitled 'The Case for the Ancient Astronauts'. I was contracted as a Researcher, which was my first television job. I was originally supposed to be the subject of the entire programme, but the producer, Graham Massey, became more interested in discrediting Erich von Däniken, so most of the programme was devoted to that. Graham did an incredible demolition job on von Däniken; I did not prepare that material, but worked only on my own subject matter. The last 15 minutes of the programme were devoted to the Sirius Mystery, which Graham treated very fairly indeed, contrasting it as a 'respectable theory' with what he considered the nonsense of von Däniken. From the script, which I have, I see that the narration of the programme stated of myself that 'He is an assiduous, careful, and extremely knowledgeable researcher.'

While the programme was being prepared, Graham kept getting phone calls from a stranger in America. Finally Graham told me about them. He said the man was ranting and saying 'you must not let Robert Temple on television'. (Also, it appeared that the man in question was available for an interview himself at any time!) Graham told me: 'I told this annoying man that I am the producer of the programme and I make my own decisions about who appears in it and who doesn't, and would he please stop calling me all the time.' The man apparently kept mentioning that he worked for NASA, and Graham was doubly annoyed that there seemed to be the implication that the American authorities did not think I should receive media attention. The man was the same one who had phoned Arthur Clarke. NASA was never disassociated from this man's activities and attacks against me.

*****

I want to turn now to important new subjects which I have not discussed in this context before. I have some observations on the pyramids of the Giza plateau, and on the Sphinx.

It is often said that the Egyptian Sphinx is a large statue with the body of a lion and the head of a man. I can see no reason for this. People said with as much confidence a hundred years ago that the Sphinx was a large man's head sticking out of the sand. Now that it has been cleared and we can see that the head is attached to the body of an animal, everyone assumes that the body is a lion's body. But surely this is a case of the 'Emperor's New Clothes'. I cannot see any leonine features in the body of the Sphinx, unless one were to say that because it has four legs and four paws and a tail, it must be a lion.

There is no mane. There are no prominent muscles in the chest above the front legs, as are often shown in statues of lions. The tail does not have the tuft at the end which lions have, and which statues of lions also have. But most telling of all, the rear haunches do not rise up above the level of the back, bulging and prominent. The back of the Sphinx's body is straight. But if you look at an Egyptian hieroglyph of the letter 'r' you see a lion's crouching body in profile and realize that lions were portrayed in Egypt

11

with huge rear haunches rising well above the line of the back. We all say the Sphinx is a lion because we have been told it is a lion. We see with the eyes of the unknown and anonymous people who 'say' it is a lion. We have all accepted secondhand information without checking its validity.

If the Sphinx's body is not a lion's body, what kind of body is it?

It looks more like a dog's body! Representations of the god Anubis, who was portrayed as a canine – probably not actually a jackal (although he is often called a jackal) but is more probably a dog (from whom the modern Pharaoh Hound is thought to be partially descended) – show a crouching animal the line of whose back is more or less straight, like that of the Sphinx. And its tail often curls round in the same way as that of the Sphinx, and it has no tuft on the end. Furthermore, it has no mane and no muscled chest.

To me it makes much more sense to suggest that the Sphinx was Anubis, and that originally he was guarding the sacred precinct of the pyramids at Giza. If, as has often been suggested, the head was recarved by a megalomaniac Pharaoh in his own likeness, it may have been recarved from an Anubis head. The current head of the Sphinx is dispro-portionately small in comparison to the body, as many people have pointed out. It certainly does appear to have been substantially cut down from a much larger original head. But be that as it may, the body of the Sphinx could well be a dog's body, not a lion's.

I believe it is inevitably the case that the pyramid complex at Giza has symbolic celestial importance. And if this be so, then the Guardian of the complex should be the Egyptian Guardian par excellence – Anubis.

There is another aspect of the Sphinx, about which so much has been said in recent years by other authors, which seems to me a red herring. John Anthony West has become the central figure in this debate, which concerns the water erosion which is so evident at the Sphinx. As far as I know, I was the first person to publish West's theories on this subject. From 1978 to 1980 I was co-editor of an American magazine called *Second Look*, and my co-editor Randy Fitzgerald and I agreed to publish West's interesting article 'Metaphysics by Design. Harmony and Proportion in Ancient Egypt', in which West first aired the matter of the water erosion. I recently gave a copy of this to West, who had none and had forgotten all about it. The article appeared in the June 1979 issue.[7] Later in the same year, West's book *Serpent in the Sky: The High Wisdom of Ancient Egypt* appeared.[8] West's book was very badly edited and constructed, as I have told him personally, and it did not make the impact it should have done with the public. A surprisingly large proportion of the book consisted of disconnected quotations from a variety of books which were not inte-grated into the text nor subject to any kind of comment; these were all placed in a very large margin which ran throughout the book. A large amount of material about the Dogon appeared in this fashion, and two pages of marginalia relating to *The Sirius Mystery*.[9] Though suggestive, all of this material was not marshalled towards any kind of a thesis. It is best therefore to give West's actual thesis in his own words: '. . . the earliest calculation would place the founding of Egypt around 30,000 BC, the latest around 23,000 BC . . . "Atlantis" can no longer be ignored by anyone seriously interested in the truth.'[10] West therefore suggests that Egyptian civilization cannot be less than 25,000 years old, and may be 32,000 years old.

In his book, West states that the Egyptian civilization did not develop, but was a legacy. I am inclined to agree with him, and that is an elegant way of putting it. I also agree with him so far as to say that an origin could well go back to 4240 BC (the commencement of something called the First Sothic Cycle, connected with the heliacal* rising of Sirius),[11] and in any case *must* go back to approximately 3500 BC. However, at that point we diverge, because West makes it very plain that he believes the legacy came from a lost 'Atlantis'-type of early civilization native to this planet, and he dismisses people who drag in 'extra-galactic' origins to explain the Egyptian civilization. West and I are in agreement about many things, such as admiration for the Egyptologist Schwaller de Lubicz and enthusiasm for Pythagorean studies. We tend to agree about many aspects of pyramid measurements, and a host of such things. Also, he is well aware that I always suggested in *The Sirius Mystery* that an 'Atlantis'-type of explanation was certainly an alternative possibility to the extraterrestrial hypothesis. The trouble is that I do not personally believe in the viability of the 'Atlantis' theory as presently articulated: it implies an *absence* of extraterrestrial contact. A number of people including West cannot bring themselves to think seriously about extraterrestrials, because their minds do not run that way, I suppose. This is a kind of natural divide which I believe rests more on psychological disposition than intellectual choice. I am friendly with a number of authors who currently advocate the 'Atlantis' hypothesis of a high civilization in the Earth's past where all advanced science was purely of human origin and there was no contact with beings from any other world. I do not support this, and we have had perfectly amicable discussions about our variance of interpretation of origins. At least one of them sees perfectly clearly the strength of the extraterrestrial hypothesis, and realizes he might one day have to amend his interpretation to accommodate it.

I certainly believe that there is much undiscovered – possibly under the silt and mud of the Nile Delta – concerning the high civilization of Predynastic Egypt. But the 'Atlantis' which is postulated today is too far back, and it leaves *several thousand years* of 'nothingness' in between it and Egypt and Sumer. John Anthony West's suggestion leaves a 'blank' of between 22,000 and 27,000 years! I cannot accept such suggestions. Nor can I accept that the Sphinx is 12,500 years old, even though I believe it and the pyramids were probably built long before the lifetimes of the

---

* With or just before the sun – this is discussed later.

13

Pharaohs Cheops and Khephren. But these things are all a matter of degree. In my view, there was ancient extraterrestrial contact with Earth. And I believe that the period of interaction with extraterrestrials and the founding of Egyptian and Sumerian civilization with their help probably fell between 5000 and 3000 BC. We can call the time of this interaction, whenever it was, the Contact Period. I believe that the pyramids and the Sphinx were probably built by the extraterrestrials themselves during the Contact Period, and that the Step Pyramid of Saqqara was a later and magnificent attempt by men working unaided under the human architect Imhotep – since the extraterrestrials had long since vanished – to match those mysterious earlier achievements and show that humans could do such things too. Many of the other Egyptian pyramids then imitated the Step Pyramid, but it can be seen that a lot of them have crumbled into dust and were not very well constructed. Eventually the Egyptians gave up trying to build large pyramids and the so-called 'Pyramid Age' ended altogether.

Without going into it all here, I must note that several authors have discussed extraordinary artifacts which have survived from antiquity, indicating an advanced scientific knowledge. The ancient tradition of maps depicting an Antarctica before it was covered in ice, represented by the Peri Reis Map for instance, is extremely important. In the 1960s I used to discuss these maps for hours with the late Charles Hapgood, the first man to publish anything about them. I believe that these ancient maps do preserve such important ancient knowledge, and they are priceless evidence of advanced science in antiquity. But I do not interpret them as evidence of 'Atlantis'; I see them as yet more survivals of knowledge left by visiting extraterrestrials, who were able to map the Earth from space, and who were able to detect the true continental outline of Antarctica *through the ice* by orbiting space observations in the same way that we can do today. This knowledge was meant to be part of the legacy left behind when the extraterrestrials departed. The whole point is that some of this evidence from the Contact Period was meant to survive and be recognized by men at such time as we developed enough science and technology to be able to do so. I am convinced that *we are meant to piece together the mystery ourselves* from the few clues which have survived. The extraterrestrials do not want to return until we have figured out that they are there. For they are worried about our morale. They do not want to announce themselves without warning – they want *us* to detect *them*. Then they will come. It is all part of the ethics of galactic species interaction.

Now to return to discussing Egypt: West relegated to the end of his book a section entitled 'Egypt: Heir to Atlantis', so that his main point was rather buried, and was easily overlooked by people who did not bother to read his book thoroughly. It was in this section that West emphasized the water erosion at the Sphinx, to which attention had first been called by the late Schwaller de Lubicz. In order to consider the history of how this subject first arose, I give the comments made by Schwaller de Lubicz himself in his book *Le Roi de la Théocracie Pharaonique* (English title: *Sacred Science*) in 1961. In discussing the Sphinx in general, he speaks of 'that Sphinx whose leonine body, except for the head, shows indisputable signs of aquatic erosion'. To this passing remark he appends a footnote which states: 'It is maintained that this erosion was wrought by desert sands, but the entire body of the Sphinx is protected from all desert winds coming from the West, the only winds that could effect erosion. Only the head protrudes from this hollow, and it shows no signs of erosion.'[12] These were the remarks which sent the very observant John Anthony West forth on his quest. West is somewhat at variance with Schwaller de Lubicz about the winds, since the latter stresses that the prevailing desert winds come from the west, but West is more concerned about the seasonal *khamsin* winds which he says blow from the south ('the fierce desert wind blowing from the South in the month of April').[13] In any case, West is at pains to assure us that the Sphinx is entirely sheltered from this wind by the Sphinx Temple,[14] so all is well.

Where this subject has gone awry is in what I believe to be the mistaken insistence that the obvious water erosion around the Sphinx can only have been caused by rain at an earlier period of wet weather before Egypt became dry, more than 10,000 years ago – something which is now stated by various authors. This argument is unjustifiably used as evidence for the belief that a high civilization (equivalent to 'Atlantis') existed on Earth about 10,000 BC or thereabouts. I do not propose to go into the details of this theory, except to consider the Sphinx erosion. Other aspects of the theory are a separate discussion into which I have never entered, and I do not intend to start now, apart from what I said about the ancient maps a moment ago. I published discussions of the technology of the Olmecs (the pre-Maya inhabitants of Mexico and Guatemala) in the 1970s, and in the 1960s I was corresponding with the widow of Arthur Posnansky about Tiahuanaco in Bolivia; I knew Peter Allan, who did the studies of the Tiahuanaco 'Sun Gate', personally. I was puzzling over the Nazca Lines in Peru by 1963. I am familiar with many of these fields even though I have not mentioned them here. I have thought about them for more years than many current authors have been active. I do not dismiss them at all lightly as evidence of an 'Atlantis'. Nor is there any reason to believe that there will not be extraordinary further discoveries in relation to Tiahuanaco, for instance.

But these things must not be allowed to distract us from realizing the strong evidence in favour of a Contact Period. The Dogon and the Egyptians spoke of civilization coming from the Sirius System, and the Babylonians spoke of it coming from the heavens; the Dogon and the Babylonians agreed on the amphibious nature of the beings who did this.

The information which has been preserved is astrophysically accurate to an uncanny degree. Its precision is such that the onus is really on those who do not wish to accept the consequences to try and disprove it. So far nobody has been able to do this. My collected replies to various critics may be read in a separate pamphlet for reviewers published with this new edition. But the discovery of Sirius C has in any case rendered most criticism obsolete.

As far as the 'Atlantis' hypothesis is concerned, I believe that the 'evidence of the Sphinx' is nonexistent, as I shall explain in a moment. I do not intend my observations to be discourteous to any individuals, with whom I have friendly relations, and if their theories did not exist I would still be writing about this subject, because it concerns my own work. Let me stress once again, therefore, that I am not making the following points as part of any argument or dialogue with anyone else.

Opposed to John Anthony West and his supporters are the orthodox Egyptologists, who are – as one might expect – horrified at the notion that the Sphinx might be 12,500 years old. However, I believe that both sides are probably in error.

The Egyptologists are in error because in order to counter West's argument, they have been led to deny the existence of the water erosion at the Sphinx. But anyone can see that there is water erosion at the Sphinx, so all the members of the public who see that with their own eyes think, quite rightly, that the Egyptologists on that point at least must be wrong.

West and his supporters are so astonished at the 'blindness' of the Egyptologists that they are encouraged to make more and more impassioned criticisms of the Egyptologists, thereby driving the harassed Egyptologists ever further into their desperate corner from which they issue supercilious snarls, which the public generally ignore.

This goes to show the lack of resourcefulness of the Egyptologists, and their rather limited capacities. Just as a man who lays the bricks for a beautiful wall is rarely the architect who has designed that wall, so the archaeologists with spade in hand are rarely capable of interpreting the vast array of findings made by their entire professional class, or to make sweeping historical observations, much less to formulate grand theories about their field. I am amazed that the Egyptologists have fallen so readily into the trap of denying the water erosion at the Sphinx, thinking thereby to rid themselves of the heinous notion of a Sphinx 12,500 years old. For they have in that way put a noose around their own necks.

It seems to me that the debate about the Sphinx cannot move forward one inch on either side until we dispense with the assertion of the Egyptologists that there is no water erosion at the Sphinx. It is there for all to see – so we have to accept it! However, it is not at all necessary to assume that if you acknowledge the existence of water erosion at the Sphinx, you have to admit that it was caused more than 10,000 years ago by rain in a previous, less dry era!

There is one obvious thing that both sides in this dispute have overlooked. Anyone visiting the Sphinx or looking at a sufficient number of photos of it can readily see that the Sphinx sits in a deep pit carved out of the rock. We know for certain that that pit has often been filled with the shifting sands of the desert. Indeed, only in our own time has the pit been cleared out again so that we can see the whole figure of the Sphinx once more. There are still people alive who remember when the Sphinx was only a head sticking out of the sand. The Sphinx had to be cleared in 1816, in 1853, and in 1888,[15] but was half-covered again by 1898, as I see from a photo of that date which I found amongst my grandmother's papers. In 1916 it was again fully covered by sand except for the head.[16]

And here is my helpful suggestion: What if we consider that the pit was once filled with water! I have seen on an archaeologists' plan the indication of an ancient well in either the Sphinx Temple or the Valley Temple which is beside it, and the presence of water on the Giza Plateau was substantiated also by the excavation of a number of stone water conduits in 1995 and 1996 (which have now been covered over again, but were photographed before that was done). We also know from ancient texts that the Nile used to rise very high indeed, causing floods nearly to the level of the Giza Plateau, in ancient times.

There is some very intriguing evidence for substantial quantities of water on the Giza Plateau to be found in the *History* of Herodotus, the Greek 'Father of History' who lived in the fifth century BC and spent a long time in Egypt, of which he left a substantial account which survives today.[17] In his Book II, Herodotus discusses the pyramids at some length but does not mention the Sphinx at all. It is therefore practically a certainty that the Sphinx was buried in sand at the time of his visit. This is an important point to remember when we attempt to interpret the remarks which he recorded about water on the Giza Plateau. First, in considering the environs of the Great Pyramid, Herodotus strangely states that he was told the following by his Egyptian informants:

> They worked in gangs of a hundred thousand men, each gang for three months. For ten years the people were afflicted in making the road whereon the stones were dragged, the making of which road was to my thinking a task but a little lighter than the building of the [Great] Pyramid, for the road is five furlongs long and ten fathoms broad, and raised at its highest to a height of eight fathoms, and it is all of stone polished and carved with figures. The ten years aforesaid went to the making of this road and of the underground chambers on the hill whereon the pyramids stand [i.e., the Giza Plateau]; these the king meant to be burial-places for himself, and encompassed them with water, bringing in a channel from the Nile.[18]

This passage has been largely ignored by Egyptologists. But before we consider its implications, let us consider three further passages in Herodotus:

> Chephren also built a pyramid, of a less size than his brother's [Cheops was his elder brother]. I have myself measured it. It has no underground chambers [we now know this to be false], nor is it entered like the other [the Great Pyramid] by a canal from the Nile, but the river comes in through a built passage and encircles an island, in which, they say Cheops, himself lies.[19]

And further:

> Thus far I have recorded what the Egyptians themselves say. Now . . . I will add thereto something of what I myself have seen.[20]

And further still:

> [The Egyptians] made a labyrinth, a little way beyond the Lake Moeris and near the place called the City of the Crocodiles. I have myself seen it, and indeed no words can tell its wonder; were all that the Greeks have builded and wrought added together the whole would be seen to be a matter of less labour and cost than was this labyrinth, albeit the temples at Ephesus and Samos are noteworthy buildings. Though the pyramids were greater than words can tell, and each one of them a match for many great monuments built by Greeks, this maze surpasses even the pyramids. It has twelve roofed courts . . . There are also double sets of chambers, three thousand altogether, fifteen hundred above and the same number under ground. We ourselves viewed those that are above ground, and speak of what we have seen; of the underground chambers we were only told; the Egyptian wardens would by no means show them, these being, they said, the burial vaults of the kings who first built this labyrinth, and of the sacred crocodiles. Thus we can only speak from hearsay of the lower chambers; the upper we saw for ourselves, and they are creations greater than human. The outlets of the chambers and the mazy passages hither and thither through the courts were an unending marvel to us as we passed from court to apartment and from apartment to colonnade, from colonnades again to more chambers and then into yet more courts. . . . Hard by the corner where the labyrinth ends there stands a pyramid forty fathoms high, whereon great figures are carved. A passage has been made into this underground.
>
> Such is this labyrinth; and yet more marvellous is the Lake Moeris, by which it stands. This lake has a circuit of three thousand six hundred furlongs, or sixty schoeni, which is as much as the whole seaboard of Egypt. Its length is from north to south; the deepest part has a depth of fifty fathoms. That it has been dug out and made by men's hands the

lake shows for itself; for almost in the middle of it stand two pyramids, so built that fifty fathoms of each are below and fifty above the water; atop each is a colossal stone figure seated on a throne. Thus these pyramids are a hundred fathoms high; and a hundred fathoms equal a furlong of six hundred feet, the fathom measuring six feet and four cubits, the foot four spans and the cubit six spans. The water of the lake is not natural (for the country here is exceeding waterless) but brought by a channel from the Nile; six months it flows into the lake, and six back into the river.[21]

And finally:

When the Nile overflows the land, the towns alone are seen high and dry above the water, very like to the islands in the Aegean sea. These alone stand out, the rest of Egypt being a sheet of water. So when this happens folk are ferried not, as is their wont, in the course of the stream, but clean over the plain. From Naucratis indeed to Memphis the boat going upwards passes close by the pyramids themselves; the usual course is not this . . .[22]

From all of these passages we can see quite clearly that in the fifth century BC, when Herodotus was an eye-witness, large stretches of water were far more important in Egypt than we assume today. The amazing account of the Great Labyrinth, of the three unidentified pyramids of considerable size adjoining it, and of the artificial lake, are astonishing in themselves, and have never been satisfactorily explained to my knowledge. Certainly the huge artificial lake sounds like a very good base for visiting amphibians, and is the sort of thing amphibians rather than men would have constructed. But since no one today seems to have much idea of where on earth the ruins of all of this are to be found (although the Egyptologist Sayce thought it might be near the Pyramid of Hawara[23]), we shall not detain ourselves with speculations on that subject here. I have mentioned it in order to gather together Herodotus's various statements about substantial hydraulic engineering works bringing Nile water in by channels to dry places, and the extent to which the flooded Nile and a huge lake spread water over Egypt to the foot of the pyramids.

Let us now analyse exactly what it is that Herodotus says about the water brought into the Giza Plateau. The account is somewhat garbled, and the fact that Herodotus did not know of the existence of the Sphinx (other than, possibly, a head sticking out of the sand, which he didn't bother to mention; and who is to say even that it was visible?) must be borne in mind. He mentions 'the underground chambers on the hill whereon the pyramids stand; these the king meant to be burial-places for himself, and encompassed them with water, bringing in a channel from the Nile'. The first thing to be pointed out is that the testimony explicitly contradicts any notion that King Cheops intended himself to be buried inside the Great Pyramid! Herodotus clearly states that the king intended himself to be buried in *the underground chambers on the hill whereon the pyramids stand*, meaning underground chambers in the Giza Plateau, not underneath or within any actual pyramid. This very clear evidence appears to have been wilfully neglected by the Egyptological community, who insist that Cheops was the builder of the Great Pyramid and that he intended it as his own tomb. But they are overtly contradicted in this by Herodotus.

The next thing to note is that the burial-places on the Giza Plateau, or at least one of them, were 'encompassed with water'; the word *encompassed* indicates that somewhere on the Giza Plateau an important site was surrounded by water. How could this be without a retaining-pit? And where is such a retaining-pit on the Giza Plateau except around the Sphinx? Now let us look at the second passage from Herodotus, where he speaks of water from the Nile which 'comes in through a built passage and encircles an island, in which, they say, Cheops himself lies'.

Is this not absolutely clear? The Sphinx *bears the face of the Pharaoh*, and if encircled by water in the retaining-pit, the *Pharaoh lies there*, just as the Egyptians said, in an island surrounded by water. Whether the face is of Cheops or his brother Khephren matters little, and the two could be easily confused. Although Herodotus says it is Cheops who lies in the island surrounded by water, he does so in the section where he is really discussing Khephren, having already dealt with Cheops, and immediately afterwards he states: 'Chephren, they said, reigned for fifty-six years.'[24]

If we disentangle all of these secondhand accounts recorded by Herodotus, we have a clear tradition in the fifth century BC in Egypt that somewhere on the Giza Plateau (a place where the body of the Sphinx could not then be seen) there was at the time of Cheops and Khephren an island surrounded by water in which the Pharaoh lay. Since the body of the Sphinx would be covered by water and only the head of the Pharaoh would protrude from the water at that time, it was literally correct to say this. The Pharaoh did indeed lie on an island surrounded by water, if the retaining-pit of the Sphinx was full of water, which we suggest that it was. If it were not, then *where is the island on the Giza Plateau? Does anybody know of any other candidate?*

My suggestion is, therefore, that the Sphinx was surrounded by water originally, and for a significant portion of its history. And furthermore, the record of this fact has been sitting there in the text of Herodotus unrecognized for 2,500 years. As for how the water got there, the raising of water by simple wooden devices called norias is very ancient and survives today throughout the Nile Delta. I suggest therefore that from the Nile, from the well in the Sphinx Temple or Valley Temple, or by the stone water-conduits excavated on the Giza Plateau in 1995 and 1996, for much of its history the pit around the Sphinx was a moat, and that the Sphinx was kept artificially surrounded by water. Apparently there is still some water beneath the Sphinx today, a fact which has puzzled modern archaeologists.

The notion of Nile water reaching the Sphinx is in any case well addressed by James M. Harrell, who writes: 'The floor of the Sphinx enclosure is 19.9 to 20.2 metres above sea level . . . The normal Nile-flood maximum at the Roda Nilometer near Cairo has ranged between 19.0 and 19.5 metres above sea level this century, with exceptional floods reaching elevations of 20.3 metres in 1938 and 21.4 metres in 1874. During the past two centuries, there have been numerous reports of flood water reaching the base of the Giza Plateau.'[25]

If the Sphinx was sitting in a moat for much of its history over thousands of years, this could explain its significant water erosion. The winds on the plateau would have whipped up the water and caused a sloshing motion on countless occasions. This could have been rendered far more erosive by the fact that sand would have blown continually into the water and, in churning with the water, would have had a significant scouring effect on the stone. The moat would have had to be dredged frequently to clear it of the sand, and in the dredging process, great quantities of raised water would pour back down along the sides, not uniformly but at certain points. This corresponds with the observation that the subsurface weathering of the limestone floor of the sphinx pit is greater in some places than others. The fact that there is less subsurface weathering at the rear of the Sphinx could also be explained by the possibility that as the space there is narrow, drifting sand may have regularly accumulated in the water there more readily and to a greater depth, faster than in the more spread-out regions in the other directions. It would have been a kind of sand-trap. And the effect would have been to insulate the limestone floor at that point from water-action. It should be noted also that the head of the Sphinx is considerably less eroded than the body; the reason for this could be that it was never submerged in water. (If the 'ancient rain' theory were true, the head of the Sphinx would be eroded to the *same* extent as the body.)

Why is it that no one has 'seen' that the Sphinx sits in a moat? And that the moat, having been filled with water for much of ancient history, at least prior to the New Kingdom, there is naturally water erosion around the Sphinx?

As I have already said, I do not subscribe to the 'Atlantis'-theory of a high civilization having existed 12,500 years ago. And I certainly do not believe we can invoke the weathering of the Sphinx to try and prove that the Sphinx dates from that time. I believe that the extraordinary things which happened on our planet occurred much more recently than that. It may be shocking to some people, but to me there is nothing unusual in postulating that an extraterrestrial visitation was responsible for kick-starting high civilization on the Earth. It is not really unusual if you believe that the Universe must be filled with life, some of it intelligent. And I believe that that visitation to our planet came from the system of the star Sirius, as the ancient peoples as well as the Dogon have tried to tell us. And since the accounts are of aquatic beings from a watery planet there, it may well be that the reason why the Sphinx – which I believe to have been a statue of Anubis – was sitting in water, was *because the visitors from the planet in the system of the star Sirius were amphibious.* If the chambers said to have been discovered by geologists beneath the Sphinx are filled with water, this may be no accident. If it be true that they are filled with indications or records of some kind, as many enthusiasts of the 'Hall of Records' idea believe (a suggestion made in this book in 1976, by the way), it would make sense that aquatic beings would prefer to leave some traces of that kind in watery chambers rather than dry ones. And the moat around the Sphinx might then be seen as a simple but brilliant protection device, since only with diving-suits could tomb-robbers hope to break in and steal anything preserved in water-filled chambers beneath the Sphinx moat. These chambers, on the other hand, could readily be entered by amphibians. So I put forward the possibility that this was all done by design.

This is not the place to survey the many attempts to find significance in the measurements of the Great Pyramid: such efforts fill many books. Certainly some are the work of fanatics, especially in the cases where Biblical or prophetic messages are sought in pyramidal proportions. But I believe that some of the geophysical, astrophysical, and mathematical correspondences make sense, and that some of the measurements of the Great Pyramid do represent aspects of the size of the Earth for instance. It has been suggested by many writers that the Great Pyramid represents the Earth's Northern Hemisphere, and that is quite likely to be one of the things it represents. It also appears to incorporate or express the values of *pi* (3.1416) and another natural constant, *phi* (1.618), which is connected with the Golden Section and a series of numbers called the Fibonacci Series. All of this has been discussed by many previous investigators. I am suggesting new insights into the pyramids which should be viewed as additional to those I have just mentioned, and which do not rule out any of the above.

I now see in retrospect that in *The Sirius Mystery* I pioneered a strange kind of thinking whereby stellar constellation patterns were seen as represented on the ground in Egypt. I concentrated on the constellation of Argo, as the reader may see in Chapter Six (a pattern of the key stars of Argo is shown as represented geodetically in Figure 19 in Chapter Six). To me this was a normal way to think, but to most people it was unusual. Robert Bauval, who has paid generous tribute to my work on many occasions, readily fell in with this manner of thinking and also looked for a stellar pattern displayed on the ground. The result forms the basis for his fascinating book *The Orion Mystery* (1994), in which he points out that the layout of the three main pyramids at Giza corresponds with the three stars of Orion's Belt.[26] Orion and Argo, which we see to have these symbolic presences on Egyptian soil, are the two constellations most associated with Sirius.

However, an enigma remains. Surely there are direct associations with Sirius itself – but what are they? Bauval explains how the southern shaft of the so-called King's Chamber of the Great Pyramid in ancient times pointed to the constellation of Orion; he then worked out that the southern shaft of the so-called Queen's Chamber pointed directly at the star Sirius.[27]

I have now discovered a further association, which I suspected in the 1970s, when the existing astrophysical measurements were imprecise so that my instinctive hunch could not be confirmed, Now, however, the astrophysical measurements available since the publication of the new figures in *Astrophysical Data* in 1992 make it possible for me to suggest this correspondence, which I had been disappointed that I could not make earlier because the figures appearing in the former reference book *Astrophysical Quantities* in 1973 were, it now turns out, inaccurate and did not yield the intuitively sensed correspondence which I strongly felt at that time.

I am referring to the strange fact that the Great Pyramid stands beside another pyramid which is nearly but not quite the same size. This always seemed to me very peculiar, and I felt that it must symbolize something – but what? I look upon the Great Pyramid as being associated with the Sirius cult and I felt that it must represent the star Sirius B. I knew that our own sun had a mass nearly but not quite that of Sirius B; or perhaps (according to the obsolete 1973 figures) it was the other way around. Couldn't the two pyramids represent by some key measurement of theirs the relative masses of our sun and Sirius B? However, it was not possible to pursue this notion in the 1970s because at that time the mass of Sirius B was incorrectly believed to be 0.98 that of our own sun,[28] and such relative measurements did not correspond to the two pyramids. However, that situation has now changed. According to the new figures, Sirius B has a mass 1.053 that of our sun.[29] The new figures also suggest that Sirius B has a radius 0.0078 that of our sun.[30]

It is now possible to make a correlation whereby the Great Pyramid may be seen to represent Sirius B and the Pyramid of Khephren may be seen to represent our sun.

If we follow this line of reasoning, we find a correlation accurate to two decimal points. The way I have arrived at it is this: according to the leading authority on the pyramids, Dr I. E. S. Edwards, the measurement of each side of the base of the Pyramid of Khephren was originally 707.75 feet.[31] As for the Great Pyramid, Edwards says that the original measurements of the four sides of the base were: North: 755.43 feet, South: 756.08 feet, East: 755.88 feet, and West: 755.77 feet.[32] The mean of these four measurements is 755.79 feet. If we compare the mean side of the base of the Great Pyramid with the side of the base of the Pyramid of Khephren, we find that the larger measurement is 1.0678 that of the smaller. We know from the new astrophysical data that the mass of Sirius B is 1.053 that of our sun. The correspondence is thus accurate to 0.014. However, even this tiny discrepancy may be highly significant. For 0.0136 (which rounded off is 0.014) is the precise discrepancy between the mathematics of the octave and the mathematics of the fifth in harmonic theory, where 1.0136 is referred to as the Comma of Pythagoras, and was known to the ancient Greeks who are said to have obtained knowledge of it from Egypt.

A value of the Comma of Pythagoras computable to an astonishing nine decimal places appears in the form of an arithmetical fraction preserved in the ancient Greek Pythagorean treatise *Katatomē Kanonos* (Division of the Canon).[33] There we are told that the number 531,441 is greater than twice 262,144. Twice 262,144 equals 524,288, though this number is not actually stated. The ratio is not computed in the text either, but if we carry out the division we obtain the number 1.013643265, namely, the Comma of Pythagoras expressed to nine decimal places. The Greek text is coy in the extreme, giving the information in such an obscure manner that only someone initiated into its significance could be expected to have any idea what was being said. The only explanatory comment earlier in the passage is: 'Six sesquioctave intervals are greater than one duple interval.' One has to be fairly well educated in these matters to have any idea at all of what the author means! André Barbera, the immensely learned modern editor and translator of this text, has apparently not noticed that this passage, which he has translated from no less than three separate versions, in fact presents obliquely the mystery of the Comma of Pythagoras. He does not mention the Comma, has evidently never carried out the necessary multiplication and division to arrive at it, and gives no indication whatever that he is aware of the special significance of the passage.[34] If Barbera, who is probably the world's expert on this text, has no inkling of its true importance, then it is no wonder that no one else until now has either.

The actual author of the strange treatise from which this comes is unknown. Certainly the material in it, according to Barbera, could have been put together in some form in the fifth century BC or at the turn of the fourth century BC,[35] and reworked some centuries later.[36] But some of the *content*, and in particular the sly reference to the Comma of Pythagoras, appear to come from very ancient and unidentified Pythagorean sources which cannot be traced today. There seems to have been an actual, and typically Pythagorean, attempt to *state but conceal* the main mystery. No overt statement of the important number is given, and even its computation requires two successive arithmetical operations, the carrying out of which would not even occur to anyone who didn't know what he was looking for in the first place. The nine-decimal value of the universal constant, the Comma of Pythagoras, is therefore concealed in this ancient text in a kind of code, but one which is entirely unambiguous once it has been recognized as such. The ancient text is so extraordinarily dry, technical and boring, that only expert musical theorists would ever have read it, and of those, only a handful of initiates would have deciphered the purposely concealed reference to one of the greatest discoveries ever made in ancient science and mathematics. The text therefore seems to have been intended, amongst its other, more mundane discussions, to preserve this secret Pythagorean (and originally Egyptian) knowledge whilst hiding it so carefully that its preservation would await discovery by the right kind of person.

I have done a great deal of work on the Comma of Pythagoras over many years, and I found it necessary to give a name to the decimal increment 0.0136 itself; I have named it the Particle of Pythagoras, which I hope will be found acceptable by others – should anyone but myself ever wish to discuss it, of course. I believe the numerical coefficient of this Particle, 136, is related to the 136 degrees of freedom of the electron discussed by the famous physicist, the late Sir Arthur Eddington,[37] and that the number plus one gives the Fine Structure Constant of nuclear physics, which is 137.[38] (The Fine Structure Constant is a universal natural constant greatly beloved by physicists, although hardly anyone else has ever heard of it.) I have discovered relationships between this natural constant and several others such as *phi*, *e*, and *pi*. However, such discussions are too lengthy and distracting for inclusion here. I mention this only so that readers will understand how important the Particle of Pythagoras really is. Essentially, one could say that it expresses the *minute discrepancy between the ideal and the real*. For the pyramid builders to incorporate it as the identical discrepancy just discussed in the Sirius and pyramid correlation should be interpreted as their way of signalling to us: 'This is a symbolic representation of a real cosmic fact.'

Musical theorists will be well aware that the discrepancy 0.0136 necessitates the tuning technique known as 'equal tempering'. I have published an account of the invention of the Equal Temperament system elsewhere.[39] As if to tease us, the builders of the pyramids appear to have left a microscopic discrepancy in the correlation precisely equal to a universal numerical constant. For the Comma of Pythagoras is implicit in the structure of the Universe itself, and is absolute throughout the cosmos.

However, another point should be made about this corrrelation. That is, the ratio of 1.053 is actually the precise value of the sacred fraction $\frac{256}{243}$ mentioned by Macrobius at the turn of the fourth/fifth centuries AD, who describes its use in harmonic theory by people who to him were 'the ancients'.[40] The fraction was also mentioned in antiquity by the mathematical, harmonic, and philosophical writers Theon of Smyrna (second century AD), Gaudentius, Chalcidius (fourth century AD), and Proclus (fifth century AD, for whom see Appendix II of this book, as he seems to have been aware of the Sirius Mystery).[41] One must ask how it is that this precise value of 1.053, which we see is astrophysically the precise ratio between the masses of Sirius B and our Sun, was mentioned so frequently in the works of writers dealing in esoteric astronomical lore in ancient times, one of whom (Macrobius) is prominently identified with the heliocentric theory, and another of whom (Proclus) appears to have been initiated into the Sirius Mystery and specifically mentioned the existence of important but invisible heavenly bodies. Especially in the case of Proclus, who appears to have known of the existence of Sirius B, to have him also mentioning this number, exact to three decimal places, specifying its mass stretches credulity beyond its limits. Surely the coincidences are multiplying to an impossible degree if we are to view this as all being by chance. (As regards him, I recently discovered the following passage in an old book about the pyramids: 'The hieroglyph for Sirius is, oddly enough, the triangular face of a pyramid. Dufeu [a nineteenth-century French author who wrote about the pyramids*] and others suppose that the pyramid may have been dedicated to this venerated star . . . Proclus relates the belief in Alexandria that the pyramid was used for observations of Sirius.'† Unfortunately, this has come to light just before going to press, and so I have not been able to locate the passage in the works of Proclus.)

But there is also this purely cosmological question: why is it that our Sun and the star Sirius B have a mass ratio of 1.053 in any event? For the fraction $256/243$ of which 1.053 is the decimal expression does appear to have a universal harmonical status. So by stumbling upon this coincidence we may have uncovered some hitherto unsuspected astrophysical harmonical value in operation between two neighbouring stars. I don't believe anyone before has found a precise numerical correlation which could extend the notion of a 'harmony of the spheres' beyond our solar system, to link it with a neighbouring one. But this appears to be the case here. Perhaps it has something to do with the inherent nature of white dwarf stars and their dimensions vis à vis normal stars like our Sun, and this ratio would thus occur throughout the Universe frequently. It makes more sense to view the correlation as one which appeals to underlying fundamentals of cosmic structures than to view it as a special case applying only to Sirius B and our Sun. But even so, the correlation is so extraordinary and so precise that it suggests whole avenues of research and offers the hope of absolute numerical expressions recurring in the cosmos where none had been suspected. And by discovering this, we can only be pleased, since it enables us to discern some scaling elements of concealed structure which may be cosmic in scope. I hope cosmologists will not neglect this observation. I believe it demonstrates that the Universe *has more structure than we thought*, and that that structure can be so precisely articulated that it can generate an

---

* Dufeu, A., *Découverte de l'Age et de la Véritable Destination des Quatre Pyramides de Gizeh, Principalement de la Grande Pyramide*, Paris, 1873.
† Bonwick, James, *Pyramid Facts and Fancies*, Kegan Paul, London, 1877, pp. 168–9.

exact value of this kind as a ratio between neighbouring stellar bodies. For Sirius B and our Sun, in terms of the cosmos, are certainly neighbours. And it all comes down to this question: how is it that two stars 8.7 light-years apart can have a mass ratio which is not random but which expresses a universal harmonic value which is precise to three decimal points? It can only be because the astrophysics of stars and their evolutionary development (such as in the formation of a white dwarf) follow certain harmonic laws which we have not yet suspected, much less expressed. And we should not overlook the fact that the universal harmonic fraction concerned is not one which today receives any attention. This in turn indicates that it is *ancient* harmonic theory that should be dusted off and studied for clues as to what is going on. Many of us have believed this for years, even without this evidence.[42] One of my 'hobbies' is trying to get to grips with ancient harmonic theory, which is why I took the fraction seriously enough to work out its decimal expression and notice its importance; needless to say, the decimal value of the fraction does not appear in Macrobius, and only someone actually doing the division and holding up the result beside the mass ratio value of Sirius B and our Sun for comparison would ever have noticed anything at all.

The implication of all of this is that different types of stars express different harmonical values in a surprisingly precise way. But why should stellar evolution *not* have a harmonical nature and structure to it? This will probably be found to be relevant to the concept of the 'stellar mass function' which astrophysicists always speculate about. It may be found, for instance, that the difficulties of star formation in the first place are regularly overcome by some kind of binary-star formation – in our own solar system we could view the planet Jupiter as an incipient brown dwarf star in the making – and in 1983 I published an account of the possible existence of another actual small and invisible star in our own solar system, which was first suggested in 1977 by the radioastronomer E. R. Harrison because of a perturbation which he discovered that our solar system was exercising on six particular pulsars in a small region of the sky.[43] Star formation might thus involve a binary process in far more cases than we think, possibly in all. Binary stars may only be able to coexist according to specific harmonic relations, just as certain musical notes when struck together are consonant when they are in specific proportions such as the musical fifth or fourth.

Fundamental to an improved theory will be a realization that star types are expressions or articulations of harmonical ratios and frequencies and that however much variance they may show, even those variations are always methodical and coherent. Any lack of method and coherence which appears in these cosmic occurrences is thus due not to any lack of structure in the Universe, but is due rather to our own lack of understanding of it. We have learned this lesson in any case by discovering that even chaos is ordered, with the marvellous development of Chaos Theory.

More important is Complexity Theory, which is still in the process of establishing itself. It deals with the sudden onset or loss of long-range order by what scientists call 'phase transitions' and 'symmetry breaking'. I should point out that the mass ratio of Sirius B and our Sun demonstrates that long-range order exists between the two solar systems, extending over a distance of 8.7 light-years, which can only be explained by conceiving of the two solar systems inhabiting the same 'cell' of space. And if that is the case, then we know from Complexity Theory that a strange form of what resembles 'instantaneous communication' subsists in such 'cells' whereby huge macro-regions of space behave as if their elements were not separated by spatial or temporal distance, and the 'cell' engages in what is called 'self-organization'. Such a 'cell' turns into what is called by scientists a 'dissipative structure' which turns disorder into order.

The 1977 Nobel laureate for Chemistry, Professor Ilya Prigogine, whom I have visited in Brussels, has stressed that the onset of complexity in a system can result in the instantaneous extension of long-range order by a magnitude of *ten million or more*, as is easily demonstrated in the onset of so-called Bénard Cells caused by thermal convection in a fluid.[44] This enormous expansion of order is equivalent to one fifth of the population of Britain suddenly and spontaneously adopting the same bodily posture at the same instant while having no direct contact with one another. Imagine ten million people suddenly standing on their heads for no apparent reason. An outside observer might call this uncontrollable turbulence, for a hairdresser doing this would start cutting toenails, drivers would lose control of their vehicles, tennis players would invariably hit the net. . . . It would be chaos. But nevertheless, it would not be denied that ten million people had stood on their heads at the same time due to some mysterious long-range ordering principle which extended across the whole country. This turbulent chaos is in fact a *spontaneous creation of complexity*. For a moment ago the ten million people had absolutely nothing in common about their posture, but now there is no denying that there is an immense complexity in existence, – a connection suddenly exists which did not previously exist – a coherence is established. Ten million simultaneous, complex, intricate and criss-crossing links exist: the ten million people have all suddenly stood on their heads *all just like each other*. This is analogous to what actually happens in a Bénard Cell, where ten million molecules instantaneously align.

The discovery of the significance of the 1.053 mass ratio between Sirius B and our Sun suggests that our solar system and the Sirius system are elements of a larger entity which is a self-organizing open system – what is called in thermodynamics a 'dissipative structure far from thermal equilibrium'. But let us give it an actual name. I propose to call it the Anubis Cell. The Anubis Cell clearly has long-range order extending over at least 8.7 light-years. Since all such structures increase their order and eliminate their disorder, a continuous ordering process must have been in operation inside the Anubis Cell since at least the formation of either our Sun or Sirius B's condensation as a white dwarf, whichever was the later. Long-range order has thus operated between the systems presumably for billions of years. Under such circumstances, both solar systems must have a shared movement in relation to the Galaxy. The two systems must also be in continuous harmonic resonance with one another. It may be presumed that a significant perturbation of one would affect the other, and that this could apply to very high frequency events including 'mental', 'thought' or 'information' events. Membership of the same cosmic cell implies the potential for the modulation of some shared field (of an unknown type, but possibly not unlike the 'quantum potential' proposed by my friend the late David Bohm to solve the Einstein-Podolsky-Rosen Paradox in physics – a subject we cannot go into here!) for purposes of communication between the systems. Let us call it here the 'cell potential'. In other words, electromagnetic amplitude modulation such as radio, for signalling in the traditional manner, may be unnecessary. The strange aspects of long-range order may mean that in some way yet to be discovered by us, instantaneous communication between the systems might be possible, which would seem to overcome the limitations of the speed of light for communication between them.[45] Psychic communication and even nonmaterial interactions of souls might be possible. The ancient Egyptians said that the Sirius system was where people go when they die. The Dogon say the same thing, and perhaps the Sirius system is the actual location of 'the Other World' in more senses than one. Inspiration may even come to humans on Earth from the Sirius system by harmonic resonance articulated by the (still undefined) Anubis Field of the Anubis Cell, and this might be instantaneously 'transmitted' not as a signal but by harmonic resonance response within the continuous Anubis Field subsisting within this cosmic cell.

We have similar phenomena throughout nature: even the lowly sponge has been found to have a physically impossible 'conduction velocity' for stimulus transmission from one end of its body to another. So bizarre were these findings that the three Canadian scientists involved in studying it were forced to suggest that a sponge was like a single giant nerve cell so that: 'the entire conduction system could act as a single neuron'.[46] If a simple sponge can defy time and space at the bottom of the sea, surely the Anubis Cell can do so within the Galaxy. The Anubis Cell may be analogous to a macroscopic 'neuron' seen from the point of view of Galactic scale. And this brings us to another possibility: *the Anubis Cell may be alive*. The vast Ordering Principle may be an Entity. Even if it were not an Entity to start with, it must long ago have spontaneously generated considerable consciousness, if only by weighted connections in parallel distributed processing.[47] And we can be sure that it has had a few billion years to do its thinking.

And if we are to be agreeable and tolerated parasites, perhaps we should give some thought to this problem. It may be that one communicates with the Entity by modulating the Anubis Field with one's thought patterns – a procedure generally known as prayer. However, I do not wish to encourage people to try and receive 'channelled inspiration' from the Anubis Field, because that immediately opens the door to all the world's crazies – every nut in California who thinks he or she is a chosen vessel for privileged communication will start spouting and pontificating in the most offensive manner and pretending to be All-Wise. I think we could adopt an unbreakable rule: *anyone who insists that what he says is true is a phoney.* The only people to whom one should ever listen are those who suggest things tentatively, as *possibly true.* Conscious of the need never to insist upon the truth of anything, I want to stress that everything in this book is hypothetical. I have never insisted on the truth of any of it. If it were all disproved tomorrow, I would be surprised but not dismayed. I believe we should never, never accept anyone's insistence upon the necessary truth of a theory which cannot be proved. To do so is to surrender your integrity as an entity yourself. That is why one should never join a religious sect or cult with a leader who says that he knows the absolute truth. There have been several very sinister cults which have adopted *The Sirius Mystery* as a recommended text, but never with my encouragement. I do not, cannot, and will not ever support such cults. Most of them have sensed that and have left me alone personally. All cults are destructive of human integrity. I feel sorry for people insecure enough to join them; the cult leaders exploit their insecurity by offering them spurious 'leadership'. And I condemn utterly anyone who attempts to make use of my writings or ideas in connection with such activities.

Returning now to our observations of the pyramid measurements, the value of 1.0678 given there may thus also be a double-tease by the builders. For not only does it vary from the precise mass ratio of Sirius B and our Sun by a tiny amount equal to one harmonic natural constant, but it varies from another harmonic natural constant by that same exact amount. One could then say that the builders were only intending to express the latter, ignorant of the astrophysical ratio, but the following additional correlations relating to the Sirius system discourage such a notion.

What about the respective radii of Sirius B and our sun? Are they indicated by the two pyramids? Turning to a different form of measure, the slope angles of the respective pyramids, we find that the sides of the Great Pyramid originally had slope angles of about 51°52′ to the ground, according to Edwards,[48] which is equal to 51.866°, whereas the Pyramid of Khephren had slightly steeper slopes of 52°20′ according to Edwards,[49] which is equal to 52.333°. The slope of the Great Pyramid is thus 0.0089 less than the slope of the Pyramid of Khephren, which yields a value equivalent to the relative radius of Sirius B to that of our sun accurate to

0.0011. The appearance of these two correspondences act as a kind of cross-correlation on each other, since one is accurate to 0.014 and the other is accurate to 0.0011. This significantly reduces the chance of coincidence being at work in these correlations, as there is not only one such correlation but a pair. However, there are two more to come.

I am not insisting that these correlations are intended, but suggesting that they may be, considering the established connections already noted between the pyramids and the Sirius cult.

From the latest information about Sirius C in their 1995 article, Benest and Duvent state that Sirius C cannot be much more than about 0.05 of the mass of our sun (and of Sirius B).[50] Using one of the simple length measures of the kind which seemed to indicate the relative masses of Sirius B and our sun, the mass of Sirius C may be indicated by the height of the missing pyramidion (top point) of the Great Pyramid. For it was 31 feet and the original total height of the pyramid was 481.4 feet, according to Edwards,[51] so that the height of the pyramidion was 0.0643 of the total height of the pyramid, corresponding to within 0.01 of the 0.05 of solar mass suggested for Sirius C in 1995.

This is thus the third Sirius astrophysical measurement correlation accurate to at least 0.01 to be found in the Giza pyramid complex.

What about the third pyramid in the Giza complex, known as the Pyramid of Mycerinus? What significance could it have in this scheme of things? Edwards says that the Pyramid of Mycerinus originally had a height of 218 feet.[52] The height of the Pyramid of Khephren was originally 471 feet, according to Edwards.[53] The ratio of these two heights is 2.160. We note from Benest and Duvent that the latest estimate of the ratio of the masses of our sun and Sirius A is 2.14.[54] The correspondence is thus accurate within 0.02. This is a fourth possible correspondence.

Can it be, therefore, that the pyramid complex at Giza is representing to us, among many other things such as the value of *pi* and the dimensions of our Earth, the relative masses of the three stars of the Sirius system? They all seem to be there, accurate to the second or third decimal. Nor is that likely to exhaust the possibilities. But any further discussions will have to be left for another time.

When the German edition of this book appeared in 1977, I added a lengthy Nachwort (which is not a sausage but an Afterword). In it I indulged in some speculations about the aliens, some of which I feel that I should mention here. I pointed out that interstellar travel cannot be easy at the best of times and any aliens capable of it would probably first have to master the technology of cryogenics (or alternatively some other form of suspended animation), so that they could go into suspended animation for the duration of the interstellar part of the voyage. I then suggested that perhaps the whole thing was so difficult that such expeditions were often one-way trips from which there was no return. And that led me to the important suggestion that perhaps the ancient visitors to our planet never really went home. All the traditions seem agreed that they 'ascended to the heavens' and left the Earth. But there is no guarantee that they went back to Sirius. In fact, anyone capable of mastering the technology of suspended animation for an interstellar voyage would find it a simple matter to re-enter that state and then simply to stay put. So that the Nommos* may very well still be somewhere in the solar system, either asleep or slowly bestirring themselves now that things are getting more interesting down here.

Is there any clue in the traditions as to where any sleeping Nommos might be? There is in the Dogon tradition. For the Dogon differentiate very clearly between the fiery, roaring landing craft which they describe as bringing the Nommos to Earth, and the new star which appeared in the sky while they were here which would seem to be a reference to their larger base parked in orbit. This is called 'the star of the tenth moon'. The Dogon do three drawings of it, showing it in different phases which seem to imply that it could be expanded and contracted as a sphere at will.

When I gave some thought to this I realized the Dogon might be suggesting that the base of the Nommos is parked in the solar system as the tenth moon of one of the outer planets. Neptune doesn't have ten moons, so that was out. It didn't take me long to realize that the tenth main moon of Saturn is anomalous in the solar system, and is the only one which seems to have a smooth surface without craters or other lumps and bumps. Its name is Phoebe. It has a retrograde orbit around Saturn wildly different from all the other Saturnian moons, so that when our space probe photographed the moons of Saturn, Phoebe was the only significant one which was not close enough to give a good photo. (At the time I suggested Phoebe as a possible artificial body it was several years before this space probe, and I was deeply disappointed that the probe was unable to produce much more information about Phoebe.) Phoebe is about 160 kilometres in diameter, but its mass seems still to be unknown, so that we cannot make statements about its composition. It orbits Saturn every 523 days, 15.6 hours. In 1982, following the *Voyager* results, I asked Brad Smith of the University of Arizona Astronomy Department about Phoebe and he said 'as far as we can see it is *perfectly* round'. He also pointed out that it was too large to be a degenerate cometary nucleus. He said it had only 3% reflectivity.

We should not forget that if aquatic amphibious beings are making an interstellar voyage, they will need fresh water in their ship in considerable quantities. In the ancient legends of the Sumerians and Babylonians about the god Enki (Ea), who was the god who warned mankind about the Deluge so that the Ark could be constructed, Enki was said to sleep in a freshwater receptacle or chamber shaped like the Ark, called the Abzu.

---

* The Nommos are discussed in detail later in the book.

Could this be a reference to an amphibian in suspended animation? There is at least one occasion in Sumerian literature (fourth to third millennium BC) where the god Enki is described as behaving like an amphibian: 'Enki, in the swampland, in the swampland, lies stretched out . . .'[55] The context indicates that this is his normal position, since he continues to lie stretched out in the swampland for a considerable time while his vizier goes in and out. There are two things which are puzzling here: why would Enki lie stretched out, and why in a swampland? If he were assumed to be one of the amphibious fish-tailed beings, that could explain both features. As far as I know, no scholar has ever addressed these problems of Enki lying stretched out in a swampland, and it has just been ignored. But as Enki was generally described as inhabiting the Abzu, which is filled with water, if you think about it, someone who actually lives in the water really does need a fishtail to get around properly.

As for the 'moon' Phoebe, perhaps it is unlikely that it is an actual interstellar ship. If it really is artificial, then it may be a thin metal shell (hence 'perfectly round') inflated or manufactured here in the solar system, which is essentially hollow, perhaps even largely empty like a balloon, or containing some water at the centre, suitably insulated and heated to prevent it becoming ice. A largely empty sphere might be needed as insulation for a watery core. Amphibians would not need artificial gravity to the extent that we would, because buoyancy in their natural medium would be familiar to them, and their natural life style would be more akin to a low-weight condition.

If Phoebe is a blown-up sphere, it will have very low density and will have an orbital precession due to solar light pressure. It could act as a 'marker' to draw our attention because of its many anomalies, and it could indicate a more important object of interest nearby or somehow in correspondence, which would be smaller and possibly invisible from Earth by ground-based telescopes. Certainly some oddities were discovered at Saturn, such as leading and trailing co-orbital satellites, plus two satellites which periodically exchange orbits with each other, as well as a satellite about the same size as Phoebe (a 'twin'?) which moves along the leading triangular libration point of the moon Dione. Phoebe was the only one of the eighteen Saturnian satellites unobserved by *Voyager One*, and it may be a long time before that situation improves. I hope it will finally be observed by the Cassini Probe which will reach Saturn in the year 2004. Phoebe is the tenth satellite of Saturn in terms of size. It is also the tenth proper satellite of Saturn, disregarding the eight small inner satellites and considering them as debris associated with the rings. In short, it might well be the 'star of the tenth moon' of Dogon tradition. If so, it might have been put into its strange orbit both to call attention to itself and to keep it away from the other moons of Saturn both for the sake of safety and to ensure that any photographic missions such as *Voyagers One* and *Two* would not crack its secret too soon, since celestial mechanics would prohibit an early probe to the planet and the other moons which could possibly study Phoebe at the same time. And the aliens would know that no one on Earth would send a probe all the way to Saturn to study Phoebe alone, until the rest of the Saturn system had first been studied. Following that logic, it could be that *Voyager One* might have triggered a local alarm by entering the Saturn system, and thus awakening the Nommos. The whole design might have been that simple and elegant. It avoids artificial or questionable criteria and sets as its absolute threshold the entering of the Saturn system by an artificial probe (of whatever kind, since this plan would enable an alarm to be triggered by an extraterrestrial as well as by an Earth probe). The entering of the Saturn system would thus constitute a tripwire which would have activated the Nommos in 1981.

It is interesting that two years after I published my thoughts about Phoebe, the astronomer D. G. Stephenson published a similar theory in the *Quarterly Journal of the Royal Astronomical Society* relating to the outer planet Pluto.[56] He said he thought that Pluto's eccentric orbit might be artificial, rather in the way I have suggested for Phoebe, and have come about as a result of the activity of extraterrestrials visiting our solar system. He also suggested the existence of 'space arks' full of extraterrestrials who never went home but continued to breed generations of descendants as they travelled for hundreds of thousands of years through interstellar space. His notion is that such an 'ark' is parked in our outer solar system and that it may have mined and largely stripped the planet Pluto for raw materials. This is eerily similar to my own suggestion. It puzzled me that Stephenson could make a suggestion similar to my own and not be held up to ridicule for it, whereas for making the same sort of suggestion I underwent years of virulent attacks. But I was delighted by Stephenson's imaginative contribution to the debate, and he makes a lot of sense.

We should not forget that the Dogon say that the Nommos will return, and when they do it will be called The Day of the Fish. The first indication of their return, say the Dogon, will be that a new star will appear in the sky – the 'star of the tenth moon' will have returned. Elements which are at the moment retracted inside this body will then re-emerge. Then the Nommos will land on the Earth again in their Ark – the landing craft which makes a lot of noise and emits fire. From this will emerge 'the mythical ancestors', namely the very same personalities who figure in all the myths. This reinforces the notion that they never died and never left the solar system. After their return, this group of Nommos 'will rule from the waters'. So there will presumably be considerable political implications to their arrival! However, it is most unlikely that they will be hostile to humans, since they will have invested so much of their efforts in trying to help this planet develop civilization thousands of years ago that they won't want to see all their work go to waste. They would doubtless be helpful, therefore, but not a little distressed. As aquatic beings, one doesn't have to be a genius to realize that the present state of the world's oceans will greatly upset them, and they might take drastic steps about that. Can you imagine yourself as a Nommo swimming in the sea, coming up for air only to have a plastic bottle bump against your nose? And number one on their list would probably be the control of oil spills at sea. Think like a Nommo: what would they want most? Clean seas, of course. They are bound to have advanced technologies for cleaning up the seas very promptly. So they will be very popular with environmentalists and will probably form alliances with the world's 'green' parties. Maybe it is the future friends of the Nommos who will be the true 'little green men'.

I speak of all this as if I believed it. Do I believe it? However much verification occurs, the hypothesis of contact with Sirians remains a hypothesis until contact is re-established, and then we don't need to wonder about it anymore because it will have become obvious. My personal opinion is that it is probably true. I don't say that it is definitely true. But the hypothesis gets more convincing all the time, and there are fewer nervous or blinkered people nowadays who wish to dismiss all extraterrestrial contact possibilities as impossible in principle. Of course I am aware of the many articles written by astronomers in such journals as that of the Royal Astronomical Society (of which, after all, I am a Fellow, so I receive it in the post automatically) suggesting that as there seem to be no extraterrestrials around or in contact, maybe we are alone in the Universe after all. But I don't believe any of that.

In the past few years we have learned of increasing numbers of planets discovered by astronomers in other solar systems. Those astronomers who by nature of their psychological dispositions are determined to be sceptical used to take refuge in saying: 'Other solar systems don't have planets.' How well I remember that! Most sensible people always thought that such sentiments were crackpot, and now it has been proved. So then the argument shifted to: 'There may be planets but they don't have any life.' That too has been called into question by what we know already about Mars. So once again the argument can be expected to shift: 'There may be life, but it can't be intelligent.' And so on. People who are determined to have negative thoughts can always find new ones.

I have mentioned the planet Mars in passing. Do I believe that there was intelligent life on Mars at one time? I would not be surprised at a Martian connection with the Sirius Mystery, as I have thought for some years. I have no idea whether the 'Face On Mars' in the region of Cydonia is really a face or not, but it looks pretty convincing, doesn't it? And I think that a lot of other people must think so too. I thought NASA was supposed to be broke, and now suddenly they are sending ten Mars missions in ten years, and the Russians are joining in. What's going on here? The announcements of the life forms in Martian meteorites seemed pretty orchestrated to me. The first announcements were that evidence of bacteria had been found. This then escalated to worms when nobody shot himself. Then we heard of ice on the far side of the Moon, of water on Europa (one of Jupiter's moons), of all kinds of possibilities of simple life forms on Mars in the distant past, and now of huge floods having swept that planet. More recently still, we are told Mars once had an ocean larger than the Pacific. Still no riots in the streets! These announcements seem to be released as if a doctor were taking the patient's temperature to see if the dose can be increased. By the time this book is in print, doubtless other levels in an escalating series of revelations will have been reached. Who is to say that the *Mars Orbiter* really broke down after all? Perhaps it sent back incontrovertible evidence to the official folk who are in charge of such information, and they pretended that the probe malfunctioned to buy time while they formulated a policy of slow leaks, carefully judged in case of public hysteria. But by now those officials will have realized that a lot of (Martian flood?) water has passed under the bridge since those heady days of 1938 when Orson Welles's radio broadcast about the Martians landing sent a nation into panic and precipitated suicides. The public is now well and truly conditioned: bring on the extraterrestrials, please!

The danger now would seem to be that the public is so used to a thrill every thirty seconds on television that they would eventually become *bored* by real extraterrestrials, as they will probably disappoint our fantasy expectations. And, of course, they may be, as the Babylonians said, physically repulsive, though unlike the Babylonians many people today are used to seeing dolphins and whales close up, and natural history films have made the public very familiar with strange-looking creatures. The only people likely to get really upset about extraterrestrial contact will probably be the religious fanatics, who are in any case always upset about something. The very people who can without the slightest qualm believe in blood oozing out of holy statues are going to be the last to accept that religious beliefs can extend beyond this planet, and they will take great exception to the religious centre of the Universe shifting in a kind of theological Copernican upheaval. On the other hand, some of us may find this concept rather comforting and exciting and draw strength from it.

So let us move on now to a much-expanded version of *The Sirius Mystery*, which contains a great deal of new information. There have never been sufficient resources to undertake much of the research that I would have liked. I hope this present version of the book proves useful to those who are interested in these matters, which may affect us all sooner than we think.

Robert Temple
August, 1997

Notes

1. There were actually three editions of *The Sirius Mystery* in 1976, with the second and third editions containing further information than the first.

2. Benest, Daniel, and Duvent, J. L., 'Is Sirius a Triple Star?', *Astronomy and Astrophysics*, Vol. 299, 1995, pp. 621–8. The article was received 11 October 1994 and accepted 8 November 1994.

3. Temple, Robert K. G., 'A Response to an Appeal from W. H. McCrea Concerning Sirius', *The Observatory*, Vol. 95, No. 52, 1975.

4. Smith, R. C., 'The Book of Job, and Stellar Dynamics', *The Observatory* Centenary Celebration Issue, Vol. 97, No. 1020, October 1977, containing a pink joke section, p. 15P (P for pink).

5. Lessing, Doris, *Shikasta*, Jonathan Cape, London, 1979.

6. Lessing, Doris, *The Sirian Experiments*, Jonathan Cape, London, 1981.

7. West, John Anthony, 'Metaphysics by Design: Harmony and Proportion in Ancient Egypt', *Second Look*, Vol. I, No. 8, June 1979, pp. 2–5.

8. West, John Anthony, *Serpent in the Sky: The High Wisdom of Ancient Egypt*, Wildwood House, London, 1979.

9. Ibid., pp. 109–10.

10. Ibid., pp. 229–30.

11. Ibid., p. 107.

12. Schwaller de Lubicz, R. A., *Sacred Science: The King of Pharaonic Theocracy*, translated by André and Goldian Vanden Broeck, Inner Traditions International, Rochester, Vermont, USA, 1982, p. 96.

13. West, *Serpent in the Sky*, op. cit., p. 202.

14. Ibid.

15. Ibid., p. 202.

16. Ibid.

17. Herodotus, translated by A. D. Godley, Loeb Classical Library, Harvard University Press, 4 vols, 1960.

18. Ibid., Book II, 124; pp. 425–7.

19. Ibid., Book II, 127; pp. 429–31.

20. Ibid., Book II, 147; p. 455.

21. Ibid., Book II, 148–9; pp. 455–9.

22. Ibid., Book II, 97; p. 385.

23. Ibid., p. 455, note 1.

24. Ibid., Book II, 127; p. 431.

25. Harrell, James M., 'The Sphinx Controversy: Another Look at the Geological Evidence', *KMT*, Vol. 5, No. 2, Summer, 1994, p. 72.

26. Bauval, Robert, and Gilbert, Adrian, *The Orion Mystery*, Heinemann, London, 1994. Although the idea that the three pyramids represent the three stars of Orion's Belt couldn't be more convenient to me, I have to mention that there is an alternative theory about the layout of the three pyramids in a manuscript that was sent to me in 1978: Rocky McCollum, Gerald J. Fraccaro, and Elmer D. Robinson – none of whom I know or have ever heard of in any other connection – wrote a treatise entitled *The Giza Pyramids: The Final Decoding*, dated 1978, and sent a typescript of it to me (any accompanying letter has been misplaced). I have never had time to read it, but I have noticed by scanning through it when going through my old Sirius files in preparation for this new edition, that on p. 31, in Figure 16, a most extraordinary diagram appears, which shows the Fibonacci spiral or 'Golden Spiral' (connected with the Golden Section) superimposed upon part of the Giza Plateau in such a way that the apexes of the three pyramids lie along that curve. I feel that I should mention this, although I have had no opportunity to study the matter owing to shortage of time. I have no idea whether the three authors ever published their work, and I only know from an introductory page that they are American because it is dated from Lincoln, Nebraska. It may well be that these authors did not actually send me their manuscript, but that I was

given it by my friend the Argentine physicist, Professor Jose Alvarez Lopez. I had wished to join him in some pyramid investigations in the late 1970s, but this never proved possible. I should also add that the builders of the pyramids were so clever that they could do more than one thing simultaneously, and it is quite possible that the three pyramids are laid out on a logarithmic Fibonacci spiral *and* represent the three stars of Orion's belt. The two are not necessarily mutually exclusive. In fact, this is just the sort of intellectual game which the pyramid builders seem to have taken such delight in. The best way to understand the mentality of the pyramid builders is to compare them to a computer genius, whose main joy in life is to construct fantastically elaborate programmes and to leave multi-layered clues, complete with many intellectual jokes.

27. Ibid., pp. 131–2, 172–4, and diagram on p. 174.
28. Allen, C. W. *Astrophysical Quantities*, 3rd edition, Athlone Press, London, 1973, p. 228.
29. Lang, Kenneth R., *Astrophysical Data: Planets and Stars*, Springer-Verlag, New York et al., 1992, p. 542.
30. Ibid.
31. Edwards, I. E. S., *The Pyramids of Egypt*, revised edition, Viking, London, 1986, p. 143.
32. Ibid., pp. 105–6.
33. Barbera, André, *The Euclidean Division of the Canon: Greek and Latin Sources*, University of Nebraska Press, USA, 1991, Greek text on pp. 146 and 148, English translation on pp. 147 and 149. The text is repeated in the later work by the third century AD Neoplatonist Porphyry (232–301 AD), in his *Commentary on Ptolemy's Harmonics 1.5*; this Greek text is found on pp. 214 and 216, with English translation on pp. 215 and 217. The Latin translation of the same passage by Boethius (480–524 AD) in his *De Institutione Musica*, 4. 1–2, is on p. 256 and the English translation on p. 257. The Greek text of the original work has further comments on pp. 164, 166, 168 and 170, translated into English on pp. 165, 167, 169 and 171, as follows: 'The diapason is less than six tones. For the diapason was proved to be duple, and the tone sesquioctave. Six sesquioctave intervals are greater than a duple interval; therefore, the diapason is less than six tones. . . . The tone will not be divided into two equal tones nor into more. . . . Therefore, the tone will not be divided into equal intervals.'
34. He merely mentions on p. 24 certain matters relating to the issue from the point of view of the proposition found in the text.
35. Ibid., p. 23.
36. Ibid., p. 28.
37. Eddington, Sir Arthur, *New Pathways in Science: Messenger Lectures 1934*, Cambridge University Press, 1935, pp. 237, 242.
38. Ibid., pp. 232, 243.
39. Temple, Robert K. G., *The Genius of China* [also: *China: Land of Discovery and Invention*], London and New York, 1986, pp. 209–13.
40. Macrobius, *Commentary on the Dream of Scipio*, Book II, Chapter 1, Section 22; translated by William Harris Stahl, Columbia University Press, New York, 1952, p. 189.
41. Ibid, footnote 30 gives those references.
42. Thinking along these lines can sometimes bring useful results. For instance, in 1971 or 1972 I noticed that the Earth's diameter exceeded that of the planet Venus by 0.0294 and exceeded that of the planet Mercury by 2.94. The same number thus recurs, differing only by a scaling factor of 100. This cannot be a coincidence. It indicates to me that the Earth, Venus, and Mercury – the three inner planets – form what I call the Inner Limb of the Sun. I do not look upon them as bits of rock hurtling round in space, I look upon them as a limb of the Sun. They are united by a specific numerical coefficient, so that their sizes are not arbitrary in their relation to one another. Just as in astronomy the distance of the Earth from the Sun is called an Astronomical Unit (AU), which is simply a computational convenience for us, here we see an actual occurrence of the size of the Earth as another kind of unit – a real unit this time – a unit of reference which acts as a kind of fundamental note in relation to which its two inner planets have formed in sizes which are in demonstrable

resonance to it. For, by the operation of a specific numerical coefficient (the innate significance of which requires further investigation), Venus and Mercury have taken on diameters bearing a fixed relationship to the Earth and to each other. This has considerable implications for any theory of planetary formation. But all of this is invisible unless you have the key – *the actual number*. As soon as one knows the number 294, and applies it, one sees the relationships between the three bodies. Otherwise they appear to be random in their size. Of course, I didn't know the number 294, I had to find it by intuitive investigation. And there are certainly other such numbers operative elsewhere in the solar system, and I expect they are all related to one another as well. Such discoveries elucidate concealed structure where none was apparent.

43. Temple, Robert K. G., *Strange Things*, Sphere Books, London, 1983, section entitled 'Are There Two Suns in Our Solar System?', pp. 81–33. The suggestions made by several astronomers including Harrison, E. L. Wright of MIT, H. F. Heinrichs, R. F. A. Staller, Serge Pineault, and Daniel Wilkins, combine to say that this star if it exists – which most of them seem to think it does – must have at least one third of the mass of our Sun but cannot be a normal uncompacted star, so therefore would be an almost undetectable neutron star or mini-black hole at a possible distance of one light-year from our Sun. This subject arose because E. R. Harrison detected evidence that the centre of gravity of our solar system is being shifted towards a particular region of the sky, in the direction of the galactic centre, and affecting the behaviour of six pulsars in that small region of sky by a perturbation. The known mass of our solar system being insufficient to account for this perturbation, the existence of a so far undetected component was suggested to account for it. We may thus live in a binary star system without being aware of it.

44. See for instance p. 13 of Prigogine, Ilya, and Nicolis, Gregoire, *Exploring Complexity*, W. H. Freeman, New York, 1989. I tried to get commissioned to write about these subjects from about 1977, but without success.

45. This is analogous to what has been found at the microscopic scale in the Aspect Experiment – named after the French physicist Alain Aspect – but this is another very complicated subject in physics which we cannot go into here. I am sorry to plunge so precipitously into all of this physics, in a book which deals with a wholly different subject, but it unexpectedly turned out to be relevant. It is however simply impossible to give full explanations of these things here, for which I offer many apologies.

46. Temple, Robert, *Strange Things*, op cit., p. 54.

47. Obviously I cannot in the space available here describe parallel distributed processing, but I have published a hundred pages on the subject in the last chapter of my book *Open to Suggestion*, Aquarian Press, Wellingborough, UK, 1989.

48. Edwards, op. cit., pp. 105–6.

49. Ibid., p. 143.

50. Benest and Duvent, op. cit., p. 625.

51. Edwards, op. cit., pp. 105–6.

52. Ibid., p. 152.

53. Ibid., p. 143.

54. Benest and Duvent, op. cit., p. 625.

55. Kramer, Samuel Noah, *Sumerian Mythology*, Harper Torchbooks, New York, 1961, p. 57.

56. Reported in the London *Daily Telegraph*, December 24, 1979. The original article is Stephenson, D. G., 'Extraterrestrial Cultures within the Solar System', *Quarterly Journal of the Royal Astronomical Society*, Vol. 20, No. 4, December, 1979, pp. 422–8.

What is the Mystery?

The question which this book poses is: Has Earth in the past been visited by intelligent beings from the region of the star Sirius?

This entire matter of the Sirius mystery first came to my attention around 1965. I was working on some philosophical and scientific problems with Arthur M. Young of Philadelphia, the inventor of the Bell Helicopter and author of many books, most of which were published after *The Sirius Mystery* first appeared (which was in January 1976). In 1972 Arthur was co-editor of and contributor to the fascinating book *Consciousness and Reality*.[1] Arthur's work was so slow to catch on that his other works did not appear until 1976, some months after mine. After many changes of title he decided to call his main work *The Reflexive Universe*.[2] It had once been called, in manuscript, *Quantum Lost, Quantum Regained*, and before that was called *The Universe as Process*. I had worked on it with him under those titles for five years (1962–1966, and from time to time for years after that) and had filled in two or three portions of his 'grid' diagram with him; strangely, he didn't acknowledge my involvement with his central work. Instead, he acknowledged me at the front of his other book of 1976, *The Geometry of Meaning*, with which I had actually been less associated.[3] Arthur's work on the Bell Helicopter is recorded in his book *The Bell Notes*.[4] When I was a very small child aged three or four there was an incident regarding myself and a helicopter with a kind of glass bubble cockpit on the Hudson River in New York State, and I have always thought it must have been Arthur paying me an early visit on one of his test flights. I was sixteen when I officially met him in 1961, in my first year as an undergraduate student at the University of Pennsylvania.

Arthur single-handedly taught me more science concurrently with my official university studies from 1961–7 than an entire university faculty might have done. For while I was ploughing my way through the Sanskrit language and other onerous subjects at the official university level, I imbibed a considerable scientific education from Arthur in company with a few friends from the university, with whom I participated for years in a series of extremely stimulating seminars and research projects supervised by Arthur Young and occasionally linked to a philanthropic foundation which he had established, entitled the Foundation for the Study of Consciousness.

During 1966 I became the Acting Secretary for this embryonic Foundation, one of its directors was the delightful archaeologist Fro Rainey, who was later to marry my distant cousin Marina; but at that time he hadn't met her yet. Arthur was furious with me for moving to England in October 1966, and for years he kept hoping I would return to live in America again and resume my work with him. He took it as a personal rebuff, although it was of course not intended as anything of the kind. We continued to have massive correspondence, exchanging philosophical ideas, and for a while planning things together. Then he moved to California where he spent half of every year and made new friends and contacts, and although our friendship always remained intact, our contacts became intermittent. It was hard for him when I told him I had had a book accepted for publication, as he had been unable to achieve this yet for himself. I didn't manage to visit Arthur's Institute for the Study of Consciousness in Berkeley until after he had died. But we saw each other over the years in England and Pennsylvania whenever we could, and the last time I stayed with him was about a year before he died, when he gave me a substantial portion of his enormous library, saying he wouldn't be needing it anymore. My last phone conversation with him was shortly before he died, when he was in too much pain to talk for more than a few sentences. He has many disciples now, and I hope his profound philosophical work will continue to grow and spread as it deserves to do. I don't know many of the new people, and many of the old people whom I did know have died (because I was unusually young when I knew them). But the lead has been taken by Chris Paine, grandson of Arthur's wife Ruth by her previous husband, and the work of the Foundation and Institute are fortunately continuing.

Arthur Young had a particular passion for reading about mythologies from all over the world, including those of obscure tribes. One day he showed me a book entitled *African Worlds*, which contained several chapters, each dealing with a different tribe, with its views of life and its customs and mythology. There was a chapter about the Dogon translated into English from the French of Marcel Griaule and Germaine Dieterlen, the eminent anthropologists.[5]

Arthur pointed out to me a passage he had just read in this chapter, in which these anthropologists were describing the cosmological theories of the Dogon. I shall quote the paragraph which I read then, which first brought to my attention this whole extraordinary question, so that the reader will begin this subject just as I did, with this brief reference:

'The starting-point of creation is the star which revolves round Sirius and is actually named the "*Digitaria* star"; it is regarded by the Dogon as the smallest and heaviest of all the stars; it contains the germs of all things. Its movement on its own axis and around Sirius upholds all creation in space. We shall see that its orbit determines the calendar.'

That was all. There was no mention by the anthropologists of the actual existence of such a star which revolves around Sirius. Now Arthur Young and I both knew of the existence of the white dwarf star Sirius B which actually does orbit around Sirius. We knew that it was 'the smallest and heaviest' type of star then known. (Neutron stars and 'black holes' were not much discussed and pulsars had not yet even been discovered.) We both naturally agreed that this was a most curious allusion from a supposedly primitive tribe. How could it be explained? I had to let the matter drop, due to other activities and concerns at that time.

Approximately two years later in London, I suddenly was struck by the irresistible urge to investigate this question. I was prompted to do so by reading the rousing futuristic essays of Arthur C. Clarke, whom I had come to know by then. By this time I could not even remember the name of the African tribe, so I wrote to Arthur Young for it. He replied and kindly sent me a photostat of the entire chapter I had seen in *African Worlds*. So, armed with the knowledge that it was a tribe called the Dogon that I was after, I bravely made my way to the Royal Anthropological Institute to see what I could find out about this peculiar tribe.

The librarian went over the catalogue listings with me and I ran into a problem: everything was in French, and I did not know French. However, I persevered and found an article listed which included the word 'Sirius' in its title. That looked promising (for nothing else did). I asked for a photostat. When I picked this up a week or two later (in early November 1967) I was unable to make any sense of it, of course. So I eventually found someone to translate it for me in return for a fee. Finally I was presented with the material in English – and it was quite as rewarding as I could have wished.[6] For this article dealt exclusively with the most secret of all the traditions of the Dogon which, after years of living with them, the anthropologists Griaule and Dieterlen had managed to extract from four of their head priests,[7] after a special priestly conference among the tribe and a 'policy decision' to make their secrets known to Marcel Griaule, the first outsider in their history to inspire their confidence.

The most secret traditions of the Dogon all concern the star which the Dogon call after the tiniest seed known to them (see Figure 1), the botanical name for which is *Digitaria*, and which is thus used in the article as the name of the star instead of the actual Dogon name, *põ*.

However, even in this article which deals exclusively with this subject, Griaule and Dieterlen only mention the actual existence of a star which really exists and does what the Dogon say Digitaria does, in a passing footnote and in this brief remark: 'The question has not been solved, nor even asked, of how men with no instruments at their disposal could know the movements and certain characteristics of stars which are scarcely visible.' But even in saying this, the anthropologists were indicating their own lack of astronomical expertise, for the star, Sirius B which revolves around Sirius, is by no means 'scarcely visible'. It is *totally invisible* and was only discovered in the last century with the use of the telescope. As

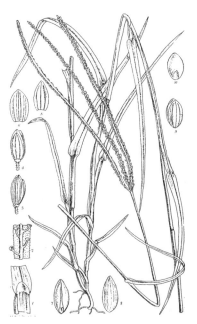

Figure 1. The plant whose botanical Latin name is *Digitaria exilis*. The Dogon call it *fonio*. It is a grass whose seeds are used for food, but it is very localized and grows only in West Africa; it does not occur at all in East Africa. Its seed is so incredibly tiny that one botanist has called it: 'This Lilliputian grain, which is described by Mr Clarke as being about the size of mignonette-seed . . .[8] However, despite the minute size of the grain, vast quantities of it are produced for food in the region. In 1976, a botanist reported that 721,000 acres of *fonio* were being harvested annually in West Africa in the region 'from Senegal to Lake Chad', and that: 'The fonios were extensively harvested as wild cereals before pearl millet was domesticated. They are still frequently grown as encouraged weeds in the fields of other crops, and provide a harvest long before pearl millet or sorghum matures . . . providing food to over three million people during the most difficult months of the year.'[9] *Fonio* is also called in the region 'hungry rice'. The Dutch botanist Henrard speaks highly of its flavour: 'It gives a delicious grain for food and Mr [Robert] Clarke* is of opinion that if the fundi grain [another name for *fonio* by other tribes than the Dogon] were raised for exportation to Europe, it might prove a valuable addition to the list of light farinaceous articles of food in use among the delicate or convalescent.'[10] H. M. Burkill says of the plant: 'Its grain is an extremely important cereal, staple of many tribes. Its origin is lost in antiquity. . . . To the Dogon it is the source of everything in the world. . . . The grain has an agreeable taste and is considered a delicacy. It is normally ground to a flour and eaten as sauce, porridge, or pap, seasoned in various ways. It is easily digested and is fed to babies. . . . The grain is often fermented to produce a beer . . .'[11]

The reason why *Digitaria exilis* is important for the Sirius Mystery is that its tiny seed, probably the world's smallest grain seed, has been chosen by the Dogon as symbolic of the star Sirius B, which being a white dwarf star is the smallest type of star that exists, due to the fact that its matter is 'superdense' – as described in the main text. When in the text we refer to the Digitaria Star of the Dogon, we are referring to Sirius B in the way that they speak of it, as the star symbolized by the tiniest seed known to them. The reason why the Dogon believe that the Digitaria seed is the source of everything in the world is that they believe that all forms of matter were emitted by Sirius B – a possible survival of a concept that matter in the Universe is ejected by exploding supernovae which leave white dwarfs like Sirius B behind as the remnant of the original star

* Mentioned above, the botanist who first recognized this plant in 1842.

Arthur Clarke put it to me in a letter of 17 July 1968, after he had suggested he would check the facts: 'By the way, Sirius B is about magnitude 8 – quite invisible even if Sirius A didn't completely obliterate it.' Only in 1970 was a photograph of Sirius B successfully taken by Irving Lindenblad of the US Naval Observatory; this photograph is reproduced in Plate 1.

In the article which I had obtained from the Royal Anthropological Institute, Griaule and Dieterlen recorded that the Dogon said the star Digitaria revolved around Sirius every fifty years. It didn't take me long to research Sirius B and discover that its orbital period around Sirius was indeed fifty years. I now knew that I was really on to something. And from that moment I have been immersed in trying to get to the bottom of the mystery.

I have before me a letter from Arthur Young dated 26 March 1968, responding to my initial article called 'The Sirius Question'. He says: 'And don't get me into it. I heard about it from one Harry Smith who[m] you met. So the credit should go to him.' I had indeed met Harry Smith at Arthur's house in Philadelphia more than once. Arthur and I often argued about him: I did not warm to him but Arthur liked him and said that he was useful. It was Harry Smith who had given to Arthur a typescript of a translation of Griaule and Dieterlen's book about the Dogon, *Le Renard Pâle* ('The Pale Fox'), by someone named Mary Beach (of whom I have never otherwise heard; this is not the translation which was eventually published: see Bibliography). It was as a result of this that Arthur was able to send it to me, as I could not read the French original. This very copy was then stolen from me by an American associated with the CIA by means of an elaborate ruse and confidence trick of breathtaking audacity: he took me to lunch in London and begged me to loan him the manuscript overnight so that he could photocopy it, and he would give it back to me first thing in the morning. But in the morning I didn't hear from him, so I went to the rented flat where he had been staying. I found the door wide open and the flat entirely empty. I asked a neighbour what had happened, and was told that the man had moved out, and had flown to California at the crack of dawn. I never heard from him again; he had clearly attempted to sabotage my work. I knew he was friendly with a well-known author who lived in America; I phoned that man and complained about the theft and asked if he could help me retrieve the manuscript. He virulently insulted me with a savage tongue-lashing and told me the theft was justified. I was not astonished when I later learned that he had once been employed by the American security services as well. I began to see who some of my enemies were! But this was in the early 1970s. To return to the chronological account:

Arthur C. Clarke was extremely helpful during the next few months. He wrote from Sri Lanka and was fairly often in London, so he and I also discussed at great length many of the mysterious facts from around the world which have since been given such public prominence by the Swiss-German author Erich von Däniken in his best-selling book *Chariots of the Gods* and its sequels. At first I found myself preparing a book on all these exciting mysteries. (No one in the English-speaking world had at that time heard of von Däniken.)[12] Arthur Clarke introduced me to one interesting professor after another – each with a pet mystery all his own. Derek Price, Avalon Professor of the History of Science at Yale University, had discovered the true nature of the now famous mechanical computer of approximately 100 BC found in the Anti-Kythera shipwreck at the turn of the century and unappreciated until it was dropped on the floor in Athens, cracked open and they saw what it was. (See Bibliography under Price.) He also had found traces of Babylonian mathematics in New Guinea and talked a lot about 'the Raffles shipwreck'.

Then there was Dr Alan McKay, a crystallographer of Birkbeck College at the University of London, who was interested in the Phaistos Disc of Crete, in a mysterious metal alloy found in a Chinese tomb, and in the wilder stretches of the Oxus River. I found that, with people like this around every corner, I was rapidly becoming distracted from my true quest by so many glittering riddles.

I therefore abandoned all those mysteries and determined to concentrate in depth on cracking the one really hard and concrete puzzle that I had been initially confronted with: how did the Dogon know such extraordinary things?

It is important that this strange material be placed before the public at large. Since learning was freed from the tyranny of the few and opened to the general public, through first the invention of printing and now the modern communications media and the mass proliferation of books and periodicals, then the 'paperback revolution' and now the Internet revolution which is even more explosive, any idea can go forth and plant the necessary seeds in intellects around the world without the mediation of any panel of approval or the filtering of a climate of opinion based on the currently accepted views of a set of obsolescent individual minds.

How difficult it is to keep in mind that this was not always the case. No wonder, then, that before such things were possible, there were secret traditions of priests which were handed down orally for centuries in unbroken chains and carefully guarded lest some censorship overtake them and the message be lost. In the modern age, for the first time secret traditions can be revealed without the danger that they will be extinguished in the process. Can it be that the Dogon came to realize something of this when, through some powerful instinct and after mutual consultations among the highest priests, they decided to take the unprecedented step of making public their highest mysteries? They knew they could trust the French anthropologists, and when Marcel Griaule died in 1956, approximately a quarter of a million tribesmen massed for his funeral in Mali, in tribute to a man whom they revered as a great sage

– equivalent to one of their own high priests. Such reverence must indicate an extraordinary man in whom the Dogon could believe implicitly. There is no question but that we are indebted to Marcel Griaule's personal qualities for laying open to us the sacred Dogon traditions. I have now been able to trace these back to ancient Egypt, and they seem to reveal a contact in the distant past between our planet Earth and an advanced race of intelligent beings from another planetary system several light-years away in space. If there is another answer to the Sirius mystery, it may be even more surprising rather than less so. It certainly will not be trivial.

It should not surprise us that there must be other civilizations in our galaxy and throughout the entire universe. Even if the explanation of the Sirius mystery is found to be something entirely different in the years to come, we should bear in mind that the Sirius mystery will have served to help us speculate along proper and necessary lines, and opened our innately lazy minds that much further to the important question of extraterrestrial civilizations which must certainly exist.

At the moment, we are all like fish in a bowl, with only the occasional leap out of the water when our astronauts go aloft. The public long ago became bored with space exploration before it had even really begun properly. We found that Congressmen needed continual injections of 'space rescues' and 'satellite gaps' in their tired bloodstreams, like a heroin fix, in order to stimulate them in their horrible state of lethargy to vote funds for the space programmes which so many of them consider a bore and lacking in excitement and suspense.

The psychological impact of photographs of the Earth from space, a giant and beautiful orb resting on nothing, pearled with clouds and sparkling with sea, has begun to send resonances down the long and sleepy corridors of our largely drugged psyches. Mankind is imperceptibly struggling to the new and undeniable realization that we are all in this game together. We are all perched on a globe suspended in what appears to be emptiness, we are made up of atoms which are mostly themselves emptiness, and above all, we are the only really intelligent creatures directly known to us. In short, we are alone with each other, with all the fratricidal implications of such a tense situation. Now the Mars explorations promise to bring us to our senses and reawaken our sense of awe and wonder regarding space – and not a minute too soon. At last we are exploring another planet, albeit by remote control, and the future can begin.

But at the same time as we are all slowly realizing these things, the inevitable conclusion which follows upon all this is beginning to make some headway with us as well. It has begun to occur to more than a handful of exceptional people (exceptionally intelligent or exceptionally insane) that if we are sitting here on this planet fighting among ourselves for lack of any better distraction, then perhaps there are lots of planets all over the universe where intelligent beings are either sitting and stewing in their own juice as we are, or where those beings have broken out of the shell and established contact with other intelligent beings on other planets. And if this is really going on all over the universe, then perhaps it will not be all that long before we find ourselves linked up with our fellows elsewhere – creatures living beside another star out in that vast emptiness which spawns planets, suns and minds.

For years I have thought that those organizations which spend millions of dollars on 'peace' and attempts to find out what is wrong with human nature that it should indulge in so perverse a thing as conflict, would be better advised to donate their entire treasuries to the space programmes, and to astronomical research. Instead of seminars for 'peace research' we should build more telescopes. The answer to the question: 'Is mankind perverse?' will be known when we can compare ourselves with other intelligent species and evaluate ourselves according to some scale other than one which we fabricate out of the air. At the moment we are shadow-boxing, chasing phantoms. . . . The answers lie out there somewhere with other stars and other races of beings. We can only compound our neuroses by becoming even more introspective and narcissistic. We must look outward. At the same time, of course, we must look back relentlessly into our own past. To go forward with no conception of where we have been makes no sense whatsoever. There is also the probability that we may discover mysteries about our own origins. For instance, one result of my research, which began harmlessly with an African tribe, has been to demonstrate the possibility that civilization as we know it was an importation from another star in the first place. The linked cultures of Egypt and Sumer in the Mediterranean area simply came out of nowhere. That is not to say that there were no people alive before that. We know there were lots of people, but we have found no traces of high civilization. And people and civilization are vastly different things. Take for instance these words by the late Professor W. B. Emery from his book *Archaic Egypt*:

At a period approximately 3,400 years before Christ, a great change took place in Egypt, and the country passed rapidly from a state of advanced neolithic culture with a complex tribal character to two well-organized monarchies, one comprising the Delta area and the other the Nile valley proper. At the same time the art of writing appears, monumental architecture and the arts and crafts developed to an astonishing degree, and all the evidence points to the existence of a well-organized and even luxurious civilization. All this was achieved within a comparatively short period of time, for there appears to be little or no background to these fundamental developments in writing and architecture.

Now, whether or not one supposes that there was an invasion of advanced people into Egypt who brought their culture with them, the fact remains that when we get back to that period of history we are faced with so many imponderables that we can hardly say anything for certain. What we do know is that primitive people suddenly found themselves living in thriving and opulent civilizations and it all happened rather abruptly. In the light of the evidence connected with the Sirius question, as well as other evidence which has either been dealt with by other authors or remains to be tackled in the future, it must be entertained as a serious possibility that civilization on this planet owes something to a visit by advanced extraterrestrial beings. It is not necessary to postulate flying saucers, or even gods in space suits. My own feeling is that this matter has not been dealt with in a sophisticated enough manner so far. But rather than enter into mere speculation as to what extraterrestrials landed in, etc., let us move on to the evidence that at least indicates that they might have been here. In Part Three we shall consider some details and clues that the extraterrestrial visitors from Sirius, whom I postulate, may have been amphibious creatures with the need to live in a watery environment. But all this gets into the speculative areas which are such treacherous ground. It has always been my policy, as well as my temperamental inclination, to stick to solid facts. We shall see as we proceed just how solid the facts are, and that is a strange enough tale for the moment. As usual, truth has proved itself stranger than fiction. The reader is advised to read Part Three of this book for some 'wild speculation'.

The book which now follows poses a question. It does not present, but merely suggests, an answer. In Part One the question is posed in its original form, and in Part Two it is rephrased. But nowhere is it answered with any certainty. The best questions are the ones which often remain unanswered for a long time and lead us down new avenues of thought and experience. Who knows where the Sirius mystery will lead us in the end? But let us follow it for a while. At the very least it will be an adventure. . . .

Notes

1. Muses, Charles, and Young, Arthur M., eds., *Consciousness and Reality*, Outerbridge & Lazard, New York, 1972. Arthur inscribed this to me: 'To Bob, Who went through the door'.
2. Young, Arthur M., *The Reflexive Universe: Evolution of Consciousness*, Delacorte Press and Robert Briggs Associates, San Francisco, 1976. Arthur inscribed this book to my (future) wife and myself 'with fond memories of past discussions and anticipation of more'.
3. Young, Arthur M., *The Geometry of Meaning*, Delacorte Press and Robert Briggs Associates, San Francisco, 1976. Arthur inscribed this one: 'To Bob Temple Whom, I believe, must be one of these beings from Outer Space –'
4. Young, Arthur M., *The Bell Notes: A Journey from Physics to Metaphysics*, Robert Briggs Associates, Mill Valley, California, 1979.
5. *African Worlds*, ed. Daryll Forde, Oxford University Press, 1954, pp. 83–110. I wish to point out to the reader that in the article in *African Worlds*, the French word *arche* is mistranslated 'arch' and should instead be rendered 'ark'.
6. The translation was, it turned out, extremely inept. The article has been entirely retranslated by a professional translator for inclusion in this book. It has also been vetted by Mme Germaine Dieterlen herself, who has kindly given permission for the publication in English of the entire article written by herself and Marcel Griaule, as Appendix I.

7. Photographs of these four tribal priests are reproduced in the colour plates. I thought it particularly important that these original native informants be seen by the reader. Apart from the fact that their faces are extremely interesting, we owe these four people a great deal. Without them the public at large might never have known anything about the Sirius mystery, and the entire tradition might, after its thousands of years on earth, actually have sunk without trace.

8. Stapf, O., 'Iburu and Fundi, Two Cereals of Upper Guinea', in *Bulletin of Miscellaneous Information, Royal Botanic Gardens, Kew*, London, No. 8, 1915, p. 383.

9. de Wet, J. M. J., 'The Three Phases of Cereal Domestication', in Chapman, G. P., ed., *Grass Evolution and Domestication*, Cambridge University Press, UK, 1992, p. 183.

10. Henrard, J. Th., *Monograph of the Genus Digitaria*, University of Leiden Press, Leiden, Netherlands, 1950, p. 238.

11. Burkill, H. M., *The Useful Plants of West Tropical Africa*, Edition 2, Vol. 2, Royal Botanic Gardens, Kew, UK, 1994, pp. 225–7.

12. Erich von Däniken entered into correspondence with me on 22 April 1976, after reading my book. He wrote to me saying: 'With great enthusiasm I have read your book *The Sirius Mystery*. I should like to congratulate you for this masterpiece! . . . One thing that among scientific circles is hardly known is the fact, that already way back in 1959/60/64 and 65 I have written several articles on the subject [of extraterrestrial visitation] which were published in various newspapers (for your information I am enclosing a copy of such an old article).' He enclosed a photostat of an article by him in German, published in 1964. My original statement that nobody had heard of von Däniken at this stage is therefore misleading, for in the German-speaking world he was already writing about extraterrestrial visitations for newspapers.

PART ONE

THE SIRIUS QUESTION IS POSED

Chapter 2

The Knowledge of the Dogon

If you look up at the sky, the brightest star you can see is Sirius. Venus and Jupiter are often brighter but they are not stars; they are planets going round our own sun, which is a star itself. Now no astronomer will tell you there is any particular reason for intelligent life to be in the area of Sirius. The reason Sirius is so bright is that it is large and close, bigger than the sun and bigger than the handful of other nearby stars. But an intelligent astronomer will tell you that perhaps the stars Tau Ceti or Epsilon Eridani, which are rather similar to our sun, have planets with intelligent life. It would be a good guess. But among the stars most frequently discussed as possibly harbouring intelligent life Sirius is not included. It is not a particularly 'obvious' choice.

Project Ozma in the spring of 1960, and, in more recent years, other radio searches for intelligent life in space, listened for meaningful signals from the stars Tau Ceti and Epsilon Eridani. But none were detected. Not that that proves anything but that these two nearby stars were thought by some sensible astronomers to be possible locations of intelligent life in our neighbourhood of space.[1] Project Ozma only listened to these two stars to see if any signals were coming from them on a certain wavelength at a certain time with a lot of energy behind them. Nothing happened. Later such attempts have more realistically widened their scope somewhat, but the astronomers are fully aware that they are waltzing in the dark, and their efforts really take on the nature of a gesture which can only be described as bravado in the face of enormous odds. They cannot be certain that they are going about the task in the right way, but are doing what they hope is their best. Since Project Ozma, the giant radio telescope at Arecibo in Puerto Rico, which is the largest in the world, has listened selectively to several stars – but not to Sirius. It is the author's hope that the evidence presented in this book will be sufficient to stimulate an astronomical investigation of the Sirius system more thorough than all those to date, and build on the studies by Irving Lindenblad.[2] I also believe that a programme should be instituted at a major radio telescope to listen to the Sirius system for indications of any possible intelligent signals.

Now the basis of speculations about intelligent life in space is always going to include the possibility that contact with life on our planet has already been made by some more highly evolved society from elsewhere in the universe.[3] It is the possibility that our planet has had contact with a culture apparently from the area of Sirius that this book will discuss. There seems to be substantial evidence that at some relatively recent time in the past – possibly between 7,000 and 10,000 years ago – this may have happened, and any other interpretation of the evidence would not seem to make enough sense.

Before we come to the evidence, I should say a little more about Sirius. About the middle of the last century an astronomer was looking rather hard at Sirius over a period of time and got annoyed because it wasn't sitting still.[4] It was wobbling. He had a difficult time figuring this out, but he finally concluded that an extremely heavy and massive star going around Sirius could make it wobble that way. The only trouble was that there wasn't any large star going around Sirius! Instead there turned out to be a tiny little thing going around it every fifty years, and so Sirius came to be called Sirius A and the little thing became Sirius B.

Sirius B was at that time unique in the universe as far as anyone knew. Over a hundred of these things have now been actually seen scattered around the sky and there are many thousands more which we cannot see even through our modern telescopes because they are so tiny and their light so feeble. They are called white dwarfs.[5]

White dwarfs are strange because although they are feeble they are strong. They do not give out much light, but they are fantastically powerful gravitationally. On a white dwarf we would not even be a fraction of an inch high. We would be flat, pulled in by the gravity. A cubic foot of the matter of Sirius B would weigh 2,000 tons. A match-box full of matter from the star would weigh a ton and a quarter. But a match-box full taken from the star's core would weigh approximately fifty tons. The star is 65,000 times denser than water, whereas our own Sun has a density about equal to that of water. The 'big' star that was necessary to make Sirius A wobble turned out to be a little thing, but it still had to be as massive and heavy as an ordinary star of much more enormous size. It is, in short, a star so dense and closely packed that it is not even made out of regular matter. It is made out of what is called 'degenerate' matter or 'superdense' matter, where the atoms are pressed together and the electrons squashed. This matter is so heavy that it cannot be thought of in any familiar terms. There is nothing in our solar system, to our knowledge, comparable to this stuff. But physicists have considered it theoretically, and in this century we are making some progress towards understanding it.

It was even claimed by some astronomers that the Sirius system has a Sirius C, or a third star. Fox claimed to see it in 1920, and in 1926, 1928 and 1929 it was supposedly seen by van den Bos, Finsen, and others at the Union Observatory. But then for several years when it should have been seen, it was not. Zagar and Volet said it was there because there were wobbles that pointed to it.[6] And as we saw in Chapter One, Benest and Dudent in 1995 confirmed the existence of the third star.

An extensive study of the Sirius system by an astronomer was carried out by Irving W. Lindenblad of the US Naval Observatory in Washington, DC. He and I corresponded, and he sent me his publications (the latest appeared in 1973) and also the photograph in Plate 1, which was taken by him in 1970 after several years' preparation and is the first photograph ever taken of the star Sirius B, which in the photograph is a tiny spot of light near the main star Sirius A, which is 10,000 times brighter.

Lindenblad's accomplishment in getting a successful photograph is described in 'Notes to the Plates'. He studied the Sirius system for seven years and found no evidence of a third star, Sirius C. He says:[7] 'There is no astrometric evidence, therefore, of a close companion to either Sirius A or Sirius B'. Another astronomer, D. Lauterborn, persisted in believing – correctly as we now know – that there is a third star in the Sirius system.[8]

Now we see that the Sirius system is rather interesting and complicated. Only in this century have we advanced towards knowing about degenerate matter and understanding white dwarfs through our researches into nuclear physics. So we would be surprised, would we not, if someone without our modern science had known as much about the Sirius system as we do?

At this point I want to quote from *Intelligent Life in the Universe* by Carl Sagan and I. S. Shklovskii. In a very sensible chapter called 'Possible Consequences of Direct Contact' Sagan says :[9]

[Matters of human evolution], while difficult for us to reconstruct from a distance of millions of years, would have been much clearer to a technical civilization greatly in advance of the present one on Earth, which visited us every hundred thousand years or so to see if anything of interest was happening lately. Some 25 million years ago, a Galactic survey ship on a routine visit to the third planet of a relatively common G dwarf star [our Sun] may have noted an interesting and promising evolutionary development: Proconsul [the ancestor of *homo sapiens*, or modern man]. The information would have filtered at the speed of light slowly through the Galaxy, and a notation would have been made in some central information repository, perhaps at the Galactic center. If the emergence of intelligent life on a planet is of general scientific or other interest to the Galactic civilizations, it is reasonable that with the emergence of Proconsul, the rate of sampling of our planet should have increased, perhaps to once every ten thousand years. At the beginning of the most recent post-glacial epoch, the development of social structure, art, religion, and elementary technical skills should have increased the contact still further. But if the interval between sampling is only several thousand years, there is then a possibility that contact with an extraterrestrial civilization has occurred within historical times.

This is a very interesting prelude to our own story, and I believe Sagan and

Shklovskii's attitude is broadly true of the entire astronomical profession. It must be a very dour and pessimistic astronomer indeed who seriously doubts that there must be countless numbers of intelligent civilizations scattered throughout the universe on other planets which are orbiting around other stars.[10] An attitude which asserts that man is the only intelligent life form in the universe is intolerably arrogant today, though in, say, 1950 it was probably common belief. But anyone who holds such an opinion today is, fortunately for those who like to see some progress in human conceptions, something of an intellectual freak equivalent to a believer in the Flat Earth Theory.

Dr Melvin Calvin, of the Department of Chemistry, University of California at Berkeley, has said: 'There are at least 100,000,000 planets in the visible universe which were, or are, very much like the earth . . . this would mean certainly that we are not alone in the universe. Since man's existence on the earth occupies but an instant of cosmic time, surely intelligent life has progressed far beyond our level on some of these 100,000,000 planets.'[11]

Dr Su-Shu Huang of the Goddard Space Flight Center, Maryland, has written: '. . . planets are formed around the main-sequence stars of spectral types later than F5. Thus, planets are formed just where life has the highest chance to flourish. Based on this view we can predict that nearly all single stars of the main sequence below F5 and perhaps above K5 have a fair chance of supporting life on their planets. Since they compose a few per cent of all stars, life should indeed be a common phenomenon in the universe.'[12]

Dr A. G. W. Cameron, Professor of Astronomy at Yeshiva University, has discussed the stars Tau Ceti and Epsilon Eridani, which are considered the two likeliest localities for intelligent life within our immediate neighbourhood of space (within five 'parsecs' of us, a parsec being an astronomical unit of distance). He has then said, however: 'But there are about 26 other single stars of smaller mass within this distance, each of which should have a comparable probability of having a life-supporting planet according to the present analysis'.[13]

Dr R. N. Bracewell of the Radio Astronomy Institute, Stanford University, has said:[14]

As there are about one billion stars in our galaxy, the number of planets would be about 10 billion. . . . Now not all of these would be habitable, some would be too hot and some too cold, depending on their distance from their central star; so that on the whole we need only pay attention to planets situated as our earth is with respect to the sun. Let's describe such a situation as being within the habitable zone.

This is not to imply that no life would be found outside the habitable zone. There may very well be living things existing under most arduous physical conditions. . . . After elimination of frozen planets and planets sterilized by heat, we estimate that there are about 10^{10} [ten thousand million] likely planets in the galaxy [for life]. ... Of the 10^{10} likely planets, we frankly do not know how many of them support intelligent life. Therefore, we explore all possibilities, beginning with the possibility that intelligent life is abundant and in fact occurs on practically every planet. In this case, the average distance from one intelligent community to the next is 10 light-years. For comparison, the nearest star, of any kind, is about 1 light-year away.

Ten light-years is a very large distance. A radio signal would take 10 years to cover the distance. ... Consequently, communicating with someone 10 light-years away would not be like a telephone conversation ... are we sure that we can send a radio signal as far as 10 light-years? A definite answer can be given to this question.

There is no need for me to continue marshalling quotations from distinguished scientists and astronomers in support of the possibility of intelligent life in space, as the situation is by now obvious. The odds against intelligent life occurring fairly frequently within our galaxy are impossible ones. Since this is established, we are faced with yet another factor: in our own history, technological development has been rapid within a short space of time. It is familiar to older members of our species today that when they were young there were no airplanes, automobiles, rockets, satellites, electricity, radio, atom bombs, computers or Internet. People were dying of diseases which today we do not take seriously, no one with a toothache could obtain modern dental treatment, the concept of elementary hygiene was a novelty. I am not reciting all these wonders merely as a ritual incantation to our new god of progress. The point to be grasped is the sudden combustible nature of progress of this kind. In the lifetime of a single person all this can come about.

'Take-off point' is probably a universal phenomenon. Intelligent societies all over the universe will probably have experienced it, or are due to. Now the lifetime of a single person is of no consequence on the great universal time scale for the development of civilizations, not to mention the formation of planets. Therefore any society in advance of our own is certain to be *very* much in advance of ours. Once intelligent societies reach take-off point, they rush so quickly upward in technological competence that a comparison between them and non-technological societies is almost absurd. It would be foolish for us to suppose that any society more advanced than ours would be just a few years ahead of us. It would more likely be just a few tens of thousands of years ahead of us. And the technology and nature of such a society are beyond our abilities to imagine. The intelligent societies existing in the universe, then, are going to be of two kinds: less advanced than ourselves, 'primitive'; and fantastically more advanced than ourselves, 'magical'. To be at the point where we are now, at the watershed between 'primitive' and 'magical', is such a rare event in the universal history, that we may be the only intelligent society in the entire galaxy which is at this moment experiencing such a stage in our evolution. We therefore should feel privileged to be witnesses of it. Of course, the nature of time comes in again with the impossibility of talking sensibly about simultaneity in the galaxy at all. But that is another subject, and one which we may ignore here.

A further thought follows upon the above observations. Granted that there are two forms of society in the universe aside from our own bizarre transition stage, the 'primitive' societies are obviously only of interest to those more advanced than themselves, for they are incapable of communicating with anybody else. They are like we were as little as a hundred years ago: provincial, quiet, probably quite murderous, and smug, with the occasional visionary who is burned at the stake or crucified causing a moral ripple. But they cannot send or receive messages between the stars. In our transition stage, aptly enough, we can receive such messages with existing equipment, but could not send any unless we constructed expensive and special means to do so. Now that means that the only societies carrying on an interstellar dialogue of any kind are the 'magical' societies. These societies will be so advanced that they probably have emerging primitives like ourselves 'taped'. They certainly have standard sets of procedures for dealing with the likes of us, and may already have commenced their operations with the long-range intent of bringing us into their club. But just as no London gentlemen's club wishes to have a savage in a g-string waving his spear and poisoned arrows about in the members' lounge, so the interstellar club is unlikely to plug us straight into the circuits as a fully-fledged member.

But what I am getting at is not merely to impress upon the reader that a pecking order is likely to exist in the interstellar club of any galaxy, at least to the extent of having restrictions on novices, but to make the point which emerges from this. And the point is, that such highly advanced societies have possibly developed to such a pitch of technological expertise that interstellar travel has become possible for them, whereby they can physically transport themselves over at least modest interstellar distances of a few light-years to their near neighbours. And if that is the case, then our own planet, which any half-witted extraterrestrial astronomer in the neighbourhood could assume as a likely place for life to exist, has almost certainly been physically visited by extraterrestrials in their travels. This could have happened at any time in our lengthy history as a planet. No doubt, at the very least, our distant ancestors the cave-men would have been observed by extraterrestrial probes, who would have made a note that something was happening on this planet – slowly happening, but nevertheless actually happening. And as Sagan and Shklovskii said in the quotation from their book: 'It is reasonable that . . . the rate of sampling of our planet should have increased, perhaps to once every ten thousand years. . . . But if the interval between sampling is only several thousand years, there is then a possibility that contact with an extraterrestrial civilization has occurred within historical times.'[15]

If this were so, it would certainly have left some impact upon man and been incorporated somehow into his traditions. But if several thousand years had elapsed between that time and the present, the traces of the impact on man's culture would have been mostly dissipated and, it would seem, nearly impossible to elucidate. Unless some specific and unmistakable survival were found to exist, in circumstances which would probably be unusual, it seems that the hope of reconstructing scattered clues and fragments of the original tradition would be futile. That there would be something there if you could find the key seems certain. Let us return to a continuation of that passage from Sagan and Shklovskii for suggestions as to how a memory of an extraterrestrial contact might have been preserved from prehistoric or early historic times on Earth, through comparison with a verifiable story of French contact made with certain American Indians in 1786, as it was told to a modern anthropologist in the form of a tribal myth:[16]

There are no reliable reports of direct contact with an extraterrestrial civilization during the last few centuries, when critical scholarship and non-superstitious reasoning have been fairly widespread. Any earlier contact story must be encumbered with some degree of fanciful embellishment, due simply to the views prevailing at the time of the contact. The extent to which subsequent variation and embellishment alters the basic fabric of the account varies with time and circumstances. [An example] relevant to the topic at hand is the native account of the first contact with the Tlingit people of the northeast coast of North America with European civilization – an expedition led by the French navigator, La Perouse, in 1786. The Tlingit kept no written records; one century after the contact, the verbal narrative of the encounter was related to the American anthropologist G. T. Emmons by a principal Tlingit chief. The story was overlaid with the mythological framework in which the French sailing vessels were initially interpreted. But what is very striking is that the true nature of the encounter had been faithfully preserved. One blind old warrior had mastered his fears at the time of the encounter, had boarded one of the French ships, and exchanged goods with the Europeans. Despite his blindness, he reasoned that the occupants of the vessels were men. His interpretation led to active trade between the expedition of La Perouse and the Tlingit. The oral rendition contained sufficient information for later reconstruction of the true nature of the encounter, although many of the incidents were disguised in a mythological framework – for example, the ships were described as immense black birds with white wings.

As another example, the people of sub-Saharan Africa, who had no written language until the colonial period, preserved their history primarily through folklore. Such legends and myths, handed down by illiterate people from generation to generation, are in general of great historical value.

I don't know why the people of sub-Saharan Africa – with whom our initial evidence deals – are mentioned at this point in the Sagan book, for they do not crop up again in this chapter and it is something of a coincidence that they are mentioned out of the blue like this. Sagan goes on to discuss some fascinating creatures credited with founding the Sumerian civilization (which sprang up out of nowhere, as many Sumerian archaeologists will unhappily admit). They are described in a classical account by Alexander Polyhistor* as amphibious. He says they were happier if they could go back to the sea at night and return to dry land in the daytime. All the accounts describe them as being semi-demons, personages, or animals endowed with reason, but they are never called gods. They were 'superhuman' in knowledge and length of life and they eventually returned in a ship 'to the gods' carrying with them representatives of the fauna of the earth. I discuss these traditions particularly in Chapter Nine, and the surviving accounts of them are to be found in Appendix III, reprinted here in their entirety for the first time since 1876.

The Sumerian culture is very important. We shall be discussing it later in this book. It formed the original basis of that Mesopotamian civilization which is better known to most people through the much later Babylonians and Assyrians who inherited much of the Sumerian culture. The actual language of the Sumerians was superceded rather early by the Akkadian language (which is Semitic; Sumerian is non-Semitic and seems to have no linguistic affinities at all). The Akkadians and the Sumerians intermingled and eventually formed a meld like that which now exists between what once were the separate Normans and Anglo-Saxons in Britain, except that the Akkadians were Semitic and the Sumerians were not, and with considerable physical differences between them. Then the city of Babylon with its Babylonians and the region of Assyria with its Assyrian warriors to the north – and later the distant region of Fars with its Persians to the east – commanded the Mesopotamian area. From the Sumerian-Akkadian milieu also evolved those Semites known as Hebrews or Jews.

It should be more widely realized that when those famous Biblical figures Noah and Abraham 'lived' there was no such thing as a Hebrew yet in existence. Indeed, Noah is merely a Hebrew name for a much more ancient flood hero discussed in ancient texts which we have now recovered from early Sumer.[17] It is these Sumerians to whom Sagan has just referred,

---

* Born circa 105 BC at Miletus, lived at Rome and wrote more than fifty volumes of history, Pythagorean lore, etc., all lost but for a few fragments.

with their legend of an amphibious creature who founded their civilization. But all this does not concern us quite yet. I will just add that the Jews and the Arabs are both traditionally said to be descendants of Abraham, and Abraham was neither a Jew nor an Arab.

Now the peoples of sub-Saharan Africa are the source of our first arresting information. The particular people are called the Dogon, and they live in the present state of Mali. The nearest cities to them are Timbuctoo* (see Figure 2), Bamako, and Ouagadougou in Burkina (formerly Upper Volta). Initial research by me on the Dogon turned up an article in an anthropological journal by the French anthropologists Marcel Griaule and Germaine Dieterlen entitled 'A Sudanese Sirius

Figure 2. A view of Timbuctoo in 1830 – the first time it was seen by the Western public. Published as the frontispiece to René Caillié's *Travels through Central Africa to Timbuctoo; and Across the Great Desert, to Morocco; Performed in the Years 1824–1828,* 2 vols, London, 1930. Caillié was the first Western explorer to reach this fabled and remote city, of which he wrote: 'The city of Timbuctoo forms a sort of triangle, measuring about three miles in circuit.' (Vol. II, p. 56.) The large building is the Great Mosque. Caillié did not penetrate as far as to meet the Dogon, but he encountered the Bambara Tribe and wrote of them: 'I scarcely ever saw so gay a people as the Bambaras. At sunset they assemble under the great bombaces, at the entrance of the village, and dance all night to music which is not unpleasant. . . . their dispositions are gentle and humane . . .' (Vol. I, p. 369)

* Frequently written now as Tombouctou.

61

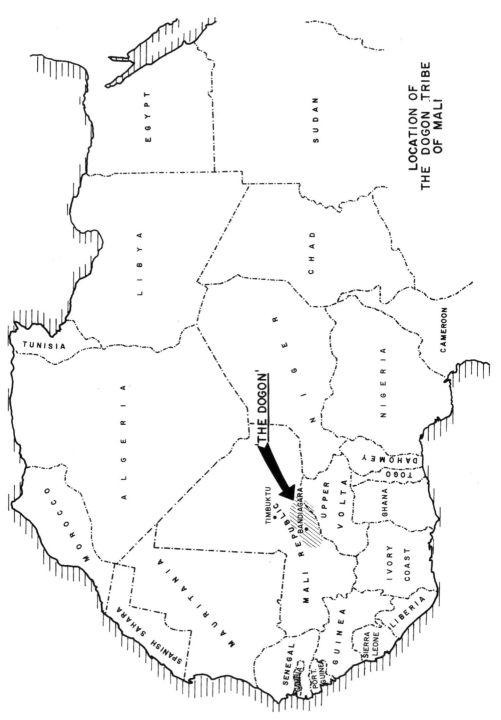

Figure 3.

System.[18] The article was written in French and an English translation of it is published as Appendix I of this book. I decided to publish the article in full because of the difficulty most interested readers would find in locating the French journal in which the original article appeared. And, of course, the original article could only be read by those who know French. The complete article, with its footnotes and all its illustrations, and in English, is therefore available for anyone who wishes to read it for himself. It is thus not necessary for me to summarize its contents.

When I first read the article (which refers to the French Sudan area, not the Republic of Sudan over a thousand miles to the east below Egypt), I could hardly believe what I saw. For here was an anthropological report of four tribes, the Dogon and three related ones, who held as their most secret religious tradition a body of knowledge concerning the system of the star Sirius, including specific information about that star system which it should be impossible for any primitive tribe to know.

The Dogon consider that the most important star in the sky is Sirius B, which cannot be seen. They admit that it is invisible. How, then, do they know it exists? Griaule and Dieterlen say: 'The problem of knowing how, with no instruments at their disposal, men could know the movements and certain characteristics of virtually invisible stars has not been settled, nor

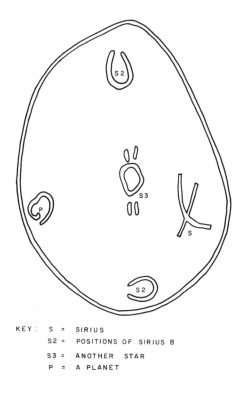

KEY : S = SIRIUS
      S2 = POSITIONS OF SIRIUS B
      S3 = ANOTHER STAR
      P = A PLANET

Figure 4.

even posed.' But even in saying this, Griaule and Dieterlen imply that Sirius B is only 'virtually invisible', whereas we know it is totally invisible except through a powerful telescope. What, then, is the answer?

Griaule and Dieterlen make clear that the large and bright star of Sirius is not as important to the Dogon as the tiny Sirius B, which the Dogon call *põ tolo* (*tolo* meaning 'star'). *Põ* is a cereal grain commonly called 'fonio' in West Africa, and whose official botanical name is *Digitaria exilis*. In speaking of the *põ* star, Griaule and Dieterlen call it 'the star Digitaria', or just simply 'Digitaria'. What is significant about the *põ* grain is that it is the smallest grain known to the Dogon, being extremely minute, and unknown as food in Europe or America. To the Dogon, this tiny grain represents the tiny star, and that is why the star is called *põ*, after the grain. In the article we read: 'Sirius, however, is not the basis of the system: it is one of the foci of the orbit of a tiny star called Digitaria, *põ tolo* . . . which . . . hogs the attention of male initiates.' Now, this is a most unsettling statement. The casual reader may not notice just how unusual it is for an African tribe to put it quite this way. But the orbit of Digitaria, which the Dogon elsewhere describe as egg-shaped or elliptical (see also Figures 8 and 9, as well as the illustrations to the article in Appendix I), is specifically described as having the main star Sirius as 'one of the foci of [its] orbit'. Of course, the technical term 'focus' has here been supplied by the anthropologists. But they were faithfully rendering the meaning of what the Dogon said in their own language. And what the Dogon were saying, and which they also make quite clear graphically in their drawings (see Figures 4 and 8), is that the orbit of Sirius B around Sirius A is of a kind which obeys one of Kepler's laws of planetary motion, extended to other orbiting bodies. It was Johannes Kepler (1571–1630) who first proposed that heavenly bodies do not move in perfect circular paths. He hit upon the brilliant insight that the planets in their motions around the sun were moving in elliptically shaped orbits, with the sun at one of the two foci of each ellipse. Most people I speak to have no idea that the planets don't go

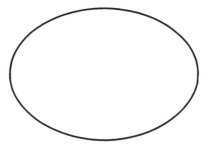

AN ELLIPSE

Figure 5.

in circles around the sun. Even if they were taught the truth at school, they have long since forgotten about things like that. And many people honestly don't know what an ellipse is unless you show them one.

An ellipse is a kind of 'stretched' circle. You can conceive of grabbing the centre of a circle and ripping the centre into two pieces, and then pulling those two portions away from each other. This would naturally make the circle flatten at the top and the bottom and bulge at the two sides, and the two pieces of the centre would fall along a straight line joining the two most distant points. These two fragments of centre each then have the name of *focus*, and the two together are 'the foci of the ellipse'. If you could get your hands on that ellipse and push at the bulging ends, you might force it back together again and make it a proper circle.

CIRCLE,ONE CENTRE   ELLIPSE,TWO FOCI

Figure 6.

But what I ask all readers to take note of is this: How did the Dogon tribe, who had no access to the theories of Kepler or his successors, know about matters like this? Although Kepler lived in the sixteenth century, we shall see that other information possessed by the Dogon originated in the West only in the late 1920s. There were no Western missionaries to the Dogon prior to Griaule and Dieterlen first visiting them in 1931. The White Fathers, the French missionary order, have confirmed this to me in correspondence. The transmission of Western knowledge to the Dogon seems to be an impossibility. How did they even get the idea in the first place that elliptical orbits existed, rather than circular – much less apply this idea to some invisible star way out in space? And also to get it right by saying that Sirius A was at one of the foci, rather than just somewhere in the ellipse? And not at the centre? Wouldn't the natural primitive idea seem to be, even if you wanted to say the orbit was elliptical, still to have Sirius itself at the centre? But no. They knew too much to make a mistake like that. For the whole point about Kepler's Law is that not only are the orbits ellipses, but the sun must always be at one of the foci; otherwise nothing will work. Now, in order to know about all this, you need not have had Kepler. Elliptical orbits are a universal truth, as true here as they are on the other side of the galaxy, or even in some other galaxy. Kepler merely discovered a natural principle. So there was no need for the Dogon to know about Kepler personally. All that is required is an explanation of how they could have learned the universal principle from any other source.

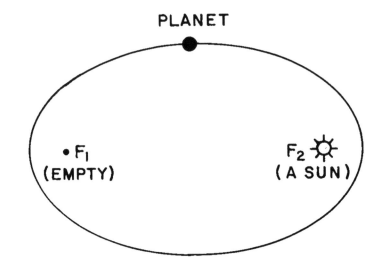

Figure 7.

In Figure 8, I compare the Dogon drawings of the orbit of Sirius B around Sirius with the modern astronomical diagrams of the same (which have been confirmed as accurate at this scale by Lindenblad's work); also there is a comparison of the same information, tribal and modern, as seen in a linear perspective, stretched through time. I do not need to claim any perfect scientific accuracy for the Dogon drawings. The similarity is so striking that the most untrained eye can immediately see that the general picture is identical, in each instance. There is no need for perfectionists to get out their calculators or measuring tapes. The fact is demonstrated, and it is that the Dogon have an accurate general knowledge of the most unobvious and subtle principles of the orbiting of Sirius B around Sirius A.

The Dogon also know the actual orbital period of this invisible star, which is fifty years. Referring to the sacred Sigui ceremony of the tribe, Dieterlen and Griaule tell us: 'The period of the orbit is counted double, that is, one hundred years, because the Siguis are convened in pairs of "twins", so as to insist on the principle of twin-ness'.

The Dogon also say that Sirius B rotates on its axis, demonstrating that they know a star can do such a thing. In reality, all stars really do rotate on their axes. How do the Dogon know such an extraordinary fact? In the

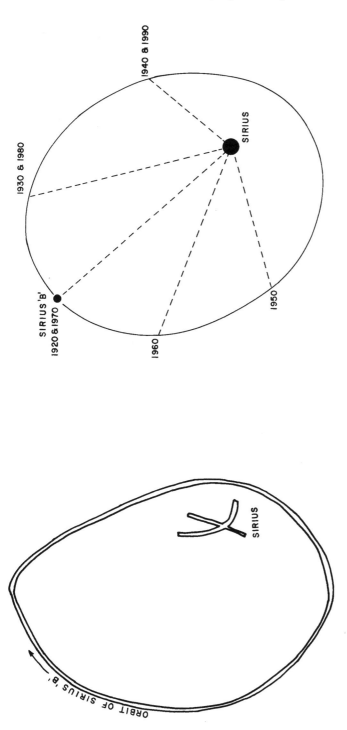

Figure 8. On left: the orbit of Digitaria (Sirius B) around Sirius as portrayed by the Dogon in their sand drawings. On right: A modern astronomical diagram of the orbit of Sirius, the years indicated being the positions of Sirius B in its orbit on those dates. Note that the Dogon do not place Sirius at the centre of their drawing but seem to place it near one focus of their approximate ellipse – which constitutes one of the most extraordinary features of their information, and matches the diagram on the right to an uncanny degree

article, the Dogon are recorded as saying: 'As well as its movement in space, Digitaria also revolves upon itself over the period of one year and this revolution is honoured during the celebration of the *bado* rite'. The Dogon believe the day of the *bado* is when a beam of rays carrying important signals strikes the Earth from Sirius B. It is not known to modern astronomy what the period of rotation of Sirius B is; the star is so small we think we are doing well to see it at all. I asked one astronomer, G. Wegner, then of Oxford's Department of Astrophysics and the University Observatory, whether one year might be a sensible estimate of the rotation period of Sirius B. He naturally replied that we had no way of determining it, but that a year could be right; in other words, it cannot be ruled out, which was all I was seeking to establish.

The Dogon describe Sirius B as 'the infinitely tiny'. As we know, Sirius B is a white dwarf and the tiniest form of visible star in the universe. But what is really the most amazing of all the Dogon statements is this: 'The star which is considered to be the smallest thing in the sky is also the heaviest: "Digitaria is the smallest thing there is. It is the heaviest star." It consists of a metal called *sagala* which is a little brighter than iron and so heavy "that all earthly beings combined cannot lift it". In effect the star weighs the equivalent of . . . all the seeds, or of all the iron on the earth . . .' (all this from the article by Griaule and Dieterlen which is Appendix I of this book.).

So we see the Dogon presenting a theory of Sirius B which fits all known scientific facts, and even some which are not known it presents as well.

All this forms the most sacred and most secret tradition known to the Dogon, the basis of their religion and of their lives. Connected with all this are statements they make about the existence of a third star in the Sirius system, which they call the *emme ya* ('Sorghum – female') star which, in comparing it to Digitaria, they say is 'four times as light (in weight), and travels along a greater trajectory in the same direction and in the same time as it (fifty years). Their respective positions are such that the angle of their radii is at right angles.' This last star has a satellite, indicating that the Dogon appreciate that bodies other than stars are satellites of stars. Of *emme ya* itself, they say: 'It is "the sun of women" . . . "a little sun" . . . In fact it is accompanied by a satellite which is called the "star of women" . . . or Goatherd . . . as the guide of *emme ya*.' It is the third star, *emme ya*, 'Sorgum Female', or the sun of women, which is the Sirius C which in 1995 was confirmed by the astronomers, as described in Chapter One.

Around the astronomical facts of this extraordinary system, the Dogon have a complicated system of mythology. Sirius B they see as 'relentlessly revolving around Sirius . . . and never capable of reaching it'. All these facts have mythological tales and personages connected with them. I have tried to extract the bare facts from the article and present them here for the reader. But the reader will by now see quite clearly why I have included the entire article in this book, for the information is so incredible that I

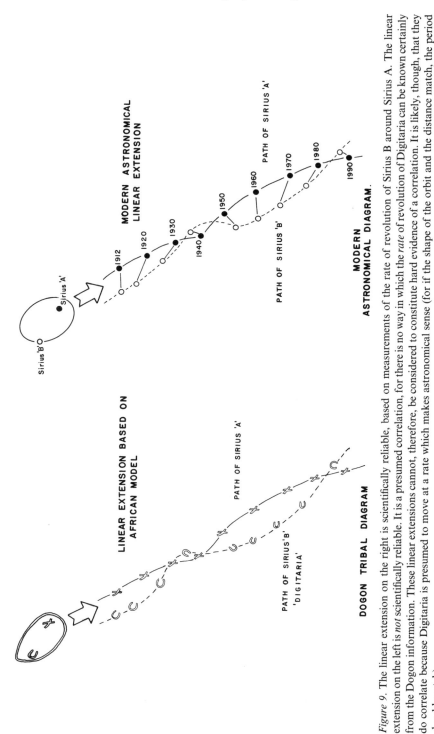

Figure 9. The linear extension on the right is scientifically reliable, based on measurements of the rate of revolution of Sirius B around Sirius A. The linear extension on the left is *not* scientifically reliable. It is a presumed correlation, for there is no way in which the *rate* of revolution of Digitaria can be known certainly from the Dogon information. These linear extensions cannot, therefore, be considered to constitute hard evidence of a correlation. It is likely, though, that they do correlate because Digitaria is presumed to move at a rate which makes astronomical sense (for if the shape of the orbit and the distance match, the period should match)

Figure 10. Dogon drawing of a planet going round Sirius C – *Emme ya*

thought the reader would simply think I had made it all up unless I presented the source for him to read through himself.

But let us move beyond the Griaule and Dieterlen article 'A Sudanese Sirius System' and consider a later and fuller publication of book length, which is obviously too bulky to include within this book as an appendix. I refer to the book *Le Renard pâle* (The Pale Fox) published in 1965.* This book, by Griaule and Dieterlen, was produced ten years after the death of Marcel Griaule himself. It contains Mme Dieterlen's latest reflections on the Sirius system of the Dogon. In this definitive compendium[19] of much of the joint findings of herself and Marcel Griaule (it is only the first such volume of theirs to appear in a planned series summing up their work), Mme Dieterlen has actually added a brief appendix on pages 529–31 which gives information about Sirius and its companion star in the form of an extract from an article by Dr P. Baize which appeared in the September 1931 issue of *Astronomie*. She says: 'The excerpts concern the discovery, orbit, period and density of the Companion of Sirius'.[20] Her curiosity has obviously developed since 1950 and the publication of 'A Sudanese Sirius System'. But like a true professional, Mme Dieterlen merely cites the astronomical facts in this way in a short appendix at the back of her book[21] without drawing any conclusions or even indicating the connection of this subject with the Dogon traditions. In fact, lest the reader assume otherwise, I must make clear that neither Marcel Griaule nor Mme Dieterlen has at any time (to my knowledge) made any claim of extra-terrestrial contact to do with the Dogon. They have not even made any direct comments on the extraordinary impossibility of the Dogon knowing all the things which they know. I could never have made discoveries such as those of Griaule and Dieterlen and merely said (as in the article): 'The problem of knowing how . . . has not been settled, nor even posed.' I do

---

* The fox of the Dogon ('Yurugu') is *Vulpes pallidus* (see Plate 2), not the fox found in Britain, which is *Vulpes vulpes*.

70

believe such restraint calls for a medal; it is so phenomenal that it is the greatest factor in favour of Griaule and Dieterlen's discoveries. If they had trumpeted their findings, I suppose I would never have taken them seriously. I would have thought them unreliable. Such are the ironies by which information can be revealed – by almost disappearing through diffidence.

I sat down and rewrote this book in the light of *Le Renard pâle*. (I read the translation in manuscript*), with its more complete information. Much of this will be found in the context of a more advanced discussion in Chapter Nine.

In *Le Renard pâle* it is possible to learn much more of the Dogon beliefs and knowledge relating to astronomy and the Sirius system. Of the moon, they say it is dry and dead like dry dead blood'.[22] Their drawing of the planet Saturn has a ring around it, and is reproduced as Figure 12 in this book. They know that the planets revolve around the sun. Planets are called *tolo tanaze*, 'stars that turn (around something)'.[23] But this does not mean turning around the Earth. The Dogon specifically say, for instance: 'Jupiter follows Venus by turning slowly around the sun.'[24] The various positions of Venus are recalled on a very large geographical space by a series of altars, raised stones, or arrangements in caves or shelters.[25] The positions of Venus determine a Venus calendar.[26] In fact, the Dogon have four different kinds of calendar. Three of them are liturgical calendars: a solar calendar, a Venus calendar, and a Sirius calendar. Their fourth is an agrarian one, and is lunar.[27]

The Dogon know of the existence of four other invisible heavenly bodies besides Sirius B and its possible companions in the Sirius system. These other four bodies are in our own solar system. For the Dogon know of the four major 'Galilean' moons of Jupiter. These four moons are called 'Galilean' because Galileo discovered them when he began to use the telescope in the autumn of 1609. The other moons of Jupiter are small and insignificant, having formerly been asteroids which were captured by Jupiter's gravitation at some unknown time in the past. (They are thought to have come from the asteroid belt between Mars and Jupiter which some astronomers think once constituted a planet which exploded.) The Dogon say: 'The mutilation the Fox [identified with the troublesome Ogo; see account of him which follows] suffered was still bloody. The blood of his genitals fell on the ground, but Amma made it ascend to heaven as four satellites that turn around *dana tolo*, Jupiter, . . . "The four little stars are Jupiter wedges" . . . When Jupiter is represented by a rock, it is wedged in with four stones.'[28] A Dogon drawing of Jupiter with its four moons is reproduced as Figure 11. Griaule and Dieterlen describe this drawing as follows:[29]

* Subsequently an English translation has appeared – by Stephen C. Infantino, published by the Continuum Foundation, Chino Valley, Arizona, USA, in 1986. It has no index.

This figure represents the planet – the circle – surrounded by its four satellites in the collateral directions and called *dana tolo unum* 'children of *dana tolo* (Jupiter)'. The four satellites, associated to the four varieties of *sene* (acacia), sprang from the drops of blood from the Fox's mutilated genitals. 'The four small stars are Jupiter's hulls'. . . . The sectors between the satellites represent the seasons. They turn around Jupiter and their movements will favour the growth of the *sene* leaves, for the *sene* moves on the ground at night like the stars in the sky; they turn on their own axes (in a year) like the satellites.

Figure 11. Dogon drawing of Jupiter with its four main moons

They add in a footnote that 'the trunks of certain varieties of *sene* are spiralled. A house is not built with *sene* wood, which would make the house "turn". The "movements" of the *sene* at night are supposed to attract the souls of the dead who "change place".'

As for Saturn, drawn in Figure 12, the Dogon specifically describe its famous halo, which is only visible through a telescope. According to Griaule and Dieterlen:[30] '. . . the Dogon affirm there is a permanent halo around the star, different from the one sometimes seen around the moon . . . the star is always associated to the Milky Way.'

Saturn is known as[31] 'the star of limiting the place' in association somehow with the Milky Way. The meaning is unclear, and Griaule and Dieterlen say the subject must be pursued further,[32] but it would seem they may be trying to convey the idea that Saturn 'limits the place' of the solar system, separating it from and acting as link with, the Milky Way itself, in which the solar system is situated. Saturn being the outermost planet which the Dogon mention, this may be their intended meaning. The Dogon realize that the Milky Way contains the Earth:[33] '. . . the Milky Way . . . is in itself the image of the spiralling stars inside the "world of spiralling stars" in which the Earth is found. In this "world of stars", the axis ("Amma's fork") around which they move, links the Polar Star . . .' and so on. The Milky Way is described as the 'more distant stars' – that is, than the planets.

Figure 12. Saturn with its ring. Dogon drawing

We are told that[34] 'For the Dogon an infinite number of stars and spiralling worlds exist'. They carefully differentiate the three kinds of *tolo* or 'stars': 'The fixed stars are a part of the "family of stars that doesn't turn" (around another star) . . . the planets belong to the "family of stars that turns" (around another star) . . . the satellites are called *tolo gonoze* "stars that make the circle".'[35] The heavenly motions are likened to the circulation of the blood. The planets and satellites and companions are 'circulating blood'.[36] And this brings us to the extraordinary point that the Dogon do know about the circulation of the blood in the body from their own tradition. In our own culture, the Englishman William Harvey (1578–1657) discovered the circulation of the blood. Strange as it may seem to us now, before his time the notion seems not to have occurred to anyone in the Western world. John Aubrey, author of *Brief Lives*, knew Harvey well, and tells us:[37] 'I have heard him say, that after his Booke of the *Circulation of the Blood* came out, that . . . 'twas beleeved by the vulgar that he was crack-brained . . .'. However, the same theory does not seem to arouse among the Dogon notions that their wise men are crack-brained. Here is an account of the Dogon theory recorded in their own words:[38]

The movement of the blood in the body which circulates inside the organs in the belly, on the one hand 'clear' blood, and on the other the oil, keeps them both united (the words in man): that is the progress of the word. The blood-water – or clear – goes through the heart, then the lungs, the liver and the spleen; the oily blood goes through the pancreas, the kidneys, the intestines and the genitals.

Postscript (1997): It was the Chinese who first discovered the circulation of the blood, although this remained unknown in the West until 1546, when Michael Servetus mentioned it (he, Giordano Bruno and two others actually preceded Harvey). The circulation of the blood is clearly described in the Chinese medical classic, *The Yellow Emperor's Manual of Corporeal Medicine*, in the second century BC, and the theory is believed to have been formulated in China no later than the sixth century BC. But this knowledge seems to have been confined to China for two millennia, and can hardly have reached West Africa.I published an account of this in my book on the history of Chinese science in 1986 (Temple, Robert K. G. *The Genius of China* (original title in the UK: *China: Land of Discovery and Invention*, Patrick Stephens, Wellingborough, 1986), Simon and Schuster, New York, 1986, and Prion Books, London, 1991, pp. 123–4.).

The Dogon say: '. . . the food you eat, the beverage you drink, that Amma changes into red blood; white blood is a bad thing'.[39] They also say: 'The essence of nourishment passes into the blood'.[40] They know that the blood passes into the internal organs 'starting with the heart'.[41] The Dogon even seem to understand the role of oxygen – or at least, air – entering the bloodstream. For they equate air with 'the word' which they say enters the bloodstream bringing 'nourishment of the interior' by 'the impulse raised by the heart'. The 'integration of the "word" (air) into the body also has to do with the food nourishing the blood. All the organs of respiration and digestion are associated with this integration.'[42]

The Milky Way, likened as I said to a circulation of the blood, is described further: '. . . the term *yalu ulo* designates the Milky Way of our galaxy, which sums up the stellar world of which the Earth is a part, and which spins in a spiral. . . . (it encompasses) the multiplication and the development, almost infinite, of the spiraloid stellar worlds that Amma created . . . (there are) spiralling worlds that fill the universe – infinite and yet measurable.'[43] Amma is the chief god, the creator, of the universe, to the Dogon. There is an interesting account of Amma and the creation: 'The active role of fermentation at the time of the creation is recalled in the present brewing of beer. . . . the fermentation of the liquid constitutes a "resurrection" of the cereals destroyed in the brewing. . . . Life . . . is comparable to a fermentation. "Many things were fermenting inside Amma"' at the creation.[44] And 'Spinning and dancing, Amma created all the spiralling worlds of the stars of the universe.'[45] '. . . Amma's work realized the universe progressively, it was made up of several stellar worlds spiralling around.'[46]

The Dogon have no difficulty in conceiving of intelligent life all over the universe. They say:[47]

> The worlds of spiralling stars were populated universes; for as he created things, Amma gave the world its shape and its movement and created

living creatures. There are creatures living on other 'Earths' as well as on our own; this proliferation of life is illustrated by an explanation of the myth, in which it is said: man is on the 4th earth, but on the 3rd there are 'men with horns' *inneu gammurugu*, on the 5th, 'men with tails' *inneu dullogu*, on the 6th, 'men with wings' *inneu bummo* [An ancient Dogon iron state of one of these 'men with wings' from the 'Sixth Earth' may be seen in Plate 9], etc. This emphasizes the ignorance of what life is on the other worlds but also the certainty that it exists.

The Dogon know that the Earth turns on its own axis. The standard way of foretelling the future for the Dogon is to draw a pattern in the sand before going to bed, and in the morning to look and see where in that pattern the fox has stopped during the night – this indicates events to come. When the fox walks over the tables of divination which have been drawn in the sand, 'the planet begins to turn under the action of (the fox's) paws'.[48] 'When the only traces that are visible are made by the tail, the image is likened to the movement of the Earth turning on its own axis; it is said: "The Fox turned with his tail; the Earth turned on its own axis".'[49] 'So the divination table represents the Earth "which turns because of the action of the Fox's paws" as he moves along the registers; while the instruction table represents the space in which the Earth moves, as well as the sun and the moon, which were placed by Amma out of his reach.'[50] The instruction table here referred to has twelve registers and constitutes a lunar calendar, with each register representing a month. It is Figure 96 in *Le Renard pâle*. These twelve months, then, are 'the space in which the Earth moves' – that is, one year's orbit around the sun. And within this orbit, the Earth's rotations on its own axis every day take place. The orbit around the sun is 'the Earth's space'.

The Dogon know perfectly well that it is the turning of the Earth on its axis which makes the sky seem to turn round. They speak of '. . . the apparent movement of the stars from east to west, as men see them'.[51] The Dogon are thus free from the illusions of our European ancestors, who thought the sky and stars wheeled round the Earth (though there was an exception to such primitive notions in Europe which no historian of science has ever reported, at least as far as I have been able to discover after a great deal of searching. I have summarized this 'secret' tradition in Appendix II and pointed out its connection with the Sirius mystery).

The placenta is used by the Dogon as a symbol of a 'system' of a group of stars or planets. Our own solar system seems to be referred to as 'Ogo's placenta',[52] whereas the system of the star Sirius and its companion star and satellites, etc., is referred to as 'Nommo's placenta'.[53] Nommo is the collective name for the great culture-hero and founder of civilization who came from the Sirius system to set up society on the Earth. Nommo – or, to be more precise, the Nommos – were amphibious creatures, and are to be seen in the two tribal drawings in Figure 52 and Figure 54 in this book.

Here is the way in which Griaule and Dieterlen record the Dogon beliefs about the two cosmic placentas I have just mentioned:[54]

> Two systems, that are sometimes linked together, intervene, and are at the origin of various calendars, giving a rhythm to the life and activities of man. . . . One of them, nearest to the Earth, will have the sun as an axis, the sun is the testament to the rest of Ogo's placenta, and another, further away, Sirius, testament to the placenta of the Nommo, monitor of the Universe.

The movements of the bodies within these 'placentas' are likened to the circulation of blood in the actual placenta, and the bodies in space are likened to coagulations of blood into lumps. This principle is also applied to larger systems: 'In the formation of the stars, we recall that the "path of the blood" is represented by the Milky Way . . .',[55] '. . . the planets and satellites (and companions) are associated to the circulating blood and to the "seeds" . . . that flow with the blood.'[56] The system of Sirius, which is known as 'land of the fish',[57] and is the placenta of Nommo, is specifically called the 'double placenta in the sky',[58] referring to the fact that it is a binary star system. The 'earth' which is in the Sirius system is 'pure earth', whereas the 'earth' which is in our solar system is 'impure earth'.[59]

The landing of Nommo on our Earth is called 'the day of the fish',[60] and the planet he came from in the Sirius system is known as the '(pure) earth of the day of the fish . . . not (our) impure earth . . .'[61] In our own solar system all the planets emerged from the placenta of our sun. This is said of the planet Jupiter,[62] which 'emerged from the blood which fell on the placenta'. The planet Venus was also formed from blood which fell on the placenta.[63] (Venus 'was blood red when she was created, her colour fading progressively'.[64]) Mars, too, was created from a coagulation of 'blood'.[65] Our solar system is, as we have noted, called the placenta of Ogo, the Fox, who is impure. Our own planet Earth is, significantly, 'the place where Ogo's umbilical cord was attached to his placenta . . . and recalls his first descent'.[66] In other words, the Earth is where Ogo 'plugged in', as it were, to this system of planets. What Ogo the Fox seems to represent is man himself, an imperfect intelligent species who 'descended' or originated on this planet, which is the planet in our solar system to which the great umbilical cord is attached. Ogo is representative of ourselves, in all our cosmic impurity. It comes as a shock to realize that we are Ogo, the imperfect, the meddler, the outcast. Ogo rebelled at his creation and remained unfinished. He is the equivalent of Lucifer in our own tradition in the Christian West. And in order to atone for our impurity it is said over and over by the Dogon that the Nommo dies and is resurrected, acting as a sacrifice for us, to purify and cleanse the Earth. The parallels with Christ are extraordinary, even extending to Nommo being crucified on a tree, and forming a eucharistic meal for humanity and then being resurrected.

We are told that the Nommo will come again. A certain 'star' in the sky will appear once more[67] and will be the 'testament to the Nommo's resurrection'. When the Nommo originally landed on Earth, he 'crushed the Fox, thus marking his future domination over the Earth which the Fox had made'.[68] So perhaps man's brutish nature has already been sufficiently subdued in our distant past. Perhaps it was those visitors whom the Dogon call the Nommos who really did 'crush the Fox' in us, who all but destroyed Ogo, and have given us all the best elements of civilization which we possess. We remain as a curious mixture of the brute and the civilized, struggling against the Ogo within us.

The Dogon comment further on the heavenly motions: '. . . the Earth turns on its own axis . . . and makes a great circle (around the Sun) . . . The moon turns like a conical spiral around the earth. The Sun distributes light in space and on the earth with its rays.'[69] The sun is 'the remainder of Ogo's placenta'[70] and the centre of our system. For some reason, which they say is the visitation to earth of the amphibious bringers of civilization from there, the Dogon centre their life and religion not on our own solar and planetary system, but on the system of a nearby star and its invisible companions. Why? Can it really be for the reason they say? And if so, will the Nommo come again? We should really investigate the details of the Dogon knowledge as fully as possible. In *Le Renard pâle*, as opposed to the earlier article reproduced here, it is said, for instance, that the star *emme ya* in the system of Sirius may have an orbital period of thirty-two years instead of the fifty years which others maintain. It is larger than Sirius B and 'four times lighter'. In relation to Sirius B, 'Their positions are straight'. It is watched over by Sirius B and acts as an intermediary, transmitting Sirius B's 'orders'.[71] We now know that such a body exists. The Dogon prognostications could thus act as evidence to be tested. Dr Lindenblad could not find evidence of a Sirius C of the kind which was presumed earlier by astronomers. But evidence has now been found of the kind of Sirius C suggested by the Dogon. And such a discovery having been made, it conclusively establishes the validity of the Dogon claims. The Dogon information about the actual orbit of Sirius C is very confused and incoherent, apparently contradictory.

Among the Dogon, an allusion to the great Creator's immortality and stability is expressed in good wishes of greetings or farewell that are addressed to a friend or relative: 'May the immortal Amma keep you seated'.[72] It is just as well that we keep our seats, for we are about to launch into the dark waters of our planet's past, which may bring quite an alteration of our normal conceptions of it. For it is not only that a culture contact between ourselves and an alien civilization from outer space may have taken place, of which we shall find more evidence from our own ancient cultures, we shall also discover that the ancient world, the further back one goes in time, tends to develop a more and more odd flavour. The mysteries become denser, the strangeness thicker and more viscous. Just as in tracing the origins of sugar one goes from lighter syrup back to the thick and pungent molasses which develops, it seems, qualities far removed from one's expectations at the beginning, so with the past. Its doors encrusted with almost solid cobwebs give off the stench of air last breathed by ancestors forgotten by us all.

Notes

1. Cameron, A. G. W., ed., *Interstellar Communication*, W. A. Benjamin, Inc., New York, 1963. See p. 75 (Calvin), p. 88 (Huang), p. 110 (Cameron), and particularly p. 176 (Drake).
2. For account see *Sky and Telescope*, June, 1973, p. 354. Publications: Lindenblad, Irving, 'Relative Photographic Positions and Magnitude Difference of the Components of Sirius' in *Astronomical Journal*, 75, No. 7 (September, 1970), pp. 841–8, and 'Multiplicity of the Sirius System' in *Astronomical Journal*, 78, No. 2 (March, 1973), pp. 205–7.
3. Sagan, C. and Shklovskii, I. S., *Intelligent Life in the Universe*, Dell Publishing Co., New York, 1966, pp. 437, 440–64.
4. The astronomer Johann Friedrich Bessel in 1834. Just before his death in 1844 he decided Sirius must be a binary system. In 1862 the American Alvan Clark looked through the largest telescope then existing and saw a faint point of light where Sirius B should be, confirming its existence. In 1915 Dr W. S. Adams of Mt Wilson Observatory made the necessary observations to learn the temperature of Sirius B, which is 8000°, half as much again as our sun's. It then began to be realized that Sirius B was an intensely hot star which radiated three to four times more heat and light per square foot than our sun. It then became possible to calculate the size of Sirius B, which is only three times the radius of the Earth, yet its mass was just a little less than that of our sun. A theory of white dwarfs then developed to account for Sirius B, and other white dwarfs were later discovered.
5. See previous note.
6. Aitken, R. G., *The Binary Stars*, Dover Publications, New York, 1964, pp. 240–1. The account of Sirius extends from p. 237 to p. 241.
7. 'Multiplicity of the Sirius System,' art. cit. (see above, Note 2).
8. *Mass Loss and Evolution in Close Binaries*, Copenhagen University, 1970, pp. 190–4. (A seminar held in Elsinore Castle, with Lauterborn as a participant.)
9. Op. cit. (Note 3 above) Chapter 33.
10. See for instance the book *Interstellar Communication*, op. cit. (Note 1 above), an anthology with contributions from nineteen astronomers and scientists.
11. Ibid., p. 75.
12. Ibid., p. 92.
13. Ibid., p. 110.
14. Ibid., pp. 232–5.
15. Op. cit. (Note 3 above), pp. 440–64.
16. Ibid.
17. See for instance Pritchard, J. B., *Ancient Near Eastern Texts relating to the Old Testament*, Princeton University Press, 1955, p. 42, the introductory remarks to trans. of 'The Deluge' and also pp. 93–5, account of the Flood.
18. Griaule, M., and Dieterlen, G., 'Un Système Soudanais de Sirius', *Journal de la Société des Africainistes*, Tome XX, Fascicule 2, 1950, pp. 273–94. An English translation of this article is Appendix I of this book.
19. Griaule, Marcel, and Dieterlen, Germaine, *Le Renard pâle* (Tome I, Fascicule 1), Institut d'Ethnologie, Musée de l'Homme, Palais de Chaillot, Place du Trocadéro, Paris 16° (75016 Paris), 1965, 544 pp.
20. Ibid., p. 529.
21. Nine references are given to Baize's publications, extending to 1938, and one given to Schatzman in *L'Astronomie*, 1956, pp. 364–9.

22. *Le Renard pâle*, p. 478.
23. Ibid., pp. 480–1.
24. Ibid., pp. 480–1.
25. Ibid., p. 486.
26. Ibid., p. 481.
27. Ibid., p. 226.
28. Ibid., p. 264.
29. Ibid., p. 329.
30. Ibid., p. 292.
31. Ibid., p. 291.
32. Ibid., p. 292.
33. Ibid., p. 321.
34. Ibid., p. 321.
35. Ibid., p. 323.
36. Ibid., p. 323.
37. Aubrey, J., *Brief Lives*, Penguin, London, 1972. See entry for Harvey, William, pp. 290–1.
38. *Le Renard pâle*, p. 348.
39. Ibid., p. 287 n. 1.
40. Ibid., p. 141.
41. Ibid., p. 141.
42. Ibid., p. 141.
43. Ibid., pp. 102–4.
44. Ibid., p. 128.
45. Ibid., p. 163.
46. Ibid., p. 168.
47. Ibid., p. 170 n. 2.
48. Ibid., p. 276.
49. Ibid., p. 279, inc. n. 4.
50. Ibid., p. 280.
51. Ibid., p. 335.
52. Ibid., p. 470.
53. Ibid., p. 470.
54. Ibid., p. 470.
55. Ibid., p. 489.
56. Ibid., p. 323.
57. Ibid., p. 384.
58. Ibid., p. 384.
59. Ibid., p. 381.
60. Ibid., p. 381.
61. Ibid., p. 381.
62. Ibid., p. 287.
63. Ibid., p. 248.
64. Ibid., pp. 248–9.
65. Ibid., p. 249.
66. Ibid., p. 219.
67. Ibid., p. 440.
68. Ibid., p. 440.
69. Ibid., p. 477.
70. Ibid., p. 477.
71. Ibid., p. 475.
72. Ibid., p. 499 n. 2.

PART TWO

THE SIRIUS QUESTION IS REPHRASED

INTRODUCTION

We shall turn now to the star Sirius in history. What was its importance, if any, in ancient religions? Is there evidence from the ancient cultures that the mysterious details of the Sirius system were known to others than the Dogon tribe? And can we discover where the Dogon got their information?

I must warn the reader that Part Two is difficult, by the nature of its subject-matter. I have tried to make it readable, but beg the reader's indulgence if I have not succeeded. It is exciting material and the reader should stick with it. I am certain he will come out at the end of the tunnel with a great deal of amazement. For the ancient cultures are far more bizarre than the ordinary person is generally led to expect.

Chapter 3

A Fairytale

Once there was a beautiful bright star named Sothis, as fine as any goddess. She had long held a dominant position in the sky and been admired by all for her beauty. But of late she had felt unwell; indeed, it distinctly seemed to her that she felt her life ebbing away. Night by night she fell further from her high, proud place in the sky – closer to the skyline and what must surely be her certain death. Failing, failing, she clung to any companion star she could find, only to discover that they too felt this deathly weakness, and were sinking into a kind of sweet sleep. What was she to do? She felt her strength going nightly; she could hardly shine the way she wished. Once she had been as glamorous, as scintillating a queen of the night sky as ever had been seen. And now she felt she was as worthless as any old woman, her position at the centre of things gone, and her beauty fading steadily. . . . Towards the end she wept bitterly and her eyes reddened with the shame of her coming eclipse. She was so ill, her discomfort so acute. She was almost glad to welcome her fate, and that terrible line of earth and hills which she had dreaded, at last devoured her brilliant presence entirely. The night came and she was no more. Beneath the earth she rested in the balm of death.

But because this queen of the sky had been good during her ascendancy and had not been too haughty or vulgar, there were many admirers of her beauty to mourn her passing. Down on the lowly earth moved less brilliant mortals. Many nights they had stood in awe of the beautiful Sothis when she was in her prime. Some, indeed, had watched her birth when, red as a baby from the womb or as the Sun when he rises daily, this bright and beautiful immortal (or so she had seemed) had first flashed the most piercing and glittering rays of her incomparable presence sideways across the earth – seeming almost to scorch the very ground with her flaming beauty. This first appearance had been brief, for immediately behind her had come the all-engrossing grandeur of the great Sun himself. Heedless of Sothis, he soon washed the sky white with his splendour. All the stars dissolved like tiny drops of milk, lost when their bowl is suddenly filled to overflowing. So great was the Sun, so irresistible his presence – he whom some compared to a great wild bull bellowing and lording it over the heavens and the earth alike. But every night the Sun retired to his resting place, and night by night the flaming goddess Sothis entranced and bewitched mortal men, as she rose steadily higher and grew to great perfection. And further and further ahead of the Sun she rose each night.

But with her absence, how barren, how bleak, the sky now seemed. The disappearance of this renowned beauty from the vault of the heavens seemed such an unbearable deprivation. How the goddess was missed! Many mortal men shed bitter tears not to see the beauty who had infatuated them with her glancing eyes, her winsome smile, her slim waist and delicate feet. Were they never again to see her light tread in the celestial round dance of the stars?

Day followed night, and the sorrow of many became soothed by time's healing wings, which slowly fold themselves around the sufferer in invisible layers of sleep, forgetfulness, and the new interests which life must bring. The beautiful Sothis, though mourned, was lost only to the sight. For all remembered her, and that image of her burned into memory was so glorious, that to expect her actual presence came to seem almost too much to ask of many-hued, shifting, and various Fate.

Seventy days had elapsed. Hope had long since been abandoned to acceptance; sorrow had become numb. A shepherd had gone out before sunrise to his lambs now fully six months old. The Sun would not long be delayed, it was approaching the time of daybreak. The shepherd looked towards the skyline in the east. And as he looked, he saw the horizon burn with a refulgent fire, and the shimmering red birth of the goddess. It was she, it must be she! No other star had that aura, such a penetrating persona. The shepherd stood transfixed; his eyes were seared by this fresh star, dripping it seemed, with the waters of life, and aflame also with the fiery resurgence of its renewed existence. As the quick Sun behind her moved up to erase Sothis's tantalizingly brief appearance, the shepherd turned and ran to the nearest settlement. 'Awake! Awake! The goddess has returned! She is reborn, immortal, come back from death!' And all the devotees assembled with excitement and renewed hope. They heard the tale, saw for themselves the next morning, and they instituted a yearly celebration. This celebration exists to this day, and many are the temples, many are the priests, who gather in the month of July throughout all our land of Egypt to witness the much-heralded yearly rebirth of the great Sothis, bestower of concord and blessings to her people. And in honour of her seventy days spent in the underworld, we have instituted the seventy-day embalming and mummification rites for our own dead, as it is pious and indeed right that we should do.

*****

I wrote this fairytale, from the point of view of an ancient Egyptian priest, in order to convey to the reader not only certain facts but also certain equally important and, unfortunately, extinct emotions. For the attitudes and feelings of ancient peoples are just as important as the dry description of what facts they believed.

Sothis was the ancient Egyptian name for Sirius as it was spelt by the Greeks, and it was by the movements of Sirius that they regulated their calender. The first appearance of Sirius on the western horizon just before the sun – after seventy days in the Duat (Underworld) – was what is called the heliacal rising (or 'with-the-sun' rising) of Sirius. This event occurred once a year and gave rise to the Sothic Calendar, whose details we need not go into.

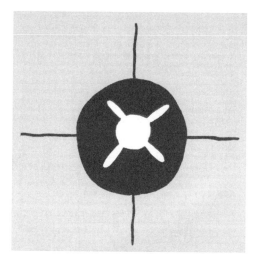

Figure 13. The heliacal rising of Sirius. Dogon drawing of Sirius and the sun joined together at this moment

The heliacal rising of Sirius was so important to the ancient Egyptians (as indeed it is to the Dogon as well[1]) that gigantic temples were constructed with their main aisles oriented precisely towards the spot on the horizon where Sirius would appear on the expected morning. The light of Sirius would be channelled along the corridor (due to the precise orientation) to flood the altar in the inner sanctum as if a pin-pointed spotlight had been switched on. This blast of light focused from a single star was possible because of the orientation being so incredibly precise and because the temple would be otherwise in total darkness within. In a huge, utterly dark temple, the light of one star focused solely on the altar must have made quite an impact on those present. In this way was the presence of the star made manifest within its temple. One such temple to the star Sirius was the temple of Isis at Denderah in Egypt. An ancient hieroglyphic inscription from that temple informs us:[2]

She shines into her temple on New Year's Day, and she mingles her light with that of her father Rā on the horizon.

(Rā is an ancient Egyptian name for the sun.)

The heliacal rising of Sirius was also important to other ancient peoples. Here is a dramatic description by the ancient Greek poet Aratus of Soli of the rising of Sirius[3] (often known as the Dog Star as it is in the constellation Canis, or 'Dog'):

> The tip of his [the Dog's] terrible jaw is marked by a star that keenest of all blazes with a searing flame and him men call Sirius. When he rises with the Sun [his heliacal rising], no longer do the trees deceive him by the feeble freshness of their leaves. For easily with his keen glance he pierces their ranks, and to some he gives strength but of others he blights the bark utterly.

We see that this dramatic description of the rising of the star indicates an event which was certainly noticed by ancient peoples. Throughout Latin literature there are many references to 'the Dog Days' which followed the heliacal rising of Sirius in the summer. These hot, parched days were thought by that time to derive some of their ferocity and dryness from the 'searing' of Sirius. Traditions arose of Sirius being 'red' because it was in fact red at its heliacal rising, just as any other body at the horizon is red. When making rhetorical allusion to the Dog Days, the Latins would often speak of Sirius being red at that time, which it was.

We tend to be unaware that stars rise and set at all. This is not entirely due to our living in cities ablaze with electric lights which reflect back at us from our fumes, smoke, and artificial haze. When I discussed the stars with the late well-known naturalist Seton Gordon, I was surprised to learn that even a man such as he, who had spent his entire lifetime observing wildlife and nature, was totally unaware of the movements of the stars. And he was no prisoner of smog-bound cities. He had no inkling, for instance, that the Little Bear could serve as a reliable night clock as it revolves in tight circles around the Pole Star (and acts as a celestial hour-hand at half speed – that is, it takes twenty-four hours rather than twelve for a single revolution).

I wondered what could be wrong. Our modern civilization does not ignore the stars only because most of us can no longer see them. There are definitely deeper reasons. For even if we leave the sulphurous vapours of our Gomorrahs to venture into a natural landscape, the stars do not enter into any of our back-to-nature schemes. They simply have no place in our outlook any more. We look at them, our heads flung back in awe and wonder that they can exist in such profusion. But that is as far as it goes, except for the poets. This is simply a 'gee whiz' reaction. The rise in interest in astrology today does not result in much actual star-gazing. And as for the space programme's impact on our view of the sky, many people will attentively follow the motions of a visible satellite against a backdrop of stars whose positions are absolutely meaningless to them. The ancient mythological figures sketched in the sky were taught us as children to be quaint 'shepherds' fantasies' unworthy of the attention of adult minds We are interested in the satellite because we made it, but the stars are alien and untouched by human hands – therefore vapid. To such a level has our technological mania, like a bacterial solution in which we have been stewed from birth, reduced us.

It is only the integral part of the landscape which can relate to the stars. Man has ceased to be that. He inhabits a world which is more and more his own fantasy. Farmers relate to the skies, as well as sailors, camel caravans, and aerial navigators. For theirs are all integral functions involving the fundamental principle – now all but forgotten – of orientation. But in an almost totally secular and artificial world, orientation is thought to be unnecessary. And the numbers of people living at home doped on tranquilizers testifies to our aimless, drifting metaphysic.

We have debased what was once the integral nature of life channelled by cosmic orientations – a wholeness – to the enervated tepidity of skin sensations and retinal discomfort. Our interior body clocks, known as circadian rhythms,* continue to operate inside us, but find no contact with the outside world. They therefore become ingrown and frustrated cycles which never interlock with our environment. We are causing ourselves to become meaningless body machines programmed to what looks, in its isolation, to be an arbitrary set of cycles. But by tearing ourselves from our context, like the still-beating heart ripped out of the body of an Aztec victim, we inevitably do violence to our psyches. I would call the new disease, with its side effect of 'alienation of the young', *dementia temporalis.*

When I tried to remedy my own total ignorance of this subject originally, I found it an extremely difficult process. I discovered that I was reading coherent explanatory matter which I 'understood' but did not comprehend. For comprehension consists of understanding from the inside as well as understanding from the outside. Things that do not really matter to us, or into which we do not imaginatively project our own consciousness, remain strange to us; we understand them outside (like a man feeling the skin of an orange) but we have no inherent relation with the thing, and hence are ultimately divorced from its reality. This increasing isolation and alienation, a cultural blight of which there is almost universal complaint in the 'civilized' world, is yet another consequence of *dementia temporalis.* For how can you get inside anything in the end if you have ceased to be inside your own local universe with its cycles and natural events? To be outside nature is to be an outsider in all things.

With these observations in mind and a child's fairytale to help guide us

---

* i.e. daily rhythms; the word 'circadian' means 'about a day' because the rhythms are not exactly twenty-four hours.

into the anteroom of the Egyptian psyche, let us prepare to take a plunge over a waterfall in the certainty that there is no chance of drowning. I have been over this particular waterfall before, and I assure you that the thrill is absolutely delicious if you just let yourself go. But there is no question about the fact that you will have to swim pretty hard. We're off . . . and immediately we are in the frothing rapids where names and basic guidelines must be established quickly. Professors Neugebauer and Parker, experts in such matters as these, tell us:[4]

> The Egyptian calendar-year on which the diagonal star clocks (hitherto called 'diagonal calendars') were constructed is the well-known civil or 'wandering' year which consisted of twelve months of three ten-day weeks, divided into three seasons of four months each, followed by five epagomenal days, called by the Egyptians 'the days upon the year'. The total of 365 days did not vary and as a consequence the Egyptian year moved slowly forward in the natural year by, on the average, one day in four years. As we shall see later . . . this was a continuously vexing complication in keeping the star clocks adjusted.
>
> The basis of these clocks was the risings of the stars (conventionally referred to as 'decans') at twelve 'hour' intervals through the night and in ten-day weeks through the year.

The main star or decan was Sirius. The four decans immediately before it in order comprise the constellation Orion. The last portion of Orion rises above the horizon one 'hour' before Sirius. It was for this reason that Orion took on significance in the Egyptian mythology and religion. The Egyptians were so concerned with Sirius, the star whose rising formed the basis of their entire calendar, that the decan immediately preceding it came to be looked on as Sirius's 'advance man'. Sirius itself was known to the Egyptians as *Śpd* or *Śpdt* (a 't' ending is feminine). This is sometimes spelt S*ept* and pronounced thus. Orion was known to the Egyptians as S₃*ḥ* which is transliterated as S*aḥ* or S*ah*, and pronounced thus.

Now that we have established a few names and facts, we have to consider the next fundamental point. We must establish, on the professors' word for it, that the star Sirius was actually identified (as Sothis) with the famous goddess Isis, the head of the Egyptian pantheon.

The heliacal rising of Sirius is called in Egyptian *prt Śpdt*. Neugebauer and Parker say:[5] 'We offer the suggestion that Śpdt was in origin a nisbe of śpd referring to Isis as "the one of śpd". That śpd and śpdt Sothis are both identified with Sirius is one of the rare certainties in Egyptian astronomy. Sothis is a goddess firmly identified with *Śpdt* and residing there. Sothis is also identified with the goddess known to us as Isis but whose actual Egyptian name is transliterated as *Ȧst*.

Professor Wallis Budge was practically the founding father of modern Egyptology. He makes this interesting observation:[6] 'The throne or seat,

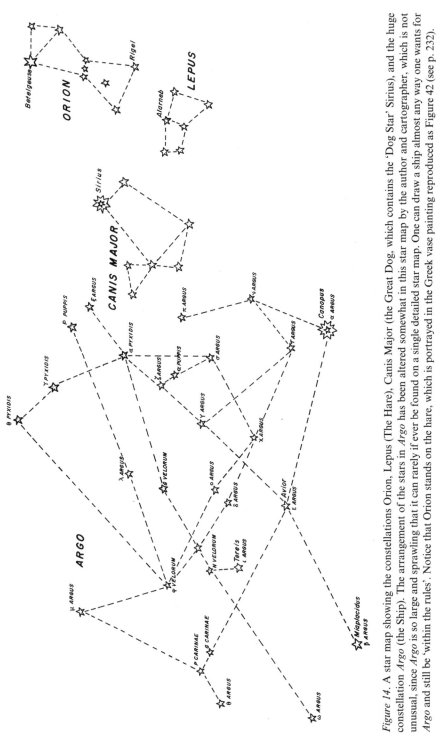

Figure 14. A star map showing the constellations Orion, Lepus (The Hare), Canis Major (the Great Dog, which contains the 'Dog Star' Sirius), and the huge constellation *Argo* (the Ship). The arrangement of the stars in *Argo* has been altered somewhat in this star map by the author and cartographer, which is not unusual, since *Argo* is so large and sprawling that it can rarely if ever be found on a single detailed star map. One can draw a ship almost any way one wants for *Argo* and still be 'within the rules'. Notice that Orion stands on the hare, which is portrayed in the Greek vase painting reproduced as Figure 42 (see p. 232).

⨎ , is the first sign in the name of Ȧs-t, ⨎◠ , who is the female counterpart of Osiris, and it is very probable that originally the same conception underlay both names.' Osiris as the husband of Isis was identified with the constellation Orion.

Wallis Budge also said, after giving the following hieroglyphic forms of Osiris:[7]

Osiris, ⬯ , Ȧs-Ȧr, or

From the hieroglyphic texts of all periods of the dynastic history of Egypt we learn that the god of the dead, *par excellence*, was the god, whom the Egyptians called by a name which may be tentatively transcribed Ȧs-Ȧr, or Us-Ȧr, who is commonly known to us as 'Osiris'.

The oldest and simplest form of the name is ⨎ ,

that is to say, it is written by means of two hieroglyphics the first of which represents a 'throne' and the other an 'eye', but the exact meaning attached to the combination of the two pictures by those who first used them to express the name of the god, and the signification of the name in the minds of those who invented it cannot be said.

There is a great elaboration of what Ȧs-Ȧr does *not* mean, referring to the use of puns which particularly delighted Egyptian priests, etc. Two pages later he winds up by saying: 'The truth of the matter seems to be that the ancient Egyptians knew just as little about the original meaning of the name Ȧs-Ȧr as we do, and that they had no better means of obtaining information about it than we have.'

The Bozo tribe in Mali, cousins to the Dogon, describe Sirius B as 'the eye star', and here we see the Egyptians designating Osiris by an eye for reasons which are not clear. And Osiris is the 'companion' of the star Sirius. A coincidence? The Bozo also describe Sirius A as 'seated' – and a seat is the sign for Isis.

A little later Budge adds: '. . . in some passages (Ȧs-Ȧr or "Osiris") is referred to simply as "god",

without the addition of any name. No other god of the Egyptians was ever mentioned or alluded to in this manner, and no other god at any time in Egypt ever occupied exactly the same exalted position in their minds, or

was thought to possess his peculiar attributes.' He adds:[8] 'The plaqu
Ḥemaka[†] proves that a centre of the Osiris cult existed at Abydos under
Ist Dynasty, but we are not justified in assuming that the god was f
worshipped there, and . . . it is difficult not to think that even under the Ist
Dynasty shrines had been built in honour of Osiris at several places in
Egypt.*

Thus we see the immense antiquity of the recognition of Ȧst and Ȧs-Ȧr
(Isis and Osiris), going back well before the dynastic period in Egypt.

Wallis Budge says:[9] 'The symbol of Isis in the heavens was the star Sept,

which was greatly beloved because its appearance marked not only the
beginning of a new year, but also announced the advance of the
Inundation of the Nile, which betokened renewed wealth and prosperity
of the country. As such Isis was regarded as the companion of Osiris,
whose soul dwelt in the star Saḥ,

i.e. Orion . . .'

Wallis Budge also says :[10]

ȦST, 𓊨 , or 𓊨𓏏 , or 𓊨𓏏𓁐 , ISIS

Notwithstanding the fact that Ȧs, or Ȧst, i.e. Isis, is one of the
goddesses most frequently mentioned in the hieroglyphic texts, nothing
is known with certainty about the attributes which were ascribed to her
in the earliest times. . . . The name Ȧst has, like Ȧs-Ȧr, up to the present
defied all explanation, and it is clear from the punning derivations to
which the Egyptians themselves had recourse, that they knew no more
about the meaning of her name than we do. . . . The symbol of the name

of Isis in Egyptian is a seat, or throne, 𓊨 , but we have no means of

connecting it with the attributes of the goddess in such a way as to give
a rational explanation of her name, and all the derivations hitherto
proposed must be regarded as mere guesses. . . . An examination of the
texts of all periods proves that Isis always held in the minds of the
Egyptians a position which was entirely different from that of every
other goddess, and although it is certain that their views concerning her

---

* Excavated in 1935, this inscribed wooden label was thought to come from the tomb of
Ḥemaka, Chancellor of Egypt, but is now known to be from the tomb of King Udimu of the
First Dynasty (*circa* 3000 BC).
† Emery estimates the First Dynasty as commencing around 3200 BC.

varied from time to time, and that certain aspects or phases of the goddess were worshipped more generally at one period than at another, it is correct to say that from the earliest to the latest dynasties Isis was the greatest goddess of Egypt. Long before the copies of the Pyramid Texts which we possess* were written the attributes of Isis were well defined, and even when the priests of Heliopolis assigned her the position which she held in the cycle of their gods between BC 4000 and BC 3000 the duties which she was thought to perform in connexion with the dead were clearly defined, and were identical with those which belonged to her in the Graeco-Roman period.

I had begun to suspect that the sister-goddess of Isis, who is called Nephthys, represented a possible description of Sirius B, the dark companion star that described a circle around Sirius. (For we have just seen that Isis was identified with Sirius quite precisely by the Egyptians, a fact which no Egyptologist would ever dream of disputing, as it is quite undeniably established as we have seen.) But I must confess that I was not prepared to discover this following passage:[11]

> On the subject of Anubis Plutarch reports (44;61) some interesting beliefs. After referring to the view that Anubis was born of Nephthys, although Isis was his reputed mother, he goes on to say, 'By Anubis they understand the horizontal circle, which divides the invisible part of the world, which they call Nephthys, from the visible, to which they give the name of Isis; and as this circle equally touches upon the confines of both light and darkness, it may be looked upon as common to them both – and from this circumstance arose that resemblance, which they imagine between Anubis and the Dog, it being observed of this animal, that he is equally watchful as well by day as night.

This description could be taken to be one of the Sirius system. It clearly describes Isis (whom we know to have been identified with Sirius) as 'the confines of light' and 'the visible', and her sister Nephthys is described as being 'the confines of darkness' and 'the invisible', and common to both is the horizontal circle which divides them – the horizontal circle described, perhaps, by the orbit of the dark companion about the bright star? And here, too, is an explanation of the symbolism of the dog which has always been associated with Sirius, which has borne throughout the ages the name of the 'Dog Star'.

Anubis is variously represented as jackal-headed and dog-headed in Egyptian art. Wallis Budge adds:[12] 'Thus much, however, is certain, that in ancient times the Egyptians paid the greatest reverence and honour to the Dog. . . .'

---

* Wallis Budge believes those of the Vth and VIth Dynasties to be copies of earlier writings including those of the Ist Dynasty; see p. 117 of his book.

Anubis was also variously represented as the son of Nephthys by Osiris and as being really identical with Osiris himself. A famous tale has him embalm the corpse of Osiris. Osiris was known as Anubis, though, at Oxyrhynchus and Cynopolis.[13]

A name similar to Anubis (which is really Anpu in Egyptian) and which is also associated with Isis-Sothis is Anukis, a fellow-goddess who, along with the goddess Satis, sails in the same celestial boat with Sothis in the Egyptian paintings. There are thus the three goddesses together, possibly a description of Sirius A, Sirius B, and Sirius C, and emphasizing that the Sirius system is really thought to be a three-star system. Just to underline the point, Neugebauer specifically states:[14] 'The goddess Satis, who like her companion Anukis is hardly to be taken as a separate constellation but rather as an associate of Sothis.'

The goddess Anukis holds two jars from which she pours water, possibly indicating two watery planets around her star? All the references to the Sothic heavens are to a watery, reed-growing paradise. Many archaeologists have surmised that this refers to some specifically Egyptian locale. But no one is sure. What is known is that heaven is almost invariably associated with the Sirius system and is described as being prolific of vegetation and watery.

In Plutarch's famous and lengthy treatise 'Isis and Osiris' (356) we read: '. . . Isis was born in the regions that are ever moist.' In the Loeb Library edition of this, the translator F. C. Babbitt adds a footnote at this point saying: 'The meaning is doubtful. . . .' In other words, no one is really sure what is meant by all these references to Isis-Sothis and the 'moist regions', which are supposed by most scholars quite sensibly to be projections of local Egyptian conditions around the Nile into an ideal celestial region. But most scholars admit that this is mere conjecture. The 'moist regions' could just as well be an attempt to describe some watery planets. It is worth pointing out that in the event of planets in the Sirius system being watery, we must seriously consider the possibility of intelligent beings from there being amphibious.

Perhaps 'the sirens' are, figuratively, a chorus of mermaids recalled from earlier times. By coincidence, in zoology a siren is 'one of a genus (Siren) of eel-shaped amphibians having small forelimbs, but destitute of hind legs and pelvis, and having permanent external gills as well as lungs'. It would be interesting to see how far back in time these creatures were called by their name. As for the singing sirens who lure sailors to the rocks, they are called in Greek *Seirēn* (singular), *Seirēnes* (plural) and are first mentioned in Homer's *Odyssey*. Homer knew of two sirens, but later there was a third, and some added a fourth. (Plato decided there were eight because of that number matching the number of musical notes in the octave.) It is interesting that in Greek Sirius is *Seirios*. Liddell and Scott in their definitive Greek lexicon give a meaning of the previous *Seirēn* as 'a constellation, like Seirios, Eust. 1709. 54'.

Another similar word *Seistron* became in Latin *sistrum* and Liddell and Scott define it as '*A rattle* used in the worship of Isis. . . .'

Let us now turn our attention to a remarkable book, *Star Names, Their Lore and Meaning* by Richard Hinckley Allen. In this book, under a discussion of the constellation Canis Major (The Dog), which contains Sirius,[15] on p. 130, is a description of the star of the constellation represented by the Greek letter δ (delta): It is the 'modern Wezen, from (the Arabic) Al Wazn, Weight, "as the star seems to rise with difficulty from the horizon," but Ideler calls this an astonishing star-name.'

Before leaving the star, it is worth noting that Allen says the Chinese knew it as well as some stars in Argo as 'Hoo She, the Bow and Arrow', and that the bow and arrow is a variation motif associated with the Sirius system by the Egyptians. In Neugebauer we read:[16] 'The goddess Satis, who like her companion Anukis is hardly to be taken as a separate constellation but rather as an associate of Sothis. In Dendera B, the goddess holds a drawn bow and arrow.'

More information regarding Al Wazn, 'Weight', is found in Dr Christian Ludwig Ideler's *Untersuchungen ueber den Ursprung und die Bedeutung der Sternnamen* (Investigations Concerning the Origin and the Meaning of Star Names) Berlin, 1809, which Allen describes as 'the main critical compendium of information on stellar names – Arabic, Greek, and Latin especially. It is to him that we owe the translation of the original Arabic text of Kazwini's *Description of the Constellations*, written in the 13th century, which forms the basis of the *Sternnamen*, with Ideler's additions and annotations from classical and other sources. From this much information in my book is derived.'

Ideler might well comment that Al Wazn is 'an astonishing star-name'. To call a star in the same constellation as Sirius 'too heavy to rise over the horizon with ease' looks suspiciously like an attempt to describe a 'heavy star' such as Sirius B.

Could this reference to a 'heavy star' be a reference to Sirius B by people who have inherited a slightly garbled version of the tradition of its being a super-dense star invisible to the unaided eye – resulting in their seizing on one of Sirius's apparent companions (as seen from the Earth) and giving it a description properly applying to its actual companion? The Arabs do not mention '480 ass loads' to describe its weight in the quaint fashion of the Dogon, but the substance of the idea seems to be present. It is well known that ancient Arabic astronomical lore derives from Egypt and is found in Arabic traditions in a degenerate form. Obviously the search must now be on for this concept of a super-heavy star in Egyptian traditions! I had also always suspected that this most secret tradition of the Dogon reached them from Egypt. It will not be easy for us to discover, as it must have been an extremely esoteric and secret teaching of the Egyptians, just as it was the most secret teaching of the Dogon. In searching for this, it will be helpful for us to look at the Greek traditions for greater clarification, as well as to turn to ancient Sumer.

A further use of the name Wazn is its loose application to the star Canopus in the constellation Argo.[17] Allen, in describing the Argo, quotes the ancient Greek poet Aratos, in a passage showing us something of the relation Argo bears to Canis Major, the Great Dog:

Sternforward Argo by the Great Dog's tail
Is drawn . . .

Argo is the constellation representing both Jason's ship with its fifty Argonauts and Noah's ark.

Jason's *Argo* 'carried Danaos with his fifty daughters from Egypt to Rhodes', as Allen puts it. He adds: 'The Egyptian story said that it was the ark that bore Isis and Osiris over the deluge; while the Hindus thought that it performed the same office for their equivalent Isi and Iswara.'

Allen's old-fashioned spelling 'Iswara' is a reference to the word 'Ishvara'. There are some interesting facts to be gleaned from perusing the meanings of the Sanskrit word *ishu*, which basically means 'an arrow'. Recall the connection of the bow and arrow with Sirius among both the Egyptians and the Chinese. (Further examples are given in the book *Hamlet's Mill* by Santillana and von Dechend, along with interesting illustrations.) Now note from Monier-Williams's definitive Sanskrit dictionary that *ishu* means not only 'arrow' but 'ray of light'. *Ishvasa* means 'a bow' or 'an archer'. Remember the three goddesses and note this: that *Ishustrikanda*, which literally means 'the threefold arrow', is specifically meant to be the name of a constellation! Monier-Williams says it is 'perhaps the girdle of Orion' (which has three prominent stars). The interested reader must refer to *Hamlet's Mill* for a great deal of discussion of Sirius the Bow Star. *Hamlet's Mill* is one of the most fascinating books about ancient astronomical lore. In Plate 25 a Babylonian cylinder seal shows the heliacal rising of Sirius, with Sirius portrayed graphically as the Bow Star!

We have previously encountered this idea of the celestial boats in Egypt where their gods sailed through the waters of the heavens. The three Sirius-goddesses: Sothis, Anukis, and Satis, were all in the same boat. So it is interesting to see that *Argo* was a boat connected with Isis and Osiris, for a concept which seems to be peculiarly stubborn in attaching itself to *Argo* is the number fifty. It is my suspicion that this is a remnant of the concept of Sirius B taking fifty years to complete an orbit around Sirius A. This suggestion is not as far-fetched as it may seem at first sight. Indeed, the reader will discover as he proceeds that the suggestion will become more and more obvious. We must realize that in Egyptian terms the orbit of Sirius B around Sirius A could have been expressed in terms of a celestial boat. Now since *Argo* is the boat of Isis and Osiris, what better way to express the fifty-year orbit than by giving the boat fifty oarsmen? And that is what *Argo* has – in the tradition there are fifty rowers, or Argonauts.

In order to fortify my argument I shall quote Allen's precise way of describing this:[18] 'Mythology insisted that it was built by Glaucus, or by Argos, for Jason, leader of the fifty Argonauts, *whose number equalled that of the oars of the ship . . .*' In other words, it is not the men but the *number of oars* laid out in line around the ship that is important. A ship (an orbit) with fifty oars (fifty 'markers' or yearly stages)!

But before moving on, it is worth giving an illustration of the concept of 'the rower' in the celestial barque from an ancient Egyptian coffin text 'The Field of Paradise'.[19] '. . . in the place where Re (the Sun) sails with rowing. I am the keeper of the halyard in the boat of the god; I am the oarsman who does not weary in the barque of Re.' (Re is another form of the more familiar Rā.)

The first person in this text refers to the deceased Pharaoh. This is one of the examples of the common Egyptian conception that when a Pharaoh died he became a celestial rower. It should be obvious, then, how the concept of 'fifty rowers' by fifty positions, or oars, came to be important as symbols in ancient Greece. It harks back to this Egyptian motif.

Now we must turn to the Sumerian civilization (which later developed into the Babylonian civilization). Sumer-Akkad was roughly contemporaneous with ancient Egypt, and the lands are known to have been in contact. In a major source we read[20] of the Sumerian word Magan: 'The land Magan is usually identified either with Arabia or with Egypt.'

But whatever contact the two civilizations may have had, we must first investigate the Sumerian religion and mythology. For this we rely primarily on the excellent work of the late Professor Samuel Noah Kramer of the University of Pennsylvania. Kramer accepted me as a special student there in the 1960s, but our association was terminated by a severe heart attack which forced him into temporary retirement. He eventually lived into his nineties.

The Sumerian heaven-god is called Anu. (In Sanskrit *anupa* means 'a watery country'.) I had a considerable shock when I discovered that Alexander Heidel says in *The Babylonian Genesis*: '. . . just as the departed spirits of Enlil and Anu were pictured as the wild ass and the jackal, respectively'.[21] Anu is represented by the jackal. Well, of course, the jackal is the symbol (interchangeable with the dog) of the Egyptian Anpu (Anubis)!

I shall explain later why I consider Anu to be related to the Sirius question, apart from this obvious parallel. At the moment I shall deal with further related parallels which I consider amazing. Anu is the king of some attendant deities called the Anunnaki. Note the recurrence in Sumer of 'Anu' in both Anu and the Anunnaki, and in Egypt with both Anpu (Anubis) and Anukis. In all these cases Sirius is involved. The jackal or dog is common as a symbol to the 'Anu' in both countries. There are other parallels, but we shall come to them in due course.

In Sumerian the word *an* means 'heaven' and Anu is the god of heaven. Wallis Budge says[22] that the Egyptian god Nu was often identified with Nut, which is 'heaven'.

Significantly, he expressly states:[23]

It is surprising therefore to find so much similarity existing between the primeval gods of Sumer and those of Egypt, especially as the resemblance cannot be the result of borrowing. It is out of the question to assume that Ashur-banipal's editors borrowed the system from Egypt, or that the literary men of the time of Seti I borrowed their ideas from the *literati* of Babylonia or Assyria, and we are therefore driven to the conclusion that both the Sumerians and the early Egyptians derived their primeval gods from some common but exceedingly ancient source. The similarity between the two companies of gods seems to be too close to be accidental . . .

I had come to all these conclusions myself before seeing this passage by Wallis Budge.

But to return to Anu. Osiris is sometimes known as An.[24] In a hymn to Osiris[25] he is called the 'god An of millions of years . . .' and also 'An in An-tes, Great One, Ḥeru-khuti, thou stridest over heaven with long strides'. Therefore this designation as An is specifically connected with heaven and the long strides mean heavenly motion.

In considering An and Anu we must look again at Anubis. But as we do so we shall take a glance at the Sanskrit. Recall that Anubis in Plutarch's account seemed to refer specifically to the *orbit* of Sirius B. In Sanskrit the word *anḍa* means 'ellipse', and the word *anu* means 'minute, atomic, "the subtle one", an atom of matter' and *animan* means 'minuteness, atomic nature, the smallest particle, the superhuman power of becoming as small as an atom'. The first word could describe an orbit. Since Kepler, we have known that our planets move in elliptical orbits rather than circular ones, and the orbit of Sirius B is that of an ellipse. As for the next two forms *anu* and *animan*, they seem to have meanings perilously peripheral to an account of that level of matter (the atomic) where the nature of Sirius B is manifested. (We shall see later in this book that other similarities exist between certain Sanskrit terms relevant to the Sirius question and like terms in Egypt and the Near East; they will be shown to have considerable importance.)

Wallis Budge says of Anubis:[26] 'His worship is very ancient, and there is no doubt that even in the earliest times his cult was general in Egypt; it is probable that it is older than that of Osiris.' Also he points out here, as elsewhere, that the face of the deceased human becomes identified with Anubis, and it is just the head of Anubis which is symbolically represented by the jackal or dog. I have already pointed out that he is described as the circle or orbit separating the dark Nephthys from the light Isis or Sirius. In other words, I take Anubis to represent the orbit of Sirius B around Sirius A. We also find him described as 'time',[27] a particularly intelligent way of looking at an orbit as progressive and sequential in time. 'Time the devourer', a motif common to us all, is no stranger to the Egyptians. It should not surprise us that Anubis is also represented as a devourer! More specifically, he is accused of devouring the Apis bull. The Apis bull is the animal into which the dead Osiris was sewn and transported, according to a late legend which is widely known. But more basically, the 'Apis Bull' (the deity known under the Ptolemies as Serapis) is Āsar-Ḥāpi. It is Osiris himself! In *The Gods of the Egyptians*, we read 'Apis is called "the life of Osiris, the lord of heaven"' and 'Apis was, in fact, believed to be animated by the soul of Osiris, and to be Osiris incarnate'.[28] So consequently, when Anubis devoured Apis, he was eating the husband of Isis! It is very colourfully represented in these dramatic mythological terms, but the meaning is clear. We read later:[29]

'Others again are of the opinion that by Anubis is meant Time, and that his denomination of *Kuon* [the Greek word for 'dog'] does not so much allude to any likeness which he has to the dog, though this be the general rendering of the word, as to that other significance of the term taken from *breeding*; because Time begets all things out of itself, bearing them within itself, as it were in a womb. But this is one of those secret doctrines which are more fully made known to those who are initiated into the worship of Anubis.'

Exactly. A secret doctrine! What one would give for a fuller account! This is the trouble with most of our sources; they give away little except by inference. Secret doctrines are not scribbled down too frequently and left for posterity. The most secret doctrine of the Dogon was only revealed with great reluctance after many, many years, and following a conference by the initiates. The Egyptians were no fools, and we can hardly expect them to have left papyri or texts specifically revealing in so many words what they were not supposed to reveal. We can only try to piece together clues. But we will see our clues eventually turn into a veritable avalanche.

The last passage from Wallis Budge was a quotation by him from Plutarch's 'Isis and Osiris'. Many Egyptologists have remarked on the irony that we have nowhere in Egyptian sources a full, coherent account of Isis and Osiris, not even in all the sources put together! And we are forced to rely on Plutarch, who did preserve a long account which he wrote in his native Greek. Plutarch (first century AD) was a priest at Delphi for the last thirty years of his life. One of his best friends was the priestess Clea at Delphi. His treatise 'Isis and Osiris' is dedicated to Clea and addressed to her. It begins with these words: 'All good things, my dear Clea, sensible men must ask from the gods; and especially do we pray that from those mighty gods we may, in our quest, gain a knowledge of themselves, so far as such a thing is attainable by men.' This gives some indication of what Plutarch was like as a man.

The Introduction to the Loeb edition of Isis and Osiris by F. C. Babbitt says: '[Plutarch] once visited Egypt, but how long he stayed and how much he learned we have no means of knowing. It is most likely that his treatise represents the knowledge current in his day, derived, no doubt, from two sources: books and priests.' It is certain that Plutarch, who was so important at Delphi as a priest, would have had ample introductions to the leading priests of Egypt. This sort of thing was standard practice – as with the study of Egyptian religion and astronomy undertaken centuries earlier by the Greek scholar Eudoxus (colleague of Plato and Aristotle), who was given a letter of introduction to the last of the native Pharaohs, Nectanebo, by the Spartan general Agesilaus, and who in turn sent him off to associate with his priests. So, no doubt Plutarch did with the Egyptian priests what Griaule and Dieterlen did with the Dogon – drew some secret traditions out of them. It is thus not surprising that Plutarch's essay is more respected by Egyptologists than by classicists.

Plutarch says: 'Some are of the opinion that Anubis is Cronos.'[30] Chronos, of course, was the Greek 'time the devourer', spelt with an *h*. Cronos in Latin is Saturn. There is a considerable debate among scholars whether Cronos (Saturn), the former chief god prior to Zeus (Jupiter), has any definite relation to the word *chronos* spelt with the *h* and sometimes used as a proper name for Time. From this latter word we derive *chronology*, *chronicle*, etc. The Sumerian god Anu is quite similar to the Greek Cronos because both Cronos and Anu were 'old' gods who were displaced by younger blood – by Zeus and Enlil respectively. Thus another possible link between Anu and Anubis, if one be willing to grant that Cronos and Chronos are not entirely separate words and concepts in ancient pre-classical Greece.

Wallis Budge continues with reference to Plutarch:

Referring to Osiris as the 'common Reason which pervades both the superior and inferior regions of the universe', he [Plutarch] says that it is, moreover, called 'Anubis, and sometimes likewise Hermanubis (i.e. Ḥeru-em-Ȧnpu); the first of these names expressing the relation it has to the superior, as the latter, to the inferior world. And for this reason it is, they sacrifice to him two Cocks, the one white, as a proper emblem of the purity and brightness of things above, the other of a saffron colour, expressive of that mixture and variety which is to found on those lower regions.'

Here is what I take to be a possible reference to the white Sirius A and the 'darker' Sirius B. But also, the 'lower regions' are the horizons, where white heavenly bodies at their 'births' and 'deaths' become saffron-coloured.

There is a clearer translation by Babbitt in the precise description of Anubis as 'the combined relation of the things'[31] rather than as 'the common Reason which pervades' the light world and the dark world. A circular orbit is just that – 'a combined relation' between the star revolving and the star revolved around. In order to make this more firmly established less as fancy than as fact, I shall cite Plutarch's words from his next paragraph (Babbitt's translation): 'Moreover, they (the Egyptians) record that in the so-called books of Hermes (the Trismegistic literature? – see page 103) it is written in regard to the sacred names that they call the power which is assigned to direct the revolution of the Sun Horus . . .' This is important because we see here that they specifically call the orbit of the sun by a god's name. If they can call the revolution of the sun by a god's name, they can call the revolution of Sirius B (assuming they really knew about it) by a god's name. We are dealing with a precedent. Now we resume this quotation because it is interesting for other reasons: '. . . but the Greeks call it Apollo; and the power assigned to the wind some call Osiris and others Serapis; and Sothis in Egyptian signifies "pregnancy" (cyesis) or "to be pregnant" (cyein): therefore in Greek, with a change of accent, the star is called the Dog-star (Cyon), which they regard as the special star of Isis.'

A further piece of information from Plutarch about Anubis is:[32] 'And when the child (Anubis, child of Nephthys by Osiris) had been found, after great toil and trouble, with the help of dogs which led Isis to it, it was brought up and became her guardian and attendant, receiving the name Anubis, and it is said to protect the gods just as dogs protect men.'

If Anubis is conceived of as an orbit around Sirius, then he would indeed be attendant upon Isis! He would go round and round her like a guard dog.

Plutarch provides us with an important crucial clue linking Isis with the *Argo* and the Argonauts and demonstrating a probable derivation of an idea that has puzzled classicists enormously: 'Like these also are the Egyptian beliefs; for they oftentimes call Isis by the name of Athena, expressive of some such idea as this, "I came of myself," which is indicative of self-impelled motion.'[33]

It must be remembered that the Greek goddess Athena, the goddess of the mind and of wisdom, was reputed to have sprung full-fledged from the brow of Zeus. She was not born. She came of herself. However, the quotation must be continued to make the point:

Typhon, as has been said, is named Seth and Bebon and Smu, and these names would indicate some forcible and preventive check or opposition or reversal.

Moreover, they call the lodestone the bone of Horus, and iron the bone of Typhon, as Manetho records. For, as the iron oftentimes acts as if it were being attracted and drawn toward the stone, and oftentimes is rejected and repelled in the opposite direction, in the same way the salutary and good and rational movement of the world at one time, by persuasion, attracts and draws towards itself and renders more gentle that harsh and Typhonian movement, and then again it gathers itself together and reverses it and plunges it into difficulties.

Figure 15. An engraving from 1675 showing 'Jupiter Dodonaeus' – the god Zeus in his sacred grove at the Oracle of Dodona. Behind him, an oak tree is shown with an anthropomorphic trunk because its leaves 'speak the oracles' with a rustling voice like the wind. On Zeus's shoulder sits an oracular dove, although it is badly drawn with a tuft on its head; the original Latin caption confirms that it is meant to be a dove nevertheless. According to Herodotus in the fifth century BC, the Egyptians of his day claimed that the Oracle of Dodona was founded by two doves which flew from Thebes in Egypt and came to rest on that spot. As I have explained at length in my book *Conversations with Eternity* (Rider, London, 1984), where I have gathered together all the ancient textual evidence, the oracular doves of the oracle centres were carrier pigeons who carried messages over hundreds of miles in a day, enabling the oracular priests and priestesses to make 'predictions' based on instant reports of distant events. This secret carrier pigeon network was the real basis for the political power of the oracle centres. 'Carrier-swallows' were also used. From the sacred oak in this picture hangs a garland dedicated by someone who has consulted the oracle and departed. Zeus has his arm protectively around a smaller figure perhaps intended to represent one of the *Selloi* – the oracular priests who slept on the ground beneath the oak trees on beds of leaves. This was a practice which they presumably discontinued during the winters, when Dodona can hardly have been 'open for business', although the actual oak leaves themselves would not have fallen at that season – the oaks at Dodona would have been holm oaks, which are evergreen

The identification of Isis with Athena here in connection with lodestones and 'self-impelled motion' brings to mind the placing by Athena of a cybernetic* oak timber from the holy sanctuary of Dodona (supposedly founded by Deukalion, the Greek Noah, after his ark landed) in the keel of the *Argo* (see Figure 15). H. W. Parke in his books *Greek Oracles* and *The Oracles of Zeus* refers to this: 'Athena when the *Argo* was built took a timber from the oak tree of Dodona (the oracular centre of Zeus) and fitted it into the keel. This had the result that the *Argo* itself could speak and guide or warn the Argonauts at critical moments, as it actually is represented as doing in our extant epics on the subject. The original epic is lost, but there is no reason to doubt that this miraculous feature went back to it, and, if so, was at least as old as the *Odyssey* in which the *Argo* and its story are mentioned.' (The oracle at Dodona and its oak leaves are also mentioned in the *Odyssey*.) Parke then emphasizes most strongly that it is the timber itself that acts as guide. It is self-actuating and not merely an oracular medium. Thus we see that the *Argo* had a unique capacity for 'self-impelled motion' which was built into it by Athena (whom Plutarch identifies with Isis).[34]

We leave the fifty Argonauts and their magical ship to turn our attention to what appears to be a rather precise Egyptian description of the Sirius system preserved in an unusual source. The source is G. R. S. Mead (who was a friend of the poet Yeats and is mentioned by his nickname 'Old Crone' in Ezra Pound's *Cantos*), whose three-volume *Thrice Greatest Hermes*[35] contains a translation of, with extensive prolegomena and notes to, the obscure and generally ignored ancient 'Trismegistic literature' of the Hermetic tradition.† These writings are largely scorned by classical scholars who consider them Neoplatonic forgeries. Of course, ever since the wild Neoplatonic boom in the Italian Renaissance period when Marsilio Ficino translated and thereby preserved for posterity (one must grant the Medicis the credit for finding and purchasing the manuscripts!) such Neoplatonists as Iamblichus, as well as these Trismegistic writings, the Neoplatonists have been in the doghouse.

But most readers will not be familiar either with the term 'trismegistic' or with the Neoplatonists. So I had better explain. The Neoplatonists are Greek philosophers who lived long enough after Plato to have lost the name of Platonists as far as modern scholars are concerned (though they were intellectual disciples of Plato and considered themselves Platonists). Modern scholars have added the prefix 'Neo-' to 'Platonist' for their own convenience, in order to distinguish them from their earlier predecessors,

---

* Norbert Wiener in *Cybernetics*, the pioneer textbook of computer theory, said: 'We have decided to call the entire field of control and communication theory, whether in the machine or in the animal, by the name *Cybernetics* . . . (from the Greek for) *steersman.*'
† The epithet 'Thrice Greatest' has not been definitely explained, but may refer to the three degrees of initiation in the Egyptian mysteries.

those Platonists who lived within 150 years of Plato himself. The Platonic Academy existed for over nine centuries at Athens. In actuality, scholars talk about 'Middle Platonists', 'Syrian Platonists', 'Christian Platonists' 'Alexandrian Platonists', and so on. I suggest the reader look at my Appendix II, which will tell him a lot about the Neoplatonists and their connection with the Sirius mystery, and which deals primarily with the Neoplatonist Proclus.

G. R. S. Mead, at the beginning of his work *Thrice Greatest Hermes*, explains fully what 'the 'Trismegistic Literature' is. He calls it 'Trismegistic' instead of by its earlier designation 'Hermetic' (from the name of the Greek god Hermes) in order to distinguish it from other less interesting writings such as the Egyptian Hermes prayers and also the 'Hermetic Alchemical Literature'. The Trismegistic writings are now fragmentary and consist of a large amount of exceedingly strange sermons, dialogues, excerpts by Stobaeus (an anthologist of the early fifth century AD) and the Fathers of the Church from lost writings, etc. I hesitate to give a brief summary of them and suggest that the interested reader actually look into this subject himself. There are some matters which defy summary, and I consider this to be one of them. The writings contain some 'mystical' elements and certainly some sublime elements. Old Cosimo de Medici was told by Ficino that he could translate for him either the Hermetic Literature or the dialogues of Plato, but not both at once. Cosimo knew he was dying. He said something like: 'If only I could read the Books of Hermes, I would die happy. Plato would be nice but not as important. Do the Hermes, Ficino.' And Ficino did.

As I explain fully in Appendix II, the Neoplatonists are so thoroughly despised through the bias of the moment, however one cares to define that bias, that the Trismegistic literature suffers with Neoplatonism under the onus of being considered too far removed from reality and logic and being inclined towards the mystical. This does not fit well with the hard rationalism of an age still bound by the (albeit decaying) fetters of nineteenth-century scientific deterministic prejudice. The sublime irony is, of course, that proven and authentic Egyptian texts are obviously mystical, but that is considered all right. However, as long as there is a belief that the Trismegistic literature is Neoplatonic it will be despised because it is mystical.

The Trismegistic literature may be Neoplatonic. But that does not make what it has to say about Egyptian religion any less valid *per se* than the 'Isis and Osiris' by the Greek Plutarch, who was only slightly earlier in time than the Neoplatonist Greeks. It is time for scholars to pay some attention to this sadly neglected material. Much of the Trismegistic literature probably goes back to genuine sources or compilations such as Manetho's lost *Sothis*. (Manetho, High Priest of Egypt *circa* 280 BC, wrote a history of Egypt and other works in Greek, of which fragments survive.) Or the literature may be quite ancient, in which case some of it cannot, in its present form, be earlier than the Ptolemaic period when the Zodiac as we know it was introduced into Egypt by the Greeks who in turn had it from Babylon. (I cannot here discuss the matter of earlier forms of zodiac, such as at Denderah.)

Mead quotes an Egyptian magic papyrus, this being an uncontested Egyptian document which he compares to a passage in the Trismegistic literature: 'I invoke thee, Lady Isis, with whom the Good Daimon doth unite, He who is Lord in the perfect black.'[36]

We know that Isis is identified with Sirius A, and here we may have a description of her star-companion 'who is Lord in the perfect black', namely the invisible companion with whom she is united, Sirius B.

Mead, of course, had no inkling of the Sirius question. But he cited this magic papyrus in order to shed comparative light on some extraordinary passages in a Trismegistic treatise he translated which has the title 'The Virgin of the World'. In his comments on the magic papyrus Mead says: 'It is natural to make the Agathodaimon ("the Good Daimon") of the Papyrus refer to Osiris; for indeed it is one of his most frequent designations. Moreover, it is precisely Osiris who is pre-eminently connected with the so-called "underworld", the unseen world, the "mysterious dark". He is lord there . . . and indeed one of the ancient mystery-sayings was precisely, "Osiris is a dark God." '

'The Virgin of the World' is an extraordinary Trismegistic treatise in the form of a dialogue between the hierophant (high priest) as spokesman for Isis and the neophyte who represents Horus. Thus the priest instructing the initiate is portrayed as Isis instructing her son Horus.

The treatise begins by claiming it is 'her holiest discourse' which 'so speaking Isis doth pour forth'. There is, throughout, a strong emphasis on the hierarchical principle of lower and higher beings in the universe – that earthly mortals are presided over at intervals by other, higher, beings who interfere in Earth's affairs when things here become hopeless, etc. Isis says in the treatise: 'It needs must, therefore, be the less should give place to the greater mysteries.' What she is to disclose to Horus is a *great* mystery. Mead describes it as the mystery practised by the arch-hierophant (chief priest). It was the degree (here 'degree' is in the sense of 'degree' in the Masonic 'mysteries', which are hopelessly garbled and watered-down versions of genuine mysteries of earlier times) 'called the "Dark Mystery" or "Black Rite". It was a rite performed only for those who were judged worthy of it after long probation in lower degrees, something of a far more sacred character, apparently, than the instruction in the mysteries enacted in the light.'

Mead adds: 'I would suggest, therefore, that we have here a reference to the most esoteric institution of the Isiac tradition . . .', Isiac meaning of course 'Isis-tradition', and not to be confused with the Book of Isaiah in the Bible (so that perhaps it is best for us not to use the word-form 'Isiac').

It is in attempting to explain the mysterious 'Black Rite' of Isis at the highest degree of the Egyptian mysteries that Mead cited the magic papyrus which I have already quoted. He explains the 'Black Rite' as being connected with Osiris being a 'dark god' who is 'Lord of the perfect black' which is 'the unseen world, the mysterious black'.

This treatise 'The Virgin of the World' describes a personage called Hermes who seems to represent a race of beings who taught earthly mankind the arts of civilization after which: 'And thus, with charge unto his kinsmen of the Gods to keep sure watch, he mounted to the Stars'.

According to this treatise mankind have been a troublesome lot requiring scrutiny and, at rare intervals of crisis, intervention. For the significant passage, now, here is the entire paragraph: 'To him (Hermes) succeeded Tat, who was at once his son and heir unto these knowledges [this almost certainly implies a priesthood]; and not long afterwards Asclepius-Imuth, according to the will of Ptah who is Hephaestus, and all the rest who were to make enquiry of the faithful certitude of heavenly contemplation, as Foreknowledge (or Providence) willed, Foreknowledge queen of all.'

Now this is a really striking passage. We have the mysterious 'Hermes' succeeded by an Egyptian priesthood of Thoth who were initiates into the celestial mysteries. Then 'not long afterwards' we have someone called Asclepius-Imuth 'according to the will of Ptah'. This is Imhotep! The extraordinary Imhotep, a brilliant genius, philosopher, doctor, and Prime Minister (to use our terms) during the Third Dynasty in Egypt *circa* 2600 BC under King Zoser, whose tomb and temple he constructed and designed himself. (This is the famous step-pyramid at Sakkara, the first pyramid ever built by men and the world's earliest stone building according to some.) Imhotep was over the centuries gradually transformed into a god and 'a son of Ptah'. One reason why the process of his deification may have been retarded for some thousands of years is that writings by him survived, rather like the survival of the *Gathas* by Zarathustra (Zoroaster), making it impossible to claim that a man who left writings could in fact have been a god. Just like Mohammed and Zoroaster, Imhotep remained a sort of 'prophet' through his surviving writings. Ptah – known to the Greeks as Hephaestus, god of fire and the forge, and husband of Aphrodite – was considered the father of Imhotep in late Egyptian times. In fact, it is interesting that this text avoids the late form 'son of Ptah' to describe Imhotep. Imhotep was known to the Greeks and provided the basis for their god Asclepius (the Greek god of medicine, corresponding to Imhotep's late form as Egyptian god of medicine). Imhotep is also spelled Imouthes, Imothes, Imutep, etc.* Hence the form in this treatise 'Asclepius-Imuth'.

There is absolutely no question that Imhotep is being referred to here.

---

* Egyptian hieroglyphs can be transliterated in different ways, but in this case there seem to be variant forms of the Greek version of the name as well.

And in the light of that, certain other statements in this passage become quite interesting.

It has already been mentioned that in a treatise like 'The Virgin of the World', where gods' names are thrown round like birdseed, the authors were exceedingly restrained to have avoided labelling Asclepius-Imhotep as 'a son of Ptah-Hephaestus'. This may, indeed, point to a genuine early source from the time before that when the Egyptians ceased to regard Imhotep as a mortal.

Hurry says:[37]

For many years Egyptologists have been puzzled to explain why Imhotep who lived in the days of King Zoser, *ca.* 2900 BC, was not ranked among the full gods of Egypt until the Persian period, dating from 525 BC. The apotheosis of a man, however distinguished, so many centuries after his life on earth seems mysterious. The explanation appears to be that first suggested by Erman, viz. that Imhotep, at any rate during a large part of the interval was regarded as a sort of hero or demigod and received semi-divine worship. Erman suggested that this rank of demigod was bestowed on him at the time of the New Kingdom, i.e. about 1580 BC, but more recent evidence seems to indicate that this demigod stage was reached at a much earlier period.

Here a bit of chronology helps. 'The Virgin of the World' correctly described Imhotep as 'not long afterwards', following upon the creation of the Egyptian priesthood, presumably in the First Dynasty after Menes (*circa* 3300 BC), in the form in which it would be known after the unification of Egypt. Imhotep lived in the Third Dynasty, at the beginning of the Old Kingdom. I. E. S. Edwards[38] estimates this as commencing about 2686 BC. He puts the start of the First Dynasty about 3100 BC. Imhotep is thus literally 'not long afterwards'. Whoever wrote 'The Virgin of the World' knew his Egyptian chronology and also did not call Imhotep 'son of Ptah'.

There is another point. Looking at this statement from 'The Virgin of the World': '. . . and all the rest (i.e. after Imhotep) who were to make enquiry of the faithful certitude of heavenly contemplation . . .', we find that we have a reference to successors of Imhotep who 'enquired' into the riddles of the universe and also a description of Imhotep's own activities as an 'enquirer'. This reflects considerable knowledge of the subject. For Imhotep is often described as the first genuine philosopher known by name. And on p. 30 of his book, Hurry refers to apparent successors mentioned in an Oxyrhyncus papyrus (in Greek, edited by Grenfell and Hunt) which relates that 'Imhotep was worshipped as early as the IVth Dynasty, and his temple was resorted to by sick and afflicted persons'. Hurry further says: 'The other persons are Horus son of Hermes, and Kaleoibis son of Apollo (Imhotep being a son of Ptah); it is not known who these were.' Could they have been successors of Imhotep at 'enquiring'?

Hurry refers to the Trismegistic (Hermetic) literature as follows: 'If the references to Imhotep in Hermetic literature can be trusted, he was also interested in astronomy and astrology, although no special observations are associated with his name. Sethe gives various references to that literature, showing that Imhotep was reputed to have been associated with the god Thoth (Hermes) in astronomical observations.'[39] Obviously Imhotep, as chief priest under King Zoser, was associated with Thoth (Tat) in the form of the priesthood previously mentioned who had the 'Dark Rite' as their highest mystery. Here is actual confirmation, then, that it was astronomical matters with which they dealt.

Inscriptions in a temple at Edfu (in the far south of Egypt, near to Aswan) built by Ptolemy III Euergetes I (237 BC) describe Imhotep as 'the great priest Imhotep the son of Ptah, who speaks or lectures'. Hurry says 'Imhotep enjoyed the reputation of being "one of the greatest of Egyptian sages";[40] his fame for wisdom made so deep an impression on his country-men that it endured as a national tradition for many centuries.

'As regards his literary activities, he is said to have produced works on medicine and architecture, as well as on more general subjects, and some of his works were extant at the dawn of the Christian era. . . . his eminence as a man of letters led him to be recognized as the "patron of scribes".'

In other words, he was the first great philosopher. And he obviously 'spoke and lectured' in his lifetime. Perhaps he was the first classical Greek in prototype. We also have something to look forward to – his tomb has yet to be discovered. It is thought to be at Sakkara (a little south of Giza, on the same side of the Nile), and the late Professor Emery more than once thought he had come close to discovering it in his excavations there. Its discovery would be the most important in archaeological history, beside which the minor and later tomb of a boy Pharaoh named Tutankhamen would entirely pale by comparison. But perhaps the most interesting thing about the possible forthcoming discovery of Imhotep's tomb is that it will almost certainly be full of books. Would a man like Imhotep be buried without them?

It is interesting to read this passage in 'The Virgin of the World' following shortly upon that previously quoted:

> The sacred symbols of the cosmic elements were hid away hard by the secrets of Osiris. Hermes, ere he returned to Heaven, invoked a spell on them, and spake these words: . . . 'O holy books, who have been made by my immortal hands, by incorruption's magic spells . . . (at this point there is a lacuna as the text is hopeless) . . . free from decay throughout eternity remain and incorrupt from time! Become unseeable, unfindable, for every one whose foot shall tread the plains of this land, until old Heaven doth bring forth meet instruments for you, whom the Creator shall call souls.'

Thus spake he; and, laying spells on them by means of his own works, he shut them safe away in their own zones. And long enough the time has been since they were hid away.

In the treatise the highest objective of ignorant men searching for the truth is described as: '(Men) will seek out . . . the inner nature of the holy spaces which no foot may tread, and will chase after them into the height, desiring to observe the nature of the motion of the Heavens.

'These are as yet moderate things. For nothing more remains than Earth's remotest realms; nay, in their daring they will track out Night, the farthest Night of all.'

We 'will chase out into the height' of space to 'observe the nature of the motions of the Heavens', says this old (indeterminately old) treatise. How correct it was. We have now landed on the moon, which is 'chasing out into the height' with a vengeance. And we are indeed 'observing the nature of the motion of the Heavens'. And the treatise is also right in saying that 'these are yet moderate things'. For, as everyone knows, the people in the space programme feel as if they have only just begun. Man will only pause properly again when he has made the entire solar system his familiar and his own. Then we shall be faced with the limitations of our solar system and the barrier that separates it from the stars. What then? Yes, what we have done to date certainly deserves the description of 'yet moderate things'. Vasco da Gama may have congratulated himself on his brilliant navigational accomplishments, but as we can clearly see in his case, a beginning is only a beginning. It is 'yet moderate things'.

According to the treatise, after these moderate things we shall 'in our daring' even learn the greatest secret . . . we shall discover 'Night'. And the meaning of the 'Dark Rite' will become clear. And as this rite and this mystery concern Isis and the star Sirius and by the context of this prophecy clearly concern the heavens, can we be accused of sensationalism in making the suggestion that nothing would shake up the human race more than having the discovery of intelligent life elsewhere in the universe proven for the first time? And what if the dark companion of Sirius really does hold the answer to this mystery? What if the nearest centre of civilization really is based at the Sirius system and keeps a watchful eye on us from time to time? What if this is proven by our detecting on our radio telescopes actual traces of local radio communications echoing down those nine light years of space in the vast spreading ripple of disintegrating signals that any culture remotely near to us in development would be bound to dribble forth into the surrounding universe? What if this happens? It will be like the sky falling in, won't it?

Notes

1. *Le Renard pâle*, p. 325. Figure 109 in that book shows it, drawn as 'the meeting of Sirius with the Sun'. We have reproduced it here as Figure 13.

2. Mariette, *Denderah*, Vol. I, p. 206.
3. Aratus, *Phaenomena* 331–6. English translation in Loeb Library series, in volume with Callimachus and Lycophron. See Bibliography.
4. Vol. I, p. 1, of *Egyptian Astronomical Texts*, Otto Neugebauer and Richard Parker, Brown University Press, USA, 1960–7.
5. Ibid., Vol. I, p. 25.
6. *The Gods of the Egyptians*, London, 1904, Vol. II, p. 114.
7. Ibid., Vol. II, p. 113.
8. Ibid., Vol. II, p. 117.
9. Ibid., Vol. II, p. 215.
10. Ibid., Vol. II, pp. 202–3.
11. Ibid., Vol. II, p. 264.
12. Ibid., Vol. II, p. 265.
13. Ibid., Vol. II, p. 139.
14. Neugebauer and Parker, op. cit.
15. *Star Names, Their Lore and Meaning*, R. H. Allen, Dover Publications, New York, 1963, p. 130.
16. Neugebauer and Parker, op. cit.
17. *Star Names, Their Lore and Meaning*, p. 68.
18. Ibid., p. 65.
19. *Ancient Near Eastern Texts relating to the Old Testament*, ed. by James B. Pritchard, Princeton University Press, USA, 1955, p. 33.
20. Ibid., p. 41.
21. Alexander Heidel, *The Babylonian Genesis*, University of Chicago Press, USA, 1965, p. 86.
22. Wallis Budge, op. cit., Vol. I, p. 284.
23. Ibid., Vol. I, p. 290.
24. Ibid., Vol. II, p. 154, and Vol. I, p. 446.
25. Ibid., Vol. I, p. 154.
26. Ibid., Vol. II, p. 261.
27. Ibid., Vol. II, pp. 264–5.
28. Ibid., Vol. II, pp. 195–200.
29. Ibid., Vol. II, pp. 264–5.
30. 'Isis and Osiris', Loeb edition, p. 107.
31. Ibid., p. 145.
32. Ibid., p. 39.
33. Ibid., p. 147.
34. *The Oracles of Zeus*, H. W. Parke, p. 13.
35. *Thrice Greatest Hermes*, G. R. S. Mead, John Watkins, London, 1964.
36. Ibid., Vol. III, p. 95. He quotes from Wessley, *Denkschr d. k. Akad.* (1893), p. 37, l. 500.
37. See *Imhotep, the Vizier and Physician of King Zoser and afterwards the Egyptian God of Medicine*, by Jamieson B. Hurry, Oxford University Press, 1926.
38. I. E. S. Edwards, *The Pyramids of Egypt*, Penguin, 1970.
39. Hurry, op. cit., p. 20.
40. Ibid., p. 40.

SUMMARY

Sirius was the most important star in the sky to the ancient Egyptians. The ancient Egyptian calendar was based on the rising of Sirius. It is established for certain that Sirius was sometimes identified by the ancient Egyptians with their chief goddess Isis.

The companion of Isis was Osiris, the chief Egyptian god. The 'companion' of the constellation of the Great Dog (which includes Sirius) was the constellation of Orion. Since Isis is equated with Sirius, the companion of Isis must be equated, equally, with the companion of Sirius. Osiris is thus equated on occasion with the constellation Orion.

We know that the 'companion of Sirius' is in reality Sirius B. It is conceivable that Osiris-as-Orion, 'the companion of Sirius', is a stand-in for the invisible true companion Sirius B.

'The oldest and simplest form of the name' of Osiris, we are told, is a hieroglyph of a throne and an eye. The 'eye' aspect of Osiris is thus fundamental. The Bozo tribe of Mali, related to the Dogon, call Sirius B 'the eye star'. Since Osiris is represented by an eye and is sometimes considered 'the companion of Sirius', this is equivalent to saying that Osiris is 'the eye star', provided only that one grants the premises that the existence of Sirius B really was known to the ancient Egyptians and that 'the companion of Sirius' therefore could ultimately refer to it.

The meanings of the Egyptian hieroglyphs and names for Isis and Osiris were unknown to the earliest dynastic Egyptians themselves, and the names and signs appear to have a pre-dynastic origin – which means around or before 3200 BC, in other words 5,000 years ago at least. There has been no living traditional explanation for the meanings of the names and signs for Isis and Osiris since at least 2800 BC at the very latest.

'The Dog Star 'is a common designation of Sirius throughout known history. The ancient god Anubis was a 'dog god', that is, he had a man's body and a dog's head.

In discussing Egyptian beliefs, Plutarch says that Anubis was really the son of Nephthys, sister to Isis, although he was said to be the son of Isis. Nephthys was 'invisible'. Isis was 'visible'. (In other words, the visible mother was the stand-in for the invisible mother, who was the true mother, for the simple reason that the invisible mother could not be perceived.)

Plutarch said that Anubis was a 'horizontal circle, which divides the invisible part . . . which they call Nephthys, from the visible, to which they give the name Isis; and as this circle equally touches upon the confines of both light and darkness, it may be looked upon as common to them both.'

This is as clear an ancient description as one could expect of a circular orbit (called 'Anubis') of a dark and invisible star (called 'Nephthys') around its 'sister', a light and visible star (called 'Isis') – and we know Isis to have been equated with Sirius. What is missing here are the following specific points which must be at this stage still our assumptions: (a) The circle is actually an orbit. (b) The divine characters are actually stars, specifically in this context.

Actually, Anubis and Osiris were sometimes identified with one another. Osiris, the companion of Isis who is sometimes 'the companion of Sirius' is also sometimes identified with the orbit of the companion of Sirius, and this is reasonable and to be expected.

Isis-as-Sirius was customarily portrayed by the ancient Egyptians in their paintings as travelling with two companions in the same celestial boat. And as we know, Sirius does, according to some astronomers, have two companions, Sirius B and Sirius C.

To the Arabs, a companion-star to Sirius (in the same constellation of the Great Dog) was named 'Weight' and was supposed to be extremely heavy – almost too heavy to rise over the horizon. 'Ideler calls this an astonishing star-name,' we are told, not surprisingly.

The true companion-star of Sirius, Sirius B, is made of super-dense matter which is heavier than any normal matter in the universe and the weight of this tiny star is the same as that of a gigantic normal star.

The Dogon also, as we know, say that Sirius B is 'heavy' and they speak of its 'weight'.

The Arabs also applied the name 'Weight' to the star Canopus in the constellation Argo. The *Argo* was a ship in mythology which carried Danaos and his fifty daughters to Rhodes. The *Argo* had fifty oarsmen under Jason, called Argonauts. There were fifty oars to the *Argo*, each with its oarsman-Argonaut. The divine oarsman was an ancient Mediterranean motif with sacred meanings.

The orbit of Sirius B around Sirius A takes fifty years, which may be related to the use of the number fifty to describe aspects of the *Argo*.

There are many divine names and other points in common between ancient Egypt and ancient Sumer (Babylonia). The Sumerians seem to have called Egypt by the name of 'Magan' and to have been in contact with it.

The chief god of Sumer, named Anu, was pictured as a jackal, which is a variation of the dog motif and was used also in Egypt for Anubis, the dog and the jackal apparently being interchangeable as symbols. The Egyptian form of the name Anubis is 'Anpu' and is similar to the Sumerian 'Anu', and both are jackal-gods.

The famous Egyptologist Wallis Budge was convinced that Sumer and Egypt both derived their own cultures from a common source which was 'exceedingly ancient'.

Anu is also called An (a variation) by the Sumerians. In Egypt Osiris is called An also.

Remembering that Plutarch said that Anubis (Anpu in Egyptian) was a circle, it is interesting to note that in Sanskrit the word Aṇḍa means 'ellipse'. This may be a coincidence.

Wallis Budge says that Anubis represents time. The combined meanings of 'time' and 'circle' for Anubis hint strongly at 'circular motion'.

The worship of Anubis was a secret mystery religion restricted to initiates (and we thus do not know its content). Plutarch, who writes of Anubis, was an initiate of several mystery religions, and there is reason to believe his information was from well-informed sources. (Plutarch himself was a Greek living under the Roman Empire.) A variant translation of

Plutarch's description of Anubis is that Anubis was 'a combined relation' between Isis and Nephthys. This has overtones which help in thinking of 'the circle' as an orbit – a 'combined relation' between the star orbiting and the star orbited.

The Egyptians used the name Horus to describe 'the power which is assigned to direct the revolution of the sun', according to Plutarch. Thus the Egyptians conceived of and named such specific dynamics – an essential point.

Plutarch says Anubis guarded like a dog and attended on Isis. This fact, plus Anubis being 'time' and 'a circle', suggests even more an orbital concept – the ideal form of attendance of the prowling guard dog.

Aristotle's friend Eudoxus (who visited Egypt) said that the Egyptians had a tradition that Zeus (chief god of the Greeks whose name is used by Eudoxus to refer to his Egyptian equivalent, which leaves us wondering which Egyptian god is meant – presumably Osiris) could not walk because 'his legs were grown together'. This sounds like an amphibious creature with a tail for swimming instead of legs for walking. It is like the semi-divine creature Oannes, reputed to have brought civilization to the Sumerians, who was amphibious, had a tail instead of legs, and retired to the sea at night.

Plutarch relates Isis to the Greek goddess Athena (daughter of Zeus) and says of them they were both described as 'coming from themselves', and as 'self-impelled motion'. Athena supervised the *Argo* and placed in its prow the guiding oak timber from Dodona (which is where the Greek ark landed, with the Greek version of the Biblical Noah, Deukalion, and his wife Pyrrha). The *Argo* thus obtained a distinctive 'self-impelled motion' from Athena, whom Plutarch specifically relates to Isis in this capacity.

The earliest versions of the *Argo* epic which were written before the time of Homer are unfortunately lost. The surviving version of the epic is good reading but relatively recent (third century B.C.)

The Sumerians had 'fifty heroes', 'fifty great gods', etc., just as the later Greeks with their *Argo* had 'fifty heroes' and the *Argo* carried 'fifty daughters of Danaos.'

An Egyptian papyrus says the companion of Isis is 'Lord in the perfect black'. This sounds like the invisible Sirius B. Isis's companion Osiris 'is a dark god'.

The Trismergistic treatise 'The Virgin of the World' from Egypt refers to 'the Black Rite', connected with the 'black' Osiris, as the highest degree of secret initiation possible in the ancient Egyptian religion – it is the ultimate secret of the mysteries of Isis.

This treatise says Hermes came to earth to teach men civilization and then again 'mounted to the stars', going back to his home and leaving behind the mystery religion of Egypt with its celestial secrets which were some day to be decoded.

There is evidence that 'the Black Rite' did deal with astronomical matters. Hence the Black Rite concerned astronomical matters, the black Osiris, and Isis. The evidence mounts that it may thus have concerned the existence of Sirius B.

A prophecy in the treatise 'The Virgin of the World' maintains that only when men concern themselves with the heavenly bodies and 'chase after them into the height' can men hope to understand the subject-matter of the Black Rite. The understanding of astronomy of today's space age now qualifies us to comprehend the true subject of the Black Rite, if that subject is what we suspect it may be. This was impossible earlier in the history of our planet. It must be remembered that without our present knowledge of white dwarf stars which are invisible except with modern telescopes, our knowledge of super-dense matter from atomic physics with all its complicated technology, etc., none of our discussion of the Sirius system would be possible; it would not be possible to propose such an explanation of the Black Rite at all – we could not propound the Sirius question. Much material about the Sumerians and Babylonians has only been circulated since the late 1950s and during the 1960s, and our knowledge of pulsars is even more recent than that. It is doubtful that this book could have been written much earlier than the present. The author began work in earnest in 1967 and finished the original edition of the book in 1974. Even so, he feels the lack of much needed information: sites remain unexcavated, texts untranslated from various ancient languages, astronomical investigations are perpetually incomplete. The author has also found it difficult to master material from so many different fields and wishes he were much better qualified. The Sirius question could not realistically have been posed much earlier, and future discoveries in many fields will be essential to its full consideration. The situation has not greatly changed at the end of 1997.

Chapter 4

The Sacred Fifty

'The Virgin of the World' is quite explicit in saying that Isis and Osiris were sent to help the Earth by giving primitive mankind the arts of civilization:

And Horus thereon said:
'How was it, mother, then, that Earth received God's Efflux?'
And Isis said:
'I may not tell the story of (this) birth; for it is not permitted to describe the origin of thy descent, O Horus (son) of mighty power, lest afterwards the way-of-birth of the immortal gods should be known unto men – except so far that God the Monarch, the universal Orderer and Architect, sent for a little while the mighty sire Osiris, and the mightiest goddess Isis, that they might help the world, for all things needed them.
' 'Tis they who filled life full of life. 'Tis they who caused the savagery of mutual slaughtering of men to cease. 'Tis they who hallowed precincts to the Gods their ancestors and spots for holy rites. 'Tis they who gave to men laws, food and shelter.' Etc.

They are also described as teaching men how to care for the dead in a specifically Egyptian way: ' 'Tis they who taught men how to wrap up those who ceased to live, as they should be.'
Now anyone knows this is Egyptian and not Greek practice. What Neoplatonist would include such a statement unless it were actually taken from an early source which he used, and which had been written by someone actually living in Egypt?
The treatise ends this long section with:

' 'Tis they alone who, taught by Hermes in God's hidden codes, became the authors of the arts, and sciences, and all pursuits which men do practise, and givers of their laws.
' 'Tis they who, taught by Hermes that the things below have been disposed by God to be in sympathy with things above, established on the earth the sacred rites over which the mysteries in Heaven preside.
[The absence here of a blatant propaganda for astrology argues a pre-Ptolemaic date for this treatise; after the Greek and Babylonian influx a mild statement like this would have been almost impossible to make

114

without the author dragging in all the paraphernalia of the astrology-craze of late Egypt.]

"'Tis they who, knowing the destructibility of (mortal) frames, devised the grade of prophets, in all things perfected, in order that no prophet who stretched forth his hands unto the Gods, should be in ignorance of anything, that magic and philosophy should feed the soul, and medicine preserve the body when it suffered pain.

'And having done all this, my son, Osiris and myself perceiving that the world was (now) quite full, were thereupon demanded back by those who dwell in Heaven . . .'

And in the treatise Isis claims that the 'Black Rite' honours her and 'gives perfection'. It is also concerned with the mysterious thing called 'Night' – 'who weaves her web with rapid light though it be less than Sun's'. It is made plain that 'Night' is not the night sky because it moves in the Heaven along with 'the other mysteries in turn that move in Heaven, with ordered motions and with periods of times, with certain hidden influences bestowing order on the things below and co-increasing them'.

We must scrutinize the description of what is labelled 'Night' in this treatise. This description makes it perfectly clear that 'Night' is not 'night', but a code word. For it is said to have 'light though it be less than Sun's'. The dark companion of Sirius is a star and has light, though less than the sun. Also 'Night' is said 'to weave her web with rapid light' which specifically describes the object as being in motion. Since Sirius B orbits Sirius A in fifty years, it moves more rapidly even than three of our sun's planets in our own solar system – Pluto, Neptune, and Uranus. Of these three, Uranus is the most rapid, and its orbit about the sun takes eighty-four years. So here is a star orbiting more rapidly than a planet! That may indeed be said to constitute 'weaving a web with rapid light.'

Now to return to the Sumerian culture, or, more properly, the Sumero-Akkadian culture. It was roughly contemporaneous with ancient Egypt and I had already suspected its basic religious concepts to be so similar to those of Egypt that I imagined they might have a common origin. Then I discovered that Wallis Budge thought the same thing from his point of view as a distinguished Egyptologist. I am not aware of any Sumerologists having dealt with this particular problem. Far more attention has been given to the known trading links which existed between Sumer and the Indus Valley civilization, and also to the problem of deciding where Dilmun was located. (To the Sumerians, Dilmun was on the one hand a real foreign country or region from which they obtained timber, but on the other hand, it seems to have represented the 'Other World' – but *not* the Underworld – a 'clean place', 'a pure place', 'a bright place'.) Kramer thinks Dilmun was the Indus valley; Bibby follows Peter B. Cornwall and thinks it was the island of Bahrein in the Persian Gulf. But to the Sumerians this land, which lay in a direction seemingly other than that of

Egypt, had immense importance. Consequently, it has tended to monopolize the attention of modern scholars investigating Sumerian geographical references. Kramer thinks that the land 'Magan' was probably Egypt and that Sargon even sent his armies there.

The basic Egyptian astronomy and the basic Sumero-Akkadian astronomy are identical. For the multitude of variations at a less basic level, one may consult Professor Otto Neugebauer's *The Exact Sciences in Antiquity*. But Neugebauer's interests lie with late material, as he admits, and he does less than justice to the earlier material, skimming over it quickly and making little of some things which are important. Here is an example of his attitude expressed in his own words near the beginning of Chapter Five: 'Our description of Babylonian astronomy will be rather incomplete. The historical development will be given in bare outline. As in the case of Egypt, a detailed discussion of the few preserved early texts would require not only too much room but would also unduly exaggerate their historical importance. For the late period, however, the opposite situation prevails.' Well, at least Professor Neugebauer is honest about his preferences. We turn to E. A. Speiser's translation[1] of the Akkadian creation epic know as the *Enuma Elish* from the first two words of the text which mean 'When on high . . .'. At the very beginning of this text we read:

> He constructed stations for the great gods,
> Fixing their astral likenesses as constellations.
> He determined the year by designating the zones:
> He set up three constellations for each of the twelve months.
> After defining the days of the year [by means] of (heavenly) figures,
> He founded . . ., etc.

In other words, the text gives a system identical with that recorded in the Egyptian star clocks. Twelve months composed of three ten-day weeks each, resulting in thirty-six constellations or 'decans' designating astral likenesses of gods. The text specifically states that there are twelve months consisting of three periods each (unless one strains the point enormously and maintains on no grounds whatsoever that these three periods are unequal, they must be of ten days each – hence 'ten-day weeks' as in Egypt), and that a constellation or 'zone' of the sky applies to each of these 'weeks'. Since three times twelve equals thirty-six, we have thirty-six decans, each of which is 'designated' by a constellation. And also as in Egypt, each decan is an 'astral likeness' of a great god. It is surprising that no scholar has seen that this passage in the *Enuma Elish* describes the Egyptian star-clock system down to the last detail.

No doubt also the five 'epagomenal' days left over in order to fill out this resulting 360-day year to a 365-day year are referred to in the line: 'After defining the days of the year of (heavenly) figures,' which is again identical with the Egyptian tradition where the five left-over days are each assigned to five different gods or heavenly figures and thus defined. In Egypt these five left-over days are called 'the days upon the year'. These five days are also extremely important in Maya astronomy.

We can see that the astronomical systems in Egypt and Sumer were absolutely identical in their fundamentals. Now these similarities between Egypt and Sumer are a far different matter from similarities of names of gods and religious concepts. One can always maintain that people in different parts of the globe spontaneously produce identical sounds when awe-struck by divine concepts. 'Everybody around the world says "Ma!" to Mother,' as we have all heard many times. But an astronomical system of this kind is a complex set of specific data. The fact that this Akkadian text tentatively dated by Speiser at the Old Babylonian period (i.e. the early part of the second millennium BC) records an astronomical system of this complexity which is identical with that of the Egyptian star clocks can be said to point to either contact between these two civilizations or a common derivation for the system. And it suggests a date which could serve as an upper limit. Culture contact during which this information was shared could not have been any later. Let any latest date accepted for the writing of the *Enuma Elish* serve as an upper limit. If this be done, we find the first millennium BC as the upper limit, even for those who require incontrovertible physical proof. The contact between Egypt and Sumer must have been considerably earlier if direct, or it may not have been a contact, but rather a common derivation (which was Wallis Budge's favoured idea).

The Egyptian star clocks date from at least the reigns of Seti I (1303–1290 BC) and Ramses IV (1158–1152 BC) of the XIXth and XXth Dynasties respectively, on the walls of whose tombs they are found. Therefore these star clocks are at least as old as 1300 BC and seem to go back to the very origins of Egyptian culture. By the first millennium BC they had been changed and a fifteen-day week substituted for the ten-day week. Other innovations took place as well at later dates, and the system fell into a considerable decay and became, it seems, a relic. I should imagine that a rise in the popularity of the sun god Ra made stars and especially Sirius seem less important. In any case, the innate integrity of the Sirius system in Egypt began to rot away and be ignored by the first millennium BC, as it was superseded by ideas more obvious and less esoteric to impatient priests. Perhaps when this began to happen some purists may have gone off to other places where they hoped to retain the traditions without interference from decadent Pharaohs. We shall return much later to this idea, with some surprising information.

But let us return to Sumer and continue in hot pursuit. In Tablet VI* of the *Enuma Elish* we find an interesting passage. In it are mentioned the

---

* For those texts which survive on baked clay tablets, it is conventional to refer to Tablet number.

Anunnaki, who were the sons of An (An means 'heaven'), also known as Anu the great god. These Anunnaki were fifty in number and were called 'the fifty great gods'. Nearly always these Anunnaki were anonymous, the emphasis being on their number and their greatness and their control over fate. No certain identification of any important Sumerian god with any one of the Anunnaki exists except peripherally (as I shall describe later). In fact, all Sumerologists have been puzzled by the Anunnaki. They have not been 'identified' and no one knows exactly what is meant by them. They recur often throughout the texts, which makes it all the more annoying that nowhere are they explicitly explained. But their apparent importance to the Sumerians cannot be questioned.

In an early Sumerian fragment (from a time long before the civilization of the Babylonians) of the material concerning the epic hero Gilgamesh, entitled 'Gilgamesh and the Land of the Living', we find an antecedent to the tradition of the Argonauts of the Greeks. This fragment appears in a translation by Kramer.[2] In fact, I feel it is safe to say that this Sumerian fragment is the earliest known form of the story of that hero who was later to be named Jason. In the story from this fragment, the hero, Gilgamesh, wishes to go to the 'land of the living', which is described as being in the charge of the sun god Utu. In the story of Jason and the Argonauts, the hero, Jason, wishes to search for the golden fleece, which is known to be a solar symbol. In the Sumerian fragment we also find the surprising line: 'The hero, his teeth are the teeth of a dragon.' In the Jason story, the hero, Jason, sows the dragon's teeth! (So does Cadmus in another Greek tale which we shall examine later.)

In the Jason story, Jason is accompanied on his quest by the fifty Argonauts. In the Sumerian fragment, Gilgamesh is accompanied by fifty companions also! Here is the relevant passage (in which Gilgamesh is speaking):

'Who has a house, to his house! Who has a mother, to his mother!
'Let single males who would do as I (do), fifty, stand by my side.'
Who had a house, to his house; who had a mother, to his mother,
Single males who would do as he (did), fifty, stood at his side.
To the house of the smiths he directed his step,
The . . ., the . . . -axe, his 'Might of Heroism' he caused to be cast
    there.
To the . . . garden of the plain he [directed] his step,
The . . . -tree, the willow, the apple tree, the box tree, the . . . [-tree] he
    [felled] there.
The 'sons' of his city who accompanied him [placed them] in their
    hands.

The fifty companions are mentioned several times. The fragmentary text is extremely broken and confused. Further light on the motif of sowing the dragon's teeth seems to come from a passage where Gilgamesh, who has for some unknown reason been asleep, was awakened, girded himself, stood like a bull on the 'great earth' and: 'He put (his) mouth to the ground, (his) teeth shook.' Note that it is at least open to question that the mouth and the teeth are actually his, and the word 'his' is both times in parentheses, put thus by the translator. But here is the entire passage:

> He put (his) mouth to the ground, (his) teeth shook.
> 'By the life of Ninsun, my mother who gave birth to me, of pure
>   Lugulbanda, my father,
> 'May I become as one who sits to be wondered at on the knee of
>   Ninsun, my mother who gave birth to me.'

Apart from the fact that Gilgamesh's desire to sit on the knee of his mother, the goddess Ninsun, is similar to Horus sitting on the knee of his mother, the goddess Isis, as a constant motif in Egyptian art, there seems to be here an obscure but significant reference to the fact that if the hero puts his mouth to the ground and his teeth shake, he can invoke a kind of rebirth in strength. I suspect that the translation needs to be worked on further, but it is difficult, as there are so many words in Sumerian whose meanings are not precisely understood. Whether or not it is Gilgamesh's own mouth and teeth that are being discussed here, the fact is that Gilgamesh seeks strength by putting some teeth to the ground – either his or someone else's. As previously in the same tale, there has been the clear statement: 'The hero, his teeth are the teeth of a dragon', we may assume that Gilgamesh's own teeth are probably being referred to – *his own teeth which have previously been described as being dragon's teeth!*

Now in the lines following the putting of the teeth to the ground, we learn that Gilgamesh needs to summon strength by putting his teeth to the ground because he needs to fight. In the story of the *Argo*, Jason sows the dragon's teeth in the ground, and from them spring up armed soldiers who begin to fight – as is also the case in the story of Cadmus, legendary king of Greek Thebes, born at Tyre (see later, pp. 232–6 and Figure 42). So we see that in the two Greek myths, as also in this Sumerian fragment, the dragon's teeth go to the ground and a fight ensues where the hero has acquired superhuman strength. Later in this book we shall see the precise explanation of where this curious jumble originated, that it is specifically derived from an Egyptian sacred pun, and what it all means.

Meanwhile we must stay at our present level of enquiry. This book is an anabasis, or journey upward.

Let us look a little closer at the story of Jason and the golden fleece. The golden fleece was given to Phrixus and Helle by the god Hermes. The Egyptian god Anubis became known to the Greeks as their own Hermes. Furthermore, the first-century-BC Greek historian Diodorus Siculus (IV, 47), and Tacitus, the first-century-AD Roman historian (*Ann.* VI, 34), explain the golden fleece's origin by saying that Phrixus and Helle (who flew away on the golden ram's back to Colchis, Helle falling in the Hellespont on the way and giving that body of water its name) really sailed in a ship with a ram's head on the prow, rather than having ridden on the magical ram of the story. The fact that the more widespread myth which had an actual ram in the story maintained specifically that they *flew* on the golden ram, could refer to the idea of a celestial boat.

In any case, this boat would definitely have been a boat of Egypt, which to the Sumerians would have been called a 'Magan-boat', if we accept what Kramer and others believe, namely, that Magan is Egypt. And the boat was a 'gift from Hermes' – in other words from Anubis. No wonder, then, that the Sirius-related fifty is connected with the golden fleece as well as Anubis. It is worth mentioning also that the fifty Argonauts were also called the Minyae, as they were all related to each other and of the same family, descended all of them from Minyas, who had been the king of the Minyan city of Orchomenus in Boeotia, in Greece. So Jason and the Argonauts, fifty in number, all shared a kind of shadowy anonymity somewhat reminiscent of the fifty Anunnaki of Sumer, as they were often referred to simply as 'the Minyae' – a group of fifty related oarsmen in a celestial boat. The 'fifty' were eventually given personalities by later writers such as Apollonius Rhodius, as I shall discuss later.

Later on we shall look extremely closely at the *Argo* story and also at the connections between the land Colchis, the object of its quest, and ancient Egypt, as attested for us by the historian Herodotus. But we must complete our look at the story of Gilgamesh and the Land of the Living. For even a boat is mentioned in that fragment, corresponding to the *Argo*. My equating a moment ago of the *Argo* with an Egyptian celestial barque must now be seen in conjunction with the following passage in which Gilgamesh's boat is specifically referred to as the 'Magan-boat'! I might add that the trees which Gilgamesh cut down and which his fifty companions 'placed in their hands' according to the text were probably their oars! (The text is too broken for anything at all to be certain, even punctuation, among the fourteen lines which follow that particular passage.) Here, then, is the passage about the boat:

'For me another will not die, the loaded boat will not sink,
The three-ply cloth will not be cut,
The . . . will not be overwhelmed,
House (and) hut, fire will not destroy.
Do thou help me (and) I will help thee, what can happen to us?
After it had sunk, after it had sunk,
After the Magan-boat had sunk,
After the boat, "the might of Magilum", had sunk,
In the . . . , the boat of the living creatures, are seated those who come out of the womb;

Come, let us go forward, we will cast eyes upon him,
If we go forward,
(And) there be fear, there be fear, turn it back,
There be terror, there be terror, turn it back,
In thy . . . , come, let us go forward.'

I must emphasize that there is confusion here. In a footnote Kramer emphasizes that from the line 'After it had sunk' it is no longer certain that Gilgamesh is still speaking. It is not clear whether the Magan-boat has really sunk or whether this is a statement injected by Gilgamesh's 'faithful servant' who immediately before the passage just quoted had told Gilgamesh:

'O my master, journey thou to the "land", I will journey to the city,
I will tell thy mother of thy glory, let her shout,
I will tell her of thy ensuing death, [let her] shed bitter tears.'

What seems to happen is that Gilgamesh here tells his frightened servant (who just previously in the text is described as 'terror-stricken') that no other will die for him and that 'the loaded boat will not sink'. Then the servant would seem to break in again in his terror with his hypothetical tale to Gilgamesh's mother with 'After it had sunk . . .' Then Gilgamesh again speaks, beginning with, 'Come, let us go forward . . .'

The phrase 'those who come out of the womb' to describe those who are seated in the Magan-boat may be meant to refer to those who are children of the goddess Nintu, also known as Ninmah, Ninhursag, and Ki – 'earth'. This, combined with the strange reference to teeth ('His teeth shook' – see page 119), seems to refer to the children of the earth-goddess springing from the womb of the earth – for Ki, the earth-goddess (*ki* means 'earth' in Sumerian) is also Nintu or 'the goddess who gives birth'. (Ninmah means 'the great goddess' and Ninhursag means 'the goddess of the hill', a *hursag* or hill having been erected by her son – and she was named after it by him in commemoration of a significant mythical event; in Egypt Anubis is also called 'Anubis of the Hill', about which I shall have much to say later on, but suffice it here to note that if the Sumerians were to speak of 'Anubis of the Hill' they would call him Anpu-hursag.)

Basically in the goddess who gives birth, and also in the earth-goddess, we thus find antecedents to the soldiers springing up from the dragon's teeth sown in the earth, and also the throwing over his shoulder of the 'earth's bones' (stones) by Deukalion, the Greek Noah, with the stones becoming men much as the teeth did in the other stories. (And teeth are bones!)

In fact there are several points of contact other than this one between the Deukalion and Jason stories. For the ark of Noah is a concept which is identical with that of the ark of Deukalion, and both are magical ships in which sit 'those who come out of the womb', in the sense that they repopulate the world after the deluge. And both arks, but particularly that of Deukalion, are concepts related to the *Argo*. (As anyone who has read the full *Epic of Gilgamesh* will know, the ark of Noah in the Middle East before either the Hebrews or the name Noah even existed, was the ark of Ziusudra or the ark of Utnapishtim, and it occurs as an established element of the mythical background brought into the *Epic*.) For the ark of Deukalion rested on the mountain by the sacred oracle grove of Dodona, from which the *Argo* received its cybernetic guiding timber. Also, of course, the origin of the story of the flood and the ark (containing as it does 'archetypes' of all living creatures in pairs, and the word *archē* in Greek being definitely related to *ark*, as we shall see much later in this book) is Sumerian at least, if not even before that something else (which we shall also see in due course). But it was from this early source that the Greeks obtained their Deukalion and the Hebrews their Noah – both of which are extremely late forms of an exceedingly ancient story, which existed thousands of years before there were such things as either Greeks or Hebrews in existence. (Anyone really interested in the origins of Greek and Hebrew civilizations should read Professor Cyrus Gordon's brilliant book *The Common Background of Greek and Hebrew Civilizations*.[3])

Now the point of going into all this is really to show that the Argonaut motif of fifty heroes in a boat on a heroic quest exists in Sumer and forms a complement to the 'fifty great gods'. For if the Magan-boat's fifty heroes are seated, as the Anunnaki usually are, and are 'those who come forth out of the womb', and thus children, so to speak, of Nintu, 'the goddess who gives birth', then they may be directly equated with the Anunnaki. For the Anunnaki, as the children of An, would also be the children of An's ancient consort Ki or Nintu. In other words, the fifty heroes are heroic counterparts of the celestial Anunnaki. The corollary of this is, that the fact that there are fifty Anunnaki is not so likely to be a coincidence as might have been thought. This brings out all the more the immense significance of the number fifty.

The number occurs also in 'Gilgamesh, Enkidu, and the Nether World'. There Gilgamesh dons armour which weighs 'fifty minas'. And in this tale also Gilgamesh has fifty companions. In the later Babylonian version the fifty companions are omitted from the story. At that date the true nature of the symbolism of fifty must have been forgotten.

In his book *The Sumerians*, Kramer points out[4] that cultic and symbolic weapons, maces with fifty heads, were fashioned by the ruler Gudea (*circa* 2400 BC).

If we return for a moment to the intriguing *hursag* of the Sumerians, the strange 'hill', we must recall that Ninhursag the goddess of the hill is identical with Nintu the goddess who gives birth. Those are two separate names for the same deity. Now it is interesting to note that in Egyptian the word *tu* means 'hill', so that if we take the word *nin* which means 'goddess' and add the Egyptian *tu* we have 'the goddess of the hill', which in fact is a synonym.

This is by no means the end of this interesting investigation. For if we note that the Egyptian form of Horus (the son of Isis and Osiris) is Ḥeru (which is a bit like Hero, isn't it?) and the traditional usage in Egyptian is to speak continually of Ḥeru-sa-*something* which means Horus-the-son-of-*something*, then we shall note that the strange and puzzling word *hursag* might really be the Egyptian Ḥeru-sa-Agga, which means 'Horus the son of Agga'. It so happens that Agga is an Egyptian synonym for Anubis. And 'Anubis of the Hill' has already been mentioned. What is more, the word *hursag* in its older Sumerian form is indeed *hursagga*, as may be seen in *The Babylonian Genesis*, Chapter Two, by Alexander Heidel, 'A Sumerian Creation Account from Nippur', where we read of the goddess Ninhursagga.

It also happens that Agga is in fact a reputable Sumerian name. There is in translation a short 115-line text entitled 'Gilgamesh and Agga' from the Sumerian period.[5] In line eighty of this text is the mention of a 'magurru-boat', which is referred to in much the same way as the Magan-boat in 'Gilgamesh and the Land of the Living'. Just as in that previous text the Magan-boat was being discussed as to whether or not it would sink, so in this latter text the '*magurru*-boat' is being discussed as to whether or not it would have its prow cut down. Curiously, as in the other tale, in this one also the boat is described as having had the worst fate actually occur, for in line ninety-eight we learn that 'the prow of the *magurru*-boat was cut down', just as in the previous text we read: 'After the Magan-boat had sunk,/After the boat, "the might of Magilum", had sunk.'

The connections between Egyptian and Sumerian words in sacred contexts become so multifold that it is impossible to ignore the continuities between the two cultures. Let us look, for instance, at the curious phenomenon of the cedar which Gilgamesh is always being claimed to have cut down. In 'Gilgamesh and the Land of the Living' Gilgamesh says: 'I would enter the land of the cut-down cedar' and later he is described as he 'who felled the cedar', etc. That is an early Sumerian text. In the actual *Epic* proper, as we have it, Gilgamesh goes to the Cedar Mountain and slays the monster Humbaba (or Huwawa) in 'the cedar mountain, the abode of the gods'. In the Fifth Tablet we read:

Gilgamesh gripped the axe
And with it felled the cedar.
Huwawa, hearing the sound of this,
Fell into a fury and raged:
'Who is it who has come –
Come, and interfered with my trees?
My trees which have grown on my own mountains?
And has also felled the cedar?'[6]

In Chapter 22 of *Hamlet's Mill,* Santillana and von Dechend identify Huwawa with the planet Mercury. Now, remembering that Huwawa is also the god of the cedar forest, it is interesting to note that in Egyptian the word *seb* means 'cedar' and also means 'the planet Mercury'! The subject is far more complicated than that, but I wanted to note the further source of an Egyptian pun for yet another crucial Sumerian motif. In other words, Huwawa is connected with both Mercury (the planet) and the cedar, because the planet Mercury and the cedar are both called by the same name in Egyptian – namely, *seb.*

Let us now put aside the enigmatic monster-god Huwawa and turn to the *Epic of Gilgamesh* for another purpose. But in doing so let us note Kramer's opinion in his essay 'The *Epic of Gilgamesh* and Its Sumerian Sources',[7] that 'the poem was current in substantially the form in which we know it, as early as the first half of the second millennium BC.'

Let us recall that, in an early Sumerian fragment, Gilgamesh's mother was the goddess Ninsun 'who is versed in all knowledge', and upon whose knee he wanted to sit (like Horus on the knee of Isis). In the First Tablet we read:

And so Gilgamesh rose from his bed
And to his mother, in revealing his dreams, said:
'Mother, I saw in a dream last night
That there were stars in heaven.
And a star descended upon me like unto
The essence of Anu who is God of the Firmament.
I tried to lift it up but it was too heavy for me,
I tried to move it away but it would not be moved.
The land of Uruk was around it,
The land was placed round about it.
All the people were pressing towards it,
All the nobles also came round it,
And all my friends kissed its feet.
I was drawn towards it as to a woman
And laid it at your feet.
And you said it was my equal.'[8]

There is another version of this at the beginning of Tablet II in the Old Babylonian version which is older than the above Assyrian version and preserves more of the original significance:

And so Gilgamesh arose from his bed
And to his mother, in revealing his dreams, said:
'Mother, in the time of night
I was joyful; I walked about
In the midst of the nobles.

124

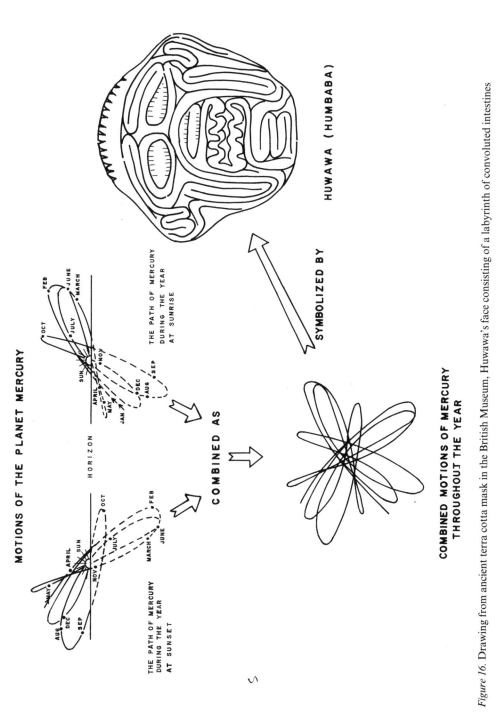

MOTIONS OF THE PLANET MERCURY

THE PATH OF MERCURY DURING THE YEAR AT SUNRISE

THE PATH OF MERCURY DURING THE YEAR AT SUNSET

HORIZON

COMBINED AS

HUWAWA (HUMBABA)

SYMBOLIZED BY

COMBINED MOTIONS OF MERCURY THROUGHOUT THE YEAR

Figure 16. Drawing from ancient terra cotta mask in the British Museum, Huwawa's face consisting of a labyrinth of convoluted intestines

The stars assembled themselves in the heavens.
The star-essence of Anu descended towards me.
I tried to lift it up but it was too heavy for me!
I tried to move it away but it would not be moved!
The land of Uruk was around it,
The land was placed round about it.
All the nobles also came round it
And they kissed its feet.
As the strap strained against my forehead,
I pulled it, and they supported me.
I raised it and brought it to you.'[9]

Kramer translates the two versions somewhat differently.[10] One of the most important changes occurs in his translation of what Heidel (another modern scholar) before him had rendered as 'the host of heaven'.[11] Kramer renders '*An*' not as 'heaven' but as An (or Anu), the god who was the father of the Anunnaki. And the word which Heidel renders as 'host' he comments on in a footnote at considerable length:

As regards *ki-sir*, there are too many possible meanings. Furthermore, the one adopted for this passage ('the *ki-sir* of Ninurta' earlier than our passage) should also apply to . . . the war-god Ninurta, and the sky-god Anu, Enkidu, and something that fell down from heaven. The common assumption that the author may have used in these passages the same term in more than one sense is unsatisfactory.

In the earlier edition I tried to justify for *kiṣru* the rendering 'liegeman' for the several passages in question. I now withdraw that suggestion. The correct sense, I believe, is indicated by the use of the term in medical contexts as 'concentration, essence'.* 'Essence', or some nuance of this term, could well be applied to deities as well as to missiles from heaven. Our poet had in mind, no doubt, some specific allusion, but the general meaning appears clear enough.

Kramer, then, renders 'the host of heaven' as 'the essence of An'. He says: 'Like the essence of Anu it descends upon me.' He adds another footnote to comment on the word 'it' in this sentence: 'One of the stars?'
Kramer also changes the last lines in the first version:

'[I] was drawn to it as though to a woman.
And I placed it at [thy] feet,
For thou didst make it vie with me.'

The emphasis here on being 'drawn to it' may be important. He continues:

* cf. E. Ebeling, *Journal of Cuneiform Studies*, IV (1950), 219.

[The wise mother of Gilgamesh, who] is versed in all knowledge,
Says to her lord;
[Wise Ninsun), who is versed in all knowledge,
Says to Gilgamesh:
'Thy rival, – the star of heaven,
Which descended upon thee like [the essence of Anu];
[Thou didst seek to lift it], it was too stout for thee;
[Thou wouldst drive it off], but couldst not remove it;
[Thou didst place] it at my feet,
[For it was I who made] it vie with thee;
Thou wert drawn to it as though to a woman –*

Let us look once again at part of the second version, this time as Kramer gives it:[12]

'My mother, in the time of night
I felt joyful and I walked about
In the midst of the nobles.
The stars appeared in the heavens.
The essence of Anu descended towards me.
I sought to lift it; it was too heavy for me!
I sought to move it; move it I could not!'

All this, which we have examined here in two translations each of two versions, was worth seeing from these several angles. It helps us cover all the possibilities of meaning. The reference is clearly to a star connected with 'the essence of Anu' which 'draws him towards it' and is in the area of the (fifty) heroes – and is super-heavy.

Thus we see that in Sumer both the concepts of the heavy star (later *al Wazn*) and of the figure 'fifty' associated somehow with that star are present. Does this look familiar?

In Tablet VI of the *Enuma Elish* we read[13] about the Anunnaki and something called 'the Bow Star' which is their brother and is in the midst of them as they are seated in the celestial regions. This Bow Star is also the daughter of Anu, who raises it up in their midst. (Remember 'the essence of Anu'.) What is being referred to seems to be Sirius. Remember the Egyptian goddess Sati (or Satis) with her bow, who was one of the three goddesses (one was Sothis and the third was Anukis) riding in the celestial barque of Sothis (Sirius). Also recall the other connections of the bow with Sirius, even in China. (Here one must refer to *Hamlet's Mill* for many examples.[14]) Now with particular reference to the three goddesses which Neugebauer claims are versions of Sothis ('The goddess Satis, who like her

---

* With these Tablet texts, sections broken off the clay tablets or now illegible have been filled in by Kramer, hence the frequent square brackets.

companion Anukis is hardly to be taken as a separate constellation but rather as an associate of Sothis'), note the following emphasis on three names for the star, only one of which is 'Bow Star':

The fifty great gods took their seats.
The seven gods of destiny set up the three hundred [in heaven].
Enlil raised the bo[w, his wea]pon, and laid (it) before them.
The gods, his fathers, saw the net he had made.
When they beheld the bow, how skilful its shape,
His fathers praised the work he had wrought.
Raising [it], Anu spoke up in the Assembly of the gods,
As he kissed the bow: 'This is my daughter!'
He mentioned the names of the bow as follows:
'Longwood is the first, the second is [. . .];
Its third name is Bow-Star, in heaven I have made it shine.'
He fixed a place which the gods, its brothers, [. . .].

A footnote says of the word 'its' in the last line: 'Referring to the Bow, as indicated by the feminine possessive prefix in line 94.' (In Egyptian the word *Sept*, which is the name of the star Sirius, also has the meaning 'a kind of wood', though whether this could be 'longwood' or not is anyone's guess.) We continue:

After Anu had decreed the fate of the Bow,
And had placed the exalted royal throne before the gods,
Anu seated it in the Assembly of the gods.

The phrase 'the Assembly of the gods' invariably refers to the seated assembly of the fifty Anunnaki. So it is clearly stated, we see, that this 'Bow Star' – the daughter of An – was placed by An on the exalted royal throne in the midst of the fifty Anunnaki. In Egypt, Isis as Sothis was also pictured as seated on a white royal throne in the heavens. She too was the daughter of the sky god. Recall also that the hieroglyph for Ast (or Isis) is a throne. And the hieroglyph for her husband Asar (or Osiris) is a throne above an eye.

Before proceeding, we had better see who 'the seven gods of destiny' are. They are often referred to as the seven Anunnaki of the underworld. This, we shall see, also relates to the Sirius question. But the use of Anunnaki in this way underscores the total anonymity of the term 'Anunnaki'. None of these seven Anunnaki is ever identified as an individual god. They are always 'the seven' underworld gods who determine destiny. The strictly celestial Anunnaki are also known as the Igigi (the precise meaning of which is unknown). No Sumerologist has satisfactorily explained all this. It is terribly imprecise and confusing – unless one had a structure to supply which fits under the cloth and matches the contours and can thereby be accepted as a tentative basis of explanation.

Now let us try to think of what we know is connected with the celestial Anunnaki and Sirius which also fits into this idea of there being seven Anunnaki-gods in the underworld. Remember that in both Sumer and Egypt each god of significance in astronomical terms has his own ten-day period or 'week'. If we multiply seven (gods) times ten days we get seventy days. Is there any basis for this length of time being of significance for the underworld in either Sumer or Egypt?

Parker and Neugebauer say[15]: 'It is here made clear that Sirius (Sothis) gives the pattern for all the other decanal stars.' Sirius was, astronomically, the foundation of the entire Egyptian religious system. Its celestial movements determined the Egyptian calendar, which is even known as the Sothic Calendar. Its heliacal rising marked the beginning of the Egyptian year and roughly coincided with the flooding of the Nile. (Plutarch says the Nile itself was sometimes called Sirius.) This heliacal rising was the occasion of an important feast. One can imagine a kind of New Year-cum-Easter. The heliacal rising was the occasion when Sirius again rose into visibility in the sky *after a period of seventy days of being out of sight*, during which time it was conceived as being in the Duat, or underworld. A further connection with Anubis comes in here, as Anubis was conceived of as embalming Sothis for these seventy days in the Duat. An embalmed mummy is supposed to come alive again. And this is what happens to the mummy of Sothis. Sothis is reborn on the occasion of her heliacal rising. Parker and Neugebauer also say:[16] 'During the entire time of its purification it (Sothis, the star) was considered dead and it was only with its rising again out of the Duat that it could once more be considered as living.'

The Egyptians stubbornly clung to the traditional seventy days as the prototype of an underworld experience, despite its inconvenience, and, as we have already seen, 'Sirius gives the pattern for all the other decanal stars'. In fact, it was the practice through all of Egyptian history for there to be a period of precisely seventy days for the embalming of a human mummy – in imitation of Sirius. Even during the late Ptolemaic period, the embalming process invariably lasted the precise period of seventy days.

Thus we find the explanation of the seven Anunnaki of the underworld! It is also interesting to note that in Mexico before the Spanish Conquest the underworld was thought to have seven caves.

It is worth noting too the Sumerian story *Etana*,[17] about the legendary King Etana. He was an early Sumerian ruler, a shepherd king who was said to have ruled for 1,560 years. Etana was supposed to have lived in the early third millennium bc, not long after the Great Flood. He had to ascend to heaven in order to have infertility treatment! As a result he was able to have a son and heir when he returned to Earth. This tale mentions 'the divine Seven' and describes them specifically as Igigi. This emphasises the apparent interchangeability of the terms Igigi and Anunnaki. In the same tale, 'the great Anunnaki' are described as 'They who created the regions, who set up the establishments'.

In the 'Descent of Ishtar to the Nether World' (a long poem which survives in both the Sumerian and Akkadian languages)[18] the Anunnaki are described as being brought forth (they are referred to as if they were stuffed animals being brought out of a closet, dusted off, and displayed in a taxidermists' contest) and seated on thrones of gold. Once more the throne concept appears. It seems all the Anunnaki ever do is sit and be symbolic.

Good little Anunnaki, like poodles, sit and smile at Anu. They are never given personalities, poor fellows. I might mention that in this story the nether world is described as having seven gates leading to seven successive rooms (or caves). It is obvious that the period of seventy days during which Sirius was 'in the underworld' to the Egyptians led to a breaking down of the seventy days into ten-day weeks, each with a god, giving seven gods. But these seven gods of the underworld must not have personalities lest there be the distraction of personal qualities to detract from the purely numerical significance of the concept. And of course the seven rooms of the seven gods are successive, leading from 'week' to 'week' until Sirius again rises. So we see yet another essential link between the early Sumerian concepts and the Egyptian concepts.

In later times the god Marduk usurped the central position of the pantheon from all the other gods in Babylon. (Marduk was a god of the Semitic Babylonians, not a Sumerian God. His ascendancy came about as a result of the mixture of cultures.) The *Enuma Elish* is largely a description of this process and is basically written to Marduk, telling of his honours. This was quite an innovation, a real centralization of power. 'The black-headed people', which is how the Sumerians usually referred to themselves in their writings (when the context is sufficiently pious they meekly call themselves 'the beclouded'; it is also interesting to note that the Egyptians were known as 'the *melampodes*' or 'the black-*footed* people' to the Greeks!) obviously didn't take to the rise of Marduk with unanimous acclaim. In many ways the *Enuma Elish* is a blatant propaganda tract for Marduk, alternately trying to convert and to denounce the people. Here we see the author trying to woo them:[19]

Let his sovereignty be surpassing having no rival.
May he shepherd the black-headed ones, his creatures.
To the end of days, without forgetting, let them acclaim his ways.

Here, however, we see a more authoritarian approach, where the sugary smile dissolves:

May he order the black-headed to re[vere him],

But the next moment, compromise comes again in the form of a mock-tolerance:

Without fail let them support their gods!
Their lands let them improve, build their shrines,
Let the black-headed people wait on their gods.

In other words, the author despairs and goes into a sulk. For his next words indicate the sentiment, 'We don't need them, we'll go it alone':

As for us, by however many names we pronounce it, he is our god!
Let us then proclaim his fifty names!

In other words, the supporters of Marduk thought the best way to glorify their god was to give him fifty names. Then, with any luck, he would be omnipotent.

As Marukka, Marduk 'gladdens the heart of the Anunnaki, appeases their [spirits]'. All the fifty names are given, along with short comments following each. In a footnote Speiser says, revealingly, that: 'The text etymologizes the names in a manner made familiar by the Bible; the etymologies, which accompany virtually every name on the long list are meant to be cabalistic and symbolic rather than strictly linguistic, although some of them happen to be linguistically sound.'
The list ends and we read in the text:

With the title 'Fifty' the great gods
Proclaimed him whose names are fifty and made his way supreme.

This final note adds a last flourish of emphasis to the importance to the supreme god of the title 'Fifty' as well as the designation by fifty names.
There is one cluster of names among the fifty given which is of particular interest. They are Asaru, Asarualim, Asarualimnunna, and the group of three centred round the similar name Asaruludu (the other two being Namtillaku and Namru). I suspect these names of being related to the Egyptian Asar (Osiris). We have already seen how the An of Egypt was known in Sumer not only as An but as Anu, picking up a 'u' ending. It is therefore not so senseless to see in Asaru a Sumerian form of Asar, with the same 'u' ending added. But the Egyptians themselves also had an Asaru, or more precisely, an Asar-uu, whom Wallis Budge describes as 'a form of Osiris worshipped in lower Egypt'.
Since Asaru in Sumer corresponds to Asar-uu in Egypt, what about the Sumerian Asaruludu? In Egyptian a vegetative Osiris would be known as Asar-ruṭu but the liquid 'r' and 'l' are in Egyptian entirely interchangeable (this is a linguistic commonplace and the contemporary Chinese do this when speaking English) and represented by the same hieroglyph. So Asar-ruṭu could just as well be Asar-luṭu, and the lingual 't' as opposed to a dental 't' is pronounced rather like a 'd', being a softer sound. If we merely

transliterate it thus, we have Asar-ludu. It would mean, 'Osiris of the growing plants'. And in fact, in the Sumerian text, we find Asaru described as 'bestower of cultivation . . . creator of grain and herbs, who causes vegetation to sprout'.

Immediately after one of the Asaru-names of Marduk in the *Enuma Elish* we find that his thirteenth name is Tutu. It so happens that Tutu is the name of an Egyptian god. Wallis Budge describes him as 'a lion-god, son of Neith'. (Wallis Budge says that Neith was: 'One of the oldest goddesses of Egypt. She was the goddess of hunting and weaving, but was identified with many other goddesses such as Isis, Meh-urt, and their attributes were assigned to her.'[20]) There is even an Egyptian precedent for the use of Tutu as one name of a god who has many names. The Egyptian monster of darkness, Apep, 'possessed many names; to destroy him it was necessary to curse him by each and every name by which he was known. To make quite sure that this should be done effectively, the Papyrus of Nesi-Amsu adds a list of such names, and as they are the foundation of many of the magical names met with in later papyri they are here enumerated . . .'[21] And one of these is Tutu. Surely this almost identical preoccupation with the need to enumerate every one of the magical names of a god in both countries must have common origins – especially as the name *Tutu* is in the lists of both countries.

It is important to look even closer at the Egyptian god Tutu. In Heidel's translation of the *Enuma Elish* he gives for Asaruludu the early Sumerian epithet *namshub* as opposed to the late Babylonian form *namru* – both meaning 'bright', and in the text further explained as, 'The bright god who brightens our way'. In a footnote Heidel explains: 'The poets are here apparently playing on the Sumerian term *shuba*, which is equated with the Babylonian words *ebbu*, *ellu*, and *namru*, all of which mean "bright".' Now, what is so interesting is that in Egyptian the word *shu* means 'bright' and also describes the sun god – who is indeed a 'bright god who brightens our way'. So we see that *shu* in Egyptian means the same as *shuba* in Sumerian. Furthermore, both are made to apply to a description of the sun. Also the Sumerian *shuba* is made to refer to Asarluhi, and we may now take note of the further surprising fact that the Egyptian god Tutu is, according to Wallis Budge: 'a form of the god Shu, whose symbol was a lion walking'.[22]

So as we examine the material we find an increasingly complex weave of common patterns in Egypt and early Sumer both linguistically and in religion-astronomy. Later in the book we shall see this all reach a meaningful climax.

POSTSCRIPT (1997)

The mythological motif of 'fifty' is so widespread that Wilhelm Roscher wrote an entire book about it. It is entitled *Die Zahl 50 in Mythus, Kultus, Epos und Taktik der Hellenen und Anderer Voelker Besonders der Semiten* (The Number 50 in Myth, Cult, Epic and Tactics of the Greeks and Other Peoples, in Particular the Semites).[23] In his learned survey, Roscher discusses the fifty daughters of Danaus (the Danaids), the fifty sons of Aegyptus, the fifty Argonauts, the fifty daughters of Nereus, the various fifty-headed, fifty-armed, or hundred-headed and hundred-armed monsters, the fifty daughters of Thespios, the fifty sons of Orion, the fifty sons of Priam, the fifty sons of Lykaon, the fifty sons of Pallas, the fifty daughters of Endymion, the fifty heads of the Hydra, the fifty heads of the dog Cerberus, the fifty heads of Typhon, the fifty cows stolen by Hermes from Apollo, and so on, just to give some of the Greek examples. Roscher's books only came to my notice just before the original publication of this book, so I had no time available to expand my account of the significance of 'fifty' using his extensive material. Now the reprint of this book has come about so suddenly that once again there is no opportunity to do justice to Roscher's material or to many other matters. However, I would call special attention to Roscher's section on the fifty sons of Orion,[24] because Orion is the companion constellation of Sirius and in Egypt was identified with Osiris.

Ultimately the whole point of the constellation Orion is that it is the *visible* companion of Sirius, and as such was a substitute and representative of the *invisible* companion, which is Sirius B. It is therefore extremely important to come across ancient evidence that Orion was said to have 'fifty sons', since that is a clear acknowledgement from antiquity that there was a 'fifty-ish' aspect to the visible companion of Sirius just as there is of the invisible companion, with its orbit of fifty years.

We should never lose sight of the fact that Orion's importance is that of a substitute for an invisible counterpart. The significance of Orion is thus derivative, not intrinsic. Sirius B was represented amongst the stars by the visible substitute of Orion, and was represented in the solar system by a 'local substitute', the planet Mercury.

Notes

1. In Pritchard, *Ancient Near Eastern Texts.*
2. Also in Pritchard, ibid.
3. Pub. by W. W. Norton & Co., New York, 1965. An earlier edition of this book had a different title: *Before the Bible.*
4. *The Sumerians*, University of Chicago Press, 1963, p. 67.
5. Also in Pritchard, op. cit.
6. Temple, Robert K. G., *He Who Saw Everything: A Verse Translation of the Epic of Gilgamesh*, Rider, London, 1991, p. 45.
7. *Journal of the American Oriental Society*, 64 (1944), p. 11.
8. Temple, op. cit., p. 11.
9. Temple, op. cit., p. 15.
10. Pritchard, op. cit.
11. Heidel, Alexander, *The Gilgamesh Epic and Old Testament Parallels*, University of Chicago

133

Press, USA, 1970.

12. Pritchard, op. cit.
13. Ibid. Also see p. 514, Addenda: New Text Fragments, in same vol.
14. de Santillana, Giorgio, and von Dechend, Hertha, *Hamlet's Mill*, Macmillan & Company Ltd., London, 1969.
15. *Egyptian Astronomical Texts*, Vol. I, p. 74.
16. Ibid., p. 73.
17. Pritchard, op. cit., p. 114.
18. Ibid., p. 106.
19. In Pritchard, ibid.
20. *Book of the Dead*, trans. by Wallis Budge, p. 176, n.
21. Wallis Budge, *The Gods of the Egyptians*, Vol. I, p. 326.
22. Ibid., Vol. I, pp. 463–4.
23. The book is Vol. 33, No. 5, of the *Abhandlungen der Philologisch-Historischen Klasse der Koengl. Saeschsischen Gesellschaft der Wissenschaften*, Leipzig, 1917.
24. Ibid., pp. 57–9.

SUMMARY

'The Black Rite' concerned something called 'Night' which was apparently an object that moves in heaven along with 'the other mysteries in turn that move in heaven, with ordered motions and periods of times'. It has less light than the sun and it 'weaves a web with rapid light'.

Sirius B moves in heaven with ordered motion and period, has less light than our sun, and distinctly weaves a web with its rapid motion, since it revolves round Sirius A in much less time than the planets Uranus, Neptune, and Pluto revolve around our own sun.

'Night' may thus refer to Sirius B, just as may 'black Osiris' and 'invisible Nephthys'.

In really early times the basic concepts of Egyptian astronomy and Sumerian astronomy were identical. Later many differences appeared. Authorities on ancient astronomy tend to give short shrift to the earlier times, hence the similarities between the two cultures in this particular field have tended to go unremarked.

In Egypt and Sumer (Babylonia) there were identical systems of dividing the calendar year into twelve months each composed of three weeks which lasted ten days apiece. Each week had a constellation of the night sky associated with it (which in modern parlance we might describe as 'being a kind of zodiac'). Thirty-six of these weeks added up only to 360 days, which was less than a year, so the 365-day year was obtained by adding on five extra days at the end.

Identical systems of such complexity in these two cultures mean that the relationship between Egypt and Sumer must be explored further.

In Sumer the 'fifty great gods' called the Anunnaki were anonymous as individuals and only ever spoken of as 'the fifty great gods' with the emphasis on their number. They were literally restricted to the level of being a numerological cipher. They are continually invoked and are of importance – but they never did anything but sit on their thrones and 'be fifty'.

In an early Sumerian tale of their epic hero Gilgamesh, we find him accompanied in his adventures by fifty heroes, reminiscent of the fifty Argonauts who accompanied Jason. 'His teeth are the teeth of a dragon', we are told – reminiscent of Jason sowing the dragon's teeth. And Gilgamesh also puts his teeth to the ground (that much we can gather, but the passage is obscure and he may really be sowing teeth). Each of his fifty heroic companions carries a specially felled tree for the journey – and the only reasonable purpose to go around carrying a tree seems to be that these trees were used as oars, especially as there is an association with a boat. This again is like the Argonauts. We thus seem to have found a Near Eastern tale from which the tale of the Argonauts was derived two thousand years or so later by the Greeks.

Gilgamesh somehow derives strength from putting his teeth to the ground. In the Greek tale, Jason sows the teeth and they spring up as strong soldiers – another parallel.

Anubis, who is now familiar to us from Egypt, was identified by the Greeks with their own god Hermes (known in Latin as Mercury). Hermes turned the Golden Fleece to gold originally, in the Greek myth. It was this same Golden Fleece that Jason and the Argonauts sought in their quest, and which they succeeded in seizing and taking away with them.

In the early Gilgamesh tale of the Sumerians, Gilgamesh and his fifty proto-Argonauts have some connection with a ship (the text is tantalizingly fragmented) called 'the Magan-boat'. It should be remembered that Magan is the Sumerian name for Egypt. Hence the boat is connected with Egypt.

All the Greek Argonauts were related to one another and more or less anonymous as individuals – reminiscent of the earlier Sumerian 'fifty heroes' accompanying Gilgamesh and also the 'fifty great gods' known as Anunnaki.

The Greek ark of Deukalion came to rest after the Flood at Dodona, from where the *Argo* received its guiding timber. The ark and the *Argo* apparently were related in other ways too.

Professor Cyrus Gordon has written an important book on common origins of Greek and Hebrew cultures from the Egyptian-Sumerian milieu of the cosmopolitan world of the ancient Mediterranean (see Bibliography).

The 'fifty great gods' of Sumer, the Anunnaki, are invariably seated. Sacred oarsmen or Argonauts are all, of course, invariably seated while they are rowing. 'The fifty who sit' and 'the fifty who sit and row' seem to be a motif.

The other element besides the eye in the Osiris-name hieroglyph is the throne, which is the hieroglyph for Isis as well. The throne is a divine seat. The Sumerians frequently intoned of the Anunnaki that they were 'they who are seated on their thrones'; or sometimes for a bit more drama, 'the fifty great gods took their seats'. (Of course they did nothing even then.)

The Egyptian Anubis (Anpu) was a god 'of the hill'. The Sumerian god Anu's wife was a goddess 'of the hill'.

The older form of the Sumerian word for hill, *hursagga*, may be derived from the Egyptian Ḥeru-sa-agga, where 'agga' refers to Anubis (who was 'of the hill'). There are many other word and name similarities between Egypt and Sumer.

In the *Epic of Gilgamesh* a dream of Gilgamesh is described where he encounters a heavy star that cannot be lifted despite immense effort. This star descends from heaven to him and is described as connected with Anu (who is the god of heaven). Thus we find 'the heavy star' concept in Babylonia long before the Arabs even existed and were to have their star in the Great Dog (and the other in Argo) called 'Weight' and described as 'the heavy star'.

Gilgamesh is drawn to this heavy star irresistibly, in a manner described in a way that seems to hint at a kind of gravitational attraction (to those, that is, who are conscious of a 'heavy star' like Sirius B being gravitationally powerful as well as 'heavy').

The *Epic of Gilgamesh* refers to 'the essence of Anu' possessed by the star. The word rendered as 'essence' is used elsewhere in medical contexts referring to 'concentration, essence' – an intimation of super-dense matter? This 'concentrated star essence of Anu' was too heavy for Gilgamesh to lift in his dream.

It must be recalled that Gilgamesh had his fifty companions in the early versions of the *Epic* (they were discarded later, by Babylonian times). Hence connected with Gilgamesh we find:

(a) Fifty anonymous companions seemingly important only as a numerological element in the story and in later times discarded as useless.

(b) A super-heavy star connected with An (also an Egyptian name of Osiris, husband of Isis who was identified with Sirius).

(c) A description of the star as being composed of a 'concentrated essence' and of having extreme powers of attraction described in a manner reminiscent of gravitational attraction.

These elements comprise almost a complete description of Sirius B: a super-heavy gravitationally powerful star made of concentrated super-dense matter ('essence') with the number fifty associated with it (describing its period?) – and connected with An (Anu), which we know to be linked in Egypt (and Gilgamesh's 'Magan-boat' seems Egyptian) with Sirius.

Chapter Five

The Hounds of Hell

Since Sirius is the Dog Star, let us turn to the dog-headed Sumerian goddess Bau. According to a leading Assyriologist, Thorkild Jacobsen,[1] 'Bau seems originally to have been goddess of the dog and her name, Bau, to have constituted an imitation of the dog's bark, as English "bow wow"'.* Bau was also the daughter of An. So here the dog-goddess is the daughter of An, where as in Egypt the dog-god was himself An-pu (Anubis). Since An is connected with Sirius, we should thus not be surprised that he has a dog-goddess for a daughter in Sumer. Sirius as the Dog Star was a tradition which was not thought to have existed in Sumer, however, before now.

Since the fifty Anunnaki were children of An, and Bau is a daughter of An, it is not far-fetched to see in Bau a survival (for she is an old goddess who faded into obscurity in later times) of the concept of a dog-star goddess equivalent to Isis as Sothis. And it is interesting that she was dog-*headed*. For Anubis was not entirely a jackal or dog, he was merely jackal- or dog-*headed*.

Bau's husband Ninurta was the son of Enlil. Just as Marduk usurped the position of chief god, at a somewhat earlier time Enlil had usurped this position from An. (The situation is analogous to Greek mythology where Cronos usurped the position of Uranus and was in turn overthrown by Zeus.) There is an interesting 170-line hymn to Enlil[2] which seems to describe a stellar abode for the god. The 'lifted eye' or 'lifted light' scanning and searching the lands sounds reminiscent of the Dogon concept of the ray of Digitaria which once a year sweeps the Earth. In any case, a 'lifted light' which searches and scans is definitely a beam or ray, and is in its own right an interesting concept for the Sumerians to have had as situated in the celestial abode. I must emphasize in advance for the reader that lapis lazuli was considered by the Sumerians to represent the night sky. Here then are significant excerpts from the hymn:

Enlil, whose command is far-reaching, whose word is holy,
The lord whose pronouncement is unchangeable, who forever decrees
    destinies,

* In Egyptian a word for 'dog, jackal', is Áuàu, which probably has the same 'dog's bark' derivation as the Sumerian Bau.

Whose lifted eye scans the lands,
Whose lifted light searches the heart of all the lands,
Enlil who sits broadly on the white dais, on the lofty dais . . .

The lofty white dais of Sothis-Sirius is an Egyptian concept. It is Ast (Isis). It is also Asar (Osiris), with the addition of a hieroglyphic eye. Later we find in this hymn from Sumer, the city of Nippur's* temple in comparison:

Nippur - the shrine, where dwells the father, the 'great mountain',
The dais of plenty, the Ekur which rises . . . ,
The high mountain, the pure place . . . ,
Its prince, the 'great mountain', Father Enlil,
Has established his seat on the dais of the Ekur, lofty shrines;
The temple – its divine laws like heaven cannot be overturned,
Its pure rites, like the earth cannot be shattered,
Its divine laws are like the divine laws of the abyss, none can look upon them,
Its 'heart' like a distant shrine, unknown like heaven's zenith. . . .

And:

The Ekur, the lapis-lazuli house, the lofty dwelling place, awe-inspiring,
Its awe and dread are next to heaven,
Its shadow is spread over all the lands
Its loftiness reaches heaven's heart.†

These mentions of the lapis lazuli aspect of Enlil's abode and also that it reaches heaven's heart make quite clear that we are not merely dealing with a solar description. It is not the sun but a stellar abode that is being distinctly described. Hence the references to the ray or beam are all the more curious as they do not refer to the sun's light, as might have been thought from a superficial reading. We continue:

Heaven – he is its princely one; earth – he is its great one,
The Anunnaki – he is their exalted god;
When in his awesomeness, he decrees the fates,
No god dare look on him.

Here we see Enlil has been called the exalted god over the Anunnaki (in other texts his son Enki, or Ea, boasts that *he* is their 'big brother' and

---

* Nippur was in the centre of Sumer, beside the River Euphrates.
† The most important temple in Sumer was the Ekur at Nippur, the temple of Enlil, chief god of the Sumerian pantheon.

leader). Here Enlil has also himself been given the power of decreeing the fates, which the Anunnaki traditionally do themselves. In the fourth line from the end above, 'heaven' is An and 'earth' is Ki, An and Ki were married. The compound *an-ki* is Sumerian for 'heaven-earth' and is the word meaning 'universe'. Note the similarity between *an-ki* and the name of the Egyptian goddess Anukis who is identified with Sothis-Sirius. Also, of course, the similarity to the name Anunnaki.

So above we find stellar descriptions of Enlil, the father-in-law of the dog-headed goddess we tentatively identify with Sirius. And we find those fifty irrepressible Anunnaki creeping in again. They manage to turn up everywhere, given half a chance, when the subject of Sirius comes up.

Now the many similarities between Sumer and Egypt which we have so far noted (with more to come), which have led us to consider the possibility of the two nations having been in some way linked, may be referred to in a most interesting passage from the Jewish historian of the first century AD Josephus,[3] in which 'the children of Seth' are mentioned. Many ancient writers supposed Seth to have been Hermes Trismegistus.

This fact may suddenly be more important in the light of what we have begun to suspect about a scantily surviving authentic Hermetic tradition (maligned and obscured by a welter of useless, trivial co-survivals from later times). Here is the passage:

> 'The children of Seth' were the inventors of that peculiar sort of wisdom which is concerned with the heavenly bodies, and their order; and that their inventions might not be lost before they were sufficiently known, upon Adam's prediction, that the world was at one time to be destroyed by the force of fire, and at another time by the violence and quantity of water, they made two pillars, the one of brick, the other of stone. They described their discoveries on them both, that in case the pillar of brick should be destroyed by the flood, the pillar of stone might remain, and exhibit those discoveries to mankind, and also inform them that there was another pillar of brick erected by them. Now this remains in the land of Syria or Seirad to this day.

This passage calls forth many comments. The point which immediately springs to one's notice is that there is a 'pillar of brick' in the land of Syria, or in the land of Sumer-Akkad-Babylonia. Well, this is the very land of brick! It is the land of the brick ziggurat or 'great mountain' – a giant pillar if you like. But where is the land of stone? Why, it is obviously Egypt, the land of the great stone pyramids. Here, then, is a description of two linked cultures, one building brick edifices and the other building stone edifices. In Egypt we have the Great Pyramid, which so many people have believed to contain in its basic construction the proportions and measurements to demonstrate that it was constructed by highly advanced and civilized men. The great ziggurats of Babylon and other cities, too, though in a more ruinous state, seem to embody in their construction much that is profound. Can it be that Josephus has preserved a tradition of the link between Egypt and Sumer and their respective types of building? He says the link was an astronomically-defined one. 'The children of Seth' first possessed 'that peculiar sort of wisdom which is concerned with the heavenly bodies'. Well, we have already discovered for ourselves that the fundamental astronomical and astronomical-religious concepts were common to earliest Egypt and Sumer. And here is Josephus telling us the same thing, and what is more, telling us what the treatise 'The Virgin of the World' would have us know: that it all began with Hermes Trismegistus – in the way we have already discovered in the previous two chapters.

But now let us pursue other relevant ramifications of Egypt found elsewhere. And let us do so by returning to the subject of the *Argo* and the fifty Argonauts, who were all Minyae (descendants of Minyas), who were led by Jason (also a descendant of Minyas) in the quest for the golden fleece at the mysterious land of Colchis, which actually existed and was just about as strange a locale as one could wish. For if you sail through the Hellespont (named after Helle, who fell from the golden ram) into the Black Sea (called the Euxine Sea by the Greeks), and follow the coast of present-day Turkey until you come to the region of the border with Georgia of today, you will have come to Colchis. It is a pretty strange place for the Greeks to attach so much importance to. It sits at the foot of the formidable Caucasus Mountains and not far away are the Georgian people who live in their mountains to such amazing ages as a hundred and ten, with a culture peculiarly their own. Not far to the south is that strange place, Mount Ararat, where the ark of Noah landed after the Flood. Surely this is a most unusual land, and far removed from the Greek world. Or is it?

Minyas had a great-grandson called Phrixus. Phrixus had four sons who lived in Colchis, to which he had fled on the back of the golden ram and where he gave the golden fleece to the local King of Colchis, and in return was made welcome and married the king's daughter. It is obvious that these four sons were only half-Colchian and would feel some loyalty towards their father's homeland which was in mainland Greece. Sure enough, on his deathbed Phrixus asked his sons to return to Orchomenos, his home in Greece, to reclaim their birthright there. This they agreed to do. For Phrixus's father had been the King of Orchomenos (as had Minyas) and these sons should be able to claim what honour and position (not to mention more material matters) was rightly theirs. However, they knew that setting things straight might be a bit difficult, as their father and his sister Helle (who fell into the Hellespont) had left in rather a hurry on the golden ram with the blessing of Hermes, but not with too many tears being shed in Orchomenos at the time.

So these four sons set out and were shipwrecked but were fortunately picked up and rescued. Who rescued them? None other than our fifty

Argonauts who were just passing. In fact, these Argonaut cousins of theirs were at that moment just happening by on their way to Colchis where their mission was to try to get that fleece back. The four young fellows had no objection to such a plan, especially as they were also descended from Minyas. The Argonauts had been losing some of their men (for instance, Hercules and Hylas had vanished; Hylas was dragged down into a stream by a passionate water nymph and Hercules went berserk and wandered off into Turkey calling his name in vain, later founding cities and doing various Herculean things). So these four fellows from Colchis were just the thing to recharge the ranks.

But what about this place Colchis? Perhaps if we examine it we shall find some Egyptian connections. Anything seems to be possible in a magical land like this.

In fact if we look at the *Histories* of Herodotus[4] we read : 'It is undoubtedly a fact that the Colchians are of Egyptian descent. I noticed this myself before I heard anyone else mention it, and when it occurred to me I asked some questions both in Colchis and in Egypt, and found that the Colchians remembered the Egyptians more distinctly than the Egyptians remembered them. The Egyptians did, however, say that they thought the Colchians were men from Sesostris' army.' This Sesostris is identified tentatively by scholars with Ramses II (thirteenth century BC). Herodotus continues:

My own idea on the subject was based first on the fact that they have black skins and woolly hair (not that that amounts to much, as other nations have the same), and secondly, and more especially, on the fact that the Colchians, the Egyptians, and the Ethiopians are the only races which from ancient times have practised circumcision. The Phoenicians and the Syrians of Palestine themselves admit that they adopted the practice from Egypt, and the Syrians who lived near the rivers Thermodon and Parthenius, learnt it only a short time ago from the Colchians. No other nations use circumcision, and all these are without doubt following the Egyptian lead. As between the Egyptians and the Ethiopians, I should not like to say which learned from the other, for the custom is evidently a very ancient one; but I have no doubt that the other nations adopted it as a result of their intercourse with Egypt, and in this belief I am strongly supported by the fact that Phoenicians, when they mix in Greek society, drop the Egyptian usage and allow their children to go uncircumcized.

And now I think of it, there is a further point of resemblance between the Colchians and Egyptians: they share a method of weaving linen different from that of any other people; and there is also a similarity between them in language and way of living.*

* Circumcision is absolutely fundamental to Dogon culture for religious reasons.

So here we see a probable (indeed, almost entirely certain) explanation for the connection of Colchis with the Argonaut story. No wonder the Hermes-given (which is to say, Anubis-given) golden fleece was at Colchis. For Colchis was a thoroughly Egyptian country. But because the heroes of a Greek tale must be Greeks and not Egyptians, the Argonauts are all Minyae from Greece. The familiar anonymity of 'the fifty' witnessed by us with the Anunnaki of Sumer, prevails here among the Argonauts as well. Different epic poets who treated of the tale chucked in various epic heroes. In the main surviving *Argonautica* by Apollonius of Rhodes, Orpheus and Herakles (Hercules) are among the crew, though Hercules is left behind as I have just said. In fact, Hercules was so obviously borrowed for his 'box-office draw' as a 'guest star' in a cameo performance that we can't really take the matter seriously.

On with the story and those Argonauts. I said that Orpheus was included in the cast by that great film producer Apollonius of Rhodes. But another competing film producer, Pherecydes, insisted that Orpheus was not an Argonaut. Diodorus Siculus, a great supporter of women's lib, maintained that Atalanta* was an Argonautess. Apollonius says pointedly that super-star Theseus was in Hades at the time and otherwise engaged (with another contract), but Statius (who was obviously with the other studio) later made Theseus an Argonaut anyway. H. W. Parke has pointed out that the Apolline seers (who prophesied the future) were apparently injected into the Argonaut story as a propaganda effort by the rising power of the Delphic Oracle which was trying to squeeze out the premier oracle of Dodona and achieve first place for itself in the eyes of the Greek public.

Parke has shown how the really central oracular elements in the Argo story were all related to Dodona, not Delphi. (Dodona is shown on the map, Figure 17, later in this chapter.) Delphi was quite an upstart in the centuries immediately preceding the classical period (which ended with Alexander the Great), and initially was not more important than Dodona, though it was to become so and held precedence by the time of Socrates and the classical Greeks. Parke concludes that all the Delphic and Apolline elements in the *Argo* story are late accretions from the time after Delphi had usurped the primacy of Dodona. They would not have been in the *Argo* epic referred to by Homer, who proves the antiquity of the *Argo* saga by his mention in the *Odyssey* (XII, 69–72) of 'the celebrated *Argo*' and of Jason and the Clashing Rocks. Significantly, no other Argonaut is mentioned by name by Homer. It is obvious, in fact, from what I said above, that the Argonauts were primarily noted for being fifty in number and related (a comfortable kind of anonymity – cousins!). Outstanding

---

* Atalanta was a mythological figure, a woman who was a great huntress and wrestler, and who announced that she would only marry a man who could beat her in a foot race. Melanion beat her, but by trickery.

Hellenic heroes were thrown into their ranks by the caprices of successive epic poets to provide recognizable colour. With the exception of Jason there is total disagreement among everyone concerned about just who were the Argonauts. And according to Robert Graves in *The Greek Myths*, Jason was originally Hercules. And Hercules was originally Briareus (a more archaic figure; for an account of him, see pp. 217–20 and 238). Of course, the answer is that they were not individuals and were not meant to be.

They were fifty and they were related and usually seated and they sailed in a magic boat. Just like the Anunnaki, and just like the fifty anonymous companions of Gilgamesh! And in the Gilgamesh fragments from the early Sumerian times, the boat mentioned is a 'Magan-boat', or Egyptian boat. It must be remembered also that Sumer is located between Egypt and Colchis.

We are now beginning to get down to the bare bones of the *Argo* story. I don't believe that the earliest levels of this ancient tale have ever previously been reached.

Not only Herodotus, but Pindar (518–438 BC) as well, describes the Colchians as dark. In his IVth Pythian Ode, which is largely about the Argonauts, Pindar says (212): 'Among the dark-faced Kolchians, in the very presence of Aeetes'. Pindar therefore confirms Herodotus on this point.

It remains to attempt a dating. If Herodotus is correct and the Colchians were Egyptian soldiers dating from the reign of Sesostris (Ramses II), then they would have gone to Colchis at some time during the years 1301–1234 BC, which is estimated by John A. Wilson[5] as the period of the reign of Ramses II. This dating is only of use as an indicator of the general antiquity of the origins of our material. There does not seem to be any archaeological information of any kind from the undiscovered site of Aea, the capital city of Colchis, which is on the coast of the Black Sea (just by a river known anciently as the Phasis), just across the border of Georgia from Turkey. I would suspect the site of Aea has never even been sought! It would certainly make an interesting site for excavation. It would presumably offer an unusual amount of Egyptian-style material mixed with Armenian-Caucasian styles. It should be extraordinarily interesting from the point of view of ancient art, almost certainly being quite rich in precious metals and beautiful metal-working, particularly gold. We shall see later in this book that it was near a famous ancient metallurgical centre. And, of course, there should be finds which would confirm Herodotus's account.

Here is a description of the site, for those who wish to seek it: 'They reached the broad estuary of the Phasis, where the Black Sea ends . . . and then rowed straight up into the mighty river, which rolled in foam to either bank as it made way for *Argo*'s prow. On their left hand they had the lofty Caucasus and the city of Aea, on their right the plain of Ares and the god's sacred grove, where the snake kept watch and ward over the fleece, spread on the leafy branches of an oak.' (Another hint of Dodona, with the oak and the grove. This similarity will be seen to become extremely relevant later on.)

To return to the question of dates (also bearing in mind Homer's early casual reference to 'the celebrated *Argo*'), we'll recall my mention of dates when I showed the identical nature of the Sumerian and Egyptian astronomical systems in their essential details. I pointed out then that the Babylonian tablets were dated from the second millennium BC, giving us an upper limit on time in the Sumerian region. The Egyptian star clocks to which they bear such total resemblance calendrically had already altered (such as by the introduction of a fifteen-day week instead of a ten-day one, indicating the advanced degeneration of the traditions) in Egypt in the first millennium BC.

Hence we see that the Egyptian star clocks no longer existed in the necessary form by the first millennium, giving us an upper limit date in Egypt of the end of the second millennium BC, identical with the upper limit we have in Sumer. I am tempted now to steal a phrase of the physicists and remind the reader that these dates are of an order of magnitude comparable with the date of Ramses II's reign adopted tentatively for the settlement at Colchis of Egyptian colonists. Surely these three dates cannot coalesce accidentally round the same material! We have no choice but to adopt the approximate date of 1200 BC as the upper limit for the spread (and subsequent degeneration) of our Sirius-related material throughout the Mediterranean area, from whichever source it originated.

It may perhaps be of some relevance that this coincides roughly with the end of Minoan domination of the Mediterranean. From the point of view at least of the spread of the Sirius material, I would connect it with what seems to me an obvious fact: that when Minoan sea power, based on Crete, collapsed, the Egyptians and inhabitants of the Near East could and did expand their own maritime activities to fill the vacuum left by the disintegration of the Minoan fleets. (An alternative but unlikely suggestion is that fleeing Minoans dispersed their culture with them as they settled in exile in different areas of the Mediterranean following the collapse of their nation; but I do not believe they alone were the source of the Sirius material.)

I am inclined to believe the increasingly strong and accumulating evidence that the Minoan culture was dealt a death blow by eruptions of the volcano Thera. F. Matz, in 'Minoan Civilization: Maturity and Zenith' in the *Cambridge Ancient History*, says: 'The peaceful transfer of power in Crete from the Minoans to the Mycenaeans is difficult to explain.' But not, surely, if volcanic eruptions had enfeebled the Minoans. The Minoan cities had no walls. On their island the Minoans relied, it seems, on their unchallenged sea power to keep enemies at bay, just as the Spartans in their unwalled city of Sparta in mainland Greece relied on their unchallenged land power to keep enemies at bay in late classical times. For the Cretan island could not be reached by enemies on foot, and as the Minoans had total naval superiority they could not be threatened at home. The latest conclusions about Thera seem to be that the towns on that small volcanic island near Crete were first evacuated due to earthquakes some years before the final volcanic eruption which destroyed Minoan civilization.

Herodotus in Book I of his *Histories* gives us a good illustration of how hopeless it is for a land power to challenge a sea power on the sea, when he shows the landlubber Lydians abandoning their plans to build ships and extend their conquests to the islands because they are aware they just don't know what they're doing. If the Minoan fleets had been sunk in great tidal waves following volcanic eruptions, the Minoans would have had no choice but to come to an understanding with the Mycenaeans. Any other possibility would have meant suicide. Probably they made a graceful and dignified pact or series of pacts which made the inevitable seem voluntary. And if the Mycenaeans were traditionally a good bit in awe of the more sophisticated Minoans, so much the better for the Minoans who 'condescended' to come to terms like gentlemen.

But the 'spheres of influence' of the sea-going Minoans could not be taken over immediately by the Mycenaeans, who lacked the maritime skill (not to mention ships) to complement on the waves their success in overrunning most of the island of Crete, probably leaving certain areas to the native Minoans according to the pacts I have suggested. It is not that the Mycenaeans would have lacked the energy or will, but the Minoan fleets would have been destroyed and even the most willing Minoan sailors could not sail non-existent ships for the Mycenaean invaders. Furthermore, the work of consolidating power on the recently taken island would have been a protracted and distracting matter for the Mycenaeans. So, for all these reasons, the new Cretan rulers could not attain to the full stature of their predecessors and be in complete command of the Mediterranean Sea.

The Mycenaeans had been competing with the Minoans (and raiding them, apparently under Theseus) as best they could for some time before the cataclysm. In fact F. H. Stubbings[6] informs us that the Minoans made a 'disastrous Sicilian expedition' against the Mycenaean trading interests in the central Mediterranean. This is reminiscent, of course, of the famous Athenian expedition to Sicily which was a total disaster and caused Athens to lose the Peloponnesian War. Sicily was thus responsible for two great historical disasters that altered the course of events to an unknown extent elsewhere than in Sicily.

So we see the Minoan power may already have been declining. Stubbings says: 'All that is really certain, however, is that the fall of Crete laid the way clear for a vastly increased Mycenaean activity.' And, we may be sure, for a vastly increased Egyptian maritime activity as well. Egypt, which is known to have traded heavily with Crete under the Minoans, must have found itself without choice: expanded maritime activity on her own account or a severe starvation of imported goods. There may even be a possibility that the name Minyas (and, hence, Minyae for the Argonauts) may have some connection with Minos (which gave us the word Minoan). After all, the Minoans were in considerable contact with the Egyptians and were the best sailors of their day.

It has been worth while to go into all this about the Minoan collapse at about the time of the upper limit dates (1200 BC – see p. 144) which we have arrived at in other ways. For with the disappearance of Minoan supremacy at sea, vast numbers of other people were free to ply the sea lanes and no doubt did so, bringing a proliferation of variegated contacts between cultures which the uniform Minoan sea traffic had ironed flat and featureless. Enterprising folk from almost anywhere – ethnics from mainland Greece, sophisticates from riverine Egypt, and clever Semites from Lebanon, Canaan, Palestine, all with their eyes on the main chance, could find something that would float and have a go.

All these folk suddenly let loose on the high seas brought an inevitable cross-fertilization at the cultural level, even if piracy must have increased alarmingly. There must have been an amazing amount of syncretism, during which our Sirius material must have leaked out into wider currency beyond the confines of Egypt and Sumer. Two millennia earlier, or even before that, the Egyptian and Sumerian cultures had shared many secrets: now these secrets were let out of Pandora's box and entered what was to become the Greek culture through synthesis in the white heat of warlike Mycenaean exploits at Troy and elsewhere. The Heroic Age was beginning, *aretē* (the classical Greek ideal of *excellence* in all things) was to be forged by blood and iron in the *Iliad*, with the subsidiary sources of the great *Odyssey* and what remains of the *Argo* tales, as well as many other ancient epics of which only fragments survive. Deeply imbedded like subtle dragon's teeth sunk in tough battle flesh, the bony outline of our Sirius material was to peer through the membrane of Greek epic tradition, to spring forth now in our century as the armed men of controversy. They have re-entered the field, we must face them. Rather than enter into combat, let us question these strangers about their origins. We are faced with the living fossils of a world almost entirely beyond our modern comprehension. These creatures are shaggy with the cobwebs of the centuries that preceded even classical Greece, and came before even Hesiod and Homer. These ghosts are antique in a sense which we rarely encounter except inside the tombs of Egypt or the burials at Ur.

To continue with elucidations of the Argonaut complex, we turn now to that invaluable compendium of all that is strange and wonderful about the world of the Greeks, Robert Graves's superb work *The Greek Myths*. There we find:[7] 'Aeaea ("wailing") is a typical death island where the familiar Death-goddess sings as she spins. The Argonautic legend places it at the head of the Adriatic Gulf; it may well be Lussin near Pola. Circe means "falcon", and she had a cemetery in Colchis, planted with willows, sacred to Hecate.' In the *Argonautica*, we recall, Jason offers a sacrifice to the goddess Hecate at Colchis at the suggestion of Medea. We shall see later that Hecate is a degenerate form of Sothis, or Sirius. But let us examine the above information from Graves. First we note that Circe, who figures so prominently in the *Argonautica*, has the meaning of 'falcon'. This brings to mind the prominent Egyptian symbolic 'falcon of Horus', which was the symbol of rising from the dead, or resurrection. The hawk or falcon of Horus presided over the Egyptian necropolis at Memphis, so it is quite obvious that it could have presided over the Egyptian necropolis at Colchis.

Naturally, the Greeks would have thought of the falcon in terms of their death-goddess Hecate.* There was no reason for them to preserve the masculine gender of a Horus of whom they knew nothing. But the falcon of Horus could have had a powerful effect on them as a symbol and have been transferred to a feminine figure of Greek myth. In fact, this cemetery of Circe in Colchis is almost undoubtedly an Egyptian cemetery surviving from Herodotus's Egyptian Colchians, and presided over by the falcon of Horus which in Greek was called Circe, and eventually became a female figure. The springing up from the earth of the magically sown soldiers in the *Argonautica* must partially refer to the Egyptian soldiers buried in 'the cemetery of Circe' who were meant to rise from the dead under the auspices of the Egyptian god of resurrection, Horus, whose symbol was the falcon, or 'circe'. (Excavations could unearth the Colchian necropolis some day.)

Circe lived on the island of Aea, which has the same name as the city which Jason visited in Colchis and from where Medea came. In Greek mythology, Circe is the daughter of Helios and Perse and the sister of King Aeetes, the king of Colchis. She is therefore Medea's aunt (Medea eloped with Jason). As for the 'island' of Aea, I believe it was a holm, or river-island, in the Phasis River near the city Aea. The Circe episode in the *Odyssey* is so obviously an interpolation into the original and central epic *The Homecoming of Odysseus* – an insertion of some archaic material in a fairly undigested fashion – that any geographical conclusions are unwarranted. If anything, the island of Aea portrayed there seems to be the North Atlantic, North Sea, or Baltic Sea!

Circe's father Helios is the sun, who rose every morning from his magnificent palace near Colchis where he slept and stabled his horses

---

* 'Hesiod's account of Hecate shows her to have been the original Triple-goddess, supreme in Heaven, on earth, and in Tartarus; but the Hellenes emphasized her destructive powers at the expense of her creative ones ... Lion, dog, and horse (were) her heads ... the dog being the Dog-star Sirius': Robert Graves, *The Greek Myths*, 31.7. Hesiod, who lived *circa* 700 BC, wrote *The Theogony*, a long poem dealing with the origins and genealogies of the gods. In it, he says (*Theogony* 416): 'In starry heaven she has her place, and the immortal gods greatly respect her'.

147

overnight. And likewise the father of the Egyptian Horus was the sun, and Horus himself represents the rising sun. The Greek word κιρκη (*kirkē* latinized as *circe*) revealingly means 'an unknown bird', if we consult (as we shall do from now on) Liddell and Scott's definitive Greek lexicon. In the form κιρκος (*kirkos*) the meaning is 'a kind of hawk or falcon', 'a kind of wolf', 'a circle' (which in Latin became *circus*) or 'ring', and 'an unknown stone'. Κιρκαια (*kirkaia*) means 'an uncertain plant'. Of these only the proper noun Κιρκη (*Kirkē*) has the specific meaning of Circe the Enchantress, although the same word in general is 'an unknown bird'. How appropriate a reaction for the Greeks to the falcon of Horus – a bird symbol unknown to them. But in trying to be more precise they make κιρκος (*kirkos*) 'a kind of hawk or falcon', as that is obviously what it is from its appearance, though its especial symbolic value makes the Greeks doubt precisely what the Egyptians intended. It looked like a kind of hawk or falcon but the Greeks weren't prepared to insist on exactly what species – because it was an Egyptian, not a Greek, idea.

On a point such as this we must 'take advice' as from a lawyer. It is not sufficient merely to cite Liddell and Scott's lexicon. For this subject we turn to D'Arcy Thompson's definitive source-book *A Glossary of Greek Birds*.[8] Under the entry there for *kirkos* we read: 'A poetic and mystical name for a Hawk: the sacred Hawk of Apollo; in the main an astronomical, perhaps solar, emblem. . . . In Homer, the bird of Apollo . . . *Od.* xv. 525. . . . The bird is not identifiable as a separate species, and is so recognized by Scaliger and others. Neither the brief note as to its size in a corrupt passage of the ninth book of the History of Animals, nor the mystical references to its alleged hostilities and attributes in Aristotle, Aelian, and Phile, are sufficient to prove that the name indicated at any time a certain particular species. The word is poetical . . . The chief allusions to κιρκος are obviously mystical, though the underlying symbolism . . . is not decipherable.'

Under another entry, for *Hierax*, Thompson gives some further interesting information. The word *hierax* is a generic term for all hawks. It too seems to partake of overtones of Horus, as Thompson specifically notes when he refers to the 'Worship of Hawks in Egypt', citing Herodotus and Aelian, and says: 'In the Rig-Veda* the sun is frequently compared to a hawk, hovering in the air. . . . Their heart is eaten, to obtain prophetic powers, Porph. *De Abst.* ii. 48.[9] . . . The Hawk entered in Egypt into innumerable hieroglyphics . . . (as) Horus and Hat-Hor, the latter being the ὁικος Ωρου of Plutarch. According to Chaeremon, fr. 8 ψυχη– 'ηλιος–θεος = ἱεραξ. On the sanctity of hawks in Egypt, and the solar symbolism associated with them there, see also . . .' etc., referring to Porphyry, Plutarch, Eusebius and Clement of Alexandria. The scholarly reader who wishes to pursue all this must go to Thompson directly.

---

* The oldest Sanskrit text, dating to 1300–1200 BC.

Kirkos also means 'an unknown stone'. Here again we come upon the stone motif which we encounter with Deukalion (the Greek Noah) and elsewhere. The stones of Deukalion spring up as men – men born from the earth just as the dead of the Colchian cemetery are meant to be born again from the earth.

A further connection of Circe with the Sirius complex lies in the fact[10] that the island of Circe was the place where Orion met his death. Orion as a constellation was identified (as Sah, its Egyptian name) with Osiris, the husband of Isis, who was identified, of course, with Sirius.

The stone motif in its recurring forms seems to have had a particular connection with the Minyae, as I discovered from that invaluable duffle-bag of information, the ancient Greek author Pausanius (flourished 150 AD), whose *Guide to Greece* is a real 'experience'. The Minyan city was traditionally that of Orchomenos in Boeotia, and it will be recalled that all the Argonauts were Minyae and descended from Minyas, King of Orchomenos.

All my references to Pausanius will be to Peter Levi's excellent translation published in two volumes by Penguin in 1971 with extensive notes and comments by that learned Jesuit translator, who has travelled over most of the terrain described by Pausanius and attempts a running commentary on the present state of the ruins and sights (and sites).

In Book IX, 34, 5, we read: 'Over from Mount Laphystion is Orchomenos, as famous and glorious as any city in Greece.' Levi's footnotes tell us: 'No one knows which mountain this was: probably the one above Hagios Georgios and the modern Laphystion' and: '(Orchomenos is) at the north-west corner of the old Kopaic Lake.'

At Orchomenos 'there are graves of Minyas and of Hesiod' (38, 3). At Mount Laphystion near by was (34, 4) 'the sacred enclosure of Laphystian Zeus . . . The statue is stone. They say Athamas was about to slaughter Phrixos and Helle here when Zeus sent the children a ram with a golden fleece and they ran away on the ram.'

Now note what Pausanius says (38, 1) about the Minyae of Orchomenos: 'Orchomenos has a sanctuary of Dionysos, but the most ancient one is consecrated to the Graces. They pay particular worship to rocks, saying they fell out of heaven for Eteokles: finely-made statues were dedicated in my time but even these were in stone.' Levi adds: 'The ruins of these sanctuaries are on the site of the old monastery (now itself in ruins).' Now, I believe this singular observation on the Minyae's preoccupation with stones ties in with all the recurring stone motifs in our material. And now we shall see a further recurrence which ties back in another way (38, 4): 'The Orchomenians had a legend about Aktaion. *An apparition with rocks in its hand* was devastating the countryside: when Delphi was consulted the god ordered them to find anything that was left of Aktaion and cover it with earth, and then make a bronze image of the ghost and rivet it with iron to a rock. I have seen this riveted statue; once a year they burn offerings to Aktaion as a divine hero' [the italics are mine].

Aktaion happened to see the goddess Artemis (known to the Romans by her Latin name of Diana) of the silver bow bathing naked. Artemis then hunted him down, with fifty hounds, transformed him into a stag, and killed him with her bow (not only are hounds connected with the Dog Star, but the bow is a familiar symbol connected also with Sirius, which was so often known in ancient times also as the Bow Star). This scene is portrayed in Figure 18, from an ancient Greek vase painting from approximately 470 BC.

Not only were the hounds of Hades who chased Aktaion fifty in number, but Robert Graves tells us 'Actaeon was, it seems, a sacred king of the pre-Hellenic stag cult, torn to pieces at the end of his reign of fifty months, namely half a Great Year...'[11] Note the application of the number 'fifty' here to a period of time. The orbit of Sirius B around Sirius A is fifty years; the reign of a sacred stag-king was fifty months. We know how often in ancient traditions the numerical quantity of time periods remains stable while their quality (as individual durations) varies. The classic examples are in the Bible, where the seven days of creation refer to seven aeons, and the 'years' of life of the Hebrew patriarchs such as Methusaleh are not correctly interpreted as solar *years* but as lunar *months* or 'lunar years' a month long (since by late times the area of the New East which had by then produced the people known as Hebrews had succumbed to a lunar calendrical craze – literally 'moonstruck' – and everything was a lunar rather than a solar period of time to those people in that area).

Note further the reference to a 'Great Year' of twice fifty months, consisting of two reigns. This would be one hundred months. And it should not surprise us to learn now that the name of the Greek goddess Hecate literally means in Greek 'one hundred'.*

Perhaps something of the true meaning of the myths is now becoming evident. The ancient peoples were not concealing information from us out of spite. Their purpose in disguising their secrets was to see that those secrets could survive. In fact, so successful were the ancient Egyptians in accomplishing their purpose, that the Greeks often preserve earlier Egyptian secrets in total ignorance of their true meaning, retaining only through an innate conservatism certain peculiar archaic details which we

---

* The Dogon tribe often describe the fifty-year orbital period of Sirius B by saying: 'The period of the orbit is counted double, that is, one hundred years, because ... (of) the principle of twinness' (see Appendix 1). Here we have the same custom in operation among the Greeks, of 'twinning' their sacred durations for 50 × 2 = 100. Hecate ('one hundred') unites them. Of *both* Sirius B and Sirius C have 50-year orbits around Sirius A (C of course having its own orbit around B in addition), the 'twinning' could refer to the fact that these are *two* stars which simultaneously share the 50-year orbital period. This would explain the 50 × 2 = 100 tradition.

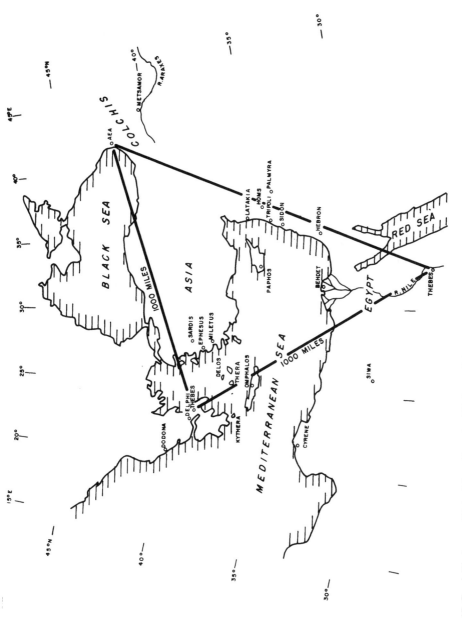

Figure 17. Greek Thebes equidistant from Egyptian Thebes and Aea

151

now find to be so important. Not only are the stories mythical and symbolical in that they are not meant to be taken at face value, but they even involve 'characters' and 'events' which have a strictly numerical significance. But this should have been quite obvious to the reader since we began to study the Anunnaki. It is, admittedly, difficult for those of us who have been brought up in our strictly literal civilization, where there is no such thing as a hidden meaning and everything is on the surface, to think in such a way as to understand the ancient myths. It was, after all, only a century ago that supposedly intelligent people were maintaining that the Earth was created in 4004 BC, on the basis of what the Bible was reputed to have said! And it was only in the 1930s that the courts of Tennessee, in the famous Scopes trial, decided that the theory of evolution was not only unholy but illegal and could not be taught in the schools. During the 1970s, 1980s and 1990s the fantastically stupid 'Creationist Movement' has grown in America – ignorance carried to supreme height. We mistakenly assume that because we have superlative technology and science we must also be extremely civilized and come from a subtle background of sophisticated thinkers. But this is all a base illusion.

Figure 18. The goddess Artemis sets the hounds of hell upon Aktaion and slays him. She holds the bow of Sirius the Bow Star. The hounds are the hounds of Sirius the Dog Star. She is herself, in this guise, a Greek version of Sirius the goddess. But the tradition has become confused and fragmented by the Greeks, broken down into elements which are used to construct other myths. Artemis is not generally a representation of Sirius, but of the moon. The bow and the dogs are here merely left-over trappings from an earlier forgotten symbolic system. (From a red-figured vase in the Berlin Museum *c.* 470 BC)

In fact, we are on a low rung of the ladder of evolutionary intelligence, and in many ways (such as ethics and aspirations to excellence) we have gone backward since those early mutants in our paltry intellectual history on this planet, Confucius, Socrates, the Buddha, and the others of whom every reader may substitute his own favourites.

But this book is not meant to be a sermon on the evils of a vacuous civilization. We are meant to be examining the names of some of the principal characters of the *Argonautica*, and it is best that we pretend to ourselves that we are rational creatures and supremely moral, and turn back to the subject again.

The name Jason means 'appeaser' in Greek, which is in accordance with his vacillating character (see Rieu's introduction to his Penguin translation of the *Argonautica* for some caustic comments on Jason).[12] 'Medea' means 'cunning'. 'Aeetes' means 'mighty' or 'eagle', and he was Medea's father, the King of Colchis from whom Jason stole the fleece.

Now we have seen that Aktaion was associated with Minyan Orchomenos, with a rock-throwing ghost (echoes of Deukalion), with fifty hounds of Hades, and with a reign of fifty months. The connections go even further. From Pausanius (34, 4) we learn that on Mount Laphystion is the place described thus: 'Higher up (from the spot where the ram with the golden fleece leapt into the air and took off) is Fire-eyed Hercules where the Boeotians say Hercules came up with the dog of Hades.' Now, this 'dog of Hades' is Cerberus, who originally had fifty heads! (Later the simplification of three heads, as for Hecate who was also of Hades, was adopted for Cerberus, when fifty must have seemed to make no sense and was probably too difficult to paint on vases. But of course three is significant too. The Egyptians portrayed three goddesses in the Sothis-boat: Sothis, Anukis, and Satis.)

Graves informs us[13] that, 'Cerberus was, at first, fifty-headed, like the spectral pack that destroyed Actaeon (see 22.1); but afterwards three-headed like his mistress Hecate (see 134.1).' (The three-headed Hecate is the three Sothis-goddesses blended in one and is an underworld counterpart, just as with the Sumerian 'Anunnaki of the underworld'.)

What of the fleece itself? There are obvious connections of the golden fleece and Colchis with the common golden-yellow dye which comes from saffron (*crocus sativus*). The crocus with its saffron is even today confused with 'meadow saffron' (*colchicum*) which takes its name, obviously, from Colchis, which was its chief area of production. The colchicum plant which somewhat resembles the crocus in its flowering stage was terribly important to the ancient world. It was the only known medicine against the disease of gout (and indeed still is). It is known to have been used to treat gout in ancient Egypt and all over the ancient Mediterranean. As Colchis was the place to find colchicum that may explain why the Egyptians first settled there! (I have seen immense plains and hills covered in colchicum near the Atlantic coast of Morocco, but these would only have been accessible in ancient times to the Egyptians by sailing out into the Atlantic and follow-ing the coast southwards, taking rivers inland of the proper point, and then returning safely. This was evidently an almost impossible task in ships with square sails, lacking both proper rudders and fore-and-aft rigging.)

It is probable that the crocus and ordinary saffron was present in Colchis in abundance, along with the false or meadow saffron, colchicum, and that the two became as confused with each other in ancient times as they are today. Indeed, it is only modern botany which proclaims a difference between the two to the extent that we no longer confuse them officially. As real saffron produced a much valued dye, it is not surprising that a golden fleece dyed golden yellow by saffron dye would be said to exist in Colchis! And indeed, Medea's famous herbal knowledge was well suited to Colchis, which produced the only cure for one of antiquity's most dreaded diseases, a disease which causes terrific pain and discomfort and could only be relieved by the magic herb from the mysterious distant land of Colchis. I. Burkill[14] gives interesting information on the early history of saffron. He says that sun-worshippers speaking an Aryan language spread to India from Turkey and made the saffron crocus an object of veneration and found ways of using its colour.[15] This information, given by Täckholm and Drar,[16] offers a great deal of support to my contention.

Richard Allen[17] discusses Aries (the ram) and says that the Egyptian stellar ram's stars were called the Fleece. He adds that the god Zeus-Amen (Ammon-Jupiter) 'assumed the Ram's form when all the inhabitants of Olympus fled into Egypt from the giants led by Typhon'. And in this discussion of Aries, Allen mentions 'some of its titles at a different date being applied to Capella of [the constellation of] Auriga'. This is the sort of process we shall encounter again and again – titles and descriptions of stars being applied to neighbouring or similar stars as the original traditions become confused. It is particularly evident in the application of the description of 'heavy' or 'weight' to different stars associated somehow with Sirius, as the original object to which this description was meant to apply, Sirius B, was not visible and so tradition, being conservative, kept the description and applied it to other stars related to Sirius which could actually be seen. As with numerical traditions like that of 'fifty', when the true significance was forgotten, the symbol or concept was merely given a new, impromptu explanation.

Aries was definitely identified with the golden fleece. Allen gives much information regarding this:

> It always was Aries with the Romans; but Ovid called it *phrixea ovis*; and Columella *pecus athamantidos helles, phrixus*, and *portitor phrixi*; others *phrixeum pecus* and *phrixi vector*, Phrixus being the hero-son of Athamas, who fled on the back of this Ram with his sister Helle to Colchis. . . . On reaching his journey's end, Phrixus sacrificed the creature and hung its fleece in the Grove of Ares, where it was turned to

154

gold and became the object of the Argonauts' quest. From this came others of Aries' titles: *ovis aurea* and *auratus*, *chrysomallus*, and the Low Latin *Chrysovellus*.

As the fleece was a solar symbol, it is just as well that we look at the concept of Horus once again. Horus in Egyptian is Ḥeru. And from Wallis Budge we learn that Ḥeru is 'the ancient name of the Sun-god'.[18] The word *ḥeru* also has the meaning of 'face'.[19] But let us consider the following: Ḥeru (Horus) and his hawk/falcon presided over the Colchian cemetery and gave the name to Circe (which means 'hawk/falcon') who was Medea's aunt. The Greek sun-god Helios was said to stable his horses at Colchis and have a magnificent palace there, from which he arose every morning. Also Colchis was the place of residence of the solar golden fleece.

Now, we recall that in Egyptian the letter 'l' and the letter 'r' are entirely interchangeable and have the same hieroglyph. Consequently, Ḥeru could just as reliably be Ḥelu. If one takes Ḥelu and puts a Greek ending on it one gets Helios! And the same word means the sun-god in both the Egyptian religion (early) and the Greek religion (early). In both lands the name was eventually superseded, in Greece by Apollo, for instance. So here we have a further connection between the Greek tradition as centring round Colchis and the Egyptian tradition as settled there, only this time the evidence is linguistic.

It seems that the curious Greek word *hero* comes also from *ḥeru*, though a word similar to *hero* exists in Sanskrit, the language of ancient India after 1200 BC. The word in Sanskrit which has the meaning of 'hero' is the related *Vīra*. It is used in the precise sense of 'hero (as opposed to a god)' in the early *Rig-veda* and is thus attested at the time of the first migrations of Aryans into India. There is no question that the two words are cognates of each other. However, I propose for them (and we shall see more examples of this later in the book) a common derivation: from the Egyptian *ḥeru*.

The word *ḥeru* is given a meaning by Wallis Budge[20] almost identical with that of *hero* and *vīra* and is described as follows: 'applied to the king as the representative of the sun-god on earth'. This is a precise meaning applying to a human being on earth who is neither god nor daemon, but *hero*. Liddell and Scott make clear that the word was not used solely for those warriors who were prominent in battle, but was used to describe the minstrel Demodocus, the herald Mulius, and even (in the *Odyssey*, 7, 44) 'the unwarlike Phaeacian people are so called'. In Homer 'the heroes were exalted above the race of common men', but particularly in Pindar the poet, we find the word used to describe a race 'between gods and men', in precisely the sense that we should expect the word *ḥeru* to survive in another language. This Egyptian application of the word to their Pharaohs survived almost without change in Greek and Sanskrit and later in Latin and the later Indo-European languages.

It is interesting to note in the account of the word Helios as given by Liddell and Scott, Homer used the term in reference to 'the rising and setting, light and darkness, morning and evening'. In Egypt the precise application of Horus as sun-god was in his activity as rising and setting. He was the child who was born afresh each morning (and to the Greeks Helios was born afresh every morning at Colchis). Homer has thus used the *heru*-derived Helios in precisely the manner which we might have expected of an Egyptian, rather than a Greek, poet.

In Liddell and Scott we find the listing immediately after Helios of Helio-Serapis, which is 'an Egyptian divinity'. I leave the reader to draw his own conclusions regarding this clear use of the word Helio to preface a description of Serapis. Serapis was the Greek form of Àsàr-Hep, Hep being what is known in Greek as Apis the Bull. Àsàr is, of course, Osiris. In Egyptian it was quite common for there to be references to 'Horus-Osiris' combining Ḥeru and Àsàr. Here in Greek we find this, if we accept my thesis of the derivation of Helio from *helu* or *heru*.

The reader is by now presumably immune to shock at the endless 'surprises' which arise in the course of this enquiry. Hence he will no doubt be prepared to learn that if we shorten the 'e' (from eta to epsilon) in Greek, we have the *heru*-derived word (which has dropped the aspirate, probably in connection with the shortening of the vowel) *erion*, which means – 'woollen fleece'!

There is a possibility that Herakles ('the glory of Hera'), the original captain of the *Argo* according to Graves, and his protectress the goddess Hera (wife to Zeus and Queen of the gods) are derived from *heru* and they are known to be related to the word Seirios which gave us Sirius and the Sanskrit *svar, suryas*, etc. In Sanskrit *Sūra* means 'hero', indicating that these words may relate also. Liddell and Scott believe this complex of words to be separate from the Helios-complex, but their opinion is only an opinion. *Sūrana* means 'fiery', just as Seirios can in the sense of 'scorching' (due to the supposed 'scorching' of the Dog Star, etc.).

Back to our fleece. We find that the Greek word for a woollen fleece is related to the Egyptian word for Horus, the Greek word for sun, etc., etc. So much for the puzzling nature of that now moot question: Why a fleece? Back to sacred puns again, which besiege us endlessly.

Let us not forget the Sumerians. Let us look again at that list of the fifty names of Marduk. One of them is the name Nebiru. It is commonly taken to be the name of the planet Jupiter, but there is confusion there, and the word is discussed in *Hamlet's Mill* and many other places as one of the infuriating Sumerian words which we would like to understand. Where did it come from? What does it mean? Why is it one of the fifty names?

Immediately after this forty-ninth name, Marduk is called 'Lord of the Lands' (its Akkadian form, which has no significance for us, is Bēl Mātāti; I do not know the Sumerian form, which might be of interest to us). Then, after this supposed fiftieth name comes another name, namely Ea (Enki). Then Marduk is described as being of fifty names. It seems not to make perfect sense, since he has just been given fifty-one names. One way in which to make it sensible is to treat 'Lord of the Lands' (which is given in English in Speiser and Heidel, unlike all the other names) as a synonym of Nebiru. If we do this, then Ea is the fiftieth name and everything is all right.

Now, let us look at the Egyptian language once again. We find that the word *Neb* is extremely common and is used in many combinations and means 'Lord'. Without further ado, let me make clear that I believe the Sumerian Nebiru to be derived from the Egyptian Neb-Heru. If we treat Heru in its older Egyptian sense as the sun, then the descriptions of Nebiru in the Babylonian *Enuma Elish* could read as a perfect description of Neb-Heru – 'the Lord the sun': 'Nebiru shall hold the crossings of heaven and earth. . . . He who the midst of the Sea restlessly crosses,/Let "Crossing" be his name, who controls its midst,' etc., though overlaid with this, as with the traditional Horus, is a strictly stellar element which is behind the more obvious solar element. However, I do not wish unduly to confuse the issue by peeling off too many layers at once. Suffice it to recall the previously mentioned associations of Horus with the Sirius system and note that there is a Heru-ami-Sept-t 'Horus of Sothis' and Heru-Sept 'Horus the Dog Star' and then to note, again in association with Nebiru which is supposed to have been Jupiter, that there is in Egyptian a Heru-sba-res 'Horus, star of the south, i.e. Jupiter', and Heru-up-Shet, 'the planet Jupiter'; also in the *Enuma Elish* Nebiru is clearly described as 'a star'. Horus also exists as Heru-ami-u which is 'a hawk-headed crocodile with a tail terminating in a dog's head'. The dog is related to Sirius. Heru-ur-shefit is a jackal form of Horus, *heru* is also the name of a sceptre and of a jackal-*headed* standard in the other world. A form of Horus using the common word Neb is Heru-Neb-urr-t, meaning 'Horus as possessor of the supreme crown'. Another of several is Heru-Neb-pāt, meaning 'Horus, lord of men'. Heru-Neb-taui is 'Horus, Lord of the Two Lands'. Recall our synonym for Nebiru – 'Lord of the Lands'!

We are getting deeper and deeper into the legend of the golden fleece, of origins of Greek and Middle Eastern ideas in Egypt, along with key words and names, etc. All these centre round the curious Sirius complex. What more will we uncover? Perhaps we need a break from all these Egyptian words. There are many other aspects of our subject, and it leads us ever closer to the solution of our mystery – which is the origin of the subject.

Notes
1. *Toward the Image of Tammuz and Other Essays*, Harvard University Press, USA, 1970.
2. Kramer, S. N., *History Begins at Sumer*, Doubleday Anchor Book, New York, 1959, pp. 91–4.
3. *Antiquity of the Jews*, Book I, Chapter 2.
4. *Herodotus*, trans. A. de Selincourt, Book 2, 103.

5. In Pritchard, *Ancient Near Eastern Texts*, p. 8.
6. 'The Rise of Mycenaean Civilization', *Cambridge Ancient History*.
7. Graves, Robert, *The Greek Myths*, 2 vols., Penguin Books, London, 1969, 170.5.
8. Thompson, D'Arcy Wentworth, *A Glossary of Greek Birds*, Oxford, 1896.
9. Porphyry, *On Abstinence from Animal Food*, for those who are not familiar with the traditional abbreviations. Porphyry was an early Neoplatonist, a student of Plotinus, who transcribed the *Enneads*. Thomas Taylor translated much of what survives of Porphyry's own writings, including *On Abstinence*, in *Select Works of Porphyry*, London, 1823.
10. Graves, op. cit., 170.6.
11. Ibid., 22.1.
12. Robert Graves takes the view that Jason means 'healer'.
13. Graves, op. cit., 31.3.
14. The reference is to I. Burkill (1935) but I have not been able to trace the publication concerned and have gone to immense pains over it. Burkill was a noted botanist. A botanical publication of his for 1936 is not the correct reference. See Note 15 for source.
15. Täckholm and Drar, 'Flora of Egypt'. Vol. III, *Bulletin of the Faculty of Science*, No. 30, Cairo University Faculty of Science, Cairo University Press, 1954.
16. See Note 15.
17. S*tar Names*, op. cit. See entry under Aries.
18. Wallis Budge, *Hieroglyphic Vocabulary to the Theban Recension of the Book of the Dead*, London, 1911. See entry for *Ḥer*, p. 273.
19. Ibid., p. 271.
20. Ibid., p. 273, entry for *Ḥer*.

SUMMARY

The Sumerian god An had a daughter, Bau (representing the sound of a dog barking, as does the ancient Egyptian word for 'dog', *auau*), who was a dog-headed goddess. The Egyptian god Anubis (Anpu) was a dog-headed god.

The Sumerian Bau, as a daughter of An, is a sister of the fifty great gods (Anunnaki) who are also children of An. Since Bau may be a goddess of the Dog Star Sirius, the fact that she is the sister of 'the fifty' is significant, as Sirius B has an orbital period of fifty years.

The golden fleece was situated at Colchis in the Black Sea, where Jason and his Argonauts went to see it. Colchis was an ancient Egyptian colony before 1200 BC.

Herodotus emphasizes that the Egyptians originated the practice of circumcision, which survived also among the Colchians, whom he visited (the Hebrews acquired circumcision from the Egyptians while in bondage). It is noteworthy that the Dogon ceremony of the Sigui, which is connected with the Dogon Sirius-mysteries, centres largely round rites of circumcision.

Prominent in the story of the *Argo* is the female character Circe (whose name means 'falcon' or 'hawk'). Horus, son of Isis and Osiris, was symbolized by a falcon or hawk. Circe presided over the Colchian cemetery (which was originally Egyptian, Colchis having been an Egyptian colony). Horus, who presided over the cemetery of Memphis in Egypt, would have presided also over the one at Colchis while Egyptian influence was still directly exercised. Circe is obviously a Greek derivation of Horus.

The word *kirke* (Circe) in Greek (which we customarily write 'Circe' due to our habit of changing Greek k's into Latin c's) specifically means 'a kind of hawk or falcon' or 'an 'unknown bird' – just the sort of confusion we should expect among the Greeks with regard to a concept derived from Egyptian culture and imperfectly understood.

Aktaion, representing a sacred stag-king, was hunted down by fifty hounds (the dog motif joined to fifty) and killed with a silver bow (Sirius has also traditionally been known as 'the Bow Star', and in Egypt the goddess Sirius holds a bow).

The sacred king, such as Aktaion represented, had a 'sacred reign' of fifty months. It is arguable that 'fifty months' is a shorthand version of 'fifty years', but we now see undeniable ancient traditions connecting Sirius with fifty intervals of time (whether months or years) comprising 'a reign'. And of course the orbital period of Sirius B is fifty years comprising 'an orbit', which in mythological parlance could quite easily be considered 'a reign'.

As is explained in Chapter Seven, the fifty-month period later became applied to the Olympic Games when they were established. It defined the interval of time separating them – approximating four solar years. In fact, the Olympic Games were actually separated by alternating intervals of 49 months, then 50 months, then 49 months, etc. This suggests even further an attempt more closely to approximate the $49\frac{1}{2}$ years of Sirius B's orbit in 'month-code'. For by doubling up in this way, using the nearest two whole numbers in alternation, the exact correspondence was obtained, for 49 plus 50 gives the same as $49\frac{1}{2}$ plus $49\frac{1}{2}$. Robert Graves has offered the only previous theory to explain the 'fifty months' in ancient Greece, but his lunar theory does not explain the alternation between 49 and 50, or other mysterious aspects. It is probable that the true explanation based on the Sirius mystery was later overlaid by a lunar tradition which was offered as an 'explanation' to non-initiates, despite its obvious flaws.

It was customary in ancient times also to group together two sacred reigns of fifty months each to form a 'Great Year' of one hundred mouths. (In practice, as with the Olympic Games, 99 months were actually used, but in theory one used the round figure of 100 months conceived of as 'two reigns'.) The name of the Greek goddess Hekate (Hecate) literally means 'one hundred'. She was involved with the *Argo* tale and specifically identified by Robert Graves with Isis, and in other ways linked to Sirius as an 'underworld version'. Since both Sirius B and Sirius C may share a fifty-year orbit around Sirius A, we can possibly understand the 'twice-fifty years' as an esoteric reference to that.

The fifty hounds of hell who pursued Actacon have a counterpart in Cerberus, the hound of hell who had fifty heads in the earlier tradition. These fifty heads were later discarded in the tradition, like Gilgamesh's original fifty companions, and Cerberus was said to have three heads. But originally he had fifty, as Hesiod describes him. This is thus yet another dog-motif connected with fifty (Sirius being the Dog Star), and linked to Sirius in various ways, such as through the goddess Hekate as an underworld version of Sirius. (The fifty Sumerian Anunnaki also had their counterparts in the underworld. Fifty in the underworld as 'death-counterparts' or shadows to fifty in heaven makes one hundred – the very meaning of Hekate.)

The only known cure for gout (a serious ancient Egyptian complaint) is a substance taken from the plant colchicum, named after Colchis where it grew. This may explain a colony at Colchis. Colchicum is also called 'meadow saffron' and resembles true saffron (which also grows along the Black Sea coasts), which gives a golden dye, perhaps explaining the 'golden' fleece. A golden fleece is a solar symbol. Horus was a solar god. The letters 'l' and 'r' are interchangeable phonetic liquids. The Egyptian form of Horus, Ḥeru, can become Ḥelu and give us the Greek solar god's name Helios. Helios was supposed to stable his horses at Colchis. The Greek word for 'woollen fleece' is *erion*, a word similar to Ḥeru with a dropped aspirate ('h').

Chapter Six

The Oracle Centres

A consideration of the ancient oracle centres will now be useful in our quest. These centres in the Middle East seem at a casual glance to be dotted around apparently at random. However, there is actually a pattern in their distribution which we will find bears some relation to our subject, and which indicates a highly advanced science of geography and related disciplines in the ancient world. Examination of the oracle centres will be seen to have a connection with the ship *Argo* and will help us to fill in some of the missing background to the entire system of the ancient religious mysteries. The oracle centres were the main places where religion was practised in the ancient world. It makes sense that their occurrence would not be the product of pure chance, and certainly not of convenience. What place could be more out of the way than Dodona in Greece? It was geographically outside the sphere of the civilized world of the Greeks – somewhat more north and more west than any Greek could call comfortable. Why was such an important and senior place of worship in the wilds? Indeed, for that matter, why did Noah's ark land on a mountain nobody ever visits and which is far more remote than even Dodona? The ark and *Argo* and their connections with the Sirius mystery will now be seen to have an intimate connection with the entire geographical structure of the practice of religion in the ancient Mediterranean world. It is important that we explore these extraordinary ramifications fully.

Now we are about to consider a most difficult and complex web of ancient practice. Let us look at the ship *Argo* as if it were spread over the surface of the globe by projection. This may seem a curious idea, but the reader must bear with me. After all, the boat is celestial, so why not a projection on the earth's surface from above? Most prominent in the constellation is the star Canopus which was called 'the Rudder', *pēdalion*, by Aratos, Eudoxus, and Hipparchos (the leading Greek astronomical figures before Ptolemy), as we are informed by Allen.[1] The use of the word 'rudder' is actually incorrect, because there were no real rudders at this time; technically, one should say instead 'steering-oar'.

There was a place named Canopus on the northern coast of Egypt, which was quite a famous city to the Greeks, and Allen describes it thus: 'Ancient Canopus is now in ruins, but its site is occupied by the village of Al Bekūr, or Aboukir, famous from Lord Nelson's Battle of the Nile, 1 August 1798,

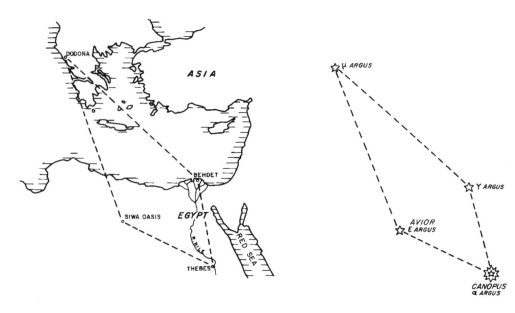

Figure 19. The above geodetic pattern (left) seems to match a stellar pattern of Argo (right)

and from Napoleon's victory over the Turks a year afterwards; and it is interesting to remember that it was here, from the terraced walls of the Serapeum, the temple of Serapis, that Ptolemy made his observations.' In his book *Hellenistic Civilization*, W. W. Tarn comments on Canopus after Alexander the Great had founded Alexandria near it, that from Alexandria 'the gardens of the wealthy extended to Canopus, Alexandria's playground'. To the Greeks, Canopus was the most famous Egyptian city on the northern coast before the foundation of Alexandria. In earlier times the fame of Canopus was held by a city called Behdet, which was a pre-dynastic capital of Egypt before the unification of Egypt and the transferring of the capital to Memphis further south. So, just as Canopus became superceded by Alexandria, Canopus had itself superceded the extremely ancient Behdet which existed before 3200 BC as the most important city on the Egyptian coast. In our discussion which follows, we must realize that in the times just preceding and during the classical period in Greece the fame that had once attached to Behdet had shifted to Canopus, along with many traditions which were in actuality native to Behdet, which was by then a neglected place which no Greek knew.*

---

* Behdet is on the same latitude as Hebron on the west bank of the River Jordan. In Chapter Four of *The White Goddess*, Graves tells of '. . . the Philistines, who captured the shrine of Hebron in southern Judaea from the Edomite clan of Caleb; but the Calebites ("Dog-men"), allies of the Israelite tribe of Judah, recovered it about two hundred years later . . .'. 'The Dog-men' are probably connected with Sirius the Dog Star and Hebron is the eastern counterpart of Behdet.

Richard Allen says further of the city of Canopus: 'Our name for it is that of the chief pilot of the fleet of Menelaos, who, on his return from the destruction of Troy, 1183 BC, touched at Egypt, where, twelve miles to the north-eastward from Alexandria, Canopus died and was honoured, according to Scylax,* by a monument raised by his grateful master, giving his name to the city and to this splendid star, which at that time rose about 7½° above that horizon.' Sir Norman Lockyer in *The Dawn of Astronomy* describes ancient Egyptian temples oriented to the rising of the star Canopus.[2]

Note in the above story of the pilot Canopus that the names of the city and the star are specifically said to have the same origin and that it is from a famous pilot of a fleet, the man at the helm who steers the steering-oar in the lead ship. Once again, in another way, the star (and the place) are identified with the steering-oar, which was the other name for the same star.

Allen brings forward another interesting aspect of the star's name, which will be something familiar to us:

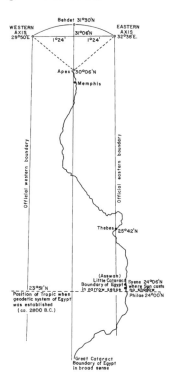

Figure 20. Plan of ancient Egyptian geodetic schema based on Behdet

* Scylax was a remarkable voyager and explorer of the fourth century BC, who sailed down the Indus river to its mouth and thence to the Isthmus of Suez and wrote a book about it, quoted by Aristotle.

The foregoing derivation of the word Canopus is an early and popular one; but another, perhaps as old, and more probable, being on the authority of Aristides, is from the Coptic, or Egyptian, *Kahi Nub*, Golden Earth. Ideler, coinciding in this, claimed these words as also the source of other titles for Canopus, the Arabic *Wazn*, Weight, and *Ḥaḍar*, Ground; and of the occasional later Ponderosus and Terrestris. Although I find no reason assigned for the appropriateness of these names, it is easy to infer that they may come from the magnitude of the star and its nearness to the horizon; this last certainly made it the Περιγειος [*Perigeios* – 'near the earth'] of Eratosthenes.

Notice how the irrepressible *Al Wazn*, 'Weight', and its Latin form *Ponderosus*, keep springing up whenever there seems to be a connection with Sirius.

Allen mentions that 'The Hindus called (Canopus) Agastya, one of their Rishis, or inspired sages, and helmsman of their Argha . . .' which is in striking agreement with the Mediterranean concepts.

Further in line with our previous discoveries, it will be interesting to note what Allen says of another of the stars of Argo, the star η (*eta*): '(Jensen) claims it as one of the (Babylonian) temple stars associated with Ea, or Ia [*], of Eridhu, the Lord of the Waves, otherwise known as Oannes, the mysterious human fish and greatest god of the kingdom.'

Here we have the amphibious creature Oannes (see later discussion especially in Appendix III, for this Babylonian equivalent of Nommo), identified with the god Enki, who in Sumerian myth did indeed reside at the bottom of the Abzu, or Abyss, in fresh (not salt) water. It was, in fact, the god Enki who assisted man before the flood came by warning the proto-Noah of the Sumerian deluge story to build his ark. He thus fulfilled the function of the special presiding deity of the Hebrews, the Jehovah of the Old Testament. How many Jews know that their god was originally amphibious?

This early Noah or proto-Noah, whom the god Enki warned, was called either Ziusudra (Sumerian) or Utnapishtim (Babylonian), depending on which period of pre-Biblical literature one consults. In the early deluge stories, the proto-Noah in his ark sends forth birds to seek dry land just as does Noah in his ark and rather as Jason sends forth birds to find the way through the clashing rocks. H. W. Parke in his book *The Oracles of Zeus* specifically associates the birds sent forth by Jason with Dodona. Both Dodona and Delphi claimed the 'Greek Noah' Deukalion as having landed his ark on the mountain tops at their locations. Noah himself landed his ark on Mount Ararat, which his bird found for him. We shall see in a little while the importance of these birds and the locations espied

---

* Ea was his Akkadian name, Enki was his Sumerian name; Eridu was his geodetic city, which was the southernmost of all the Sumerian cities.

Figure 21. The only original excavation drawing which is still preserved in the British Museum of the Assyrian Oannes sculptures excavated at Kouyunjik (in Iraq) by Austen Henry Layard in the mid-nineteenth century. This one shows the bottom half of a large broken bas relief described as 'Fish Deity' by the excavators. The figure, whether intended actually to represent Oannes or a priest dressed up as Oannes, holds the usual mysterious basket, apparently made of reeds. No one knows what was in the basket! Probably this drawing was preserved because it was omitted from reproduction by the publishers of Layard's books, whereas they took delivery of the rest, which disappeared after being engraved

by them. But recall now the connections between Dodona and Mount Ararat implied by a common tale of their having both been found by a 'Noah' in an ark who sent forth a bird who found the mountain. It is true that one tale is purely Greek and the other tale purely Hebrew. Naturally, there cannot be any real connection between Dodona and Mount Ararat. After all, they are probably purely arbitrary locations. It is all myth and fable, isn't it? The Jews and the Greeks were never in contact. There could have been no liaison between them. It is all separate hermetically sealed cultures with vague fairy-tales and nonsense. Isn't it? Can anyone challenge such a view? Of course not.

So it is interesting that Dodona and Mount Ararat are on the same parallel and have the same latitude.

Furthermore, Mount Ararat has a centre associated with it which served much the same function to the Caucasians as Dodona did to the Greeks. It is called Metsamor. Here is a description of it by Professor David Lang and Dr Charles Burney:[3]

Archaeological research during the past half century [they were writing in 1971] has materially altered our concept of the history of literature, science, and learning in Transcaucasia. A key site here is the village of Metsamor, a few miles to the west of Echmiadzin, and within sight of Mount Ararat and Alagöz. Close to the village is a massive rocky hummock, perhaps half a mile in circumference, with outcrops of craggy stone. The hummock is riddled with caves, underground storage vaults, and prehistoric dwellings, and is now seen to have been a major scientific, astronomical and industrial centre, operating in the fields of metallurgy, astrology and primitive magic from a period hardly less than five thousand years ago.

The Metsamor 'observatory' is covered with mysterious, cabbalistic signs. Indeed, hieroglyphic writing in Armenia goes back to very early times, perhaps to the New Stone Age. All over Armenia, we find pictograms or petroglyphs, carved or scratched on rocks, caves and cliff faces, and showing simplified human and animal figures. There is little doubt that these served as means of communication, as well as of ritual and artistic self-expression.

They also describe Metsamor's wide-ranging contacts with the outside world:[4]

Sumerian achievements as pioneers in copper and bronze metallurgy must not be underestimated. ... The early Transcaucasian cultural zone, though geographically within the Near East, was divided only by the high but narrow Caucasus from the northern steppes; and, once there, nothing could prevent the traders reaching the central European copper-working centres. Thus Georgia, with its neighbouring regions, was perhaps open as much to influences from Europe as to those from the Near East. Transcaucasia may have been not so much an original centre as a region into which metal-working arrived from two different directions, and where, though present in earlier periods in a modest way, it took root and from the late third millennium BC began to develop along distinctive lines, no longer owing its forms to external inspiration. ... Metsamor gives a hint that, just as earlier in Europe, once foreign merchants had arrived seeking sources of metals, bringing their copper and later their bronze products with them, and explaining, by choice or otherwise, their techniques to the local population, it was no time before a local industry began to arise. If present evidence indeed points to Armenia as the oldest centre of metallurgy in Transcaucasia, it points also to a Near Eastern inspiration.

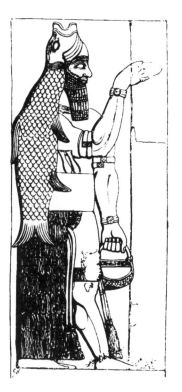

Figure 22. (a) (left) The Babylonian semi-daemon Oannes, a fishtailed amphibious being from the heavens who, according to the Babylonians founded civilization on earth. *From Nimrud. (b) (above)* An Assyrian wall carving of Oannes, from the royal palace of King Sargon II (reigned 721–705 BC) at Khorsabad (in modern Iraq). Reproduced from Figure 54 of Joseph Bonomi's *Nineveh and Its Palaces* (London, 1875). He calls it Dagon, using the Philistine name for Oannes. The original carving shows Oannes surrounded by waves of the sea, which are omitted in the engraving

Many years ago, a reader sent me photocopies of various archaeological reports about Metsamor in Armenian and Russian, but I have never gone to the expense of having them translated. He did tell me, however, that the site contained a religious centre oriented towards the heliacal rising of Sirius, and that the American and Russian archaeologists had concluded that Metsamor was a centre of 'the worship of the star Sirius'. This is one of the many subjects in need of proper funding for an investigation.

It is extraordinary that if you place a compass point on Thebes in Egypt you can draw an arc through both Dodona and Metsamor.

We now return to Allen and his further remarks[5] about Oannes: 'Berōssōs described Oannes as the teacher of early man in all knowledge; and in mythology he was even the creator of man ... and some have regarded him as the prototype of Noah.'

Allen also describes the star Canopus in this way: 'And, as the constellation (of Argo) was associated on the Nile with the great god Osiris, so its great star became the Star of Osiris. ...' He gives a further application of the title 'heavy': *'The Alfonsine Tables** had (for Canopus) Suhel Ponderosus ("Among the Persians Suhail is a synonym for

* Astronomical tables compiled in 1252 in Spain under the future King Alfonso X.

167

wisdom . . ." and there was also, therefore, a "Suhel Sirius"), that appeared in a contemporary chronicle as Sihil Ponderosa, a translation of Al Suhail al Wazn.' Allen then gives several tales indicating that this designation was once applied to another star 'formerly located near Orion's stars' and 'had to flee south', being an apparent admission that Canopus is being called by another star's title. Canopus is south of Sirius (which is 'near Orion's stars'), and so obviously the description of the invisible Sirius B 'fled south' to a likely visible star, Canopus.

Now to return to our projection of the *Argo* on the earth's surface. We put the centre of the stern of the ship at the obvious place – Canopus. (But really slightly altered eastwards to the original city Behdet.)

Now we must consider Dodona. We are told that oak from Dodona was placed 'in the middle of the keel' of *Argo* by Athena. It obviously ran the whole length of the ship. It is also referred to as being in the prow. Allen says of this:

> Mythology insisted that (the *Argo*) was built by Glaucus, or by Argos, for Jason, leader of the fifty Argonauts, whose number equalled that of the oars of the ship, aided by Pallas Athene, who herself set in the prow a piece from the speaking oak of Dodona; the Argo being 'thus endowed with the power of warning and guiding the chieftains who form its crew'. She carried the famous expedition from Iolchis in Thessaly to Aea in Colchis, in search of the golden fleece, and when the voyage was over Athene placed the boat in the sky.

Figure 23. An ancient Greek gem carving of Argus shaping a piece of the sacred oak of Dodona for the prow of the ship *Argo*

In measuring with the *Argo*'s projection one does so from the site of Behdet which is a bit east of Canopus on the northern Mediterranean coast of Egypt, but it was common classical Greek practice to think of Canopus in place of the forgotten Behdet, as for instance with 'the Canopic Hercules' who went to Delphi and is mentioned by Pausanius as predecessor to the Greek Hercules from Tiryns (an ancient town on a rocky hill in the Argive Plain of Greece, finally destroyed by Argos *circa* 470 BC) who was of much later date. (It is important that the original Hercules was admitted by the Greeks to have been an Egyptian.) In fact, the Delphic oracle itself compares the Greek Hercules most unfavourably with the original Egyptian one – and remember it is said that in the earliest versions of the story it was Hercules, not Jason, who led the Argonauts.

Also, it is well accepted today among scholars that Hercules was in many ways a survival of Gilgamesh, with particular motifs and deeds being identical in both heroes.

Well, if we project the *Argo* on the earth with the centre of its stern at Canopus (really Behdet) we put the other end at Dodona because the oak in the prow came from there. Canopus-Behdet is named after the stern, and Dodona produced the prow. Therefore we are not merely fantasizing when we project the image of the *Argo* in such a way that the stern is at the stern on earth and the prow is at the earthly source of the prow.

If we then keep the stern at the same spot and swing the boat over a map so that the prow which touched Dodona points towards Metsamor, we discover that the angle made is exactly a right-angle of 90°.

Now we get into geodetics, a fearsome subject that involves a bit of bother. It concerns latitudes and longitudes, and most people would run a mile upon hearing those mentioned (sailors and pilots of aircraft excepted). In fact no one is more likely to flee with terror from the subject than an archaeologist. There is almost nothing an archaeologist likes less than being reminded how little he may know about the Earth as a body in space and about astronomy. The average archaeologist is almost bound to be ignorant of even the most elementary astronomical facts. There are many caustic comments on this state of affairs to be found in *The Dawn of Astronomy*, written by the distinguished Victorian astronomer and friend of Sir Wallis Budge, Sir Norman Lockyer,[6] and more recently some severe remarks have been made also by Santillana and von Dechend in *Hamlet's Mill*.

But we must come now to some extremely interesting further discoveries. Egypt is 7° long – in latitude – from Behdet to the Great Cataract. I have reasons for believing that the ancient Egyptians thought of distances of 7° as an octave, by analogy with music. Most readers will know that an octave contains eight notes on a scale over a space of seven intervals (five tones and two semitones actually, but let us think only of the seven intervals).

Ancient Mediterranean peoples did indeed know the principles of our musical octave. In the London *Times*[7] an article appeared describing the work of Dr Richard L. Crocker, Professor of Music History, and Dr Anne D. Kilmer, Professor of Assyriology and Dean of Humanities, both at the University of California, Berkeley. The article quoted Dr Crocker as saying: 'We always knew there was music in the earlier Assyro-Babylonian civilization. But until this, we did not know that it had the same heptatonic diatonic scale that is characteristic of contemporary Western music and Greek music of the first millennium BC.' After fifteen years of research, Crocker and Kilmer demonstrated that some clay tablets from Ugarit on the coast of present-day Syria, dating from about 1800 BC, bore a musical text based on our familiar octave. Dr Kilmer summed it up by saying: 'It is the oldest "sheet music" known to exist.' The two professors even

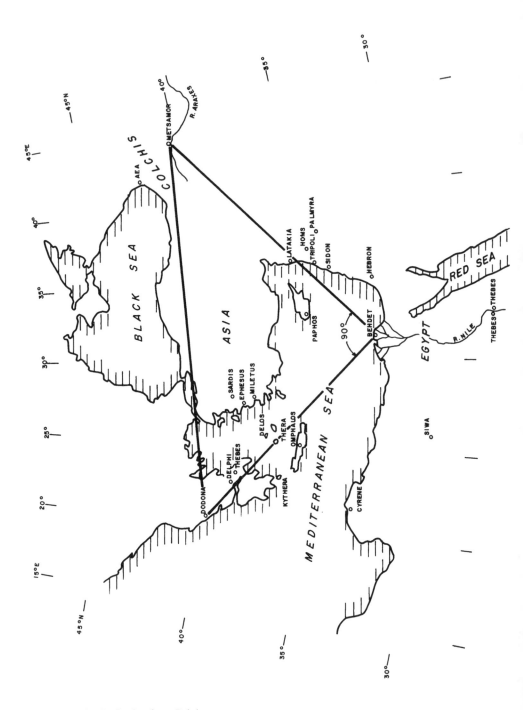

Figure 24. Projection from Behdet

recorded the tune on a reconstruction of an ancient lyre in public, after an interval of only 3,700 years.[8] (A commercial record album plus accompanying booklet, entitled *Sounds From Silence: Recent Discoveries in Ancient Near Eastern Music* by Anne Kilmer, Richard Crocker and Robert Brown, was put on sale in 1976 by Bit Enki Publications and Records (BTNK 101), California. The recordings are fascinating.)

I believe that the Egyptians laid out a 'geodetic octave' commencing at 1° north of Behdet (to emphasize its separateness from Egypt) and culminating at Dodona. For Dodona is precisely 8° north of Behdet in latitude, and the related oracle centre of Delphi is exactly 7° in latitude north of Behdet. (These last two facts were discovered by Livio Stecchini, as will be explained somewhat later.) As we have seen, octaves go back at least to the Sumerians.

I have arrived at this sequence for a geodetic oracle octave (see Fig. 26):

8. Dodona
7. Delphi (with its famous *omphalos*, a stone navel)
6. Delos, the famous shrine of Apollo, once an oracle centre (also with an omphalos)
5. Kythera (Cythera), a site on the north-east coast (see later); or Thera (Santorini)
4. Omphalos (Thenae) near Knossos on Crete (on the Plain of Omphaleion)
3. Undiscovered site on Southern or South-western coast of Cyprus? (Paphos?) (Cape Gata?)
2. Lake Triton (or Tritonis) in Libya
1. El Marj (Barce or Barca)

The ones which I have identified are spaced apart by one degree of latitude from each other in sequence and are integral degrees of latitude from Behdet, which we shall see was the geodetic centre of the ancient world (akin to Greenwich in the modern world) and was also a pre-dynastic capital of Egypt.

What justification have I for speaking of a link between the oracle centres and the musical octave? I have several reasons, and it would be just as well for me to give some slight indications here to make the reader who is justifiably puzzled at this point a little less so.

Graves[9] informs us of some interesting facts about Apollo, who was official patron god of Delphi and Delos (two of the centres on our list): 'In Classical times, music, poetry, philosophy, astronomy, mathematics, medicine, and science all came under Apollo's control. As the enemy of barbarism, he stood for moderation in all things, and *the seven strings of his lute* were connected with the seven vowels of the later Greek alphabet, *given mystical significance*, and used for therapeutic music. Finally, because of his identification with the Child Horus, a solar concept, he was

Figure 25. The god Apollo sits on his tripod at the Oracle of Delphi, in this ancient Greek vase painting. Beside him the Delphic laurel is growing. In his right hand he holds the mantic bowl into which the priestess, who approaches him with a gesture of welcome, will gaze as she goes into trance. A female attendant stands with a jug of water to refill the bowl as it becomes necessary. The bowl was filled with a hot steaming liquid containing powerful decoctions of narcotic herbs such as henbane, thorn apple and black and white hellebore, which helped induce a prophetic frenzy in the self-hypnotized priestess. The terrible smell was explained away to the public as 'fumes from the rotting corpse of the monster Python', supposedly oozing up through a chasm under the temple (although modern excavators have proved that there was no chasm). For a lengthy account of how these proceedings worked, of the drug plants, and of the oracular institutions, see my book *Conversations with Eternity*, Rider, London, 1984; on pp. 53, 58 and 59 of that book further illustrations are to be found which relate directly to this one

worshipped as the sun, whose Corinthian cult had been taken over by solar Zeus. . . .' (The italics are mine.) Note also the reference to Horus, whose falcon would have presided over the Colchian dead in their hope of resurrection. In fact, one meaning of *kirkos* (Circe – 'falcon'), which I did not elaborate on earlier, is 'ring'. I wish to comment in passing that not only was the ring traditionally a solar symbol (as was the golden fleece, and as was the falcon), but the Cyclopes who were one-eyed were really one-ring-eyed. Cyclopes means 'ring-eyed', in fact. Graves says:[10] 'One-eyed Polyphemus . . . can be traced back to the Caucasus. . . . Whatever the meaning of the Caucasian tale may have been, A. B. Cook in his *Zeus* (pp 302–23) shows that the Cyclops's eye was a Greek solar emblem.'

The following remarks by Graves then tend to dissociate Cyclops from Cyclopes, but perhaps this should not be done, in the light of all these new insights. After all, the older Cyclopes were three, wild, and ring-eyed, and sons again of Gaia the Earth goddess just as were the three fifty-headed monsters (there is to be much discussion of this later). They would, according to my 'system', be solar too, and 'ring', 'falcon', 'earth-born of Gaia' and solar seem always to go together in the schema. Gaia, indeed, preceded the solar Apollo as presiding deity at Delphi. Not surprising, as Deukalion's ark landed on Mount Parnassus above Delphi (according to Delphic propaganda) and his 'mother' was Gaia, whose 'bones' he threw behind him to people the desolated Earth once again.

It is not only Deukalion's ark that is connected with Delphi. There are connections also with the *Argo*, as we learn from Godfrey Higgins:[11] 'In the religious ceremonies at Delphi a boat of immense size was carried about in processions; it was shaped like a lunar crescent, pointed alike at each end: it was called an Omphalos or Umbilicus, or the ship *Argo*. Of this ship *Argo* I shall have very much to say hereafter. My reader will please to recollect that the os minxae or Δελφυς (Delphys) is called by the name of the ship *Argo*.'

Other matters which Higgins connects with Delphi are the sacred syllable *om* of the Indo-Europeans which he says 'is not far from the *divina vox* of the Greek. Hesychius,* also Suidas† in voce, interprets the word *omph* to be Θεια χληδων (*theia chlēdōn*), the sacred voice, the holy sound – and hence arose the ὀμφαλος (*omphalos*), or place of *Omphe*.' He relates all this with sacred music and the traditional sacred name of God which consists of the seven vowels spoken in sequence to form one word, which is the '*not-to-be-spoken* word'. He says: 'As a pious Jew will not utter the word Ieue,* so a pious Hindu will not utter the word Om.' But whether this is strictly true or not, the sacred quality of the names is undisputed.

Higgins says φη, *phē*, is the verb root in Greek of *phaō* 'to speak or pronounce' and *phēmi*, 'to say'. (I might add that φηγος, *phēgos*, is the word for oak, as at Dodona, and φημη, '*phēmē*, literally means 'oracle'. Hence *Omphē* means 'the speaking of Om'. (At the *phēmē* Dodona the *phēgos* literally practised *omphē* because the oak spoke there.)

Delphi was said to be the *omphalos*, 'navel', of the world. But it was in fact only one of many.[12] In Figure 26 the reader can see that there is an Omphalos near Knossos in Crete which is one of the octave sequence of oracle centres laid out in geodetic integral degrees of latitude from Behdet, pre-dynastic capital of Egypt. A photograph of the omphalos stone of Delos may be seen in Plate 21 as well. The seven vowels, the seven strings of Apollo's lyre, the seven notes of the octave (the eighth being a repetition one octave higher of the first, as most people will know), the eight oracle centres in the 'northern octave' of oracles, the seven degrees of latitude marking the official length of ancient Egypt itself, the mystic and unspeakable name of God consisting of the seven vowels run together in one breath – all these are part of a coherent complex of elements forming a system, which also involves cosmic bodies.

Before going much further, I should justify my tentative selection of a

* Alexandrian lexicographer, fifth century AD.
† Now correctly called Suda – a lexicon, not an author, compiled about the end of the tenth century AD at Byzantium.
‡ i.e. Yahweh.

site on the island of Kythera (Cythera), which is off the southern coast of the Greek Peloponnese, as possibly being associated with the fifth in my series of geodetically sited oracle centres. I found the necessary information while reading Professor Cyrus H. Gordon's remarkable book, *The Common Background of Greek and Hebrew Civilizations*.[13] At the end of Chapter II, Gordon tells us the following:

Sometimes cultic centres attracted people from remote areas. Probably the most common cause for such magnetism was an efficacious priesthood, that earned a reputation for helping people in need of practical advice, psychological guidance or medical aid. Cythera began to attract foreigners as early as the Pyramid Age. A stone cup, with the name of a Fifth Dynasty [the chronology of Richard A. Parker gives the dates 2501–2342 BC for the Fifth Dynasty] solar temple [of Pharaoh Userkaf at Abusir] (sp-rᶜ) inscribed in Egyptian hieroglyphs, has been found on Cythera. Early in the second quarter of the second millennium, a Babylonian inscription of Naram-Sin, King of Eshnunna, was dedicated on Cythera 'for the life' of that Mesopotamian monarch. [This is one of the reasons for believing that both texts were sent to Cythera in antiquity. Modern deception is unlikely because the Naram-Sin text was found on Cythera in 1849 before the decipherment of cuneiform.] The interesting thing is that both of these texts found on Cythera are religious in character. Herodotus (1:105) relates that the Phoenicians erected a temple on Cythera to the goddess of the heavens. Finally in classical times, Cythera was a great centre of the cult of Aphrodite. The ancient temples were built in the vicinity of Palaiopolis around the middle of the eastern shore. I visited the site in 1958 and found it extensive and promising for excavation. ... Egyptians, Babylonians and Phoenicians came to worship the great goddess there. [At that time the great goddess, Gaia, was also in charge of Delphi, before the usurpation by Apollo.] Ancient cultic installations, carved out of the living rock, can still be seen on a high place at the north end, near the shore. A well, cleared some years ago, had, at its bottom, ancient statuary ... [there are] ancient stone walls. ... The whole area is covered with ceramics that show the site was occupied in Middle Minoan III (*c.* 1700–1570), Late Minoan I–III (*c.* 1570–1100) [Note: 'Late Minoan III (*c.* 1400–1100) is the Mycenaean Age'] and subsequently in classical times (5th–4th centuries BC).

The problem posed by ancient Cythera has not yet been answered. The island is rather remote from Egypt and Asia for men to have sailed there, for religious purposes alone. And yet it is hard to discover any more practical reason. Cythera is not remarkable for its natural resources. ... Meanwhile we must reckon with Cythera as a site where all the evidence so far points to its importance as a religious centre with international attraction. ... Such shrines have remained well known

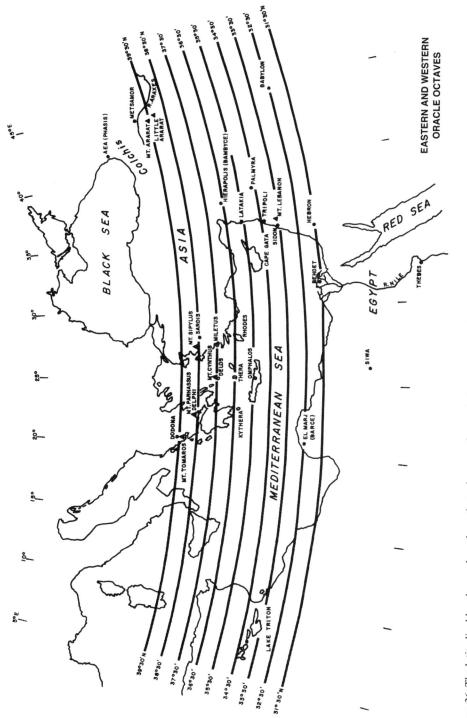

Figure 26. The latitudinal bands – such as those that criss-cross the omphalos stones (see Plate 21 and Figure 33) – graphically demonstrate the oracle octaves descending from Dodona to Behdet and from Mount Ararat to Hebron

throughout the ages. In classical antiquity, the oracle at Delphi was sought within a wide radius. Today Lourdes attracts from every continent people in need of help that they have not succeeded in finding nearer home.

Cythera thus became a centre for Egyptians and Semites and still other people, from Abusir along the Nile to Eshnunna beyond the Euphrates. Such visitors brought their influence to bear upon the Aegean, and on returning home, carried some Aegean culture with them. ... It is gratifying that Cythera is now being excavated by Professor George Huxley for the University of Pennsylvania Museum. [Gordon was writing in 1964.]

So much for Cythera; an alternative possible site is on the island of Thera. Or the two may be linked. Some justification for my guess that site number three would be in the south of Cyprus comes from the famous references

Figure 27. Engravings of five copper coins of the Roman era showing the omphalos stone at the oracle centre of Zeus Kasios, whose name is written on the bottom of the three coins shown in the top row. This oracle centre was at Mount Kasion, near Latakia, and marked the eastern site of the oracle octave for 35°30'. These engravings are reproduced from *Zeus* by A. B. Cook, Cambridge, Vol. II, Part 2, 1925, p. 982. Cook comments: 'Coppers struck by Trajan and Antoninus Pius have on the reverse a shrine with pyramidal roof resting on four pillars and enclosing a sacred stone, which is filleted.' The depiction of a filleted omphalos stone is well known from Delphi and Cook stresses that the stone shown on these coins is definitely not a meteorite or 'thunder-stone'. This site is a remote one: 'Mt Kasion, a barren sand-dune adjoining Lake Sirbonis, was famous for its sanctuary of Zeus *Kasios* . . .'; there was another Mount Kasion in Egypt. And according to Servius, the ancient commentator on Virgil, the sanctuary was founded by a Cretan named Kyparissos. This tallies with the Minoan associations with Dodona, Delphi, and Delos. There is nothing definitely known about the origin of the name Kasios. It was to this site that the rebellious fish/serpent-tailed Typhon (Greek name for the Egyptian Set) was pursued by Zeus in their cosmic conflict, according to the ancient writer Apollodorus (second century BC)

to 'Aphrodite Kytherean, even as far as Cyprus', in the ancient literature. Also, Herodotus (Book I, 105) refers to the temple of Aphrodite Urania at Ascalon in Syria and says: '[it is] the most ancient, I am told, of all the temples of this goddess. The one in Cyprus the Cyprians themselves admit was derived from it, and the one in Cythera was built by the Phoenicians, who belong to this part of Syria.' In the latter (unquoted) part of his last footnote given above, Gordon mentions that 'Phoenicians' is Herodotean language inclusive of the Minoans.

In passing, I might mention that a little island opposite Cythera is called Anti-Cythera and there a famous shipwreck was recovered from which came the miniature mechanical computer dated from the first century BC (concerning which Professor Derek Price of Yale University has written a good deal, including a 'cover story' for the *Scientific American* and his definitive book *Gears from the Greeks: The Antikythera Mechanism – A Calendar Computer from ca. 80BC*, Science History Publications, Neale Watson Academic Publications, New York, 1975). This little computer is one of many survivals of ancient times which demonstrate conclusively that the conventional attitudes today to ancient technology are inadequate, and that we seriously underestimate the early peoples.

Now as for the site of Delos, I will give information here from H. W. Parke's authoritative book *Greek Oracles*[14] which will indicate its importance as an oracle centre in my postulated 'northern octave' of geodetic centres:

> The other point which Dodona could urge against Delphi in its favour was that it was the oracle of Zeus himself. Apollo was at most the son of Zeus, inserted somewhat awkwardly into the Greek pantheon. On the face of it his prophecies could not be as significant as the utterances of the father of gods and men. Delphi replied with an elaborate piece of theological propaganda. While not attempting to detract from the supreme position of Zeus, it was argued that Apollo was his chosen prophet. This doctrine appears first in the Homeric *Hymn to Apollo*, but not in the sections connected with Delphi. It is in the Delian hymn where the infant god bursts from his swaddling clothes and cries: 'May the harp and the bending bow be my delight, and I shall prophesy to men the unerring will of Zeus.' In the rest of the same poem there are other references to Delos as an oracle-centre, a function which had lapsed in the classical period. But this part of the Homeric Hymn with its description of the Delian festival evidently dates back to an early stage of the archaic period – probably about 700 BC.
>
> The concept of Apollo as the prophet of Zeus may, then, have started in Delos, but it was certainly taken over and largely developed by Delphi.

Also '. . . Delos, though later mainly famous as [Apollo's] birthplace, evidently once had been a centre of divination.'[15]

Figure 28. An engraving by Romain de Hooghe, published in 1688, showing his conception of the Delphic priestess seated on her tripod and intoxicated by the billowing fumes which arise from the chasm beneath

The island of Delos was known as 'the sacred Isle' and was traditionally meant to be immune from war or conquest. As the great scholar W. W. Tarn expressed it, in his article on 'The Political Standing of Delos': 'Now there is no doubt that the tiny island of Delos, which held a special position in religious life as being the birthplace of Apollo, was for centuries considered a "holy place". . . . the whole island of Delos was considered holy. . . . In the third century [BC] Callimachus' *Hymn to Delos* calls it the most holy of islands: it is immune from war, and needs no walls, for its wall is Apollo. . . . Delos then was a holy place from the sixth to the second century [BC]; possibly tradition made it so from time immemorial, *i.e.* from the birth of Apollo . . .'[16]

The historian Diodorus Siculus (first century BC), drawing upon very archaic historical material compiled by his predecessors, records important consultations of the Oracle of Apollo at Delos which prior to the seventh century BC were carried on in the same way that consultations of Delphi were in the later periods which are more familiar to us. For instance:

. . . when the land of Rhodes brought forth huge serpents, it came to pass that the serpents caused the death of many of the natives; consequently the survivors dispatched men to Delos to inquire of the god how they might rid themselves of the evil. And Apollo commanded them to receive Phorbas and his companions and to colonize together with them the island of Rhodes . . . and the Rhodians summoned him as the oracle had commanded and gave him a share in the land. And Phorbas destroyed the serpents, and after he had freed the island of its fear he made his home in Rhodes . . . At a later time than the events we have described Althaemenes, the son of Catreus the king of Crete, while inquiring of the oracle regarding certain other matters, received the reply that it was fated that he should slay his father by his own hand. So wishing to avoid such an abominable act, he fled of his free will from Crete . . . Shortly before the Trojan War Tlepolemus, the son of Heracles, who was a fugitive because of the death of Licymnis, whom he had unwittingly slain, fled of his free will from Argos; and upon receiving an oracular response regarding where he should go to found a settlement, he put ashore at Rhodes together with a few people, and being kindly received by the inhabitants he made his home there. And becoming king of the whole island he portioned out the land . . .[17]

It is not necessary to know who the above personalities were or to understand the incidents – these examples are merely mentioned to indicate the manner in which the Oracle of Delos held a position similar to that of Delphi.

As regards Omphalos in Crete, another archaic site on our oracle octave, Diodorus Siculus records the following:

> . . . Rhea . . . when she had given birth to Zeus, concealed him in Ide, as it is called . . . And many instances of the birth and upbringing of this god remain to this day on the island. For instance, when he was being carried away, while still an infant, by the Curetes, they say that the umbilical cord (*omphalos*) fell from him near the river known as Triton, and that this spot had been made sacred and has been called Omphalos after that incident, while in like manner the plain about it is known as Omphaleium.[18]

The goddess Athena, who was said to have been born at Lake Triton in Libya (also on our oracle octave), was also said to have been born at the River Triton in Crete, either near to or actually at the site of Omphalos. We know this tradition from Diodorus Siculus: 'Athena, the myths relate, was likewise begotten of Zeus in Crete, at the sources of the river Triton, this being the reason why she has been given the name of Tritogeneia. And there stands, even to this day, at these sources a temple which is sacred to this goddess, at the spot where the myth relates that her birth took place.'[19] Athena thus seems to have been born at *two* oracle octave sites, but the important point is that her two 'births' are geodetically related to one another and are two degrees of latitude apart.

My contention that the oracle centres of Dodona, Delphi, Delos, Cythera, Knossos, and Cyprus are linked as a series – apart from the obvious facts that they are all separated from each other by a degree of latitude and are integral degrees of latitude from Behdet in Egypt and have demonstrable connections with Egypt in tradition or archaeology – is further cemented by another passage in H. W. Parke's book:[20]

> At Delphi, namely the site of the classical shrine of Athena Pronaia on the east of Castalia ... as excavation has shown, there was not a settlement, but a cult centre going back to Mycenaean times. .... It is interesting archaeologically that a number of important finds from the earlier archaic periods show clear affinities or actual derivation from Crete. For, as we have mentioned, the Homeric *Hymn to Apollo* ends by describing how 'Phoebus Apollo then took it in mind whom he would bring of men as his worshippers who would serve him in rocky Pytho.* Then while pondering he was aware of a swift ship on the wine-dark sea, and in it were good men and many – Cretans from Minoan Knossos who offer sacrifices to the lord Apollo and announce the oracles of Phoebus Apollo of the golden sword whatever he speaks in prophecy from the laurel-tree ...' ... Some scholars have seen in the evident archaeological links between early archaic Delphi and Crete a basis of fact behind this facade of legend, and it is possible that the cult of Apollo was introduced by sea from Crete. ...

In the Homeric *Hymn* quoted we find it specifically stated that Minoan Cretans (contemporaneous with ancient Egypt, of course, and who traded with the Egyptians) from Knossos took Apollo to Delphi, the site of an omphalos. And these Knossians are stated to respect oracles. And near Knossos is a site called Omphalos which is one degree of latitude south of the site of Kythera, which is one degree south of Delos, which is one degree south of Delphi.

Parke gives further information.[21] He mentions the connections well known to have existed *between Delos and Dodona* through what are known as 'the Hyperborean gifts' (see below), which were sent to Delos by way of Dodona from the mysterious northern Hyperboreans, whose land is thought by many to have been Britain. In Book II of Diodorus Siculus one finds a description of the Hyperboreans observing celestial objects

Figure 29. Detail of mural from Pompeii reproduced by W. H. Roscher. The omphalos resembles the one at Delos (see Plates 15 and 18). Here the friendly omphalos-serpent is being harassed by a python

* Delphi.

through what sounds to me and some other scholars distinctly like a telescope. In a forthcoming book I have a very great deal to say about the use of crystal and glass lenses in antiquity, and their possible juxtaposition as simple telescopes. But they couldn't have observed Sirius B!

Parke tells us: 'In the Cyclades Delos had once had an Apolline oracle of importance. . . . One can suppose that this institution existed . . . at the end of the eighth century [BC], and may have dwindled away in the seventh century [BC]. . . . By the time when Pisistratus and Polycrates in the latter half of the sixth century [BC] revived the sanctity of Delos, the oracle appears to have already ceased and was not restored.'[22]

It is worthwhile giving some details of the 'Hyperborean gifts', because an account of them is one of the strangest tales to survive from ancient Greece, and it relates directly to our subject. One of the longest studies of them was written by Rendel Harris.[23] Here is a part of what he had to say:

The people who send [Apollo] gifts are real people who have a genuine connexion with him: they have lost him, they have not forgotten him, they find him again by holy embassies and sacred gifts. . . . the gifts . . . came such long distances over land and sea, carefully packed in straw, and hidden from the intruding eyes of all except those to whom they were sent. The box was labelled carefully, *Apollo, Delos,* and it was taboo. . . . Now let us see what Herodotus says about the sacred gifts that came to Delos in his day [Herodotus, 'the father of history', lived in the fifth century BC]. He tells us (his information being derived from the priests at Delos) that the sacred things were brought by the Hyperboreans, wrapped in straw, to the Scythians, and that then they passed from tribe to tribe westward to the Adriatic; from thence they are carried south to Dodona, where they pass into Greek hands; from Dodona they are carried eastward again to the Malian Gulf, and so across to the island of Euboea, and from town to town to Karystos, the people of which town take them to Tenos (passing by Andros); and the people of Tenos take them to Delos. [Herodotus, IV, c. 33.]

This is a very roundabout pilgrimage, but some of the repetition and prolongation of the journey is due to an attempt to avoid mountain ranges. Mt Cithaeron, for example, is avoided by crossing to Euboea, and working down to the most southerly point of the island at Karystos, where Andros is in sight and Delos close at hand.

The story which Pausanius gives [second century AD] shows much variation. He tells us that 'at Prasiai (on the coast of Attica) there is a temple of Apollo. Here the first fruits of the Hyperboreans are said to come. The Hyperboreans, I am told, hand them over to the Arimaspians, and the Arimaspians to the Issedones; from thence the Scythians convey them to Sinope: from thence they are borne by Hellenes [Greeks] to Prasiai; and it is the Athenians that bring them to Delos. These first fruits, it is said, are hidden in wheaten straw, and no one knows what they are.'

Pausanius knows, however, that the offerings were of the nature of first fruits; and his reference to the bringing of the offerings into Attica is at once explained by the fact that Athens had acquired suzerainty over Delos, so that a deflection of the route from Euboea would be natural. What surprises one is that the offerings are now brought across the Black Sea to Sinope (shall we say from Olbia?), and that from Sinope they pass coast-wise to the Bosphorus and so onwards. This is quite different from the route described [700 years earlier] by Herodotus. Yet it is so detailed that it can hardly be set aside, and moreover it makes the sacred route pass through Scythia to the Euxine [Black Sea] along the amber way. It also puts the Hyperboreans further off, by interpolating two tribes between themselves and the Scythians. If, however, we say that in Pausanius' time the offerings came to Delos by the eastern amber road, it is equally clear that the offerings which Herodotus describes are being carried along the western amber way down to the Adriatic.

An explanation of the change of route was offered by Prof. Ridgeway and endorsed by Frazer . . . He has made it highly probable that from very remote ages there was a regular trade-route from the Black Sea up the Danube, and across to the head of the Adriatic . . . This route is the one indicated in the account which the Delians gave to Herodotus of the route by which the offerings came from Southern Russia to Delos. But with the establishment of Greek colonies in Southern Russia this long circuitous route would be exchanged for the direct one through the Bosphorus, the Hellespont and Aegean. This newer and shorter route appears to be the one indicated by Pausanius. He says, indeed, that the offerings came from Scythia (Russia) by way of Sinope, an important Greek colony situated on the southern shore of the Black Sea opposite to the Crimea.[24]

Another factor overlooked by the scholars who have tried to explain the alternative routes is that during the seven centuries between the time of Herodotus and that of Pausanius, the importance of Dodona dwindled, so that a difficult travel diversion in the route which had existed for religious reasons connected with the oracle octave was abandoned because the religious establishment at Dodona under the Romans had fallen into desuetude and had no remaining significance. Of course the later route was the easier and more direct – but the question is: Why was the more difficult route taken in the first place? It is because the scholars considering this matter have not realized the important archaic connection between Dodona and Delos that they have never been able to make sense of the original route of these mysterious gifts which were transported for thousands of miles across difficult terrain.

It is a daunting prospect to try to set forth at proper length all the complex tangle of information concerning the 'northern octave' and its many links with the Sirius tradition. It is impossible for me to do justice in this book to the subject of the astronomical knowledge of the ancients.[25]

From *Hamlet's Mill* we have a passage which is now relevant. The reader will have to accept on trust that the seven notes of the octave and the seven planets of ancient times were thought of in connection with one another. We cannot here take on the debate concerning early Pythagoreanism versus Neo-Pythagoreanism and the genesis of different concepts of 'harmony of the spheres'. Here is the passage: 'And Aristotle says (*Rhet.* 2.24, 1401a15) that, wishing to circumscribe a "dog" one was permitted to use "Dog star" (Sirius) or Pan, because Pindar states him to be the "shape-shifting dog of the Great Goddess [Gaia]" . . . The amazing significance of Sirius as leader of the planets, as the eighth planet, so to speak, and of Pan, the dance-master (*choreutēs*) as well as the real *kosmokrator*, ruling over the "three worlds", would take a whole volume.'[26]

Now this reference to Sirius as 'the eighth planet, so to speak' is an extremely interesting clue. (In fact, there is some evidence to suggest that the ancients knew of the existence of the eighth planet Uranus because the Egyptians could just have managed to observe it in the way suggested by Peter Tompkins in *Secrets of the Great Pyramid*.[27] And I believe both that this was probably the case and that Uranus was sometimes compared to Sirius B because they were both 'invisible'. Also, Sirius B orbits Sirius A as a planet orbits a sun, as I have mentioned before, for its orbital period is less than that of our own planets Uranus, Neptune, and Pluto. The fact that Sirius B, a star, moves faster than Uranus, a planet, is an additional reason for the two to be thought of as similar. Sirius B was additionally compared in some obscure way to the innermost tiny planet Mercury, the nature of whose orbit was symbolized by the human intestines – see Figure 16 for this – and Uranus was the 'octave' expression of Mercury.)

Consider this 'eighth planet' theme in relation to the oracle centres. Dodona is the eighth oracle centre of the 'northern octave'. In music, the eighth note closes the octave by repeating the first note an octave higher. The octave of a note is double its frequency – if you play C on the piano and then play the succeeding seven notes you reach a higher C, double the frequency of the original C – its octave. The 'eighth planet' would therefore repeat the first planet which was Hermes (in Latin, Mercury). Now it was Hermes (Mercury) who supplied the golden ram to Phrixus so that he could make his getaway to Colchis. And it was the oak of Dodona which was fitted into the prow of the *Argo* which returned the golden fleece. During the interval of the fleece's stay in Colchis the fleece rested 'in the grove of Ares [Mars]'. The important points to note are that the fleece went to Colchis under the auspices of the first planet, rested there under the auspices of (the planet?) Mars, and returned under the auspices of Sirius the 'eighth planet' with the oak of the eighth oracle centre in the *Argo*'s prow. And we have already seen how *Argo*, if swung through a 90° angle, touches its prow first at Dodona and then points directly at

Metsamor near Mount Ararat. But if an extended *Argo* has its prow touch Dodona and its stern at Egyptian Thebes, the *Argo* may be swung to Ararat/Metsamor and touches its prow there too.

Parke says: 'On Asia Minor Didyma near Miletus is the only oracle-centre for whose activity we have some evidence in the sixth century.'[28] Miletus seems to be on the same parallel as Delos, just as Sardis is on the same parallel as Delphi.[29] And we have seen that Mount Ararat (having its associated centre at Metsamor) is on the same parallel as Dodona. There is thus a 'north-eastern octave' to correspond to the 'northern octave'. But we shall see later that geodetic points exist over great stretches of territory, marked out from Behdet, the ancient Greenwich. (For instance, an arc swung through Aea in Colchis would pass through Mecca as well, if the compass point were on Behdet. A line from Egyptian Thebes to Dodona intersects the vicinity of Omphalos and Knossos on Crete. The lines connecting Thebes, Dodona, and Metsamor, form an equilateral triangle. A line from Behdet to Dodona intersects Thera. Also, a straight line passes through the three points Behdet, Mecca, Dodona. As for Mecca, I doubt that many Moslem scholars will be at all surprised to learn of these aspects of their holy centre. They know very well that the centre has geodetic aspects and the central shrine of the Kaaba dates from prehistoric times; they say it was established by the prophet Abraham.)

Associations of Delphi with the Sirius tradition are not limited to the Canopic Egyptian Hercules's visit, the carrying of an *Argo* in procession, and the desire to claim the ark of Deukalion instead of Dodona's claiming it (the centres then being rivals for power and attention, as I have said).

Other Sirius-tradition elements present in connection with Delphi are concerned with the *Argo* and the Minyae. It was an oracle from Delphi which stated the golden fleece would have to be brought back to Iolchus from Colchis. It was a series of insistent oracles from Delphi that were ultimately responsible for our knowing the Sirius tradition from the Dogon today, as we will see near the end of the book. For Delphi determined the later fate of the Minyae, and it is their tradition which survives today in the former French Sudan. The explanation of this will be left to somewhat later.

Now, as to the omphalos stone and also Behdet. For these subjects we must turn to the amazing book published in 1971 *The Secrets of the Great Pyramid* by Peter Tompkins (with a scholarly appendix by Livio Stecchini). Tompkins tells us:[30]

The prime meridian of Egypt was made to split the country longitudinally precisely in half, running from Behdet on the Mediterranean, right through an island in the Nile just northeast of the Great Pyramid, all the way to where it crossed the Nile again at the Second Cataract. ... Cities and temples, says Stecchini, were deliberately built at distances in round figures and simple fractions from

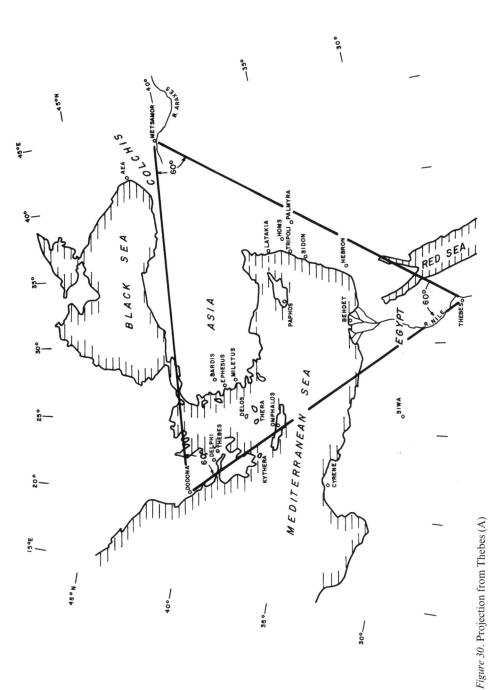

Figure 30. Projection from Thebes (A)

the tropic or the prime meridian. The predynastic capital of Egypt was set near the mouth of the Nile at Behdet, right on the prime meridian, at 31° 30'. . . . Memphis, the first capital of united Egypt, was again laid out on the prime meridian and at 29° 51', precisely 6° north of the tropic. . . . As each of these geodetic centres was a political as well as a geographical 'navel' of the world, an omphalos, or stone navel, was placed there to represent the northern hemisphere from equator to pole, marked out with meridians and parallels, showing the direction and distance of other such navels. In Thebes the stone omphalos was placed in the main room of the temple of Amon, where the meridian and parallel actually cross. . . . For the ancient Egyptians to have laid out an absolutely straight meridian of 30° of latitude from the Mediterranean to the equator, over 2,000 miles, and drawn two more, equidistant, east and west, as boundaries of the country [see Figure 20 in this book], must have required an enormous amount of personnel and careful astronomical sightings. Even more sophisticated was their method of establishing longitude, as reconstructed by Stecchini.

With the aid of an elementary system of telegraphy, consisting of a series of beacons, the Egyptians, says Stecchini, were able to note what star was at its zenith at a certain moment, and flash the data, via a string of flares, to other observers, so many degrees to east and west. . . . Because of the advanced geodetic and geographic science of the Egyptians, Egypt became the geodetic centre of the known world. Other countries located their shrines and capital cities in terms of the Egyptian

Figure 31. This representation of the sacred basket found at Khorsabad (a modern village in Iraq, site of the ancient palace of the Assyrian king Ashurnasirpal) is important evidence connecting Oannes with the omphalos stone tradition. The basket, which was invariably carried by Oannes, is seen here with the two doves with heads turned away – motif of the omphalos. The basket-work is also seen to resemble the mesh which usually covers the omphalos

meridian 'zero', including such capitals as Nimrod, Sardis, Susa, Persepolis, and, apparently, even the ancient Chinese capital of An-Yang.

All of these localities, says Stecchini, were set and oriented on the basis of the most exact sightings. The same applies to the centres of worship of the Jews, the Greeks, and the Arabs.

According to Hebrew historians the original Jewish centre of worship was not Jerusalem, but Mount Gerizim, a strictly geodetic point 4° east of the main axis of Egypt. It was only moved to Jerusalem after 980 BC.

The two great oracular centres of Greece – Delphi and Dodona – were also geodetic markers according to Stecchini. Delphi is 7° and Dodona 8° north of Behdet, the northernmost part of Egypt, on the prime meridian of Egypt.

From this brilliant observation of Stecchini's I got the original idea for my 'northern octave'.

Readers who have pondered the strange story of Pharaoh Tutankhamen – whose previous name had been Tutankhaten – and his father-in-law, Akhenaten and mother-in-law Nefertiti – might do well to note that a geodetic-religious dispute lay behind Akhenaten's desire to build a new geodetic capital city, which he did, but outraged the priests in the process. Why were the boundary stones of this city later ferociously mutilated? Because the Pharaoh had tried to establish a variation on the geodetic system of Egypt, and those marker stones represented it quite literally!

In Plates 14 and 16 the reader may see for himself the omphalos stones of Delphi and of Miletus[31] – both of which are spread with 'nets' representing a latitudinal and longitudinal geodetic mesh.[32] It is this mesh which is probably carried at all times by Oannes (see Figures 21, 22 and 31 and Plates 34, 38 and 39) as a 'basket'. For the 'warp and woof' of the sacred basket of Oannes/Dagon – surviving as the *lyknos* basket of Greek Demeter (the Goddess who governed the fruits of the earth, particularly corn (and was mother of Persephone) and who succeeded the Philistine fish-tailed Dagon as agricultural deity, keeping Dagon's 'basket') – represent perfectly the warp and woof of latitude and longitude. The Dogon have traditions of the religious and mythological importance of 'warp and woof' in weaving, and of sacred baskets 'which are not baskets', all of which may be found described in many places in *Le Renard pâle*. For other images of the omphalos stone and its 'basket', see Figure 33.

Figure 32 shows the omphalos stone found by Reisner in the great temple of Amon at Thebes in Egypt. This stone was placed in the main room of the temple where the meridian and parallel actually cross.[33] In Figure 36 is a reproduction of a figure from an Egyptian papyrus of omphalos stones with two doves perched on top. These two doves are the standard glyph meaning 'to lay out parallels and meridians'.[34] They are the 'two doves' who flew to Dodona from Thebes according to the account of

Figure 32. An Egyptian omphalos stone found in the temple of Amon at Napata in Nubia. (See *Journal of Egyptian Archaeology*, Vol. III, Part IV, 1916, page 255.) This drawing is reproduced by W. H. Roscher in *Der Omphalosgedanke*, Leipzig, 1918, as Figure 6. Roscher says of the stone: 'On the 21st of April, 1917, I received a letter from Professor Gunther Roeder, now Director of the Pelizaeus Museum in Hildesheim saying that Reisner (Harvard University) had, in excavations for the Boston Museum at Gebel Barka (Napata) in the Sudan, found a stone in a temple of the Nubian-Meroitic kings which was the omphalos of the Amon-oracle of Napata. . . .'

Herodotus.[35] Of course, the two doves are in fact carrier-pigeons. To keep in touch over such enormous distances, and to maintain prompt communication between oracle centres which was essential to the successful operation of a coherent 'world-wide' religious network spread over thousands of miles, the only available means were carrier-pigeons. I am informed that carrier-pigeons could fly from Thebes to Dodona in about a day. To travel such a distance oneself by sea and land would take months. Daily communication between the Egyptian religious centre of Thebes and all its oracle 'colonies' would have been transacted by the very carrier-pigeons whom we see plainly depicted on omphalos stones by both Greek (see Plate 21) and Egyptian (see additionally Figure 37) representations and documented clearly by Herodotus. Also, I should imagine such instantaneous 'news coverage' would surreptitiously find its way into the oracular pronouncements at the various centres and exercise a considerable political influence. For after all, there was hardly a king or potentate anywhere in the ancient world who would disregard an oracular order 'from the gods'. Probably the political forces were totally ignorant of the 'hot news line' ticking away secretly in the local oracle centre's temple complex.

Since the original appearance of this book, I have published another book entitled *Conversations with Eternity,* which deals with these matters at considerable length.[36] There is a great deal of textual evidence for networks of carrier-pigeons and carrier-swallows as well, and I describe the way they worked in my chapter on 'The Oracular Establishments' in that book.[37]

I might in passing also mention the remarkable beacon-signalling system described in Aeschylus's play, the *Agamemnon,* first produced in 458 BC at Athens, which purports to describe how the result of the Trojan War was signalled back to Argos in Greece by a chain of beacon fires on mountain tops. A lengthy study of this was written by J. H. Quincey, and he even published a large map showing that section of the amazing beacon system which extended from Mount Athos to Argos. The bonfire signal went from Mount Athos across the Thracian Sea to Mount Pelion, was relayed from there to Mount Othrys, from there to Mount Messapion, thence to Mount Cithaeron, from there to Mount Aegaleos, from where it was transmitted to Arachnaeon and finally to Argos.[38] This practical use

Figure 33. Several depictions of omphalos stones encircled by the oracular guardian serpent. Numbers 1, 3 and 5, which are Etruscan, are of particular interest because they show clearly the intersecting latitude and longitude lines which were marked on the globe by the oracle centres. Number 2 is Roman, excavated in the baths of Titus, by which time depictions of omphalos stones were mere subjects for art, as is the case with Number 4 from Pompeii, for which see Figure 29. Reproduced from *Neue Omphalosstudien* [New Omphalos Studies] by Wilhelm Heinrich Roscher, Leipzig, 1915, Plate IV

of mountain tops also serves as a salutary reminder of just how important mountain tops were to the ancient peoples. If it were not for the evidence preserved indirectly by the playwright Aeschylus, this particular mountaintop signalling network would forever have been unknown to us. Equally, the oracular mountaintop networks had been forgotten until now, with their importance for the measuring of the globe by marking latitude lines and their religious importance as 'navels of the earth' which connect the above with the below – so important to ancient religions.

I realize that acknowledgement of all these facts is bound to evoke howls and cries of anguish from any of those archaeologists to whom a drastic revision of their ideas is more painful than would be an amputation of all their limbs without an anaesthetic. Such are the hazards which go with the addictive and opiate pleasures of submersion in a body of orthodox theory.

As the philosopher David Hume pointed out concerning the revolutionary discovery of the circulation of the blood by William Harvey: 'It is remarked that no physician in Europe who had reached forty years of age ever, to the end of his life, adopted Harvey's doctrine of the circulation of the blood; and that his practice in London diminished extremely from the reproach drawn upon him by that great and signal discovery. So slow is the progress of truth in every science, even when not opposed by factions or superstitious prejudices!'[39]

It should be strongly emphasized that Dodona and Metsamor/ Ararat are equidistant from Egyptian Thebes. The Greek ark landed at Dodona and the Hebrew ark landed at Ararat. The process of 'landing an ark', therefore, consists of starting at Thebes and going north to either of the two places which are 8 degrees of latitude northwards and which are joined to each other by a distance equal to their distances from Thebes. That may sound complicated. The fact is that an equilateral triangle is formed by the lines joining Thebes with Dodona and Ararat. These facts cannot possibly be an accident. There cannot be supposedly separate Greek and Hebrew traditions giving the landing points of the ark in their respective regions of the world, which then both turn out by chance to be equidistant from Thebes and the same distance from each other, as well as on the same latitude. Since Mount Tomaros at Dodona and Mount Ararat are both 'landing sites' for an ark, this must mean that the tip of the prow of the ark literally does touch either of them when projected on the globe from Thebes. This may be seen clearly drawn by a cartographer in Figure 30.

Also founded from Thebes by flying doves, according to Herodotus,[40] was the Oracle of Ammon in Libya, known to be at the Oasis of Siwa. In Figure 19 we may even see a comparison of the line patterns made by joining Thebes, Dodona, and Siwa with each other, with the line patterns formed by joining certain stars in the constellation of Argo together. The pattern is seen to be identical. The site of Siwa may have been chosen simply to display this. In both instances we have the helm of the *Argo* as the starting point: in the celestial pattern we start from the star Canopus, identified with the *Argo*'s helm; and in the geodetic pattern we start with Thebes, which is the site for the global *Argo*'s helm when projected either to Dodona or Ararat. But there is another means of projecting the Argo, using Behdet, to convey other meanings – bearing in mind always the interconnecting relationships of the sites, with Behdet equidistant from both Siwa and Thebes, and also on the northernmost point of Egypt and (see Figure 20) on the prime meridian dividing Egypt as demonstrated by Livio Stecchini.[41]

When the helm of the *Argo* is placed at Behdet (near the geographical Canopus) rather than at Thebes, with the prow touching Mount Ararat, if we swing the prow across to Dodona through an arc of exactly 90° (a right angle), we find that the prow is then too long and must be shortened. In fact, for this extraordinary point, documentary evidence actually exists in a Babylonian text. In Chapter Four we cited the passage in another context, and I will here return to it. It is from the brief Sumerian epic poem 'Gilgamesh and Agga', of extreme antiquity, the surviving tablets preserving it dating from the first half of the second millennium BC. This Sumerian poem contains, within the framework of what seems to be a local political diatribe, a certain bizarre core of material which no scholar has ever satisfactorily interpreted.[42] (The political aspect of the poem has, in my opinion, been over-emphasized due to Jacobsen and Kramer's understandable excitement at finding in the poem actual evidence of the existence 4,000 years ago of a bicameral parliament, which Kramer wrote up as one of the world's 'firsts' in his excellent book, *History Begins at Sumer*.)[43]

The poem mentions (line 104) a 'fleeing bird' which I believe may be a reference to the carrier-pigeon network which we have just discussed. But the most important elements in the poem seem to me to be two apparently contradictory statements:

(1) 'The prow of the *magurru*-boat was not cut down.' (line 80)
(2) 'The prow of the *magurru*-boat was cut down.' (line 98)

In Chapter Four I discussed why the *magurru*-boat and the *magan*-boat of another poem were in fact that boat which was later known as the *Argo*.

I believe that statement (1) refers to the *Argo* as projected from Behdet to Ararat, and that statement (2) refers to the projection of the *Argo* from Behdet to Dodona. The latter requires the cutting down or shortening of the prow lest the *Argo* extend beyond Dodona.

As long as the prow was not cut down in 'Gilgamesh and Agga', we find that 'The multitude did not cover itself with dust' in mourning. For the projection was still extended over the north-west of Mesopotamia, the Sumerian homeland being at least in the general vicinity. The Behdet–Ararat line actually intersects the famous oracle centre of Hierapolis (the name means 'priest city')[44] which I propose as the fifth eastern oracle centre at 36° 30'.

Figure 34. (left) The design carved on to the Babylonian omphalos. Rawlinson suggested that the design was of a zodiac. He thought it obvious that the figures were of constellations. It would seem definitely to be a star-map, but it is not necessarily true that the intention is to represent the sky accurately. Attempts to interpret such complex maps (the Egyptian zodiac of Denderah being a notorious example) usually fall short, so I will not here tempt the fates

Figure 35. (right) A Babylonian omphalos stone (from Rawlinson). A flattened view of its entire conical design is seen in Figure 34

The poem says also, as long as the prow is not cut down, that 'The people of all the foreign lands were not overwhelmed'. In other words, the projection did not fall over foreigners such as those living in Greece. It did not literally 'overwhelm' people of foreign lands, meaning overshadow or pass over them.

However, when the prow was shortened, the projection of *Argo* left Mesopotamia altogether, and then 'The multitude covered itself with dust' and the people of foreign lands were overwhelmed. It is at this point that Gilgamesh says to Agga, 'O Agga, the fleeing bird thou hast filled with grain' (in other words, fed the carrier-pigeon in preparation for his flight to another and different oracle centre – namely, Dodona rather than Metsamor). The entire poem is based round a repeated refrain which Kramer calls 'a riddle',[45] and which concerns the digging and completing of wells, of 'the small bowls of the land', and wishes 'to complete the fastening ropes'. At this point only a Sumerian scholar can tell us whether there are any other shades of meaning or alternative readings which might make the passage clearer, following the clue that 'the fastening ropes' may refer to the rope-like mesh which we see, for instance, on the omphali of Delphi and Delos. Can 'the small bowls of the land' be either geodetic points or their markers, the omphalos stones themselves, which are like small bowls? Could 'small bowls' be an accepted expression for omphali in Sumerian parlance? Answers to these questions are entirely beyond the competence of any but a dozen or so scholars. Even experts in the Akkadian language cannot help us here, with non-Semitic Sumerian. And even answers from one of the experts might be wrong through human error. Sighing, therefore, at the difficulty of our subject-matter, let us look again at Egypt.

Stecchini says:[46] 'Because Egyptologists have ignored the issue of geodetic points and of the linear units, the figure of the revolutionary Pharaoh Akhenaten has turned out to be the most mysterious and controversial in the long history of the Egyptian monarchy.' He then makes some extremely critical remarks about the archaeologist Cyril Aldred (author of *Akhenaten, Pharoah of Egypt: a New Study*, London, 1968) and others and continues:

Because they have resisted accepting the solidly documented facts, established scholars have devoted their energies to debating theories such as that Akhenaten was impotent, was a practising homosexual, or a woman masquerading as a man; there are historians who profess to be informed about the intimate relations between him and his wife, the beautiful Nefertiti. Since the picture of Akhenaten has remained indefinite and blurred, scholars have used it to project their own emotions. Those who do not like Akhenaten present him as a psychopath and dispute about the clinical definition of his illness. . . . If instead of trying to imagine what were the hieroglyphic notes of the psychoanalyst of the royal family, we consider the documented facts, the most important action in the revolutionary reign of Akhenaten proves to be the establishment of a new capital for Egypt, the city of Akhet-Aten, 'Resting-point of Aten'. The miles-long remains of the buildings of this city have been found and excavated in the locality known today as Tell el-Amarna. During the reign of Akhenaten a substantial percentage of the national resources was dedicated to the construction of this city.

Scholars of the last century, who had not yet adopted the psychologizing fashion, at least recognized the political meaning of the shift in the location of the capital of Egypt. Akhenaten intended to cut at the root of the power of the priests of the Temple of Amon in Thebes, who through their control of the national oracle, identified with the god of this temple, had usurped the royal functions. But what these scholars did not know is that the Temple of Amon was the geodetic centre of Egypt, the 'navel' of Egypt, being located where the eastern axis (32° 38' east) crosses the Nile, at the parallel which is at $^2/_7$ of the distance from the equator to the pole (25° 42' 51" north), and that the god Amon was identified with the hemispheric stone which marked this point.

The new city which was intended to replace Thebes as the capital and geodetic centre of Egypt was planted in a position which seems undesirable in terms of what we would consider the function of a capital city. Some scholars have interpreted this fact as further evidence of the mental derangement of its founder. . . . The new capital for the god Aten, who was raised to the status of the one true god, was set at latitude

193

27° 45′ north, at the middle point between the northernmost point Behdet and the southern limit of Egypt at latitude 24° 00′ north. . . . Akhenaten wanted to prove that Thebes could not properly claim to be the geodetic centre of Egypt and that he had chosen the geodetic centre conforming to an absolutely rigorous interpretation of *maet*, the cosmic order of which the dimensions of Egypt were an embodiment. In order to follow absolutely exact standards of measurement, he reverted to the pre-dynastic geodetic system which counted in geographic cubits starting from Behdet. . . . In terms of the system based on the pre-dynastic capital of Behdet, there could be no question that Akhet-Aten is the 'true and just' navel of Egypt.

This conclusion implies that one should re-evaluate the entire historical role of Akhenaten, taking as the starting-point what he himself considered the initial step in his program to establish true and just conformity with *maet*. There is a possibility that his revolutionary reforms, which extended from religion to art and family relations, were understood as a general return to pre-dynastic ideas and practices.

Note the fact that Thebes had established itself as the 'navel' of Egypt but not on the basis of the 'Behdet system' which Akhenaten apparently tried to revive. It shows how ancient the 'northern octave' must be if it were based on the 'Behdet system' whereas Thebes was not. The clear involvement of Thebes in the 'northern octave' system is not exclusive but is complementary to that of Behdet. In Herodotus, Book Two (54) we find this significant tale:

At Dodona . . . the priestesses who deliver the oracles have a . . . story: two black doves, they say, flew away from Thebes in Egypt, and one of them alighted at Dodona, the other in Libya. The former, perched on an oak, and speaking with a human voice, told them that there, on that very spot, there should be an oracle of Zeus. Those who heard her understood the words to be a command from heaven, and at once obeyed. Similarly the dove which flew to Libya told the Libyans to found the oracle of Amon – which is also an oracle of Zeus. The people who gave me this information were the three priestesses at Dodona – Promeneia the eldest, Timarete the next, and Nicandra the youngest – and their account is confirmed by the other Dodonaeans who have any connection with the temple.

It is really interesting to see how chummy Herodotus was with the priestesses of Dodona. Just how vividly accurate the Dodonaean story really is, will in a moment become even more clear. But as for the question of Thebes versus Behdet, tied in as it is with the Akhenaten question, I beg to bow out of that controversy. Put me down as having 'no opinion'.

We must note Stecchini's remarks about Delphi as follows:[47]

The god of Delphi, Apollo, whose name means 'the stone', was identified with an object, the *omphalos*, 'navel', which has been found. It consisted of an ovoidal stone. . . . The *omphalos* of Delphi was similar to the object which represented the god Amon in Thebes, the 'navel' of Egypt. In 1966 I presented to the annual meeting of the Archaeological Institute of America a paper in which I maintained that historical accounts, myths, and legends, and some monuments of Delphi, indicate that the oracle was established there by the Pharaohs of the Ethiopian Dynasty. This is the reason why the Greeks portrayed Delphos, the eponymous hero of Delphi, as a Negro.

Stecchini also explains his theory that the oracles originally functioned through the operations of computing devices:

An object which resembles a roulette wheel, and actually is its historical antecedent, was centred on top of the *omphalos*. The spinning of a ball gave the answers; each of the thirty-six spokes of the wheel corresponded to a letter symbol.

In studying ancient computing devices, I have discovered that they were used also to obtain oracular answers. This is the origin of many of the oracular instruments we still use today, such as cards and ouija boards. . . . The roulette wheel of Delphi originally was a special kind of abacus for calculating in terms of angles.

The following information from Stecchini is also both surprising and informative with regard to the story of the *Argo*, Colchis, etc.:[48]

Very revealing is that a base line was marked along parallel 45° 12' north on the north side of the Black Sea. This base line started from the mouth of the Danube, cut across the Crimea, and ended at the foot of the Caucasus. Beginning from this base, Russia was surveyed for a length of 10 degrees, along with the three meridians which formed the three axes of Egypt, up to latitude 55° 12' north. The river Dnieper was understood to be a symmetric counterpart of the Nile, running between the same meridians. Key positions along the course of the Dnieper were identified with corresponding key positions along the course of the Nile, up to the point of transferring Egyptian place names to Russia. The information about the existence of this geodetic system is provided by the description of a map of Russia which is based on it. The description of the map indicates that it was used at the end of the sixth century BC, but the map may be older; in any case there are other sources of information about the base line which indicate that it was marked in very early times.

In Tompkins and Stecchini's marvellous book[49] there are some first-rate photographs and drawings of stone omphalos navels which are extremely helpful in trying to understand all these matters. It makes all the difference to see the fantastic nature of these objects, representative as they are of a highly developed ancient science which until recently was completely unknown. These are reproduced here in Figures 36 and 37 and Plates 14–19.

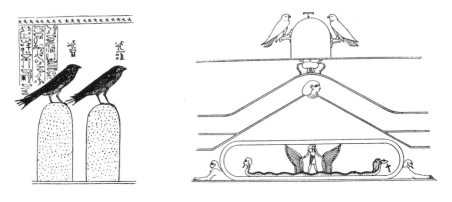

Figure 36.   *Figure 37.*

It is also interesting to note, by way of relation with the ark of Noah, the ark of Ziusudra (or Utnapishtim), the ark of Deukalion, and the *Argo* – all of whom sent forth birds over the water (like those birds from Thebes as well) – that the standard Egyptian hieroglyph for the act of laying out of parallels and meridians is, as we have seen, two pigeons facing each other. Stecchini says: 'In the religion of the Old Kingdom (of Egypt), Sokar is an important god of orientation and of cemeteries. The god and the geodetic point were represented by the stone object which the Greeks called *omphalos*, 'navel'; it is a hemisphere (the northern hemisphere) resting on a cylinder (the foundations of the cosmos). Usually on top of Sokar, as on top of any *omphalos*, there are portrayed two birds facing each other; in ancient iconography these two birds, usually doves, are a standard symbol for the stretching of meridians and parallels.'

Hence we see even further Egyptian connections with the Greek and Near Eastern tales in which the birds are let fly and the ship finds the oracle centre's mountain.

Associated with oracle centres was probably also a 'tree-code'. Dodona had its oak. Delphi was associated with laurel. And we learn from the *Elegies* of the sixth-century BC poet Theognis (5–8) and from the Homeric *Hymns* that the oracle centre of Apollo at Delos was specifically associated with the palm tree. Any site in the Lebanon, of course, such as Mt Lebanon and its possibly related centre of Sidon, would be associated with the famous cedars, known to us also from the *Epic of Gilgamesh* as intimately connected with Gilgamesh's exploits at 'Cedar Mountain' in the Lebanon. In putting together a schema of trees we are faced with considerable problems, but this is at least a beginning. A great deal of information on 'tree alphabets' is to be found in Robert Graves's books *The Greek Myths*[50] and even more so in his *The White Goddess*.[51] The willow was associated with the Colchian cemetery and with the island of Aeaea of Circe (the location of which is not known), but particularly it is connected with the island of Crete in tradition. But this subject will have to be tackled at some other time, lest I blow this book up into a puff ball of miscellaneous odds and ends. We do know from Robert Graves that the oracle centre of Hebron – which is on the same latitude as Behdet and seems to be its eastern counterpart, was connected with the tree *sant*, or wild acacia, 'the sort with golden flowers and sharp thorns. . . . It is . . . the oracular Burning Bush in which Jehovah appeared to Moses.' Graves adds: 'The acacia is still a sacred tree in Arabia Deserta and anyone who even breaks off a twig is expected to die within the year.'[52]

Its symbolism for the Sirius Mystery is an act of pure genius, and is graphically elucidated by Theophrastus:[53] 'There are two kinds, the white and the black; the white is weak and easily decays, the black is stronger and less liable to decay . . .' A perfect symbol of the two stars, the 'black' Sirius B being 'strong' for its size compared with the white Sirius A. Also of the willow (fourth centres), Theophrastus tells us:[54] 'There is that which is called the black willow . . . and that which is called the white . . . The black kind has boughs which are fairer and more serviceable . . . There is a (dwarf) form.'

Figure 38. A mythological scene set at an oracle centre, from a painting on an amphora excavated at Ruvo. At the top right, the god Apollo sits with his bow, indifferent to the fact that the young warrior, Neoptolemos (centre, sword in his hand), son of Achilles, has been wounded and is about to be dealt his death-blow in a quarrel. The palm tree motif of Delos/Miletus, rather than the laurel of Delphi, is prominent on the right, and in the background stands a temple with its decorated ivory doors open. A woman, probably a Pythian priestess, top left, starts back in horror. The main interest of the scene is the detailed depiction of the Delphic omphalos stone in the centre foreground. It is covered ('filleted') with a drapery of strands to represent the longitudes and it is horizontally divided into eight evenly graduated latitude bands, corresponding with the oracle octave scheme. It sits in a mount representing what is evidently metal curling leaves, as if it were a bud which had arisen from the Earth

CHART OF THE ORACLE OCTAVES

WESTERN CENTRE	EASTERN CENTRE	TREE-CODE	'PLANET'-CODE	DIVINE BIRTHS
8. Dodona (Mt Tomaros)	Metsamor (Mt Ararat)	oak (phēgos)	Saturn?	Mankind born from stones ('bones of Earth') at Dodona
7. Delphi (Mt Parnassus)	Sardis (Mt Sipylus)	laurel	Sun?	(Mankind born from stones at Delphi according to rival tradition)
6. Delos (Mt Cynthus)	Miletus (Didyma, also known as Branchidae, its associated oracle centre) Mt Latmus	palm	Moon (Artemis was born first, not Apollo)	Artemis (Diana) and Apollo born on Delos
5. a. Somewhere on north-east coast of Cythera? b. Rhodes? c. Thera on Island of Thera? (If so, destroyed by the volcano)	Hierapolis (Bambyce)	?	Mars?	?
4. Omphalos (Thenae) near Knossos on Crete	Mt Kasion (near Latakia) seat of Zeus Kasios; coins survive showing an omphalos there (A. B. Cook, II, 982)	willow (according to Pliny, a willow grew out of the Cretan cave where Zeus was born)	Jupiter	Zeus (Jupiter) was born on Crete
3. Somewhere on south coast of Cyprus? (associated with Paphos? Akrotiri?) Cape Gata?	near Tripoli? Palmyra?	cypress (the word cypress is derived from Cyprus)	Venus	Aphrodite (Venus) born at Cyprus
2. Lake Tritonis (also known as Lake Triton) in Libya/Tunisia	Sidon (Mt Lebanon)	cedar	Mercury (*seb* in Egyptian means both 'cedar' and 'the planet Mercury')	Athena (Pallas) born at Lake Tritonis
1. El Marj (Barce) Libya	Babylon	?	?	?
0. Behdet	Hebron	wild acacia	Earth?	—

Note: At one degree of latitude north of Dodona and Ararat is the mystery centre of the Cabeiroi on the island of Samothrace.

Notes

1. *Star Names*, op. cit., p. 67.
2. Lockyer, Sir Norman, *The Dawn of Astronomy*, London, 1894. (Reprinted in the 1960s by MIT Press in U.S.A., introduction by Prof. de Santillana.)
3. *The Peoples of the Hills, Ancient Ararat and Caucasus*, London, 1971, p. 226.
4. Op. cit., p. 73.
5. Allen, *Star Names*, op. cit., p. 73.
6. See Note 2.
7. 7 March 1974.
8. A week later, on 14 March, a letter appeared in *The Times* from Brian Galpin claiming that his father, Canon F. W. Galpin, had previously established the certain antiquity of the heptatonic diatonic scale in his book *Music of the Sumerians, Babylonians, and Assyrians*, Cambridge University Press, 1937. A month after this, on 15 April 1974, a letter appeared in *The Times* from Dr Crocker and Dr Kilmer themselves, in California, which was long and not particularly clear. It seemed to be trying to acknowledge Professor Gurney of Oxford for some assistance and condemning Canon Galpin for reaching his conclusions on a different basis from themselves. Crocker and Kilmer obviously aimed at clearing up some misunderstandings, but only succeeded in muddying the waters (at least the letter befuddled me).
9. *The Greek Myths*, 21, 10.
10. Ibid., 170.3.
11. Higgins, Godfrey, *The Anacalypsis*, New York, 1927, Vol. I, Book III, Chapter 2, Section 4.
12. According to the Dogon: 'Sirius is the navel of the world.' See *Le Renard pâle*, pp. 324–5.
13. Op. cit.
14. Parke, H. W., *Greek Oracles*, Hutchinson (paperback), London, 1967, p. 38.
15. Ibid., p. 32.
16. Tarn, W. W., 'The Political Standing of Delos', *The Journal of Hellenic Studies*, London, Vol. XLIV, 1924, p. 143.
17. Diodorus Siculus, *The Library of History*, Book V, 58–9, translated by C. H. Oldfather, Loeb Classical Library, Harvard University Press, Vol. III, 1970, pp. 257–61.
18. Ibid., Book V, 70, pp. 285–7.
19. Ibid., Book V, 72, p. 293.
20. Parke, op cit., pp. 33–4.
21. Ibid., pp. 94–5.
22. Ibid., p. 94.
23. Harris, Rendel, 'Apollo at the Back of the North Wind', *The Journal of Hellenic Studies*, London, Vol. XLV, 1925, pp. 229–42.
24. Ibid., pp. 233–6.
25. I refer the reader who suffers from a desperate urge to purge his ignorance to that magnificent work by Sir Norman Lockyer, *The Dawn of Astronomy*. His book should be required reading in all schools, even though it becomes quite technical in places (which the non-technical reader is well advised to skim over quickly). This book was published in 1894 in London by Cassell, but at the instigation of Professor Santillana, has been brought out again by MIT Press in America in the 1960s (see Note 2).

    Of course another excellent, perhaps essential, book on the subject is Santillana and von Dechend's *Hamlet's Mill* (see ch. 4, n. 14). Though it is a long book, the authors admit it amounts only to a preliminary essay, and it is a good deal more confusing to read than it should be. In fact, the authors have frankly let their material overwhelm them; but they were coping with material on a far grander scale than Lockyer, and it was like trying to hold back a tidal wave. They have opened up an entirely new field for modern scholars and they may wear the badge of the pioneer and perhaps the pioneer's smile as well.
26. *Hamlet's Mill*, op. cit., p. 286.
27. Tompkins, Peter, *Secrets of the Great Pyramid*, Harper and Row, New York, London,

1971. Appendix by Livio Stecchini.

28. Parke, op. cit., p. 95.

29. Livio Stecchini mentions: '. . . a number of Greek accounts which associate Delphi with Sardis, the capital of the kingdom of Lydia in Asia Minor, which is on the same parallel (38° 28' north)', p. 349 (Stecchini's Appendix) in Tompkins, op. cit. I believe that the mountain associated with this geodetic centre is Mount Sipylus, north-east of Smyrna (now Izmir). See Pausanius III, xxii. 4 and p. 13 of Garstang, John, *The Syrian Goddess*, London, 1913. Mt. Sipylus boasts an extremely ancient gigantic carving from the living rock of the Great Goddess whose main centre came to be Hierapolis, another oracle centre in the series. The Great Goddess as Gaia (to the Greeks) was the original patroness of Delphi before the usurpation by Apollo. ('. . . the earth-goddess was the original female deity . . . in Late Mycenaean times . . . there may have been an oracle as part of the cult. . . . the arrival of Apollo as a god of divination was originally a hostile intrusion . . .' p. 36, Parke, op. cit.) I believe that Malatia (Malatya), further inland than Sardis on the same parallel, may be connected somehow with Delphi and Sardis as well (obviously more with Sardis than Delphi). For this, see Garstang, pp. 14–15.

30. See Notes 27 and 29.

31. See also Appendix V.

32. It is such a mesh to which the Dogon presumably refer when they speak of 'the basket which is not a basket'. See *A Sudanese Sirius System* by Griaule and Dieterlen (Appendix I).

33. Tompkins, op. cit., p. 182.

34. Ibid., p. 298.

35. Herodotus. *The Histories*, Penguin paperback, London, 1971, p. 124. (Textual reference: Book II, 54–9.)

36. Temple, Robert K. G., *Conversations with Eternity: Ancient Man's Attempts to Know the Future*, Rider, London, 1984.

37. Ibid., pp. 32–71.

38. Quincey, J. H., 'The Beacon-Sites in the *Agamemnon', The Journal of Hellenic Studies*, London, Vol. LXXXIII, 1963, pp. 118–32.

39. Hume, David, *The History of England*, Porter and Coates, Philadelphia, undated (nineteenth century), 5 vols. p. 57, Vol. V (end of Chapter 62). See also John Aubrey, *Brief Lives*, entry for William Harvey; Hume got much of this from Aubrey. (Hume is not always to be trusted; he does misrepresent General Monk's motives shamelessly despite Aubrey's explicit account. Perhaps the reader uninterested in seventeenth-century English history will forgive this aside.)

40. See Note 35. The famous oracle of Ammon in Libya, visited by Alexander the Great following his conquest of Egypt (if a fruit falling on one's head is a conquest), was at the Oasis of Siwa, where some ruins are still preserved. Also see maps in this book.

41. Tompkins, op. cit., p. 181.

42. Pritchard, op. cit., p. 44 ff. (Scholarly references, including Jacobsen, on p. 45.)

43. Kramer, S. N., *History Begins at Sumer* (originally entitled *From the Tablets of Sumer*, 1956, before revision), Doubleday Anchor Book (paperback), New York, 1959.

44. See Garstang, John, *The Sirian Goddess* translation by Professor Herbert A. Strong of the *De Dea Syria* of Lucian, ed. with notes and introduction by Garstang, London, 1913.

45. See Note 43.

46. Tompkins, op. cit., p. 336.

47. Ibid., p. 349.

48. Ibid., p. 346.

49. See Note 27.

50. Op. cit.

51. Graves, Robert, *The White Goddess, A Historical Grammar of Poetic Myth*, Vintage paperback, New York, undated (originally copyright 1948 by Graves).

52. Ibid. See pages listed under *acacia* in index. (I leave this to the reader because my edition of this book is undated and will probably not match the reader's in pagination.)

53. Theophrastus, *Enquiry into Plants*, Book IV, ii, 8., trans. by A. F. Hort, Loeb Classical Library, William Heinemann Ltd., London, and Harvard University Press, U.S.A., 2 vols. (This ref. vol.1, p. 299). Theophrastus was the 'father of botany', and succeeded his friend Aristotle as Head of the Peripatetic School at the Lyceum in Athens. He lived 370–*c*. 285 BC, and at the peak of his teaching career actually had 2,000 students.
54. Ibid., Book III, xiii, 7 (Vol. I, p. 249).

SUMMARY

The other Arabian star named 'Weight' was in the constellation Argo. But we see the *Argo* was associated with Sirius, as was the first star named 'Weight' which was in the Great Dog constellation and a visible companion of Sirius.

If an *Argo* is projected on the globe with its helm near the ancient Egyptian city Canopus on the coast of the Mediterranean (the star Canopus forms the helm of the *Argo* in the sky) and with its prow at Dodona (from where the oak came which was placed in the *Argo*'s prow), if we hold the stern firmly on Canopus but swing the ship eastwards at the top, so that the prow points towards Mount Ararat, where Noah's ark was supposed to have landed, we find that the arc thus described is a right-angle of 90°.

Instead of Canopus we must really use the neighbouring site of the now entirely vanished city of Behdet, which was the capital of pre-dynastic Egypt prior to the foundation of Memphis.

Dodona is exactly 8° of latitude north of Behdet. Delphi is exactly 7° north of Behdet. Delos (another important early oracle centre, vanished by classical Greek times) is exactly 6° north of Behdet. Behdet was the Greenwich of the ancient world prior to 3200 BC and was used as a geodetic headquarters.

Associated with near-by Mount Ararat as a mystery-centre was the now little-known site of Metsamor. Mt Ararat is 8° north of Behdet and on the same parallel as Dodona.

A site on Kythera is known to have connections with early dynastic Egypt as a religious centre and is about 5° north of Behdet. The island of Thera may, however, have been an oracle centre. It was destroyed by a famous volcanic eruption in Minoan times.

All these sites were revealed as a pattern now termed a 'geodetic octave' by the projection on the globe of the *Argo*, which is connected with Sirius. Sirius was not only the element of the most sacred traditions of the Dogon and the ancient Egyptians, but apparently of the entire civilized and cosmopolitan Mediterranean world prior at least to 3000 BC and probably well before 3200 BC.

The amphibious creature Oannes, who brought civilization to the Sumerians, is sometimes equated with the god Enki (Ea) who ruled the star Canopus of the *Argo*. Enki is a god who sleeps at the bottom of a watery abyss, reminiscent of Oannes who retired to the sea at night. Enki is also the god responsible for the ark in those early tales of the Sumerians and Babylonians from which the Biblical ark and deluge story was derived.

The 'Greek ark' was claimed to have landed at both Dodona and Delphi. An 'ark' was carried in procession at Delphi.

At Delphi and at Delos are surviving omphalos ('navel') stones. Omphalos near Knossos in Crete is 4° north of Behdet. We know from the Homeric *Hymn to Apollo* that Minoans (before 1200 BC) 'from Knossos took Apollo to Delphi'.

The Egyptian Pharaoh Akhenaten's reform was really at least partially a geodetic one, explaining the move of his capital city. He may have wished to return to the 'pure' system of pre-dynastic times.

Herodotus tells us that Dodona (according to its priestesses, whom he knew) was founded from Egypt – specifically Egyptian Thebes. Thebes is equidistant from both Dodona, where the Greek ark landed, and Mount Ararat, where the Hebrew ark landed. The three points, when joined, form an equilateral triangle on the globe. Also according to Herodotus, the Oasis of Siwa, with its oracle of Ammon, was founded from Thebes. This oasis centre and Thebes are both equidistant from Behdet. Geodetic surveys of immense accuracy were thus practised in ancient Egypt with a knowledge of the Earth as a spherical body in space and projections upon it envisaged as part of the institutions embodying Sirius lore for posterity.

SUPPLEMENT (1997)

There is no aspect of the Sirius Mystery which I have a greater interest in researching further than the geodetic aspect, including the Oracle Octaves. I did push this subject forward some more by writing a section on oracle centres in my book *Conversations with Eternity*, which appeared in 1984.[1] A few further aspects concerning it were addressed also in the notes to my translation of the Epic of Gilgamesh.[2] But most of my further work has not been published and is incomplete, owing to the lack of funding for expeditions to farflung places. For instance, I now believe that I know the true original location of the first Oracle of Dodona, which is some distance further up the mountain than the classical site (just as the original site of Delphi is two miles higher up than the place visited by tourists). But to inspect it would require more than just a casual visit, and should involve at least a small team.

In 1979, my friend Randy Fitzgerald and I set up an American foundation to solicit funds for, among other things, a proper investigation of ancient geodetics. But we were not successful and the foundation closed down. At that time some highly qualified experts were prepared to help us, but we could not even cover their expenses. From time to time eccentric multi-millionaires have wasted my time toying with the notion of paying for some Sirius Mystery research, but they have always turned out to be hopeless characters. Most of them have been egomaniacs. One in particular wasn't, but he was as useless in the end as the rest. There is something about very rich people that makes them a complete waste of time, like over-endowed birds of paradise who show their colourful feathers only in some remote forest where only the monkeys can see them. And the strangest thing of all is that every time I have ever had any dealings with a very rich person, I have always ended up poorer. They have some way of sucking money out of your pocket by a vacuum mechanism, and the money never gets replaced. They start by offering some advantages, perhaps a free fare to see them, or something of that kind. But this always turns into the need to spend money on them, instead of the other way around.

So, I'm afraid that most of my further work on these matters remains in an incomplete state owing to the inability to carry out the appropriate investigations. You simply cannot study geodetics without making extensive travels, and these need to be with the right people, such as a surveyor for instance. It would be pointless to apply to a foundation for support, because all such bodies would throw their hands up in horror like outraged virgins about to be raped, owing to the connection with that unrespectable subject, extraterrestrials, the very mention of which is meant to condemn all scholarly work as absurd and the author to be branded insane. (Several of my stuffier friends dropped me completely after the publication of *The Sirius Mystery* because discussions of extraterrestrial life are not socially acceptable and I was clearly a dangerous madman.)

There is one crucial addition to this subject which I propose to make here, however, although to investigate it fully the amount of necessary travelling would instantly double that needed to get to grips with these issues. It concerns China, and by considering it we can really 'get a handle on' the Mediterranean Oracle Octaves.

When I wrote *The Sirius Mystery* I had not yet commenced my long and fascinating association with Joseph Needham, and hence I was entirely unaware of what I am about to discuss. Indeed, only a tiny handful of people in the West – or even in China, for that matter – will ever have heard of the subject I am about to raise.

About 1982, I first met Joseph Needham of Cambridge, although I had first read some of his writings in 1963 and knew very well who he was from that time. He has died now, but he was perhaps the greatest scholar in any field since Edward Gibbon, author of *The Decline and Fall of the Roman Empire*. Joseph's mammoth work *Science and Civilisation in China* has reached nearly twenty volumes by now, and unpublished portions are still being readied for publication by a huge team of collaborators. My association with Joseph was rather different from those of the official 'collaborators'. They tended to be academics, often in remote universities in a variety of countries, and fulltime Sinologists. I had a more free-wheeling relationship with Joseph and his Chinese collaborator Lu Gwei-Djen, who was eventually to become his second wife. In fact, I had a closer friendship with Gwei-Djen than I did with Joseph, because Joseph was a more distant type of person, whereas Gwei-Djen and I shared a mischievous sense of fun and were always laughing together. She was truly wonderful. We had such fun when we all travelled to China together in 1986. She died before Joseph did, having lived for two decades with only half of one lung, so that she was always short of breath in a wheezing sort of way, and her laughter as a result was always semi-breathless.

She loved to tease people whom she thought were being stupid or self-important, and this made my life more difficult because she often teased and taunted some of her more pompous colleagues about not being able to keep up with Robert Temple, which of course made them hate me. Worst of all was the late Colin Ronan, who as he was in charge of all the photos and illustrations stored at the Needham Research Institute, spitefully refused me access to them when I was compiling an illustrated book with Joseph! And when my own photos were published by Joseph, Colin would erase my photo credit. That is how petty and pathetic he was. Fortunately, I had the help of the young librarian at that time, Carmen Lee, who sneaked the photos and illustrations to me after Colin had gone home in the evenings, and immensely enjoyed scheming to get round his roadblocks to my work. Gwei-Djen's reaction to all this was simply to taunt and abuse Ronan all the more, having contempt for how low he could stoop at pettiness, thus increasing his determination to thwart me at all costs. Sometimes one's friends really know how to make things worse for one! Even though it was all so unpleasant, it had the advantage of being hilariously funny as well, because Ronan's efforts to block my work were really a kind of Marx Brothers farce. Rather like watching a beetle rolling a dung ball uphill, I never ceased to be amazed at the phenomenal energy that Ronan put into his entirely negative project – which consumed a large proportion of his waking hours. It is truly amazing how people can become obsessed with enmity to the exclusion of productive work.

Even when I am the victim of these campaigns, which I have so often been, I still cannot help laughing at the ridiculousness of the people engaged in such a waste of their time. However, it has taught me that there is a widespread perversity in human nature whereby it is not uncommon for someone to dedicate himself not to constructive activity, but only to destructive activity. For those of us who are builders rather than destroyers, this demented mentality will always remain incomprehensible, but we ignore it at our peril. The root of the problem is personal vanity: if *I* can't do it, nobody else will! Or: I may be inferior, but I'll see to it that I level anything higher, so that I am not shown up so badly. *Vanity*, pure *vanity* is at the basis of much that is wrong with the world. And those of us who can laugh are the ones who have managed to free ourselves to greater or lesser extent from this suffocating human failure. Gwei-Djen, for instance, was as lacking in vanity as a mountain spring is lacking in sea salt. And the same was true of Joseph, whose laughter may have been quieter, but he would rock with it like a giant toppling boulder about to fall down the hillside, and one sometimes feared for his chair. Gwei-Djen would dig him in the ribs with her fingers and provoke him to even greater mirth, and his face would crack like a chestnut: 'Isn't it, Joseph? Isn't it?' He would turn his eyes fondly on her and agree that indeed it was, indeed it was, beaming with love and laughter as she mocked the follies of the people they knew mercilessly and he, who would not normally have taken the time out from his work to do so, vicariously enjoyed this mischievous digression. But enough of Joseph and Gwei-Djen. I just wanted to paint the picture of what it was I was doing.

My task was to write the popular book about the history of Chinese inventions and discoveries which Joseph had announced as early as 1946 he intended to write, but which he never had time to do. Gwei-Djen was the greatest advocate of getting me to do this, pointing out to Joseph, who accepted it, that he was well up in his eighties and simply would never do it himself. And thus it was that I set about reading everything Joseph had ever written (except for his earlier work in embryology), including his unpublished manuscript material. I know I must have read at least eight and a half million words of Joseph's. There was no time to take notes, so I just remembered it all, which was so much simpler. But it meant I had to remember 'tracking data' as well, since I had to be able to open to the right page of the right volume to piece together the fragments for every subject that came up, as Joseph's organizational principle was wholly incompatible with mine. (It was like going between two different computer languages, I suppose.) The result was my book, originally entitled in Britain *China: Land of Discovery and Invention* and in America *The Genius of China*. The book was later reissued in Britain under the title *The Genius of China*.[3]

In the course of going through all Joseph's material, I came across one of Joseph's most obscure articles, published in 1964. Entitled 'An 8th-Century Meridian Line: I-Hsing's Chain of Gnomons and the Pre-History of the Metric System', it was written jointly with Gwei-Djen, another Sinologist, and three astronomers.[4] I had some discussion with Joseph about this amazing subject and he agreed that if we (but by then 'we' could not include him, as he was too old for such travel) could visit the sites and do a proper study on the ground of the geodetic phenomena, it would be an incredible project which would yield a great deal of fascinating findings. Joseph had wanted to do this since the 1960s but never had the opportunity, because of course the ten years' madness of the Cultural Revolution got in the way at that time, and travel in the Chinese countryside was absolutely impossible even for him, despite being a friend of Chou En-Lai. After Joseph discovered the Meridian Line it was to be nearly twenty years before a geographical investigation of it could be even remotely possible, and by that time Joseph was getting too old for such an exhausting project.

The great eighth-century mathematician and astronomer I-Hsing is one of my and Joseph's favourites in the history of Chinese science. But I shall transform the spelling of his name into the modern Pinyin system, and call him Yixing here. (In my book on Chinese science I preserved the old spellings of the Wade-Giles system, because they match Joseph's own volumes and most scholarly publications.) In quoting from the article by Joseph, Gwei-Djen, and their co-authors, I shall change all Chinese names into Pinyin below. I shall also alter Joseph's quirky use of dates, since he refused to use AD and BC but insisted upon plus and minus signs instead, which only serves to confuse people!

Here, then, are some excerpts from the article, and practically all the explanatory remarks made about the purposes and uses of the system could apply equally well to the Mediterranean Oracle Octaves:

The fundamental significance of the introduction of the metric system lies in the fact that it was the first great attempt to define terrestrial units in terms of an unvarying cosmical quantity. . . . this system took its origin in the need imposed by the development of scientific thought for immutable and at the same time conveniently related units of physical measure. And they imply that this need was not satisfied until the last decade of the eighteenth century AD. This may be true enough for Europe but . . . an approach was made to such an immutable unit in China in the first decade of that century. Moreover, as in the case of many post-Renaissance developments, there were earlier historical aspects of this celestial-terrestrial bond; indeed, we can find already in the eighth century AD in China a large-scale attempt to establish it.

A great step forward was taken when the idea arose of fixing terrestrial length-measures in terms of astronomical units. That this could have occurred to the scholars at all was due to the fact that the Sun's shadow thrown by an 8-foot gnomon at Summer Solstice had a very convenient length (about 1.5 feet) at the latitude of Yang-cheng, the 'centre of the Central Land'. [The Chinese name for China means 'Central Kingdom'.] From ancient times use had been made of the 'gnomon shadow template' (*tu gui*), a standard rule made of pottery, terracotta, or jade, equivalent in length to the solstitial shadow. This was used to the determination of the exact date of the solstice each year.

It was a long-standing idea that the shadow-length increased one inch for every thousand *li* [a *li* was a common measure of distance in China, like the mile or kilometre to us, but unfortunately it varied at different times in Chinese history, which causes historians of science lots of headaches] to the North of the 'Earth's centre' at Yang-cheng, and decreased in the same proportion as one went to the South. After the end of the Han period (third century AD), measurements made as far south as Indo-China soon disproved this numerically, but it was not until the Tang Dynasty (eighth century AD) that a systematic effort was made to cover a great range of latitudes.

This effort aimed at correlating the lengths of terrestrial and celestial measures by finding the number of *li* which corresponded to 1° change in the altitude of the Pole Star (giving the geographic latitude of the observer's position) and thus, in effect, fixing the length of the *li* precisely in terms of the Earth's circumference. The meridian line set up for this purpose takes its place in history between the meridian line of Eratosthenes (*circa* 200 BC) and those of the astronomers of the Caliph al-Ma'mun (*circa* 827 AD). Its detailed examination is the subject of this paper.[5]

Here we can already sense the importance of the Chinese project, and its relation to our earlier Oracle Octaves, of which by the way Joseph knew nothing whatever. For anyone encountering the Oracle Octaves must immediately wonder: '*Why?*' – Why go to all those distant mountains tops and remote regions, why mark out such a lengthy series of latitude lines, why go to such incredible trouble – what was it all for?

When we look at the matter from the point of view given by Joseph about the Chinese project of the eighth century, we suddenly realize that perhaps the determination of the number of 'miles' (or whatever land measure you like) in a degree of latitude, an exact measure of the Earth's circumference, and a precise correlation of 'the lengths of terrestrial and celestial measures', to use Joseph's words, was considered worth it. But there was a great deal more involved, as we shall see:

When Liu Chuo, in the early part of the seventh century AD, realized the fallacy of the statement that a change by 1 inch in the length of the Sun's shadow corresponded to a change of 1,000 *li* in distance, he wrote to the Emperor as follows:

'We beg Your Majesty to appoint water-mechanics and mathematicians to select a piece of flat country in Henan or Hebei, which can be measured over a few hundred *li* to choose a true North-South line, to determine the time with water-clocks, to [set up gnomonsl on flat places [adjusting them with] plumb-lines, to follow seasons, solstices and equinoxes; and to measure the shadow of the Sun [at different places] on the same day. From the differences in these shadow-lengths the distance in *li* can be known. Thus the Heavens and the Earth will not be able to conceal their form and the celestial bodies will not prevent us from knowing their measurements.'

His advice was not adopted by the Sui Emperor.[6]

Although this was the first suggestion of a national network of which a textual record fully survives, the issue goes back many centuries earlier in China. Needham and Lu translated a relevant section from the *Record of Institutions of the Zhou Dynasty* (*Zhou Li*) which was compiled no later than the second century BC, but contains material from the Zhou period several centuries earlier than that. It speaks of:

> . . . the method of the gnomon shadow template to measure 'the depth of the Earth' and to establish correctly the sun-shadows in order to find the centre of the Earth. . . . The place where the shadow at [Summer] Solstice is 1 ft. 5 in. is called the centre of the Earth. This is where Heaven and Earth unite, where the four seasons intermingle, wind and rain join together, where the Yin and the Yang combine. Then all things prosper and the royal territory may be established there.[7]

By the second century AD, Zheng Xüan stated that the Sun shadow differed by one [Chinese] inch for every 1,000 *li* on the Earth's surface [going north or south]. 'From the place where the shadow is 1 ft. 5 in. it would be [he thought] 15,000 *li* to the South to the place directly below the Sun [i.e., at the Equator]. The Earth makes its four excursions and the stars rise and fall within a range of 30,000 *li* so by taking the half of this one gets the centre of the Earth.'[8]

We are now beginning to see what was needed: samples of solar shadow lengths taken over a huge stretch of territory to the north and to the south, along a series of ascending and descending latitude lines. This is precisely what must have been involved with the Oracle Octaves. The oracle centres of the Mediterranean were also places 'where Heaven and Earth unite', as the second-century BC Chinese document so beautifully expressed it. The Mediterranean region's 'navels of the Earth' were intended precisely as that.

When the French excavators excavated the older of the Delphic omphalos stones, they found the name Gaia ('Earth') written on it together with the symbol 'E' (see Appendix V). But they also discovered that this ancient omphalos stone had a hole in the top as if a thin metal post had protruded from it at one time. I would suggest that it either represented or actually functioned as a gnomon, which is a thin upright to cast a shadow to be measured. (This is the origin of the Egyptian obelisks – gnomons to cast measurable shadows.) This is all a bit like very sophisticated sun-dials, but instead of measuring the time of day, far greater considerations were at stake, such as the circumference of the Earth.

How far did the Chinese take this, then? The full system was finally organised between the years 721 and 725 AD under what was by then the Tang Dynasty. As Needham and Lu and their colleagues say:

> . . . the required expeditions were organised under the direction of the

Astronomer-Royal, Nangong Yüeh, and a Buddhist monk, Yixing, one of the most outstanding mathematicians and astronomers of his age. Our sources of information about them are quite extensive. . . . The sources tell us that at least eleven stations were established where simultaneous measurements of shadow lengths were made, using identical 8-foot gnomons. The latitude of these stations ranged from 17.4° (at Lin-Yi [near Hue in present-day Vietnam] . . .) up to 40° (at Wei-zhou, an old city near modern Ling-chiu, near the Great Wall in northern Shanxi, and almost at the same latitude as Peking). And there was even another place still farther North, the country of Tieh-lo (Tölös) horde of Turkic nomads near Lake Baikal . . . Yang-cheng was a place which had been for centuries the seat of the central imperial observatory of China. Although it did not belong to the measured central chain of stations, it is the only place where one of the original gnomons of Yixing and Nangong Yüeh is still preserved . . . On the South side this bears an inscription terming it 'Zhou Gong's Tower for the Measurement of Sun Shadows', and it is known to have been erected . . . in 723 AD. The construction is such that at the Summer Solstice of that time the shadow just extended to the top of the pyramidal base, the slope of the North side of which corresponded exactly with the edge of the shadow. In later times, Guo Shou-Jing, Astronomer-Royal of the Yuan [Mongol] Dynasty, made shadow measurements at Yang-cheng with a gnomon of forty feet in height and a measuring-scale of some 120 feet. This was about 1270 AD, and there still remains intact at the place the massive tower and scale constructed in Ming times following his methods.[9]

Here are some more portions of the Tang Dynasty (eighth-century) text:

. . . if one went South from Yang-cheng along a road as straight as a bowstring to the point directly below the Sun [the Equator] it would not be as much as 5,000 *li*. The Commissioners for Shadow Measurements, Daxiang and Yuan-Tai, say that at Jiao-zhou if one observes the pole it is elevated above the Earth's surface only a little more than 20°. Looking South in the eighth month from out at sea Canopus is remarkably high in the sky. The stars in the heavens below it are very brilliant and there are many large and bright ones which are not recorded on the charts and the names of which are not known. . . . [on the other hand] there are the Guligan people who live to the North of the Uighurs, dwelling North of Han-hai [Lake Baikal] where grass is plentiful and there are many herbs, and where fine horses are produced capable of going several hundred *li* [in a day]. To the North of that there is still some distance to the Great Sea [the Arctic]. The days are long and the nights are short. After the Sun has set the sky is still half lit and if you cook a sheep the outside is hardly done before the dawn begins to appear in the East. . . . In the 13th year of Kaiyuan reign-period [725 AD] Nangong Yüeh the Astronomer-Royal selected a region of level ground in Henan and using water-levels and plumb-lines set up 8-foot gnomons with which he made measurements. Beginning at Baima Xien in Hua-zhou he found the Summer Solstice shadow to be 1 foot 5.7 inches. Proceeding South from the observation station at Hua-zhou 198 *li* 179 *bu* [a fraction of a *li*] they reached the old observation station at Jün-Yi Bien-zhou with its gnomon: there the Summer Solstice shadow was found to be 1 foot 5.312 inches. Again, going South from Jün-Yi for 167 *li* 281 *bu* they reached the gnomon at Fukou Xien in Xü-zhou, which gave a length of 1 foot 4.4 inches at the Summer Solstice. Then 160 *li* 110 *bu* South of Fukou there was another gnomon at Wujin near Shangtai in the district of Yüzhou, which gave a shadow of 1 foot 3.65 inches at Summer Solstice. In all, therefore, in a distance of 526 *li* 270 *bu*, the difference in shadow length was a little more than 2 inches. This completely disagreed with the opinion of the ancient scholars that for a distance of 1,000 *li* in the royal territory there would be a variation of 1 inch in the shadow's length.'

The passage goes on and on like this at enormous length and then concludes:

Thus the differences in the Sun Shadows vary as between the Winter and Summer Solstices and also as between northern and southern latitudes. But the ancient scholars equalized the differences everywhere with a fixed value in terms of *li*, and so failed to give a true account. Accordingly the monk Yixing prepared the 'Da Yen' diagram and also the 'inverted square diagram' covering the range from the furthest South to the furthest North. He also made twenty-four diagrams in order to investigate the computations of the eclipses of the Sun, and to establish the lengths of the indicator-rods of the night clepsydra [water-clock]. Here we record the shadow lengths in feet and inches of all the observation centres. ... [skipping all of this] ... On the basis of the northern and southern Sun shadows, Yixing made comparisons and estimates. He used the 'right-angle triangle' method to calculate them. Roughly speaking, the distance between the North and South poles was found to be scarcely more than 800,000 *li*.[10]

That is enough about the details of the visits to the stations, the measurements, etc. I gave that much in order for the reader to get a feel for the kind of mentality at work with early scientists visiting a long string of measuring-stations. These expeditions of working-parties of scientists are similar to what can be imagined visiting the Mediterranean centres. But let us see some of Needham and Lu's conclusions:

The accuracy achieved is uncanny. It can easily be seen that the computed shadow lengths which are quoted to 3 significant figures are indeed accurate . . . to 0.1 inch or nearly 1 part in a thousand. . . . To enable divisions of this smallness, i.e. of about 2 minutes of arc, to be read off with any certainty they would have to be separated by, say, 1 cm. This magnification would have required a circle of radius exceeding 17 metres, or a room at least the size of a large palace hall. . . . While the length of the central series of stations was some 150–215 kilometres, that of the whole series was as much as 2,500 kilometres, and if the most northerly place is included, a line of no less than 3,800 kilometres was considered. This work must therefore surely be regarded as the most remarkable piece of organised field research carried out anywhere in the early Middle Ages. Even if the ground distances of the furthest stations were not measured, there can be no doubt that observations of Sun shadow lengths were systematically made at them.[11]

We now begin to see what a gigantic enterprise this was, and that it rivalled in extent the Oracle Octaves of the Mediterranean. 3,800 kilometres is a huge distance over which to string a series of observational stations at successive latitudes. This amazing eighth-century project therefore serves as a significant example to us of what the construction and use of the Oracle Octaves must have been like. Imagine all the Chinese records of the project which we have just described being lost – there is just the Yangcheng gnomon and a few scraps of evidence at other sites of the observation stations (whereas in fact we know that there is none). All the texts have been destroyed. How would we ever have known about this incredible project strung out over 3,800 kilometres? And if someone had come along like myself and claimed that there had been such a project, no one would have believed him. Because it seems too incredible to be true. And yet we know that it is because we have the texts to prove it, even though they only came to light as recently as 1964. This is similar to the situation with the Oracle Octaves. I have gathered huge amounts of circumstantial evidence, so massive that it is enough to convict for murder. But we do not possess the official reports such as the Chinese ones which survive. However, this Chinese example gives us heart. It shows us that such huge projects were indeed mounted by early empires, and what the motivations were. I omit here all the further details such as the availability or otherwise of trigonometric tables, of the use of 'shadow-catcher' devices to refine the edges of blurred Sun-shadows because the Sun is not a point-source of light but a disc (which in any case I shall explain in my next book, which touches on such matters), and so forth. There is no need here for any further detail.

Needham and Lu also came to the edge of their available evidence: 'Did Yixing attempt to derive from his measurements a value for the circumference of a spherical Earth? It is impossible to say. . . . Although no record remains in the texts that Yixing made any calculations to obtain from his data the dimensions of a spherical Earth, certain Chinese cosmological schools had from antiquity onwards assumed its sphericity. This would have been very well known to him ... Moreover, his acquaintance with Indian and Hellenistic astronomy, gained as an outstanding Buddhist scholar, may well have informed him of the previous estimates of the Earth's circumference. There is thus no reason why Yixing should have hesitated to use in this way the data which his observers collected. Besides, it is hard to see how he could have given a constant *li* per degree, if he had not had at least some previous notion of a curved Earth's surface.'[12]

And thus we leave China. At the time I originally wrote *The Sirius Mystery*, I had no idea whatever of the Yixing project in eighth-century China. And another major source of information was also unavailable then – the English translation of Claudius Ptolemy's *Geography* (written in the first century AD). The only translation had been published in New York in 1932, but in an edition limited to 250 copies. However, in 1991 Dover Publications brought out a magnificent large-format paperback of it at a very modest price, so that now it is available to everyone.[13] It is a strange and unsatisfactory book. Ptolemy was a querulous, whingeing sort of character. He starts out hypocritically paying lip service to the achievements of his predecessor Marinus, but soon commences tearing him to shreds and scoring points off him. Most of the actual text of the book is devoted to this sustained attack on Marinus, who was guilty of every fault, and the posturing of Ptolemy who wishes us to believe he is the first sensible geographer who has ever lived. The rest of the book is largely just page after page of data. It seems that Ptolemy was indeed more scientific and rigorous than Marinus in many ways, and did bring about some scientific improvements. On the other hand, I thought that there were some occasions when Marinus was right and Ptolemy was clearly wrong. But since we do not possess Marinus's work, we can never carry out a true comparison.

There are several points in Ptolemy's work which are very interesting from the point of view of the Oracle Octaves. I have suggested that the latitude line of Rhodes, which cut through the destroyed Minoan island of Thera, was an oracle centre line. I couldn't help but note that Ptolemy many times speaks of the latitude of Rhodes. He leaves us in absolutely no doubt that this parallel was one of the fundamental parallels in ancient geography. For instance, in Book I, he mentions the parallel many times and says:

The parallel passing through Rhodes must be inserted because on this parallel many proofs of distances have been registered and inserted in right relation to the circumference of the greatest circle, following in this Marinus who followed Epitecartus. By thus doing we shall insure that the longitude of our earth, which is the better known, will be in right proportion to the latitude. We will now show how this may be done, treating first, as far as is necessary, of the properties of a sphere.[14]

And on another occasion:

Only the parallel through Rhodes has [Marinus] kept in right proportion to its meridian and the circumference of the equatorial circle.[15]

Many of Ptolemy's latitudes and longitudes are numerically incorrect, as might be expected. But the fact that we see 'the parallel of Rhodes' used centrally in this way, with at least two named predecessors who laid emphasis upon it, gives some comfort to us in believing that the Oracle Octave scheme was indeed meant to be used as a system of latitudinal reference for just such purposes. The kind of uses referred to by Ptolemy are similar to the preoccupations of Yixing.

The amount of data marshalled for Ptolemy's book is absolutely gigantic, and is obviously drawn from centuries of reports by travellers – hundreds of them. There must have been, for a very long time before Ptolemy, vast repositories of (often conflicting) geographical data. He seems to have shovelled it into his book by the spadeful with very little commentary. It is not the exactness of the data nor even its organization which is of particular interest, but its sheer bulk. Ptolemy was clearly drawing upon information in a raw form and many other attempts to organise it by a long series of predecessors. He also had to hand a huge quantity of maps, portalans (coastal port maps from sea captains), and cartographic aids. But what strikes me is that this vast mass of data, which had been garnered over so long a time, was preserved without any accompanying or informing structure. It is as if one had come upon a huge pile of lamb chops and from them tried to imagine what a lamb might have looked like.

I believe that the huge body of data indicates a long and continuing accumulation of geographical information which had gone adrift and lost its anchorage. In a much, much earlier time, this type of information had been harnessed to a system of surpassing ingenuity; brilliant schemes such as the Oracle Octaves had given shape to every particular. But that system had been lost entirely. From the flotsam and jetsam that survived, combined with the late reports of travellers (including much which resulted from Alexander's conquest of the known world, of course), latecomers such as Marinus and Ptolemy struggled to construct something using only their geometrical notions and such ingenuity as they could muster. But it is clear that by their time, the tradition was gone, and they were wading knee-deep in place names, whilst upon the waves floated

213

latitude and longitude numbers – bobbing like corks. They tried with greater or lesser success to estimate distances from numbers-of-days travelled, and so forth (Ptolemy was always subtracting from these, very sensibly, stressing that crossing deserts was not easy, etc.), but they were not operating within a grand scheme anymore. They were improvising. They were actors without a script, possessing only a few throwaway lines and plenty of costumes. It pays to read Ptolemy if only to see what a fellow could do with masses of data and no organising principles other than a few geometrical insights and a heady dose of scepticism. Not bad. But not particularly good either.

I offer these further reflections in the hope that they will be helpful. If fortune wills, time will bring more upon its returning tide.

Notes

1. Temple, Robert K. G., *Conversations with Eternity*, Rider, London, 1984. This book was only published in English in the British Commonwealth and in Polish; part of it was published in German. No American edition ever appeared, and very rude things were said to me about the supposed incapacity of the American public to take an interest in or have the intelligence to understand such matters, with which I could never agree. But in the 1980s it is perhaps true that people everywhere were obsessed with economics and the struggle to survive in the face of a very serious worldwide economic depression. That decade also coincided with the final collapse of the traditional Western value system.
2. Temple, Robert K. G., *He Who Saw Everything: A Verse Translation of the Epic of Gilgamesh*, Rider, London, 1991. This book was never published outside the British Commonwealth.
3. Published in 1986 in English, and in a large number of foreign languages subsequently. A wonderful Chinese edition was prepared by the Chinese Academy of Sciences using a team of thirty-four specialist translators.
4. Beer, A., Ho Ping-yü, Lu Gwei-Djen, Needham, J., Pulleyblank, E. G., and Thompson, G. I., 'An 8th-Century Meridian Line: I-Hsing's Chain of Gnomons and the Pre-history of the Metric System', *Vistas in Astronomy*, Pergamon Press, Oxford etc., Vol. 4, 1964, pp. 3–28.
5. Ibid., pp. 3–4.
6. Ibid., p. 4.
7. Ibid., p. 9.
8. Ibid.
9. Ibid., pp. 8–9.
10. Ibid., pp. 10–13.
11. Ibid., pp. 18–19 and 14.
12. Ibid., p. 25.
13. Ptolemy, Claudius, *The Geography*, translated and edited by Edward Luther Stevenson, Dover, New York, 1991.
14. Ibid., p. 40.
15. Ibid., p. 39.

Chapter Seven

Origins of the Dogon

We shall now return to Hercules and the number fifty. A connection between them arises in Pausanius, Book IX (27, 5), when Pausanius is discussing a city in Boeotia, which is the region where Orchomenos is. The city is called Thespiai 'below Mount Helikon', as he says. He continues:

> They have a sanctuary of Herakles [Hercules] where a virgin priestess serves until she dies. They say this is because Herakles slept with all the fifty daughters of Thestios in the same night, except for one. She alone refused to mate with him. Thinking she was insulting him he sentenced her to be his virgin priestess all her life. I have also heard another legend about it: that Herakles went through all Thestios's* virgin daughters on the same night and they all bore him male children, but the youngest and the eldest bore him twins. But I am quite unable to believe that other story, that Herakles could behave so arrogantly to the daughter of a friend. Besides, even when he was on earth he used to punish arrogant outrages, particularly if they were against religion: so he would hardly have founded his own temple and set it up with a priestess like a god. But in fact this sanctuary seemed to me older than the days of Herakles son of Amphitryon, and to belong to the Idaian Daktylos called Herakles, whose sanctuaries I also discovered at Erythrai in Ionia and at Tyre. Actually even the Boiotians† knew the name, since they say themselves that the sanctuary of Mykalessian Demeter has Idaian Herakles as patron.

Levi adds in a footnote that the sanctuary at Tyre is mentioned by Herodotus (2, 45), and gives other references as well.[1]

To return to the amorous labour of Hercules: I hope it will be noted that Pausanius had here elucidated a Middle-Eastern connection for this tale with the important city of Tyre, the site of which is off the coast of present-day Lebanon. Here, at least, we have a bit of evidence from ancient times bearing direct witness to the connections between these endless curious traditions in Greece about the fifty and their Middle-Eastern counterparts, or at least Middle-Eastern locale.

* A mythical figure.
† Boeotians.

It would now be worth while for us to see what Robert Graves has to say about this tale. Graves calls Thestios by the name of Thespius and spends some time pondering the meaning.[2] He says it means 'divinely sounding', but wishes he could find another meaning. I am inclined to be happy with 'divinely sounding', because of what I believe to be the heavy emphasis on music, sound and harmony among the ancients. The Greeks were reputed, for instance, to have considered music the highest art; and the Pythagoreans made harmony and number into an actual religion. We have already come across the use of the octave as a relevant theme in our considerations and we have seen the possible connection of *omphalos* and *om* – the latter being the Indo-Aryan sacred syllable chanted for its 'divinely sounding' qualities and surviving in Christianity and Islam as 'Amen'. Since if we were to look for a Greek word to describe the sacred syllable *om* we could choose the appropriate name meaning 'divinely sounding', it seems that this meaning is by no means unsatisfactory.

Graves tells us the following:[3]

King Thespius had fifty daughters by his wife Megamede [mega-*Medea*?] daughter of Arneus, as gay as any in Thespiae. Fearing that they might make unsuitable matches, he determined that every one of them should have a child by Heracles* [Hercules], who was now engaged all day in hunting the lion; for Heracles lodged at Thespiae for fifty nights running. [Notice fifty applied here as a succession of *days*: days, months, years. They can become blurred as long as *fifty* remains.] 'You may have my eldest daughter Procris as your bedfellow,' Thespius told him hospitably. But each night another of his daughters visited Heracles, until he had lain with every one. Some say, however, that he enjoyed them all in a single night.

It is interesting to note that the name Procris of the eldest daughter means 'chosen first'. *Prokrossoi*, which is a closely related form of the same stem means, 'ranged at regular intervals like steps'. Now, what could be a more obvious name for the eldest daughter than one with such overtones and signification if it were clearly intended, as it obviously was, to emphasize that the daughters were not meant to be thought of as individuals but as successive expressions of fifty successive periods of time – in this case, twenty-four-hour periods, or days? But the intention obviously was to highlight the sequence of fifty time periods, personified as 'daughters' enjoyed by our ubiquitous Hercules who is connected in so many ways with the Sirius complex.

Graves adds:[4] 'Thespius's fifty daughters – like the fifty Danaids, Pallantids, and Nereids, or the fifty maidens with whom the Celtic god Bran (Phoroneus) lay in a single night – must have been a college of

---

* Some authors and translators have used Herakles, others Heracles.

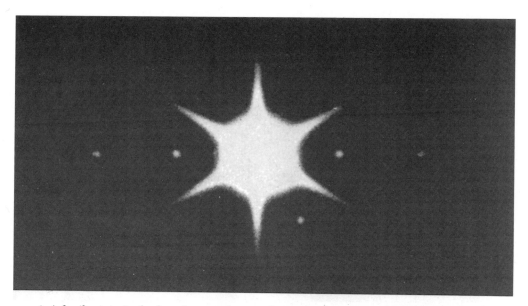

1. A family portrait: the first photograph ever taken (1970) of Sirius B, which is the tiny dot to the lower right of the large star, Sirius (small multiple images of Sirius itself are seen here extending off to left and right). See Notes to the Plates.
© *Irving Lindenblad, US Naval Observatory*

2. The 'pale fox' (*yurugu*) of Mali, *Vulpes Pallidus*. It only emerges from its lair at night and is never seen in the daytime.

The four Dogon priests who revealed the Sirius traditions to anthropologists.

3. Manda D'Orosongo

4. Ongnonlou

5. Innekouzou

6. Yébéné

7. *(Above)* Dogon dancers in Sanga. © *A Costa*

8. *(Below)* One of the Dogon initiates is being adorned with an earring prior to the Sigui ceremony. © *A Costa*

9. An ancient Dogon iron statue, probably at least 300 years old, depicting 'the men with wings' who are reputed to live on 'the sixth Earth' – a planet in yet another nearby star system, neither our own nor that of Sirius. The Sirians know them but they have not taken part in the Sirian project on Earth and leave us to the care of the Nommos. We live on 'the fourth Earth' and 'men with horns' live on the third, while 'men with tails' live on a fifth. In all, the Dogon claim that there are five or six solar systems with intelligent life in our vicinity.
From the Lester Wunderman Collection, New York. Photo by Lester Wunderman

10. The only known Dogon iron statue of the Nommo from Sirius, believed to be three or four hundred years old. Here the tail is more serpent-like rather than fish-like, and there are legs and arms without any knees or elbows, and both feet and hands designed for swimming.
From the Lester Wunderman Collection, New York. Photo by Lester Wunderman

11. Krater [Cup] Number E466 in the British Museum. The scene portrays the heliacal rising of Sirius. Orion is in the centre, turned backwards in his customary pose with his right arm raised as in the configuration of the constellation, and with his pelvis at the angle made by the stars of the 'belt of Orion'. Beneath his right foot is Canis Major, the dog of Sirius, who has just risen. On the right of the scene, Eos, the winged goddess of dawn is chasing Sirius and Orion away, as it is now time for daybreak. (On the other side, out of our sight in this photo, the sun god in a four-horse chariot is holding his impatient horses back while Eos clears the way for rising.)

12. The towering mass of Mount Ararat in Turkey, where the Biblical ark landed.
© *Sonia Halliday*

13. The nearby site of Metsamor, a major religious cult centre and astronomical observatory which has never been satisfactorily studied (all relevant publications are in the Russian and Armenian languages).
© *Mrs Charles Burney*

Omphalos ('navel of the world') stones from three ancient cultures: Greek, Egyptian and Mesopotamian. See Notes to the Plates.

14. Delphi © *Scala*

15. Delos

16. Miletus – it shares the palm motif with Delos, which is on the same latitude.

17. Babylonian © *Michael Holford*

18. Delos

19. Egyptian

20. The magnificent site of Delphi in Greece, with ruins of the oracle shrine, the Temple of Apollo. © *Alinari*

21. *(Opposite page)* Bas reliefs and coins showing evidence of oracle centres and use of omphalos ('navel') stones. Two coins, bottom, from Delphi show the famous 'E' suspended in the centre of the entrance to Delphi's Temple of Apollo (See Appendix V). The two coins immediately above them show the Temple of Apollo at Delphi with the statue of the god. See Notes to the Plates. © *Bodleian and British Museum*

22. Jason, Medea and the teeth of the dragon, from an ancient vase painting. See Notes to the Plates. © *Mansell*

23. An ancient Babylonian cylinder seal which may show the sowing of the serpent's/dragon's teeth. See Notes to the Plates. © *Oriental Institute, University of Chicago*

24. Jason and Medea with a living fleece being transmuted alchemically into gold . See Notes to the Plates. © *Michael Holford*

25. A Babylonian cylinder seal in the British Museum (Number 89,110) which depicts the heliacal rising of Sirius. See Notes to the Plates for full explanation.

26. An ancient representation of the construction of the ship *Argo*. On the left the goddess Athena bestows the oak timber of Dodona. Argus is hard at work on the prow, which will contain the oak beam. An oak tree graces the scene, with a branch pointedly missing. © *Alinari*

27. Argus (*Argos*), who had a hundred eyes all over his body, being murdered by Hermes at the command of Zeus. See Notes to the Plates.

28. A Greek painting on ceramic of the 'Old Man of the Sea', Nereus. He had daughters called the Nereids, who were either fifty (according to Hesiod and Pindar) or one hundred (according to Sophocles) in number. He thus combined the Oannes tradition with the fifty/one hundred tradition, as did the similarly amphibious Typhon, who was said to have fifty heads. Nereus began to be represented in Greek art in the early sixth century BC. However, it is believed that he was the original sea god of the Greeks, and that the more famous Poseidon displaced him from his position at an early date.

29. An ancient vase painting showing the fish-tailed female monster, Scylla (*Skylla*), with a dog's head protruding from her waist. According to Homer, Scylla lived in a cave opposite the whirlpool Charybdis and ate sailors as they went past her. She was said to bark like a dog. The Greek name for dogfish was *skylion*. The name Scylla probably came from *skylax*, which means a 'young dog'. In her attributes and name, Scylla thus combined the dog motif of Sirius the Dog Star with the fish-tailed and human-headed nature of Oannes.

30. A painting from an Etruscan amphora formerly in the Royal Museum of Berlin, whereabouts now unknown. The subject is called Dagon (i.e. Oannes) by Lenormant and de Witte, from whose *Élite des Monuments Céramographiques*, Paris, 1858, Vol.III, Plate 35, this is reproduced. However, it is probably more correct to identify it as Tyrrhenus, the Etruscan Oannes, god of the Tyrrhenian Sea.

31. These two cult objects from the worship of the goddess Isis during the Graeco-Roman era were excavated at the Greek city of Cyzicus, in ancient Phrygia, opposite Byzantium. Both show the goddess Isis with a serpent's tail, and the bronze statue on the right shows her with her tail entwined with that of her husband Serapis (a later name for Osiris). See Notes to the Plates.

32. (*Far left*) The goddess Isis, showing the small fishtail in her headress.

33. (*Left*) Votive Stela from the Temple of Tanith at Carthage. At bottom, two oracular doves flank a pointed stone or pyramid topped by a symbol of the navel of the earth.

34. *(Above left)* The remains of a giant statue of Oannes found at Kouyunjik.

35. *(Above right)* A pottery representation of Oannes, or of a priest dressed in an Oannes costume. A fish head surmounts a human head, a fin protrudes from the back, 12.6 cm high. Believed to have been excavated at Nineveh by Layard in the mid-nineteenth century. British Museum Dept of Western Asiatic Antiquities, Inventory No. 91,837.

36 and 37. Two views of another Oannes figure, No. 91836, also 12.6cm high, found with the other, presumably at Nineveh. From the side this figure seems to be entirely a fish standing upright, but from the front we see the human face and in one hand the sacred basket is held. Such figures would have been buried together as a foundation dedication for an important building or temple. Their Babylonian name is *apkallu*; there were usually seven in all, and they were the original 'Seven Sages' who founded civilisation.

38 and 39.
Further repre-
sentations of the
amphibious
heavenly being,
Oannes, from
Assyrian cylinder
seals.
© *Pierpont
Morgan Library/
Staatliche
Museum zu
Berlin*

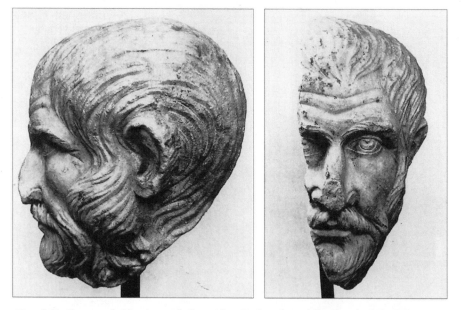

40 and 41. Front and side views of a bust identified as that of the Greek philosopher
Proclus, for whom see Appendix II; see also Notes to the Plates. © *Athens Museum*

priestesses serving the Moon-goddess, to whom the lion-pelted sacred king had access once a year during their erotic orgies around the stone phallus called Eros ('erotic desire'). Their number corresponded with the lunations which fell between one Olympic Festival and the next.'

Here is Graves's irrepressible moon-goddess – and here are her lunations! She carries them about with her wherever she goes. But unfortunately, Graves's brave attempt to find a lunar rationale for the fifty is not sufficient. The Olympic Games were, as they are now, held every four years, and the Olympiads or four-year periods were understood to have commenced in 776 BC, which is an extremely recent date compared with the extreme antiquity of 'the fifty' in all its myriad occurrences. For instance, there were no Olympiads in Homer's day when 'the tale of the *Argo* was on everybody's lips', and the fifty Minyae were on their way into literary immortality in what was to become the Western world. Much more likely that a period of fifty lunations was modelled after a long-established tradition – the esoteric fifty-*year* period. Thus the fifty-month and fifty-day sequences were probably derived in emulation.

I assume that the cycle of fifty lunations which Graves mentions here is identical to his fifty-month period of the reign of a sacred king, which is supposed to be 'half of a Great Year of a hundred months'. Can it be that fifty, as half of one hundred, is meant to represent by its reduplication the two-to-one ratio as a means of signifying the concept of the musical octave with its two-to-one ratio?*

And can this be why the *Argo* is supposed to be 'whole in the sky' (Aratos) and yet the constellation is also supposed to represent only the latter half of a ship? Can this apparent double-talk be yet another way of signifying the two-to-one ratio?

It also seems significant that each fifty-month period is carefully specified to constitute 'one reign', even though it is only half of 'the Great Year'. Can 'one reign' be analogous to 'one orbit' and the 'Great Year' of two orbits be contrived to communicate the two-to-one harmonic ratio of the octave? Or does it refer to a shared fifty-year orbit of two stars, Sirius B and Sirius C? Or *both* concepts at once?

Another occurrence of fifty and a hundred together is with the three monsters born to Uranus the sky and Gaia the earth. Their names were Cottus, Briareus, and Gyges. ' "From their shoulders sprang a hundred invincible arms and above these powerful limbs rose fifty heads attached to their backs." For this reason they were called the Hecatoncheires or the Centimanes,' as we are reliably told.[5]

These monsters resemble the monster Cerberus, the hound of Hades who originally had fifty heads, but later became simplified and had only

---

* The frequency of a note is doubled when it is raised an octave – hence a ratio of 2 to 1. This may be demonstrated visually on a single string and does not require the modern measurements of frequency.

three heads – presumably for the same reason that these monsters are three in number, and also the reason that Hecate (whose pet Cerberus was, and who was a form of Isis-Sirius and whose name literally means 'one hundred') had three heads or forms, and that the boat of Sirius in ancient Egypt had three goddesses together in it. In other words, probably the same reason that the Dogon insist that there are three stars in the Sirius system. (For some years the astronomical evidence went against the existence of a third star, with the conclusion that if there is a third star, it does not produce the perturbation which had been claimed for it before the seven years' observations by astronomer Irving Lindenblad.[6] However, the situation has now changed drastically with the apparent confirmation of the existence of Sirius C. See p. 3.)

We will recall that originally Hercules is supposed to have led the expedition of the *Argo*. In the version of Apollonius Rhodios he accompanies the expedition. In Graves we may read of another traditional exploit of Hercules in the Black Sea.[7] He went 'in search of Hippolyte's girdle in the Black Sea' and 'the girdle belonged to a daughter of Briareus ("strong"), one of the Hundred-handed Ones . . . ,' who was of course a fifty-headed one as well. And note his name: Strong! The word βριαρός (*briaros*) means 'strong', and another form is βριᾱρότης (*briarotēs*) which means 'strength, might', and a related form βρίθος (*brithos*) means 'weight', and βριθοσύνη (*brithosynē*) means 'weight, heaviness'. Where have we encountered this idea before?

We should note that Hippolyte means simply 'letting horses loose'. And it was from Colchis that the horses of the sun were let loose every morning, for it was there that they were stabled, according to Greek tradition. There is also a really peculiar use of the word *hippopedē*, which has the normal mundane meaning of 'a horse fetter', in a cosmic sense. It appears from Liddell and Scott that this word was used by the astronomer Eudoxus (the one who went to Egypt and who was mentioned earlier) as the word for the curve described by a planet. We know this from Simplicius on Aristotle's *De Caelo* and Proclus on Euclid.* Two sources are better than one. There is probably more to this than we can ever discover, for the necessary texts are lost.

If we examine the name Gyges, who was one of the other three monsters which included Briareus, we find its meaning has the same origins as *gygantelos*, which in English became 'gigantic', but the meaning of this word was not by any means simply 'giant'. Graves gives Gyges the meaning of 'earth-born', another concept we have come to expect in connection with our Sirius-complex of myths. Just as the stones Deukalion and his wife Pyrrha threw over their shoulders had been torn from their mother earth, Gaia, and were her bones turning into men to repopulate the

---

* Simplicius and Proclus are despised by the orthodox mentalities because they were *Neoplatonists*. See Appendix II.[8]

earth after the flood and the voyage of the Greek ark, and just as Jason (and also Cadmus) sowed the teeth and they sprang up as 'earth-born men', so we find that Gyges is also 'earth-born'.

And just as Gilgamesh sought *strength* from the earth when 'his teeth shook' in the earth, so we discover that *gygas* means 'mighty' or 'strong', and is also used in Hesiod to refer to 'the sons of Gaia (Earth)', which is as specific as we could wish, for it gives an undeniable and conscious connection between 'the children of Gaia' of Deukalion, 'the offspring of Gaia' of the Colchian teeth, and 'the sons of Gaia' who were a race of giants, and Gyges, whose mother was Gaia.

And we are not to forget that Gyges, like Briareus, can mean 'strength' and 'might', though with the particular shade of meaning added that it is strength and might drawn from the earth, which could be one way of describing a super-dense body of degenerate matter. After all, super-dense matter is 'strong earth'. We must also remember that Gyges has fifty heads.

As for the name Cottus, the third of the three monsters, Graves tells us that it is not Greek. Graves says (3, 1): 'Cottus was the eponymous [name-giving) ancestor of the Cottians who worshipped the orgiastic Cotytto, and spread her worship from Thrace throughout North-western Europe. These tribes are described as "hundred-handed", perhaps because their priestesses were organized in colleges of fifty, like the Danaids and Nereids; perhaps because the men were organized in war-bands of one hundred, like the early Romans.'

The Cottians might possibly derive their name from an Egyptian word.

Perhaps it was *qeṭi*, which means 'oarsmen' and has

been applied to 'divine oarsmen'. With a different determinative and when not applied to a man, the word means 'orbit', 'revolution', 'to go around'. And the word in Egyptian was also applied to a group of specific people in a specific region. The *Qeṭu* were the natives of Qeṭi, which Wallis Budge says was 'The Circle', that is, 'the North Syrian coast about the Gulf of Issus and the deserts between the Euphrates and the Mediterranean'.

There was also an Egyptian precedent for applying the same name to a god. Qeṭi is 'a god of the abyss', and a reduplicated version of the name which repeats the 't' as Cotytto does is Qeṭqeṭ, who is significantly one of the thirty-six decans. In addition, Qeṭshu refers specifically to 'the "nude" or Syrian goddess',* which seems clearly to be an orgiastic element, for Graves says that Cotytto was an orgiastic goddess. It seems fairly clear, then, that Cottus is of Egyptian origin and originally applies to the orbit of Sirius B, and in the Egyptian era the particular term came to be

---

* The great goddess of Hierapolis (one of the oracle centres) must be intended by this 'Syrian goddess'. See note 44 to Chapter Six, reference to Lucian's *De Dea Syria*, and Garstang; also see Bibliography.

associated with a people of Syria who moved to Thrace, and even in Egyptian times the name had all its applications to a foreign people, a foreign orgiastic goddess, and Sirius-related concepts including both oarsmen and an orbit, two ideas which I have frequently connected before. Here in Egyptian we find an orbit called by a name which applies equally well to divine oarsmen. And the word survives in the fifty-headed Cottus! Fifty oarsmen, fifty years in the orbit, fifty heads to the Sirius-monster. How simple, how elegant.

I am indebted to my friend the late Michael Scott, who once rowed at Oxford, for the fine suggestion that there could hardly be a better analogy of any symbol with its intended meaning of 'a specific interval both of space and time' than the oar-stroke. Rowing is a precisely paced discipline when practised in earnest, as it was in ancient times when it was one of the two principal means of navigation at sea, and the only reliable one if the winds failed, as they so often did. It also represents a self-reliance which illustrates the self-impelled motion of a body in space which is orbiting (or what seems to be self-impelled).

I should point out here that the earliest name for the figure known to us as Hercules was, according to Robert Graves in *The Greek Myths* (132. h.), none other than Briareus. And we also have learned that the earliest form of Jason was Hercules (whose earliest form was Briareus). We thus find that Briareus, with his fifty heads, was the earliest captain of the fifty-oared *Argo*. Briareus, whose name means 'weight'. And whose brother's name means both 'oarsman' and 'orbit'.

Apart from the three monsters each with fifty heads, Gaia also gave birth to Garamas, who was not only earth-born, but who 'rose from the plain' like the earth-born men of Colchis. Graves says:[9] 'The Libyans, however, claim that Garamas was born before the Hundred-handed Ones and that, when he rose from the plain, he offered Mother Earth (Gaia) a sacrifice of the sweet acorn.' The acorn of the oak – the oaks being representative of Dodona, of the piece of the *Argo*'s prow, and of the Colchian grove!

It is in the footnote of Graves[10] that we learn something of really immense significance to us: 'Garamas is the eponymous ancestor of the Libyan Garamantians who occupied the Oasis of Djado [see top portion of Figure 40], south of the Fezzan, and were conquered by the Roman General Balbus in 19 BC. They are said to have been of Cushite-Berber stock, and in the second century AD were subdued by the matrilineal Lemta Berbers. Later they fused with the Negro aboriginals on the south bank of the Upper Niger, and adopted their language. They survive today in a single village under the name of Koromantse.'

I need hardly point out to the alert reader that the southern bank of the Upper Niger is the home of the Dogon! What should be investigated on the spot is the relations which subsist between this sad shaggy remnant of the Garamantians and the surrounding Dogon and other tribes. Also, the villagers of Koromantse might be discovered to possess the Sirius lore themselves.

On the most detailed French map of this area there is a village called Korienze only sixty miles from Bandiagara and in the heart of Dogon country. It is on the south bank of the Upper Niger and is presumably the place Graves means.

In line with this important discovery I should point out that Herodotus says in Book Two (103 and 106): 'It is undoubtedly a fact that the Colchians are of Egyptian descent . . . the Colchians, the Egyptians, and the Ethiopians are the only races which from ancient times have practised circumcision. The Phoenicians and the Syrians of Palestine themselves admit that they adopted the practice from Egypt, and the Syrians who live near the rivers Thermodon and Parthenius, as well as their neighbours the Macronians, say that they learnt it only a short time ago from the Colchians. No other nations use circumcision, and all these are without doubt following the Egyptian lead.'

Circumcision is fundamental to Dogon culture and forms the central part of the ritual of the Sigui which the Dogon hold every sixty years – and though I have pointed all this out earlier, it does no harm to repeat it.

We shall recall if we read the *Argonautica* that the Argonauts were blown off course to Libya, where they were stranded for some time. In his book *Herodotean Inquiries*,[11] Seth Benardete speaks of the Garamantes to whom he gives an alternative name, the Gamphasantes. They are described in Herodotus, Book Four (after 178) as inhabitants of 'Further inland to the southward, in the part of Libya where wild beasts are found'. At 179 Herodotus connects Jason and the Argonauts' visit to Libya with the eventual foundation in Libya 'of a hundred Grecian cities'. Benardete's comments (p. 122) in his book connect the *Argo*'s visit to Libya and the Libyan city of Cyrene:

Herodotus first indicates how closely Libya, Egypt, Scythia, and Greece are joined. The ancestors of Cyrene's founders were descendants of Jason's companions, who sailed to Colchis, originally an Egyptian colony on the eastern shore of the Black Sea; and the third generation from these Argonauts were expelled from Lemnos by the very same Pelasgians who later abducted Athenian women from Brauron, where a cult of Artemis-Iphigeneia was practised, just as among the Taurians in the Crimea; and Jason is said to have been carried off course to Libya. Cyrene is the melting-pot of Egyptian, Libyan, and Scythian things. Its founding suggests the Scythian account of their origins. They said that golden objects fell from heaven, which flashed fire when the two older brothers of Kolaxais approached them, but Kolaxais himself was able to take them home. To these celestial ποιήματα [*poiēmata*] there here correspond the oracular verses of Delphi which, in both the Theban and Cyrenaic versions, prompted the sending of a colony to Libya.

Robert Graves got his information[12] on the Garamantians going to the
Upper Niger by way of Libya from a series of books by Eva Meyrowitz,
an anthropologist who spent many years studying the Akan tribe of
Ghana, directly south of the Dogon.[13] Graves paraphrases her books: 'The
Akan people result from an ancient southward emigration of Libyo-
Berbers – cousins to the pre-Hellenic population of Greece – from the
Sahara desert oases (see 3, 3) and their intermarriage at Timbuctoo with
Niger River Negroes.' Timbuctoo – or Timbuctu – is the nearest big city
to the Dogon. Graves continues: 'In the eleventh century AD they moved
still further south to what is now Ghana.' I might point out that the path
of migration from Timbuctu to Ghana goes straight through the country
of the Dogon, whose territory is directly south of Timbuctu. So it is quite
clear by now that peoples intimately connected with the Sirius tradition
came from Greece to Libya and thence south to the Libyan oases of the
Sahara, thence further south-west past the Sahara to Timbuctu and the
region of the Dogon, where they mingled with Negroes of the Dogon
region and took their local language for themselves, eventually becoming
indistinguishable from the local African population in appearance and
speech, but retaining their old traditions as their most secret doctrines. The
migration route is shown in Figure 40.[14]

There is something incredible in the survival of the Argonauts in the
obscure reaches of the French Sudan. These people, which I assume must
include the Dogon as well as their immediate southern neighbours (and the
Dogon sell onions to Ghana as part of their livelihood), seem to be direct
descendants of Lemnian Greeks who claimed to be the grandsons of the
actual Argonauts. It almost seems too amazing to be true, that we should
have begun this book by considering a strange African tribe, then
considered similar Sirius traditions in the Mediterranean stemming from
ancient Egypt, and then be led back again to the African tribe whom we
discover to be directly descended from the Mediterranean peoples privy to
the Sirius complex!

Later, I shall mention a bit more about the Pelasgians, who lived in
Arcadia and, so Herodotus informs us, were not conquered by the Dorian
invaders of Greece in pre-classical times. They have been among the main
continuers of the Sirius tradition as, apparently, have the people they
displaced by force. But I mention them now to give more relevant
information for this Libyan connection. Graves says:[15] 'According to the
Pelasgians, the goddess Athene was born beside Lake Tritonis in Libya',
and: 'Plato identified Athene, patroness of Athens, with the Libyan
goddess Neith . . . Neith had a temple at Sais (in Egypt), where Solon was
treated well merely because he was an Athenian . . . Herodotus writes (IV,
189): "Athene's garments and aegis were borrowed by the Greeks from the
Libyan women ..." ... Ethiopian girls still wear this costume ...
Herodotus adds here that the loud cries of triumph, *olulu, ololu*, uttered in
honour of Athene above (*Iliad*, vi. 297–301) were of Libyan origin. *Tritone*

Figure 39. Distribution of Libyan tribes according to Herodotus

means "the third queen".' Again the reference to the three goddesses. And recall that in Libya was the shrine of Ammon equivalent to the Dodona oracle of Zeus, where the other of the two birds flew from Egyptian Thebes. And Athene, the daughter of Zeus, is equivalently the daughter of Ammon, who is identified with Zeus.

Athene was also known as Pallas Athene, for reasons given in Graves. He adds that 'the third Pallas' was father of 'the fifty Pallantids, Theseus's enemies (see 97.g and 99.a), who seem to have been originally fighting priestesses of Athene'. Once again the fifty.

Graves gives some interesting information:[16] 'Pottery finds suggest a Libyan immigration into Crete as early as 4000 BC; and a large number of goddess-worshipping Libyan refugees from the Western Delta seem to have arrived there when Upper and Lower Egypt were forcibly united under the First Dynasty about the year 3000 BC. The First Minoan Age began soon afterwards, and Cretan culture spread to Thrace and Early Helladic Greece.'

While again on the subject of the fifty, I want to note more information concerning Cerberus, the fifty-headed hound of Hades. Graves says:[17] 'Echidne bore a dreadful brood to Typhon: namely, Cerberus . . .', etc. Recall that Typhon was identified with Python[18] in the Homeric *Hymn to Apollo* and elsewhere; Python was the particular monster, slain by Apollo according to legend (as depicted in Figure 41), whose rotting corpse lay directly under the oracle of Delphi.

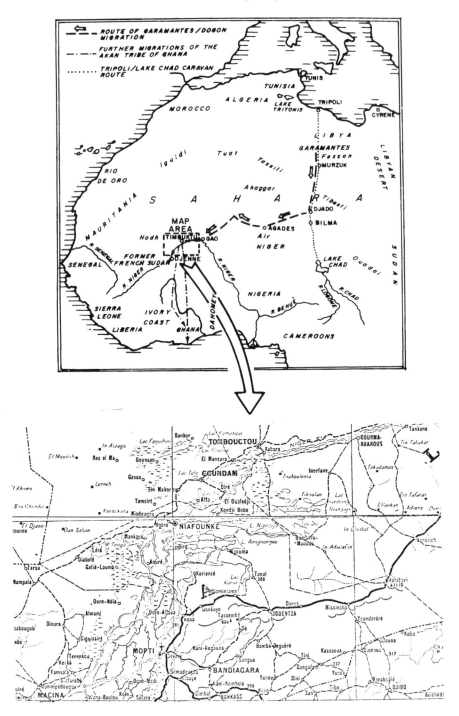

Figure 40. Migration route of the Dogon

224

Figure 41. Artemis stands by as the infant Apollo, held by their mother Leto, lets fly an arrow at the Python. This scene is not Delphi but Delos, for the palm trees are the 'tree-code' of Delos. This Attic vase painting provides important confirmation that the story, which was supposed to have occurred at Delphi, was also linked with Delos. If Python was not only at Delphi but at Delos as well, then Python is a concept rather than a creature. This is all further evidence for the geodetic oracle-octave which includes both Delphi and Delos, which are one degree of latitude apart. Delos had ceased to have any function as an oracle centre by about 600 BC, which helps one appreciate the antiquity of the system, since Delos had no oracular functions at all by the time of classical Greece, when Socrates was gadding about the agora in Athens

Graves continues :[19] 'Cerberus, associated by the Dorians with the dog-headed Egyptian god Anubis who conducted souls to the Underworld, seems to have originally been the Death-goddess Hecate, or Hecabe; she was portrayed as a bitch because dogs eat corpse flesh and howl at the moon. . . . Orthrus, who fathered [various creatures] on Echidna* was Sirius, the Dog-star, which inaugurated the Athenian New Year. He had two heads, like Janus, because the reformed year at Athens had two seasons, not three.' The three heads of Hecate, of Cerberus in his simplified form, etc., possibly all represent the old, original year which had three seasons and originated in Egypt with the the seasons of their (1) inundation, (2) sowing, (3) harvesting, which were traditional there. But it seems unlikely. For why would the three goddesses sail in their Sirius boat in Egyptian representations which have absolutely nothing to do with a calendar? In short, the three goddesses and the three-headedness always to do with Sirius are not calendrical at all. But by the extremely late (post-Classical) times of Athens, calendrical explanations may have become fashionable for what could not otherwise be explained.

In the above passages I hope the reader will note the specific information that connects Anubis (which much earlier I identified on altogether

* Mother of the dog Cerberus and wife of Typhon – see later, p. 287.

separate grounds with the orbit of Sirius B) with the Greek version of Anubis, Cerberus, with his fifty heads. In the Egyptian tradition I hadn't found any specific connection between Anubis and fifty. It is true that we have found the Egyptian word *qeṭi* means both 'oarsman' and 'orbit', and as there were always fifty oarsmen in the Sirius-related boats, both in Greek and Sumerian saga, we were on our way to an identification on solid grounds. But here at last a specific connection has come to light, and would seem to be a splendid confirmation of my identification! And furthermore, we see that the dog Orthrus who was the brother of Cerberus, was specifically identified with Sirius. We thus have found in the Mediterranean world all the elements of the description of the Sirius system which were possessed by the Dogon. And we have also traced the Mediterranean Sirius lore to the Dogon by way of Libya, then the Saharan oases, then Timbuktoo, and finally the south bank of the Upper Niger and the Dogon region. Thus, through thousands of miles and thousands of years, we have discovered the source of that strange tradition still intact among a tribe deep in Africa. But there is more to be learnt. We must examine the Mediterranean tradition more closely, and particularly its oldest Egyptian origins in the shadowy pre-dynastic world of Behdet (which seems not to have been excavated and has presumably been lost in the mud of the Nile delta).

The father of Orthrus the Sirius-dog and his brother Cerberus the fifty-headed dog was the monster Typhon whom we mentioned a moment ago (see Figure 49, later on). And it is worth while for us to see what Liddell and Scott's *Greek Lexicon* has to say about the meaning of the name Typhon and also related forms of this word.

One meaning of *Tῡφῶν* (*Typhon*), curiously enough, is 'a kind of comet' – in other words, a moving star. Another form is either Typhoeus or Typhos and specifically refers to the youngest son of Gaia, who was mother also of the three fifty-headed monsters and of Garamas. *Typhlos* means 'smoke, vapour', and also 'conceit, vanity (because it clouds or darkens a man's intellect)'. *Typhlos* means 'blind' and specifically 'in the sense of misty, darkened'. The verb *Typhloō* means 'to blind, make blind' or 'to blind, baffle'. It also means 'to wrap in smoke'.

Since Typhon is specifically said to be the father of Sirius (Orthrus) and one of its unexplained definitions is a description of a moving star, and its son has fifty heads, I take all the references to obscurity and invisibility to mean that Typhon represents Sirius B which is the dark companion of Sirius and is invisible to us. In other words, we are *typhlos* (blind) to Typhon because it seems as if it were obscured or *typhloo*'d by *typhos* (vapour, smoke), and we are baffled, blind (*typhlos*) in the sense of the subject being darkened (*typhloō*).

A possible origin of the word Typhon may be the Egyptian word *tephit* or *ṭeph-t*, both of which have the meaning of 'cave, cavern, hole in the ground'. This Egyptian word describes perfectly the chasm at Delphi in which Python was supposed to lie rotting, his corpse giving off the fumes out of the earth. And, as we have seen, Python was equated with Typhon in early times.

If we take the Egyptian word *tep* we discover that it means 'mouth' and in the form *tep ra* it means 'mouth of the god' literally, but in fact the real meaning of this is 'divine oracle'. *Tep* is an unaspirated *teph*. Hence the *tep* of Delphi has a *tephit*, or cavernous abyss beneath it. Later I shall consider the Egyptian word *tep* in its further ramifications. But for the moment it is sufficient to see that Typhon almost certainly originates from the Egyptian word describing a cavern or hole in the earth, as the Egyptians founded the *tep* or oracle at Delphi and naturally used their own word to describe the cavern. As Delphi passed into Greek culture and the Egyptians became forgotten in all but vague legends (such as the famous visit of the Canopic Herakles to Delphi, etc.), the original word to describe Delphi's cavern would have been retained through the natural conservative inclinations of religious organizations who retain antique words and language for notoriously long periods of time, forgetting their origins. Hence a Greek who had no knowledge of Egyptian culture or that it had ever penetrated to his homeland in earlier days would nevertheless call the cavern at Delphi which produced the sulphurous fumes the den of Typhon after its original Egyptian designation of *tephit*. It has been noted by people other than myself and with greater knowledge that the Sumerian word for cavern, *abzu*, survived in Greek as *abyssos*, leading to the English 'abyss'.

The fumes arising from the Delphic cavern obviously gave rise to the usage of forms of the word for 'obscuring with smoke, dark', etc. And the fact that the personified Typhon became closely associated with Sirius was obviously due to the fact that this word which had entered Greek usage and been extended to considerations of 'darkness, obscurity', was useful in the traditional Sirius lore as adopted in Greece. The other meanings for the word then developed from there, except for the obvious popular usages, such as applying the word to a description of 'vanity' because vanity clouds a man's intellect – a really superb extension of the meaning for use in poetic and common expression.

It is probably due to considerations such as the Typhonic in the sense of Sirius B's association with darkness and obscurity, and hence with cavernous blackness, that some of the Sirius-related divinities were reputed in later times to live in the dark underworld. The prototype of these is quite specifically Anubis, the embalmer of mummies. Anubis was not originally meant to be a death god *per se* and his association with mummies and the underworld has been previously explained. Egyptian mummies were, as I have said, embalmed over a period of seventy days, to correspond with the number of days each year when the star Sirius was 'in the Duat, or Underworld', and was not visible in the night sky. Hence the seventy-day 'death' of Sirius each year was the fundamental and earliest underworld aspect of the Sirius lore. Of course, Anubis, as the expression of the orbit of Sirius B, was invisible all the time, and not only for seventy days a year. Hence the permanent Typhonic darkness could be even further extended in later lore and a heightened sense of the importance of the underworld aspects could arise. This concept of invisibility and darkness must have become more and more important as time went on and the grasp of the nature of the mysteries became weakened by successive generations of initiates who were further and further from the original sources of information, though the Dogon even down to our time have maintained the information in a remarkably pure state. So there developed the underworld nature of the fifty-headed Cerberus-Anubis in Greek times. With the earlier Egyptians, as always with them, the underworld concept had been on more than one level. To the public the underworld aspect seemed to be entirely explicable by the disappearance of Sirius for seventy days – a fact which anyone could notice – and its reappearance following that period at dawn on the occasion of the star's heliacal rising. But the priests knew that the dark companion of Sirius was *never* visible.

It would be worth while now to look a little more closely at the dog Orthrus, who was Sirius. Orthrus is the dog of Eurytion (the herdsman of the triple-bodied monster Geryon, who lived on the island of Erytheia in the far west, father of one of the Hesperides. Herakles was told to steal his cattle). Graves interestingly compares this Eurytion with the Sumerian Enkidu, the companion of Gilgamesh who was hairy and wild and came from the steppes and was imbued with incredible strength:[20] 'Eurytion is the "interloper", a stock character . . . The earliest mythical example of the interloper is the same Enkidu: he interrupted Gilgamesh's sacred marriage with the Goddess of Erech [Uruk], and challenged him to battle.' It is particularly interesting to find the Greek companion of Sirius compared by Graves to the Sumerian Enkidu, whom I also have identified with the companion of Sirius. For 'companion of Sirius' is precisely what Eurytion is; if Orthrus is Sirius and Eurytion the herdsman accompanies him, then Eurytion is the 'companion of Sirius'. And Enkidu is the strong hairy wild man who endured a trial of strength against Gilgamesh and became his companion after their wrestling match. Both Eurytion and Enkidu are hairy and rustic characters, and they seem to be related also to the god Pan, whose hairy and rustic nature classes him with them.

The motif of 'interloper' and 'interrupting' and of challenging to a test of strength has to do with the fact that the bright star Sirius is challenged by its strong companion star. Graves adds: 'Another interloper is Agenor' and Agenor means 'very manly'. He interrupted the wedding of Perseus with Andromeda. Perseus was the son of Danae, great-granddaughter of Danaos, who had fifty daughters. As we learn in Graves,[21] Danae herself had connections with an ark. Her father 'locked her and the infant Perseus in a wooden ark, which he cast into the sea'. Later companions of Perseus in his exploits were 'a party of Cyclopes'.[22] This is yet another familiar ingredient.

Perseus fell in love with Andromeda, the daughter of Cassiopeia (Queen of Ethiopia). Graves says:[23] 'Cassiopeia had boasted that both she and her daughter were more beautiful than the Nereids, who complained of this insult', etc. And, of course, the number of the Nereids was fifty. Of them, Graves says:[24] 'The fifty Nereids seem to have been a college of Moon-priestesses'. Graves explains the recurring fifty in relation to moon lore. It is a brave but, again, unconvincing solution.

It is interesting in the light of our knowledge of Danaus having fifty daughters to read the opening of Pindar's tenth Nemaean* Ode[25] which is written largely about the city of Argos (a name related to Argo just as was the name Argus of the Argo's builder and as was the word 'ark'):

The city of Danaos
And his fifty daughters on shining thrones,
Sing of it, Graces,
Of Argos, home of Hera, fit for the gods.

Perseus and Danae also have a connection with Argos. And as for the Graces here mentioned, their worship was first instituted at Orchomenos. The Graces are often associated with Hermes and called 'the Graces of Hermes' which occurs especially in a work such as *The Lives of the Philosophers*[26] by the historian Eunapius. He tells us something extremely interesting about the area of Behdet and Canopus in Egypt. In speaking of Antoninus, the son of the remarkable and brilliant woman Sosipatra (fourth century AD), Eunapius says: 'He crossed to Alexandria, and then so greatly admired and preferred the mouth of the Nile at Canobus,† that he wholly dedicated and applied himself to the worship of the gods there, and to their secret rites.'[27] And also: 'Antoninus was worthy of his parents, for he settled at the Canobic mouth of the Nile and devoted himself wholly to the religious rites of that place'.[28] This is interesting, that there were rites peculiar to Canopus to which one could exclusively devote oneself. A little later,[29] Eunapius mentions that the Christians destroyed the temples in the vicinity and demolished the Serapeum at Alexandria, and settled their black-robed monks on the spot of Canopus in order to supplant paganism there. Hence, we see that that particular place had a unique importance. Surely it should be excavated. The pagan mysteries of the place, eventually destroyed by the Christians, probably continued the Behdet tradition and were related to our Sirius question.

But back now to the quotations from Pindar given above. What is so especially significant about this passage of Pindar's is the expression 'and his fifty daughters on shining thrones'. It will be remembered that the

throne 𝕁 is the hieroglyph for Ast or Isis identified with Sirius, and that the fifty

---

* Odes celebrating the Nemaean games, held at the city of Nemaea.
† The alternative spelling to Canopus of Canobus is sometimes used by other authors.

Anunnaki of Sumer were on thrones. All through the earlier traditions there has been a great deal of emphasis on the throne in connection with the Sirius material, and here in the late Pindar we find the same. By describing him as 'late' I do so on our Sirius time-scale, for of course he was at the very earliest portion of the Greek classical age.

There are further connections between the Sirius system and Argos and Danaos. Connections with the Minyan Libyans are many. The father of Danaos was himself 'the son of Libya by Poseidon'.[30] Danaos was also 'sent to rule Libya'.[31] However, the connection with Egypt is also strong. Danaos's twin brother was called Aegyptos, of whom we read:[32] 'Aegyptus was given Arabia as his kingdom; but also subdued the country of the Melampodes [the 'black-footed people' – the Egyptians], and named it Egypt after himself. Fifty sons were born to him of various mothers: Libyans, Arabians, Phoenicians, and the like.' So we see Danaos's twin brother had fifty sons. And Danaos had fifty daughters. This finally abolishes Graves's argument that they must refer to a college of fifty moon-priestesses, and emphasizes the connection with the fifty male companions of Gilgamesh, fifty male Argonauts, fifty male Anunnaki, etc. Notice the two related but also quite definitely separate groups of fifty here. Together they add up to a hundred – a *hecate* – and have the same grandparents, but they are basically two separate fifties. Not only do they have separate parents and especially separate fathers, but they are separately distinguished by sex. In this connection we should remember that Sirius C is called by the Dogon 'the star of women'. Its 50-year orbit around Sirius A could be symbolized by 50 daughters, while the male Sirius B's orbit would be symbolized by 50 sons.

Danaos learns that his brother wishes to marry his fifty sons to Danaos' fifty daughters with the aim of their killing the fifty daughters after marrying them. So Danaos and his daughters all take flight to Rhodes* and then to Greece where they land and Danaos announces that he is divinely chosen to become the King of Argos. Note that he chooses Argos. This and his connection with fifty are especially important later when I give the derivation of the words Argo, Argos, etc. And it is particularly interesting that when Danaos flees his brother, he does so in a ship which he built with Athena's assistance – exactly the case with the Argonauts, who built the *Argo* with Athena's assistance.

The way in which Danaos became King of Argos was that a wolf came down from the hills and killed the lead bull of the city and the Argives accepted the omen. 'Danaus, convinced that the wolf had been Apollo in disguise, dedicated the famous shrine to wolfish Apollo at Argos, and became so powerful a ruler that all the Pelasgians of Greece called themselves Danaans. He also built the citadel of Argos, and his daughters

---

* This may be an indication that Rhodes, at latitude 36° 30′, does indeed belong in the sequence of oracle centres as was only tentatively suggested in the chart at the end of Chapter Six.

brought the Mysteries of Demeter, called Thesmophoria,* from Egypt and taught these to the Pelasgian women. But, since the Dorian invasion, the Thesmophoria are no longer performed in the Peloponnese, except by the Arcadians.'[33]

It is well known that the Pelasgians survived in Greece only in remote Arcadia after the Dorian invasion of *circa* 1100–1000 BC. This is why some of the older traditions continued in that strange region after they had ceased to exist elsewhere in Greece. Arcadia was in a sense the Wales of Greece. The Pelasgians considered themselves 'earth-born', as I shall discuss in a moment. Note that there is a specific reference to Egyptian mysteries being transplanted in Greece among the Pelasgians. When Danaos fled from Egypt to Argos, he is specifically said to have brought Egyptian mysteries, the Thesmophoria. Presumably the Sirius-complex was thus transplanted. (Herodotus tells of Danaos bringing the Thermophoria to Greece in Book II, 171.)[34] The element of the wolf, sometimes substituted for the dog in the Sirius tradition of the Dog Star, is important. It is an obvious European substitute for the jackal of Anubis. With no jackal in Europe, the wolf was the candidate. Wolfish Apollo is jackalish. It was from this changing of the jackal into the wolf through adaptation to the European clime that those peculiar wolf traditions arose in wild Arcadia which developed in pre-classical times into the werewolf concepts. Human blood-sucking vampires, the use of garlic for protection against them, and lycanthropy or werewolves all luxuriated in the wilds of Arcady among the Pelasgian survivors in pre-classical Greece after the Dorian invasion. The phenomenon is rather like the plethora of fairy-tales and 'Celtic twilight' to be found in Ireland, with the multitude of fantastic stories and creatures. What is a werewolf? It is a man's body with a wolf's head. That is exactly what Anubis became when transferred to Greece; instead of a man's body with a jackal's head, he was a man with a wolf's head because there was no jackal in Greece. And the temples of Wolfish (or Lycian) Apollo, were not altogether rare in Greece. Aristotle's famous school at Athens, the Lyceum, was in the grounds of the Lycian Apollo's temple just outside the Athens Gate of Diochares. The name 'Lyceum' comes from the Lycian Apollo, which is the Wolfish Apollo.

It is extremely interesting, incidentally, to read in Pausanius (Book II, 38, 4) that near Argos 'are the Landings, where they say Danaos and his sons first landed in the Argolid'. (The Argolid was a region of Greece around Argos.) Here we read that Danaos had sons, not daughters. This is a strong indication that what was really meant to be significant about Danaos's progeny was not their sex but their number of fifty. And from Pindar we see that they were on fifty thrones. The fact that Aegyptus of

---

* *Thesmophorus* in Greek means 'law-giving'. By Classical times the Thesmophoria was an annual festival at Athens held by women in honour of 'Demeter Thesmophorus' because she founded the institution of marriage.

Egypt had fifty sons as well and that Danaos's daughters (or sons) taught the Egyptian mysteries to the Greeks all indicates that what transpired was a transplanting from Egypt to Greece of the all-important tradition to be common to both countries from then on – the fifty as linked with the Dog Star Sirius and as celestial thrones. In other words, the mystery of the orbit of Sirius B around Sirius A in its fifty celestial steps.

According to Graves,[35] the serpent's teeth sown by Jason were 'a few left over from Cadmus's sowing at Thebes'. Graves says of the latter:[36] 'A small tribe, speaking a Semitic language, seems to have moved up from the Syrian plains to Cadmeia in Caria – Cadmus is a Semitic word meaning "eastern" – whence they crossed over to Boeotia towards the end of the second millennium, seized Thebes, and became masters of the country. The myth of the Sown Men . . .' But before continuing his explanation I shall quote his description of the events. Figure 42 depicts an ancient Greek vase painting of Cadmus standing above a hare, just as Orion 'stands' on Lepus, the Hare, in the night sky.

Figure 42. An extremely important representation, in the Louvre, of Cadmus of Greek Thebes, slaying the serpent/dragon. Its teeth are almost more prominent than it is. Cadmus seems to represent the constellation Orion, for beneath his feet figures prominently a hare which appears to be meant as the constellation Lepus. As if to emphasize the stellar symbolism, on either side of Lepus are what appear to be stars. The serpent itself, to the left and slightly lower than Cadmus, would therefore correspond with the position in the sky of Sirius. (Figure 14, earlier in this book, shows a star map of this area of the sky which will help in visualizing the constellations, though the conventional figures of a man, a hare, etc., are not drawn in.) Since we know that Cadmus and Jason were the two heroes who sowed the serpent's teeth, and this serpent has prominent rows of teeth (notably not fangs, the emphasis instead being upon the rows), and the serpent is placed in the position of the star Sirius in this pictorial star-map, we have evidence (if we accept the star-map interpretation) that the Greeks must have been conscious of the Egyptian pun whereby 'serpent's tooth' in hieroglyphics is a synonym for 'the Goddess Sirius'. The doves and the shrine with serpents are both elements of the oracle centres associated with the Sirius tradition in Greece

Graves tells us:[37]

Cadmus sailed with Telephassa to Rhodes [where Danaos also stopped in his flight to Argos], where he dedicated a brazen cauldron to Athene of Lindus, and built Poseidon's temple, leaving a hereditary priesthood behind to care for it. [Like Danaos, Cadmus instituted religious rites where he went.] They next touched at Thera [the place from which the Minyae later left their settlements there to go to Libya], and built a similar temple, finally reaching the land of the Thracian Edonians, who received them hospitably. Here Telephassa [who was Cadmus's mother and whose name means 'far shiner'; her husband and Cadmus's father was 'Agenor, Libya's son by Poseidon and twin to Belus (who) left Egypt to settle in the Land of Canaan, where he married Telephassa, otherwise called Argiope ("bright- face"), who bore him Cadmus', etc. And notice the name Argiope, related as it is to what we will discuss in a moment as the *Argo*-complex of words and the related meaning of *argent*, silver, taken here as the shade of meaning from this large *Argo*-complex.] died suddenly and, after her funeral, Cadmus and his companions proceeded on foot to the Delphic Oracle. When he asked where Europe (his lost sister) might be found, the Pythoness* (of Delphi) advised him to give up his search and, instead, follow a cow and build a city wherever she should sink down for weariness. . . . at last (the cow) sank down where the city of Thebes now stands, and here (Cadmus) erected an image of Athene, calling it by her Phoenician name of Onga. Cadmus, warning his companions that the cow must be sacrificed to Athene without delay, sent them to fetch lustral water from the Spring of Ares [Mars], now called the Castalian Spring, but did not know that it was guarded by a great serpent. This serpent killed most of Cadmus's men, and he took vengeance by crushing its head with a rock. No sooner had he offered to Athene the sacrifice than she appeared, praising him for what he had done, and ordering him to sow the serpent's teeth in the soil. When he obeyed her, armed Sparti, or Sown Men, at once sprang up, clashing their weapons together. Cadmus tossed a stone among them [just as Jason later did] and they began to brawl, each accusing the other of having thrown it, and fought so fiercely that, at last, only five survived; Echion, Udaeus, Chthonius, Hyperenor, and Pelorus, who unanimously offered Cadmus their services. But Ares demanded vengeance for the death of the serpent, and Cadmus was sentenced by a divine court to become his bondsman for a Great Year.

Note here that the serpent's teeth motif is again linked with the concept of fifty. For the Great Year is a hundred months long and consists of two

---

* Another name for the Sibyl at Delphi.

separate cycles of fifty months, as I have mentioned before. It is just as well for us that Hyginus and Apollodorus have preserved this interesting bit of information which Graves has passed on from them. The 'Spring of Ares' resembles 'the grove of Ares' where the golden fleece was hung, and both were guarded by serpents. And in both the story of the *Argo* and this story the hero throws a stone in the midst of the sown men – the stone motif again, a thrown stone being central to the Deukalion story and to the Orchomenos ghost, etc. (see page 149). And it was a stone with which Cadmus crushed the serpent's head as well.

The cow in the Cadmus story is also reminiscent of the Egyptian sacred cow Hathor, who was identified with Isis. *Hathor* is the form we use for the original Egyptian *He-t-Her*, which means 'the House of Horus'. (Horus is, of course, our form for the Egyptian *Heru*, or *Her*.)

It is interesting that the cow Hathor – 'House of Horus' – is identified with Isis, who, as Sothis, is the star Sirius and who is also the Mother of Horus. Hathor seems to be meant to represent the actual Sirius system, the 'house' or area in the celestial regions. And significantly the sister of Isis, Nephthys, whom I have earlier identified with Sirius B, the dark star of the system, is our form for the original Egyptian *Neb-t-He-t*, which means 'Lady of the House'. The reader will recall a previous discussion of the word *Neb* meaning 'Lord'. *Neb-t* is merely the female form of the word, and means 'Lady'. And presumably the house of which Nephthys is the Lady is the House of Horus. In other words, the lady is just as much a resident of the area of Sirius as is Sirius herself. Just because she is the dark sister does not mean that she is not quite as much at home in the House of Horus as Isis.

So much for the cow who led Cadmus to the serpent's teeth. It will all make even more sense as we go along. Wait till we find out what 'serpent's teeth' really means.

Now to resume Graves's commentary on all these Cadmean adventures at Thebes:[38] 'The myth of the Sown Men and Cadmus's bondage to Ares suggests that the invading Cadmeans secured their hold on Boeotia by successfully intervening in a civil war among the Pelasgian tribes who claimed to be autochthonous ['sprung from the earth']; and that they accepted the local rule of an eight-year [one hundred months according to Graves's lunar theories, but it really comes to only ninety-six] reign for the sacred king. Cadmus killed the serpent in the same sense as Apollo killed the Python at Delphi (see 21.12). The names of the Sown Men – Echion ("viper"); Udaeus ("of the earth") . . .'

At this point I shall interrupt him once again.[39] Let us look at this strange name Udaeus. We should note that the similar word 'οδαξ (*odax*) means 'by biting with the teeth' and comes from the verb root ΔAK (*dak*) and its infinitive *dakein* which means 'to bite – of dogs'. Perhaps this is a clue as to the importance of *teeth*, since in Greek there was this word 'to

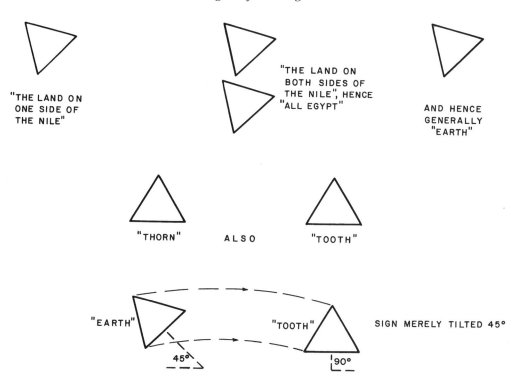

Figure 43. Hieroglyphics for tooth and thorn

bite' which specifically referred to the biting of dogs and it may be that this aspect of dogs was incorporated at a pre-Hellenic early date into the lore of the Dog Star by one of those many puns which proliferated in all the high civilizations of the Mediterranean. We must, in order to understand the ancient inclinations to punning, rid ourselves of our modern prejudice against puns as a form of humour. Puns in the ancient world had no direct humorous intent. In a milieu where codes and allegories were sorely needed, puns provided the 'handles' to new ways of cloaking truths by use of synonyms. If it was a game, it was a sacred game, a *ludens*. For Thebes was the site of the Castalian Spring, as just mentioned a moment ago, and was intimately part of the milieu of the *ludi* of the ancient world.

Also, where *circe* meant 'rings', so does *daktylios* – which specifically means 'anything ring-shaped'. Thus we see another meaning in common in our complex of interweaving terms connected with Sirius traditions. A possible further example of this is in the hieroglyphics of Egypt. Wallis Budge informs us in *Egyptian Language*, in his list of hieroglyphs,[40] that the sign for 'thorn' (which is the tooth of a plant) is almost identical with the sign for Sothis-Sirius. The same sign tilted 45° represents *àteb*, the land on one side of the Nile, and if placed one on top of another, forming a pair, means 'all Egypt'. The very same sign is incorporated in the sign for *ārt* meaning 'jawbone with teeth'. Remember Gilgamesh with his jaw to the earth 'and his teeth shook'. Certainly this all seems to mean something. In fact, the same single sign which means 'the land on one side of the Nile' and looks like a tilted tooth, also has the general meaning of 'earth', which latter concept is so important in all the later Greek Sirius-traditions. It may well be that all these puns on the determinative hieroglyphic sign for Sirius came, in the usual way with the pun-loving Egyptian priests, to form a complicated body of Sirius doctrine involving teeth, Earth-born, ring-shaped, falcon or hawk (Circe), etc., etc. It should therefore not surprise us in the least to learn that the ancient Egyptian word for 'tooth', *ābeh*, has exactly the same hieroglyph as the word for Earth. Hence the origin, almost without question, of the connection between teeth and the Earth: in ancient Egypt they were written by the identical sign, which were tilted forms of the same sign used to represent Sirius!

Notes

1. Peter Levi's translation of Pausanius, op. cit.
2. Graves, *The Greek Myths*, op. cit., 120.1.
3. Ibid.
4. Ibid., 120.1.
5. Larousse *Encyclopaedia of Mythology*, Paul Hamlyn, London, 1965, pp. 90–1.
6. Lindenblad, op. cit. (see Note 2 to Chapter Two). See also further discussion in Chapter Nine.
7. *Greek Myths*, 131.g. and 131.2.
8. Proclus on Euclid's *Elements*, op. cit.: two translations, one by Thomas Taylor (1792) and one by Glenn Morrow (1960s). A translation by Thomas Taylor of much of Simplicius's commentary on Aristotle's *De Caelo* (*On the Heavens*) may be found in *The Works of Aristotle*, London, 1806–12, 9 vols., all trans. by Thomas Taylor and 'printed for the translator'. However, only fifty copies were printed and not a single volume of this work is to be found either in the British Museum Library or in the Bodleian Library at Oxford. The publication was financed originally by William and George Meredith, patrons of learning at the beginning of the nineteenth century. Patrons of this kind of learning seem thin on the ground these days, since the Bollingen Foundation in New York has ceased its benefactions.
9. *Greek Myths*, 3.c.
10. Ibid., 3.3.
11. Benardete, Seth. *Herodotean Inquiries*, The Hague, 1969, p. 126.
12. See the end of his Introduction to *Greek Myths*, op. cit.
13. The four books by Eva Meyrowitz are now out of print. In the fourth book of the series (see Note 14) the author describes the series: 'This is the fourth volume of the series of which the first, *The Sacred State of the Akan* [1951], gives a picture of the old Akan civilization. The second, *Akan Traditions of Origin* [1952], deals with the early history of the people who now call themselves Akan. The third, *The Akan of Ghana, their Ancient Beliefs* [1958, originally entitled *The Akan Cosmological Drama*], showed the development of their religion. The fourth, here presented, attempts to show that Akan religion, which includes the cult of the divine king and the main features of their social organization, is largely derived from Ancient Egypt.' Eva Meyrowitz is an anthropologist from Cape Town who worked in the Gold Coast (now Ghana) from 1936–45 studying the peoples of that country. The third

volume mentioned above (1958) contains a final chapter which is entitled 'Analogies to Akan Beliefs and Customs in Libyan North Africa'. As for the Akan peoples, they speak languages of the Twi branch of the Kwa sub-family of the Western Sudanic linguistic stock and inhabit the eastern part of Ivory Coast, the southern half of Ghana, and parts of Togo. The majority are in Ghana, where they settled in successive waves between the 11th and 18th centuries. All of Meyrowitz's books above, and the fourth mentioned in Note 14, were published by Faber in London.

14. *The Divine Kingship in Ghana and Ancient Egypt* (originally entitled *The Akan of Ghana, the Akan Divine Kingship and Its Prototype in Ancient Egypt*), Faber, London, 1960. Went out of print in February 1963. The map is adapted from one in this book.
15. *Greek Myths*, op. cit., 8.
16. Ibid., 8.2.
17. Ibid., 34.
18. Ibid., 21.2.
19. Ibid., 34.1. and 34.3.
20. Ibid., 143.5.
21. Ibid., 73.c.
22. Ibid., 73.p.
23. Ibid., 73.j.
24. Ibid., 33.3.
25. *The Odes of Pindar*, trans. by C. M. Bowra, Penguin paperback, 1969, p. 176.
26. Eunapius, *Lives of the Philosophers and Sophists*, trans. by W. C. Wright, in Vol. No. 134 of Loeb Library Series (*Philostratus and Eunapius*), Heinemann, London; Harvard University Press, U.S.A., 1961.
27. Ibid., p. 419 (text, 471).
28. Ibid., p. 417 (text, 470).
29. Ibid., pp. 421–5 (text 472): 'Next, into the sacred places they imported monks, as they called them, who were men in appearance but led the lives of swine, and openly did and allowed countless unspeakable crimes. But this they accounted piety, to show contempt for things divine. For in those days every man who wore a black robe and consented to behave in unseemly fashion in public possessed the power of a tyrant, to such a pitch of virtue had the human race advanced! All this however I have described in my *Universal History*. They settled these monks at Canobus also, and thus fettered the human race to the worship of slaves . . .' Among the unspeakable crimes being referred to was the destruction by Bishop Theodosius of the Great Library of Alexandria because it contained 'heathen literature'. Hence, the loss of the hundreds of thousands of books from the ancient world, which everyone laments so often, took place at the hands of a fanatical Christian bishop attempting to wipe out all trace of history before Christ, and not as the result of an accidental fire from the time of Mark Anthony, as the story is usually told.
30. Graves, *Greek Myths*, op. cit, 60.a.
31. Ibid., 60.b.
32. Ibid., 60.b.
33. Ibid., 60.f.
34. Loeb Library, p. 483, Herodotus, Vol. I, trans. A. D. Godley, Harvard University Press, 1960.
35. Graves, *Greek Myths*, op. cit., 152.e.
36. Ibid., 58.5.
37. Ibid., 58.e–g.
38. Ibid., 58.e–g.
39. I will complete the quotation from Graves here: '. . . Chthonius ("of the soil"); Hyperenor ("man who comes up") and Pelorus ("serpent") – are characteristic of oracular heroes. But "Pelorus" suggests that all Pelasgians, not merely the Thebans, claimed to be born in this way; their common feast is the Peloria (see 1.2.)'. The remaining three names are thus seen to be quite as one would expect.

40. Wallis Budge, E. A. *Egyptian Language*, Routledge, Kegan Paul Ltd., London, 1951, pp. 43–94.

SUMMARY

In Greek mythology there were fifty daughters of King Thestios (or Thespius) with whom Hercules (in Greek, Herakles), who is said to have been the predecessor of Jason as leader of the *Argo* and who is demonstrably derived in part from Gilgamesh, had sexual intercourse on fifty successive nights. Again, the number fifty is seen as related to intervals of time – in this instance days instead of months – and again in connection with the complex of myths concerning Sirius.

The monsters Cottus, Briareus, and Gyges of Greek mythology each had fifty heads. Briareus was the original name of the figure later called Hercules, and as Hercules was the original Jason, it is seen that the original commander of the fifty-oared *Argo* was a fifty-headed gentleman. The name Briareus is derived from words meaning 'strength' and 'weight'. Gyges also means 'strength'. As for the name Cottus, Robert Graves says that it is not Greek. In fact, it seems to be derived ultimately from Egyptian *qeṭi* meaning 'oarsmen' (not surprising, since Briareus was the original commander of the fifty oarsmen), and also 'orbit'. The fact that in Egyptian the words for 'oarsman' and 'orbit' are the same may explain why fifty oarsmen are symbolic of a fifty-year orbit. Oar-strokes are ideal constant intervals of time combined with constant intervals of space (distance traversed) and thus perfect symbols of intervals of an orbit. In Greek the Egyptian word meaning both 'orbit' and 'oarsmen' seems to survive as the name of a fifty-headed monster. The conclusion: an orbit of fifty intervals (years) concerned somehow with Sirius and with something called 'Weight' (already known to be assigned by the Arabs to a visible companion of Sirius) – obviously, the fifty-year orbit of Sirius B is being referred to.

Garamas, a brother of the three above-named monsters, is a name also adopted by the Garamantian people. These Garamantians were Libyan residents who migrated from there by way of Algeria to the banks of the Niger River in Mali where they intermarried with local Negroes.

The *Argo* was reported to have stopped in Libya for some time, which resulted in the foundation in Libya of 'a hundred Grecian cities'. The Libyans from whom the Garamantians came are reputed to be 'descended from the Argonauts' through migrant Lemnian Greeks who settled in Libya. These same Garamantians over hundreds – indeed, thousands – of years in their migration to Mali obviously brought to that region as the most secret and holy of all their sacred traditions the sacred Sirius tradition now propounded by the Dogon, who are presumably their descendants. (The Dogon themselves insist that they were definitely not

238

originally native to their present homeland in Mali.)

The Libyan version of the Greek goddess Athena had 'fifty Pallantids' as priestesses, with evident association at an early time with the Garamantians.

The dog Orthrus, brother of the god Cerberus who had fifty heads, was specifically identified by the Greeks with the star Sirius. Robert Graves equates Anubis, Cerberus, and Hecate with each other. This brings together Anubis-the-orbit with Cerberus the fifty-headed dog, and Hecate meaning 'one hundred', as well as Orthrus who is Sirius the Dog Star.

The father of Orthrus was Typhon, one meaning of which is 'a kind of comet' or a 'moving star'. Another meaning is 'blind' or 'darkened'; that is, we see it could refer to a moving but invisible star. And his son Orthrus is clearly identified with Sirius, and had a brother with fifty heads.

Orthrus (Sirius) was the dog of the herdsman Eurytion whom Robert Graves compares with Enkidu, the companion of Gilgamesh. It is possible the name Orthrus may be derived from the Egyptian *urt* meaning 'the setting of a star'. We see this same word used in Chapter Eight in reference to the Sirius complex.

The *Argo* carried the fifty daughters of Danaos, who was 'sent to rule Libya' and had a twin brother Aegyptos, king of Egypt (which got its name from him), who had fifty sons. Sometimes Danaos is said to have fifty sons instead of fifty daughters. It was obviously their number which mattered, not their sex.

'The old man of the sea', named Nereus to the Greeks, had fifty daughters called the Nereids (who are enumerated by Hesiod in his *Theogony*, 241). An 'old man of the sea' is reminiscent of Oannes and Enki – of amphibious wise men generally.

The Greek poet Pindar (fifth century BC) describes the fifty Danaids as 'on shining thrones', reminiscent of the fifty Anunnaki on their shining thrones, of Isis on her shining throne. (The throne is the hieroglyph of Isis who is identified with Sirius.) Danaos is also associated with the wolf- or dog-motif, and that motif refers to the Dog Star, Sirius.

Chapter 8

The Rising of 'Serpent's Tooth'

It would now do to elaborate further on the points so recently made. It should be noted that in Egyptian the hieroglyph *tchet* of a serpent means both 'serpent' and 'body'. The cobra hieroglyph *ārā* means both 'serpent' and 'goddess'. Elsewhere we encounter *ārā* frequently having the common general meaning of 'goddess'. The frequent incorporation of the serpent into late Sirius-lore among the Greeks probably stems from a pun or corruption of the Egyptian determinative form for 'goddess' in reference to the goddess Sothis-Isis (Sirius). In fact, if an Egyptian were to write 'the Goddess Sirius' in hieroglyphs, the result would be:

which can also (by pun) be read quite literally as: 'serpent's tooth'! In addition to this Egyptian pun, there is a Greek pun connected with the story of Jason sowing the teeth. In Greek the word which describes the growing of a tooth from the gum is *anatolē*; a variant is *anatellō*. These words would describe the growing from the ground of the teeth, and 'to make to rise up' or 'to give birth to' is their basic meaning. However, these words are also used to describe the risings of stars and constellations. Hence, if one wanted to say that the star Sirius was rising at the horizon, one could pun and say: 'The tooth is growing up from the ground as from a gum, that is, the ground is giving birth to a tooth.' Hence all the many 'earth-born' creatures linked to the stars, and especially Sirius. As a matter of fact, in translating the now lost early *Argo* tales from Greek into English it is problematical whether instead of saying 'the teeth in the ground gave birth to . . .', etc., one should really have considered the equally literal translation 'Sirius namely "the tooth", rose over the horizon.' In short, when does a pun cease to be a pun and merely consist of a mistranslation based on ignorance of the true subject-matter?

It may be that some of the puns taken over from Egyptian into Greek might have involved the same misunderstandings that ours could do with regard to translating the Greek into English. There may thus be a double layer of obfuscation between English readers and the true subject-matter. Those experts in Greek mythology who may feel safe in discussing 'earth-born' mythological creatures as being sprung from the earth in a direct

240

sense, mud and grime no doubt still caking their hides as they pop up into the air, may be better advised to take into consideration that these creatures were not meant really to be described as coming out of holes in the ground so much as rising over the horizon, due to the fact that they are stars and constellations. And if they are such cosmic figures their peculiar shapes and characteristics become immediately less bizarre and, instead, more meaningful.

We know that Colchis was the place where Helios stabled his horses and rose each morning, according to Greek mythological tradition. Since Colchis was thus the archetypal eastern rising point to the Greeks, being at the far eastern end of the Black Sea and being 'as far east as you can get' to a Greek, it actually represented 'the East'. Thus it makes sense that Jason should have sowed the serpent's teeth there. For the growing of the teeth from the ground at that precise point was symbolic language for: 'The star (goddess) Sirius, known in code as "serpent's tooth", is rising heliacally on the eastern horizon which is symbolically represented by Colchis.' And since the sun follows immediately upon the star at its heliacal rising, all the more reason that 'Serpent's Tooth' should spring up at the place where the Sun, Helios, spends the night and then rises.

The reason why the only other example of serpent's teeth being sown took place at Greek Thebes, when Cadmus sowed them there, is that Egyptian Thebes and Aea at Colchis are equidistant from Greek Thebes (see Figure 17). Hence, a probable reason for the name of Thebes being used in Greece. Greek Thebes is in a sense a 'code' for Colchis, since an action performed there may be understood as taking place within the symbolic framework of the Thebes – Colchis–Thebes triangle (Figure 17). To go to Thebes in Greece was symbolically to step on to the Colchis axis. To sow the teeth at Greek Thebes was to perform the Colchian action on Greek soil because of the knowledge of their geodetic interrelation. This kind of thinking is based on a theory of correspondences such as the Dogon exhibit in all their most minute daily acts.[1] In my opinion, a mind is healthy which can perform symbolic acts within mental frameworks which are not immediately obvious. A mind is diseased when it no longer comprehends this kind of linkage and refuses to acknowledge any basis for such symbolic thinking. The twentieth century specializes in producing diseased minds of the type I refer to – minds which uniquely combine ignorance with arrogance. The twentieth century's hard core hyper-rationalist would deride a theory of correspondences in daily life and ritual as 'primitive superstition'. However, the rationalist's comment is not one upon symbolic thinking but merely one upon himself, acting as a label to define him as one of the walking dead.

Greek Thebes Phthiotides – quite distinct from the main Greek Thebes – almost adjoins Iolchus in Thessaly, a few miles away, from which port Jason and the Argo sailed to Colchis. The voyage of the *Argo* may be seen as a symbolic journey. For to travel from Greek Thebes – either the proper one or a nominal substitute – to Colchis was equivalent to travelling from Greek Thebes to Egyptian Thebes: the distance was the same. Greek Thebes, where 'serpent's teeth' were sown, is equidistant from Colchis, where 'serpent's teeth' were sown, and Egyptian Thebes, where 'Serpent's Tooth' was worshipped. And a ship travelling on one of the lines in effect travels on both. The voyage of the *Argo*, a later form of the *magan*-boat, or 'Egypt-boat', was both to Colchis and to the equidistant Egyptian centre of Thebes, where the prime omphalos was placed in the temple of Ammon.

The name of Danaos who fled Egypt with his fifty daughters (or sons) and went to Argos seems to be derived from Δανάη (Danaē) which is 'the mythological name for *Dry Earth*', according to Liddell and Scott, 'whose union with the fructifying air is expressed in the fable of Zeus and Danae'. And Danae, as we have seen, is associated with the Sirius complex and was also set adrift in an ark. It may or may not be relevant that the Egyptian hieroglyph for wind or air, with which Danae is supposed to have united, is a boat's sail.

The word 'ark' itself is an interesting one worth investigating. We already know that the related word *Argo* was the ship of fifty oars which we believe symbolized Sirius B in its fifty-year orbit. Could this word 'ark' also have a tie-in with the other characteristic of Sirius B, namely its strength? In this we are not disappointed. The Greek verb ἀρκέω (*arkeō*) has the meaning, according to Liddell and Scott's lexicon, of 'to be strong enough'!

Figure 44. Odysseus (Ulysses) returns home to Ithaca after all his wanderings, and is greeted by his faithful dog, Argus, the only one to recognize him. After doing so, Argus dies. This represents both *the completion of a cycle* (which is a meaning of the Egyptian word *arq*, from which Argus derives), and also the ability of the dog to recognize the truth to which men are blind. The dog is the symbol of Sirius, the Dog Star, because Sirius represents a higher level of perception beyond the normal senses of humans, and also a higher truth which we cannot recognize

The word Argus has even applied to a dog. It was the name of the old hunting hound of Odysseus (Ulysses) who recognized his master Odysseus when he finally returned from his voyages, and died as it greeted him. No one else had recognized Odysseus after twenty years' absence except for the faithful old dog, who upon greeting his long-lost master, expired on the spot, as shown in Figure 44.

Argus has also been used by the Greeks as their name for the hundred-eyed monster set by Hera to watch over Io. And it was Io the cow who led Cadmus from Delphi to Thebes where he sowed the serpent's teeth.

If the words ark, *Argo*, Argus, etc., could be construed as having an actual linguistic derivation from the ancient Egyptian (which would have had to precede by some time the Aryan invasion of India *circa* 1500 BC, as the word exists in Sanskrit, as we shall see shortly), then it might ultimately be from *ārq* and *ārqi* which are

These related words have various curious meanings in Egyptian and can be written many ways other than the simplest given above. *Ārq* means 'to complete, to finish', in the sense of a cycle. It also means 'the last' or 'the end of anything'. For instance, *ārq renpet* means 'the festival of the last day of the year'. *Ārqit* means 'the conclusion of a matter'. All these meanings are reminiscent of the meaning of 'Argus' in Homer – to represent the dog who witnesses Odysseus's return and immediately dies, having seen his master's face once again after so many years. The great cycle was completed – Odysseus was home. And immediately Argus dies. Here in the earliest Greek literature we see 'Argus' used as a synonym for the Egyptian *ārq*.

The Egyptian *ārqi* is even more significant. Note the final determinative

(picture not used as a letter) sign ☉ which is a circle with a dot in the

middle. The meaning of this word is 'the end of a period, the last day of the month'. This term, then, has calendrical usage. It can be applied as well to any culmination of a period. Hera's monster Argus has a hundred eyes, and there are a hundred months (comprising two sets of fifty) to a Great Year. Here 'Argus' is a poetic synonym in early Greek tradition for *ārqi*, 'the end of a period' – its culmination, its total when completed.

Our suspicion that there is a distinct reference to an orbital period of Sirius B is hinted at by the additional meaning of *ārq* – 'girdle', representing as it does something around a centre. *Ārq* has the further verbal meaning of 'to bind around', implying specifically a revolution. The Latin *arcere* means 'to enclose' and our present-day word 'arc' carries on the circular motion idea.

Not surprisingly, an *ārqu* is 'an educated man, a wise man, an expert, an

adept'. It is not difficult to realize that anyone privy to the mysteries of *ā
rq* would have to be an adept, an initiate and wise man. Hence this
meaning for someone who knows about *ārq*, an *ārqu*.

In Wallis Budge we find[2] a description (taken from Mau) of an
Egyptian-influenced Italian temple of the first century BC which contained
'seven large paintings representing Egyptian landscapes, and Io watched
by Argus, and Io received by Isis in Egypt. In this room the Mysteries of
Isis were probably acted.' – So we have specific archaeological evidence
that Argus of the hundred eyes was pictured on the wall of the inner
sanctum of an Isis temple, and Isis was, as we know, identified with Sirius.
Also pictured there was Io, whom I earlier compared to the Egyptian
Hathor (see p. 234) who was identified with the Sirius system, and it was
of course this same Io who led Cadmus to the Greek Thebes (there being
an Egyptian Thebes as well, as the reader well recalls).

What were these mysteries of Isis? Well, they seem to have been related
to the Thesmophoria Mysteries which the daughters of Danaos were said
to have brought from Egypt to Argos. For in Liddell and Scott we find
that the name Thesmophoros ('law giving') was a name given to Isis. The
name was most commonly applied to Demeter, a Greek goddess, but was
also the name of Isis in Greece. In short, Isis was represented as Demeter
in connection with these mysteries, but in the Italian temple referred to
above was obviously represented as herself. The 'fifty' and 'hundred',
connected as we have seen with Danaos, are found again here in the ruins
of this Italian temple, where hundred-eyed Argus is portrayed in the inner
sanctum of the Isis temple. The name Thesmophoros should not distract
us too much. It comes from Thesis, with a meaning including our *thesis* of
today – and *thesmos* means 'that which is laid down or established, or
instituted'. And *thesmōdeō* is a verb meaning 'to deliver oracular precepts',
once again a meaning which should not surprise us.*

In Wallis Budge we read[3] from an Egyptian text of 'the star Septet
(Sothis, the Dog Star), whose seats are pure', which is a specific reference
to there being *seats* around Sirius – and, of course, there are fifty seats as
we know, which led to the fifty thrones of the Anunnaki, the fifty oarsmen
of the *Argo*, etc.

In Wallis Budge we also read[4] excerpts of Egyptian texts speaking of
holy emanations proceeding from Sirius and Orion which 'vivify gods,
men, cattle, and creeping things . . . both gods and men', and are a pouring
out of the seed of the soul. Of course, the Dogon maintain the same thing
in almost precisely the same terms. To them the seed which energizes the
world pours forth from the Sirius system.

In Wallis Budge we find also a particularly interesting bit of further

---

* Plutarch in 'Isis and Osiris' (378 D) informs us: 'Among the Greeks also many things are done
which are similar to the Egyptian ceremonies in the shrines of Isis, and they do them at about
the same time. At Athens the women fast at the Thesmophoria sitting upon the ground.'[5]

information.[6] There we learn that the deceased spirit of a man 'goes to Nephthys' and the celestial boat. We have much earlier identified the dark Nephthys with Sirius B. It is therefore interesting to learn that as soon as the deceased visits Nephthys and his 'double' (*ka*) is recorded in heaven, he immediately 'revolves like the sun' – which I think is a pretty specific astronomical description. As he *revolves* he 'leads on the Ṭuat (underworld or heaven)', which is a curious turn of phrase implying a round dance or at least motion which is purposeful, 'and is pure of life in the horizon like Saḥu (Orion) and Sept (Sirius, the Dog-star)'. I hope it will be noticed that the phrase here reads '*in* the horizon' – and much earlier I said I believed the term 'the horizon' applied specifically to the orbit of Sirius B. Here we have the deceased revolving like a sun in a purposeful way in 'the horizon'. I don't think the Egyptians could possibly have been more specific and clear than this. Wallis Budge comments: 'The mention of Orion and Sothis is interesting, for it shows that at one time the Egyptians believed that these stars were the homes of departed souls.'

Having learned this (a belief held as well by the Dogon, as we know), let us return to our word *ārq* which I believe to be the origin of *ark* and *Argo* and *Argus* in Greek, all of which I claim are related to Sirius. Perhaps the reader will not be too amazed if by now I inform him that *ārq ḥeḥ* is a 'necropolis' and *ārq-ḥeḥtt* is 'the Other World' – which we have just this moment learned was located by the early Egyptians at the star Sirius! (Also remember that the guardian of the necropolis in Greek was a *circe* in the *Argo* story.)

Ārq has the further meaning of 'a measure', possibly because spirits are normally measured in *Ārq-ḥeḥtt*.

And for final touches of mystery, I will add that *ārq* can mean 'to wriggle (of a serpent)' – from 'binding around' – and *ārq ur* is the word for that mystery of mysteries, the Sphinx!

The same word means also 'silver', and Wallis Budge claims that the Greek ἄργυρος (*argyros*) is derived from it, which gave us our heraldic term argent and the country's name Argentina. Since this term in Greek is derived from *ārq ur* (*ur* means 'chief' or 'Great'), in the opinion of an eminent expert, I believe there is no objection then to my suggestion that the other Greek words came from *ārq* and its forms.* But, as I said, this derivation is one which entered Indo-European from Egypt before the Aryan invasion of India, for in Sanskrit *ārksha* means 'stellar, belonging to or regulated by the stars or constellations', and *ārksha-varsha* is 'a stellar year or revolution of a constellation'. This is very similar to the meaning in Egyptian of 'the end of a period', and a calendrical application to the end of a month. In Sanskrit again *ārka* means 'belonging or relating

* In discussion with Professor Oliver R. Gurney of Oxford, who was sceptical of Egyptian origins of Indo-European words, I found that he considered Wallis Budge's suggestion possible on two bases: (1) The word is a technical one, (2) my explanation of the Colchian connection as providing a geographical forum for such linguistic influence.

to the sun'. *Arkam* means 'as far as the sun, even to the sun inclusively'. *Ārki* has become a name for Saturn, thought at that time to be the most distant planet. *Arc* means 'to shine, be brilliant', and can mean 'to cause to shine'. *Ārkin* means 'radiant with light'. *Arka* means 'a ray' and is also a religious ceremony. An *arka-kara* is a 'sunbeam'. *Arkaja* means 'sun-born, coming from the sun', and it and *arkanandana* can be applied to the planet Saturn. *Arkaparna* is the name of a snake demon. *Arka-putra* is also Saturn. Forms of the word relate also to various specific astronomical events and the Arka ceremony and the arka plant which has 'a grain of fruit' of some importance,* reminding one of all the grains of the Dogon (which one learns about by reading more about the Dogon than I have given in this book), particularly the grain Digitaria which gave its name to Sirius B among the Dogon – in their own language, of course.

Arcā means 'worship, adoration'. *Arjuna*, besides being the famous Hindu mythical personage, means 'white, clear' and 'made of silver' – this latter being clearly a form of *ārq ur*, the Egyptian variant form of *ārq* meaning 'silver', which I mentioned a moment ago and which, according to Wallis Budge, has the cognate in Greek which was just mentioned, *argyros* meaning 'silver'.

And as Argo is a constellation in the sky, it should not be a surprise to us to find that in India the Sanskrit *Arjuna* refers to a specific Vedic constellation. (The Vedas were the earliest Sanskrit texts, and gave their name to the initial Aryan residence in India.) The actual name of the constellation is *Phalgunī*. *Phala* means 'grain' or 'seed'. The *Phal-grantha* is a work describing the effects of celestial phenomena on the destiny of men.

There is also a connection of the Sanskrit with an expression involving a thigh; in Greek, *Arktos* became a name for our constellation Ursa Major, which was known to the Egyptians as 'the thigh' – the Egyptians often drew pictures of it as a bull's thigh.

There has not been room either in the original edition or in this revised (1997) edition to publish my appendix entitled 'An Explanation of the "Laryngeal Theory" of Hittite'. However, I have worked out an explanation for this celebrated linguistic problem which was originally suggested by the problem which we have just discussed, of the *ark* words. The Hittite cognate for *argyros* 'silver' is the word *ḫarki* 'white'. (The Tocharian cognate is *ārki*, the Sanskrit is *ārjuna*.) I became interested in the strange Hittite letter which was a mysterious lost guttural sound called 'a laryngeal'. After a time, this laryngeal sound disappeared from Hittite, and it is not known in any other of the Indo-European languages. I therefore made a survey of eight examples of Hittite words containing the laryngeal and was able to demonstrate that all of them appear to have had origins from Egyptian words containing strange guttural sounds which the Hittites had tried to accommodate with their laryngeal *ḫ*. The Hittite words were:

---

* *Calotropis gigantea*, of the family *Asclepidaceae*, closely resembling the Dogbane family.

ḫarki, išḫai/išḫiya ('to bind'), *paḫš* ('to protect'), *newaḫḫ* ('renew'), *ešḫar* ('blood'), *ḫaštai* ('bone', from which comes osteopathy!), *paḫḫur* ('fire', from which comes pyre), and *ḫanti* ('in front of' from which comes 'anti-'). The Egyptian origins of all of these terms are: *ārq ur* ('silver'), *m'shaiu* ('bindings of a bow'), *pa-āa-n-ursh* ('guardian'; Coptic is *panourshe*), *n'uatch* ('to be young and new on account of'), *tesher* ('blood'), *qes/qas* ('bone'), *pā-u* ('flames'), and *khenti* ('in front of'). I suggested that a military force from Egypt had come into prolonged contact with the Hittites and most of these words such as 'blood', 'bone', 'flames', 'protect', 'bind', 'occupying a front position', formed part of a common idiom for soldiers and had been adopted into Hittite as a result. From thence they made their way into most of the Indo-European language before the Aryans migrated to India. The laryngeal sound, I suggested, was adopted by the Hittites to try and pronounce such weird Egyptian sounds as deeply-breathed *a* and *u* vowels and gutturals like the Egyptian *q* and *kh* sounds. I worked out this solution to the laryngeal theory of Hittite in about 1973, and only now 24 years later am I mentioning it in this brief form, which is better than not mentioning it at all, I suppose. It seems to me notable that the solution to the problem emerged from the position which I took on the *ark* words as being derived from Egyptian, and I look upon it therefore as an unexpected confirmation of the soundness of that viewpoint.

If the reader can bear some other words, I propose to consider a few which are important in other ways. I beg to refer again to the work of Wallis Budge, which is becoming rather familiar to us now,[7] since I have cited it so frequently in recent pages. The reader must realize that we are nearing the end of the matter and summon his last reserves of patience for the final trudge across hieroglyphic soil, craggy though it may be.

In Wallis Budge, then,[8] we find a passage from one of the Pyramid Texts[*] where Osiris is described in his role of husband of Sothis (Sirius) and implored: 'Be not wroth in thy name of Tchenṭeru'. This plaintive plea must be examined. What on earth is so terrible about this 'Tchenṭeru'? Well, to begin an explanation, the word *tchentch* means 'wrath, anger'. So that is obviously the meaning of the word. But we have to continue to pursue this.

Shortly afterwards in the same Pyramid Text we read of the birth of Horus the son of Osiris, by Sothis: 'Horus-Sepṭ [Horus-Sirius] cometh forth from thee in the form of "Horus, dweller in Sepṭ [Sirius]". Thou makest him to have a spirit in his name of "Spirit, dweller in Tchenṭeru".'

Here we have an interesting new light on this Tchenṭeru which seemed so important for no reason which was immediately apparent. It is something to do with Sirius. What, then? Obviously the close association of the place Tchenṭeru and the Sirius system led me to investigate the word and its related forms.

---

[*] Texts inscribed on the walls of passages in some of the Pyramids. The archaic language – thou, etc. – is an affectation of the translator.

I found that *tchentha* means 'throne'. I found that *tchenḥ-t* means 'beam (of a ship)' – second significant meaning. And I discovered a third. Namely, that *tchens* means 'weight, heavy'! This was just too much to be coincidence. We first have the Sirius system described as being the place Tchenṭeru and then discover that that word in related forms means three strictly Sirius-related things: 'throne', 'beam of a ship', and 'weight, heavy'. Tchenṭeru is 'the place of weight or heaviness' and is identified by the Egyptians with the Sirius system! I also discovered that Tchenti is a two-headed god (later this name became one of the seventy-five names of Ra and lost its original importance). Now, a two-headed god with each head representing one orbit and having fifty eyes, gives us a hundred-eyed god, and the hundred-eyed monster of the Greeks was Argus.

Wallis Budge says another form of *tchens*, 'weight', is *ṭens*, which also means 'weight, heavy'. And the very next word in the giant dictionary is *ṭeng* which means 'dwarf'! We thus see an apparent variation of the same word meaning 'heavy' and 'dwarf', and this word is specifically applied to the Sirius system.

But just in case there are any sceptics left (and there always are), a look at the Egyptian word *shenit* will be helpful. This word means 'the divine court of Osiris'. The same word *shenit* means 'circle, circuit', and *shent* means 'a circuiting, a going round, revolution'. *Shenu* means 'circuit, circle, periphery, circumference, orbit, revolution', and there is a specific expression written:

$$\Omega \ \Omega$$

which Wallis Budge gives, and which means 'the two circuits' – and of course twice fifty is a hundred, giving us the Great Year. *Shen ur* means 'the Great Circle' or 'the circuit of the Great Circle' or 'the islands of Shen-

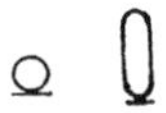

Figure 45. Left: the Egyptian symbol *shen*; *right:* the cartouche sign inside which it became habitual to write the name of the Pharaoh and other proper names. As E. A. Wallis Budge says in *Egyptian Magic* (Routledge & Kegan Paul, London, 1899/1972, pp. 61–2: '[Shen] . . . is intended to represent the sun's orbit, and it became the symbol for an undefined period of time, i.e. eternity; it was laid upon the body of the dead with the view of giving to it life which should endure as long as the sun revolved in its orbit in the heavens. In the picture of the mummy chamber the goddesses Isis and Nephthys are seen kneeling and resting their hands on *shen*. . . . The . . . cartouche has been supposed to be nothing more than *shen* elongated . . .' The cartouche is an ellipsoid shape, and I believe that this 'stretched' or 'elongated' *shen* is specifically meant to represent an *elliptical* orbit. The fact that the sisters Isis and Nephthys, representing Sirius and her 'dark companion', have their hands placed upon *shen*, and the reason why *shen* is often represented as double, is in reference to the binary star system at Sirius. And the fact that there was an elliptical form of *shen* which became the receptacle for names is in reference to the esoteric knowledge that heavenly orbits are really elliptical and not circular, as specifically stated by the Dogon tribe

ur', which last is interesting in that it indicates that this place of the Great Circle is not only 'the divine court of Osiris', who is the husband of Sothis (Sirius), but is also a place with islands (stars or planets) where one can presumably live. It does seem that the Egyptians had quite as clear a conception of the Sirius system as the Dogon have.

The verb *shenu* means 'to go round, to encircle', but the verb *shen* means 'to hover over', and presumably the great orbit is above us in the sky, hovering over us in space.

The Egyptian word *khemut* means 'hot parching winds, the khamāsin, or khamsin, i.e. winds of the "fifty" hot days'. This is rather interesting. Arabic *khamsin*, 'fifty' and Hebrew *khamshin*, 'fifty', are obviously derived from this Egyptian source. In late times 'the dog days' about the time of the rising of Sirius and called 'dog days' from 'the Dog Star' were supposed to be hot and scorching. There are many references to this in writers like Pliny and Virgil. Here is an earlier tradition of hot days incorporating the Sirian number *fifty*. This same word *khemut* has familiar meanings in its related forms. *Khemiu-urțu* means 'the stars that rest not'. *Khemiu-ḥepu* means 'a class of stars'. *Khemiu-ḥemu* also means 'a class of stars'. In short, *khemiu* means 'stars'. So *khem* (though apparently not used on its own in surviving texts) really means 'star', as well as referring to fifty days. *Khem* also has the meanings 'shrine, holy of holies, sanctuary', and 'little, small', also 'he whose name is unknown, i.e. God', also 'god of procreation and generative power', also 'to be hot', and 'unknown'. All these meanings are relevant to the Sirius mysteries. The Sirius system was held to be the source of generative and procreative power as we have already seen, Sirius B was of course 'unknown', and was 'little, small', and was a star that rests not. And which star rests not unless it be Sirius B? For only the planets, which were well known and differentiated by the ancient Egyptians, 'rested not' with the remarkable exception of Sirius B. Comets and meteors apart, and they too were well classed to themselves.

There is a 'Hymn to Osiris' preserved on a stele in the Bibliothèque Nationale, Paris, which dates from the XVIIIth Dynasty around 1500 BC, and which we find in Wallis Budge. We find *khem* used in this interesting hymn in the following passage:[9]

àukhemu — seku
The stars which never diminish

kher àst
are under
the throne

ḥrà-f
of his face,

àst –
his thrones

f

pu
are

àukhemu-urțu
the stars which never rest.

249

This passage is extremely interesting because of the recurrent theme of 'thrones' (which word as a proper noun in the singular is the name of Isis) as applied to the celestial region of Osiris – which, as we know, is the Sirius system. Of course, in the superficial view this passage may seem merely to describe some vague kind of reference to a great god who is in the sky somewhere or other, and has a heavenly throne and has a lot of stars twinkling here and there around him for added glamour. But a close inspection of the way things are said here won't let that kind of interpretation stand up. The fact is that the Egyptians were incredibly precise in what they said. One cannot just gloss over inconvenient precise statements which seem unintelligible and tempt one to brush them aside in order to 'get on with it'. In the above passage describing the *khem* or stars, we find them associated with – indeed identified with – thrones, which are quite separate from the throne of Osiris himself. Now, this is precisely equivalent to the description of the throne of Anu and the thrones of the Anunnaki which surround it, as we meet in Sumer. And here too the context is both celestial and related to Sirius. And here too the thrones are 'stars which never rest' – which could be a description of the movement of Sirius B, with the familiar meaning of each year's 'step' in the orbit equated with a 'throne'. The same word, *khemut*, however, refers to fifty days; and to Sirius!

There is another Egyptian word which can shed some light on our subject. A possible explanation of serpent's teeth and their springing up as soldiers may result from a pun on the Egyptian word *meni*. This word means both 'soldier' and 'to plough, to till the earth, to cultivate'. A combination of the two meanings yields the strange idea of soldiers resulting from ploughing. And in the Jason story, Jason has to yoke the bulls and plough the field – only after which can he sow the serpent's teeth. Anyone who has read the *Argonautica* will know this. Jason didn't just walk into some field, throw some serpent's teeth about like birdseed, stand back and presto! He had to plough the field. He had to practise *meni* in order to produce *meni*.

Now we must turn our attention to the mysterious Egyptian word *tchā m*. A general meaning of *tchām* is 'sceptre', possibly because the meaning of *tchām en Ànpu* is the name of 'the magical sceptre of Ànpu (Anubis)'.

Tchāmti are 'bowmen' and Sirius is the Bow Star, as we know. Now, the really intriguing meaning of *tchām* is 'a kind of precious metal'. There are various expressions in the literature such as 'the finest *tchām*', 'real *tchām*', and '*tchām* from the hill-top'. The impression one gets is that this *tchām* is a pretty special commodity. Presumably Anubis's sceptre, which is the *tchām* sceptre, is made of this *tchām* material. A sceptre is an object which exercises rule and force. The fact that there is '*tchām* from the hill-top' could either have a mundane meaning to the effect that the stuff is a metal mined in the hills or more likely is connected with Anubis, not only through his sceptre, but through the hilltop as the residence of the god in the ziggurat sense such as one finds in Sumer. For Anubis was known as 'Anubis of the hill'.

In Wallis Budge we find more information from Pyramid Texts about *tchā m*.[10] The references are entirely stellar. There is a description of the deceased Pharaoh, in this case Pepi I. Pepi's father is Tem 'the great god of An (Heliopolis) and the first living Man-god; the creator of heaven and earth'. In Sumer too the great god of An was the creator of heaven and earth, but there was not, as far as we know, a city named after him as was the Egyptian city of An which came to be known to the Greeks as Heliopolis.

Of Pepi we read in the text that 'the appearance of this god in heaven, which is like unto the appearance of Tem in heaven'. This is all gross flattery – typical for the texts mourning the dead Pharaohs. Every Pharaoh looks like the great god of An and every other great god and does every conceivable celestial thing. The Pharaoh is dead, long live the Pharaoh!

Now various gods, including the Governor of the Land of the Bow and Sept (Sirius) 'under his trees', carry a ladder for Pepi. Pepi then 'appeareth on the two thighs of Isis, Pepi reposeth on the two thighs of Nephthys'. Tem puts Pepi at the head of all the gods, and 'Pepi setteth out in his boat', with Horus. He then stands 'among the imperishable stars, which stand up on their *tchām* sceptres, and support themselves on their staves'. This seems to make clear that the metal *tchām* is also a specifically stellar material which supports the stars!*

Then we read:[11] 'This Pepi liveth life more than your sceptres *āu*.' The word *au au* means 'dog, jackal', and I suspect a connection with 'dog star' and Anubis who is jackal/dog. Also the *àu-t en àthen* is the *àu-t* of the sun, or 'the course of the sun'. But, to resume:

> O ye gods of the Sky, ye imperishable ones, who sail over the Land of Tehenu [the Tehentiu are 'the sparkling gods, the stellar luminaries' from *tehen* which means 'to sparkle, to scintillate'] in your boats, and direct them with your sceptres, this Pepi directeth his boat with you by means of the *uas* sceptre [Uasàr is a variant form of Asàr, the name of Osiris, and *uas-t* is 'a kind of animal, dog (?)'[12]] and the *tchām* sceptre, and he is fourth with you. [indicating that he joins a group of three stars!] O ye gods of heaven, ye imperishable ones, who sail over the Land of Tahennu, who transport yourselves by means of your sceptres, this Pepi transporteth himself with you by means of the *uas* and *tchām*, and he is the fourth with you. . . . This Pepi is the *ànes* matter which cometh forth from Nephthys. . . . Pepi is a star . . . Pepi is Sept, under his *sebt* trees . . . The star Septet (Sothis) graspeth the hand of Pepi. Pepi plougheth the earth . . . Osiris [Pepi is addressed by the name), thou art the double of all the gods. [Uas is also the Egyptian name of Thebes.]

---

* The Greeks had a tradition of 'the strongest metal' and called it *adamant*. Kronos used it to castrate Ouranos (Uranus); mythically it was the strongest metal.

Here we see the dead Pharaoh Pepi's celestial after-death experiences described. He goes to the stellar regions and joins three stars, becoming 'the fourth'. He uses three sceptres for power, the *āu* (similar to a word for dog/jackal), the *uas* (also the name of Thebes, similar to another word for dog, and related to a variant form of the name of Osiris), and the *tchām* (a mysterious metal and the sceptre of the dog/jackal-headed god Anubis). The star Sirius is specifically described as taking his hand. Pepi himself is transformed into a star, as clearly stated: 'Pepi is a star.' He becomes a star and his hand is taken by the star Sirius, which can only mean that he becomes a star in the Sirius system, and he 'becomes fourth with them'. He then is identified in turn with the three other stars of the Sirius system, which are Isis-Sothis, Nephthys, and Osiris. The first emits '*ànes* matter', the second is the female Nephthys, which may be identical with the 'female Sorgho' or Sirius C of the Dogon (though sometimes Nephthys refers to Sirius B in other contexts), and the third is called 'the double of all the gods' – being the circling companion and the archetypal 'double' of many figures from Isis to Gilgamesh. This is quite obviously Sirius B.

And there is *tchām*, the mysterious, potent stellar 'metal' which is said to be the power of Anubis, whom we have earlier identified as the personification of the *orbit* of Sirius B. And *tchām* is quite similar to the word we dealt with earlier, *tchens*, meaning 'weight', and its related forms *tens* 'heavy, weight', *tensmen* 'to be heavy' and the similar word *teng* 'dwarf'. If we spoke of something described only by a series of these apparently related words, namely: *tchens tens teng tchām*, the meaning would be, quite literally, allowing for the absence of proper grammar, 'the weight (of) heavy dwarf star-metal', remembering that *tchām* is also specifically identified as the power of the god Anubis whom we have identified previously as the orbit of Sirius B, the dwarf star composed of super-heavy 'star-metal'.

Concerning this star-metal it is as well to take notice that in 'Isis and Osiris' (376 B), Plutarch says of the Egyptians:[13] 'Moreover, they call the lodestone the bone of Horus, and iron the bone of Typhon, as Manetho records' (Manetho fragment 77.) Recall that 'the bones of Earth' in ancient tradition are stones. It is interesting that a heavy metal is 'the bone' of Typhon which we have earlier determined as a description of Sirius B. And magnetized iron or lodestone is 'the bone' of Horus, the son of Isis and Osiris. This is exactly the sort of tradition one would expect.

We must recall that Anubis is our form of writing the actual Egyptian word Ànp or Ànpu. The verb *ànp* means 'to wrap around', obviously connected with Anubis's role as sacred embalmer. It is significant that *Ànp heni* is 'a jackal-headed god who guarded the river of fire, a form of Anubis'. We have already postulated that 'the river of fire' may be a way of describing the orbit of the star Sirius B, so it is quite interesting to see that Anubis, whom we have already identified as representing the orbit, is specifically said to be the guardian of the same river of fire. And 'wrap around' could have an orbital meaning as well as its obvious meaning of 'swathe'.

We recall that a special description of *tchām* given in Wallis Budge's *Dictionary*[14] was '*tchām* from the hill-top'. Also we have just equated *tchā m* with Anubis. So it should not surprise us that a title of Anubis is *Tepi ṭu-f* 'he who is on his hill'. As I mentioned a moment ago, this seems to be a ziggurat-concept such as one finds in Mesopotamia. The *tepi* complex of words is quite interesting and bears examination.

Tepi means 'the foremost point of the bow of the ship, the hindmost part of the stern' – extremely specific and exactly fitting my specification of what was important about the ship *Argo. Tepi* also means 'the first day of a period of time', and I maintained earlier that the tip of the prow and the tip of the stern of *Argo* (with fifty oar-places between them) was a symbol of the orbit of Sirius B. Also we will recall that *ārqi* means 'the last day of a period of time'. So any period of time has a first day called *tepi* and a last day called *ārqi* in Egyptian. And *tepi* describes the *Argo* just as *ārq* is the origin of the very word *Argo*. And *Tepi* is part of a crucial descriptive title of Anubis whom I have equated with the *Argo*. There is even a further connection between *tepi* and the Sirius-complex. The word *tep ra* means 'the base of a triangle' and the words *sepṭu* and *septch* both mean 'triangle' – Sepṭit is Sirius and the triangle is its hieroglyph.

The basic meaning of *tep* is 'mouth' (hence the meaning *tep ra sebek* ' "crocodile's mouth" – a disease of the eye') and even more fundamentally 'beginning or commencement of anything'. It is interesting for the study of concepts of geometry to note that the Egyptians thought of the base of a triangle as its 'mouth' or beginning.

Now, the link-up which takes place between *ārqi* and *tepi* – that is, the end of a cycle and the beginning of the next – could lead to some confusion without much trouble. If the last day of the old cycle is the *ārqi* and the first day of the new cycle is the *tepi*, it would be easy to begin to think of the *ā rqi* as the beginning — after all, it and the *tepi* are adjoining each other and amount to practically the same thing. In a sense one could say that the true end of a cycle *is* the beginning of the next. For us, New Year's Day is represented by a combination of an old man with a sickle or scythe walking away and a baby, representing the New Year. The two figures are together. Similarly, the *ārqi* and the *tepi* are inescapable companions. As time passed and traditions decayed a bit, it must have been an easy thing to think of *ārqi* as the actual beginning of a new cycle, since it was the end of the old. And it is this which I presume happened in Greek, for the verb *archōmai* means 'one must begin' or 'one must make a beginning'. And it is related to *archē*, which means 'beginning, starting-point', etc., and which survives in our *architecture* and *archetype*. So here is further evidence that the 'ark' words in the Indo-European languages derived from the Egyptian *arq* words.

Another link of the 'ark' words complex with the Argonaut story is found in a strange place. One of the most peculiar of all treatises to survive from ancient times is the curious *Of the Names of Rivers and Mountains and of such Things as are to be found therein*.[15] This treatise survived in the corpus of Plutarch's writings but is obviously not by him. Plutarch lived in the first century AD, but this treatise seems a little later than that. In fact, the treatise strikes me as basically a wild satire on a type of writing which was then common. One of the rivers discussed in this treatise is the Phasis, up which Jason sailed to Aea in Colchis. Of this river we read: 'It was formerly called Arcturus . . .'. Without elaborating on this point, I merely wish to note that the very river at Colchis once may have had a name which may be related to the 'ark' word complex. Arcturus supposedly means 'bear-ward', referring to the ward of the bear known to us as Ursa Major, the Big Dipper. Arcturus in the constellation of Bootes is conceived of as its companion according to Allen, who says it had connections with Osiris and possibly Horus. This is probably another of the many confusions arising from 'companions' who are compared to each other. But as I said, I do not wish to be led astray by elaborating on the question of the name Arcturus and all that that would involve. I merely note the fact that the Phasis was once the Arcturus and leave it at that.

The name Phasis had connections with birds, such as with an expression 'the Phasian bird'. Recall the *kirke* or Circe connections with Colchis. It is interesting then to note that the *phassa* in Greek is 'the ringdove'. Forms of this word refer to doves and doves are, as we have seen previously, intimately associated with omphalos-oracle centres marked out from Behdet. And we know that Aea in Colchis, which is on the River Phasis and has such associations with the *Argo* and the oracles, is related to doves in this way and also because of the doves let fly from the arks and *Argo*. So the fact that *Phasis* and *phassa* are connected is no surprise. This river, whether named Phasis or Arcturus, seems to be aptly designated. It is also to be noted that in Greek a *phasso-phonos* or 'dove-killer' is the name of a kind of hawk. And *kirke* is likewise!

Before leaving Plutarch behind, we might note also that in 'Isis and Osiris', he tells us that a name for Osiris was *Omphis*. An interesting tie-in with the oracles, attested by Plutarch as current in Egypt in his day.

To return to *tepi*, we note that *tep ra* means not only 'the base of a triangle' but 'divine oracle', which is also quite relevant. I have postulated that the oracles are connected with the *Argo* as representative of the orbit of Sirius B, the beginning of which I designate by *tepi*, and we discover that the name in Egyptian for 'oracle' is *tep ra*.

Tepi ā became the word for 'ancestors', due to the connection of *tepi* with the *beginnings* of things. And the *tepi-āui-qerr-en-pet* were 'the ancestor-gods of the circle of the sky', which is again significant. Visitors, perhaps?

Gods of the circle in the sky seem to be referred to by Plutarch's account of the Persian religion in 'Isis and Osiris' (370 A–B). The Persian religion

254

prior to Islam was Zoroastrianism, which survives today as the religion of the Parsees of Bombay in India, to which city they fled from their Persian homeland when it was being conquered by the Moslem invaders. The Persians are not Semitic Arabs but are Indo-European, with a language and original religion closely related to the Aryan Indians and to Sanskrit. In fact, the earliest form of Sanskrit, which is called Vedic, is very little different from the earliest form of Persian, which is called Avestan.

Zoroaster* (also known as Zarathusthra) is known to have postulated two basic divine principles: Ahura Mazda the principle of light and goodness, and Ahriman the principle of evil and darkness. These two principles are also known by the names of Oromazes and Areimanius, which are the names used for them in Plutarch's treatise. If we recall Plutarch's description, cited by us earlier, that Anubis was the circle dividing the light from the dark in Egyptian religion, it will be interesting to note that in 369 E–F he equates with this concept, by describing it in similar terms, the Persian god Mithras who mediates between the darkness and the light. Then in 370 we find this remarkable passage: '(The Persians) also tell many fabulous stories about their gods, such, for example, as the following: Oromazes, born from the purest light, and Areimanius, born from the darkness, are constantly at war with each other; and Oromazes created six gods, the first of Good Thought, the second of Truth, the third of Order, and, of the rest, one of Wisdom, one of Wealth, and one the Artificer of Pleasure in what is Honourable. But Areimanius created rivals, as it were, equal to these in number.' These twelve gods would seem to be zodiacal. But it is the following passage, immediately after this, which becomes really interesting: 'Then Oromazes enlarged himself to thrice his former size, and removed himself as far distant from the Sun as the Sun is distant from the Earth, and adorned the heavens with stars. One star he set there before all others as a guardian and watchman, the Dog-star. Twenty-four other gods he created and placed in an egg. But those created by Areimanius, who were equal in number to the others, pierced through the egg and made their way inside; hence evils are now combined with good.' A footnote to the Loeb edition adds: 'It is plain that the two sets of gods became intermingled, but whether the bad gods got in or the good gods got out is not clear from the text.'

This passage is really deserving of some attention. We find a quite specific description of all this taking place in a region meant to be distinct from our solar system. The Persians seem to have quite clearly understood the fixed stars to have been beyond the system of the sun. This, at least, is what they seem to be trying to convey – a distinction of locale. In any case, the 'light' god Oromazes and the 'dark' god Areimanius each create twenty-five gods, which gives fifty. And they are placed in an egg, which is

* The prophet Zoroaster, who founded Zoroastrianism, the religion of Persia/Iran until the Mohammedan conquest, is of uncertain date, but certainly seems to have lived prior to 600 BC.

an elliptical shape just as in an orbit. One of the twenty-five gods created by Oromazes is by a slight garbling said to be Sirius, but in any case, there were created by Oromazes the Dog Star Sirius plus twenty-four other gods which makes twenty-five and a corresponding twenty-five created by Areimanius – and they mingle in the shape of an egg. What does that sound like? And Sirius is specifically stated to be the chief one. And as Areimanius was the 'dark' god and his creations were 'dark', then his creation in opposition to Sirius would be a 'dark' Sirius, wouldn't it? And as for the fifty gods arrayed round Sirius (speaking strictly from this text one would have to say the forty-nine gods arrayed around Sirius, but I speak of garbling of the tradition because, from what we already know from other such descriptions from elsewhere, Sirius should really be the fifty-first element) they obviously represent the fifty years of the orbit of Sirius B in an egg shape around the Dog Star as its 'guardian and watchman'.

There are further examples of a wavering between forty-nine and fifty in the ancient traditions. Graves has these interesting remarks:[16] 'Chief priestesses were chosen by a foot race (the origin of the Olympic Games), run at the end of the fifty months, or of forty-nine in alternate years.' Apart from the fact that Graves here speaks of 'the fifty months' as antecedent to the Olympiads, a point which we discussed much earlier, we see the alternative use of forty-nine and fifty as a quantitative time measurement. This is rather like the shilly-shallying between forty-nine and fifty in the above Persian description. There is also this example from the Bible, in Leviticus 25, 8–13:

You shall count seven sabbaths of years, that is seven times seven years, forty-nine years, and in the seventh month on the tenth day of the month, on the Day of Atonement, you shall send the ram's horn round. You shall send it through all your land to sound a blast, and so you shall hallow the fiftieth year and proclaim liberation in the land for all its inhabitants. You shall make this your year of jubilee. Every man of you shall return to his patrimony, every man to his family. The fiftieth year shall be your jubilee. You shall not sow, and you shall not harvest the self-sown crop, nor shall you gather in the grapes from the unpruned vines, because it is a jubilee, to be kept holy by you. You shall eat the produce direct from the land.

The above words and many which follow them, but which I will not quote (as anyone can refer to the Bible for the full account), were spoken by God to Moses on Mount Sinai, and are Jehovah's directions as to what the Israelites must do. It is even more significant that Jehovah is made to say much later in the same speech, all of which has been devoted to his talk of his fifty-year jubilee and what must be done about it by the Israelites: '. . . for it is to me that the Israelites are slaves, my slaves whom I brought out of Egypt. I am the Lord your God.' Remember that Egypt as the source of the Sirius tradition had had 'brought out' of it the Sirius mysteries and traditions by Danaos to Argos, etc. It seems the Israelites too are part of this, though there will probably not be a single rabbi unshaken by such a suggestion.

A lengthy appendix, 'The Sirius Mystery: Questions for Judaism', has had to be omitted from this edition (as it was from the original edition) because of lack of space, and has thus never been published. I was able to find some fascinating material in the Kabala, and I had much to say about the Hebrew Jubilee of fifty years.

What, then, of the forty-nine versus the fifty? Perhaps for explanation we should return to Robert Aitken's book *The Binary Stars.*[17] In discussing the length of time of the orbit of Sirius B around Sirius A he says: 'Thus, Volet's orbit, computed in 1931, which differs very little from my own, published in 1918, has the revolution period 49·94, whereas Auwers gave 49·42 years' – the point being that the orbit of Sirius B takes between forty-nine and fifty years and is somewhat less than fifty.'

The Aitken book also firmly informs us that the orbit is an ellipse, as are the orbits of all heavenly bodies. But of course, when speaking generally of the orbit of Sirius B one does not say 'the ellipse', one says 'the circle'. We say in common parlance: 'The planets circle round the sun,' even though we know their orbits are elliptical. And most mentions of the orbit of Sirius B in our sources are to 'the circle'. But, naturally, the Dogon draw a specific ellipse in the sand to represent the orbit of Digitaria (Sirius B). Figure 8 clearly compares the Dogon tribal diagram of the orbit of Sirius B around Sirius A with a modern astronomical diagram of the same.

We have already seen near the beginning of the book how the Dogon not only know that the orbit of Sirius B around Sirius A is an ellipse, but they also know the astounding principle of elliptical orbits whereby that body around which the orbit takes place inevitably tends to be at one of the two foci of the ellipse. For the Dogon specifically say: 'Sirius . . . is one of the centres of the orbit of a tiny star Digitaria'. Kepler first formulated this principle as a law of planetary motion – a revolutionary step forward in Western science. The Dogon also describe the orbit of the 'Star of Women' (a planet around Sirius C) as forming an ellipse with Sirius C at one of the centres.

Now, in light of the dithering over forty-nine and fifty just referred to, and the references to seven times seven equals forty-nine, seen in the light of the fact that the orbital period of Sirius B is between forty-nine and fifty years, which can be well accommodated as Graves says of the Sacred Year, 'fifty months, or of forty-nine in alternate years', thereby balancing out to a close approximation to reality by alternating the count successively as fifty years, then forty-nine years, then fifty years . . . etc., one can understand why the orbit of Sirius B around Sirius A is 'counted twice to be a hundred years', as the Dogon say and as was done in Egypt and in

Greece, and which led to the double-Sacred Year of one hundred and the Greek goddess Hekate which means 'one hundred', and the hundred-handed ones of Greek mythology, etc. It was because orbits of Sirius B had to be counted in pairs in order better to approximate a whole number. And the fact that this was the case among the Dogon and the people of the Mediterranean area seems to confirm beyond all doubt that the Sirius tradition of the Dogon is a survival of the Mediterranean (namely, Egyptian) tradition brought by the ancestors of the Dogon from the Garamantes Kingdom of Libya where it had been taken by the Minyan immigrants.

It is also significant and conclusive that the Dogon specifically say: 'The period of the orbiting of Digitaria is about fifty years and corresponds with the first seven reigns of seven years each of the first seven chiefs . . .' And: 'This rule was in operation for forty-nine years for the first seven chiefs who thus nourished the star and enabled the star to periodically renew the world. But, the eighth chief having discovered the star . . .', etc., combining also the sacrifice of the sacred chief concept emphasized over and over by Graves in his many references to the Sacred Year of fifty months. This passage from Griaule's account of what the Dogon told him almost reads like a straight quotation from the Book of Leviticus in the Bible. Or from *The Greek Myths* by Graves! Can there be any further doubt that the two traditions are identical? That the Dogon brought it from the Mediterranean world into an obscure wilderness area where it has survived the ravages of time and empire amazingly intact and specific? And that the Mediterranean tradition in turn really was about Sirius and the orbit of Sirius B, the *great invisible*?

The Dogon tribe are really the last of the Argonauts, from whom they are quite literally descended – being Minyans in the middle of West Africa.

Turning to the Egyptian word *henti*, one finds that it is a name for Osiris and it also is 'a crocodile-headed god in the Ṭuat', which is the Egyptian underworld, and it also means simply 'crocodile gods'.

Ḥent is specifically 'the crocodile of Set'; *hen-t* is, interestingly, a specific locality of the underworld and means 'a district in the Ṭuat'. But, more widely, *hen-t* is 'a mythological locality' which is not necessarily in the underworld. It would seem that the fabulous Ḥen-t was a locality which had an underworld counterpart and obviously is somehow connected closely with both Osiris and crocodiles.

The name of this region, Ḥen-t, when taken as a common noun rather than as a name, means 'dual'. This is a strong clue as to the nature of the fabulous region. A region intimately connected with Osiris and whose name means 'dual' is reminiscent of Plutarch's description of that circle or ellipse with its dual aspect of separating the light from the darkness. Lest the reader think this far-fetched I must hasten to add a further meaning of *hen-t* which is 'border, boundary', and another which is 'the two ends of heaven' – which all appear to refer to a circle and have the *hen-t* ('dual') nature of outside and inside and the two extremes connected by a diameter. *Hen-t* also means 'end, limit', and a *henti* is a specific period of time lasting for 120 years. Remember that the Sigui of the Dogon was every sixty-years and two Dogon Sigui make one Egyptian *henti*. In fact, a *hen-t henti* would be a Sigui or, perhaps, vice versa, depending upon one's grammatical preference. (The use of the word 'dual' can be rather ambivalent and be construed as either halving or doubling by the context.) And this dual time period is also rather like the two fifty-month periods which make the hundred-month period of that sacred Great Year connected with Sirius, which has a dual aspect.

Henti also has the meaning 'endless' – and the endless circling of Sirius B around Sirius A could be referred to here. Some such idea must be at work, otherwise how can the same word have the meaning of 'endless' and also of '120 years'? It must be a reference to an 'endless' cycling of perhaps the orbit of Sirius B or of the Sigui cycle's own basis. In any case, it signifies that the 120-year period was arrived at as an endlessly recurring cycle, and for that to have been the case, the 120-year period must have been quite important, which is exactly what one would anticipate. In Appendix IV there is an explanation proposed for the true nature of the Sigui . . . and of the *henti* based on certain astronomical facts.

Considering that *henti* means all this and also means 'crocodile gods', etc., it is surprising to see that *henn* means 'to plough' and a *hennti* is 'a ploughman'. One immediately thinks of Jason *ploughing* the field for the dragon's (crocodile's?) teeth. It may well be that the 'serpent's teeth' motif which was a pun for 'the goddess Sirius' was extended in another layer of pun to 'dragon's teeth' as a reference to crocodiles.

In connection with Sirius B being the hairy, bestial Enkidu-figure, we see with interest that *hen* means 'to behave in a beast-like manner' and a *henti* is also specifically 'a beast-like person'. In addition to *henti* being a name for Osiris, who is the companion of Sirius, we find it describing 'a beast-like person' who is the archetypal companion in Sirius-related legends. And additionally, we find Hathor the cow-goddess, a form of Isis-Sirius, referred to as Hennu-Neferit. (Neferit simply means 'beautiful'.) But this word *hennu* with the double 'n' has the basic meaning of 'phallus' and has a phallic determinative hieroglyph, and therefore may not be related to the *hen* words with a single 'n'.

Hen-ta significantly means 'grain' in keeping with the Dogon concept of Sirius B being a grain. *Henu* means the hawk-god Seker and his *henu* boat. This boat (echoes of celestial *Argo*) is 'the sacred boat of Seker, the Death-god of Memphis'. This reminds us of the Circe-complex and the death-god of Colchis. It must be emphasized that the hawk and the falcon are constantly being confused with each other not only in Egyptian studies, but I have asked falconers the difference between a hawk and a falcon and they vaguely suggest a difference in colour of eyes and that the falcon tends to be smallish. A hawk supposedly has golden eyes (solar?) whereas the falcon has brown eyes. But their habits are not identical and as there are various species of both hawk and falcon, confusion reigns supreme. The hawk and falcon do not seem to have been distinguished by the ancient peoples, or at least less so than the crocus and the colchicum (or 'meadow saffron'). Of course the differences were recognized in practice, but what we must realize is that in the ancient world the Aristotelian structure of genus and species for plants and animals did not obtain, and differentiation in linguistic or semantic terms did not resolve to so fine a focus. For such precision one would employ qualifying adjectives, but a systematic modern biological terminology did not exist. Hence we found much earlier that *kirke* in Greek meant 'a hawk or falcon'. In short, they are as interchangeable at the level of terminology as the 'l' and the 'r' were interchangeable in Egyptian at the level of pronunciation and symbol. It seems the Egyptians, like the Chinese of the present day with their 'flied lice' for 'fried rice' had a paralamdism and inability to differentiate the two liquid sounds. Indeed, the 'l' could be differentiated further if our ears were so trained. It is possible to pronounce a much more lingual and less dental 'l' than we use in English. But as for the French 'r', I confess to being as unable to form my tongue to pronounce that sound as Aristotle was, for instance, unable to pronounce the Greek 'rho' – this being considered by the Greeks to be a lisp.[18]

However, I have let myself digress. The subject of hawks and falcons can, it seems, be pursued to a resolution. Seton Gordon, probably the world's expert on the golden eagle, could not tell me a conclusive differentiation between them. Nor could an experienced falconer friend. I was becoming impatient at this lack of an answer until I learned from my friend Robin Baring, who had once considered becoming an ornithologist, that an extremely subtle difference between the hawk and the falcon does actually exist. According to him, on a hawk, the fourth or fifth pinion feather is longer making a rounded wing, whereas on a falcon, the second or third wing feather is longest – making a pointed wing. I am not certain whether this is fully comprehensive to all the many species. In *A Glossary of Greek Birds*,[19] D'Arcy Thompson says that the ancient Greek poet Callimachus (who was quite a scholarly gent) claimed there were ten species of hawks, and Aristotle claimed Egyptian ones were smaller than Greek ones. It looks as if people have been trying to sort out hawks and falcons since the Creation. But if the reader is as weary of these birds as the author, let us agree to drop them and face the last few remaining Egyptian words. We have survived a waterfall; can we muster the strength to pull ourselves to shore?

Ḥensekti means 'hairy one' and also Isis and Nephthys. Nephthys could be identified with Sirius B who is the archetypal 'hairy one', but it seems more likely that Nephthys varied between being a name of Sirius B and being a name of Sirius C, the female star which was also invisible. The *ḥenmemit* are, tantalizingly, 'men and women of a bygone age'. The meaning 'to plough' of *ḥenn* and 'boundary' of *ḥen-t* are linked through 'arable land' of *ḥenb-t* in the word *ḥen-b* which means 'to delimit, to measure land, to make a frontier boundary'. (This seems to connect the single 'n' words with the double 'n' words after all.) Thus, further possibilities for punning between a reference to the delimiting orbit of Sirius B and 'ploughing' in connection with the ploughing of the ground for the sowing of the serpent's teeth – serpent's teeth being a pun on the goddess Sirius, as we know. Hence a series of dizzying puns all interlocking.

Just for final measure we note that *Ḥen-b* is also a serpent god of the Ṭuat and Ḥenb-Requ is a jackal-god, bringing us into liaison with the jackal/dog Anubis and Sirius B's orbit and adding as a final flourish yet another pun on serpent.

We recall that the throne and the oar were the two most common allusions to the yearly 'steps' in the fifty-year orbit of Sirius B. Also the name of the goddess Isis (in Greek; Isios in Ionian), which in Egyptian is Àst, means 'throne', and is represented by the hieroglyph of a throne. Significantly, then, *às-ti* using the same hieroglyph of the throne, means 'one in the place of another, successor'. This is a specific reference to the sequentiality of the thrones. And the orbit which they represent, also known as Anubis, seems to be given specific recognition by the combined form Àst Ànpu, which is Isis-Anubis.

Another name for Isis as Sirius specifically is Àakhu-t. This is also the name given to the Great Pyramid! In the light of this new name it is not surprising to learn that Àakhuti is 'the god who dwelleth in the horizon'. And *àakhu-t sheta-t* means 'the secret horizon'. *Àakhuti* are 'the two spirits, i.e. Isis and Nephthys'. And the *àakhu-t* are also 'the *uraei** on the royal crown', etc., demonstrating the origin of the most central of the Pharaonic insigniae. Hence yet further demonstration of the connection of the Sirius system with 'the secret horizon' of Sirius B's orbit and its profound importance to the Egyptians.

Another form of the name of Isis, Àst, is Àas-t, which is seen as significant if we note that *àasten* means 'one of the eight ape-gods of the company of Thoth. He presided over the seven . . .' For this is a parallel to the Sirius-linked story of the Dogon, whereby the eighth chief presided over the previous seven chiefs as a means of signifying the orbital period of Sirius B commencing again with the advent of the eighth chief following the seven chiefs, each with a reign of seven years giving seven times seven or forty-nine years. This Sirius concept is here referred to in another form of the very name in Egyptian for Isis, who was identified with Sirius.

Another way of referring to Isis and to Nephthys is as Àār-ti, 'the two Uraei-goddesses, Isis and Nephthys'. There is an intimately related form

---

* Uraei were symbolic serpents heads issuing from the pharoah's own head.

of this word, Àārārut, which probably is the origin of the Sumerian goddess Aruru's name. For she was the counterpart of Isis in Sumer (and was known also as Ninhursag, Nintu, Ninmah, etc.). It is specifically in her name of Aruru that she creates the hairy Enkidu, companion to Gilgamesh. No doubt because Enkidu is related to Sirius B, she appears in this name in the *Epic of Gilgamesh* because this particular name is closely related to the Sirius lore, through its derivation from this Egyptian form. Àār-ti is a common name of both Isis and Nephthys, and Nephthys is more closely connected with the companion of Sirius. The appellation Aruru is thus closer to Sirius B, who is also represented by Enkidu, than another name for the goddess Sirius which was not specifically shared with Nephthys, the dark companion. This word also means '*uraei*' and we have just seen that the other word for the *uraei* is related to the horizon of Sirius B's orbit, as well as also being shared with Isis and Nephthys – obviously shared because the orbit described by one is described *around* the other, and as we have seen several times, the orbit was common to them both and divided their respective precincts. Therefore words connected with this orbit must be common to them both. And what more appropriate name for the Sumerians to use for the goddess in her role as creator of Enkidu, the dark companion of Gilgamesh, than a name derived from this aspect of the goddess?

Sirius the Dog Star is represented by the hieroglyph of a tooth, so it is important also to know that there is a word in Egyptian which means both 'tooth' and 'dog'. I am referring to *shaār*, 'tooth', and *sha* 'a kind of dog', *sha-t* 'female dog', *shai* 'a dog-god', and *Shaāit* which is a form of Hathor who is identified with Isis.

Also *sha-t* means 'one hundred', and is the Egyptian synonym for the Greek Hekate.

Another word for 'tooth' is *àbeḥ*, and a related form of the same word means 'jackal'. In addition *àba* means 'to make strong', and *àb-t* means 'path'. *Àpp* means 'to traverse', and *àp* means 'steps'. If I may be forgiven lack of grammar, *àpp àb-t em àp* means 'to traverse a path in steps', which is exactly what Sirius B does in its orbit. Since Anubis has been identified as the orbit of Sirius B, it is not surprising that a title of Anubis was 'the counter of hearts' with 'the counter' being the word *àpi* and *àbu* meaning 'hearts'. But if we altered that slightly to *àpi-àbt* instead of *àpi-àbu*, the meaning would be 'the counter of months', for *àbt* means 'month'. Another pun with a deeper meaning with reference to the 'hundred months' (or years) 'counted' by Anubis, who is the orbit, as he traverses his *àb-t em àp*, his 'path in steps'.

To go on examining the Egyptian language would be superfluous to our present intentions. So would a continued elucidation of Sumerian religious names from Egyptian. But it would be just as well to fill in a bit of information on that transition which brought our Mediterranean Sirius tradition south from Libya to the Niger River. Herodotus told us how the

Garamantes of Libya had been pushed further and further westwards and southwards. Graves says they were forced down to the Fezzan in the desert regions of south Libya. We find a further account in *A History of West Africa* by J. D. Fage:[20]

> Herodotus, writing about 450 BC, speaks of the Garamantes, that is the people of the oasis of Djerma in the Fezzan (who in modern terms would be accounted Tuareg), raiding the 'Ethiopians', i.e. black-skinned peoples, across the Sahara in two-wheeled chariots each drawn by four horses. About 400 years later, another great early geographer, Strabo, says much the same of the Pharusii of the western Sahara, who may perhaps be equated with ancestors of the Sanhaja. . . . The chariots of the Garamantes and Pharusii were very light fighting vehicles, unsuitable for carrying trade goods, but it is a point of considerable interest that Herodotus's and Strabo's accounts of their activities have been confirmed and given added point by the discovery on rocks in the Sahara of some hundreds of crude drawings or engravings of two-wheeled vehicles each drawn by four horses. The most significant aspect of these drawings is that they are almost all distributed along only two routes across the Sahara, a western one from southern Morocco towards the Upper Niger, and a central one running from the Fezzan to the eastern side of the Niger bend.

In *The White Goddess*, Robert Graves says also of the Garamantes:[21]

> Herodotus was right in stating on the authority of the Egyptian priests that the black dove and oracular oak cults of Zeus at Ammon in the Libyan desert and of Zeus at Dodona were coeval. Professor Flinders Petrie postulates a sacred league between Libya and the Greek mainland well back into the third millennium BC. The Ammon oak was in the care of the tribe of Garamantes: the Greeks knew of their ancestor Garamas as 'the first of men'. The Zeus of Ammon was a sort of Hercules with a ram's head akin to ram-headed Osiris, and to Amen-Ra, the ram-headed Sun-god of Egyptian Thebes from where Herodotus says that the black doves flew to Ammon and Dodona.

In his fascinating book *Lost Worlds of Africa*,[22] James Wellard in Book Three, 'The People of the Chariots', discussed the Garamantes and related topics at some length. One of the most amazing elements in the story concerns an apparently lost civilization sitting under the sands of the Sahara which once was the centre of the Garamantian empire, and which was dispersed by the Moslem Arab invaders. Wellard describes this civilization in suitably mysterious terms:

> On the track which runs across the desert from Sebha, the modern

capital of the Fezzan, to the oasis of Ghat on the Algerian border, the traveller crosses an underground water system that has few parallels for ingenuity and effort in African history. . . . Seen from inside, the main tunnels are at least ten feet high and twelve feet wide and have been hacked out of the limestone rock by rough tools, with no attempt to smooth the surface of the roof and walls. . . . How many of them actually remain is still not certain, though hundreds of them are still visible. In places they run less than twenty feet apart and their average length, from the cliffs where they originate to the oases where they terminate, is three miles. If we assume from the 230 that remain visible that there may have been as many as 300 of them in this region of the desert, we have, taking into account the lateral shafts, nearly 1,000 miles of tunnels hewn out of the rock under the desert floor.

We are still not clear as to how the system worked. First, where is the entrance to these tunnels? One can spend hours trying to find their inlet, and though the solution would seem easy at first, assuming that a particular mound is followed along its entire length, the investigator finally arrives at a jumble of rocks at the base of the escarpment without being able to tell where the tunnel has disappeared to. . . . (the system possibly) presupposes an adequate and regular rainfall, in which case we have to go back as far as 3000 BC to find such a maritime climate in the Sahara Desert. Could the *foggaras* be that old? . . . Wells are the only water sources in the Wadi el Ajal today, and they are adequate for the present population of some 7,000 people. If we compare this figure with the 100,000 or more graves so far found in the Wadi and dating from the time of the 'people of the water tunnels', we can get some idea of how populous this region was. . . . In addition, the construction of such an enormous hydraulic complex indicates an industrious and technologically advanced people who had reached a stage of culture superior to that of northern Europe before the Roman conquest.

We can, therefore, safely assume that (a) between 5000 and 1000 BC a cattle-raising and agricultural people belonging to the Negro race had occupied large areas of the Sahara Desert which they kept habitable and fertile by means of the *foggaras*; and (b) it was precisely the prosperity of these defenceless Africans that incited the white settlers along the Libyan coast to invade the Fezzan. These immigrants (originally, it seems, having come to Africa from Asia Minor) were the Garamantes, the people of the four-horse chariots – first mentioned by Herodotus, who describes them as already a very great nation in his time. They thereupon appear and disappear throughout the classical period until, around AD 700, they vanish altogether as the last of their kings was led away to captivity by the Arab invaders of the Fezzan. Their Saharan empire had lasted over a thousand years.

Yet we know almost next to nothing about the Garamantes, and the reason is obvious: with the fall of the Roman Empire, Africa became a 'lost' continent, so much so that no European traveller reached even as far south as the Fezzan until the beginning of the nineteenth century.

I should add that it was the Emperor Justinian (reigned 527–565 AD) who destroyed North African civilization, before the Moslems came.

Wellard also says that in the Garamantian territory are myriads of tombs, pyramids, fortresses, and abandoned cities lying untouched by any archaeologist's spade. For instance, he visited 'the fortress city of Sharaba which lies out there in the desert gradually sinking beneath the sand. In the first place, perhaps not more than a few score European travellers have visited the site in any case, as it lies off the caravan routes in one of the more inaccessible pockets of the Mourzouk Sand Sea. . . . In point of fact, archaeological research in the country of the Fezzan has only just begun. . . .'

After the Arab conquest of the Garamantian empire, the survivors fled south-west and 'fused with the Negro aboriginals on the south bank of the Upper Niger, and adopted their language', as Graves tells us in *The Greek Myths*,[23] and as he learned from the books of the anthropologist Eva Meyrowitz.[24]

So here is some more light on how the Dogon and related Negro tribes of the Upper Niger came to possess their amazing information. It is a tale of thousands of years, and the drama was enacted across thousands of miles, which only seems suitable considering the nature of the message they were to carry into a much different world – the global village of late twentieth-century culture. According to the Dogon, 'the shaper of the world' visited the earth and returned to the Sirius system, having given men culture. Now that our race has set foot on another heavenly body and we are looking outward to our solar system, we are prepared to give serious consideration to any neighbours who might be within a few light years of us and have solar systems of their own which they inhabit and where they pursue their lives with the same desire to know, to learn, to understand, and above all to build a genuine ethical civilization, that motivates the best of us. For if they are not so motivated it is doubtful that they will have survived their own technologies. In love one can live, but without love there is no world that will not poison itself. One must assume that any creatures living at Sirius will have come to terms with a wholesome and vital ethic. If Sirius is indeed the home of a 'shaper of the world', then it may encourage us, too, to become shapers of worlds.

Notes

1. Griaule and Dieterlen, *Le Renard pâle*, op. cit., p. 44: 'The establishment of categories, of classifications, of correspondences, constitutes an armature comparable to the framework of a construction, to the articulated bone structure of a body. What imparts life to them – gives them their own physiology – is, for the Dogon, their relationship with God and with

the order in the world he created, that is to say, with the way the universe was organized and functions today.

'It is the myth that lights up the whole. Structures appear progressively in time and are superimposed, each one with its own special meaning, also with its own interrelations which are narrowly connected. That is what lends meaning to the succession of categories and stages of classification, which give evidence of the relationships established between man and what is not of man in the universe.'

For a more complete account of how the armature of symbolic interrelationships extends even to the smallest daily action or object for the Dogon, one should read the entire section 'The Thought of the Dogon', pp. 40–50, in *Le Renard pâle*. This section expresses quite well the mentality required to function within a society grounded in reality at all levels. The one drawback to such patterns of thought is that they can ossify if over-elaborated as a baroque maze, and stultify free inquiry, as happened in the Middle Ages in Europe when the church had the answer to anything, and anyone who disagreed could go fetch his rope and stake, make a bonfire, and commit himself to his divinity. There are dangers to anything; no system of thinking is perfect. Only the constant unremitting exercise of a free will and attention can regulate that most ill-regulated of organisms, the human personality, and keep it on course. 'Systems' all are panaceas, whether of thought or society, and all equally useless to the non-vigilant individual. The doctrine of the mean expressed in all sound philosophies is the doctrine of exercise of the attention at all times; the high-wire performer is the archetype of the successful man.

2. Wallis Budge, Sir E. A., *Osiris and the Egyptian Resurrection*, 2 vols., London, 1911, Vol. II, pp. 294–5.
3. Ibid., Vol. I, p. 156.
4. Ibid., Vol. I, pp. 389–90.
5. Plutarch, op. cit. This essay in vol. discussed in my Appendix V.
6. Ibid., Vol. I, pp. 106–7.
7. *Osiris*, op. cit., Vol. I, p. 93.
8. Ibid.
9. *Gods of the Egyptians*, op. cit., Vol. II, p. 164.
10. *Osiris*, op. cit., Vol. II, p. 311.
11. Ibid., Vol. II, p. 341.
12. See Wallis Budge, Sir E. A., *An Egyptian Hieroglyphic Dictionary*, London, 1920.
13. See Note 6.
14. See Note 12.
15. In Vol. V of Goodwin's trans. (ed.) of Plutarch's *Morals*, 1874, op. cit.
16. *Greek Myths*, op. cit., 60.3.
17. *The Binary Stars*, p. 238.
18. What is so odd about the Chinese inability to distinguish the two liquids is that they have both of them more or less in their own languages. For the 'l' is extremely common and a sound rather close to an 'r' is also commonly used.
19. Op. cit, p. 65 under *hierax*.
20. Fage, J. D. *A History of West Africa*, Cambridge University Press, 1969, pp. 14–16.
21. Op. cit, p. 182 (Chapter Ten under 'D for Duir').
22. Wellard, James. *Lost Worlds of Africa*, Hutchinson, London, 1967; also reprinted by The Travel Book Club, London, 1967.
23. Op. cit., 3.3.
24. See Notes 13 and 14 to previous chapter.

SUMMARY

In ancient Egyptian, the hieroglyph and word for 'goddess' also means 'serpent'. The hieroglyph for Sirius also means 'tooth'. Hence 'serpent's tooth' is a pun on 'the goddess Sirius'. In the *Argo* story, Jason sowed the 'serpent's teeth', an idea which must originally have stemmed from this Egyptian pun. The Greek word for 'the rising of a star' also refers to 'the growing of teeth from the gum'. Therefore when the serpent's teeth were sown in the ground, they grew up from it as from a gum – that is, the star Sirius ('serpent's tooth') rose over the horizon.

Thus we see the mythological code language of sacred puns in operation. Behind the myths lay concealed meanings which are decipherable by returning to the hieroglyphics and finding synonyms which form puns.

We find explanations of the words Argo, Ark, Argos, etc., by looking for Egyptian origins. These words derive from the Egyptian word *arq*. But related words in Greek give clues as well: Argus was a dog connected with a cycle. Another Argus had one hundred eyes and watched over Io, who is connected with the Sirius traditions and Isis. The Egyptian word *arqi* refers to an end of a cycle, represented in the *Odyssey* by Argus. The Egyptian word *arq* refers to a circular concept and is the origin of the Latin *arcere* and of our arc.

A temple of Isis found in southern Italy has in its inner sanctum a painting of hundred-eyed Argus (portrayed, however, with a normal face and eyes). The mysteries of Isis were celebrated in this inner sanctum. Also the fifty daughters of Danaos traditionally brought from Egypt to Greece (and hence southern Italy) the mysteries of the Thesmophoria which according to Plutarch were Isis mysteries. So we see Isis connected intimately at the most secret and sacred levels with 'fifty' and 'one hundred' (Hekate) – and Isis was identified with Sirius.

The earliest Egyptians believed Sirius was the home of departed souls, which the Dogon also believe. The Egyptians said that when a deceased spirit 'went to Nephthys' he revolved 'in the horizon' and 'revolves like the sun'. This is a pretty specific description of the dark Nephthys as a 'sun' revolving around Sirius.

The Egyptians also maintained that emanations from the region of Sirius vivified creatures on Earth. This, too, is believed by the Dogon.

Since the Egyptians believed Sirius was the other world of departed souls, it is interesting that they called 'the other world *arq-ḥeḥtt*, using the familiar word *arq* again.

In Egyptian the region of Sirius is described by a word meaning also 'throne' and 'weight' and similar to a word meaning 'dwarf'.

The Egyptian word meaning 'fifty' (from which are derived the Arabic and Hebrew words meaning 'fifty') referred to the fifty hot 'Dog Days' of Sirius and also to 'a star that rests not' – obviously a moving star, namely Sirius B with its fifty-year orbit.

Sirius in Egypt is 'the Bow Star'. The Egyptian word for 'bowman' refers also to a heavy star metal connected with Anubis (which we have previously suggested refers to the orbit of Sirius B, which is, after all, made of 'heavy star metal'). The word for heavy star metal is similar to the words for 'dwarf' and 'weight'.

The Egyptian word for 'the beginning of a cycle' (which would join up with *arq* meaning 'the end of a cycle') means also 'oracle' and 'the front and hind tips of a ship' – a vindication of my oracle-*Argo*. The same word also means 'the base of a triangle' (and the word for 'triangle' is a variation of the name for Sirius, whose hieroglyph is a triangle). We also have geodetic triangles, connected with the ark, from Thebes and Behdet.

Plutarch gives an account of a Persian description of the Dog Star Sirius, which is said to be surrounded by fifty gods forming the shape of an egg (elliptical orbit) in which the 'light god' faces the 'dark god'.

In the Biblical Book of Leviticus, Moses commands the Hebrews to observe a jubilee every fifty years, but I have never heard of their doing so. Obviously the Hebrews did not understand the fifty-year orbit of Sirius B which Moses (who was an initiate of Egypt and 'raised by Pharoah') presumably had in mind.

In Egyptian the word for 'the secret horizon' also means 'the two spirits' – namely, the light Isis and the dark Nephthys. The same word also means 'the god who dwelleth in the horizon' and 'Isis as Sirius'. The secret horizon would seem to refer to the orbit of Sirius B in which Sirius B lives.

The Egyptian word for 'dog' also means 'tooth' (the triangle hieroglyph meaning 'Sirius' and 'tooth'), and also means specifically 'dog-god' and also 'one hundred'.

Another Egyptian word meaning 'tooth' means 'to traverse a path in steps' and 'to make strong', and is used in connection with Anubis in such a way that could be 'the counter of months while traversing the path'. A synonym means 'one hundred' and 'Sirius'. We thus have: 'counting one hundred months while traversing the Sirius path'. But Anubis who does this is 'a circle'. So we have: 'counting one hundred months while traversing the circular Sirius path'. Change months to years (as Moses might have done?) and we have two fifty-year orbital periods of Sirius B.

We see that the ancient Egyptians had the same Sirius tradition which we have encountered from the Dogon tribe in Mali. We know that the Dogon are cultural, and probably also physical, descendants of Lemnian Greeks who claimed descent 'from the Argonauts', went to Libya, migrated westwards as Garamantians (who were described by Herodotus), were driven south, and after many, many centuries reached the River Niger in Mali and intermarried with local Negroes.

The Dogon preserve as their most sacred mystery tradition one which was brought from pre-dynastic Egypt by 'Danaos' to the Greeks who took it to Libya and thence eventually to Mali, and which concerns 'the Sirius mystery'. We have thus traced back to pre-dynastic Egypt well before 3000

BC the extraordinary knowledge of the system of the stars Sirius A, Sirius B, and the now-confirmed 'Sirius C' possessed by the Dogon.

We have thus managed to rephrase, if not to answer, the Sirius question. It is no longer: 'How did the Dogon know these things?' It is now: 'How did the pre-dynastic Egyptians before 3200 BC or their (unknown) predecessors know these things?'

What is the answer to the Sirius question? We do not know. But knowing the right questions is essential to an eventual understanding of anything. The many investigations which should properly follow upon the asking of the Sirius question may give us more answers than we could at present imagine. *Added 1997:* The investigations I called for in the 1970s have still not happened and whatever attempts I made to raise funding for them failed utterly – as recently, in fact, as 1997.

Archaeologists have a difficult task trying to explain the many similarities between Sumer and Egypt, indicating some still undiscovered common origin for the two cultures – an entirely forgotten civilization whose remains must exist somewhere.

But in considering the very origins of the elements of what we can call human civilization on this planet, we should now take fully into account the possibility that primitive Stone Age men were handed civilization on a platter by visiting extraterrestrial beings, who left traces behind them for us to decipher. These traces concerned detailed information about the system of the star Sirius which is only intelligible to a society as technologically advanced as ours today. Today was the time when we were meant to discover these coded facts, I feel sure. Today is the time we should prepare ourselves to face the inevitable reality that extraterrestrial civilizations exist, and are in all probability far more advanced in culture than we ourselves – not to mention in technology which could enable them to travel between the stars!

It may be difficult for us to avoid seriously entertaining that most disturbing and also exciting of notions: that intelligent beings from elsewhere in the galaxy have already visited Earth, already know of our existence, may possibly be monitoring us at this moment with a robot probe somewhere in our solar system, and may have the intention of returning in person some day to see how the civilization they established is really getting on.

Added 1997: Alternatively, they may never have left our solar system, as I have explained in the introductory chapter to this new edition. As some form of suspended animation would be necessary for any interstellar voyage, and as their work was only half done, it is more likely that they re-entered suspended animation for a few thousand years and are preparing to re-appear from, perhaps, some base in the outer solar system. It is highly likely that our planet is currently under intensive observation by monitors too small and sophisticated for us to detect. We should really be preparing for a renewal of contact, not wasting our time insisting that it can't happen. There is nothing really strange about an extraterrestrial contact except to naive folk like us – for we are mere children in the cosmic hierarchy.

PART THREE
BEYOND THE MYSTERY

Chapter 9

A Fable

Once there was a little girl sitting by the seashore. Her mother had told her to go and play. She watched the waves and thought: 'If only something marvellous would happen to me today!' The sun was shining very hot upon the strand and the girl became drowsy. The sound of the quiet surf was like a lullaby. She began to doze.

Suddenly she awoke. The air was alive with a new coolness, a haze had lifted, everything was startlingly clear to the sight. Far out, she glimpsed a flash in the sea, then another flash, a glint of something in the sun. There it was again – something coming towards the shore and making its way through the waves. It must be a porpoise. The girl was terribly excited. Something was happening to make her day memorable. Now she would not have to sit by the seashore and be bored.

Now that the porpoise was getting nearer, it alarmed the girl. Could it be about to crash against the sand, as she had heard giant whales did from time to time in despair? Was it a dolphin actually intent on self-destruction? The girl ran hurriedly towards the spot which seemed to be the dolphin's objective. She saw its tail fin, quite close, appear for a moment. Some seaweed it seemed to be trailing with it showed through the water. It was a bright, almost shiny, porpoise . . . it was now near the sand . . . what would it do? She could see it now, through the water. It stopped. It seemed to be grovelling in the sand. Its tail splashed up, then down. It remained stationary.

The poor dolphin had crashed into the sand. Full of pity, the girl began to wade out towards it. But it moved away slightly. It wasn't stuck in the sand. It was looking up at her from under the water. What could it be trying to do? The girl went back to the shore. The fish now moved in closer again. From quite near to the fish, a woman put her head above the water. She had silver make-up on her face and eyes that went up. The little girl was worried about the fish. 'Have you got hold of the dolphin?' she asked the woman. Just beneath the woman's shoulders there was a noise like a swimming suit strap snapping against her skin. She replied to the girl with a fixed stare and a high wail which seemed to be a song. She moved towards the girl, her eyes never straying from her. Her eyes were clear blue, like the sky. It was as if there were two holes in her head and you could see the sky through them. Again her swimming suit strap snapped against her.

Her eyes were like the hot sun. The girl wanted to go to sleep. The woman's eyes were like the sound of the surf. The girl sat down in the sand and tried to make herself see the woman more clearly. The woman's face appeared to be really silver.

The woman's chest showed above the water now. Her bosom was bare. Her swimming suit strap must have snapped. The woman's bosom was a beautiful silvery green and shiny in the sun. The woman seemed unable to go any farther. She stared at the girl and remained motionless, except for a slight swaying to and fro.

'Who are you?' asked the girl. 'Have you come from a boat?' The woman gave a long wail, but the expression on her face did not change. Then there was the snapping of the swimsuit again. But this time the girl saw that above the woman's bosom were two long thin slits, which had opened and snapped shut loudly as if they were muscles flexing, just under her beautiful sleek collar-bones. The woman stirred as if she were resting uncomfortably on a high stool. She looked dissatisfied and, twisting her torso, she leapt forward and fell with a splash in the surf near where the girl sat. She had no legs. It was what the girl had thought was the dolphin. The woman was a mermaid. Her body stretched out long, sleek, shiny in the sun, with the surf rushing up past her and then retreating. She leaned on an elbow and raised her dolphin's tail slightly in the air, then tapped the shallow water, and did so several times in the way that the girl herself tapped her fingers on her desk at school sometimes.

The mermaid had no scales like an ordinary fish. Her skin was like that of the dolphins in the aquarium who jumped through hoops. But she was more silvery and more green. And there was a kind of hair streaming down her back like thin seaweed, which looked brown, or silver, or green, or grey, or even black. It was all those colours. And still the mermaid tapped her tail against the surf and stared at the girl. She was very much like a naked woman. She looked like the girl's mother did when she hurried to put on her dressing-gown before a bath.

Once again there was the snapping noise, only quieter. The girl saw the long thin slits in the woman's chest open and close instantly. Then the woman made a low, pleasant humming sound and looked sleepy. She leaned forward and an amazing series of clicks and pops were apparently made by her in her throat, which the girl could see constricting and moving.

The girl stood up and said to her, 'I've never seen a mermaid before. Can I tell Mummy?' The mermaid seemed to reply by smacking a fin against her skin somewhere behind her, rocking, and making a long, loud hum. She leaned forward more and looked at the girl and her eyes seemed to gloss over and go green. She opened her mouth, little pointed teeth showed in pink gums, and a long whispering sound came out which sounded like the sea at a distance. She then beckoned the girl to her with her arm, and her webbed fingers.

The girl stood in the surf and touched the mermaid. 'You're so soft,' said the girl, 'not like fish are. I mean fish are soft, but you're so smooth.' The girl liked the mermaid. She had never seen anyone so smooth and silvery and beautiful. 'I bet you can swim better than ordinary people. I'm going to run and tell Mummy you're here!' The girl began to walk away. 'You won't go away, will you? Wait here!' And she made every effort to smile and signal her intentions. The woman seemed to nod in agreement. The girl ran quickly, looking back often to see if her mermaid woman would wait for her. The mermaid made no attempt to move, but merely watched the girl.

From a distance the mother could see something lying in the surf, as her daughter tugged at her skirts excitedly. 'It's something from a wreck,' said the mother.

'No, Mummy, it's a mermaid!' said the little girl.

'Don't be silly darling, mermaids don't really exist. They're just in stories. Now what is it you've found?'

Then suddenly the thing in the surf moved. It was horrible, like a serpent. 'Oh! It's alive! It's moving! No!' and she turned and tried to push her little girl back home. 'I'm going to get Daddy. He'll know what to do. It may be a creature which is injured. Now come with me.'

But the little girl eluded her and ran towards the sea. 'No, Mummy, it's a mermaid! Come and see !'

Feeling sick in the pit of her stomach and apprehensive, the mother followed her daughter and feebly called after her. The girl quickly reached her friend from the sea, and the mother, seeing her standing beside the moving creature, cried, 'No! Get away! Get away from it!' She then ran and – it was a woman and fish, it was! It was silver. It was a mermaid! 'No, darling, no! Get away from it! It's horrible!' Her daughter came to her obediently and the mother stared in disgust and nausea at this awful slimy sea creature with a grotesque human frame grafted on to it – a monster, an abomination. She felt her stomach constrict, she gasped, she bent forward in the thought that she would be sick. 'God!' she gasped. 'Go home! Go home!' and pushed her daughter violently to make her run.

'What is it, Mummy?' asked the girl, who was now becoming terrified. 'Mummy!' she cried in alarm. Her mother was choking, eyes bulging, stumbling towards her with her flat palm outstretched to push her away towards home. 'Mummy! Mummy!' They heard a loud splash and turned just in time to see the mermaid slip away effortlessly at lightning speed into the deep water – gone instantly from sight.

'Oh God!' said the mother, as she clasped her head and fell to her knees on the sand.

'She's gone, Mummy. The mermaid's gone. But you saw her!'

The mother looked at her daughter as if the girl might at any moment herself turn into a mermaid. 'Oh darling, what was it? Tell me it isn't true!' said the mother, and put her head down into the hot, sharp sand.

A little story about a child and an adult and their different reactions to a strange, intelligent amphibian. To the child 'it could swim better' and was silvery and fascinating. To the mother it was repulsive and horrible.

In Appendix III the reader will find in English translation the surviving fragments of the lost *Babylonian History* by Berossus. A priest of the god Bel, and alive in 290 BC, he wrote a history of Babylon in Greek. The Creation to the Flood comprised Book One; Book Two ended at 747 BC and Book Three ended with the death of Alexander the Great. He seems to have been an acquaintance of Aristotle and drew on his own country's temple archives (which were in cuneiform, of course) to compile the history of his country from original documents. The readership would have been the cosmopolitan inhabitants of the Hellenistic world created by the conquests of Alexander.

In his work, Berossus describes his country's tradition of the origins of its civilization. And the tale is a strange one. For a group of alien amphibious beings were credited by the Babylonians with having founded their civilization. The main individual of the group of amphibians is called Oannes. We have had occasion to refer to him earlier. There are several illustrations of him throughout this book (final colour plate, Plates 34–37 and Figures 46 and 47). In somewhat later traditions than the ones Berossus drew on, Oannes became the fish-god of the Philistines known as Dagon and familiar to many readers of the Bible. By that time Oannes, as Dagon, had become an agricultural deity. In the surviving fragments of Berossus we have no reference to the Philistine tradition, and we shall probably never know whether Berossus mentioned it or not. But in the Berossus fragments preserved by the historian Apollodorus, we read that 'there appeared another personage from the Erythraean sea like the former, having the same complicated form between a fish and a man, whose name was Odacon'. This seems fairly clearly to be a corrupted form of 'Dagon'. Unless 'Dagon' is a corrupted form of 'Odacon'.[1] The

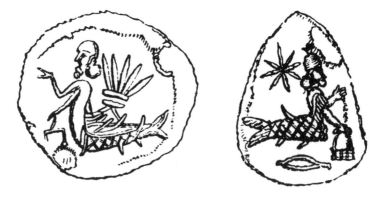

Figure 46. Fish-tailed Oannes on gems in the British Museum. The representation on the right shows a star and eye of Osiris – an Egyptian hieroglyph on a Babylonian gem

Figure 47. Fish-tailed Oannes from Assyrian cylinder seal. He stands before an omphalos stone covered in geodetic mesh with descending octaves on either side of it. The eye-star is above and a 'mouth of Nommo' is to lower left

'Erythraean sea' is that body of water known to the ancients which we today subdivide into the Red Sea, the Persian Gulf, and the Indian Ocean.

Apollodorus criticizes Abydenus (late fourth century BC; a disciple of Aristotle who wrote several historical works), for not mentioning that there were other amphibious beings besides Oannes himself. He says: 'concerning these Abydenus has made no mention'. Apollodorus, therefore, seems to have given Berossus a close attention to detail which Abydenus, for his purposes, neglected. This is an extremely important point, as we shall now see. Berossus, according to the close account of Apollodorus, calls the amphibians by the collective name of 'the Annedoti'. They are described as 'semi-daemons', not as gods. For some time I thought that 'the Annedoti' must be a convenient and tradition-sanctioned name for these creatures. I was concerned to have a name for them because, as we learn in a moment, the Dogon tribe claim that amphibious creatures with fishtails founded their civilization too, and that they came from the system of the star Sirius. If there are intelligent creatures living on a planet in the Sirius system it would seem from all evidence that they are amphibious, resembling a kind of cross between a man and a dolphin. It is therefore necessary to come up with some name for those creatures if we are to discuss them from time to time.

With this in mind, I suddenly wondered what the word 'Annedotus', which is never translated in the Cory translations of the fragments of Berossus, could actually mean. I read once again the fragment of Berossus from the careful Apollodorus and scrutinized the translation of it, which was: '. . . in whose time appeared the Musarus Oannes the Annedotus from the Erythraean sea'.

What was meant by the untranslated words 'Musarus' and 'Annedotus'? Strangely enough, until I purchased my own copy of Cory's

Ancient Fragments,[2] I had never before noticed that the words 'Musarus' and 'Annedotus' were untranslated. In libraries, with a pressure of time, one tends to overlook these details. I also had overlooked this in the account of Apollodorus quoted by Carl Sagan in his *Intelligent Life in the Universe*.[3] These are all reasons why I felt that I should include as an appendix to this book the complete surviving fragments of Berossus (excluding a couple unrelated to our concerns which may be found in the third and final, 1876 posthumous edition of Cory's book). For unless all of the material is available and easy to hand, one invariably overlooks something and neglects to make the frequent and necessary comparisons which enable one gradually to read between the lines and obtain additional insights.

It so happens that the most frequently cited version of Berossus's account is usually that preserved by Alexander Polyhistor of Miletus.*[4] But that is where problems can begin. For Alexander Polyhistor does not use the words '*annedotus*' or '*musarus*' in his account. And the version preserved by Abydenus uses the word '*annedotus*' only as if it were a proper name: '. . . in his time a semi-daemon† called Annedotus, very like to Oannes, came up a second time from the sea . . .' As for the word '*musarus*', Abydenus does not use it at all.

So I turned to the lexicon to find the meanings of these words. I assumed that Cory would have translated them into English if they had simple and obvious meanings. But to my surprise I found that their meanings were quite simple and specific. A '*musarus*' is 'an abomination', and an '*annedotus*' is a 'repulsive one'.

Now the reader may appreciate why I wrote the little fable. For the creatures credited with founding civilization in the Middle East were frankly described by the Babylonians who revered them and built huge statues of them (Plate 34) as being 'repulsive abominations'. If ever anything argued the authenticity of their account, it was this Babylonian tradition that the amphibians to whom they owed everything were disgusting, horrible, and loathsome to look upon. A more normal course for any invented tradition of the origins of civilization would have been to glorify the splendid gods or heroes who founded it. But instead we find specific descriptions of 'animals endowed with reason' (Alexander Polyhistor's account) who make their awed and thankful beneficiaries want to be sick with revulsion. And what is more, the tradition admits this freely!

The problem of revulsion is a difficult one. It seems to be partly a result of what we are taught when young. No doubt psychologists would have a great deal more to say about it. But whatever origins it may have, it seems

---

* Born *circa* 105 BC, he was taken as a prisoner of war to Rome, where he spent the rest of his life and wrote many books.
† A daemon in Ancient Greece was a semi-divine and helpful spirit; a semi-daemon was not a spirit but an embodied being with supernatural or paranormal qualities.

to be almost uncontrollable once a propensity to it has developed. If someone finds snakes or spiders repulsive, it would take a great deal of persuasion to get him to change his attitude, and hypnosis is generally required to overcome a genuine phobia. As humans, we tend to dislike all slimy creatures, creepy-crawling creatures, creatures which ooze or slither or wriggle. Indeed, people who have a pronounced fondness for such creatures often seem to be suffering from a pathological condition themselves. I once knew a girl who kept a pet boa-constrictor in her bedroom, next to her bed for 'company'. She fed it a live mouse every Thursday and she loved to watch the mouse being eaten alive. She loved more than anything to hear the snake at night in the dark when it made a curious slithering fall against the side of its tank; this excited her greatly. Sometimes she slept naked with the snake wrapped round her. [This last sentence or something like it was actually censored in my first edition, which shows how times have changed.] Now, I do not wish to criticize the girl for her strange tastes but I think most readers will agree that the girl had somehow transformed the interest in a snake into something else. And that kind of substitution is the promotion of a fantasy which can probably be classed as pathological, though possibly not dangerous to anyone (except the mice).

Granted all these circumstances of human relationships to slithery creatures and the problem of revulsion in general, it does strike me as a most superb irony that a race of intelligent beings may really exist in our near neighbourhood of space who are slimy and repulsive, and yet who have founded many of the elements of our own human civilization and have a technology sufficiently advanced to enable them to travel between the stars. Indeed, when all other pleasures in life fail, the one remaining is a delight in irony. I recommend it, both to men and Annedoti.

According to Berossus as preserved by Alexander Polyhistor, the amphibians look like this:

> The whole body of the animal was like that of a fish; and had under a fish's head another head, and also feet below, similar to those of a man, subjoined to the fish's tail. His voice too, and language, was articulate and human; and a representation of him is preserved even to this day. . . . When the sun set, it was the custom of this Being to plunge again into the sea, and abide all night in the deep; for he was amphibious.

Who was Berossus, and how reliable was he? It is best to quote Cory's own preface for the information:

> Berossus, a Babylonian, flourished in the reign of Alexander, and lived some time at Athens: and according to many wrote his Chaldaean history in the Greek language. As a priest of Belus [Bel, or Baal] he possessed every advantage, which the records of the temple and the

learning and traditions of the Chaldaeans could afford; and seems to have composed his work with a serious regard for truth. He has sketched his history of the earlier times from the representations on the walls of the temples: from written records and traditionary knowledge, he learned several points too well authenticated to be called into question; and correcting the one by the other has produced the strange history before us. ... The first book of the history opens naturally enough with a description of Babylonia. ... The second book appears to have comprehended the history of the ante-diluvian world; and in this the two first fragments ought to have been inserted.

As for two of those later writers who preserve fragments of Berossus, Abydenus the disciple of Aristotle wrote an *Assyrian History*, now lost, and Megasthenes wrote an *Indian History*, also lost. None of the four writers who have preserved Berossian fragments has had any of his own writings survive intact either. Later writers such as Eusebius, the Christian historian of the fourth century AD, and Syncellus, the ninth-century AD Byzantine historian, have preserved in turn all of the fragments of Berossus which the earlier writers had quoted in their own works. For it seems that the original of Berossus was lost long before the originals of Abydenus, Apollodorus, Megasthenes (an Ionian, *circa* 350–290 BC, who visited India and wrote a famous history, *Indika*, which is lost), and Alexander Polyhistor. And unless some obscure Byzantine monkish library or Egyptian papyrus of Hellenistic date or Babylonian tablet produces new fragments, we may never know more about Berossus than we do now at third hand. But at least my Appendix III should be a help. For it will be the first time since 1876 that the fragments of Berossus will have been published.[5]

Plutarch has an interesting tale: 'Moreover, Eudoxus says that the Egyptians have a mythical tradition in regard to Zeus that, because his legs were grown together, he was not able to walk . . .'[6] This sounds very like the amphibious Oannes of the Sumerians who had a tail for swimming instead of legs for walking.

Additional section added in 1997

I did not know at the time I originally wrote this book that Greek mythology was full of amphibious fish-tailed beings with human bodies. I thought I was fairly familiar with Greek mythology, and indeed I was, but the Greek amphibious beings had escaped my attention or I had not realized their actual significance.

What is particularly surprising is that there are so many of them. One of the oldest is Nereus (see Plate 28), who had fifty daughters – the Nereids. It is believed by scholars that he was the original Greek sea god, who was displaced by Poseidon (Neptune). He was one of the 'Old Men of the Sea'. Hesiod (eighth century BC) says of him: 'And Sea begat Nereus, the eldest of his children, who is true and lies not: and men call him the Old Man because he is trusty and gentle and does not forget the laws of righteousness, but thinks just and kindly thoughts.'[7] Another of the Old Men was Proteus. The 'Old Men of the Sea' were slippery characters who if you wrestled with them changed shape, as Hercules discovered. But they were immensely wise and knew just about everything, and could prophesy forthcoming events – if you could trick them into telling you what they knew, that is. They were quite keen on mermaids, being mermen, if you see what I mean. For they had fish tails and human bodies and could speak just like us. And they could throw their arms around a mermaid without the slightest difficulty.

Another very ancient amphibian was Cecrops (*Kekrops*). He was the founder of Athens, its first king, and he gave his name to its inhabitants, who called themselves Cecropidae before the goddess Athena came along, after which they called themselves Athenians after her. Cecrops is shown in Figure 48 with Athena, into whose care is being given the son of Cecrops, named Erichthonios. Both Cecrops and Erichthonios were fish-tailed and human-bodied (what is called 'biform'). As time went on, with many of these figures, the fish tails tended to become more and more like serpent tails. It was Cecrops who welcomed Athena to Athens in the first place, deciding in her favour in a dispute between her and Poseidon over

Figure 48. On the right is Cecrops, the fish-tailed (becoming serpent-tailed) mythical founder and first king of Athens. The large woman reaching up from below is the goddess Gaia, 'Earth', who has just borne a son to Cecrops, a baby fish-tailed being called Erichthonios, who was later to become king as well. He is being given into the custody of the goddess Athena. Cecrops holds a sprig of olive to symbolize Athens and Attica. This is thought to be the oldest surviving illustration of the Birth of Erichthonios, which was later to become a favourite subject for Athenian vase painters. It was excavated from a grave at Ilissos and dates from the middle of the fifth century BC. Before they were called Athenians after the goddess Athena, the inhabitants of Athens called themselves Cecropians (*Kekropidai*)

which one was to be the patron god of Attica, the country of Athens. There was a tradition preserved by a scholiast on Aristophanes's play *Plutus* (773) that Cecrops had come from Egypt. Diodorus Siculus (first century BC) also said the Egyptians claimed this.[8]

The fish-tailed or serpent-tailed son of Cecrops, as just mentioned, was Erichthonios. There was another form of his name, Erechtheus. Later the two names diverged and they were thought to be two separate personages. Anyone familiar with the Acropolis at Athens will know the Erechtheon, on which the philosopher Socrates worked as a stone mason. It is named after Erechtheus/Erichthonios. At one time the Acropolis had a strange salt spring, and it was said to have sprung up at the command of Poseidon; its name however was *Erechtheis thalassa*, and Poseidon was ritually invoked there by the name of Erechtheus![9] Poseidon later killed Erechtheus, however (avenging the murder of his son, Eumolpus), so there is a very curious contradiction in this early mythology. The daughters of Erechtheus were the Hyades. Diodorus Siculus said that the Egyptians claimed that Erechtheus was an Egyptian who came to Athens and became king, and introduced the Eleusinian Mysteries to Greece from Egypt.[10] There are thus traditions that both Cecrops and his son, the two mythical amphibian or half-man/half-serpent monsters who were founders of Athens, were of Egyptian origin.

Then there was Scylla, well known from Homer's *Odyssey*. She was a fearsome fish-tailed character, and from her girdle issued a dog's head, or perhaps three dogs' heads, or sometimes even more, which made her more awesome (see Plate 29). Hesiod tells us that Scylla was the daughter of Hecate, who was the underworld counterpart of Sirius.[11] Doubtless that is why she had dogs issuing from her waist, as she represented the Dog Star, and her mother had Cerberus, the fifty-headed hound of hell, to keep her company, so dogs were in the family. The fact that Scylla had dogs' heads issuing from her waist, the point where her biform nature was transformed from fish to human, is a curious fact, and I know of no mythologist who has ever explained it. So I offer a possible explanation: In his treatise on 'Isis and Osiris', Plutarch is discussing Anubis when he says:

> When Nephthys gave birth to Anubis, Isis treated the child as if it were her own; for Nephthys is that which is beneath the Earth and invisible, Isis that which is above the earth and visible; and the circle which touches these, called the horizon, being common to both, has received the name Anubis, and is represented in form like a dog; for the dog can see with his eyes both by night and by day alike. And among the Egyptians Anubis is thought to possess this faculty, which is similar to that which Hecate is thought to possess among the Greeks, for Anubis is a deity of the lower world as well as a god of Olympus.[12]

This passage, which I have discussed earlier, clearly indicates that Isis represents the visible component of Sirius (Sirius A) while Nephthys, Isis's sister, the 'dark goddess', represents the invisible component, Sirius B. As we have seen previously, 'the circle' is the orbit of Sirius B, called Anubis. Anubis was also called 'the horizon'. 'Horizon' in Egyptian is *aakhu-t*, and what has come to interest me more recently is that *aakhu-t* is also the name of the Great Pyramid. It would seem therefore that another name for Anubis was *Aakhuti*, since it was used to mean 'the god who dwelleth in the horizon', and as we have seen from Plutarch, this is Anubis. (The Egyptians sometimes spoke of Horus-who-is-in-the-Horizon, but when they do that they tend to identify him. An explanation of the strange name Horus-in-the-Horizon is too complicated to give in a small space.) In my new first chapter to this book I have explained that I do not believe that the Great Sphinx was ever meant to represent a lion, as its body has no leonine characteristics whatever (no mane, no tufted tail, no raised haunches). I believe that the Sphinx was intended to be a dog, not a lion – and that it was in fact originally a giant statue of Anubis. Either its head was originally that of Anubis and was recarved in the image of a megalomaniac pharaoh (it has often been suggested by archaeologists that the head has been recarved to represent the face of a pharaoh of later days) or the Anubis body may always have had a human head. But in any case, the lion-aspect of the Sphinx is a complete fantasy, and it astonishes me that everyone has gullibly accepted this bit of nonsense without question for so long! The body of the Sphinx has only been visible for about a century, and I wonder who originally said it was a lion. Once a mistaken notion like the Sphinx being a lion has got itself established, no one questions it. The Sphinx is really a dog, and Sirius is the Dog Star.

Under this hypothesis, then, the Giza Pyramid Complex was one where the central edifice, the *aakhu-t*, was guarded by *Aakhuti*. What could be more appropriate?

But having seen Plutarch's remarks about Anubis' connection with the division between Isis and Nephthys, whereby he was the *middle*, we can see that this was symbolized in the case of Scylla. For a dog issues from her *middle*. In Egyptian tradition, Anubis divided one female form (Isis) from another (Nephthys), whereas by Greek times, the dog divided a single female form at her middle. So, just as we have seen that the amphibians Cecrops and Erichthonios were said to be of Egyptian origin, it would appear that Scylla probably is as well. But in her strange anatomy she embodied greater secrets, and these concerned the Sirius System.

There is another possible connection here. In Egyptian the word *meh* is the name for the Egyptian measure, the cubit, said by modern scholars to be 0.525 metre, or about 20 inches. It was also called the royal cubit and was under the protection of a large number of gods including Isis, Nephthys, and Osiris. But another name for the cubit was *aakhu meh*, so perhaps part of the lore was a special connection between the cubit and the Great Pyramid (hardly surprising!) and also Anubis, who as an orbit was a measurer *par excellence*. And perhaps it should also be mentioned the *mehit* is also Egyptian for 'fish' and that *mehuiu* is Egyptian for 'the great flood that destroyed mankind'. Whether there was meant to be any connection between the royal cubit and the Great Flood, and fish or fish-men, is another subject well worth some thought. But we shall not pursue it further here. What we were particularly interested in was the unusual symbolism of Scylla's form, and its connections with the Sirius lore. She was certainly one of the strangest of the amphibians of antiquity.

Another famous Greek amphibian was Triton. In later times, he multiplied and they spoke of 'the tritons'. It was fun for the vase painters and sculptors to have lots of tritons gambolling about in the waves. It made for lovely rococo effects. But originally there was only one god Triton. Of course, he had a fishtail and the body of a man. He was another of the Old Men of the Sea. In fact, there were at least four more in addition to Nereus and Proteus who have already been mentioned: Glaucos, Phorkys, Palaimon, and Nigaion were also Old Men of the Sea. So that makes at least eight of them.

The name of Triton is important. It was also the name of the Oracle Octave centre at Lake Triton in Libya, which was the birthplace of the goddess Athena in one version of her birth. It is interesting that the Aryans took with them to India the tradition of a water god called Trita, who appears in the earliest Sanskrit texts, the Vedas.[13] This indicates the extreme antiquity of the name and the god, as it must mean that Triton/Trita was exportable by about 1500 BC to an alien people, who took him with them when they marched very far from the sea indeed, across Central Asia to India at about that time. Monier-Williams, who compiled the definitive Sanskrit dictionary, gives the Greek *tritos* as a cognate of the name *Trita*, so the relation between the names is accepted, and means 'third'.[14] Trita was a rather mysterious figure. He fought against disruptive demons and was a keeper of the nectar of the gods. He was able to prepare the magical sacred beverage, soma, which he also supplied to the gods. He was associated with the god Indra in the struggle against chaotic disorder, and was also friendly with the god Vayu, the god of the wind, and the Maruts, who were subsidiary wind deities. His other name was Aptya, 'water-deity', and he was supposed to reside in the remotest regions of the world. He could bestow long life and is said to have written part of the sacred scriptures personally. There is also a story about his being shut up in a well,[15] which might be an echo of the Sumerian Enki shut up in his Abzu (a watery chamber or 'abyss'). The fact that Triton's name means 'one third' is also very interesting from the point of view of Sumerian and Babylonian traditions, since the god Enki's (Ea's) name *Shanabi* literally means 'two thirds'. Gilgamesh was also described as being 'two-thirds god, one-third man'. Two-thirds and one-third were also part of the sacred computations regarding the orbit of the planet Mercury. And the mystical triangle symbolizing water to the Pythagoreans* also had angles of two-thirds and one-third. I have described all of these matters at some length in the notes to my translation of the Epic of Gilgamesh, so shall not repeat them here.[16] But it seems clear that the traditions of Triton/Trita preserve Sumero-Babylonian lore, and not only in that Triton is one of the Oannes-type culture-hero amphibians, or a*nnedoti.*

Hesiod's *Theogony* of the eighth century BC is the earliest text which actually mentions the name of Triton, who according to Hesiod 'owns the depths of the sea' and is a son of Poseidon.[17] Triton was well on his way to India by this time, having departed with the Aryans about 700 years before Hesiod. Daremberg and Saglio are convinced that Triton was 'originally an independent god', and assigning him to Poseidon as a son was done later; they also say:

Anciently, one finds him established in two regions of the world peopled by the Greek Aeolians, and where the Aegean civilization has left profound traces: in Boeotia and in Crete. . . . [there is also a River Triton in Boeotia] . . . In Crete at Itanos, he figures on their coins. One could ask if this Cretan divinity isn't the dolphin god Delphinios, whose name became an epithet of Apollo, and of which the cult, originally of Knossos [in Crete], spread into the Mediterranean Basin and installed itself at Delphi, where it was transformed. Similarly, on the Libyan coast, where the citizens of Itanos contributed to the foundation of Cyrene, there was a River and a Lake Triton (today Farooun, or El-Loudeah) on the banks of which are located many cosmogonic† legends. Here one cannot fail to recognize at least in the formation of the artistic type the influence of the fish-gods of the coast of Syria: Dagon, worshipped at Azoth, and at Gaza, under the form of a half-man, half-fish monster; Derceto, an analogous feminine divinity who had a temple at Askalon. It is even probable that the African Triton is a purely Libyan divinity assimilated by the Greeks as the very most characteristic of their marine gods. He played an important role in the legend of the Argonauts: he helped the heroes in their navigation, made them escape the dangers of the Syrtes [Gulf of Syrte, shallow waters near Libya] and showed them future things. The inhabitants of Attica and Euboea, the towns of Corinth, of Byzantium, of Troezen, seem equally to have known Triton at an ancient epoch. Finally, one finds him represented on the coins of Karystos, of Cyzicus, a city opposite Byzantium [one is reproduced], of Nicodemia in Bithynia, of Agrigentum, and of Skylletion.[18]

---

* The followers of Pythagoras in Classical Greece who studied sacred mathematical and musical theories, and had a secret philosophical society; several of Plato's students were Pythagorean sympathizers.
† Concerning the creation of the Cosmos.

Like Trita in India, Triton had associations with the Great Flood. Daremberg and Saglio tell us:

In the Gigantomachy,* one sees him at battle beside his father [Poseidon], 'and the terrible sound of his conch shell made the gods' adversaries flee.' It is he who made the Flood waters recede while Zeus, appeased, yielded the Earth to the human race. It seems that Poseidon delegated to him a part of his powers. He could, to his liking, with the call of his conch raise up or calm the waves of the sea. He shook the rocks with his trident, and made islands spring up from the ocean's depths. Like the other marine gods, notably Nereus and Proteus, he possessed the gift of prophecy . . . He filled beside his father the same role which Hermes fulfilled beside Zeus: he carried messages from the god, . . . he lent assistance to Theseus . . . he escorted Phrixos and Helle [in connection with the Golden Fleece], the Argonauts, and the Dioscorides. . . . Above the hips, says Apollonius of Rhodes, his body was of a shape similar to that of the bodies of the blessed gods, but below his flanks on both sides, were aligned the two extremities of the tail of an enormous sea-monster . . . originally [this type of body] belonged to the Old Man of the Sea and . . . Nereus and Glaucos. . . . As we have already said, Triton is an heir of the Old Man of the Sea, and it is he whom we must recognize in the representations of half-man, half-fish sea monsters.

Nothing supports the supposition that he originates from a purely human form . . . but we have noted the influence of Oriental models on his artistic type. The god Dagon is often figured in the reliefs of the Palace of Sargon, on Babylonian cylinder seals, on Phoenician and Persian coins, on Greco-Phoenician scarabs, with forms similar to those of the Greek Triton.[19]

Another mythological figure of great importance whose body was half-human and whose bottom half was that of a dragon or great serpent was Typhon (see Zeus fighting him in Figure 49). Typhon shared with Scylla a very unpleasant temper. Daremberg and Saglio say of him:

One of the multiple forms under which the Phoenician Set continued to live in Greek mythology. One knows that in the Egyptian legend, Set, also called Typhon [which is the name Plutarch gives Set, for instance, when writing about Egyptian mythology in Greek], is the brother of Osiris. The latter personifies light; Set is, on the contrary, the demon of the storm and of gloom. . . . The Oriental origin of Typhon seems to be well demonstrated by these resemblances. Further, most of the writers, and already Homer, place the sojourn of Typhon in Cilicia [in Asia

---

* The great battle between Typhon and Zeus.

Minor]. . . . Pindar shows us Typhon, monster of a hundred heads, . . . The artists have represented him [additionally] with wings to signify his furious leap towards the sky [as is illustrated in Figure 49]. . . . The legs of the monster are replaced by serpents . . . [he was] in conflict with Zeus and in this combat the fire of the earth carried him straightaway up to the fire of the sky. . . . The noxious winds (*vente*) were, it was said, the children of Typhon and Echidna, 'the viper' [another biform creature, human above and serpent beneath, who lived in a cavern beneath the Earth and was extremely unpleasant, with horrid breath]. One has in addition often seen in Typhon a demon of the Hurricane. From his union with Echidna, the monster had ill-omened descendants . . . [including] the Sphinx, the Harpies . . . the Hound Orthros.[20]

Here we see specific associations of Typhon with Sirius: he and his monstrous bride were the parents of the cosmic hound Orthrus, representing the Dog Star. And they were also the parents of the Sphinx, which, as I have said a moment ago, I believe was meant to represent the dog Anubis. And of course Typhon had either fifty or a hundred heads, the number of years constituting Anubis's – Sirius B's – orbit. Typhon and Echidna were also the parents of Cerberus, the fifty-headed hound of hell.

Hesiod's account of them in the eighth century BC makes hair-raising reading:

> . . . fierce Echidna who is half a nymph with glancing eyes and fair cheeks, and half again a huge snake, great and awful, with speckled skin, eating raw flesh beneath the secret parts of the holy earth. And there she

Figure 49. Zeus, wielding a thunderbolt, is seen in battle against the ferocious Typhon, leader of the rebellion against his rule, and who was said to have had fifty heads (although only one is shown here). Typhon was the Greek version of the Egyptian god Set, who murdered and dismembered Osiris. In Greek tradition, Typhon was, like Cecrops, Erichthonios, Nereus, Triton, Scylla and others, a fish/serpent-tailed monster without legs. But unlike the others, he was a chief rebel against the order of heaven. Zeus pursued him at last to Mount Kasion, one of the sacred centres of the eastern oracle octave. From a Greek vase painting.

has a cave deep down under a hollow rock far from the deathless gods and mortal men. There, then, did the gods appoint her a glorious house to dwell in: and she keeps guard in Arima [in Cilicia] beneath the earth, grim Echidna, a nymph who dies not nor grows old all her days.

Men say that Typhaon [Typhon] the terrible, outrageous and lawless, was joined in love to her, the maid with glancing eyes. So she conceived and brought forth fierce offspring; first she bore Orthrus the hound of Geryones, and then again she bore a second, a monster not to be overcome and that may not be described, Cerberus who eats raw flesh, the brazen-voiced hound of Hades, fifty-headed, relentless and strong. And again she bore a third, the evil-minded Hydra of Lerna [who had a hundred heads] . . . Echidna was subject in love to Orthrus [her own son] and brought forth the deadly Sphinx . . .[21]

Here we may have a garbled reference to the relationship between Isis and her own son Horus, who succeeded his father Osiris in importance. The Greek Sphinx was also intimately connected to the story of Oedipus, who married his mother. I would suggest that the story of Oedipus, which by classical times appears to concern human beings, has its origins in a more archaic mythological setting, perhaps that of Orthrus mating with his mother, Echidna. The Greek Sphinx is the common link between the two mother-son matings. And probably the ultimate origin of all of these tales derives from the Egyptian motif of Horus who succeeds his father Osiris as consort of his mother Isis – or at least that is how it may have appeared to the Greeks, who did not necessarily appreciate all the fine details of the Egyptian story and who may have taken a rather sensationalist, tabloid view of the situation of this son taking over his father's position like that and being just a bit too friendly with his mother.

And so, as we have seen, there was a huge cast of fish-tailed marine characters in Greek mythology derived from Oannes and Dagon, related to the Sirius tradition, often specifically said to have come from Egypt, and related to Isis, Anubis, and even the Sphinx.

In Plate 31, we see two truly remarkable effigies from Cyzicus, a city opposite Byzantium. These show the goddess Isis herself as a half-human, half-fish creature! And one of them shows her with her tail entwined with that of her husband Serapis (a later name for Osiris), who is also fish-tailed. These effigies are very late in date, being from the Greco-Roman period: that is, late centuries BC – early centuries AD. But it may be that by this time the secrets of Egyptian mysteries were coming out, having spread, as I believe that they did, into the pagan Gnostic sects and then into the Christian Gnostic sects as well. I believe that at this time the so-called Hermetic books were written up in Greek, drawing upon genuine ancient Egyptian texts in some cases, notably in the instance of 'The Virgin of the World' treatise which has already been discussed at length on p. 104. So the notion that Isis and Osiris had fish-tails may have been a dark secret in Egypt, only to emerge when the mystery traditions were dispersed after the collapse of Egypt as an independent nation. Plutarch gives a hint of this when he says in his treatise 'Isis and Osiris' that the Egyptians maintained that the Elder Horus had been 'born a cripple';[22] this seems like a reference to the fact that he could not walk because he had no proper legs. (In Greece, the limp of the god Hephaestus may have been of similar origin.) From this period the worship of Isis became widely spread as a minority cult throughout Greece, Italy, and Asia Minor, so that the goddess outlasted her pharaohs for some centuries. And some would say that she still survives under the name of the Virgin Mary, who also, you may recall, bore a sacred son. But those matters I leave to others.

The image of Isis and Serapis (Osiris) with entwined fish-tails, or serpent-tails, whichever you prefer, is remarkably similar as an iconographical motif to one found thousands of miles away at about the same time – in China! And this most certainly was something I did not appreciate when I originally wrote *The Sirius Mystery*. For it is since that time that I have become so deeply involved with China and the history of Chinese culture (for which see the recent discussion appended to Chapter Six). I shall now say something about the Chinese amphibious culture heroes and founders of civilization, to show just how widespread the 'Oannes' story really is.

The Chinese have always maintained that their civilization was founded by an amphibious being, with a man's head and a fish tail, named Fuxi (old spelling: Fu-Hsi), 伏 羲 . The date traditionally ascribed to him is 3322 BC.[23] He was the Celestial Emperor before the founding of the first, Xia (Hsia) 夏 Dynasty of China by Emperor Yü. His wife, also said to be his sister, was Nü Gua (sometimes called Nü Wa; old spelling: Nü Kua) 女 媧 They were the traditional founders of civilization, just as Oannes was to the Babylonians. Fuxi is described in the third-century-BC Great Appendix to the Chinese *Book of Change* as follows:

Anciently, when Fuxi had come to the rule of all under Heaven, he looked up and contemplated the forms exhibited in the sky, and he looked down, contemplating the processes taking place on the earth. He contemplated the patterns of birds and beasts, and the properties of the various habitats and places. Near at hand, in his own body, he found things for consideration, and the same at a distance, in events in general. Thus he devised the eight trigrams, in order to enter into relations with the virtues of the bright Spirits, and to classify the relations of the ten thousand things.[24]

Fuxi is credited with inventing the system of the trigrams and hexagrams of the *Book of Change*. These were revealed to him by another amphibious being who rose up out of the Yellow River, and who had the patterns displayed upon his back (the so-called 'Ho Diagram'; known to have been preserved at the Chinese court in a place of honour in 1079 BC).[25] The particular arrangement of hexagrams called the Fuxi Arrangement is identical to the one which Leibniz realized corresponded to the system of binary numbers (zeroes and ones), which Leibniz introduced into Europe, and which is now used as the basis of all modern electronic computing.

Fuxi and Nü Gua repaired the heavens which had been broken and were the founders of civilization after the Great Flood. In Han Dynasty times (2,000 years ago) they were often depicted with entwined fishtails holding a carpenter's square and a compass, indicating their importance for measuring and surveying (the *Book of Change* also says they invented nets, a possible reference to latitude and longitude). Joseph Needham translates a portion of the *Chou Pei Suan Ching* [new spelling: *Zhou Bei Suan Jing: The Arithmetical Classic of the Gnomon and the Circular Paths (of Heaven)*], dating from the sixth century BC and text formalized in the first century BC, often said to be the oldest surviving Chinese mathematical text:

> May I venture to enquire how Fuxi anciently established the degrees of the celestial sphere? There are no steps by which one may ascend the heavens, and the earth is not measurable with a foot-rule. . . . what was the origin of these numbers?[26]

The most ancient Chinese cosmology was also attributed to Fuxi. It is called the Gai Tian (old spelling: Kai T'ien), 盖 天 , Theory. This depicted the night sky as a hemispherical dome viewed from inside. The origin of this cosmology of a double-vault theory of the world is recorded in the Dynastic History of the Jin (old spelling: Chin) Dynasty (265 AD – 420 AD) as follows:

> The theory originated from Fuxi's setting up of degrees for the circumference of the heavens and for the calendar. . . . The sun . . . cuts across the seven barriers (declination-circles) and the six roads (between them). The diameter and circumference of each barrier . . . can be worked out mathematically by using the method of similar right-angled triangles and observing the lengths of the shadows of the gnomon. The measurements of distances of the pole, and of the motions, whether near or far, are all obtained from the use of the gnomon and the right-angled triangle which it forms.[27]

As Needham points out: '. . . a similar double-vault theory of the world existed in Babylonia. It would have been one of the culture-traits which passed both westward to the Greeks and eastward to the Chinese, to be developed in both civilizations into the theory of the celestial sphere.'[28] Needham insists correctly upon the Babylonian origins of Chinese astronomy and cosmology. We can see that Oannes was transmitted along with the astronomy and that the Chinese identified him, by the name Fuxi, as the inventor of the system.

The greatest of all the historians of China was Sima Chien. His *Historical Records* were written *circa* 91 BC. A descendant, Sima Zheng, added a preliminary chapter containing mythological lore *circa* 720 AD. In this he described Fuxi and Nü Gua. Fuxi is there given two alternative names, Taihao ('Great Brilliant'), and Paoxi. The physical description of him says: 'He had a serpent's body, a man's head, and the virtue of a sage. . . . He worked out a system of recording by tablets . . . he was called Fuxi ('hidden victims'). . . . He made the thirty-five-stringed lute.' He is also clearly associated with the first day of Spring. As the translator, Herbert J. Allen, records: 'Fuxi (by which name this worthy is best known) is said to have been born after a gestation of twelve years.' Whether this is intended as a peculiarity of the amphibians who carry their young for many years, or, as Allen believes, a reference to the orbital period of the planet Jupiter, or indeed of some other significance, is anyone's guess. According to Sima Zheng, Nü Gua also 'had the body of a serpent, the head of a man, and the virtue of a holy man.' But in this account, Nü Gua is not a female who is the wife of Fuxi, but rather Fuxi's successor: 'He came to the throne in the room of Fuxi, under the title Nüxi. . . . In his last year one of the princes named Gong Gong, whose duty it was to administer the criminal law, became violent and played the tyrant. He did not rule properly . . . He also fought with Chuyong [also called Chungli, the God of Fire] and was not victorious, when, falling into a rage, he butted with his head against the Incomplete mountain, and brought it down. The "pillar of heaven" was broken and a corner of the earth was wanting.' Nü Gua fortunately repaired this damage and then: 'After this the earth was at rest, the heaven made whole, and the old things were unchanged.'[29]

If we examine the Chinese myths, we find that there were a number of amphibious beings, in addition to Fuxi, his wife, and the being from the Yellow River who revealed the hexagrams. There was the other mythical hero in China called Gong-Gong, just mentioned, (old spelling: Kung-Kung) 共工 who was 'a horned monster with the body of a serpent', and who corresponds to the Ogo of the Dogon or the Set of the Egyptians. Gong-Gong was a rebel engaged in a cosmic struggle, who crashed against a mountain and was responsible for the Earth tilting on its axis: 'Heaven and Earth have since that time sloped toward one another in the northwest but have tilted away from one another in the opposite direction.'[30] Two other amphibians at the beginning of Chinese history were the mythical Emperor Yü 禹, first emperor of the first dynasty called Hsia (supposed to date to 2205 BC) and his father Gun (old spelling: Kun). The Chinese character for Gun 鯀 contains the element (on the left side) meaning 'fish', and that of Yü contains an element commonly used with reptiles, so that both mythical heroes were 'of non-human origins'.[31] It was Yü who conquered the Great Flood or Deluge in Chinese myth. There are various peculiarities to the myths relating to Gun and Yü. First of all, Yü was born from his father's own belly, which indicates the same androgynous aspect of the amphibians which are related by the Dogon. And after giving birth, Gun became a black fish or yellow dragon and plunged back in the sea, like Oannes. Yü was evidently not born on earth, because once he was born he 'came down from on high'. He could not walk properly and had a peculiar gait which was ever afterwards known as the 'walk of Yü', which is what one would expect of an amphibian with a fishtail. One of his prime concerns was to measure 'the dimensions of the world from east to west and north to south'.[32]

We see that there were at least six separate identifiable amphibious beings involved in the founding of Chinese civilization, according to the mythological traditions. There was a seventh as well: Fuxi was said to have had a daughter, Fu Fei, who lived in the Lo River and became its goddess.[33] We should remember that there were anywhere between six and eight amphibious Annedoti in Babylonia, and often they were referred to as 'the Seven Sages'.

A number of exceedingly strange old Chinese bone carvings bearing archaic characters which cannot be later than the third century BC, and may be a great deal older, appear to portray the amphibians, and they somewhat resemble the Dogon drawings of the Nommo. These were collected by L. C. Hopkins, who got them from a collector of Shang Dynasty oracle bones who was forced to sell up in 1910 because of political events. It is implied but not clearly stated by Hopkins that the five bone carvings which he thus acquired were also found at Anyang and were associated with the Shang material, in which case they would have been 3,500 years old rather than 2,200; the inscriptions on the carvings appear to be Shang script. I have only found a single account of these carvings, in the report of them published by Hopkins in 1913, which contains photographs of four of the objects. (These photos would not reproduce well here because they are not of very good quality.)[34] They bear either single or double (bi-form) fish or serpent tails. Vestigial legs pressed close to the body have only four toes. The heads have long beards and staring eyes. Two of the specimens indicate a small horn on the head. Hopkins records a few of the Chinese characters inscribed on what he calls his 'dragon carvings', the five main carvings, as well as on 'six miniature dragon forms acquired at an earlier date'. These include prominent occurrence of the character meaning 'rain', and on one of the large carvings the character *long* meaning 'dragon'. Another bears a typical mid-second millennium BC Shang oracle inscription: 'The king inquired as to the omens.' (The character for 'king' being *wang*, and thus preceding the unification of China.) Hopkins closes by saying: 'And there, for the time, I am fain to leave these oracular relics of an amphibious and ambiguous past . . .' I have no idea of the whereabouts of the objects today, nor have I ever seen any mention of them more recent than 1913.

The 'dragons' of archaic China were associated with the stars in a curious way. The celestial dragon, known as *chen* 辰, also represented 'beacon stars' including Orion's Belt.[35]

Water spirits, river gods, supernatural fish, and so forth have been part of Chinese folklore for millennia. Although such beliefs doubtless remain amongst the people in remote areas of the countryside (it should be remembered that 800 million Chinese live in the countryside!), it appears that the surviving traditions relating to the ancient amphibians are strongest amongst the hill tribe minorities, such as the Yao People of Guangxi Province. Many studies of the traditions have been published in Chinese, but one in English published in 1982 by Chan Ping-leung summarizes much of the contemporary Minorities folklore on the subject. The current traditions tend to stress the Great Flood and the sexual aspect of the incestuous marriage between Fuxi and Nü Gua, which led to the repopulation of the world after the Deluge. It is interesting that in the ancient legend of Fuxi he had a black dog as his companion, and his instructions to his successor Yü were to 'measure the universe'; he was 'a god with a human face and a serpentine body'.[36] It may be that certain details of the appearance of the amphibians, surviving from ancient times, are embodied in much more recent folklore of Chinese water demons. For instance, de Groot records some curious details, stressing how shocking it was that the water demons wore no clothes at all and had naked buttocks; and a man who saw one said "that neither its eyes nor eyebrows were marked with black. The creature reared itself straight up in the water, rigid, with a neck as immovable as that of a wooden image.'[37] Such details may be entirely fanciful or they may go back to the original descriptions of Fuxi and his colleagues, concerning whom most ancient texts are lost. There were still temples dedicated to the worship of Fuxi as recently as 1945, when Needham visited the chief one at Tianshui, in the remote Western Chinese province of Gansu (old spelling: Kansu) – and Needham says he noted 'the mermaid tail still iconographically prominent'.[38] Everyone who knows anything at all about China is aware of how prominent the dragon is as a symbol there, from the dragons which prowl the streets on festivals, to cushion designs, restaurant signs and company logos. It is thought that the Chinese dragon concept originated from the tradition of the amphibious beings who founded civilization. G. Willoughby-Meade, who made a specialty of studying the histories of mythical and legendary Chinese beasts and monsters, says: 'The earliest extant drawings of Chinese dragons are of rude workmanship, and very fish-like of aspect; in the next artistic stage, as exemplified by the jade funeral-objects of the Han period – roughly two centuries BC and two centuries after – the transition towards a vigorous and plastic reptile-form

Figure 50. Two of the fish-tailed founders of Chinese civilization, Fuxi and Cang Jing, from a bas relief in the Han Dynasty Wu Liang tomb dated to the second century AD. The inscription says that they governed the world within the seas, created the trigrams (the system of the *Book of Change*) and established kingship. Fuxi is holding a carpenter's and mason's square as an emblem of his role as creator of civilization. Fuxi is normally shown with his tail entwined with that of his wife, Nü Gua. Between them the two main figures hold a baby fish-tailed creature, whose two legs are separate tails, as is often seen with the Greek Triton figures. The iconography of this illustration is eerily similar to that of Plate 31, showing Isis and Serapis with entwined tails, excavated at a site thousands of miles from China. How did the image travel so far?

Figure 51. Five amphibious founders of Chinese civilization portrayed in a Han Dynasty (first century AD) tomb rubbing, published by Edouard Chavannes in his book *La Sculpture sur Pierre en Chine – Han*, Paris, 1893, Plate 24. Fuxi, the large figure on the right, as usual holds the carpenter's or mason's square with which he measured the earth. His tail is entwined with that of another amphibian, possibly his wife Nü Gua, or possibly Cang Jing. In the centre a smaller pair of amphibians with entwined tails also holds hands. On the right, a fifth amphibian looks on. To the left, the tail of a sixth amphibian seems to be represented, but we cannot see him fully. Waves and billows of the sea are represented beneath the group

is clearly shown.'[39] It seems, therefore, that the fish-tailed beings were transformed into dragons over the millennia of Chinese history, and that it is to them that we owe the now ubiquitous dragon in China.

In Figures 50 and 51 we see representations of Fuxi and Nü Gua with their fishtails entwined, as they were envisaged 2,000 years ago. It is worthwhile having given this summary of the Chinese tradition to show how widespread the story really is in the world of the founding of civilization by heavenly amphibians. However, the astonishing similarity between these Figures and Plate 31, which shows Isis and Serapis with similar entwined tails, raises the question as to how such dramatically similar representations could possibly exist several thousand miles distant from each other in wholly different cultures. A direct borrowing by the Chinese seems likely, but why would the Chinese borrow an image and then set it at the very centre of their culture, representing their own cultural origins, when it came from the Mediterranean region? It seems to me that we cannot continue to allow the issue of Fuxi and Nü Gua to languish in neglect. Their iconographical representations in dated tombs of the Han Dynasty pose a very direct problem regarding culture contacts between China and the Near East, or otherwise point to some other factor equally puzzling. In either case, a thorough study of the fish-tailed founders of Chinese civilization should be undertaken by someone capable of dealing with the highly specialized areas of Chinese mythology and folklore, Han Dynasty and earlier evidences both textual and archaeological. Probably no single person could command the expertise to do the entire study alone. But it should be done.

*****

Let us take a look now at what the Dogon tribe have to tell us about the amphibious creatures who are credited with founding their civilization as well, and who seem to have come from Sirius. In Figures 52 and 54 are Dogon tribal drawings of what the creatures actually looked like. They are credited with having descended in an ark which, in landing, looked like Figure 55 which portrays 'the spinning or whirling of the descent of the ark'. The god of the universe, Amma (whose name I feel certain is a survival of that of the god Ammon of the Oasis of Siwa), sent the amphibians to earth. They are called the Nommos. But just as the Babylonians tended to speak of Oannes, the leader, instead of always saying 'the Annedoti' collectively, the Dogon often just speak of 'Nommo' or 'the Nommo' as an individual. The Nommos are collectively called 'the Masters of the Water' and also 'the Instructors', or 'the Monitors'. They have to live in water: 'The Nommo's seat is in the water'.[40] The latter is much like the Babylonian tradition of their god Ea (Enki to the Sumerians), whose seat was also in the water, and who is sometimes connected with Oannes.

The descriptions of the landing of the ark are extremely precise. The ark

Figure 52. Dogon drawing of Nommo

is said to have landed on the earth to the north-east of Dogon country,[41] which is where the Dogon claim to have come from (originally, before going to Mande) and that is, of course, the direction of Egypt and the Middle East in general.

The Dogon describe the sound of the landing of the ark. They say the 'word' of Nommo was cast down by him in the four directions as he descended,* and it sounded like the echoing of the four large stone blocks being struck with stones by the children, according to special rhythms, in a very small cave near Lake Debo.[42] Presumably a thunderous vibrating sound is what the Dogon are trying to convey. One can imagine standing in the cave and holding one's ears at the noise. The descent of the ark must have sounded like a jet runway at close range.

Figure 53. Descent of Nommo from the sky. Dogon drawing

* The reader will recall that near the end of Chapter 2 I mentioned that 'the word' represents a concept like the *logos* to the Dogon, for it means 'air'. We may take this description to refer not only to noise but to a rushing wind.

Figure 54. Dogon drawing of Nommo

The landing of the ark is visually described:[43] 'The ark landed on the Fox's dry land and displaced a pile of dust raised by the whirlwind it caused.' For this, see Figure 53. They continue: 'The violence of the impact roughened the ground . . . it skidded on the ground.'

It is said of Nommo, or more probably of his ark: 'He is like a flame that went out when he touched the earth'. They say: 'The Nommo was "as red as fire". . . . when he landed, he became white'.[44] And consequently a bit of folklore: 'The albino is the testament on Earth of the Nommo's burns as he came down; he is said to be the "trace of the burn", the scar of the Nommo.'[45]

There seems to be a use by the Dogon of 'spurting blood' to describe what we would call 'rocket exhaust'. And let us remember that, short of anti-gravity machines (which may be impossible), rocket propulsion is likely to be used by craft landing on any planet, no matter how sophisticated and non-rocket-like the interstellar main craft, or no matter how immensely advanced the civilization may be which is making a landing on a planet. For the principle of the rocket is a simple one unlikely to be dispensed with entirely in any foreseeable future technology. Actually, the Dogon seem to make a clear differentiation between the ark in which the Nommos actually landed on earth and what we may surmise was the true interstellar spaceship hovering above in the sky at a great distance, and which the Dogon seem to describe as appearing in the sky as a new star, and leaving with the Nommos at their departure from Earth. In fact, this is the sort of arrangement one would expect. An interstellar spaceship would probably look like a bright new star, possibly visible in daytime as well as by night, and the landing craft would be simple rocket-propelled craft not so different in principle from machines which we ourselves have used for landing on the moon.

The Dogon may describe the interstellar spaceship hovering high above the Earth by what they call *ie pelu tolo*, 'star of the tenth moon'. The

Figure 55. The whirling descent of the spaceship of Nommo. Dogon drawing

Dogon say: 'As (the ark) landed, the weight of the ark caused the "blood" to spurt to the sky'.[46] This would seem to be a rocket craft landing on earth. But this 'spurting blood' (flame?) is said to be shared with *ie pelu tolo*, and 'gave the star reality and brilliance'.[47] For three different complementary tribal drawings of *ie pelu tolo*, see Figure 57. These seem to represent the 'star' in three separate conditions, differing in the amount of 'spurting blood' being emitted by it. The Dogon also describe this 'star' specifically as having a circle of reddish rays around it, and this circle of rays is 'like a spot spreading' but remaining the same size.[48]

It is said that the Nommos will come again. There will be a 'resurrection of the Nommo'. It should thus not surprise us that 'the celestial symbol of the resurrection is the "star of the tenth moon", *ie pelu tolo* . . . This star is not easy to see. . . . The ten rays, placed in pairs, are inside the circle because the star has not yet "emerged"; it will be formed when the Nommo's ark descends, for it is also the resurrected Nommo's "eye" symbolically.'[49] In other words, the 'star' is not a star, and can only be seen when the Nommo returns and his ark descends to Earth. In Chapter One

Figure 56. Dogon drawing of *ie pelu tolo*; the ten rays, in pairs, are inside the circle, having not yet 'emerged'

Figure 57. Three states of *ie pelu tolo* in the sky. Dogon drawing

I have discussed the star of the tenth moon at length and suggested that it remains in our own solar system as the tenth main moon of Saturn, Phoebe, and that is the base of the visiting Nommos who will by now have awakened from suspended animation.

The Nommo is 'the monitor for the universe, the "father" of mankind, guardian of its spiritual principles, dispenser of rain and master of the water generally.'[50] Not all the Nommos came to Earth. The 'one' called Nommo Die, or 'Great Nommo', remained 'in heaven with Amma, and he is his vicar'.[51] He manifests himself in the rainbow, which is called 'path of the Nommo'.[52] He is guardian of the 'spiritual principles of living creatures on Earth'.[53]

There are three other distinct kinds of Nommo, each personified as an individual. There is the Nommo Titiyayne, 'messenger (or deputy) of the Nommo Die . . . he (executes) the latter's great works.'[54] The Nommos who came to earth in the spaceship are presumably of this class. Figures 52 and 54 represent these beings in particular.

A third class of Nommos are represented by O Nommo, 'Nommo of the pond'. 'He will be sacrificed for the purification and reorganization of the universe . . . He will rise in human form and descend on Earth, in an ark, with the ancestors of men . . . then he will take on his original form, will rule from the waters and will give birth to many descendants.'[55] This suggests that a group of Nommos volunteered to be reincarnated as humans during the period of official absence from Earth of the Nommo Titiyayne leaders.

The fourth Nommo is the naughty disrupter named Ogo, or Nommo Anagonno. 'As he was about to be finished (being created) he rebelled against his creator and introduced disorder into the universe. Eventually, he will become the Pale Fox (*le Renard pâle*) which is the image of his fall.'[56] In many ways, the Fox resembles the Egyptian deity Set.

The name Nommo comes from a Dogon word linked to the root *nōmo*, 'to make one drink'. It is said: 'The Nommo divided his body among men

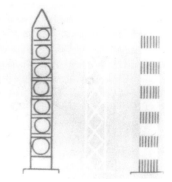

Figure 58. Sirigi designs of the Dogon

to feed them; that is why it is also said that as the universe "had drunk of his body" the Nommo also made men drink. He also gave all his life principles to human beings.'[57] He was crucified on a *kilena* tree (*Prosopis africana*, a source of charcoal) which also died and was resurrected.[58]

After the ark had landed, according to the Dogon, an interesting series of events took place which make a great deal of sense if one remembers that amphibious creatures were inside. Something described both as a 'horse' and just simply as a 'quadruped' appeared which pulled the ark with ropes to a hollow.[59] 'This stage, momentarily, transformed the ark into a chariot drawn by a quadruped with ropes.'[60] The hollow then filled with water. However, an untoward incident then occurred: 'After the first rainfall, when the water had filled the pond, the water-insect . . . entered the water . . . it wanted to "bite" the Nommo's head . . . but it was unable to reach the edge of the ark.'[61]

> The bad 'water-insect' was thus unsuccessful in wishing to do harm. When the water filled the pond, the ark floated on it like a huge pirogue [a dug-out canoe] . . . It is said: 'The great ark came out of the sky and came down. In the centre the Nommo was standing, he came down. Then he returned to the water.' . . . From then on he was called O Nommo, 'Nommo of the pond', – through respect men will not utter this name, but will call him instead *dī tigi*, 'master of the water'.[62]

Thus we see that the second and third categories of Nommo are really the same, but represent successive states. And as for the future:

> His twin who will descend later on with the Blacksmith, 'twin of the victim', will also be transformed in the pond. They will have many descendants and will always be present in the fresh 'male' water of the brooks, rivers, ponds and wells and also in the 'female' sea water.[63]

As for this reference to fresh water as male and sea water as female, it is similar to the ancient Babylonian and Sumerian tradition where Apsu (Abzu – see p. 164) was a male fresh-water deity and Tiamat a female sea-water deity. The Dogon say,[64] 'O Nommo has his seat in the waters of the earth', which could just as well be a description of Enki/Ea, whom I mentioned above.

I feel impelled to reproduce in this book as Figure 58 a Dogon drawing showing four variants of the Dogon *sirigi* mask design. Anyone can see that they look like rocket ships. Griaule and Dieterlen give[65] detailed accounts of the meanings of the lozenges, rectangles, etc. These variant designs are said specifically all to represent 'the descent and impact of the ark'.[66] The descent of the ark was like a lozenge, its impact was like a rectangle.[67] Perhaps this is why the Dogon say: 'When the ark was descending, space was four angles; when the ark was down, space had four sides.'[68] The *sirigi* design itself represents 'a "house with stories" . . . (and) indicates the ark as well as its descent.'[69] So maybe the Dogon have actually drawn a rocket ship.

The Dogon say[70] that '*po tolo* (Sirius B) and Sirius were once where the sun now is'. That seems as good a way as any to describe coming to our solar system from the Sirius system, and leaving those stars for our star, the sun. But let us now take leave of our friends the Dogon. Let us go to where Sirius and its white dwarf companion star are the suns, and where our own sun has become just another star in the sky. Let us visit the planet of the amphibians.

What are Sirius and Sirius B like as suns? We know that they revolve around a common centre, which is in fact equivalent to Sirius B revolving around Sirius A in an elliptical orbit. Sirius A, a big, bright star, has two and a half times the mass of our sun. Sirius B has – as discussed at length in Chapter One – 1.053 of the mass of our sun, but because it is made of degenerate matter and is so tiny, this is not obvious. If Sirius B with its mass were not a white dwarf, we could see it from earth as a star of magnitude 2, if it were not for the problem of parallax, which makes it impossible with the naked eye to separate it from Sirius A. In any case, if Sirius B were on its own somewhere at its distance from earth, and were not a white dwarf, it would be one of the brightest stars in the sky.

In reality, Sirius A is ten thousand times brighter than Sirius B. The luminosity of Sirius A is thirty-five and a half times the luminosity of our sun. That makes it a pretty hot number. We can be certain that our planet is not too near it. The 'habitable zone' discussed in Chapter 2 is much farther out from Sirius than it is from our sun. As for the actual size of Sirius A, its radius is a little more than one and a half times the sun's radius. This means that Sirius will be smaller in the sky than our own sun, seen from the planet. It will be a good deal smaller, but will need to have roughly the same amount of heat, which is not too difficult, considering how terribly hot and bright it is. To us it would be a strange experience to see such a small body in the sky giving out so much heat and light.

Our planet actually orbits around the small red dwarf star Sirius C, which may in turn orbit around the tiny white dwarf Sirius B, all of them orbiting round Sirius A every fifty years. I therefore speak of Sirius A as the main Sun, as it is the centre of everything.

Our planet will probably be quite hot. In fact, it will probably even be covered with a vaporous layer of cloud at most or all times. It might look something like Venus from a distance, though of course Venus does not have temperatures or clouds of the sort which living creatures are likely to find agreeable. It would seem important to keep cool on this probably rather hot and steamy planet. Therefore intelligent life is likely to have evolved as amphibious and never have taken to the land. These amphibians might easily inhabit the surface of the water, of course, for they would need to breathe atmosphere and would not have gills like fish – they would probably need to be like mammals of some kind in order to develop the brain sizes and other characteristics necessary for intelligence. They would probably spend a lot of time hanging about marshes and might have developed an indigenous way of life originally which involved the use of woven reeds for huts and transport, and so on. (They would long ago have got past that stage, of course.) But perhaps their first style of life, to which they may even look back with some nostalgia as 'the good old days of simplicity and a carefree existence', was something like that described by Wilfred Thesiger in his book *The Marsh Arabs*[71] in which the inhabitants of southern Iraq are pictured in the marshes of the lower Tigris and Euphrates (quite near where Oannes and his friends are said to have spent most of the time, one is tempted to note!).

Reeds as a building material seem to have had a profound religious importance in Sumerian and Babylonian tradition. In the *Epic of Gilgamesh*, there is a very strange and not wholly explained passage where the god Enki (Ea), who wishes to save mankind from the Great Flood, warns Ziusudra (the Noah of the Bible) in this bizarre fashion:

> Speaking through the wall of Ziusudra's reed hut:
> 'Reed hut, reed hut! Wall of the hut, wall of the hut!
> Listen, O reed hut! Consider, O wall of the hut!
> O man of Shuruppak [Ziusudra's city], O you son of Ubaru-
>   Tutu,
> Tear down your hut of reeds,
> Build of them a [reed] boat!
> Abandon things,
> Seek life.
> Give up possessions,
> Keep your soul alive!
> And into the boat take the seed of all living creatures.'[72]

It would seem that to the Sumerians and Babylonians, there was a nostalgic mystique attached to the (imagined) days when the founders of the world lived in simple reed huts. Imagine, then, that you live on your watery planet, and instead of harking back to Shaker furniture, as Americans do, or to country cottages with rosemary bushes, as the British do, in their cults of simplicity – you like to speak of the 'good old days' when even the most important people lived, like simple marsh folk, in their reed huts, without affectation.

If you were one of these creatures, you would be a good deal like a dolphin with arms and hands. (Fish seem an unpromising avenue for the evolution of intelligence due to limitations on brain size, need for gills, etc. But on Earth we see that aquatic mammals such as dolphins and whales achieve huge brain size.) You would, due to your amphibian nature, have a separate blowhole for breathing in addition to your mouth. You would be able to hold your breath for long periods, and when you did breathe through your blowhole, it would be a gasp and make a bit of noise. Your blowhole would open and close almost instantaneously and your breathing would tend to be infrequent but loud and quick. The blowhole might be placed in such a way that it consisted of one or two small slits, long and thin, just beneath your clavicles (collarbones). In fact, the Dogon have a tradition that their Nommos breathed through their clavicles.[73]

You could not go about bare-skinned in any atmosphere for long. You would require moisture on your skin after a few hours at the most; when your skin dried you would be in absolute agony – worse than a human with sunburn. Because you would frequent the surface of the water a great deal, there would inevitably be a considerable contrast between the top half of your body and the bottom half. The tradition known to us of the mermaid expresses this state of affairs quite well. Your lower extremities would be quite fishlike, but you would have articulate limbs and fingers on your

Figure 59. The Nommo breathes through air-holes in his clavicles that look like this Dogon drawing

upper half and your skin would be more capable of resisting solar radiations and hence would be more like that of a land mammal. Probably cartilaginous structures would have evolved in your head to rigidify your features beyond the simple streamlined form required for a strictly undersea life, and there would be something on your upper body resembling hair – perhaps like the hair of our own walruses.

Your teeth would probably be feeble compared with those of ferocious carnivores such as sharks. You would probably have evolved from more peaceful creatures capable of feeding on small fish in considerable numbers. Your ancestors would have travelled in packs as the dolphins do and you would be extremely sociable because you evolved in schools (packs). Nudity is probably the natural state of your species. Over-population is not one of your problems because most of your planet is water and all of the water is habitable. Even on the planet Earth, it is estimated that dolphins outnumber human beings two-to-one, and the oceans are hardly overcrowded.

As one of these creatures, you might find human beings repulsive, for many reasons. Their rough hair, dry skins, bony limbs, and particularly their pungent smells might disturb you greatly. Their sweat is not continually washed away in the way that your skin is continually cleansed by the watery medium which you inhabit. And as an amphibian you have exceedingly well-developed senses of smell and taste. You 'taste' smells or spoor-substances underwater at enormous distances and though your sense of smell is not quite as acute, it is competent enough.

One of the most disturbing sights to you is to watch human beings walking. When humans stand still with their legs together, they look almost normal. But then suddenly they 'split' into two and begin walking, which makes you slightly dizzy and upsets you. It makes you feel nervous with the thought of how dreadful it would be for you if you 'split' and thereby became a cripple in the water. You admire the agility of the humans on dry land. They can climb trees and cliffs, all of which is terribly impressive. They can go at a great speed on land with what they call 'running', and they even have a certain capacity to jump over obstacles; they are not as swift on land as you are in water, but they do passably well. You do have difficulty in seeing them sometimes because, as you are in a watery environment, your vision is not good at long range.[74] And the humans, being dry, do not stand out against their background as much as you could wish. When they move you can instantly detect motion without optical definition, but a stationary human who is even approximately camouflaged and blends with this background is impossible for you to differentiate with your unaided eye. You rely on your sense of smell, like a rhinoceros. But when the wind is against you, you have no hope. A human can easily elude your perception on dry land if he knows what he is doing and you do not have your goggles or technical aids with you.

You would have an extremely agile mathematical mind. Your ancestors developed from the primitive state by computing the intricate astronomical phenomena and radiations falling on your planet without benefit of direct optical observations. The brains of your species were thus engendered to conceive and solve vast intricate abstractions. Your powers of holding complicated mathematical structures suspended in your mind's eye while performing mathematical operations on them is extraordinary. You have a phenomenal conceptual and generalizing faculty. It is easy for you to conceive of invisible, and even imperceptible, forces, because your daily environment is a suggestive, allusive one. You taste and smell your ambience rather than see it. Your powers of telepathy may be extremely highly evolved – possibly a characteristic of your species from their earliest history.

The climate range of your planet is greater even than the Earth's because there are no ice caps, due to there being more radiation from the three stars in your multi-solar system. Your oceans are all the more extensive, therefore, for not being locked up in ice caps at the poles.

Space flight is less uncomfortable for you than for humans, as the state of weightlessness is often approximated under water (indeed, on Earth the astronauts train under water). Your blood circulation is thus better suited to the weightless condition than is the case with humans and you do not at all mind living in the gigantic water tanks orbiting your planet which constitute your many satellite space cities. It is not as difficult to simulate a watery environment in space as it is to simulate a dry land environment. Your wants are few, your existence simple. You do not eat cooked food and you do not have stoves to keep warm. Farming for you is mostly the breeding of delicious small fish, and meals are an adventure as you love a good chase and the satisfaction of catching your food. Dinner is a family sport.

Additional Comments (1997)
In 1989 some extremely bizarre discoveries were made about dolphins which may have a relevance to the Sirius Mystery and to the Nommos. Dr Margaret Klinowska of the Research Group in Mammalian Ecology and Reproduction at Cambridge University and David Goodson of Loughborough University's Sonar Research Group in Britain announced that there is something very strange about dolphins' *teeth*. They discovered that they act as highly sensitive sonar receivers. A report of these findings said:

As they move through water, dolphins emit high frequency clicks, creating echoes which tell them how far they are from any nearby objects or fish.

Until now, it has been thought the echoes were conveyed by the dolphin's lower jaw to their ears.

But now research suggests the teeth act as receivers, picking up the

305

pressure from the sound waves, and transmitting them via nerves inside the teeth to the brain stem.

'This gives us a much deeper insight into the dolphins' sonar and explains for the first time why it's so good,' said . . . Dr Margaret Klinowska . . . 'If their teeth are acting as an array of receivers, then they have 20 on each side, instead of just the one ear.' . . . Dr Klinowska, one of Britain's leading authorities on dolphins, said their teeth are very even in shape and spacing, and have little tubes in the dentine, arranged like the spokes of a wheel. She and Mr Goodson believe it is these tubes which act as pressure receivers.[75]

Perhaps this is the kind of information we have needed all along to give us the missing clues as to why *teeth* were so important in the lore concerning Sirius and the Nommos. For the tooth is the hieroglyphic sign for the goddess Sothis, and *dragon's teeth* are fundamental to the entire complex of legend. We have seen in Plate 23 a Sumerian cylinder seal showing the ploughing of dragon's teeth into the ground. Dragon's teeth were central to the Argonaut legend. And it does not take a great deal of imagination to realize that the 'dragons' were the amphibious beings. Now at last we have some hint as to why their *teeth* were so important. If dolphins' teeth are like this, it is not unlikely that the teeth of the amphibious beings from Sirius are similar.

There are oddities about the teeth of another significant earthly amphibian, the dugong. Readers have often written to me and asked me if I realized that one of the most interesting amphibious sea creatures was called a dugong. Was there any connection with the Dogon Tribe? Or at least with the god Dagon, who was amphibious? Frankly, until I started receiving these readers' letters, I had never heard of dugongs. I now have a picture of one beside me as I write – see Figure 60. A dugong is a charming creature, like a smaller manatee except that a manatee has a rounded tail, whereas the dugong has a tail exactly like that of a Dogon Nommo! (Although the Dogon Nommos are inspired by African catfish, the tail analogy holds, strangely enough.) At the time of the Gulf War, newspaper stories appeared about the danger that leaking oil slicks posed to the dugong in the Persian Gulf.[76] The dugong was called a 'Mermaid Beast'. It was only then that I realized the dugongs were once common in the Persian Gulf – just off the coast of ancient Sumer!

However, although the Persian Gulf dugong may be threatened, I understand that dugongs are absolutely thriving near the Great Barrier Reef. There was a newspaper report in 1990 about the prevalence of 'mermaids' there: 'The snub-nosed creature has a whale's tail, hide and blubber, . . . [But:] A dugong's life cycle does not allow room for complacency about its chances of survival. It lives for about seventy years, but a female has only a single calf every three to five years, is pregnant for a year and suckles the calf for about eighteen months . . .'[77]

H.Dugong.———Dugong.

Figure 60. An old engraving of a dugong, *Halicore Dugong*, which, although it looks like a whale, is actually an aquatic Pachyderm. The name dugong may come from the ancient amphibious god Dagon of the Philistines. It is interesting that Berossus describes Oannes or Dagon as being 'slimy', since the dugong is also slimy, the skin is almost naked and oily. It likes shallow water where it can feed on subaquatic vegetation. Its eyes are very small. Anatomically, the dugong is peculiar in that it has a dual heart. Dugongs are extremely passionate about their mates; the Malays have traditionally harpooned dugongs for their meat, and there have been many cases where the mate of a slain dugong has followed the boat for long distances, unwilling to part with its spouse and often being killed for this loyalty. (I cannot help but be reminded of the fanatical loyalty to the slain Osiris shown by Isis.)

Many people have written and asked if the name Dogon has anything to do with dugong and Dagon. Nobody knows, but it is entirely probable that the chief god Amma of the Dogon is none other than the god Ammon (Amun) of the Oasis of Siwa, from which region we actually know that their ancestors migrated. And having come so far bringing that name, the name Dagon which was contemporary with it – although in another location – could in theory have been part of the package, giving the name of the Dogon. So Dogon, Dagon, and dugong could be connected. As we have seen from the survival of the astronomical information, stranger things have happened!

It is the teeth of the dugong which are really interesting. A report in the journal *Biological Conservation* in 1975 only came to my attention in 1976 after the first publication of this book. According to this report:

The dugong is strange, however, in that most of its teeth seem either to be reabsorbed into the skull or worn away by use, while the so-called incisors never erupt through the bone but grow backwards into it. These incisors provide reliable material for the determination of age, but first they have to be chipped out of the bone.

Having accomplished that task with about seventy-five teeth, Dr Mitchell counted between zero, on the smallest skull, and fifty-seven and a half growth layers. Because it is not yet clear whether one or two layers are laid down each year, she can only say that dugongs have a life span just under sixty or just over thirty years.[78]

It is evident that the teeth of aquatic mammals have a tendency to be very strange indeed. The fact that the Dogon stress the pointed teeth of the

Nommos, together with all the ancient tooth traditions this seems to support the view that the Nommos have teeth with special properties, probably sonar-receivers like the dolphins', and quite possibly with a bizarre anatomical aspect such as those of the dugongs. If a tooth is like a radio and not just something with which you chomp, then it is understandable that it would take on a special significance and be referred to in myth and legend.

I should just mention the sea otter before we leave aquatic mammals. Sea otters are remarkably intelligent creatures and they have the distinction of being one of the few animals who routinely use *tools*. People who watch a lot of nature films on television may well have seen footage of sea otters doing so. The sea otters routinely turn over on their backs, floating in the sea, and crack shells open with hard objects, and thus extract the shellfish inside. They are in fact *regular* tool-users. It used to be suggested that the use of tools was the special and defining prerogative of man, as it indicated his superior intelligence. In recent times we have come to appreciate the use of tools by monkeys, some birds, and a few other creatures, even though this remains rare. But it is worthwhile realizing that there is an amphibious creature with sufficient brainpower to be a habitual tool-user. In fact, the sea otter thus joins the dolphins and the whales in the club of brainy sea-dwellers. Maybe the fact that such intelligent creatures have evolved in the earth's seas should tell us something.

But to return now to the Nommos . . .

The amphibians must have a name, and the Dogon name for them of 'the Monitors' may be the best to consider using. 'Monitor' is more specific than 'Instructor', and 'Masters of the Water' is too long. There is no point using the euphemism the 'Annedoti', knowing that it means the 'Repulsive Ones'. A more generic and neutral term, I suppose, would be simply the 'Sirians'. If we ever come into contact with them again, they will probably be called the 'Sirians' officially, and their civilization will be the 'Sirian civilization'. Their art will fall under the heading of 'Sirian culture' and their technology will be 'Sirian technology'. But what about their religion? There's a delicate point. It will be called the 'Sirian religion' and we will try to pretend it has nothing to do with us. But inevitably we will have to take into account that, whereas 'cultures' and 'technologies' can be localized, the greater problems of the nature of life itself and of an individual's relation to the universe – existential problems – are not localizable. There will in fact be no such ultimate thing as 'Sirian religion' except in the ethnographic sense. To speak of a 'Sirian' God will get us into deep waters. What do we mean when we speak of a 'Jewish' God or a 'Christian' God? There is no doubt that it is at the level of our deepest concerns – our religious and philosophical ones – that contact with an extraterrestrial civilization will make its deepest impact on us. And it is at this friable level of our preconceptions that we are most vulnerable. Here the foundations of our beliefs can crumble with the first shock wave. Here the entire edifice of our civilization can give way. Only by being prepared can we safeguard our own cultural integrity.

It is obvious from the accounts of the different Nommos which are preserved by the Dogon that many elements of both Christianity and earlier Mediterranean mystery-religions appear to be present at the very heart of Dogon religion. A closer examination reveals that the Sacrificed Nommo's body (that is, the body of O Nommo; perhaps the 'O' describing this Nommo is remembered from the name Osiris as its first syllable) was dismembered in a manner reminiscent of Osiris: it was divided into twenty-two parts and each clan (*binu*) in Dogon society corresponds to a particular part of that body. It cannot be emphasized too strongly of the Dogon that in their religion they worship 'the supreme God, Amma [presumably originally Amun/Ammon], the creator of the universe', and although there are many cults, 'all the cults, no matter what their specific nature, address themselves to the god Amma.' The fact that the Dogon religion features a crucified and resurrected Saviour from Sirius simply cannot be ignored. The different 'clans' even partake of his Body.

We should begin to realize that when we eventually come into contact with intelligent beings from other worlds, we shall have to revise our cherished religious ideas in order to accord with a truly cosmic perspective and break out of our parochial point of view. The Dogon have already done this. But it may be that we should take to heart the inspired words of Maurice Arthur Ponsonby Wood, the former Bishop of Norwich, which he spoke on the floor of the House of Lords: 'I believe that Christ has not only a terrestrial significance, but literally a galactic significance. It is good that our minds and eyes should be stretched further out into the regions of outer space because I do not believe that at any point of the universe we get beyond the hand of God.'[79]

Upon reflection over the years, I have thought that perhaps the Dogon are descended from a fundamentalist religious group of ancient Egypt who fled westwards to the Oasis of Siwa (site of the famous Oracle of Ammon, from whom the name of Amma would thus prominently survive amongst them) when compromises were being made by some pharaoh in the essentials of the Egyptian religious tradition (or perhaps on the occasion of an invasion of Egypt by 'heathen' conquerors). In this, the Dogon would have resembled the Jews, who were not prepared to compromise the essentials of their religious tradition, and were forever fleeing from pogroms and persecution rather than surrender their identity and beliefs. Previously I thought of the Dogon, despite their preserving some Egyptian traditions, as descendants of the Minyans. We should remember that the Dogon are monotheistic.

If we wish to preserve the integrity of the human race in the face of cosmic wisdom, with its overwhelming superiority to our own because of its longer duration and superior knowledge and technology – and presumably its insights – we must give some thought to how the human race can survive the blows to its pride and the challenge to its parochial religious convictions. We live at a time when religious fanaticism and religious fundamentalism of all the different religions seem to be alarmingly on the increase. People driven to extremes are becoming more violent, with intolerance reaching such fanatical levels that the extremist Taleban Government's ban on music in Afghanistan has resulted in canaries being strangled because they dare to sing. Such insanity is widely tolerated and sometimes even applauded. What are those of us who do not share such ridiculous views going to do about it? The fanatics of all religions have turned murderous, they bomb the rest of us and terrorize innocent people, blow up children, mutilate women without a qualm. For a religious fanatic, everything can be justified; non-believers are fit only for extermination. It has always been a trait of human nature to brand strangers who do not share one's opinions as *untermenschen* – the notorious Nazi word for sub-humans. Why any self-respecting extraterrestrial would want to come here I cannot imagine. But suppose they do . . . won't it be embarrassing, like having visitors enter your house and finding – as I once did at the home of a well-known writer – milk bottles with green mould growing out of them on the milk that had been left unfinished weeks before?

To religious fundamentalists I would quote the enlightened words of Archbishop Desmond Tutu of South Africa: 'It is part of the human condition to have doubt. Without it we cannot progress. It is the basis of Christianity. Even Christ on the cross had terrible doubts.' Fundamentalists are people who try to cheat by espousing a phoney certainty. We should have the courage to have doubt, and not to run away from it.

I wrote a Foreword to the 1977 paperback edition of this book from which the following remarks are worth repeating:

What will happen when a signal really is confirmed [from another world], whether it be from Sirius or from anywhere else in space for that matter? I feel certain that the day will come when all large radio telescopes will have to be surrounded by armed guards. No one seems to have realized yet that protection will have to be given to them when they become the only points of contact between ourselves and extraterrestrial civilizations. This need will become less acute when we have radio telescopes in space or on the Moon.

Passions are certainly going to be aroused. These are largely latent at the moment because our acceptance of the existence of extraterrestrial life is still only at the intellectual level. . . . Major developments are coming which will bring realizations to us which will be with us as long as we endure. Our future as a species is essentially at issue. What are we going to be? Demoralized wretches, dragging our inferiority complexes along behind us like great sacks of potatoes? Or are we going to summon up our courage and pride? Will we slink along in the galaxy, like weasels? Or are we going to roar? Roar out that we are men, that we may be very bizarre men, but that's what we are, and we like it? These alternatives lie before us as we consider how we are going to treat the news that a signal has been received and confirmed from an extraterrestrial civilization.

Once we have received such a signal, there will be no going back. Growing up, leaving childhood behind, are processes which cannot be reversed. At the moment, we are perilously close to losing our cosmic virginity. We are about to step forth from Eden. We have lived in Paradise and not known it. Life has been an idyll, but we have not realized it as such. Our descendants will look back to our day with awe and incomprehension as the time when we still snuggled in our great World Cocoon, wrapped in our dream.

'A sleeper is convinced he is awake. But then he really does awaken...'

* * * * *

As regards what I said earlier in this chapter about the Sirians and their world, we must not dismiss such speculations as idle, thinking that we will wait and see what turns up in a spaceship some day. If we are going to be coming into direct contact with amphibious extraterrestrials, we should try to get some thoughts together on their physical nature and requirements at the very least – if only to make them welcome. It is quite true, as Carl Sagan says: '... stories like the Oannes legend ... deserve much more critical studies than have been performed heretofore.'[80] The critical studies should be institutionalized by the governments of the major powers, and made official programmes. The resources of the governments which pour into programmes to prevent their countries being overrun by military invasions, chemical warfare, nuclear blasts, should also pour into programmes to prevent our planet as a whole being overrun by a sudden extraterrestrial contact which gives little warning. No matter how much care may be taken by any superior extraterrestrial civilization in dealing with us, it is really up to us to be ready for any contact. I would even venture that we may be under observation or surveillance at this very moment, with an extraterrestrial civilization whose home base is the Sirius system monitoring our development to see when we will *ready ourselves* for their contacting us. In other words, we may very possibly be allowed to control the forthcoming contact ourselves.

One wonders what any possible amphibious extraterrestrials living at Sirius would think roughly ten years later (speed of radio transmission at speed of light – across ten light years means a ten-year lag) upon receiving news from some automatic monitoring device which picked up a radio or television programme at Earth mentioning a book just published about amphibious extraterrestrials living at Sirius. Would they think that was their cue? If what I propose in this book really is true, then am I pulling a cosmic trigger?

* * * * *

In considering the material set forth in this book, I hope that serious scholars will bear in mind that the existence of amphibious beings with high intelligence and advanced civilization is not a previously unheard of idea. As far back as 1966, in their book *Intelligence in the Universe*, Roger MacGowan and Frederick Ordway wrote:[81]

Little can be said specifically about universal physical characteristics . . . life, especially the more intelligent forms, tends to be physically small, discrete, and highly mobile. . . . Humans, being land animals, tend to think in terms of land animals when considering intelligence, but we know that the sea contains a great variety of life. Moreover, all evidence points to the conclusion that the primordial seas were probably the site of the origin of life. Oceans provide an excellent environment for animal life and the competition between many species should encourage rapid evolution.

A liquid environment provides more buoyancy and support for animal bodies than does an atmospheric gas. For this reason the marine environment may be expected to develop many species that are larger than most land animal species. Knowing that larger bodies can support larger brains one might expect to find superior intelligence among the larger marine animals.

Considering this larger potential size, the great variety of life, the good stable environment of the oceans, and the competition among species, one is at first tempted to assume that the majority of intelligent extrasolar life would be marine. . . . Fins, ideal for ocean locomotion, are not well suited to developing tools (and thereby brains). However, a few ocean species have developed other appendages more suited to tool manipulation. The octopus is a very well known ocean creature which could conceivably develop tool manipulation capability with further evolution. Some other ocean floor creatures could develop the equivalent of human arms and hands. . . . The patently high intelligence of certain whales and dolphins raises the question as to whether tool manipulating appendages are really vital to the development of superior intelligence. And it makes it difficult to say whether some intelligent extrasolar life may be marine rather than land dwelling. . . . We conclude that the majority of intelligent biological species will not differ greatly in gross morphological characteristics when compared to humans. They can be expected to range from less than half the size of a human to several times larger, and they should be expected to have, in most case, two legs and two arms with hands and fingers. In a few cases centaur-like animals having four legs and two arms with hands and fingers, or elephant-like animals having four legs and one arm or a trunk might be possible. Another possibility is some form of marine life having fins and two short arms with large hands and webbed fingers.

In closing, I wish to make a final point of considerable importance. Let us assume that what I have proposed in this book really is true. Let us grant all the premises. Say that there really is an advanced civilization based at the Sirius system. No doubt we are under routine monitoring. No doubt they know by now roughly where we stand on the ladder of evolution. They have picked up our radio signals. They know we have been to the moon. Let us assume they wish us well. Let us assume even that they contact us someday when they think we are ready for it – or after we have discovered them by finding evidences of their existence.

Let us assume all this. Well, if that day comes – or if it doesn't and if some other day comes, some other civilization some day is known to us at some other star – there is one thing we must not forget. We must remember that no matter how grand and glorious *they* may be, they are still mortal beings in a universe which to them is still mysterious. They cannot and never will know all the answers. We may very well have a handful of answers that they have not. We may have some quirky skills which they cannot attain. We may have some peculiar native ingenuity which they lack, even if this is not obvious for centuries. There may be something about us that is so valuable that we are not just worthless primitives beside them. One of my pet theories is that Earth has one unique contribution to make to the galaxy: its classical music! Let us never accept a view of ourselves as recipients of cosmic charity. We are men, and for all our faults, we have a few things about us which are worth some attention. We have had some remarkable characters in our history and we will have more. Whatever one's views of what lies beyond death – extinction, reincarnation, heaven and hell – the genetic stream goes on. There will be more men, and there will be great ones. We can rise to challenges. We have demonstrated courage throughout our history. Any superior civilizations may have even more superior civilizations behind them of whom they are curious. Let us not forget the principles of hierarchy, let us never blind ourselves to the possibility of a door behind the door behind the door. And if we ever find ourselves oppressed, let us be certain that there are others – somewhere – who would free us. The universe is finite but unbounded. There are between ten and a hundred million intelligent civilizations in our galaxy alone, in all likelihood. And there is always one more to contact than the one we have already contacted.

Notes

1. The reader may wonder if the name of the Dogon tribe is in any way connected with the names 'Dagon' and 'Odacon'. This is pure speculation but not unlikely in my opinion.
2. See Appendix III, for reference.
3. With I. S. Shklovskii. Dell, New York, 1966. See Chapter 33.
4. For instance, by Kenneth Demarest in *Consciousness and Reality*, p. 351.
5. See end of Appendix III and the Bibliography. Thomas Stanley in his *The History of the Chaldaick Philosophy*, London, 1662, p. 12, notes some additional interesting information about the family of Berossus by telling us: 'A daughter of this Berossus is mention'd by Justin Martyr, a Babylonian Sibyl, who prophesied at Cumae . . .' On p. 10 Stanley describes Berossus as the man 'who first introduced Chaldaick learning into Greece'.
6. 'Isis and Osiris', Loeb edition, p. 149.
7. Hesiod, *The Theogony*, 233; translated by Hugh G. Evelyn-White, Loeb Classical Library No. 57, Harvard University Press, 1982 (originally printed 1914), p. 97.
8. Diodorus Siculus, *The Library of History*, Book I, 28. 6; translation by C. H. Oldfather, Loeb Classical Library No. 279, Harvard University Press, 1968, p. 93 and note 5.
9. See Apollodorus, III, 14, 1, and Hyginus, 164. See footnotes 16 and 17 in entry for Erechtheus in the Daremberg-Saglio mythological lexicon.
10. Diodorus Siculus, op. cit., Book I, 29; pp. 93–4.
11. Hesiod, op cit., p. 263 (Fragment 13 of the lost work *The Greek Eoiae*, preserved by the scholiast on Apollonius Rhodius).
12. Plutarch, 'Isis and Osiris' (368 E), translated by Frank Cole Babbitt, in Vol. V of *Plutarch's Moralia*, Loeb Classical Library, Harvard University Press, 1962, p. 107.
13. See entry for Triton in Daremberg-Saglio, op. cit., footnote 10 referring to Escher.
14. Monier-Williams, Sir Monier, *A Sanskrit-English Dictionary*, new edition, Oxford, 1899, p. 461, column c.
15. Ibid.
16. Temple, Robert K. G., *He Who Saw Everything: A Verse Translation of the Epic of Gilgamesh*, Rider, London, 1991, pp. 93–5 (Notes to Tablet IX).
17. Hesiod, op. cit., 930; p. 149.
18. Daremberg-Saglio, op. cit., entry for Triton. The translation from the French is by Olivia Temple.
19. Ibid.
20. Ibid., entry for Typhon. Translation by Olivia Temple.
21. Hesiod, op. cit., 205–326; pp. 101–3.
22. Plutarch, op. cit., 373c (see also 356a); p. 133 (see also p. 35): Plutarch calls the Elder Horus 'Arueris' and says he was the Greek Apollo, conceived by Isis and Osiris when they were still in the womb together!
23. James Legge, *The Yi King*, Oxford, 1882, p. 11.
24. This is from the beginning of the second chapter of Part Two of the Great Appendix. The translation is essentially that of Joseph Needham in *Science and Civilisation in China*, Vol. II, Cambridge, 1956, p. 326. In quoting from Needham I take account of the now more common Pinyin transliterations.
25. Legge, op cit., p. 14.
26. Joseph Needham, *Science and Civilisation in China*, Vol. III, Cambridge, 1959, p. 22 (spelling of Fuxi adapted to Pinyin).
27. Needham, op cit., III, p. 213.
28. Ibid., p. 212.
29. Allen, Herbert J., trans. and commentator, *Ssuma Ch'ien's Historical Records*, in *Journal of the Royal Asiatic Society*, London, April, 1894–July, 1895, pp. 269–74. In my quotations I have modernized the spelling to Pinyin.
30. Derk Bodde, 'Myths of Ancient China', in Samuel Noah Kramer, ed., *Mythologies of the Ancient World*, Anchor Books, New York, 1961, p. 388.
31. Ibid., p. 398.

32. Ibid., pp. 399–400.
33. Verne Dyson, *Forgotten Tales of Ancient China*, Shanghai, 1927, p. 286.
34. Hopkins, L. C., 'Dragon and Alligator: being notes on some Ancient Inscribed Bone Carvings', in *Journal of the Royal Asiatic Society*, July, 1913, pp. 545–52 and Plates I–III.
35. Hopkins, L. C., 'The Dragon Terrestrial and the Dragon Celestial. Part II: The Dragon Celestial', in *Journal of the Royal Asiatic Society*, January, 1932, pp. 91–7.
36. Chan Ping-leung, 'A Study of the Flood Myth of the Yao People: A Comparative Approach', in Chan Ping-Leung, et al., eds., *Essays in Commemoration of the Golden Jubilee of the Fung Ping Shan Library (1932–1982)*, Hong Kong, 1982, p. 156.
37. J. J. M. de Groot, *The Religious System of China*, Taipei reprint, 1976, Vol. V, pp. 529–30.
38. Needham, op. cit., I, p. 163.
39. G. Willoughby-Meade, *Chinese Ghouls and Goblins*, London, 1928, p. 143.
40. *Le Renard pâle*, p. 462.
41. Ibid., p. 458.
42. Ibid., p. 460.
43. Ibid., p. 440.
44. Ibid., p. 441.
45. Ibid., p. 441.
46. Ibid., p. 440.
47. Ibid., p. 440.
48. Ibid., p. 440.
49. Ibid., pp. 309–10.
50. Ibid., pp. 309–10.
51. Ibid., pp. 156–60.
52. Ibid., pp. 156–60.
53. Ibid., pp. 156–60.
54. Ibid., pp. 156–60.
55. Ibid., pp. 157–60.
56. Ibid., pp. 157–60.
57. Ibid., p. 287.
58. Ibid., p. 287.
59. Ibid., p. 444.
60. Ibid., pp. 444–5.
61. Ibid., pp. 444–5.
62. Ibid., pp. 444–5.
63. Ibid., pp. 444–5.
64. Ibid., p. 506.
65. Ibid., p. 439.
66. Ibid., p. 438.
67. Ibid., pp. 437–9.
68. Ibid., p.436.
69. Ibid., pp. 436–9.
70. Ibid., p.474.
71. *The Marsh Arabs*, by Wilfred Thesiger, Penguin Books, London, 1967; and originally Longmans Green, London, 1964.
72. Temple, *He Who Saw Everything*, op. cit., pp. 119–20.
73. *Le Renard pâle*, p. 370.
74. I may be entirely wrong in this supposition, according to a report on the bottlenosed dolphin in *Science*, Vol. 189, no. 4203, 22 August 1975, pp. 650–2. There, four joint authors from the University of Hawaii show that this dolphin has a special double-slit pupil which enables it to see very well at long distances in air. The conclusion is that 'daylight visual resolution acuity of the bottlenosed dolphin, *Tursiops truncatus* is approximately equally good in air and water'.

75. Tighe, Chris, 'Scientists Tune into Teeth of Dolphins', *Daily Telegraph*, London, 28 November 1989.

76. See for instance ' "Mermaid" Beast Faces Extinction in Dead Sea of Oil' in the *Daily Telegraph*, London, 28 January 1991, p. 3.

77. Reuters report, 'Legend Lives on as Surveys Find Dugong Is Flourishing', in the *Daily Telegraph*, London, 3 July 1990.

78. 'Science Report; Zoology: The Age of a Dugong', in *The Times*, London, 1 April 1976; source: *Biological Conservation*, 9, 21, 25 (1975). Despite the date, this was not an April Fool story.

79. These remarks have been inserted for the new edition (1997). I reported the remarks of the Bishop of Norwich – which took place in a debate to which I listened personally – in the magazine *Second Look* which I once co-edited: Temple, Robert K. G., 'House of Lords Debate UFOs', *Second Look*, Washington, DC, Vol. I, No. 6, April 1979, pp. 17–28; for the Bishop, see p. 21. The next summer (1980) I attended a Garden Party at Buckingham Palace and saw the Bishop of Norwich, so went up to him and chatted about this matter. He repeated his sentiments with great fervour. I believe he retired as Bishop of Norwich sometime in the 1980s.

80. Sagan and Shklovskii, op. cit., p. 461. (It is not true, as he says on p. 460, the previous page, that 'the idea of planets circling suns and stars is an idea which essentially originated with Copernicus', as anyone reading Appendix II will see.)

81. MacGowan, Roger, and Ordway, Frederick, *Intelligence in the Universe*, Prentice-Hall Inc., New Jersey, U.S.A., 1966, pp. 242–4.

Appendix I

A Sudanese Sirius System

by

M. Griaule and G. Dieterlen

Note: The following article is translated and published in its entirety. It is written for professional anthropologists and ethnographers, and is presented here for the reader who is sufficiently interested in the subject to wish to pursue the source material. It is, therefore, supplementary information, and is not essential for the reader who merely wishes to follow the argument.

FOREWORD

The indigenous knowledge about the Sirius System which is set forth in this chapter has been gathered from four Sudanese peoples: the Dogon in Bandiagara, the Bambara and the Bozo in Segou[1] and the Minianka in Koutiala.

The main investigation was carried out among the Dogon between 1946 and 1950, where the four major informants were:

Innekouzou Dolo, a woman aged between sixty-five and seventy, *ammayana* 'priestess of Amma', and soothsayer, living in the Dozyou-Orey quarter of Ogol-du-Bas (Lower Ogol), Sanga-du-Haut (Upper Sanga). Tribe: Arou. Language: Sanga.

Ongnonlou Dolo, between sixty and sixty-five years old, patriarch of the village of Go, recently established by a group of Arou in the south-west of Lower Ogol. Language: Sanga.

Yébéné, fifty years old, priest of the Binou Yébéné of Upper Ogol, living in Bara (Upper Sanga). Tribe: Dyon. Language: Sanga.

Manda, forty-five years old, priest of the Binou Manda, living in Orosongo in Wazouba. Tribe: Dyon. Language: Wazouba.

The system as a whole was expounded by Ongnonlou, its various details by the other informants. Although he was not responsible for drawing up the Sigui calendar, Ongnonlou was acquainted with the principles behind it and, during the periods when the investigators were there, was able to obtain further information from the Arou at Yougo Dogorou on the one hand and, on the other, from the permanent steward of the supreme chieftain of the Arou at Arou-by-Ibi.[2] Ongnonlou is in fact patriarch of the family from which the next holder of the title will be designated when the next holiday comes around.

Ongnonlou's learning, within an extremely secret body of knowledge, thus represents an initial acquaintance or, to use a Bambara expression, a 'slight acquaintance', and this point should be kept in mind. Just as, for the layman, the star Sirius is the brightest star in the sky, attracts his gaze, and plays the major role in the computation of the Sigui, so the rules of the Sirius system as revealed to the initiated in the first instance are at once simplified in some parts and complicated in others, so as to divert the attention from calculations which are more secret by far.

It must therefore be understood, once and for all, that the system described here represents one phase of the revelations permitted to initiates who are top-ranking but not specifically responsible for the calculations to do with this part of the sky.

For our part, the documents gathered together have not given rise to any original hypothesis or research. They have been simply pieced together in such a way that the accounts of the four principal informants are merged into one and the same statement. The problem of knowing how, with no instruments at their disposal, men could know the movements and certain characteristics of virtually invisible stars has not been settled, nor even posed. It has seemed more to the point, under these special circumstances, to present the documents in the raw.

THE CALCULATION OF THE TIME OF THE SIGUI

Every sixty years[3] the Dogon hold a ceremony called the Sigui (ceremony). Its purpose is the renovation of the world, and it has been described at length by them in 1931.[4] Since the beginning of this investigation, we were faced with the question of determining the method used to calculate the period separating two Sigui ceremonies. The common notion, which dates back to the myth of creation, is that a fault in the Yougo rock, situated at the centre of the village of Yougo Dogorou,[5] lights up with a red glow in the year preceding the ceremony. This fault contains various altars, in particular busts of Andoumboulou (the name given to the people of small stature who formerly lived in the rocks), and a rock painting called *amma bara*, 'god helps', to which we shall refer later. Furthermore, and before this red glow appears, a spot situated outside the village becomes covered with elongated gourds of a type which no one would have sown.

When these signs are observed, an apparently simple procedure of calculation is carried out, solely by the people of Yougo Dogorou who belong to the Arou tribe:[6] the council of elders assesses the interval by means of thirty two-yearly drinking-bouts when beer made from millet is drunk; and the eldest elder marks up each bout with a cowrie shell.

These bouts are held about one month before the first rains, sometimes in May or June, in a tent or shelter pitched to the north of the village centre.[7] But this rule is only theoretical: between the last Sigui, celebrated at the beginning of the century, and 1931[8] there has been only one bout, halfway through the period; but the two-yearly cowries were set down and gathered into a pile representing the first thirty years. From 1931 onwards, the drinking bouts took place every two years. When the second pile consisting of fifteen cowries has been collected, the second Sigui of the twentieth century will be celebrated.[9]

According to Manda, the priest, the calculation of the Sigui is recorded above the door of the sanctuary of Binou by two figures made of millet pulp representing the god Amma and his son, Nommo, Instructor of the new world.[10] The first consists of a vertical oval – the egg of the world – and its major axis, Amma in the original darkness. In the right-hand half, each year is marked with a dot, starting from the bottom. When the seventh year comes round, a kind of trident is drawn on the outside, as an extension to the line of dots. The same thing is done on the left-hand side, in the order top-to-bottom. Fourteen years are counted in this way: the seven twin years during which the world was created, and to which a unit, symbolizing the whole, is added.[11] Diagrammatically speaking, the figure shows the god's last gesture, raising one hand and lowering the other, thereby showing that sky and earth are made.

This drawing is repeated four times, making it possible to reckon a period of sixty years; it is accompanied by the figure of the Instructor,[12] composed of two vertical legs supporting a head atop a long neck. During the first thirty years which are recorded by two ovals, the figure features only the right leg. During the second thirty-year period, the left leg is made a little longer each year in such a way that when the Sigui actually occurs it is the same length as the right leg. It is by allusion to this figure that people talk about the Sigui 'getting to its feet' during this latter period.

THE CALCULATION OF THE SIGUI CEREMONIES

When it is time for the Sigui, the elders gathered in the *tâṇa tõṇē* shelter at Yougo draw a symbol on the rock with red ochre (Figure i), which represents a *kanaga* mask;[13] this, in turn, represents the god Amma; a hole is made in the ground below it symbolizing the Sigui, and thus Amma in the egg of the world. In effect these two signs should be 'read' in the opposite order: Amma, in the shadow of the egg (the hole) reveals himself to men (the red design) in his creative posture (the mask depicts the god's final gesture, showing the universe.)[14]

*Figure i.** The *Kanaga* sign, connoting the sixty-year ceremonies, at Yougo Dogorou (indigenous painting)

The hole is also interpreted as the hole which must be dug to put seeds in. From this viewpoint the holes are arranged in series of three, connoting three Siguis, placed respectively beneath the sign of three seeds, after which they are named. Thus the Sigui at the beginning of this century was called *emme sigi*, the 'sorghum Sigui'; the next one will be called *yu sigi*, the 'millet Sigui'; and the one after *nu sigi*, the 'haricot Sigui'.

In theory, then, it would seem possible to record the Siguis using this simple method. In practice, the holes become obliterated and the painting, more often than not, is touched up instead of being reproduced and thus forming part of a countable series. But there is another figure painted on the façade of the sanctuaries which reveals rather more specific data; it is called *sigi lugu*, 'calculation of the Sigui', and consists of a line of vertical chevrons, the notches of which are painted alternately black, red, and white; each colour corresponds to a seed, the first to millet, the second to the haricot and the third to sorghum (figure ii). This line can be read in two ways: Either by using just one counting system (for example the left-hand one), whereby each notch is the equivalent of twenty years; here, the notch upon which a Sigui actually falls is carried over to the following series: or, by taking the whole figure and counting twenty years for each notch, regardless of its positioning (the right column in figure ii); here, the notch upon which a Sigui falls is recounted.

More consistent evidence of the celebration of the Sigui is provided by the large wooden mask, whose carving is one of the major concrete purposes of the ceremony. This mask – usually of considerable size[15] – is seldom used, and is kept in some shelter or hideaway in the rocks, along with those which have been carved at previous ceremonies. The care with which these masks are treated – for in some ways they are the village archives – means that it is not uncommon to come across series of three or four of them, the oldest of which date back, respectively, to 1780 and

---

* As this is a direct translation of the entire article, I have kept the authors' numbering for their diagrams. My numerical sequence of figures recommences in Appendix IV.

1720,[16] give or take a year or two. In exceptional cases, when the shelter has been well selected and under constant surveillance, the series may be longer still; thus at Ibi, in 1931, nine poles were counted, and these must have succeeded three more which had been reduced to a few fragments and piles of dust and were still visible; as were the special places earmarked for them at the back of the shelter, all perfectly protected from the damp, vermin and animals. The oldest in the series of nine, which showed a continuous progression of ageing in the course of time,[17] thus date from the beginning of the fifteenth century; and if the three others are taken into account, the remnants of the earliest would date back to the first half of the thirteenth century.[18]

It is not easy to come across material evidence dating back further than the traces of these poles at Ibi. But there is another object, existing in a single edition, which is fashioned during these Sigui ceremonies and which might also be a significant milestone in the calculation process. With the festival in mind, each regional Hogon, as well as the supreme Hogon of Arou, has a fermentation stand woven out of baobab fibres; this stand is used during the preparation of the first ritual beer. This beer is distributed in small quantities to each family; it is then added to everybody's cup, and thus ensures the homogeneousness of the beer drunk by the community.

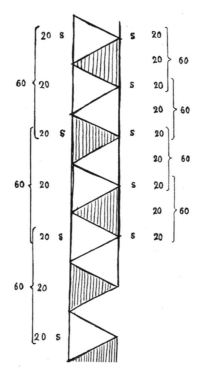

Figure ii. The calculation of the Sigui

In addition to this, all the other fermentation stands are associated, by contact, with the principal one, which is exceptionally large: the lid measures 40 cm. (16 in.) in diameter, and the four 'pompoms' are the size of the normal object. As a result, it can only enter the large jars.

These objects are kept in the Hogon's house where they are hung from the main beam, and thus form a permanent sequence. Ongnonlou saw six or seven of them in the official residence of the Hogon of Sanga; the latter, one of the oldest men in Dogon country, has it that his great-great-grandfather had seen eight others which preceded the oldest in the present series.[19] Assuming a total of fourteen objects for the Sanga chieftainry, the first – which almost certainly does not denote the first ceremony held in this region – would have been woven in the twelfth century, if one reckons on the period separating two Siguis being sixty years.

Again, Ongnonlou counted a series of eight in the house of the supreme Hogon of the Arou, at Arou-by-Ibi. But he adds that the number 'should' be twenty-four, although he cannot explain if there is an ideal series which a complete sequence would aim for, or which, conversely, would correspond to reality if the fibres had not turned to dust.[20]

The methods described above for both keeping track of the ceremonies and for calculating the intervals between Siguis are simple and tend to be mnemotechnic. For the initiate they simply act as understudies for other more complex practices and knowledge to do with the Sirius system. The Dogon names for this star – *sigi tolo*, star of the Sigui;[21] or *yasigi tolo*, star of Yasigui[22] – sufficiently indicate its relation with the ceremony of the renovation of the world which takes place every sixty years.

Sirius, however, is not the basis of the system: it is one of the foci of the orbit of a tiny star called Digitaria, *po tolo*,[23] or star of the Yourougou,[24] *yurugu tolo*, which plays a crucial role, and which, unaided as it were, hogs the attention of male initiates.

This system is so important that, unlike the systems of other parts of the sky, it has not been assigned to any particular group. In effect the Ono and Dommo tribes govern the stars, the former including Venus rising among its attributes, the latter Orion's belt. The sun should be assigned to the most powerful tribe, the Arou; but so as not to be guilty of excess, the Arou handed the sun over to the Dyon, who are less noble, and hung on to the moon. As far as the star Digitaria and the system to which it belongs are concerned, these are common to all men.

THE ORBIT OF DIGITARIA

The orbit described by Digitaria around Sirius is perpendicular to the horizon, and this position is alluded to in one of the most common ceremonies in which masks play a part:

322

> *laba ozu pǫ*
> *ozugo pǫ ya*
> (the path of the mask (is) straight (vertical)
> this path runs straight)

But if one takes the pun into account – familiar to the initiated – between *pǫ:*[25] 'straight' and *pō:* Digitaria, the translation becomes:

> the path of the mask (is the star) Digitaria
> the path runs (like) Digitaria.

A figure made out of millet pulp (fig. iii) in the room with the daïs in the house of the Hogon of Arou gives an idea of this trajectory, which is drawn horizontally: the oval (lengthwise diameter about 100 cm. = 40 in.) contains to the left a small circle, Sirius (S), above which another circle (DP) with its centre shows Digitaria in its closest position. At the other end of the oval a small cluster of dots (DL) represent the star when it is farthest from Sirius. When Digitaria is close to Sirius, the latter becomes brighter; when it is at its most distant from Sirius, Digitaria gives off a twinkling effect, suggesting several stars to the observer.[26]

This trajectory symbolizes excision and circumcision, an operation which is represented by the closest and furthest passage of Digitaria to Sirius. The left part of the oval is the foreskin (or clitoris), the right part is the knife (fig. iv).

This symbolism is also expressed by a figure used for other performances[27] (fig. v). A horizontal figure rests on a vertical axis which connects two circles: S (Sirius) and D (Digitaria); the centre of the figure is a circle T, which represents the trajectory of D. The line E is the penis, the hook B′

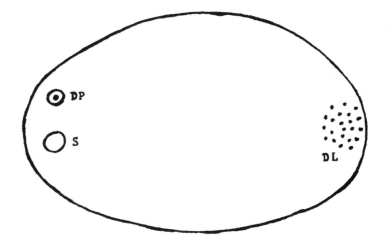

Figure iii. The trajectory of the star Digitaria around Sirius

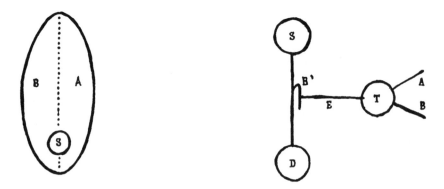

Figure iv. The symbolism of the trajectory of Digitaria. S: Sirius, A: knife, B: foreskin.
Figure v. The symbolism of Digitaria. S: Sirius, D: Digitaria, T: trajectory of Digitaria, A: knife,
E: penis, B and B': foreskin

the foreskin. Two horns hinge on the circle and reproduce once again the two parts of the trajectory (cf. fig. iv): A, the knife; B, the foreskin. Thus the Sirius system is associated with the practices of renovating people, and, consequently – in accordance with the Dogon mentality – with the ceremonies which celebrate the renovation of the world.

The period of the orbit is counted double, that is, one hundred years,[28] because the Siguis are convened in pairs of 'twins', so as to insist on the basic principle of twin-ness.[29] It is for this reason that the trajectory is called *munu*, from the root *monye* 'to reunite', from which the word *muno* is derived, which is the title given to the dignitary who has celebrated (reunited) two Siguis.

According to Dogon mythology, before the discovery of Digitaria the supreme chief was sacrificed at the end of the seventh year of his reign (the seventh harvest). This was the only computation known about; the year-unit had not then been established. The spiritual and material principles of the victim were conveyed to Digitaria – to regenerate the victim whose existence was known but whose features had not been revealed to man, because the star was invisible.

This was the rule for forty-nine years for the first seven chiefs who thus nourished the star, and enabled it to renovate the world periodically. But, having discovered the star, the eighth chief resolved to avoid the fate of his predecessors: with his son's complicity, he feigned death, lay dormant for a few months and reappeared before the chief who had succeeded him; he announced that he had been to Digitaria, knew its secrets, and that, from then onwards, every Hogon would reign for sixty years – the period which would later separate one Sigui from the next.[30] Restored to office, he raised the level of the sky which, hitherto, had been so close to the earth that it could be touched,[31] and he completely revised the method of calculating time, and the method of reckoning.

Until that time the ceremonies celebrating the renovation of the world had in fact taken place every seventh harvest;[32] the Hogon made his calculations on the basis of five-day periods, a unit which established the week as it still is today, and five harvest cycles. And as he was eighth in line, he counted eight cycles, in other words forty years, and the number forty became the basis for computation: the month had forty days, the year forty weeks (of five days each). But the Hogon lived sixty years, a number which was interpreted as the sum of forty (basis of calculation) and twenty (the twenty fingers and toes, symbolizing the person and thus, in the highest sense of the word, the chief). Thus sixty became the basis for calculations[33] and it was first applied to establish the period of time separating two Siguis. Although the orbit of Digitaria takes approximately fifty years and although it corresponds to the first seven reigns of seven years respectively, it none the less computes the sixty years which separate two ceremonies.[34]

As well as its movement in space, Digitaria also revolves (rotates) upon itself over the period of one year and this revolution is honoured during the celebration of the *bado* rite. On this occasion it ejects from its three spirals the beings and the things which it contains. This day is called *badyu*, 'surly father', because it is marked by a general movement of the world which upsets people and places them in an unsure relationship with themselves and with each other.

THE ORIGINS AND FEATURES OF DIGITARIA

The eighth Hogon instructed his people in the features of the star, and, more generally, of the Sirius system.

Sirius appears red to the eye, Digitaria white. The latter lies at the origin of things. 'God created *Digitaria* before any other star'.[35] It is the 'egg of the world', *aduno tal*, the infinitely tiny and, as it developed, it gave birth to everything that exists, visible or invisible.[36] It is made up of three of the four basic elements: air, fire and water. The element earth is replaced by metal.[37] To start with, it was just a seed of *Digitaria exilis*,[38] *pō*, called euphemistically *kize uzi*, 'the little thing',[39] consisting of a central nucleus which ejected ever larger seeds or shoots in a conical spiral motion (fig. vi). The first seven seeds or shoots are represented graphically by seven lines, increasing in length, within the sac formed in turn by an oval symbolizing the egg of the world.

The entire work of Digitaria is summarized in a drawing whose various parts are carried out in the following order:[40] a vertical line issues from the oval – the first shoot to emerge from the sac; another segment, the second shoot, takes up a crosswise position, and thus supplies the four cardinal points: the stage of the world. The straightness of these two segments symbolizes the continuity of things, their perseverance in one state. Last, a third shoot, taking the place of the first, gives it the form of an oval which is open in its lower section, and surrounds the base of the vertical segment. The curved form, as opposed to the straight, suggests the transformation and progress of things. The personage thus obtained, called the 'life of the world', is the created being, the agent, the microcosm summarizing the universe.

In its capacity as the heavy embryo of a world issued each year, Digitaria is represented in Wazouba either by a dot or by a sac enveloping a concentric circle of ten dots (the eight ancestral Nommos and the initial couple of Nommo). Its continual movement produces beings whose souls emerge at intervals from the dots and are guided towards the star Sorghum[41] which sends them on to Nommo. This movement is copied by the rhombus which disperses the creation of the Yourougou in space. Six figures are arranged around the circle, as if ejected from it (fig. vii):[42]

Figure vi. The origin of the spiral of creation (indigenous drawing actual size)

a two-pronged fork: trees;
a stem with four diagonal lines: small millet;
four dots arranged as a trapezium: cow with its head marked by a
    short line;[43]
four diverging lines starting from the base of a bent stem: domestic
    animals;
four dots and a line: wild animals;
an axis flanked by four dots: plants and their foliage.[44]

The original work is likewise symbolized by a filter-basket made of straw called *nun goro*, 'bean cap'. This utensil consists of a sheath in the form of a continuous helical spiral, the centre of which starts at the bottom.[45] The spiral supports a network of double radii.[46] The spiral and the helix are the initial vortical motion of the world; the radii represent the inner vibration of things.

326

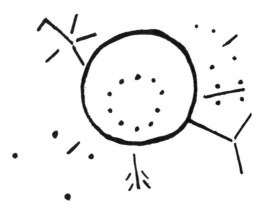

Figure vii. The star Digitaria (indigenous drawing: actual size[50])

Originally, then, Digitaria is a materialized, productive motion. Its first product was an extremely heavy substance which was deposited outside the cage of movement represented by the filter-basket.[47] The mass thus formed brought to mind a mortar twice as big as the ordinary utensil used by women.[48] According to the version told to the men, this mortar has three compartments: the first contains the aquatic beings, the second, terrestrial beings, and the third, the creatures of the air. In reality the star is conceived of as a thick oval forming a backcloth from which issues a spiral with three whorls (the three compartments).

According to the version instructed to the women, the compartments are four in number and contain grain, metal, vegetables and water. Each compartment is in turn made up of twenty compartments; the whole contains the eighty fundamental elements.

The star is the reservoir and the source of everything: 'It is the granary for everything in the world.'[49] The contents of the star-receptacle are ejected by centrifugal force, in the form of infinitesimals comparable to the seeds of *Digitaria exilis** which undergo rapid development: 'The thing which goes (which) emerges outside (the star) becomes as large as it every day.'[51] In other words, what issues from the star increases each day by a volume equal to itself.

Because of this role, the star which is considered to be the smallest thing in the sky is also the heaviest: 'Digitaria is the smallest thing there is. It is the heaviest star.'[52] It consists of a metal called *sagala*,[53] which is a little brighter than iron and so heavy 'that all earthly beings combined cannot lift it'. In effect the star weighs the equivalent of 480 donkey-loads[54] (about 38,000 kg. = 85,000 lb.), the equivalent of all seeds, or of all the iron on earth,[55] although, in theory, it is the size of a stretched ox-skin or a mortar.

* See Figure 1, earlier in this book.

THE POSITION OF DIGITARIA

The orbit of Digitaria is situated at the centre of the world, 'Digitaria is the axis of the whole world,'[56] and without its movement no other star could hold its course. This means that it is the master of ceremonies of the celestial positions; in particular it governs the position of Sirius, the most unruly star; it separates it from the other stars by encompassing it with its trajectory.

OTHER STARS IN THE SIRIUS SYSTEM

But Digitaria is not Sirius's only companion: the star *emme ya*, Sorghum-Female, is larger than it, four times as light (in weight), and travels along a greater trajectory in the same direction and in the same time as it (fifty years). Their respective positions are such that the angle of the radii is at right angles. The positions of this star determine various rites at Yougo Dogorou. Sorghum-Female is the seat of the female souls of all living or future beings.[57] It is euphemism that describes them as being in the waters of family pools: the star throws out two pairs of radii (beams) (a female figure) which, on reaching the surface of the waters, catch the souls.

It is the only star which emits these beams which have the quality of solar rays because it is the 'sun of women', *nyān nay*, 'a little sun', *nay dagi*. In fact it is accompanied by a satellite which is called the 'star of Women', *nyān tolo*, or Goatherd, *enegirin* (literally: goat-guide), a term which is a pun on *emme girin* (literally: sorghum-guide). Nominally then it would be more important as the guide of Sorghum-Female. Furthermore, there is some confusion with the major star, the Goatherd, which is familiar to everyone.

The star of women is represented by a cross,[58] a dynamic sign which calls to mind the movement of the whole Sirius system (fig. viii).

Sorghum-Female is outlined by three points, a male symbol of authority, surrounded by seven dots, or four (female) plus three (male) which are the female soul and the male soul (fig. ix).

Taken as a whole, the Sorghum-Female system is represented by a circle containing a cross (the four cardinal directions), whose centre consists of a round spot (the star itself) and whose arms serve as a receptacle for the male and female souls of all beings. This figure, called the 'Sorghum-Female pattern', *emme ya tōnu*, occupies one of the centres of an ellipse called 'the pattern of men', *anam tōnu*, consisting of a full line called the 'goatherd's course', *enegirin ozu*, flanked by two dotted lines, the outside of which is the path of the male souls, and the inside the path of the female souls (fig. x).

Figure viii. The star of women

Figure ix. The star Sorghum-Female

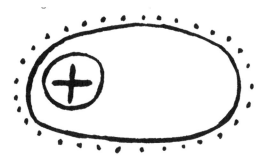

Figure x. The Sorghum-Female system

The Sirius-Digitaria-Sorghum system is represented by a 'pattern of the Sigui', *sigi tōṇu*, consisting of an oval (the world) in which one of the centres is Sirius. The two alternate positions of Digitaria at the time of the Sigui are marked and the positions at the same moment of Sorghum-Female are marked on two concentric circles encompassing Sirius.

The Sirius system as a whole is drawn at Sanga in different ways, in particular at the *bado* ceremony. On the façade of the residence of the great Hogon of Arou and inside the official houses assigned to the Hogons of Dyon, the course of these stars is represented by 'the pattern of the master of the star of the Shoemaker', *dyān tolo bāṇa tōṇu* (fig. xi), composed of a vertical axis supporting, two-thirds of the way up, a bulge, Sirius (S), and broken at its base to form an elongated foot jutting to the left at right-angles, the course of the star of the Shoemaker (C). It is topped by a semi-oval whose arms extend quite low down; the meeting-point (D) with this oval symbolizes Digitaria, whose course is traced by the right arm (F). But this arm is also the star of women whilst the left arm is Sorghum-Female (E). The lower part of the axis (SC), longer than the upper part (SD), reminds one that the Shoemaker (C) is farther than Sirius is from the other stars, and revolves in the opposite direction.

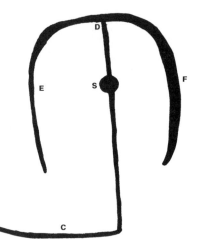

Figure xi. The course of the stars of the Sirius system

Thus it is that during the *bado* ceremony the oldest woman of the family draws, at the entrance to the house, the 'pattern of the world of women', *nyãn aduno tõṇu*,[59] or 'pattern of the top and bottom of the world', *aduno dale doñule tõṇu* (fig. xii).

It consists of an oval, the egg of the world, containing nine signs:

Da. – Digitaria. The open curve on the right indicates the acceptance of all the substances and matter placed in it by the Creator.

Db. – Digitaria in its second position. The open oval below marks the exit of the matter which spreads across the world; A and B also indicate the extreme positions of Digitaria in relation to Sirius.

E. – The star Sorghum-Female, counterpart of Digitaria. As it is the 'sun of women', it is placed at the centre of the egg, like the sun at the centre of the solar system. The oval is framed by two times two small vertical lines symbolizing the rays emitted by the star.

S. – Sirius, 'star of the Sigui' or 'star of Yasigui'. The sign, so placed that it materializes the liaison worked by Sirius between the two stars described above, consists of a kind of X with one right arm – the ant, *key* – dividing a curved arm, the lower part of which is Yasigui, and the other part the piece of the organ which is detached during excision. Although female, the ant is here depicted by a straight rod, as if it were a man. This marks its domination of Yasigui's femininity, for Yasigui is maimed.

R. – The Yourougou. A hook, made up of a circular arc and a straight segment indicates that the first movement of the Yourougou describes a curve which goes around the sky; falling short of the goal, it descended directly, as is shown by the right-hand segment which is also the piece of bared placenta.[60]

In effect, with Digitaria as the egg of the world (see earlier) this latter

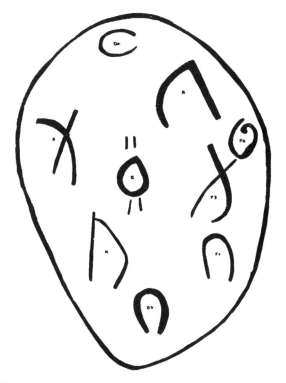

Figure xii. The Sirius system

was split into two twin placentas which were to give birth respectively to a pair of Nommo Instructors. What happened, however, was that a single male being emerged from one of the placentas; in order to find his twin, this being tore off a piece of this placenta, which became earth. This intervention upset the order of creation: he was transformed into an animal, the pale fox, *yuruga*,[61] and communicated his own impurity to the earth, which rendered it dry and barren. But the remedy to this situation was the sacrifice, to the sky, of one of the Nommo Instructors which had issued from the other placenta, and the descent of his twin to earth with life-giving, purifying rain.[62] The destiny of Yourougou is to pursue his twin to the end of time – the twin being his female soul at the same time. On the mythical level, Digitaria is thus considered to be the Yourougou held in space by Nommo, relentlessly revolving around Sirius, or Yasigui in other words, and never capable of reaching it.

N. – The figure of the Nommo consists of a vertical segment, Nommo in person, upon which, and slightly below the upper edge, rests a line broken into three unequal parts; the first is the seat of future female souls; the second the seat of the souls of the dead; and the third the seat of living souls.

Fa. – The star of Women, *nyān tolo*. An embryonic spiral calls to mind that it is the satellite of Sorghum-Female.

Fb. – The 'sign of women', *nyān tōṇu*, consists of a diagonal line, man, cut by a line which ends in a convex curve, woman. This shows the contact between the sexes.[63] The rod is upright with astonishment at the sight of creation, which started with the system of women. Woman is a heavy-bellied profile, ready to give birth.

Fc. – The sex of women is depicted by an oval which is open in the lower part, womb-world, ready for procreation, gaping downwards to spread the seeds.

THE SIRIUS SYSTEM AMONG THE BAMBARA

The Bambara call Sirius 'the star of the foundation', *sigi dolo*, which is the same term used by the Dogon, and like them they call the star Digitaria *fini dolo*.[64] The expression *fā dolo fla*, 'the two stars of knowledge', is generally attributed to it, because 'it represents in the sky the invisible body of Faro', conceived as a pair of twins.[65] This name also implies that the star is the seat of all learning.

The Sirius system is depicted on the chequered blanket called *koso wala*, 'coloured picture', consisting of ten sequences made up of some thirty rectangles coloured alternately indigo and white which symbolize, respectively, darkness and light, earth and sky, and, in Bambara mythology, Pemba and Faro. Scattered throughout there are twenty-three rectangles with different patterns of small stripes placed in the direction of the thread, alternating the indigo, white and red. Twenty of them represent stars or constellations; the other three respectively represent the rainbow, hailstones and rain. The fifth sequence in the centre, in which there is no coloured rectangle, symbolizes the Milky Way. The ninth sequence, at one end, contains five black (not indigo) rectangles which point to the 'fifth creation, in darkness, which will occur with the arrival of the waters to come'.[66]

Sigi dolo is first depicted alone 'in the cold season and in impurity' by the ninth rectangle (third sequence); it is next depicted flanked by *fā dolo fla* (two red lines) in the fifteenth rectangle (eighth sequence).[67]

In Bambara mythology, Sirius represents Mousso Koroni Koundyé, twin of Pemba, maker of the earth, a mythical woman whom he chased through space and was never able to catch. In every respect Mousso Koroni Koundyé is comparable to Yasigui.[68] She inaugurated circumcision and excision and, as a result, Sirius is the star of circumcision, for both Bambara and Dogon alike.

Appendix I

THE SIRIUS SYSTEM AMONG THE BOZO

The system is also known to the Bozo, who call Sirius *sima kayne* (literally: sitting trouser) and its satellite *toñō ñalema* (literally: eye star).

Notes
1. A member of the Bambara living in Bandiagara also confirmed the most important features of the system.
2. Various pieces of information were supplied direct by the people of Yougo-Dogorou in 1931, 1936, 1948, 1949 and 1950.
3. We ourselves accepted this figure in 1931 and it can safely be retained for the time being.
4. Cf. Griaule, *Masques Dogons*, Travaux et Mémoires de l'Institut d'Ethnologie de l'Université de Paris, vol. xxxiii (1938), chapter 1.
5. Ibid., pp.167 ff., where this fault in the rock is described in detail.
6. The Dogon are divided into four tribes, each of which had a different role at one time. The four are the Arou (soothsayers), the Dyon (farmers), the Ono (merchants), and the Dommo (who were confused in this respect with the Ono).
7. The spot is called *tâṇa tōṇo*; cf Griaule, op. cit., p. 171.
8. Or 1933.
9. Probably in 1961 or 1963, if this computation is valid. (The information came from a prominent member of the Yougo aged between fifty-five and sixty.) It is a matter of common knowledge that the next Sigui will not be celebrated for another ten years or so (we were told this in late 1950).
10. These figures are described in M. Griaule and G. Dieterlen, 'Signes graphiques soudanais' *L'Homme*, 3 (Paris: Hermann).
11. The Dogon count a week of five days as six days, just as in French a week of seven days is referred to as 'eight days' and a fortnight as 'fifteen days'.
12. For a discussion of this substitute for God the Creator cf. Griaule, *Dieu d'eau*, Paris, Editions du Chêne, 1948.
13. For a description of the mask cf. *Masques Dogons*, pp.470 ff.
14. This information came from a prominent member of the Yougo Dogorou. According to all the initiates, the *kanaga* mask represents on the one hand the static gesture of the god, and on the other hand the swastika, through the repetition of the same gestures at an angle of 90° to the first. The second figure represents the god whirling round as he comes down to earth to reorganize the world in chaos.
15. The largest known example is ten metres long. It was brought back by the Dakar-Djibouti Mission and given to the Musée de l'Homme in Paris; cf. M. Griaule, *Masques Dogons*, pp. 234 ff.
16. Thus the Yendoumman Damma niche contains three specimens; the Yendoumman Banama contains four; the Yendoumman Da, three; the Barna, four; and the Ennguel-du-Bas, three. Cf. M. Griaule, *Masques Dogons*, pp. 242 ff.
17. Ibid., pp. 245 ff.
18. For another index that enables us to establish the minimum age of some of the villages, cf. Griaule, 'Le Verger des Ogol (Soudan français)', *Journal de la Société des Africainistes*, xvii, pp. 65–79.
19. The Hogon of Sanga, who was enthroned in 1935, was thus the oldest man in the area at that date (i.e. the oldest of the Dyon). If we agree that he was born in about 1855, his great-grandfather, who, he claims, was very old when he himself was a young goatherd, was probably born between 1770 and 1780.
    Each fermenting-receptacle is evidence of the Sigui for which it was woven and is known as such. This means that these objects form a sequence that is considered by the people to be more than purely numerical.
20. The period indicated by a series of this kind would be 1,440 years by the time the next Sigui

came round. It would apparently correspond to the sequence of sixty reigns in which each Hogon appears and which itself covers a period of about 1,500 years. The supreme chiefs of the Arou tribe are in fact chosen when still young, unlike the practice current among the other tribes. The average reign is likely to be twenty-five years.

21. *Sigi dolo* in Bambara.
22. For a discussion of this mythical figure, who corresponds to the Bambaras' Mousso Koroni, see later in this article.
23. T*he põ, Digitaria exilis* is commonly called '*fonio*' in West Africa.
24. For a discussion of this mythical figure see later in text.
25. In the song the vowel becomes slightly nasal.
26. The saying that 'if you look at Digitaria it's as if the world were spinning (*põ tolo yeneñe aduno gõṇode ginwo*) was probably coined to convey this impression.
27. Cf. M. Griaule, 'Signes graphiques des Dogon', in M. Griaule and G. Dieterlen, 'Signes graphiques soudanais', *L'Homme*, 3 (Paris, Hermann).
28. In the system of notation based on the figure 80 this number is called '80 and 20'. The period of fifty years is very close to that of Sirius's companion. Cf. P. Baize, 'Le Compagnon de Sirius', *L'Astronomie* (Sept. 1931), p. 385.
29. For a discussion of this principle cf. Griaule, *Dieu d'eau*, pp.183 ff.
30. After this reform the Hogons' sacrifice was replaced by animal sacrifice.
31. This belief still obtains among the Dogon, and also among many other peoples; cf. Griaule, *Jeux Dogons, Travaux et Mémoires de l'Institut d'Ethnologie* de l'Université de Paris, vol. xxxii.
32. For a discussion of the symbolism attached to the number 7 cf. Griaule, *Dieu d'eau*, p. 60.
33. The figure 60 is the old base of the system of notation still used in the Sudan for a number of ritual calculations. In several Sudanese languages 60 is known as the 'Mandé calculation', because the system is believed to have spread from Mandé. Nowadays the various districts use 80 as a base for their calculations. Cf. G. Dieterlen, *Essai sur la religion Bambara* (Paris: PUF).
34. There is a contradiction here that has not so far been solved. On the one hand the Dogon accept that Digitaria is in orbit for fifty years and this figure governs the way the Sigui is calculated. On the other hand Siguis are held at sixty-year intervals. Nevertheless, it should be noted that the date of the last Sigui, which was celebrated at the very beginning of the twentieth century, was allegedly brought forward. Does this indicate that the date was regularly brought forward for each ceremony? The uninitiated would thus be kept going with the idea that the official period was sixty years and that, for accidental reasons, it happened to be reduced to a half-century.

    The foregoing myth is given here as an indication of the changes or combinations in the system of computation that occur in the 'history' of the black peoples.
35. *põ tolo amma tolo lā woy māṇu.*
36. According to Innekouzou, *põ tolo*, 'Digitaria star', has a hidden etymological derivation from *polo to*, 'profound beginning'.
37. See below.
38. The *Digitaria* seed is made up of four parts, only one of which, the outer casing, has a name, *kobu*. The other three are known as *yolo*.
39. This expression is always being used by Manda, whose extremely punctilious mind thus avoids even mentioning the name of one of the most basic tabus of the totemic priests.
40. For further details cf. Griaule, 'Signes graphiques des Dogons'. See also Griaule, 'L'image du monde au Soudan', *Journal de la Société des Africainistes*, xix, 2, pp. 81–9.
41. Cf. below.
42. They are counted clockwise, starting from the highest figure on the right-hand side.
43. This cow is an avatar of the Nommo.
44. It should be remembered that the Dogon, like the other black peoples, use several different symbols or even several different sequences of images to express a single idea or object. Conversely, a symbol often represents several different things.

45. The shape of this basket is roughly the same as the outline of a mortar.
46. On the system of symbols represented by this basket.
47. It is understood that Digitaria was the same shape as a basket, but was not a basket.
48. The initiates have a different idea of these dimensions.
49. *aduno kize fŭ guyoy.*
50. This drawing is executed in Wazouba inside the sanctuaries during the festival of *agu.*
51. *kize wogonode para gwãy wokuwogo dega bay tutura byede.*
52. *põ tolo kize woy wo gayle be dedemogo wo sige be.*
53. This has the same root as *sagatara*, 'strong, powerful' (native etymology).
54. The number 480 is the product of the base number 80 times the number of tens in the base number 60, which was formerly in use. It is used here to symbolize the largest number of all.
55. Versions of, respectively, Innekouzou, Manda and Ongnonlou.
56. *põ tolo aduno fŭ duduṇ gowoy.*
57. The men have two twin-souls of different sexes. Cf. Griaule, *Dieu d'eau*, pp.183 ff. The same idea is current among the Bambara, cf. Dieterlen, *Essai sur la religion Bambara*, chapter 3.
58. The figures reproduced here are used in Wazouba.
59. This figure was taught to Ongnonlou in August 1950, by the Hogon of Sanga.
60. Yourougou, who was born a single being, is fated to pursue the female soul that is his ideal twin to the end of time. In particular he tried to seize it by snatching away from his mother, the Earth, part of the placenta that emerged after he was born, because he thought it was his twin soul.
61. *Vulpes pallidus.*
62. Cf. Griaule and Dieterlen, 'Le harpe-luth des Dogon', *Journal de la Société des Africainistes*, xx, 2.
63. A man could just as well call it *anam tõṇu*, 'drawing of men'.
64. *Fini*, from which *fonio*, a word used throughout Sudanese Africa, is derived, is the same word as *põ*.
65. The expression may possibly indicate the Sirius and Digitaria grouping, or Digitaria and another companion. For Faro, or Fanro, the Bambara equivalent of the Dogon Nommo, cf. Dieterlen, *Essai sur la religion Bambara*, chapters 1 and 2.
66. Cf. ibid., chapter 1. This refers to a future world that will be heralded by flood-waters.
67. The *koso wata* blanket, which is worn by elderly initiates at the major Bambara institutions (*dyo*), belongs to a series of eight ritual blankets with patterns and colours representing mythology, cosmology and the social structure. They are used at night or worn as clothing, depending on the status, duties and aims of the wearer. Apart from their economic value, they are evidence of the wearer's knowledge. Their ritual use is plain, particularly during marriage ceremonies. The Dogon have similar blankets. The one known as *yanunu* represents a sort of very rough map of the world showing the most important stars.

    For a discussion of the way the Bambara and Dogon set great store by weaving and the various cotton strips, cf. Dieterlen, *Essai*, chapter 5, and Griaule, *Dieu d'eau*.
68. For a discussion of the parallels between Mousso Koroni Koundyé and Yasigui, cf. Dieterlen, *Essai*, chapter 1. For a discussion of Mousso Koroni Koundyé, Pemba and Faro, cf. S. de Ganay, 'Aspect de mythologie et de symbolique bambara', *Journal de psychologie normale et pathologique* (April/June 1949); Dieterlen, *Essai*, chapters 1 and 2.

Appendix II

The Moons of the Planets, the Planets around Stars, and Revolutions
and Rotations of Bodies in Space – Described by the
Neoplatonic Philosopher Proclus

'. . . . In each of the planetary spheres there are invisible stars which revolve together with their spheres . . .' So said Proclus the Platonic successor in AD 438.

The non-specialist reader may never have heard of Proclus, one of the greatest intellects in the history of philosophy, who lived from AD 410 to 485. The English translations of this Greek philosopher's gigantic output are his *Elements of Theology*[1] (which is not relevant to what we are to consider here), his *Commentary on Euclid*,[2] his *Commentary on the First Alcibiades of Plato*,[3] and one partial and one complete translation of his *Commentary on the Parmenides of Plato*.[4]

What the persistent inquirer will likely *not* be told by any compendium of information on the subject is that most of the works of Proclus were translated into English by Thomas Taylor at the turn of the eighteenth and nineteenth centuries in England and are to be found in a handful of libraries (though even the British Museum has a far from complete collection of Taylor's life's work).

Perhaps it would be as well to quote the view of Proclus held by Thomas Taylor. One should bear in mind that Taylor was the first man to translate all of Plato's works into English – a mammoth task indeed, but not as gargantuan as translating most of Proclus! Here, then, is what Taylor says of Proclus:

> To the lovers of the wisdom of the Greeks, any remains of the writings of Proclus will always be invaluable, as he was a man who, for the variety of his powers, the beauty of his diction, the magnificence of his conceptions, and his luminous development of the abstruse dogmas of the ancients, is unrivalled among the disciples of Plato.

There are many classical scholars who like to imply that the 'Golden Age' of Greece was the only significant era in Greek philosophy. Within this period one can conveniently place Socrates, Plato, Aristotle, Euripides, Sophocles, Aeschylus, Demosthenes, and the historians Herodotus, Thucydides, and Xenophon.

These brilliant names tend to blind one into accepting the false notion that Greece at any other period in its history was merely second rate in the intellects it produced. Many scholars are passionately dedicated to deriding any Greek intellects either before or after this 'Golden Age'. Some caustic comments have been made about this by other scholars, and there is no denying the tendency to ignore or belittle – even to suppress and deny – Greeks who preceded or followed the glorious 'Golden Greeks' who are most familiar to us. It certainly is an embarrassing fact, then, for certain classical scholars to have to face, that the Platonic Academy continued to function in Athens for over nine hundred years.

Regarding the Academy, George Sarton says in *A History of Science: Ancient Science through the Golden Age of Greece*:[5]

At the time when [the Emperor] Justinian closed its doors, [the Academy] might have celebrated its 916th anniversary. . . . the Academy changed considerably in the course of centuries; it is only the Old Academy that may be considered as Plato's Academy, and it lasted a century and a half or less. To this one might reply that every institution is bound to change with the vicissitudes of time and that the longer it lives the more it must be expected to change. Bearing these remarks in mind, we may put it this way: the Academy of Athens, the Academy founded by Plato, lasted more than nine centuries.

Those who find chronology difficult to comprehend without analogies might wish to ponder this: the duration of the Platonic Academy (apparently on the same site) in Athens was equivalent to the duration to date on English soil of Westminster Abbey; or, the 916 years of life of the Academy as a philosophical institution was equal to the amount of time which elapsed from the Norman Conquest of England in 1066 to the year 1982. (And even after the dismemberment, the Academy continued 'in exile' in Persia, etc.) We thus see that Plato's Academy existed longer on one spot than England has existed since William the Conqueror.

The Platonic tradition in the broader sense, with its gnostic and heretical overtones and its myriad manifestations in later ages in such bizarre and fascinating figures as Giordano Bruno, Marsilio Ficino, John Dee, and even Sir Philip Sidney and the Earl of Leicester – not to mention the troubadours of Provence, Dante in Italy, the Albigensians in France, the Knights Templar, and an infinite range of 'fringe' causes over two and a half millennia, is an agonizing and impossible problem for the orthodox mind, whatever its creed. For Platonism in the general sense is a creed which denies creed, an anti-institutional tradition known to those who adhere to it as the 'Great Tradition'. It terrifies those weaker mentalities which crave a structured belief-system; they always try to destroy it, but succeed only in destroying individuals and individual 'movements' within the larger tradition.

How can any 'intellectual establishment' conceivably admit that this undercurrent of spirituality has flowed outside the orthodox boundaries of the official religion of Christianity since the third century and the time of Origen? And how confess that Proclus, who lived seven hundred years later than Plato (429–347 BC), had a mind as luminous in his own way as Plato's? What happens to the 'hermetically sealed Greek miracle' then? If Platonism is seen to continue as a persecuted underground movement for two thousand years and more, what conclusions must we draw about the supposed openness of orthodox Western culture? If our commonly accepted pattern of civilization is seen to be based on a lie, based on the denial of the non-orthodox, the implications are so immense that nothing short of a total intellectual upheaval could result. No person with a vested interest, whether a chair at a university or a weekly newspaper, a large corporation or a television station (or a diocesan see) would be completely isolated from the results which would follow. The results need not be destructive in the sense of a political or social revolution, but they would be more fundamental, and hence more far-reaching in the end. It is fear of constructive change (which amounts to fear of the unknown) which is here involved. These indeed are problems. And they go some way to explain why the reader hears nothing of a great many subjects which have a direct relevance to the matter. One of the many such subjects is Proclus. Until recently, no one cared to discuss what Proclus really stood for and what he represents beyond his own specific ideas. Even to raise the subject of a figure such as Proclus is to bring the skeleton from the closet and rattle it with a vengeance.

Proclus does not even rate his own entry in the *Penguin Companion to Literature*, vol. 4, which deals with classical literature. He is mentioned under an entry for Neoplatonism by D. R. Dudley:

> He was a strange combination – possible in that age – of philosopher, logician, mathematician, and mystic. Neo-Platonism gave to the intellectual of the last phase of paganism a metaphysical religion. . . . The figure of the sage gazing upwards in contemplation is often found on late imperial sarcophagi.

Notice the phrase 'possible in that age', implying as it does that no person today would even consider trying to know something about so many subjects in our age of perverse over-specialization. Proclus, we are told, 'was a strange combination'. Dudley tells us nothing of what Proclus wrote, nothing of his ideas, nothing of the immense bulk of his writings, and in his bibliography refers us only to the harmless and difficult *Elements of Theology*. We are left to conclude that Proclus was an extinct species like the dodo, interesting only because he was 'a strange combination possible in that age'. There are very few historians dealing with the fifth century AD. We assume from what Dudley says that only they could be interested in a 'strange combination possible in that age'.

Surely Proclus, of whom we are told nothing of importance, is totally unimportant. Would the *Penguin Companion* mislead its readers? Such a thing is unthinkable.

Professor A. C. Lloyd of the University of Liverpool was given the task of discussing Proclus as part of his contribution to the *Cambridge History of Later Greek and Early Mediaeval Philosophy*,[6] a compendium which did not exist before 1967 and which was reprinted with corrections in 1970. The publication of this large volume of 715 pages marked the attainment of a stage in classical scholarship where many scholars were officially agreeing that they were running out of things to do in the more usual areas and had better begin compiling guidelines for a study of the long-neglected subject of the above-mentioned book. Such lonely figures as Richard Walzer, Philip Merlan, and the late I. P. Sheldon-Williams, long engaged in these arcane pursuits out of pure interest, were summoned to help delineate the bounds within which a new generation of students might have some new fields in which to do their Ph.D. theses and where some original work remains to be done by the professors who have now tidied up the Pre-Socratic field rather well and need new ground for some genuine problem-solving. This has now at last begun to happen.

But to return to Professor Lloyd, who has made an interesting attempt to describe Proclus and some aspects of his thought and writings. It is important for us to know more about Proclus the man.[7] Here is part of Lloyd's account:

Proclus was born at Constantinople in 410 or shortly afterwards. But his parents, who were patricians from Lycia in south-west Asia Minor, sent him to school in their country and then to Alexandria to study literature and rhetoric. Instead of law, which was his father's profession, philosophy attracted him, so he attended lectures on mathematics and Aristotle. The next stage was Athens.

His studies at the Platonic Academy there are then described, and it was this School of which he was to become the Head: 'It is not known when he took over the School, but he remained at its head till he died in 485. He never married and his only defects were a jealous nature and a short temper.'

His short temper seems to have extended to impatience with those who were slow to understand what he was saying or who made irritating difficulties over petty details. For instance, he begins his mammoth work *Commentary on the Timaeus of Plato* with this extraordinarily testy sentence: 'That the design of the Platonic Timaeus embraces the whole of physiology and that it pertains to the theory of the universe, discussing this from the beginning to the end, appears to me to be clearly evident to those who are not entirely illiterate.'

It is now that we begin to consider the connection which Proclus has with the larger subject of our book. We will continue with Professor Lloyd's description of Proclus:

> Proclus moved in important political circles, but like other leading Platonists he was a champion of pagan worship against imperial policy and found himself more than once in trouble. There is no doubt of his personal faith in religious practices. A vegetarian diet, prayers to the sun, the rites of a Chaldaean initiate, even the observance of Egyptian holy days were scrupulously practised. He is said to have got his practical knowledge of theurgy from a daughter of Plutarch,* and according to his own claim he could conjure up luminous phantoms of Hecate. Nor is there any doubt that he put theurgy, as liberation of the soul, above philosophy. But while his philosophy is full of abstract processions and reversions, philosophy was nothing for him if not itself a reversion, a return to the One, though achieving only an incomplete union. Its place can be seen in an almost fantastically elaborated metaphysical system: but although this system would not have been created had there not been a religion to justify, its validity does not depend and was not thought by Proclus to depend on the religion.

The connection with the mysteries of Hecate as well as Proclus's practising Egyptian and Chaldaean mysteries immediately arouses in the alert reader the suspicion that Proclus might just possibly have known something of the Sirius mystery. Could this be the case? In a moment we will consider some amazing opinions of Proclus on the heavenly bodies which no historian of science I have encountered has ever taken into account (probably because no one ever actually reads through that gigantic tome known as the *Commentary on the Timaeus of Plato* which I mentioned a moment ago). But first let us examine any further evidence than this slim fact which might link Proclus with the general milieu of our Sirius tradition. Professor Lloyd provides further interesting remarks:

> Proclus believed that his metaphysics was the true though hidden meaning of Plato and that this like all Greek 'theology' derived from the secret doctrines of Pythagoreans and Orphics. It can be studied in two works, the *Elements of Theology* and the *Theology of Plato*, with help here and there from the commentaries on the *Parmenides, Timaeus, and Alcibiades*.

It must be emphasized that in the form of such commentaries, the Neoplatonists produced much purely original and creative philosophy. It was fashionable until recently to ridicule their commentary format as derivative and inferior; a pathetic attempt to deride what cannot or will

---

* The Platonist, not the author of the *Lives*.

not be appreciated. An example may be seen in the description by Professor Robert Browning of Birkbeck College, University of London, in the *Penguin Companion* volume, of the commentaries of Proclus's later successor Simplicius as 'misconceived and pedestrian textbooks'. The word 'misconceived' is loaded, and immediately lets us know that Professor Browning disagrees with them in principle and therefore derides them. However, in my own reading of Simplicius's *Commentary on Epictetus*, for instance, I was amazed to find a luminous intellect behind the commentary, whose dissertations on free will are so startlingly contemporary that I immediately thought of comparing them with writings of our modern cybernetic age, such as the fascinating books by Norbert Weiner. In Chapter One Simplicius speaks of 'those who pretend that our opinions and desires, and generally speaking, all of our choices and intentions, are necessary and not at our own disposal, but come from exterior causes outside ourselves, not coming from us of our own volition.' He attacks the 'Behaviourists' of his day in clear and forceful terms which are not restricted in relevance to his own times by any means. Some of his reasoning is acute and his insights are profound. In recent years a huge number of Neoplatonic commentaries on Aristotle have been appearing from the British publisher Duckworth – almost forty volumes are planned, under the editorship of Richard Sorabji.

Of the works of Proclus, it is really the *Commentary on the Timaeus of Plato* (which I shall abbreviate from here on as *In Tim.*) which is the source of Proclus's views on the cosmos and of his views of the Platonic succession of an esoteric tradition from the ancient mystery religions. Professor Lloyd, in a footnote to his passage last quoted, does not give this reference on these points, but instead refers to other works by Proclus. In his entire treatment of Proclus, Lloyd gives only slight and cursory reference to the *In Tim.* However, it is to the *In Tim.* which we must now turn. Since page references to the Greek text of Lipsiae would be useless to most readers, I give page references to Taylor's English translation, vols. I and II.

At the end of Book IV of *In Tim.*, Proclus says (II, 307): 'But it is Pythagoric to follow the Orphic genealogies.* For the science concerning the Gods proceeded from the Orphic tradition through Pythagoras, to the Greeks, as Pythagoras himself says in the *Sacred Discourse*.'

The fact that he entertained this view in relation to the mystery religions is shown in his remarks about Pythagoric principles in *In Tim.*, Book V (II, 312): 'But these are Orphic traditions. For what Orpheus delivered mystically through arcane narrations, this Pythagoras learned, being initiated by Aglaophemus in the mystic wisdom which Orpheus derived from his mother Calliope.'

He attaches this view to his discussion in *In Tim.* of celestial phenomena.

* Drawn from Pythagorean and Orphic esoteric traditions.

Not long after the above passage he says: 'For Orpheus calls the moon celestial earth'. And in Book III he says: 'The Pythagoreans say . . . (that) the moon is ethereal earth'.

Taking these views, as he does, and claiming to be a devotee of Hecate specifically (a 'Hymn to Hecate' by Proclus survives in which he calls her 'Guardian of the Gates' – an ancient Egyptian title of Horus – and Mother of the Gods – an ancient title of Isis; see IV, 4, 6, of Grant's *Hellenistic Regions*),[8] Proclus seems to stand in the position as an initiate capable of knowing something of the Sirius mystery. I have found no references, and it would have been considered impious by him to make any direct references to such an esoteric doctrine. But I have found that many theories of his clearly seem to reflect on it and be based on its premise of an invisible star. These theories are so extraordinary that I feel an account of them should be made. And the primary importance of them to us is that in them Proclus speaks with full authority in insisting that certain invisible heavenly bodies definitely exist. These bodies are the moons of the planets and the planets of other stars. Furthermore, Proclus seems to have an incredibly enlightened view of celestial phenomena in many other ways as well.

In Book III of *In Tim.* Proclus says (I, 425) that the Moon is made of

celestial earth. Or why else does the moon, being illuminated, produce a shadow, and why does not the solar light pervade through the whole of it? . . . we shall find that fire and earth subsist also analogously in the heavens; fire indeed, defining the essence of them, but each of the other elements being consubsistent with it.

Shortly afterwards he says:

The elements being conceived in one way as unmingled, but in another as mingled, the first mixture of them produces the heavens, which contain all things according to a fiery characteristic. . . . For all things are in the heaven according to a fiery mode.

We know from other citations above that the theory of the moon being 'celestial earth' is a 'Pythagoric-Orphic' one which Proclus has adopted. The fact that he here extends the observation to the remarks of the general nature of the celestial bodies implies that those ideas come from the same source. The heavens are indeed of a 'fiery mode', for we now know scientifically that stars possess all the normal chemical elements in a fiery mode. Proclus's description of celestial bodies could be perfectly in harmony with our present-day scientific knowledge. It is true, as Proclus says, that the stars may be described with 'fire indeed, defining the essence of them, but each of the other elements being consubsistent with it'. For, though they are ablaze, stars are known to contain all elements.

Proclus makes absolutely clear that when he speaks of 'fire' in the heavens he is speaking figuratively. He says (page 280): 'Hence, the fire which is there (in the heavenly bodies) is light; and it is not proper to disturb the discussion of it, by directing our attention to the gross and dark fire of the sublunary region [the below-the-moon, or earthly region].' And to make it beyond the slightest possibility of misunderstanding, he adds (page 281) that fire in the heavens is 'fire which is not perfectly fire' but, rather, star-fire is more properly 'fire which is in energy'.

These conceptions are quite astounding in the light of modern science. In fact, modern theories of there being in space an interstellar medium which is of such a tenuous nature that it is barely perceivable to us but nevertheless quite extensive (*not* the old-fashioned 'aether'!), find an uncanny forerunner in Proclus's strange statement from Book III of *In Tim.* (I, 425):

> It is also necessary that the middle elements should be in the heavenly bodies, but that different elements should abound in different parts of the celestial regions. And in some places indeed, it is necessary that the fiery nature should widely scatter its splendour, on account of solidity, as in the starry bodies; but in others, that it should be concealed from us, as in the spheres that carry the stars.

No matter what interpretation one may put on these remarks by Proclus, the fact remains that he views the stars as congealed bodies in a celestial medium and that between them lies 'fiery matter' which is invisible to us. As for his references to the spheres, these are hardly the glassy globules familiar to us from more conventional ancient astronomy, as we shall see.

In Book IV of the *In Tim.* (II, 293), Proclus ridicules epicycles* and says they are valuable as 'an excellent contrivance' by which to analyse and comprehend the true simple motions of the stars,

> just as if someone, not being able to measure a spiral motion about a cylinder, but afterwards assuming a right line moved about it, and a point in the right line measuring its motions, should find what the quantity is of the motion about the spiral in a given time. To this therefore, the attention of those is directed, who employ evolvents, epicycles, and eccentrics, through simple motions, from which they discover a various motion.

We thus see that Proclus, despite his late date, is no prisoner of the Ptolemaic theory of the universe. Ptolemy lived three hundred years before him, but Proclus was a hold-out against his epicycles, preferring the views

---

* Complicated circles-around-circles postulated in the standard Ptolemaic astronomy of Antiquity to try and account for the motions of the planets as seen from Earth.

expressed above. In fact, Proclus views the spheres in a way which is extremely surprising, for in Book IV of *In Tim.* (p. 273) he says: 'Thus also the planets are moved with an advancing motion, but not the spheres of the planets'.

This is quite a clear statement that the planets move while their 'spheres' or – dare we say it? – orbits are really the spaces in which this movement takes place. However, we need not be too cautious here. Benjamin Jowett uses the word 'orbit' in his translation of the text of Plato (38–39) on which Proclus is here commenting. There is no reason why we should refrain from doing the same.

We are thus confronted with a clear description by Proclus (less obscure than Plato's own vague account) of the planets moving in orbits which themselves are clearly conceived as trajectory spaces. And this concept is so scientifically accurate and advanced, and so contrary to the then fashionable view that the 'spheres' of the planets moved and carried the planets along with them, that we must appreciate the precocity of Proclus in putting the notion forward so clearly and persistently. Plato's text may be interpreted in the same way, but it is not customary to do so, and it is too vague by far. A typical example of the standard interpretation of the passage in Plato's own *Timaeus* is that given by Professor A. C. Crombie in vol. I of *Augustine to Galileo* (though he does on page 33 describe the *Timaeus* quite starkly as a 'Pythagorean allegory', which is presumably a daring way to put it) on page 49:

> The different spheres in which the seven 'planets', Moon, Sun, Venus, Mercury, Mars, Jupiter, and Saturn, were set, revolved with different uniform velocities such as would represent the observed movements of those bodies.

This is purely an *interpretation* of a vague text. One could just as well say that Plato maintained that the spheres did not move and the planets in them were what moved, as Proclus specifically states (and as he seems to think Plato believed).

Proclus goes out of his way to say (p. 279):

> [Plato] is evidently of opinion, that the planets become through themselves, more remote from, and nearer to the earth, and that their revolutions according to breadth, are made by their own progressions, and not through being carried by other things, such as evolvents or epicycles.

This puts Proclus in a position diametrically opposite Professor Crombie in interpreting the text of Plato. I am afraid that I, for one, must come down on the side of Proclus in such a contest. In any case, Professor Crombie showed himself quick to alter a view if presented with fresh evidence on the matter, as he demonstrated on an entirely different subject in correspondence with myself about a French philosopher, Pierre d'Ailly.

Near the very end of Book IV of *In Tim.* (pp. 293 ff.) Proclus says:

> With respect to the stars, however, those that are fixed, revolve about their own centres. . . . But the planets revolve in conjunction with the inerratic sphere, and each is moved together with its sphere to the east, and revolves by itself according to breadth and depth, and about its proper centre.

It is worth while for us to examine these remarks of his closely. First of all, the 'inerratic sphere' of the fixed stars revolves around the Earth and the planets do the same in conjunction with it. That is the simplest of the motions. But on top of that are several more motions: first, the fixed stars rotate on their axes in a spin rotation; second, the planets do the same; third, the planets do more than that: each planet 'by itself' (i.e. in separate motion from all the other stars and planets as well as separate from the 'spheres') 'revolves according to breadth and depth', which obviously refers to 'becoming by itself more remote from and nearer to the earth', as seen from the previous quote. And this depth of planetary motion, which Proclus here specifically calls 'according to breadth and depth' literally adds a new dimension to any theory of planetary motion. For whereas anyone who observes the sky over long periods can see that the planets appear to get dimmer and brighter as if they were 'becoming more remote from and nearer to the earth', the formal description of planets operating in terms of a dimension at right angles to their apparent revolutions comes very close indeed to pointing to a central point of their revolutions which is something other than the Earth. There was a tradition that Plato came to believe this, which was publicly proposed by Aristarchus of Samos (an astronomer of the first half of the third century BC) and partially advocated by Plato's friend Heraclides of Pontus (fourth century BC). We know that Proclus was aware of it: 'Let Heraclides Ponticus therefore, who was an auditor of Plato, be of this opinion; for he ascribed a circular motion to the Earth' (*In Tim.* II, 288). In short – that the Earth revolves around some other centre such as the sun. '. . . But let it be admitted that Plato established it immovable' (ibid.). Thus does Proclus admit the controversy and come down on the side of caution concerning revolution about the sun.

It is phenomenal that Proclus, with an insight which is difficult for us to comprehend, attributed to all celestial bodies a spin rotation about their axes. And since the Earth is a celestial body, it is to be wondered whether Proclus gathered the appropriate conclusion – that the Earth rotates and that is what makes the sky seem to revolve about us.

In considering this point we must realize that in the *Timaeus*, Plato mentions the rotations of the heavenly bodies on their axes (40a–b): 'And (the Creator) gave to each of (the stars) two movements: the first, a movement on the same spot after the same manner ... the second, a forward movement ...'

This is an obscure way of saying the stars rotate and the sky circles. (If Plato inserted someone else's treatise into his dialogue without being fully *au fait* with the material – as has been maintained – it may explain the vagueness, though Plato does no better in the *Laws* and was a feeble astronomer; he never showed any aptitude for practical science.) In the same passage as above, Plato also clearly describes the following: 'The earth, which is our nurse, circling around the pole which is extended through the universe', which refers to the rotation of the earth itself on its axis.

Proclus apparently adds of his own volition the other motions – for Plato seems only to mention two. Furthermore, Plato's text is too brief and foggy to make it clear exactly what he did mean. The one thing of which we can be certain is that Proclus expended untold tens of thousands of words expounding Plato's meanings in all fields beyond the extent to which Plato himself managed or desired to do. On some subjects this is not particularly gripping. But with this particular subject, every scrap of evidence is essential to unravelling the intended significance of Plato's statements.

In an essay of his entitled 'Platonic Questions',[9] Plutarch provides us with essential evidence that Plato definitely abandoned his earlier geocentric ideas, despite Proclus's nervous demurral. Plutarch says in Question VIII:

> What means Timaeus [see Plato's *Timaeus*, 42D] when he says that souls are dispersed into the earth, the moon, and into other instruments of time? Does the earth move like the sun, moon, and five planets, which for their motions he calls organs or instruments of time? Or is the earth fixed to the axis of the universe; yet not so built as to remain immovable, but to turn and wheel about, as Aristarchus and Seleucus have shown since; Aristarchus only supposing it, Seleucus positively asserting it? Theophrastus writes how that Plato, when he grew old repented him that he had placed the earth in the middle of the universe, which was not its place.

(Plutarch then follows with his own opinion, which is that the earth does not move.)

Theophrastus's testimony here is unimpeachable, but was probably unknown to Proclus, by whose lifetime most of Theophrastus's works would have been lost. Theophrastus was Aristotle's successor and head of the Lyceum at Athens, and an unquestionably reliable source; and Plutarch leaves us in no doubt (see 'Against Colotes the Epicurean', 14, in *Moralia*) that he read Theophrastus's actual works attentively, making a misquotation or secondhand report impossible in this instance.

The Seleucus who is mentioned here was a mathematician and astronomer described by George Sarton[10] as follows: 'This Babylonian was a follower of Aristarchus of Samos'. Seleucus is described differently by Giorgio de Santillana, who gives him another nationality in *The Origins of Scientific Thought*, page 250: 'We know of only one [astronomer] who adopted the system [of Aristarchus] a century later, Seleucus of Seleucia, an Oriental Greek from the Persian Gulf.'

However, Plato's views on the earth's position in space are less interesting to us in themselves than as they relate to Proclus's interpretation of them, and also as they relate to modern historians of science, who tend to gloss over the possibility that Plato may have adopted a heliocentric theory of a rotating earth moving round the sun, which was obscurely expressed in the *Timaeus* and less tentatively adhered to by Plato 'when he grew old', bearing in mind that the *Timaeus* itself is no early work of Plato's.

In Plutarch's same essay, 29, we find evidence of a continuity from Plato through his student Xenocrates of the belief that the heavens contain more than one element. However, Proclus seems to transcend by far the limited theory of Plato and Xenocrates as here presented. The summary of theories of Xenocrates presumably is drawn from his lost work in six books *On Astronomy* unless from his one lost book on *Things Pythagorean.* Xenocrates was head of the Academy for twenty-five years until his death at the age of eighty-two 'from the effects of a fall over some utensil in the night', as Diogenes Laertius tells us.[11]

There is clear proof that Proclus did not himself originate the third motion at right angles to revolution which we have seen that Plato does not mention. We actually find it referred to by Plutarch in his dialogue 'Of the Face Appearing in the Orb of the Moon', 24.[12] There he says:

> Nor is the moon indeed moved by one motion only, but is, as they were wont to call her, Trivia, or Three-Wayed – performing her course together according to length, breadth, and depth in the Zodiac; the first of which motions mathematicians call a direct revolution, the second volutation, or an oblique winding and wheeling in and out; and the third (I know not why) an inequality; although they see that she has no motion uniform, settled, and certain, in all her circuits and reversions.

Plutarch's expressions 'mathematicians call' and 'as they were wont to call her' make clear that he is referring to some unidentified and now lost astronomical works. Plutarch's exposition is not as clear as we could wish, and in a succeeding passage is countered by another speaker who espouses the more fashionable theory of spheres which actually themselves move while, as for the moon: 'some supposing that she herself stirs not'. It is peripherally interesting that in this retort the speaker also cites Aristarchus of Samos as being involved in a controversy over a line from Homer's *Iliad* which Plutarch gives and which is missing from our present text of Homer, a line advocated by Crates* and opposed by Aristarchus, which correctly describes the sea as covering 'the most part of the earth'.

We must not stray too far from Proclus. In pursuit of him, however, I wish to mention his influence on Johannes Kepler, the sixteenth-century discoverer of the three laws of planetary motion (which are the only ones we possess even now). And in this I have another complaint to make. For not one major work of Kepler's has ever been translated into English.[13] This fact is enough to send one into despair. Who wants to plough through a lot of medieval Latin to read Kepler – and who can? But what has Kepler to do with Proclus? Well, Kepler was steeped – indeed, drenched – in Proclus. The interested reader may turn to the closing pages of *Harmonies of the World* in the Encyclopaedia Brittanica vol. 16, *Ptolemy, Copernicus, and Kepler*,[14] and read for himself. He will find there remarks about Proclus, after which Kepler says: 'But also I have recently fallen upon the hymn of Proclus the Platonic philosopher, of whom there has been much mention in the preceding books, which was composed to the Sun and filled full with venerable mysteries' in the context of speculation about 'what did the ancient Pythagoreans in Aristotle mean, who used to call the centre of the world (which they referred to as the "fire" but understood by that the sun) "the watchtower of Jupiter"?'

Here we see that Kepler, the great forerunner of Newton, was delighted with the 'venerable mysteries' of Proclus. In the light of what we know now and will shortly discover further, later in this appendix, about Proclus's theories, what effect did they have on Kepler's own thinking?

Was Proclus standing behind Kepler just as Aristarchus stood behind Copernicus? When will Kepler and Proclus be fully available in English so that any intelligent person can make up his own mind without first becoming fluent in often highly technical medieval Latin? But most important of all, were the greatest advances at the commencement of modern cosmological speculation made by virtue of their generation from suppressed and unorthodox ancient sources such as Proclus and Aristarchus? Did the 'secret' side of ancient astronomy from the Pythagoreans to Proclus really engender the origins of our modern cosmologies? And the corollary of this is: If so, are the possibilities of our making certain breakthroughs being stymied by the very suppression of the sources which may have engendered the earliest breakthroughs? By cutting off the root of Kepler, can we really expect the branch to continue to flower? If the facts about Proclus's theories which are being presented in this appendix really have gone unremarked by all the leading historians of science upon whom we all usually rely to tell us at second hand all the

---

* Of Mallos, dating from the second century BC. He was the first head of the Library of Pergamon.

facts which we feel we have no time to discover at first hand, then something is clearly wrong with the system. We have got to overhaul the mechanics. Otherwise we shall continue to spiral downwards and think we are rising. I am referring to means and sources of inspiration. I do not question for a moment that vast progress is made in many areas. But I do maintain most strongly that our system for deriving inspiration in theorizing about the cosmos is demented because it is incomplete, therefore unbalanced. We should by now have formulated more laws or principles of planetary motion. But it is fashionable for those who read secondhand cribs of Kepler to deride him. He was a 'nut'. We do not attempt to study his means and methods of thinking or even acknowledge the existence of many of his most important sources. And one of those sources was Proclus.

The writings of Proclus are so voluminous that I have to confess that I have not gleaned from them by any means an exhaustive survey of his views. This Appendix is merely a sampling. But of course we have not yet come to the most surprising views of all, which we must now consider:

> (The planets') adumbrations are situations according to which they darken us and other things. For the body which is arranged after another body, becomes situated in the front of that which is posterior to it. And . . . they run under each other.

Also there are 'their occultations under the sun, and their evolutions into light . . .' Significantly he here turns to the subject:

> For it is necessary to recur from the phenomena to the reminiscences of invisible natures. For as from these instruments and shadows, we are enabled to commence the contemplation of the celestial bodies; thus also from the latter, we recall to our recollection invisible circulations.

It is not an easy thing to know what Proclus is referring to. His sudden dropping of this large but obscure hint cannot be meant to be understood by everyone – not even those 'who are not entirely illiterate', as he testily warned us in the very first sentence of his huge tome. This particular work by Proclus is extremely difficult to read, and the Thomas Taylor translation has neither any index nor any form of table of contents by which to locate subjects, names or references in the text. The Lipsiae Greek text has an index, but there is no means of correlating it with the Taylor translation, which has no textual numbering.

Can this reference to 'invisible circulations' refer to the invisible circulations of the companion of Sirius? The answer to this question cannot be a final 'no', and the possibility must be seriously considered when we read these next opinions of Proclus from *In Tim.* Book IV (II, 281):

As Aristotle, however, inquires why the sphere of the fixed stars, being one, comprehends many stars, but in each of the planetary spheres, which are many, there is only one star, the solution of this conformably to his own opinion may be obtained from his writings. But we have already said something concerning this, and now agreeably to what has been before asserted, we say, that *each of the planets is a whole world, comprehending in itself many divine genera invisible to us. Of all these however, the visible star has the government . . . in each of the (planetary spheres) there are invisible stars, which revolve together with their spheres*; so that in each, there is both the wholeness, and a leader which is allotted an exempt transcendency. . . . *each of the spheres is a world*; theologists also teaching us these things when they say that there are Gods in each prior to daemons, some of which are under the government of other. . . . from all which it is evident that *each of the planets is truly said to be the leader of many Gods, who give completion to its peculiar circulation.*

Taylor, in a footnote, rightly calls this an 'extraordinary passage' of the treatise! Italics above are mine.

Elsewhere Proclus says (*In Tim.*, II, 260): 'There are, however, other divine animals following the circulations of the planets, the leaders of which are the seven planets.' Taylor adds to this in a footnote: 'And these, as we have before observed, are what the moderns call *satellites*'.

In another of his publications, Thomas Taylor writes, as introduction to his translation of Plato's *Timaeus* itself:[15]

(For) each of these spheres . . . as we have already explained, it follows that every planet has a number of satellites surrounding it, analogous to the choir of fixed stars; and that every sphere is full of gods, angels, and daemons, subsisting according to the properties of the spheres in which they reside. This theory indeed is the grand key to the theology of the ancients, as it shews us at one view why the same god is so often celebrated with the names of other gods; which led Macrobius formerly to think that all the gods were nothing more than the different powers of the sun; and has induced the superficial, *index-groping* moderns to frame hypotheses concerning the ancient theology, so ridiculous that they deserve to be considered in no other light than the ravings of a madman, or the undisciplined conceptions of a child. But that the reader may be convinced of this, let him attend to the following extraordinary passages from the divine commentaries of Proclus on the *Timaeus*. And in the first place, that every planet is attended with a great number of satellites, is evident from the following citation: 'There are other divine animals attending upon the circulations of the planets, the leaders of which are the seven planets; and these revolve and return in their circulations in conjunction with their leaders, just as the fixed stars are governed by the circulation of the inerratic sphere.' [p.279] . . . And in the same place he informs us, that the revolution of these satellites is similar to that of the planets which they attend; and this, he acquaints us a little before, is according to Plato a spiral revolution. . . . (and) 'about every planet there is a number (of satellites) . . . all of them subsisting with proper circulations of their own' [p. 275].

The reader should note that Thomas Taylor describes this knowledge as 'the grand key to the theology of the ancients'. We know from a fragment of Damascius[16] the Neoplatonist* that 'the Egyptian philosophers, who are resident among us, have explained their occult truth, having obtained it from certain Egyptian discourses. According to them, then, it appears to be this. The One principle of the Universe is celebrated as Unknown Darkness, and this three times pronounced as such . . .' But wherever the information came from, the fact is that Proclus and his Neoplatonic colleagues believed the ultimate secrets of religion concerned two things: the invisible 'Dark' and invisible circulations of certain heavenly bodies, some of which were non-esoteric enough even to be specified, namely the satellites of our planetary system. Proclus winds up a dissertation on the source of this knowledge from 'sacred rumour' which concerns 'invisible circulations' also on page 247 of *In Tim.*, II.

Since Proclus specifically describes here and in the passage from *In Tim.* II, 281, the orbits of the heavenly bodies as their 'circulations' (Taylor's choice of English), the 'invisible circulations' which he mentioned must be invisible orbits of heavenly bodies, and he also tells us that there are invisible heavenly bodies. So . . . what invisible orbitings of invisible heavenly bodies are so important that they can, as Proclus just told us, 'enable us to commence the contemplation of celestial bodies' and vice versa? Is that not a most curious thought? How can he possibly mean that there are invisible orbitings so important that they may be set against the visible orbitings for importance, the one complementing the other even to the very base of our abilities to contemplate the heavens?

The key to the paragraph from Proclus II, 281, is the expression in it: 'theologists teaching us these things'. For in those words Proclus firmly identifies these ideas with a theological as opposed to philosophical tradition, and hence one connected with one or more of his mystery religions. This is just the evidence we need. For it is these mystery religions which we know contained the essence of the Sirius mystery as their secret doctrine. And also, as we have seen earlier, Proclus sought to interpret Plato in terms of an esoteric tradition with which Proclus himself was connected directly, as an initiate.

So we see that Proclus believed that invisible 'stars' existed which

---

* Sixth century AD. He was the last head of Plato's Academy, which was forced to close in 529 AD.

accompanied the planets, and that each of the planets was a world. And the visible star, that is the planet, 'has the government' over the invisible satellites in each case. How very like the Sirius tradition this is! And as we know from Chapter Two of this book, the Dogon also knew of the moons of at least one of the planets, so that knowledge of them seems likely to have been part and parcel of the Sirius mystery. Can we then conclude that Proclus may be one further person with knowledge of the Sirius mystery?

Proclus is more specific about his planetary moons elsewhere. In his work the *Platonic Theology*, Chapter XIV of Book VII (Vol. II, pages 140–1 of Taylor's translation), we read:

But the planets are called the Governors of the world (cosmocrators), and are allotted a total power. As the inerratic sphere too has a number of starry animals, so each of the planets is the leader of a multitude of animals, or of certain other things of this kind. . . . In each of the planetary spheres, therefore, there is a number of satellites analogous to the choir of the fixed stars, subsisting with proper circulations of their own. The revolution also of these satellites is similar to that of the planets which they follow: and this according to Plato is a spiral revolution. With respect, likewise, to these satellites, the first in order about every planet are Gods; after these daemons revolve in lucid orbicular bodies; and these are followed by partial souls such as ours.

Taylor comments in a footnote in *In Tim.* Book IV (II, 299): 'For "the natures successive" to the stars, are evidently their satellites, which have more than once been mentioned by Proclus.' On the same page a second footnote adds: 'From what is here said by Proclus, it appears that the fixed stars, as well as the planets, have satellites, and that the stars which sometimes are visible, and at other times disappear, are of this description.'

This brings us extremely close to an outright statement of the principles of the Sirius mystery – but without any names. These footnotes are to the passage immediately following the one given a moment ago where we first considered Proclus's cryptic reference to the 'invisible circulations'. It is interesting to note that the passage is in the form of a commentary on a specific passage in Plato's *Timaeus* (40-c), which is not only one of the most maddeningly obscure passages in all of Plato ('Do not expect me to explain these mysteries', bewails a baffled George Sarton, p. 451, op. cit.) but a passage which Proclus quotes including missing words not otherwise known from the official text of today!

And it is even more curious that the 'missing' words quoted by Proclus are: *kai ta toutois ephexēs* of which Taylor says: 'These words, however, are not to be found in the text of Plato, but form a remarkable addition to it'. Taylor should know, as he had previously translated all of Plato's dialogues including this.

Since Proclus was head of the Academy, he may be assumed to have had a reliable copy of Plato's text in the Academy library. If he did not have a reliable copy of Plato's text in Plato's own Academy, what *did* he have a reliable text of? Hence these words must be entertained as a possibly correct version and should probably be added to the currently accepted text by classical scholars. The meaning of the words is translated by Taylor as: 'the natures successive' – that is successive to the stars. And Taylor's comment is: 'For *the natures successive* to the stars, are evidently their satellites, which have more than once been mentioned by Proclus'.

The fact that a reference to the satellites of stars was dropped from the orthodox text of Plato should come as no real surprise to us. What scribe could fathom the meaning? In copying the manuscripts over the centuries, there creep in corruptions. A reference to satellites of stars would have been too shocking, considered too bizarre. In transmission the words must have been dropped as an incomprehensible aberration or an insertion. It was only in the Academy's own library that the original words were preserved, safe and musty, in the wrappings of some really old bookrolls with which no one tampered textually. Only in the Academy would ravages against the text of the Master be forbidden.

I do not believe it is a coincidence that our search through Proclus for material relevant to the Sirius mystery has led us to a lost fragment of text of Plato's dialogue *Timaeus.* The fact that these words have been dropped from that dialogue – out of the entire body of Plato's work, which is otherwise so well documented from the myriad commentaries and citations over the centuries – illustrates the controversial nature of our subject as strikingly as any of the 'accidents' we have already encountered in our book. Our Sirius mystery is not letting us down. Every subject we have approached in connection with it has been suddenly transformed as in a distorting mirror in a fun house. Nothing that seemed staid and settled has been able to remain in its mould. Even Plato's solid text begins to quiver like a live jelly. From out of so many ossified subjects have crept mysterious little creatures, which have done disrespectful dances on their premises, indicating that these subjects do not want to lie down and be declared dead. They are living. Inside them glow sylphs and secrets. We cannot force them to turn to stone.

It seems clear that the abandoned four words of text were probably dropped in order to avoid the enormous consequences which must follow upon their being retained: that Plato himself, though not particularly well acquainted with astronomy in an active professional sense, had apparently some links to a tradition which, by being esoteric, seemed to make no sense at all outside a secret 'mystery' context. This is true whether Plato wrote the passages himself or inserted the Pythagorean treatise which has been proposed (see later).

Plato's dialogue *Timaeus* is without doubt the most difficult and bizarre of the unquestioned Platonic writings. The *Epinomis* is more bizarre, but seems to have been written by Plato's disciple Philip of Opus. It dealt with the stars as divine beings. Let us examine a few remarks concerning this strange work, taken from George Sarton (op. cit.): 'There is more Oriental lore in the *Timaios* than Greek wisdom' (p. 423, note). 'The astrologic nonsense that has done so much harm in the Western world and is still poisoning weak-minded people today was derived from the *Timaios*, and Plato's astrology was itself an offshoot of the Babylonian one. In justice to Plato it must be added that his own astrology remained serene and spiritual and did not degenerate into petty fortune telling' (p. 421). 'The influence of the *Timaios* upon later times was enormous and essentially evil' (p. 423). 'Many scholars were deceived into accepting the fantasies of that book as gospel truths. That delusion hindered the progress of science; and the *Timaios* has remained to this day a source of obscurity and superstition' (p. 430).

Those are strong words. The *Timaeus* (the more commonly used spelling in English) obviously arouses violent reactions in some! Here we see Sarton, one of the most distinguished and respected historians of science who ever lived, raving hysterically that the 'evil' *Timaeus* was responsible for 'hindering the progress of science'. Sarton's views of Plato in general are incredibly violent and hostile, though many of his criticisms of Plato are quite valid and reasonable if it were not for the purple prose. It is certainly true that there were many faults to Plato's theories, particularly his political ones which Aristotle rightly found so repulsive, and these rouse Sarton to a fury surpassing his slurs on the poor *Timaeus*. But this is common among expert scholars. They have to restrain themselves most of the time for purposes of professional poise and 'objective treatment'. But the mask can fracture and a raw nerve protrudes.

But as for the perplexity or ire which the *Timaeus* seems alternatively to arouse in so many of those who attempt to study it, we should realize that the tradition is probably true which says that the major portion of the dialogue, which consists of a lengthy speech by the character named Timaeus on the nature of the universe, is really not written by Plato, but was inserted by him as the words of an apparently imaginary character (or a disguised one). For many ancient sources maintained that this part of the dialogue was in reality a Pythagorean treatise which Plato obtained during one of his visits to Sicily. Rather than see the treatise disappear into obscurity, Plato is said to have entered it as the contribution of a character in a dialogue, using the discussion of the other characters as a means of setting it off to proper advantage. And it is this supposed Pythagorean treatise which contains all the material of interest to us in connection with the Sirius mystery. And as for the Pythagoreans, they represented a sacred community and a mystery tradition with roots in Egypt and Babylon (of both of which countries Pythagoras himself was said to be an initiate into the mysteries).

I owe it to the reader to review the evidence that the passage in the

Timaeus which is of such concern to us, and on which Proclus's commentary is based as it concerns the heavenly bodies, was not even written by Plato. I therefore quote from Book VIII, 85, of the *Lives of Eminent Philosophers* by Diogenes Laertius of the first half of the third century AD (the Loeb Library translation):

> Philolaus of Croton was a Pythagorean, and it was from him that Plato requests Dion to buy the Pythagorean treatises. . . . His doctrine is that all things are brought about by necessity and in harmonious inter-relation. He was the first to declare that the earth moves in a circle (round the central fire), though some say it was Hicetas of Syracuse.
>
> He wrote one book, and it was this work which, according to Hermippus, some writer said that Plato the philosopher, when he went to Sicily to Dionysius's court, bought from Philolaus's relatives for the sum of forty Alexandrine minas of silver [an 'equivalent value', for this was before Alexander], from which also the *Timaeus* was transcribed. Others say that Plato received it as a present for having procured from Dionysius the release of a young disciple of Philolaus who had been cast into prison.
>
> According to Demetrius in his work on *Men of the Same Name*, Philolaus was the first to publish the Pythagorean treatises, to which he gave the title *On Nature*, beginning as follows: 'Nature in the ordered universe was composed of unlimited elements, and so was the whole universe and all that is therein.'

In line with this tradition that the treatise embodied into the Platonic *Timaeus* was of Pythagorean origin – and presumably from thence derived itself from Egypt and Chaldaea (Babylonia) – we may read the following interesting remarks of Proclus from *In Tim.* Book IV (II, 273):

> The Egyptians prior to (Hipparchos and Ptolemy), employing observations, and still prior to the Egyptians, the Chaldaeans (Babylonians), being taught by the gods, prior to observations, were of a similar opinion to Plato, concerning the motion of the fixed stars. For the Oracles not once only but frequently speak of the advancing procession of the fixed stars.

Note the pointed expression 'taught by the gods, prior to observations'. This highlights the aspect of the tradition as one imparted to men 'by the gods' and then later carried on in concert with observations by the ancient Egyptians. Without my going into a minute discussion of Pythagoreanism, Orphism, and what Proclus calls 'the Oracles', I hope the reader will have gathered sufficient idea of the gist of the matter.

We see that Proclus, using a slender but nevertheless substantial basis of Plato's apparently ancient Pythagorean book *On Nature*, as it is preserved in his *Timaeus*, insisted that the planets had moons, that stars also had satellites, that there were invisible bodies in space with invisible orbits which were somehow of immense importance to us, that 'the gods' instructed the ancient peoples of the Middle East in these astronomical facts which were preserved as 'Pythagorean and Orphic' traditions in the Greek world, that epicycles and other fashionable devices to explain astronomical motions were total nonsense, that the 'spheres' did not revolve but only the planets in them, and hinted at the rotation of the Earth on its axis.

Proclus was, furthermore, a known initiate of the mystery cults of the Egyptians and Babylonians and had a particular connection with rites involving Hecate, the goddess whom we know to be a form of the star Sirius. We may, therefore, conclude that Proclus is of possible interest to us in our relentless pursuit of the Sirius mystery. For he may have known its secrets and made use of the principles of that secret tradition through the indirect means of his more general writings – by hinting broadly at 'invisible orbits' without specifying all of them, and insisting on their importance without giving any really satisfactory reasons. He seems to have been trying to get the principles across without breaking sacred vows against the revealing of the specifics of the case. As he was extremely religious, we know from his character that he would honour such vows. But as he was passionately devoted to making known the general principles of the universe, he would have done exactly what it seems he did do – tell us the story without giving the names of the characters.

A closer study of Proclus in the future would certainly be rewarding. (This has now been done by someone who read my plea. See 'Postscript, 1997, II' at the end of this Appendix.) There are certainly other relevant passages in his works which remain to be dealt with. But we have seen that we must now re-examine Plato as well, for his *Timaeus* has been shown by Proclus to be a more mysterious work than even the most exasperated scholars had ever suspected.[17] And the net of the Sirius mystery is meanwhile seen to spread ever wider through the ancient traditions and literature of all eras.

Two contemporaries of Proclus, named Macrobius and Martianus Capella, also wrote advanced astronomical theories, and both were also in the Neoplatonic tradition. They advocated the notion that the Earth went around the sun. When three people in one tradition at one time write and discuss such advanced material, then a milieu may be said to exist.[18] But, of course, the historians of science have not yet got around to noticing this inconvenient little thing. Nor have they bothered to let us know much about Johannes Scotus Eriugena (otherwise known as John the Scot or Erigena, which is a misspelling) of the ninth century AD, who promulgated the theories of Macrobius and Martianus Capella at the court of Charles the Bald, and wrote a mammoth philosophical work titled *Periphyseon* of half a million words. The latter is now being published slowly in English by the Irish Government, who have decided that Eriugena (which means 'Irish-born') was one of their great native sons and they had better make the most of him. Alas. If only Proclus too had been born in Ireland. Perhaps this is the only way to get these things into print – or even into English. Can't someone invent some more little countries looking for famous sons, and then allocate the sons? That way we might have something of a cultural revival. The Renaissance was due to the rediscovery of the Platonic tradition by the Florentines. When will we discover it?

(This appendix was referred to by two Oxford scientists in the *Quarterly Journal of the Royal Astronomical Society* in 1993 in an article about impacts with cometary debris in the inner solar system, where Proclus's observations are discussed in a fascinating new context.[19])

Postscript, 1997 I
The works of Macrobius have been available in English for a long time: Macrobius, *Commentary on the Dream of Scipio*, translated by William Harris Stahl, Number XLVIII of the Records of Civilization: Sources and Studies, Columbia University Press, New York, 1952 (this is the work relevant to our subject; Stahl's Appendix A is about the heliocentric theory and gives many references to this disputed subject); *The Saturnalia*, translated by Percival Vaughan Davies, Columbia University Press, New York, 1969 (a fascinating work, but not relevant to heliocentric astronomical theories). In 1983 I published a discussion of 'The Dream of Scipio' and Macrobius's Commentary as the Introduction to *The Dream of Scipio* (*Somnium Scipionis*), Studies in Hermetic Tradition, Volume 5, The Aquarian Press, Wellingborough, UK, 1983, pp 7–17; I should like to take this opportunity to correct a misprint by pointing out that the publication of Stahl's translation was wrongly given there as 1955, whereas it was really 1952.

The works of Martianus Capella have also now appeared in English, having been published the year after *The Sirius Mystery* first appeared. The first volume of commentary had already appeared before publication of this book: Martianus Capella, *Martianus Capella and the Seven Liberal Arts*, Vol. I, by William Harris Stahl. (Commentary), Number LXXXIV of the Records of Civilization: Sources and Studies, Columbia University Press, New York, 1971; Vol. II, *The Marriage of Philology and Mercury* (Translation), translated by William Harris Stahl and Richard Johnson with E. L. Burge, Columbia University Press, 1977.

Three volumes of Eriugena have now been published. Iohannis Scotti Eriugenae, *Periphyseon (De Divisione Naturae)*, Book I, edited and translated by I. P. Sheldon-Williams with Ludwig Bieler, The Dublin Institute for Advanced Studies, Dublin, 1968 (Vol. I); Book II (Vol. II), 1972; (Vol. III) subsequently, but I do not have it.

A book on Heraclides (contemporary with Aristotle, fourth century BC) has also been published: Gottschalk, H. B., *Heraclides of Pontus*, Oxford University Press, 1980. In this book, Gottschalk refers to the heliocentric theory as 'the Philolaic system' (p. 83), after the Pythagorean philosopher Philolaus (born *circa* 470 BC in southern Italy), who was the first Pythagorean to publish the theory that the earth was not at the centre of the Universe but revolved round a central 'fire'. As mentioned earlier, it has often been suggested that the famous dialogue the *Timaeus* of Plato was mostly written by Philolaus, and that Plato merely took Philolaus's lengthy cosmological treatise and embodied it in a dialogue of his own, not intending this at the time as an act of actual plagiarism but more as an act of homage and to get the ideas more widely circulated. However well the true facts were understood by the members of Plato's Academy at the time (and our earliest record of their being publicly discussed is by Aristotle's pupil Aristoxenus), misunderstandings certainly arose later, when on the one hand the admirers of Plato did not wish to admit that Plato would have borrowed anything from anyone, and on the other hand ill-wishers used this to blacken Plato's name by accusing him of plagiarism. Heraclides believed that the Universe was infinite, and suggested that the stars were complete worlds each with an 'earth' surrounded by an atmosphere, and Gottschalk believes (p. 82) that Heraclides probably suggested these 'earths' were all inhabited, although those comments are lost, since the works of Heraclides survive only in fragments; Heraclides is recorded, however, as having claimed – whether seriously or in jest we do not know – that 'a man fell from the moon' (p. 82). He also believed that the Earth rotated on its own axis once in a synodical day (four minutes less than a solar day), and that the planets Mercury and Venus revolve round the Sun (p. 82). Gottschalk gives many references.

Interpretations of the ancient statements vary greatly. But nothing could be more specific than the statements of Martianus Capella: '. . . but Venus and Mercury do not go about the earth. . . . Venus and Mercury, although they have daily risings and settings, do not travel about the earth at all; rather they encircle the sun in wider revolutions. The centre of their orbits is set in the sun.'[20]

It is impossible to say that Martianus Capella means anything other than what he states: that Mercury and Venus have the sun at the centre of their orbits. Macrobius is a bit more vague. He says: 'The sphere in which the sun journeys is encircled by the Sphere of Mercury, which is above it, and by the higher sphere of Venus as well,'[21] But it is obvious that he is referring to the same theory, that the planets Mercury and Venus orbit the Sun.'

The dialogue *Epinomis* which has survived in the collection of Plato's dialogues also contains a reference to the planets Mercury and Venus orbiting the Sun, although this is not often noticed by historians of science. The *Epinomis* was, frankly, written by somebody who couldn't write. It is awkward and clumsy and does not succeed well at all in presenting what it wants to say. But it was written by some earnest follower or admirer of Plato with strong Pythagorean leanings, possibly during Plato's lifetime. Benjamin Jowett, the chief Plato translator, excluded it from his translation of the *Collected Works of Plato* because it was so obviously by someone else. But a translation of the *Epinomis* may be found in the Victorian edition of the *Works of Plato* in English published by Bohn's Classical Library (a forerunner of the Loeb Classical Library of today).[22] The German scholar Boeckh suggested that the *Epinomis* had been written by a member of Plato's Academy named Philip of Opus (or Opuntium).[23] This has generally been accepted. Ostensibly, the *Epinomis* was meant to be a continuation of Plato's last work, the *Laws*. The scholar J. N. Findlay is even prepared to believe that Plato really did write the *Epinomis* just before he died, and that Philip of Opus edited it.[24] Possibly Philip, who was no writer, put it together on the basis of some notes Plato had made, and added his own 'angle'. Findlay points out that the dialogue has one very profound suggestion: it suggests the use of irrational numbers in mathematics.[25] Another interesting feature of the dialogue is its preoccupation with the stars and planets and its insistence that they are divine, living beings, and the dialogue states: 'Now to show that we are justly saying they possess a soul, let us consider first their size. For they are not in reality so small, as they appear to be; but each of them is of immense bulk, as is worthy to be believed; for this is admitted by competent demonstrations. For it is possible to conceive correctly that the whole Sun is larger than the whole earth, and that all the stars, which are borne along [he seems to mean the planets, although later he makes it clear that he believes all the stars are large as well] possess a wonderful size.'[26] But for our purposes, the most interesting passage speaks of 'the star which revolves with an equal velocity with the Sun and [Venus] has the name . . . of Mercury'.[27] By which the writer is referring, somewhat clumsily, to the theory of Venus and Mercury being heliocentric. I thought it worthwhile to point this out because it is often missed.

Notes

1. *Elements of Theology*, ed. and trans. by E. R. Dodds, Oxford, 1963.
2. *Commentary on the First Book of Euclid's Elements*, trans. by Professor Glenn Morrow, Princeton University Press, 1970.
3. *Commentary on the First Alcibiades of Plato*, trans. by W. O'Neill, The Hague, 1965.
4. *Corpus Platonicum Medii Aevi* Series, ed. by R. Klibansky; Vol. III of *Plato Latinus* (*Parmenides, Proclus in Parmenidem*). Includes English translation by G. E. M. Anscombe and L. Labowsky. Warburg Institute, London, 1953. Obtainable: as Kraus Reprint, Nendeln, Liechtenstein, 1973 (translation of Book Seven only); *Proclus's Commentary on Plato's Parmenides*, translated by Glenn R. Morrow and John M. Dillon, Princeton University Press, 1987.
5. See Bibliography. Ref. page 400.
6. *The Cambridge History of Later Greek & Early Mediaeval Philosophy*, ed. by A. H. Armstrong, Cambridge, 1970.

7. There is a Life of Proclus written by his student and successor Marinus. It was translated by Thomas Taylor and appears in Volume I of *The Philosophical and Mathematical Commentaries of Proclus on the First Book of Euclid's Elements*, London, 1792. A more recent publication of it in English may be found in *The Philosophy of Proclus* by L. J. Rosan, Cosmos, New York, 1949.

8. *Hellenistic Religions*, ed. by F. C. Grant, in Library of Liberal Arts series, Bobbs-Merrill, Indianapolis and New York, 1953. English translations of four hymns by Proclus are found on pp. 170–2. (In all, seven hymns and a fragment of an eighth by Proclus survive today.)

9. In vol. V of *Plutarch's Morals*, ed. by W. W. Goodwin, Boston, 1874. The translation of 'Platonic Questions' is by R. Brown and on pp. 425–49.

10. *History of Science*, see note 16, page 159.

11. See Life of Xenocrates in Diogenes Laertius, *Lives of Eminent Philosophers*, 2 vols., trans. by R. D. Hicks, Loeb Library series; Heinemann, London; Harvard University Press, U.S.A., 1966.

12. Translation included in the same volume as in note 9 above. Also in Loeb Library.

13. Three short complete works of Kepler are in English: *Kepler's Dream*, trans. with full text and notes, of *Somnium, Sive Astronomia Lunaris*, by John Lear and P. F. Kirkwood, University of California Press, Berkeley and Los Angeles, 1965. *Kepler's Conversation with Galileo's Sidereal Messenger*, trans. by Edward Rosen, no.5 of 'Sources of Science' series, Johnson Reprint Corp., London and New York, 1965. Also there is a brief treatise by Kepler on the *Six- Cornered Snowflake*, trans. by Colin Hardie and L. L. Whyte, Oxford University Press, 1965. Two chapters (IV and V) of *Kepler's Epitome of Copernican Astronomy* and one chapter (V) of his *Harmonies of the World* are in English, trans. by C. G. Wallis in vol. 16, *Ptolemy, Copernicus, Kepler*, of the 'Great Books of the Western World' series, Encyclopaedia Britannica, Inc., Chicago, London, Toronto, 1952. A second translation of Kepler's *Dream* has appeared: *Kepler's Somnium*, trans. and commentary by Edward Rosen, University of Wisconsin Press, 1967.

14. See previous note.

15. *The Cratylus, Phaedo, Parmenides and Timaeus with notes on the Cratylus*, English trans. of Plato by Thomas Taylor with notes, London, 1793. The quotation is from p. 388, in Taylor's Introduction to the *Timaeus*. The copy of this book which I consulted once belonged to the poet Percy Bysshe Shelley, and may be found in the Shelley collection at the Bodleian Library in Oxford.

16. Preserved and trans, in Cory, *Ancient Fragments*, 2nd ed., p. 320.

17. Marinus, in his Life of Proclus, tells us that Proclus was twenty-eight years old when he wrote *In Tim.*, which gives the date AD 438 at the beginning of this appendix.

18. I did not think it right to take space here to enter into a full discussion of the generally ignored ancient heliocentric theories of Macrobius, Martianus Capella, Julian the Emperor (Apostate), Nicholas of Cusa, and so on. As an example of this tradition (which Proclus mentioned and rejected, mistakenly thinking that Plato had done so), I quote a passage from the Fourth Oration (to Helios) of the Emperor Julian the Apostate, 146 C–D, which may be found in the Loeb Library series, which publishes the works of Julian in three vols: 'For it is evident that the planets, as they dance in a circle about (the Sun), preserve as the measure of their motion a harmony between this god and their own movements. . . . To the Greeks what I say is perhaps incomprehensible – as though one were obliged to say to them only what is known and familiar.' This indicates a distinctly esoteric tradition which was imbibed from Julian's friend and teacher the Neoplatonist Iamblichus, a predecessor of Proclus. For just before this passage, Julian had said: 'Iamblichus of Chalcis, who through his writings initiated me not only into other philosophic doctrines but these also . . . (he is) by no means inferior to (Plato) in genius . . .' I also refer the reader to 135 B of the same oration by Julian for further exposition of Julian's heliocentric ideas, all of which we may treat as fragments of lost writings of Iamblichus. All of the surviving fragments of Iamblichus have been published: Iamblichi Chalcidensis, *In Platonis Dialogos Commentariorum Fragmenta* [The Fragments of Commentaries on Platonic Dialogues by

Iamblichus], edited and translated by John M. Dillon, E. J. Brill, Leiden, 1973. I also suggest consulting Thomas Whittaker's *Macrobius*, Cambridge, 1923. On page 75 we find him summarizing Macrobius's beliefs: 'Mercury and Venus (have) orbits . . . in which they follow the sun as satellites'.

19. Asher, D. J., and Clube, S. V. M., 'An Extraterrestrial Influence during the Current Glacial-Interglacial', *Quarterly Journal of the Royal Astronomical Society*, Vol. 34, No. 4, December 1993, pp. 481–511. *The Sirius Mystery* is cited on page 502.

20. Martianus Capella, *The Marriage of Philology and Mercury*, Book VIII ['Astronomy'], 854–858, translated by William Harris Stahl, Vol. II of *Martianus Capella and the Seven Liberal Arts*, Columbia University Press, New York, 1977, pp. 332–3.

21. Macrobius, *Commentary on the Dream of Scipio*, Book I, Chapter 19, 6; translated by William Harris Stahl, Columbia University Press, New York, 1952, p. 163.

22. [Pseudo-Plato], *The Epinomis*, translated by George Burges, in Vol. VI of *The Works of Plato*, George Bell and Sons/Bohn's Classical Library [these two competitors merged], London, 1891, pp. 1–36.

23. Ibid., p. 2.

24. Findlay, J. N., *Plato: The Written and Unwritten Doctrines*, Routledge & Kegan Paul, London, 1974, pp. 23, 67,.343.

25. Ibid., p. 343.

26. *Epinomis*, op. cit., Chapter Six, p. 19.

27. Ibid., Chapter Nine, p. 27.

SUMMARY

What Proclus Knew

1. The Ptolemaic theory of the heavens is totally wrong.

2. The moon is made of 'earth' which is placed in a celestial situation, hence 'celestial earth'.

3. The planets themselves revolve, rather than their 'spheres'. They do so 'within their spheres (or orbits)'.

4. The stars all rotate on their own axes.

5. The planets all rotate on their own axes.

6. The planets become 'more remote from and nearer to the earth' in their revolutions.

7. The heavens contain all the four elements in varying proportions but tend to do so according to a 'fiery mode'. The 'fire' in the stars is different from earthly fire and is more properly 'energy'. (Earthly fire is a dark and debased form of true fire, or as Proclus expresses it: 'the dregs and sediment of fire'.)

8. The heliocentric theory of Heracleides Ponticus is mentioned by Proclus, but rejected by him on the grounds that Plato rejected it. (Although we know from Theophrastus that Plato did accept it when old, Proclus did not know this.)

9. The planets have invisible satellites which revolve around them.

10. Certain fixed stars have invisible satellites too.

11. These invisible orbitings are as important as the visible ones to us, and

can 'enable us to commence the contemplation of celestial bodies'.

12. Each planet or star is 'a world'.

13. Proclus was initiated into the Egyptian and Babylonian mysteries and would thus have known about the Sirius mystery.

14. (*Added 1997*:) Proclus discussed the sacred fraction $^{256}/_{243}$, the decimal expression of which is 1.053. The revised figure for the ratio of the mass of Sirius B to our own Sun is precisely 1.053, according to the reference book *Astrophysical Data*, published in 1992. (See discussion of this correlation accurate to three decimal places in Chapter One to this new edition of *The Sirius Mystery*.)

Postscript, 1997, II

When I wrote the preceding Appendix (as Appendix I of the first edition of this book), Proclus was really receiving no attention at all. The climate of opinion has now changed considerably: the field of classical studies has become far less stuffy. This is partially because one generation of scholars has died off and been replaced by a more open-minded one.

A young man named Lucas Siorvanes read this Appendix in the late 1970s and decided to investigate the mystery of Proclus's astronomical knowledge. This led to Lucas studying Greek and in the end doing a thesis on Proclus. I believe I got to know Lucas about 1979 after he wrote to me, and I encouraged him strongly to get to the bottom of the subject. For many years he struggled to find a publisher for his study of Proclus, and initially I persuaded my friend Colin Haycraft, the head of Duckworth, to agree to publish the book. However, years of frustration still lay ahead for Lucas, and Colin did not publish as he was supposed to. It was only in 1996 that Lucas finally had his book published by Edinburgh University Press. As he says in his Introduction, it is the first book about Proclus published since 1949. Entitled *Proclus: Neo-Platonic Philosophy and Science*, it is a very extensive survey of Proclus's work. The only place where I was mentioned was at the end of footnote 4 on p. 312, where *The Sirius Mystery* is sheepishly cited.

The subject of the invisible satellites inevitably got rather swallowed up in a study of the whole of Proclus's work, but the section in Lucas's book which deals with the matter is on pp. 268–71 (two and a half pages out of 340!). Lucas includes fresh translations and further passages, as well as some discussion. He states:

The planets and the fixed stars are not the only objects in space. According to Proclus, the planets have satellites, companions normally invisible to the naked eye because the brilliance of the celestial body to which they are attached overshadows them. This is the essence of one of Proclus's most remarkable conclusions. It seems to mean that he had anticipated, long before Galileo's pioneering observation of Jupiter's moons, the existence of satellites.[1]

He adds:

> The satellites are said to be eclipsed by the brilliance of their leading star. . . .The existence of satellites in the heavens, circulating around the planets, stands as one of the mysteries of metaphysical speculation. . . . Proclus gives to the planets a spin-rotation on their own axis, in addition to their orbital revolution.[2]

Proclus was very advanced in his notions about cosmic bodies in general:

> Proclus rejects physical solid spheres, whose combined revolutions can produce the desired orbits. His celestial objects are dynamic. . . . the spheres are not solid bodies at all, but regions of space. . . . the celestial bodies move by themselves. They move by their own power. The celestial bodies travel entirely unhindered through, but also physically unsupported by, the celestial medium. They do not need any crystalline spheres, or epicycles, to carry them around. In this respect, Proclus' theory of celestial motion . . . anticipates the birth of modern celestial dynamics.[3]

Although Lucas gives only passing attention to the matter of the invisible satellites which had originally inspired his quest, his researches do clarify one further startling aspect of the issue. It had not been evident from Thomas Taylor's translations that Proclus had made clear that cosmic satellites are eclipsed by the light from the nearby brilliant stars. This is a most amazing statement, more amazing than the suggestion that planets have moons. For it appears to refer directly and specifically to Sirius B, a satellite (albeit a stellar one) eclipsed by the brilliance of the star Sirius A. And Proclus also explicitly states, like the Dogon, that the satellites of which he speaks are *invisible to the naked eye*.

It may safely be said, therefore, that the plot thickens!

Notes

1. Siorvanes, Lucas, *Proclus: Neo-Platonic Philosophy and Science*, Edinburgh University Press, 1996, p. 268.
2. Ibid., pp. 270–1.
3. Ibid, pp. 298, 282.

Appendix III

The Surviving Fragments of Berossus, in English Translation

Note: The following fragments are published here for the first time since 1876 in order to make them readily available to the reader. Regrettably, the original Greek text is not here included, but may be found in Cory, *The Ancient Fragments* (for which, see Bibliography).

These ancient fragments give accounts of the Babylonian tradition that civilization was originally founded by amphibious beings known as Oannes, Musari, or Annedoti (in Greek). This tradition is in striking agreement with the Dogon tradition of the amphibious Nommos, or 'Monitors', who came from the system of Sirius to found civilization on earth.

FRAGMENT OF BEROSSUS
FROM APOLLODORUS

Of the Chaldaean Kings

This is the history which Berossus has transmitted to us. He tells us that the first king was Alorus of Babylon, a Chaldaean; he reigned ten sari [a saros equals 3,600 years]: and afterwards Alaparus, and Amelon who came from Pantibiblon: then Ammenon the Chaldaean, in whose time appeared the Musarus Oannes the Annedotus from the Erythraean sea. (But Alexander Polyhistor anticipating the event, has said that he appeared in the first year; but Apollodorus says that it was after forty sari; Abydenus, however, makes the second Annedotus appear after twenty-six sari.) Then succeeded Megalarus from the city of Pantibiblon; and he

Appendix III

reigned eighteen sari: and after him Daonus the shepherd from Pantibiblon reigned ten sari; in his time (he says) appeared again from the Erythraean sea a fourth Annedotus, having the same form with those above, the shape of a fish blended with that of a man. Then reigned Euedoreschus from Pantibiblon, for the term of eighteen sari; in his days there appeared another personage from the Erythraean sea like the former, having the same complicated form between a fish and a man, whose name was Odacon. (All these, says Apollodorus, related particularly and circumstantially whatever Oannes had informed them of: concerning these Abydenus has made no mention.) Then reigned Amempsinus, a Chaldaean from Laranchae; and he being the eighth in order reigned ten sari. Then reigned Otiartes, a Chaldaean, from Laranchae; and he reigned eight sari. And upon the death of Otiartes, his son Xisuthrus reigned eighteen sari: in his time happened the great deluge. So that the sum of all the kings is ten; and the term which they collectively reigned an hundred and twenty sari. – *Syncel. Chron.* 39. *Euseb. Chron.* 5.

FRAGMENTS OF BEROSSUS
FROM ABYDENUS

Of the Chaldaean Kings and the Deluge
So much concerning the wisdom of the Chaldaeans.

It is said that the first king of the country was Alorus, who gave out a report that he was appointed by God to be the Shepherd of the people: he reigned ten sari: now a sarus [*saros*] is esteemed to be three thousand six hundred years; a neros six hundred; and a sossus sixty.

After him Alaparus reigned three sari: to him succeeded Amillarus from the city of Pantibiblon, who reigned thirteen sari; in his time a semidaemon called Annedotus, very like to Oannes, came up a second time from the sea; after him Ammenon reigned twelve sari, who was of the city of Pantibiblon: then Megalarus of the same place eighteen sari: then Daos, the Shepherd, governed for the space of ten sari; he was of Pantibiblon; in his time four double-shaped personages came out of the sea to land, whose names were Euedocus Eneugamus, Eneuboulus, and Anementus: after these things was Anodaphus in the time of Euedoreschus. There were afterwards other kings, and last of all Sisithrus: so that in the whole, the number amounted to ten kings, and the term of their reigns to an hundred and twenty sari. (And among other things not irrelative to the subject, he continues thus concerning the deluge:) After Euedoreschus some others reigned, and then Sisithrus. To him the deity Cronus foretold that on the fifteenth day of the month Desius there would be a deluge and commanded him to deposit all the writings whatever that he had, in the city of the Sun in Sippara. Sisithrus, when he had complied with these commands,

365

instantly sailed to Armenia, and was immediately inspired by God. During the prevalence of the waters Sisithrus sent out birds, that he might judge if the flood had subsided. But the birds passing over an unbounded sea, and not finding any place of rest, returned again to Sisithrus. This he repeated. And when upon the third trial he succeeded, for they then returned with their feet stained with mud, the gods translated him from among men. With respect to the vessel, which yet remains in Armenia, it is a custom of the inhabitants to form bracelets and amulets of its wood. – *Syncel.* 38. – *Euseb. Praep. Evan.* lib. 9. – *Euseb. Chron.* 5. 8.

Of the Tower of Babel

They say that the first inhabitants of the earth, glorying in their own strength and size, and despising the gods, undertook to raise a tower whose top should reach the sky, where Babylon now stands: but when it approached the heaven, the winds assisted the gods, and overturned the work upon its contrivers: and its ruins are said to be at Babylon: and the gods introduced a diversity of tongues among men who till that time had all spoken the same language: and a war arose between Cronus and Titan: but the place in which they built the tower is now called Babylon, on account of the confusion of the tongues; for confusion is by the Hebrews called Babel. – *Euseb. Praep. Evan.* lib. 9. – *Syncel. Chron.* 44. – *Euseb. Chron.* 13.

FRAGMENTS OF BEROSSUS
FROM ALEXANDER POLYHISTOR

Of the Cosmogony and Causes of the Deluge

Berossus, in his first book concerning the history of Babylonia, informs us that he lived in the time of Alexander the son of Philip. And he mentions that there were written accounts preserved at Babylon with the greatest care, comprehending a term of fifteen myriads of years [15 times 10,000 equals 150,000 years]. These writings contained a history of the heavens and the sea; of the birth of mankind; also of those who had sovereign rule; and of the actions achieved by them.

And in the first place he describes Babylonia as a country which lay between the Tigris and Euphrates. He mentions that it abounded with wheat, barley, ocrus [okra], sesamum [sesame]; and in the lakes were found the roots called gongae [gongyllis is Greek for turnip], which were good to be eaten, and were in respect to nutriment like barley. There were also palm trees and apples, and most kinds of fruits; fish too and birds; both those which are merely of flight, and those which take to the element of water. The part of Babylonia which is bordered upon Arabia, was barren, and without water; but that which lay on the other side had hills, and was fruitful. At Babylon there was (in these times) a great resort of people of various nations, who inhabited Chaldea, and lived without rule and order like the beast of the field.

In the first year there made its appearance, from a part of the Erythraean sea which bordered upon Babylonia, an animal endowed with reason, who was called Oannes. (According to the account of Apollodorus) the whole body of the animal was like that of a fish; and had under a fish's head another head, and also feet below, similar to those of a man, subjoined to the fish's tail. His voice too, and language, was articulate and human; and a representation of him is preserved even to this day.

This Being in the day-time used to converse with men; but took no food at that season; and he gave them an insight into letters and sciences, and every kind of art. He taught them to construct houses, to found temples, to compile laws, and explained to them the principles of geometrical knowledge. He made them distinguish the seeds of the earth, and shewed them how to collect fruits; in short, he instructed them in every thing which could tend to soften manners and humanize mankind. From that time, so universal were his instructions, nothing has been added material by way of improvement. When the sun set, it was the custom of this Being to plunge again into the sea, and abide all night in the deep; for he was amphibious.

After this there appeared other animals like Oannes, of which Berossus promises to give an account when he comes to the history of the kings.

Moreover Oannes wrote concerning the generation of mankind; of their different ways of life, and of their civil polity; and the following is the purport of what he said:

'There was a time in which there was nothing but darkness and an abyss of waters, wherein resided most hideous beings, which were produced of a two-fold principle. Men appeared with two wings, some with four and with two faces. They had one body but two heads; the one of a man, the other of a woman. They were likewise in their several organs both male and female. Other human figures were to be seen with the legs and horns of goats. Some had horses' feet; others had the limbs of a horse behind, but before were fashioned like men, resembling hippocentaurs. Bulls likewise bred there with the heads of men; and dogs with fourfold bodies, and the tails of fishes. Also horses with the heads of dogs: men too and other animals, with the heads and bodies of horses and the tails of fishes. In short, there were creatures with the limbs of every species of animals. Add to these fishes, reptiles, serpents, with other wonderful animals, which assumed each other's shape and countenance. Of all these were preserved delineations in the temple of Belus at Babylon.

'The person, who was supposed to have presided over them, was a woman named Omoroca ; which in the Chaldaic language is Thalatth; which the Greeks express Thalassa, the sea: but according to the most true computation, it is equivalent to Selene, the moon. All things being in this situation, Belus came, and cut the woman asunder and out of one half of her he formed the earth, and of the other half the heavens; and at the same time destroyed the animals in the abyss. All this (he says) was an allegorical description of nature. For the whole universe consisting of moisture, and animals being continually generated therein; the deity (Belus) above-mentioned cut off his own head: upon which the other gods mixed the blood, as it gushed out, with the earth; and from thence men were formed. On this account it is that they are rational, and partake of divine knowledge. This Belus, whom men call Dis, divided the darkness, and separated the Heavens from the Earth, and reduced the universe to order. But the animals so lately created, not being able to bear the prevalence of light, died. Belus upon this, seeing a vast space quite uninhabited, though by nature very fruitful, ordered one of the gods to take off his head; and when it was taken off, they were to mix the blood with the soil of the earth; and from thence to form other men and animals, which should be capable of bearing the light. Belus also formed the stars, and the sun, and the moon, together with the five planets.' (Such are the contents of the first book of Berossus.)

(In the second book was the history of the ten kings of the Chaldeans, and the periods of each reign, which consisted collectively of an hundred and twenty sari, or four hundred and thirty-two thousand years; reaching to the time of the Deluge. For Alexander, following the writings of the Chaldaeans, enumerating the kings from the ninth Ardates to Xisuthrus, who is called by them the tenth, proceeds in this manner:)

After the death of Ardates, his son Xisuthrus succeeded, and reigned eighteen sari. In his time happened the great Deluge; the history of which is given in this manner. The Deity, Cronus, appeared to him in a vision, and gave him notice that upon the fifteenth day of the month Daesius there would be a flood, by which mankind would be destroyed. He therefore enjoined him to commit to writing a history of the beginning, procedure, and final conclusion of all things, down to the present term; and to bury these accounts securely in the city of the Sun at Sippara; and to build a vessel, and to take with him into it his friends and relations; and to convey on board every thing necessary to sustain life, and to take in also all species of animals, that either fly or rove upon the earth; and trust himself to the deep. Having asked the Deity, whither he was to sail? he was answered, 'To the Gods:' upon which he offered up a prayer for the good of mankind. And he obeyed the divine admonition: and built a vessel five stadia in length, and two in breadth. Into this he put every thing which he had got ready; and last of all conveyed into it his wife, children, and friends. After the flood had been upon the earth, and was in time abated, Xisuthrus sent out some birds from the vessel; which not finding any food, nor any place to rest their feet, returned to him again. After an interval of some days, he sent them forth a second time; and they now returned with their feet tinged with mud. He made a trial a third time with these birds; but they returned to him no more; from whence he formed a judgment, that the surface of the earth was now above the waters. Having therefore made an opening in the vessel, and finding upon looking out, that the vessel was driven to the side of a mountain, he immediately quitted it, being attended by his wife, his daughter, and the pilot. Xisuthrus immediately paid his adoration to the earth: and having constructed an altar, offered sacrifices to the gods. These things being duly performed, both Xisuthrus and those who came out of the vessel with him disappeared. They, who remained in the vessel, finding that the others did not return, came out with many lamentations, and called continually on the name of Xisuthrus. Him they saw no more; but they could distinguish his voice in the air, and could hear him admonish them to pay due regard to the gods; and likewise inform them that it was upon account of his piety that he was translated to live with the gods; that his wife and daughter, with the pilot, had obtained the same honour. To this he added that he would have them make the best of their way to Babylonia, and search for the writings at Sippara, which were to be made known to all mankind: and that the place where they then were was the land of Armenia. The remainder having heard these words, offered sacrifices to the gods; and taking a circuit, journeyed towards Babylonia.

The vessel being thus stranded in Armenia, some part of it yet remains in the Corcyraean* mountains in Armenia; and the people scrape off the bitumen, with which it had been outwardly coated, and make use of it by way of an alexipharmic and amulet. In this manner they returned to Babylon; and having found the writings at Sippara, they set about building cities, and erecting temples: and Babylon was thus inhabited again. – *Syncel. Chron.* 28. – *Euseb. Chron.* 5. 8.

FRAGMENTS OF BEROSSUS
FROM JOSEPHUS, ETC.

Of Abraham
After the deluge, in the tenth generation, was a certain man among the Chaldaeans renowned for his justice and great exploits, and for his skill in the celestial sciences. *Euseb. Praep. Evan.* lib. 9.

Of Nabonasar
From the reign of Nabonasar only are the Chaldaeans (from whom the Greek mathematicians copy) accurately acquainted with the heavenly motions: for Nabonasar collected all the mementos of the kings prior to himself, and destroyed them, that the enumeration of the Chaldaean kings might commence with him. – *Syncel. Chron.* 207.

* Or Cordyean mountains – *Corduarum montibus*; Ea. Ar.

Of the Destruction of the Jewish Temple

He (Nabopollasar) sent his son Nabuchodonosor with a great army against Egypt, and against Judea, upon his being informed that they had revolted from him; and by that means he subdued them all, and set fire to the temple that was at Jerusalem; and removed our people entirely out of their own country, and transferred them to Babylon, and it happened that our city was desolate during the interval of seventy years, until the days of Cyrus king of Persia. (He then says, that) this Babylonian king conquered Egypt, and Syria, and Phoenicia and Arabia, and exceeded in his exploits all that had reigned before him in Babylon and Chaldaea. – *Joseph. contr. Appion.* lib. I. c. 19.

Of Nebuchadnezzar

When Nabopollasar his (Nabuchodonosor's) father, heard that the governor, whom he had set over Egypt, and the parts of Coelesyria and Phoenicia, had revolted, he was unable to put up with his delinquencies any longer, but committed certain parts of his army to his son Nabuchodonosor, who was then but young, and sent him against the rebel; and Nabuchodonosor fought with him, and conquered him, and reduced the country again under his dominion. And it happened that his father, Nabopollasar, fell into a distemper at this time and died in the city of Babylon, after he had reigned twenty-nine years.

After a short time Nabuchodonosor, receiving the intelligence of his father's death, set the affairs of Egypt and the other countries, in order, and committed the captives he had taken from the Jews, and Phoenicians, and Syrians, and of the nations belonging to Egypt, to some of his friends, that they might conduct that part of the forces that had on heavy armour, with the rest of his baggage, to Babylonia; while he went in haste, with a few followers, across the desert to Babylon; where, when he was come, he found that affairs had been well conducted by the Chaldaeans, and that the principal person among them had preserved the kingdom for him: accordingly he now obtained possession of all his father's dominions. And he ordered the captives to be distributed in colonies in the most proper places of Babylonia: and adorned the temple of Belus, and the other temples, in a sumptuous and pious manner, out of the spoils he had taken in this war. He also rebuilt the old city, and added another to it on the outside, and so far restored Babylon, that none, who should besiege it afterwards, might have it in their power to divert the river, so as to facilitate an entrance into it: and this he did by building three walls about the inner city, and three about the outer. Some of these walls he built of burnt brick and bitumen, and some of brick only. When he had thus admirably fortified the city with walls, and had magnificently adorned the gates, he added also a new palace to those in which his forefathers had dwelt, adjoining them, but exceeding them in height, and in its great splendour. It would perhaps require too long a narration, if any one were to describe it: however, as prodigiously large and magnificent as it was, it was finished in fifteen days. In this palace he erected very high walks, supported by stone pillars; and by planting what was called a pensile paradise, and replenishing it with all sorts of trees, he rendered the prospect an exact resemblance of a mountainous country. This he did to please his queen, because she had been brought up in Media, and was fond of a mountainous situation. – *Joseph. contr. Appion.* lib. I. c. 19. – *Syncel. Chron.* 220. – *Euseb. Praep. Evan.* lib. 9.

Of the Chaldaean Kings after Nebuchadnezzar
Nabuchodonosor, after he had begun to build the above-mentioned wall, fell sick, and departed this life, when he had reigned forty-three years; whereupon his son Evilmerodachus obtained the kingdom. He governed public affairs in an illegal and improper manner, and by means of a plot laid against him by Neriglissoorus, his sister's husband, was slain when he had reigned but two years.

Upon his death Neriglissoorus, who had conspired against him, succeeded him in the kingdom, and reigned four years.

His son Laborosoarchodus inherited the kingdom though he was but a child, and kept it nine months; but by reason of the evil practices he exhibited, a plot was laid against him by his friends, and he was tortured and killed.

After his death, the conspirators assembled, and by common consent put the crown upon the head of Nabonnedus, a man of Babylon, and one of the leaders of that insurrection. In his reign it was that the walls of the city of Babylon were curiously built with burnt brick and bitumen.

But in the seventeenth year of his reign, Cyrus came out of Persia with a great army, and having conquered all the rest of Asia, he came hastily to Babylonia. When Nabonnedus perceived he was advancing to attack him, he assembled his forces and opposed him, but was defeated, and fled with a few of his attendants, and was shut up in the city Borsippus. Whereupon Cyrus took Babylon, and gave orders that the outer walls should be demolished, because the city had proved very troublesome to him, and difficult to take. He then marched to Borsippus, to besiege Nabonnedus; but as Nabonnedus delivered himself into his hands without holding out the place, he was at first kindly treated by Cyrus, who gave him an habitation in Carmania, but sent him out of Babylonia. Accordingly Nabonnedus spent the remainder of his time in that country, and there died. – *Joseph. contr. App.* lib. 1. c. 20. – *Euseb. Praep. Evan.* lib. 10.

Of the Feast of Sacea
Berossus, in the first book of his Babylonian history, says; That in the eleventh month, called Loos, is celebrated in Babylon the feast of Sacea for five days; in which it is the custom that the masters should obey their

domestics, one of whom is led round the house, clothed in a royal garment, and him they call Zoganes. – *Athenaeus*, lib. 14.

FRAGMENT OF MEGASTHENES
FROM ABYDENUS

Of Nebuchadnezzar

Abydenus, in his history of the Assyrians, has preserved the following fragment of Megasthenes, who says: That Nabucodrosorus, having become more powerful than Hercules, invaded Libya and Iberia, and when he had rendered them tributary, he extended his conquests over the inhabitants of the shores upon the right of the sea. It is moreover related by the Chaldaeans, that as he went up into his palace he was possessed by some god; and he cried out and said 'Oh! Babylonians, I, Nabucodrosorus, foretell unto you a calamity which must shortly come to pass, which neither Belus my ancestor, nor his queen Beltis, have power to persuade the Fates to turn away. A Persian mule shall come, and by the assistance of your gods shall impose upon you the yoke of slavery: the author of which shall be a Mede, the foolish pride of Assyria. Before he should thus betray my subjects, Oh! that some sea or whirlpool might receive him, and his memory be blotted out for ever; or that he might be cast out to wander through some desert, where there are neither cities nor the trace of men, a solitary exile among rocks and caverns, where beasts and birds alone abide. But for me, before he shall have conceived these mischiefs in his mind, a happier end will be provided.'

When he had thus prophesied, he expired: and was succeeded by his son Evilmaluruchus, who was slain by his kinsman Neriglisares: and Neriglisares left Labassoarascus his son: and when he also had suffered death by violence, they made Nabannidochus king, being no relation to the royal family; and in his reign Cyrus took Babylon, and granted him a principality in Carmania.

And concerning the rebuilding of Babylon by Nabuchodonosor, he writes thus: It is said that from the beginning all things were water, called the sea (Thalatth?): that Belus caused this state of things to cease, and appointed to each its proper place: and he surrounded Babylon with a wall: but in process of time this wall disappeared: and Nabuchodonosor walled it in again, and it remained so with its brazen gates until the time of the Macedonian conquest. And after other things he says: Nabuchodonosor having succeeded to the kingdom, built the walls of Babylon in a triple circuit in fifteen days; and he turned the river Armacale, a branch of the Euphrates, and the Acracanus: and above the city of Sippara he dug a receptacle for the waters, whose perimeter was forty parasangs, and whose depth was twenty cubits; and he placed gates at the entrance thereof, by opening which they irrigated the plains, and these they call Echetognomones (sluices): and he constructed dykes against the irruptions of the Erythraean sea, and built the city of Teredon against the incursions of the Arabs; and he adorned the palace with trees, calling them hanging gardens. – *Euseb. Praep. Evan.* lib. 10. – *Euseb. Chron.* 49.

FRAGMENT OF JULIAN THE EMPEROR
(REIGNED AD 360–3)

From Cyril's *Contra Julianum* V, 176 (Migne), we have this fragment of Julian's lost work *Against the Christians*:

> That God, however, has not cared for the Hebrews only, but rather that in His love for all nations He hath bestowed on the Hebrews nothing worth very serious attention, whereas He has given us far greater and superior gifts, consider from what will follow. The Egyptians, counting up of their own race the names of not a few sages, can also say they have had many who have followed in the steps of Hermes. I mean of the Third Hermes who used to come down to them in Egypt. The Chaldaeans also can tell of the disciples of Oannes and of Belus; and the Greeks of tens of thousands who have the Wisdom from Cheirion. For it is from him that they derived their initiation into the mysteries of nature, and their knowledge of divine things; so that indeed in comparison the Hebrews seem only to give themselves airs about their own attainments.

This translation (with some gaps supplied) may be found in G. R. S. Mead's *Thrice Greatest Hermes*, vol. III, page 199 (1964).

FRAGMENT OF HELLADIUS
PRESERVED BY PHOTIUS
(C. AD 820–C. 893)
PRESERVED IN THE FORM OF A SUMMARY
(CODEX 279)

(Helladius) recounts the story of a man named Oe who came out of the Red Sea having a fish-like body but the head, feet and arms of a man, and who taught astronomy and letters. Some accounts say that he came out of a great egg whence his name, and that he was actually a man, but only seemed a fish because he was clothed in 'the skin of a sea creature'.

I am indebted to Kenneth Demarest for bringing attention to this obscure fragment from the Byzantine Patriarch Photius in his essay 'The Winged

Power'. I also quote a portion of his own remarks following it:

Helladius' account is extremely valuable, the more so because it is confirmed by the extant pictorial representations of this wise being (called 'the Egg-Born') who exited in a strange suit from some kind of vessel – likened to an egg – that 'fell' into the sea. Hyginus, Manilius and Xanthus all furnish other corroborating details, speaking of gods in honor of whom the fish-form is sacred, who plunged from the sky into the waters of the Euphrates. In another variant (found in the commentary in Germanicus' edition of Aratus) the power of a holy fish pushed ashore on the banks of the Euphrates near Babylon, the 'egg' out of which the 'deity' appeared. Before it landed in the waters, the egg-like vessel was of a luminous appearance. Thus the historian Sozomen tells us that the same type of deity descended into the Euphrates as 'a fiery star' from the sky. . . . Just as these visitant capsules in the water were remembered as 'eggs' from which higher men in fish-garb emerged, so the capsules, when they were in the sky were metaphorically described as great fiery birds or griffons . . . or, again, as winged figures or deific men flying in a winged ring or capsule . . . 'Space visitors' we would call them today.

Appendix IV

Why Sixty Years?

The Sigui ceremony of the Dogon is celebrated every sixty years. What precedents for such a period of time, given religious importance, are to be found in the ancient world?

The Egyptians had such a period associated with Osiris.[1] We also find the sixty-year period reduplicated by them in a manner familiar from the reduplications of the fifty-year period of Sirius B, and also in the Dogon custom of speaking of 'uniting two Sigui': 'The *henti* period consisted of two periods, each containing sixty years.' And this period is described in a *Hymn to Osiris*:[2] '. . . most terrible is his name of "Asar" (Osiris). The duration of his existence is an eternal *henti* period in his name of "Un-Nefer".'

The *henti* period may, by pun, have had some association with the phallus, *henn.* I only suggest this because of the connection of circumcision with the Sigui ceremonies of the Dogon. It is pure speculation. *Henti* is also a title of Osiris, presumably arising from the fact that the duration of Osiris's existence is said to be 'an eternal *henti* period'.

My own predilection, when considering the period of sixty years, is to think in terms of a synchronization of the orbital periods of the two planets Jupiter and Saturn, for these come together in nearly sixty years. The orbital period of Jupiter is approximately twelve years and that of Saturn approximately thirty years. Five times twelve is sixty and two times thirty is also sixty. Sixty years is the great period which brings into synchronization the movements of the two great outer planets which can be seen by the eye. I have no doubt that this sixty-year period has been of considerable importance in ancient times, and the sharp-eyed Egyptians would have been well aware of it.

In speaking of the revolutions of Jupiter and Saturn, the Neoplatonist philosopher Olympiodorus* has written:[3] 'That of Jupiter . . . is effected in twelve years. And . . . that of Saturn . . . is completed in thirty years. The stars, therefore, are not conjoined with each other in their revolutions except rarely. Thus, for instance, the sphere of Saturn and the sphere of

---

* Alexandrian, born between 495 and 505 AD and still teaching in 565 AD. He was a pagan, not a Christian, by his own admission, despite his late date. He was equally concerned with both Plato and Aristotle.

Jupiter are conjoined with each other in their revolutions, in sixty years. For if the sphere of Jupiter comes from the same to the same in twelve years, but that of Saturn in thirty years, it is evident that when Jupiter has made five, Saturn will have made two revolutions: for twice thirty is sixty, and so likewise is twelve times five; so that their revolutions will be conjoined in sixty years. Souls, therefore, are punished for such like periods.'

These observations of Olympiodorus, from his Commentary on Plato's *Gorgias* in the form of scholia, are cited by Thomas Taylor as comment on a passage by Apuleius (best known as author of *The Golden Ass*) in one of his Platonic essays:[4] 'For in order that the measures and revolutions of times might be known, and that the convolutions of the world might be visible, the light of the sun was enkindled; and vice versa, the opacity of night was invented, in order that animals might obtain the rest which they naturally desire. Month likewise was produced, when the moon, having completed the revolution of her orb, returns to the same place from whence she departed. And the spaces of the year were terminated when the sun had passed through the four vicissitudes of the seasons, and arrived at the same sign. And the numerations of these circulations, returning into, and proceeding from, themselves, was discovered by the exercise of the reasoning power. Nevertheless, there are certain circuits of the stars, which perpetually observe a legitimate course, but which the sagacity of men can scarcely comprehend. . . . the supreme of all of them (is that of the fixed stars) . . . the second is given to Saturn, the third to Jupiter . . .'

This esoteric cycle conjoining the motions of Saturn and Jupiter would have seemed of immense importance to all ancient astronomers who had a good grasp of their subject. A cycle of sixty years is so long that no single person can live long enough to verify its recurrence a second time. The knowledge of such a cycle required a continuing tradition of observation which implies a priesthood with astronomical inclinations. The discovery and verification over more than one generation of an esoteric cycle joining the two great outer planets would appear as exciting to the ancient priests as discovering DNA has been to modern biochemists. To 'crack' the mysteries of the motions of the two outer planets is quite an achievement. No wonder, then, that the Dogon maintain that a priest who 'united two Sigui' is really rather special. Apart from the fact that no one lives 120 years very easily, and thus 'uniting two Sigui' is accepted as having celebrated two Sigui ceremonies in a lifetime, the reduplication of the cycle may be taken to signify that only by checking to see if it happens a second time can the cycle be verified. To unite two of the cycles is to achieve a *henti*, which we have just seen the Egyptians describe both as 120 years and as 'eternal'. How can 120 years be 'eternity'? This can be so when eternity is seen to consist of a cyclical construction. In other words, eternity is not a straight line to infinity but is rather an endless series of coils of the same size compressed into a great spring, known as time, and with the impetus of *happening*.

By chance, I found in an extremely obscure old book[5] from early in the nineteenth century a reference to a sixty-year period in the ancient world. The book is primarily a meandering of speculations concerning Stonehenge and British stone circles. It points out that Stonehenge has sixty stones in its outer circle. Then we read: '. . . (this) outer circle is the oriental cycle of Vrihaspati, 60'.[6] The author later adds:[7] 'The great temple of Rolrich, in Oxfordshire,[8] is surrounded with 60 upright stones; the cycle of Vrihaspati, an example not far distant from the others.' Later the author adds: 'the number 60 is the base of the famous cycle called the Saros of 3,600 years of the Chaldees or Culdees of Babylon . . .' and he mentions also that it is the decimal part of the 600-year cycle of the Neros period from the ancient Near East. But as for the 'famous Indian cycle of Vrihaspati', he seems upset that Indian brahmans explained it 'by saying that it arose from 5 revolutions of the planet Jupiter . . .'[9]

Passing beyond our quaint old source book, we may investigate this rumoured Indian cycle of Vrihaspati. We soon discover that it does indeed exist in Indian tradition, where it is more properly known as that of Brihaspati. The name Brihaspati (or Vrihaspati) is the name of the planet Jupiter in Sanskrit, and the cycle which takes its name from this planet is a sixty-year cycle.

Looking further into the matter of Brihaspati, I discovered that a Brihaspaticakra has two specific meanings: the Hindu cycle of sixty years, and also 'a particular astrological diagram'. I have not been able to locate a design of this diagram. But the fact that such a diagram exists indicates to me even further that the coincidence of five orbits of Jupiter with two of Saturn may be intended here. For it is by means of a particular astrological diagram that one traditionally computes the relative positions of Saturn and Jupiter. I reproduce two such diagrams in Figures 61 and 62. These diagrams were prepared by Johannes Kepler, discoverer of our three laws of Planetary Motion, and whom I discussed slightly in Appendix II.[10]

In reference to these very diagrams, Santillana and von Dechend tell us in *Hamlet's Mill*,[11] 'A "mighty conjunction" thus corresponds to the revolution of one angle or corner of the trigon of Jupiter–Saturn conjunctions – built up in sixty years (more correctly: 59.6 years) – through the whole zodiac . . .' And further: '. . . (in) Greece, where we have – besides the wrestling of Kronos and Saturn at Olympia – also the *Daidalia*, held in the interval of sixty years – sixty-year cycles in India, or in the West Sudan, are not likely to be understood, if the scholars prefer to inhibit the trigon of the Saturn-Jupiter conjunction . . .' And this trigon must be diagrammatically presented.

We thus see that Santillana and von Dechend specifically identify sixty-year cycles of the West Sudan, where the Dogon live, with the Jupiter–Saturn synchronism over sixty years. This was not known to me when I assumed the same thing: the reader will appreciate that such a concurrence of opinion urged me to think this idea correct.

The Dogon associate a sixty-year period with the creation of the world by Amma.[12] In the light of this, it is interesting that in the Western astrological tradition, Saturn 'gives the measures of creation' to Jupiter specifically through the interconnection of their orbits in the way which we have been describing. Santillana and von Dechend explain this quite well[13] and Johannes Kepler's works *De Stella Nova* and *De Vero Anno* are relevant to the subject.[14] See also Figures 61 and 62 for the diagrams by which Saturn gives the (temporal) measures of creation to Jupiter. There is a Great Conjunction of Jupiter and Saturn every twenty years, as the diagrams show. The Dogon seem to be aware of the twenty-year subdivision of the sixty-year period too. If the reader turns back to the Griaule and Dieterlen article (Appendix I), and studies Figure ii accompanying it, and the relevant text, he will see that the Sigui sixty-year computation is broken down into twenty-year segments.

The act of circumcision, to the Dogon, symbolizes the orbit of Sirius B around Sirius A. It may well be, then, that such a tendency to use genital symbolism in connection with heavenly motions explains the 'castration' of Saturn by Jupiter in Greek mythology. Figure xii of the Griaule and

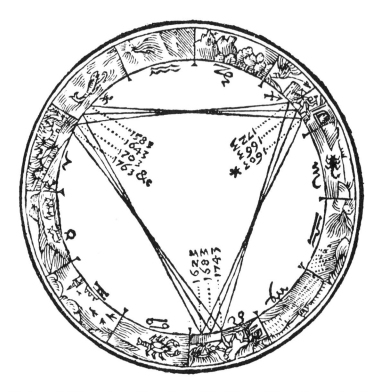

Figure 61. A detailed illustration of the motions of the Trigon of Great Conjunctions from 1583 to 1763

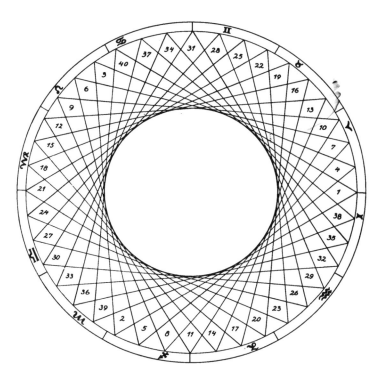

Figure 62. Scheme of the Great Conjunctions of Saturn and Jupiter, and their leap through the eighth sign and transit through all four of the triple Zodiac

Dieterlen article in this book records the 'mutilating domination of Sirius over the femininity of Yasigui' (see pp. 47–8). In *Le Renard pâle* one reads a great deal about genital mutilation, castration, circumcisions, female circumcisions, and so on. These strange conceptions of genital violence associated symbolically to heavenly movements obviously came to the Dogon along with the rest of their ancient traditions, and survive as well in the Mediterranean region indigenously. The mutilation of Saturn by Jupiter, and the various creations which sprang from the resulting blood and seed, are of the same current of tradition as all the elements of a similar kind to be found among the Dogon, and which are related to these comparative orbitings of Saturn and Jupiter, as well as other heavenly bodies. The placenta comes back into the picture too. We have seen in the main text of the book that the placenta is the symbol, for the Dogon, of a planetary system, and the system of our sun and its planets is a placenta. It is therefore interesting that the Dogon say that sixty is the count of the cosmic placenta.[15] For this specifically identifies the sixty years as a count defining our planetary system, and sixty years as the coordination between Saturn and Jupiter's movements can be seen as doing just that. For any system may be seen as defined by its boundaries, and as Saturn and Jupiter are recognized by the Dogon as their outermost planets for our system, their conjoinment would strictly speaking define our cosmic placenta, our solar system, for them. The Dogon even break 60 down themselves into '5 series of 12'[16] and twice thirty, which seems a fairly specific indication that our hypothesis has a sound basis. For the last point, the drawing above the door of the Dogon sanctuary of Binou[17] reinforces these ideas. This drawing is used for the computation of the Sigui. Accompanying this drawing is a drawing of the Nommo which is broken down into two major portions: his right 'leg' marks the first thirty years and his left 'leg' the second thirty years. The legs are joined to represent that only taken together do these two thirty-year periods have significance. And, as we know, Nommo did not actually have legs. He had a fish-tail extremity. The fact that each 'leg' represents a period of years is made quite clear by the information given that 'the left leg is made a little longer every year in such a way that it is the same length as the other (leg) by the time of the Sigui.' This process recalls Plutarch's remark, noted much earlier in the book, that Zeus (Jupiter) had his legs joined together.

In short, Jupiter's legs were joined together because each of his 'legs' represented one of the thirty-year orbital periods of his father Saturn, and it was on his father that he stood. For Saturn upheld Jupiter's creation by providing him with the temporal measures, as Santillana and von Dechend explain.[18] And the Dogon are the people who preserve this intricate tradition most fully, which should not surprise us. They say that sixty is the 'number of the placenta', and indeed it is. Without sixty we could not define our solar system according to the traditional view of it – and this traditional view is the one resting on the capabilities of observation, which is sensible. For us to define our system today by saying it is bounded by the motions of a tiny body called Pluto doesn't mean anything to anybody. For us to ground ourselves in the weighty and ponderous motions of those two observable planets Saturn and Jupiter, and define our solar system – perhaps 'poetically' – by their motions as extremities, we would be striking a deep chord in that music of the spheres of which we have all heard fanciful tales, but of which today we know nothing. But music which cannot be heard is not necessarily lost to the inner ear. Music, after all, is not necessarily audible sound. Harmony transcends the sensibly perceptive. The observance of a celestial harmony in the ancient cultures helped keep a sane perspective. To acknowledge the deep resounding bass of the sixty-year cycle was the ultimate poetic myth of the solar system, expressed in that vast mythological fabric woven around all the heavenly bodies, a whole cloth binding together both man and planets in a cosmic unity which gave man dignity and meaning in a world whose periods and cycles he had defined and celebrated in his religious festivals.

Even today we do this, but have lost consciousness of it; Easter is defined by the moon. But who notices that? The cosmic bodies make their silent music but we have stopped our ears. We do not wish to be integrally related to our cosmic environment by observances of the great motions above us. All the reader need do is to take the cotton wool out of his ears and listen. He will hear silence. And the cycles and periods of that silence are the beautiful music of the cosmos. But as long as we keep our ears stopped, we will be deafened by our inner noise and will have those tortured 'modern' looks on our faces.

POSTSCRIPT (1997)

Since the publication of the first edition of this book I have received a great deal of correspondence on the subject of the sixty-year period. I have also accumulated more information on the subject myself. The decision to reprint was taken so suddenly that I have time here only to note two articles of which I bought offprints some years ago when I was working on Chinese astronomy. They are both by Dr Herbert Chatley, who was concerned to explain the prominence of the sixty-year period in China.

The sixty-year period in China is called the *jia zi* (using modern Pinyin), although in the old style of the Wade-Giles transliteration system it is spelled *chia tzu*. The Chinese characters are 甲 子

Chatley says of it:

After the well-known annual changes of altitude of the Sun and the monthly changes of 'phase' of the Moon, the most *regular* celestial phenomena of a comparable nature are the motions of Jupiter and Saturn and the mutual conjunctions of these two great planets. Jupiter moves round the 'ecliptic' (the path of the Sun) once in twelve years . . . and Saturn once in thirty years . . . They thus come into conjunction, as seen from the Sun, every twenty years . . . and in sixty years (actually 59.5779 is the mean value) they meet again in almost the same place in the sky (actually 8.1° in advance). The times of conjunction as seen from the Earth are approximately the same and this period of about sixty years is the famous 'Soss' of the Chaldaeans and is approximately equal to the Chia-tzu (甲 子) of the Chinese. . . . The ancients attached very great chronological importance to these conjunctions. . . . In 3,535 years the motions of Jupiter and Saturn are repeated with remarkable accuracy, as after 3,534.96 tropical years they are conjoined within a fraction of a degree and have made integral numbers (298 and 120 respectively) of revolutions about the Sun. This period is possibly the 'Saros' of 3,600 years of which the Chaldaeans wrote . . . The ancients believed in apocatastatic (complete restoration) periods when all the planets would return to certain points and world crises would recur. These periods would be the least common multiples of the individual periods of return . . .[19]

In another and longer article, Chatley examines the possible origins of the sixty-year cycle in China. He mentions that in the famous Wu family tomb of the Han Dynasty in Shandong Province the sixty-year cycle was used to specify the tomb date of 147 AD. So clearly the cycle had achieved a very high prominence indeed by that time. Chatley mentions that there was a traditional belief that the cycle was very ancient indeed, but he challenges this 'in spite of the popular Chinese belief that this practice goes back to the days of Huang Ti [the mythical Yellow Emperor] and an era of 2637 BC.' Although Chatley believes the cycle of sixty as applied to days, rather than years, may have existed at that time in China, he is inclined to date the prominence of the sixty-*year* cycle to some time between 66 BC and 85 AD (Han Dynasty). He admits that the importance of the twelve-year cycle of Jupiter was important in China no later than the seventh century BC. He believes the sixty-year cycle count commenced as from 4 AD, but points out that the famous astronomer I Xing (I Hsing) in 724 AD reckoned backwards to a presumed commencement in 1017 BC. However, Chatley thinks that in 4 AD 'The convenience of a numerator of years caused the true Jupiter year to be dropped . . . and so a regular cycle of sixty tropical years came into being.'[20]

I thought it best to widen the discourse by bringing in China, and should point out that the prominence of the Babylonian sixty-year cycle in China at the time of the Han Dynasty evidently coincided with the prominence of the fish-tailed amphibious culture heroes Fuxi, Nü Gua, and the others illustrated in Figures 50 and 51 and discussed on p. 289ff, which also are presumably Babylonian in origin. We might assume, therefore, that there was some cultural diffusion whereby Han Dynasty China experienced influence by 'Chaldaean' traditions no later than the first century BC. On the other hand, much more ancient traditions of these things may simply have come into fashion in China at that time, as part of the Han Dynasty defining itself culturally. The Babylonian influence may well have been much earlier, as is thought to be the case with the general astronomical concepts of the Chinese, which are known to emanate from Babylonian sources. However, it would be too much of a digression to pursue that matter here. I refer readers to my book *The Genius of China* (also entitled in an earlier edition *China: Land of Discovery and Invention*), originally published in 1986 and based upon the researches of Joseph Needham, with whom I first visited China.

The cycle of sixty years also has associations with the crocodile, of which the Dogon say that the fifth part of the dismembered body of the sacrificed Nommo 'was transformed not into trees but into crocodiles which, since the time of the arrival of the Ark [Nommo's ship which descended to Earth], entered the ponds in pursuit of the Supervisors [the eight 'Monitor' Nommos who came to supervise humanity].'[21] This seems to be an oblique reference to the fact that the Nommos found the crocodiles troublesome, and that as they swam in rivers, the crocodiles were 'in pursuit of them'. In

Chapter One I have noted that the amphibious visitors seem to have constructed a huge artificial lake in Egypt, called by Herodotus Lake Moeris, and one reason for this may have been that the Nile was so infested with crocodiles (and hippopotami) that a 'secure base' was needed where the aliens would not continually be molested. The irony is, therefore, that after the departure of the aliens, it was at this very Lake Moeris (see below) where the crocodile was later elevated to sacred status. Despite being a nuisance to the amphibians, in the eyes of humans this other great watery creature achieved an association with them, especially after the aliens' departure, when only the crocodiles remained for people to see.

In his fascinating essay 'On Isis and Osiris', the first century AD writer Plutarch, who was a priest of Delphi in Greece, records sacred Egyptian traditions of the crocodile as follows: 'The crocodile, certainly, has acquired honour which is not devoid of a plausible reason, but he is declared to be a living representation of God, since he is the only creature without a tongue; for the Divine Word has no need of a voice . . . They say that the crocodile is the only animal living in the water which has a thin and transparent membrane extending down from his forehead to cover up his eyes, so that he can see without being seen; and this prerogative belongs also unto the First God. . . . They lay sixty eggs and hatch them in the same number of days, and those crocodiles that live longest live that number of years: the number sixty is the first of measures for such persons as concern themselves with the heavenly bodies.'[22] When Plutarch speaks of sacred mysteries he tends to be a bit obscure for reasons of piety, and this passage is no exception. However, it is clear that the cycle of sixty years was regarded by the Egyptians of Plutarch's time as 'the first of measures' relating to astronomy. And the crocodile was a symbol of it.

Herodotus (fifth century BC) is the one who records that the crocodile was especially sacred in Egypt in the vicinity of the Lake Moeris which (see my Chapter One) he insists was an artificial lake, and which I have pointed out seems to have been a watery base made for the visiting amphibious beings during their stay in Egypt. Herodotus says: 'The dwellers about Thebes and the lake Moeris deem them [crocodiles] to be very sacred. There, in every place one crocodile is kept, trained to be tame; they put ornaments of glass and gold on its ears and bracelets on its forefeet, provide for it special food and offerings, and give the creatures the best of treatment while they live; after death the crocodiles are embalmed and buried in sacred coffins . . . It is the only animal that has no tongue. Nor does it move the lower jaw. It is the only creature that brings the upper jaw down upon the lower.[23]

The irony of the crocodile as a religious Nommo-substitute is considerable, especially as it would seem that there was nothing a crocodile wanted more than a good juicy bite of a Nommo for its next meal. It is all the more remarkable that the Dogon have kept the real tradition intact and have recorded that the crocodiles in the ponds were *in pursuit of* the Nommos – a fact already wholly disregarded in Egypt 2,500 years ago! But by that date, as Herodotus has also recorded, the ancestors of the Dogon, the Garamantes, were far away in Libya, and were to take the real tradition with them through the sands of the Sahara to West Africa, where it would await our discovery. As for the association of the crocodile with the astronomical cycle of sixty years, it was a symbolic numerical correlation, as Plutarch has explained, but it also probably echoes an earlier association of that cycle with the amphibious aliens, a tradition also preserved by the Dogon despite all the ravages of time.

Notes

1. Wallis Budge, *Osiris and the Egyptian Resurrection*, op. cit., Vol. II, p. 67.
2. Ibid.
3. From his Scholia Commentary to Plato's *Gorgias*, translated by Thomas Taylor, and given by Taylor in a footnote to Apuleius's essay on the Doctrines of Plato, 'On Natural Philosophy', p. 333 in the book cited in next note.
4. Apuleius, *The Metamorphosis or Golden Ass and Philosophical Works*, trans. by Thomas Taylor, London, 1822. This book contains four of Apuleius's essays of which three are otherwise unobtainable in English translation; one is on 'The God of Socrates' and three are on the philosophy of Plato; the first of these three is relevant here; pp. 333–4. (The one on Socrates was also translated for Bohn's library.)
5. Higgins, Godfrey, *The Celtic Druids*, London, 1827.
6. Ibid., p. 240.
7. Ibid., p. 241.
8. The monument which Higgins calls Rolrich is now known as Rollright.
9. Higgins, op. cit, p. 244.
10. These figures come from Santillana and von Dechend, *Hamlet's Mill*, op. cit, and are found there opposite page 134 and opposite page 268.
11. Ibid., Appendix 23.
12. Griaule and Dieterlen, *Le Renard pâle*, op. cit., pp. 83–4.
13. See Note 11.
14. Ibid. These works of Kepler's are discussed by Santillana and von Dechend.
15. *Le Renard pâle*, p. 177.
16. Ibid., p. 185.
17. See Appendix I: 'A Sudanese Sirius System'.
18. See Note 11.
19. Chatley, Herbert, 'The Sixty-Year and Other Cycles', *China Journal*, Vol. XX, No. 3, March 1934. Unpaginated offprint of two pages' length.
20. Chatley, Herbert, 'The True Era of the Chinese Sixty-Year Cycle', *T'oung Pao*, Leiden, Vol. XXXIV, Parts 1–2, pp. 138–45.
21. Griaule, Marcel, and Dieterlen, Germaine, 'Le Harpe-Luth des Dogon', *Journal de la Société des Africainistes*, Tome 20, Fascicule 2, 1950, p. 212.
22. Plutarch, *Peri Isidos kai Osiridos* ('On Isis and Osiris'), translated by Frank Cole Babbit, in Plutarch's *Moralia*, Loeb Classical Library, Harvard University Press, U.S.A., Vol. V, 1962, pp. 173–5.
23. Herodotus, Book II, 68–9, translated by A. D. Godley, Loeb Classical Library, Harvard University Press, U.S.A., Vol. I, 1960, p. 357.

Appendix V

The Meaning of the E at Delphi

Plutarch wrote a fascinating essay entitled 'The E at Delphi',[1] actually in the form of a dialogue, featuring Plutarch himself and several other speakers. It is to be remembered that Plutarch was a high priest of Delphi, and he knew much and always sought to learn more about the nature and history of the oracles not only of Delphi but elsewhere as well. He was most interested of all in Delphi itself, for he was one of the two priests of Apollo there.

The central subject of the discussion is the letter E which was a prominent inscription at the Delphic shrine. (That is, the letter E was carved in stone quite on its own at Delphi and was a subject of much curious speculation to the classical Greeks, who retained no tradition of the meaning of the ancient inscription of this single letter – see Plate 21.) F. C. Babbitt, in his Introduction to the dialogue, says:[2]

Plutarch, in this essay on the E at Delphi, tells us that beside the well-known inscriptions at Delphi there was also a representation of the letter E, the fifth letter of the Greek alphabet. The Greek name for this letter was EI, and this diphthong, in addition to being used in Plutarch's time as the name of E (which denotes the number five), is the Greek word for 'if', and also the word for the second person singular of the verb 'to be' (thou art).

In searching for an explanation of the unexplainable it is only natural that the three meanings of EI ('five', 'if', 'thou art') should be examined to see if any hypothesis based on any one of them might possibly yield a rational explanation. ... Plutarch puts forward seven possible explanations of the letter. ... Attempts to explain the letter have been also made in modern times by Göttling ... and by Schultz ... Roscher ... C. Robert ... O. Lagercrantz ... W. N. Bates, in the *American Journal of Archaeology* xxix (1925), pp. 239–46, tries to show that the E had its origin in a Minoan character E ... later transferred to Delphi. Since the character was not understood, it, like other things at Delphi, came to be associated with Apollo. This character has been found on the old omphalos discovered in 1913 at Delphi in the temple of Apollo.

Interesting are the two coins reproduced in Imhoff-Blumer and P. Gardner, *A Numismatic Commentary on Pausanius*, plate X nos. xxii and xxiii (text p. 119), which show the E suspended between the middle columns of the temple. Learned scholars should note that the letter represented is E, not EI: therefore such explanations as are based on the true diphthong are presumably wrong.

The second explanation offered by Plutarch seems to me the correct one. This is how Plutarch suggests it:

> Ammonius smiled quietly, suspecting privately that Lamprias had been indulging in a mere opinion of his own and was fabricating history and tradition regarding a matter in which he could not be held to account. Someone else among those present said that all this was similar to the nonsense which the Chaldaean visitor had uttered a short time before: that there are seven vowels in the alphabet and seven stars that have an independent and unconstrained motion; that E is the second in order of the vowels from the beginning, and the sun the second planet after the moon, and that practically all the Greeks identify Apollo with the Sun.

The facts that Delphi is the second descending centre in the geodetic octave, and that it is symbolized by the second vowel E, would seem to go well together. The seven vowels (each corresponding to one of the oracle centres) were uttered in succession as the holy 'unspeakable' name of God by Egyptian priests. Demetrius of Phalerum, the student of Aristotle's Lyceum and who founded the famous great library of Alexandria when later in life he was exiled to Egypt, tells us in his surviving treatise *On Style*: 'In Egypt the priests sing hymns to the gods by uttering the seven vowels in succession, the sound of which produces as strong a musical impression on their hearers as if flute and lyre were used.'

In Chapter XVI of *The White Goddess*, Robert Graves discusses this too, and there quotes Demetrius. Graves also refers to an eight-letter version of the sacred name. It may be that if one wants to count the base oracle centre (which in musical analogy is the octave expression of the top centre) one should have an eight-letter version. This version of the name is:

JEHUOVAŌ.
Note that E is the second letter.

We are faced with archaeological evidence that the second vowel, E, was prominently associated with the second oracle centre in descending order. (See Plate 21.) And we know from Herodotus that Dodona, the top oracle centre, was said to be founded by Egyptian priestesses from Thebes in Egypt. We also know that certain Egyptian priests sang the seven vowels (or eight vowels, including an aspirate) in succession. We have already seen that the geodetic oracle centres seem to have an octave structure. And as this book went to press [in 1976] a discovery became known which demonstrated the existence of the heptatonic, diatonic musical scale in the ancient Near East. We may even make a presumption that the uttering of the seven vowels in succession may possibly have corresponded to the seven notes of the octave (but we may never know that for certain). And it is most important to emphasize that, however bizarre to us, the association of a vowel with an oracle centre is not our invention or surmise. The E may not only be read about in Plutarch but seen on ancient coins and on the omphalos stone itself (for both of which see Plate 21). And this association of the second vowel with Delphi has never been explained by anyone.

So granted all the above, what follows? If each oracle centre had a vowel associated with it, then the second vowel being associated with the second centre would seem to imply a corresponding arrangement for the other centres. And if that is the case, it would seem that the entire system would be associated with and actually comprise a geodetic spelling-out, over eight degrees of latitude, of the unspeakable holy name of God, known commonly to the Hebrews as 'Jehovah'.

It is most important that anyone intrigued by this possibility should keep a wary eye for any further evidence. We should be on the lookout for representations of or associations of other vowels at the other centres. These may already be known to specialists in the field or there may be evidence of this sort languishing unclassified and unexplained in the basement of some museum. Or this sort of evidence may come to light at any time in the future. One place to begin looking would, it seems to me, be with an examination of the omphalos stone from Delos, which is to be seen in Plates 15 and 18. Does this omphalos stone have a single letter inscribed on it similarly to the Delphi omphalos stone? And what of all the other omphalos stones, such as the one from the Temple of Amon in Egypt (see Plate 19). Are any of these well enough preserved to show a puzzling single hieroglyph of a vowel? I have not carried out any investigation of this sort myself at the present time.

In closing, it would seem that the E at Delphi must fall into some coherent system of the kind I suggest, and the explanation of the enigma must be connected with Plutarch's lightly advocated second explanation – that to do with E being the second vowel. (Babbitt's exclusion of the diphthong on the basis of the ancient coins to be seen in Plate 21 is therefore crucial and to my view conclusive.)

Notes

1. The dialogue 'The E at Delphi' is to be found in English in Volume V of Plutarch's *Moralia* (altogether 15 vols) published in the Loeb Classical Library series; London: William Heinemann Ltd., and U.S.A.: Harvard University Press. The volume first appeared in 1936, and the translation is by Frank Cole Babbitt. Other works of Plutarch in the same volume are 'Isis and Osiris', 'The Oracles at Delphi No Longer Given in Verse', and 'The Obsolescence of Oracles'.
2. Ibid. See Plate 21.

Appendix VI

Why the Hittites were at Hebron in Palestine

We read in Genesis 23:7 that 'Abraham stood up and then bowed low to the Hittites, the people of that country'. The only trouble about this is that, according to our extremely sound archaeological knowledge, there should not have been any Hittites in 'that country' – namely, at Hebron in Palestine. The Hittite conquests never extended that far south. So what do we do with this riddle?

In his book *The Hittites*, Professor Oliver Gurney has an entire section (pp. 59–62) entitled 'The Hittites in Palestine'. In it he says:

> We have now to deal with the paradoxical fact that, whereas the Hittites appear in the Old Testament as a Palestinian tribe, increasing knowledge of the history of the ancient people of Hatti has led us ever farther from Palestine, until their homeland has been discovered in the heart of the Anatolian plateau. Moreover, the preceding outline of Hittite history will have shown us that before the reign of Suppiluliumas there was no Hittite state south of the Taurus; that the Syrian vassal states of the Hittite Empire were confined to the area north of Kadesh on the Orontes; and that although Hittite armies reached Damascus, they never entered Palestine itself. Of the neo-Hittite states there was none south of Hamath, and the latter did not include any part of Palestine within its territories, being separated from it by the Aramean kingdom of Damascus.
>
> The presence of Hittites in Palestine before the Israelite conquest thus presents a curious problem. So far from explaining it, all our accumulated knowledge of the people of Hatti [the Hittites] has only made it more perplexing.

References in the Bible include Genesis 23 (entire), Genesis 26:9–11, 34–5; 27:46 (where Rebecca says to Isaac: 'I am weary to death of Hittite women! If Jacob marries a Hittite woman like those who live here, my life will not be worth living!'), and 36:1–3. Further crucial reference to the

Hittites appears in the Book of Numbers 13:29. There Moses is told by some men he had sent at the Lord's command to explore Hebron (and we are told in Numbers 13:22–3, that Hebron 'was built seven years before Zoan in Egypt' – which is a curious remark, implying a connection between Hebron and Egypt and also that there was something special at Hebron which could be described as 'built'), that at Hebron they had seen the Hittites.

We thus find clear evidence in books of the Bible for the Hittites residing in Palestine. And their settlements were specifically in the hills at Hebron. Gurney says: 'Who, then, were these Hittites of the Palestine hills? A very ingenious answer has been put forward by E. Forrer.' The gist of this is that, considerably before 1335 BC, some Hittites from the city of Kurustamma in the north-east of Anatolia had gone to Egypt, of which documentary evidence exists:

> However surprising it may seem, the text here quoted states explicitly that during the reign of Suppiluliumas some men from this obscure northern city entered the 'land of Egypt', a term which would include all territory under Egyptian rule. The text leaves the circumstances under which this occurred obscure, but the reference to the Weather-god of Hatti as the instigator of the move is in favour of a deliberate act of state rather than a flight of fugitives from the Hittite conquest, as suggested by Forrer. However that may be, we have here one certain instance of a group of Hittites (i.e., subjects of the King of Hatti) entering Egyptian territory, and the possibility of their having settled in the sparsely populated Palestinian hills is not to be ignored . . . (But) emigration of Anatolian Hittites to Palestine cannot have been a frequent occurrence. . . . (and) there is some hope that further excavation [of texts] among the archives of Boghazköy will bring enlightenment.

It should be pointed out that the reign of Suppiluliumas during which the above emigration took place covered the years 1380–1346 BC. It was to him that the widow of Tutankhamen, the Egyptian Queen Ankhesenamun, third daughter of Pharaoh Akhenaten, sent a plaintive letter asking for one of his sons to become her husband. He sent a son, but the son was ambushed on the way to Egypt and killed, probably by Hor-em-heb, who seized the throne of Egypt and forced Ankhesenamun to marry him in order to legitimize his usurpation. This is a sad story but does not really concern us here. I mention it merely to bring to life the chronology of the emigration to Hebron, and also because it demonstrates the close links possible at that time between the Hittites and Egypt. Those who wish to read the letter in full and follow up this interesting tale of personal tragedy are referred to *Ancient Near Eastern Texts* (ed. Pritchard, see Bibliography), pp. 319, 395.

However, the Hittite emigration in the reign of Suppiluliumas cannot have been the original Hittite settlement at Hebron. For if Abraham met Hittites when he arrived at Hebron, then there must have been Hittites there for several hundred years before the reign of Suppiluliumas which extended 1380–1346 BC. We learn from George Roux in his book *Ancient Iraq*, p.242: 'Abraham and his family came from Ur in Sumer to Hebron in Canaan, probably about 1850 BC, and there are good reasons for placing Joseph's migration to Egypt during the Hyksos period (1700–1580 BC).' Despite the fact that there can be a case made for Abraham's Ur being a different Ur, the main point is the date, for Abraham went to Hebron and met Hittites already there five hundred years before the emigration which Gurney mentions. Roux repeats his dating, and gives references, on page 215 of his book.

It is likely that, half a millennium after Abraham, the Hittite emigration of which we have proof during the reign of Suppiluliumas went to Egyptian territory, and quite probably to Hebron, to reinforce the Hittite community which had already been there for many centuries, but which was facing hard times. One has only to read the Amarna Letters in translation in *Ancient Near Eastern Texts* – vivid, compulsive, desperate documents – to know the anarchy into which the region of Palestine was plunged during this period. The prince of the Hebron region, Shuwardata, first fought the rapacious Apiru raiders who swarmed over the countryside and then joined them, rebelling against the Pharaoh before whom, in his correspondence, he had shortly before been 'bowing seven times and again seven times, both prone and supine'. But Egypt was weak, and Palestine degenerated into chaos. It is no wonder that during this period there was a Hittite migration to what was titular Egyptian territory. No Hittite settlement at Hebron could have felt itself entirely secure. But what was the reason for the Hittite settlement at Hebron in the first place?

In the light of our earlier elucidation of the geodetic oracle octaves, it seems clear that the presence of the Hittites at Hebron can be explained on religious grounds. For we know that Hebron was the 'base oracle' centre of the eastern geodetic oracle octave. The top centre of this same octave was Metsamor at Ararat, to the north and east of Hittite territory, and is probably the reason why the Hittites who migrated to 'Egyptian territory' during the reign of Suppiluliumas were from an obscure north-eastern city (because this was the closest Hittite region to Ararat). The area of Ararat was later to become the kingdom of Urartu, and we know that this kingdom and the Hittites were not altogether strangers, for we learn from Gurney, pp. 44–5: 'The North Syrian Hittite states . . . may have felt a certain racial or cultural affinity with Urartu . . .'

Since we have documentary evidence that it was a divine command which made the Hittites of the fourteenth century BC go to what we assume was possibly Hebron, we can see that they were obeying an oracular injunction. This is natural if their activity was connected with the oracle centres. Indeed, they could not have gone without a divine command on such exclusively divine and non-imperial business. Gurney may be quite right in saying that the journey was a deliberate act and not a flight of fugitives. It was as deliberate as the 'doves who flew to Dodona'.

We have distinct evidence that Hebron really did have an oracle centre, apart from its being on the same latitude as Behdet. To investigate this, we turn to *The White Goddess* by Robert Graves, where in Chapter IX he discusses Hebron a great deal.

> But Caleb . . . conveyed the Holy Spirit to Hebron when, in the time of Joshua, he ousted the Anakim from the shrine of Machpelah. Machpelah, an oracular cave cut from the rock, was the sepulchre of Abraham, and Caleb went there to consult his shade . . . it is likely that neither Isaac nor Jacob nor their 'wives' were at first associated with the cave. The story of its purchase from Ephron . . . and the . . . Hittites, is told in Genesis 23. Though late and much edited, this chapter seems to record a friendly arrangement between the devotees of the goddess Sarah, the Goddess of the tribe of Isaac, and their allies the devotees of the Goddess Heth (Hathor? Tethys?) who owned the shrine: Sarah was forced out of Beer-Lahai-Roi by another tribe and came to seek an asylum at nearby Hebron (p.162).

Graves states (p.164) that 'Abraham' was in fact a tribe, and that this tribe also came down from Armenia (vicinity of Ararat). He says: ' "Abraham" being in this sense the far-travelled tribe that came down into Palestine from Armenia at the close of the third millennium BC.' In fact, we must give some thought to 'the chosen people' – later known as Hebrews – being 'chosen' in the sense that they were particularly connected with tending an oracle centre or centres. Did Abraham go to Hebron for the same reasons that the Hittites did?

Graves says (p. 164):

> J. N. Schofield in his *Historical Background to the Bible* notes that to this day the people of Hebron have not forgiven David for moving his capital to Jerusalem ('Holy Salem') which they refer to as 'The New Jerusalem' as though Hebron were the authentic one. There is a record in the Talmud of a heretical sect of Jews, called Melchizedekians, who frequented Hebron to worship the body (consult the spirit?) of Adam which was buried in the cave of Machpelah.

In fact, these Melchizedekians, though considered heretics, may have been adherents of a purer undistorted form of worship. And it may be that David was the great perverter of Judaism by moving Holy Salem away from Hebron. Graves continues:

> For Adam, 'the red man', seems to have been the original oracular hero

of Machpelah; it is likely that Caleb consulted his shade not Abraham's, unless Adam and Abraham are titles of the same hero. Elias Levita, the fifteenth-century Hebrew commentator, records the tradition that the teraphim which Rachel stole from her father Laban were mummified oracular heads and that the head of Adam was among them. If he was right, the Genesis narrative refers to a seizure of the oracular shrine of Hebron by Saul's Benjaminites from the Calebites.

Caleb was an Edomite clan; which suggests the identification of Edom with Adam: they are the same word, meaning 'red'. But if Adam was really Edom, one would expect to find a tradition that the head of Esau, the ancestor of the Edomites, was also buried at Hebron; and this is, in fact, supplied by the Talmud ... that Esau's body was carried off for burial on Mount Seir by his sons; and that his head was buried at Hebron by Joseph.

Elsewhere (page 167) Graves says:

> It is possible that though the Calebites interpreted 'Adam' as the Semitic word Edom ('red') the original hero at Hebron was the Danaan Adamos or Adamastos, 'the Unconquerable', or 'the Inexorable', a Homeric epithet of Hades, borrowed from the Death Goddess his mother.

Graves says that according to the tradition (p.161): 'Hebron may be called the centre of the earth, from its position near the junction of two seas and the three ancient continents.' How similar this 'centre of the earth' epithet is to Delphi's, as 'the navel of the world'. All the main oracle centres were navel or *omphalos* centres of the earth. Hebron's description as such is what one would have predicted. The traditions of the creation of Adam at Hebron and of its being the site of the Garden of Eden, as Graves tells us in this chapter, make sense also when it is realized that Hebron was the base of the entire eastern geodetic octave of oracle centres. It was the eastern counterpart of Behdet itself.

Graves tells us at the beginning of Chapter Four of the later history of Hebron:

> A confederacy of mercantile tribes, called in Egypt, 'the People of the Sea' ... invaded Syria and Canaan, among them the Philistines, who captured the shrine of Hebron in southern Judea from the Edomite clan of Caleb; but the Calebites ('Dog-men'), allies of the Israelite tribe of Judah, recovered it about the same time. These borrowings were later harmonized in the Pentateuch with a body of Semitic, Indo-European and Asianic myth which composed the religious traditions of the mixed Israelite confederacy.

In closing, we should note with a minimum of surprise, that the guardian tribe of the shrine of Hebron, the Calebites, were 'Dog-men'. Dogs are guardians, and preserve the secrets of the Dog Star Sirius, particularly as expressed in the ancient geodetic oracle octaves.

As for the Hittites, they were at Hebron – and only at that specific place in Palestine – because of its oracle centre. That is why they were 'sent by divine command', centuries later, presumably to reinforce that very place against the dangers of a turbulent time when Egyptian control under Akhenaten had collapsed.

Appendix VII

The Dogon Stages of Initiation

The following description of the Dogon system of graduated initiation into the mysteries of tribal religion is taken from *Le Renard pâle* by Marcel Griaule and Germaine Dieterlen:

> The Dogon, who have classified everything, have established a layered hierarchy of their teachings they give to the initiates. Their knowledge is staggered in four degrees, that are, in the order of their importance, the *giri so*, the *benne so*, the *bolo so*, and the *so dayi*.
>
> The *giri so*, 'word at face value', is the first knowledge implying simple explanations where the mythical characters are often disguised, their adventures simplified and invented, and are not linked together. It has to do with invisible deeds, concerning the ordinary rituals and materials.
>
> The *benne so*, 'word on the side', includes 'the words in the *giri so*' and a thorough study of certain parts of the rites and representations. Their coordination only appears within the great divisions of learning which are not completely revealed.
>
> The *bolo so*, 'word from behind', completes the preceding learning, on the one hand, and on the other hand furnishes the syntheses that apply to a vaster whole. However, this stage does not yet include instruction in the truly secret parts of the tradition.
>
> The *so dayi*, 'clear word', concerns the edifice of knowledge in its ordered complexity.
>
> But initiation is not merely an accumulation of learning, nor even a philosophy, nor a way of thinking. It has an educational character, for it forms the individual, moulds him, as he assimilates the knowledge it imparts. It is more than that, because of its vital character; as it makes him understand the structure and system of the universe, it brings the initiate progressively towards a way of life which is as aware and complete as possible within his society, in the world, as he was conceived and created by God.
>
> Thus, a 'fourth dimension' is introduced into the life of the Dogon, peculiar to the myth and symbol which is as necessary to their existence as food and drink, in which they move with ease and flexibility, but also with

the deep sense of the immanent presence of the invisible thing they are invoking . . . at a given moment, for such and such a ceremony, they know to what sequence of the myth and to which connections (their) act belongs . . .

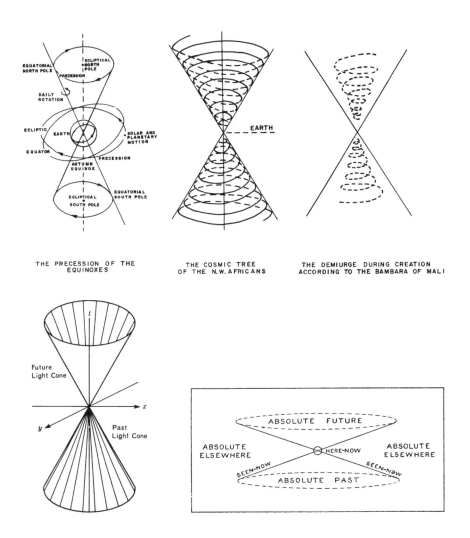

THE PRECESSION OF THE
EQUINOXES

THE COSMIC TREE
OF THE N.W. AFRICANS

THE DEMIURGE DURING CREATION
ACCORDING TO THE BAMBARA OF MALI

Figure 63. The precession of the equinoxes is a phenomenon whereby the Earth spins slowly on its axis like a top once every 25,920 years. It is for this reason that people speak of the 'coming Age of Aquarius', since every two thousand years or so, the constellation that rises just before the Sun on the first day of spring (the Spring Equinox, as it is called) shifts. And soon the constellation of Aquarius will do this, replacing the constellation of Pisces. An interesting comparison may be drawn of a modern diagram of the precession of the Earth and a diagram drawn by a neighbouring tribe of the Dogon showing the Earth in a similar configuration, complete with indications of spinning above and below. They call it the 'Cosmic Tree'. The Bambara Tribe of Mali, immediate neighbours and cousins of the Dogon, and whose culture is also based upon the secret Sirius Mystery knowledge, draw a similar diagram. For comparison I also give a scientific diagram showing 'light-cones' emanating from the Earth showing the restriction to our communication with the rest of the Universe imposed upon us by the finite velocity of light. (What this means is that if we send a signal to another star, because it cannot arrive instantaneously, its progress in time is depicted as travelling as a line on a cone rather than sticking out sideways as an instantaneous signal would have been shown.) And finally, as an extension of these concepts, a similar diagram of light-cones shows how they represent the only future and past we can know; the regions outside the cones which we cannot reach because our communications are not instantaneous are forever an 'absolute elsewhere'.

The latter two diagrams are given not because they have anything to do with the precession of the equinoxes, but because the African drawings may refer to light-cone concepts rather than to precession, especially as they are concerned with creation. Since creation is meant to have emanated from Sirius, unless there are instantaneous modes of communication in the 'Anubis Cell' (see Chapter One), such emanations would have had to travel no faster than the velocity of light, and would therefore be represented in a scientific diagram by a light cone. Consequently, the tribal drawings may preserve such knowledge. This information was left out of the original edition of *The Sirius Mystery* by the publisher, and I have restored it, as I think readers will find it interesting. Like so much else which concerns the advanced knowledge preserved by these tribes, it would repay much further and deeper investigation.

Appendix VIII

A Note about Freemasonry

Due to the fact that a garbled account of myself, Sirius and their connection with Freemasonry has appeared in a recent book and contains some inaccuracies, I thought it best to put a correct account on record, lest any false impressions be too widely circulated. I have a very friendly acquaintance with Christopher Knight and Robert Lomas, whose second book *The Second Messiah* (Century, London, 1997) contains nearly a page about me (p. 216). Unfortunately, Chris and Bob did not inform me that they intended to publish anything about me and did not show it to me beforehand. Because they remembered a conversation with me imperfectly, the account contains several inaccuracies. For instance, they believe that only if I became a 33° Mason myself could I have held the further conversations about Sirius with the man who was my grandfather's Masonic protege, and who became Lieutenant Grand Commander (second highest ranking, immediately under Supreme Grand Commander) of the Supreme Council of Freemasonry in Washington (which is also the Mother Supreme Council of the World). This is inaccurate; he only wanted me to become 3° to commence the conversations, for only then does one 'become a Mason'; going through the much higher degrees would, he said, be accelerated, but was not necessary to begin holding meaningful dialogue.

They also stated that I am a direct descendant of George Washington. As much as I admire old George, I have never claimed to be his descendant! My great-great-great grandfather John Leonard was at Washington's side for many years, and that is the person I mentioned to them. He was originally, as a very young man, a mounted dragoon under Major Bartholomaeus van Heer in 1776, along with his three brothers. The Leonard Brothers were exceptionally tall and phenomenally strong. They were excellent horsemen, and as a result of their background were among the handful of people fighting on the side of Washington who knew anything about being soldiers. They had one other advantage: they had grown up and had early military training in Hesse and were personally acquainted with some of the Hessian officers now fighting as mercenaries for the British, so that they could advise Washington on the personalities and tactics of his worst adversaries. The brothers were the sons of an English officer who had gone to Kassel in Hesse (called in those days

'Hesse-Cassel') as one of the commanders of the English expeditionary force sent to defend the Protestant cause under the Landgrave of Hesse against the assaults of the Austrians and other Catholics. Their parents appear to have died while the boys were youths, so instead of returning to England or Wales where their relations had iron mines in which they could hope for no personal share (being a younger branch of the Leonards of Herstmonceux Castle, who had originally opened iron mines in Sussex and were one of the few aristocratic families subsidizing their grand lifestyle by industry), the brothers made their way to America, where they had relations who had much earlier founded the first iron foundry in America (at Taunton, Massachusetts). They had an uncle, the Rev. Abiel Leonard, who happened to be the chaplain to a chap named George Washington in a spot of bother called the Revolutionary War. So they threw in their lot with their uncle. (A moving testimonial letter about the Rev. Abiel Leonard survives in George Washington's published correspondence, saying that he kept up everyone's spirits during the terrible winter at Valley Forge, and without his encouragement Washington might not have stuck it out.) Washington selected eight of van Heer's dragoons to be his personal life guard, to ride surrounding him when travelling and to act as his bodyguards at all times; four of these eight were the Leonard Brothers. They were the last soldiers to leave Washington's side, parting with him only on the day of his inauguration as President of the United States, when his status changed from General to President. After that they retired as soldiers, and they were the last American Revolutionary soldiers to do so. They received grants of land in the new territory of Ohio, as did many others who had fought in the War.

Since *The Sirius Mystery* is concerned with teeth and with Greek heroes, I cannot refrain from mentioning a peculiarity of John Leonard which he shared with the mythological figure of Hercules. Hercules was reputed to have had, and John Leonard certainly had, a third set of teeth. Growing a third set of teeth in ancient times was meant to be a sign of a supernatural hero. As Edward Samson the dental historian has written: '. . . it is probably the tales of Hercules, half-god, half-man, which laid the foundation of the idea that men of more than usual strength would grow more than the usual two sets of teeth.'[1] John Leonard was, coincidentally, abnormally large and physically strong, according to the information about him which survived within the family. So perhaps there is a very rare genetic syndrome – whereby a man of abnormal size and strength with a third set of teeth occurs in the population; this could be part of the rational background to the lore concerning Hercules and Gilgamesh ('The hero, his teeth are the teeth of a dragon' as we have seen on p. 119 from a Sumerian account). My forebear was, according to the family account, very depressed when his teeth starting falling out when he was in late middle age. But everyone was amazed when they were replaced by a completely new set! Dentists of whom I have enquired speculate that this happens to approximately one person out of every hundred million or so, being one of the rarest phenomena in the lore of human anatomy. In fact it seems to be much rarer than that, probably by a factor of ten or more. The irony regarding John Leonard is complete when we recall that George Washington's notoriously square jaw was not anatomically natural either but is known to have been the result of wearing a remarkable complete set of wooden false teeth – which still survive, apparently. But so much for teeth and heroic figures!

I am certain that the Leonard Brothers must have taken part in Masonic lodge meetings with George Washington, if only due to the fact that by virtue of their jobs they could not leave his side for years on end. Whether they were Masons before they came to America is something we will never know. However, my forebear's male descendants for two generations were, I believe, *all* senior Masons and Masters of Lodges in Pennsylvania and Ohio, where he settled after Washington's inauguration. Masonic comradeship appears to have been involved also in the close personal friendship between my forebear's (John Leonard's) grandson, George Washington Leonard, and Jefferson Davis, the President of the Confederate States of America, who was also a distant cousin of ours by marriage (through his wife and the Agnews).*

Meanwhile, by a bizarre coincidence, a discontented Jew named Adam Mond and his equally discontented Christian wife Catherine Emmert left Kassel in Hesse for America in the 1830s to escape religious bigotry, where their son ended up in Ohio married to John Leonard's granddaughter. They were my great-grandparents. Their families had lived in the same German city, presumably unknown to one another, and had to travel to Ohio on the other side of the world to meet and marry. The Monds are well known in Britain, as Adam Mond's nephew settled in England and with his son Alfred (later Lord Melchett) founded the company ICI (Imperial Chemical Industries). The Monds changed their name in America to Miller to avoid anti-Semitism, as they settled in the most German and most anti-Semitic city in the United States at that time, Cincinnati. Now, this great-grandfather was a 32° Mason ('Sublime Prince of the Royal Secret', to use the official title). (And this great-grandmother was not content merely to be a Mason's wife; she was a pioneer in female Freemasonry, and she founded a lodge of her own for women (in America female Masonry is called The Order of the Eastern Star).

Meanwhile *another* family, the Temples, entered the scene, and they

---

* Since Abraham Lincoln's stepmother, a Johnston, was a distant relation of the Temples, a curiosity of history which might be mentioned is that I am one of perhaps half a dozen people alive who has connections by marriage with the presidents of the two opposing sides of the Civil War, between whom there are no other personal links.

were all senior Masons as well, including my great-grandfather and his three brothers. All of my great-great-uncles and great-uncles of all these families were Masters of their lodges, several of them were 32° Masons, my Grandmother Temple was also Matron of her own (Eastern Star) lodge, and for good measure my mother was a member of Eastern Star although not very active. Another great-uncle, Charles Kitts, was a 32° Mason, and my great-aunt Sallie Miller Kitts was also Matron of her lodge. I am also descended from the Kyle family (including a Colonel under George Washington), and they were all senior Masons as well.

Rarely has anyone been born into such a welter of family Freemasonry. I believe that amongst my immediate relations, there must have been at least a dozen 32° Masons, and at least thirty Masters and Matrons of lodges. And it is certainly true to say, as Knight and Lomas did, that my family have been prominent Masons for more than 200 years. In my dinner speech after my own initiation to the third degree I pointed out that the members of my family who had been Masons would, if they could all be called back to life again, exceed in number the large body of men present at the dinner.

But to return more particularly to the story told by Knight and Lomas and how it relates to *The Sirius Mystery*. The most important Mason in my family from my point of view was my grandfather, who was also called Robert Temple. He was a 32° Mason and so highly respected in Masonry that he was asked to become a 33° Mason, which is the highest degree possible (called a Grand Inspector-General). This involves administration of the entire Movement in America as well as most of the world from the base called The Supreme Council and Mother Supreme Council of the World, at 1733 Sixteenth Street, NW, Washington, DC. However, he had to decline this invitation because it takes up so much time and in those days was also extremely expensive, and he had lost his money in the Great Depression. But he sponsored into Freemasonry a young man whom he liked very much called Ted Webber. And Ted Webber went on to become a very active and important 33° Mason, and a close friend and colleague of the Sovereign Grand Commander Henry Clausen, as well as of those other prominent 33° Masons, President Gerald Ford and American Astronaut Colonel 'Buzz' Aldrin, who carried a Scottish Rite flag to the Moon, emphasizing the interest the highest level of Freemasonry takes in worlds beyond our own.

So it was Charles E. ('Ted') Webber, not an elderly relative, who approached me about *The Sirius Mystery*. Because I had moved to England, I did not see Ted as an adult until I made a visit to Virginia when I was in my thirties. Apart from my mother, all of my Masonic relatives were dead by then or were cousins whom I never saw. Ted knew that I had no obvious route into Masonry and did what Masons are not supposed to do, actually recruited me. Masons are only supposed to join if they seek to do so, never be persuaded. Although he felt 'fraternal loyalty' (to use Masonic terms) towards me, his reason was not sentimental but practical. He said quietly to me: '*We* are very interested in your book *The Sirius Mystery*. We realize you have written this without any knowledge of the traditions of Masonry, and you may not be aware of this, but you have made some discoveries which relate to the most central Masonic traditions at a high level, including some things that none of us ever knew. We would very much like to get you to exchange some ideas and research with some of the people in our headquarters. But unfortunately because you are not a Mason we cannot discuss any of these matters with you, as it is forbidden.' I asked him what sort of connection there was and he did mention specifically that it was my work on ancient Egypt, on Isis and Osiris, and the ancient traditions of the star Sirius.

Ted asked me if I would like to become a Mason, and if so, he would arrange it immediately. 'After you pass through what we call the three degrees, which is the basic initiation, you become an official Mason, and then we will be able to talk with you about these things, which we cannot do until then.' So, out of curiosity and a vague family sentimentality, and because I liked Ted so much, I agreed reluctantly to become a Mason, despite the fact that it was against my nature to want to be part of a secret society. I would never have sought it on my own initiative.

Ted wrote to Commander M. B. S. Higham, RN, Grand Secretary of the Grand Lodge of England in London on 23 August 1984, saying 'I have known the Temple family for more than fifty years. They are very loyal American citizens. Robert has been living in England for a number of years and has published a number of books. I will appreciate it very much if you will have some of your brethren get in touch with him . . .' He requested that I be admitted immediately as a candidate for initiation at the lodge nearest to me, without any sponsor. I believe this was practically unprecedented, and well might one imagine the astonishment of the local lodge who contacted me and said they had had a request for my admission from Brother Higham – a man whose name is known from Masonic circulars but no one ever seems to meet him.

It takes some time to go through the three separate initiation ceremonies called the three degrees, as several months have to elapse between each one. It was a year and a half or two years before I completed this. At the end, I was given a certificate pronouncing me a 'Master Mason', which sounds a very grand term but merely means you have gone through the basic initiations. In Masonic correspondence, I can now sign myself 'Robert Temple, 3°', by way of identifying my status, if corresponding with, say, a really important Mason or making clear I am not still just a candidate. I discovered that the vast majority of Masons know nothing whatever of the higher degrees of Masonry, and are never invited to attain to them. Some vaguely know that what are called 'Mark Masons' – a separate order within the movement where, I was told, a great deal of beer-drinking takes place – is also a fourth degree. But few Masons seem to be intellectuals pursuing ancient mysteries – most of them seem content with jolly dinners, collections for charity, and fraternizing with one another in a hearty manner. By the time I had become eligible for conversation on 'Sirius' matters, Ted was pretty aged and I never returned to Virginia. So no further discussions on these issues ever happened. Ted died, a pillar of his community and of American and World Scottish Rite Freemasonry, noted for his rectitude and kindliness. And that was that. I haven't been to any further lodge meetings.

Knight and Lomas have done a good job of demonstrating what many people including myself had long assumed, that Freemasonry is directly descended from, and is a continuation of, the Knights Templar. Although the Knights Templar were suppressed in England and France, they continued in Scotland (hence 'the Scottish Rite'; manuscript records of sixteenth-century Scottish lodge meetings survive) and by the seventeenth-century spread back into England again. English Freemasonry likes to pretend that the Masonic Movement was founded in 1717, but that can be proved to be complete nonsense.

As for the Sirius Mystery and Freemasonry, there are some further speculations. After the publication of my book, various people wrote to me and asked me whether I knew the writings of Alice Bailey, who produced many volumes of mystical works supposedly inspired by 'Higher Beings', communicated to her in trance. Much of what she wrote concerned a kind of cosmic Freemasonry. I had no familiarity with this material but tried to look into it. My friend, the late Sir John Sinclair, Bart., had met Alice Bailey as a child and was involved in her literary estate through something called the Lucis Trust. He attempted to search for Sirius references for me. I discovered that Miss Bailey had maintained that 'the Great White Lodge' of Freemasonry was based at the Sirius System, and that it is always beaming helpful rays to the poor people of Earth who wallow in appalling ignorance, violence, and oppression. We earthlings are looked upon as a dangerous lot, and the Sirians have tried hard to civilize us without much success. Freemasonry is meant to be one of their civilizing forces here. (Of course the corrupt Masonic lodges such as the P-2 of Italy would form no part of this.) Amongst material handed to me by John before he died, not all of it by Alice Bailey, and much of it odd photocopied pages without proper referencing information, I find comments such as these:

Each star in the heavens is a solar system with a light-producing sun and revolving planets. Our solar system in which our Earth exists is one of them. There are millions of stars but, among them all, only the star Sirius has a direct link with the Earth and with humanity. Much was known to the Ancients about Sirius, now largely lost but recoverable.

... Masonic tradition has it that the first three degrees of our Blue Lodge [I haven't the faintest idea what the Blue Lodge is] are equivalent to the first degree of Freemasonry on the star Sirius. Pondering upon the implications of this statement is fascinating because it lifts the whole concept of Masonry as a spiritual quest on to a higher plane than ever known before. It gives meaning and depth to the question: Why Masonry? It will be no detriment to Masonry if we use the 'as if' technique of philosophy which does not hesitate to deal with that which is as yet unproven. More Masons are asking more fundamental questions about Masonry these days ... Among such questions is: Where did Masonry originate? Because the star Sirius is older than the Earth, Masonry could have existed there long before our Earth Masonry began. By implication there is human life on Sirius ... Our solar system receives energy from three main sources. There are three great waves of energy which sweep cyclically through our solar system, one of which comes from Sirius.

There are seven paths of progress open to man when he has learned all that human evolution on Earth can teach him. One is the path to Sirius. He arrives there in consciousness as a perfected human being. It follows that there is therefore a type of life on Sirius which includes the essential of human life on Earth. This includes Masonry and he finds that great spiritual fraternity already there. Life on Sirius is therefore the destiny of the majority of humanity who then, if they are Masons, continue as Masons. ... Great as Masonry has been in the past, it has before it a still more glorious and useful future as it moves from Speculative to Spiritual Masonry. That inevitable change is already dimly seen. It will be more important than the change from Operative to Speculative Masonry. It is towards this end that Masonic Research should direct its efforts.

I don't know whether Alice Bailey herself actually wrote that. But she certainly wrote the following:

One great fact to be borne in mind is that the initiations of the planet or of the solar system are but the preparatory initiations of admission into the greater Lodge on Sirius. ... The first four initiations of the solar system correspond to the four 'initiations of the Threshold', prior to the first cosmic initiation. The fifth initiation corresponds to the first cosmic initiation, that of 'entered apprentice' in Masonry: and makes a Master an 'entered apprentice' of the Lodge on Sirius. The sixth initiation is analogous to the second degree in Masonry, whilst the seventh initiation makes the Adept a Master Mason of the Brotherhood on Sirius.

A Master, therefore, is one who has taken the seventh planetary initiation, the fifth solar initiation, and the first Sirian or cosmic initiation.[2]

Alice Bailey also said quite explicitly: '... in the secret of the sun Sirius are hidden the facts of our cosmic evolution, and incidentally, therefore, of our solar system.'[3] This might almost serve as a motto for my own book! And yet these insights reached Miss Bailey by means of some strange 'automatic writing' which she apparently produced, like someone in trance. And I only found out about it after I worked my own way along what might be called by the Hindus 'the path of knowledge'; Miss Bailey seems to have taken some kind of short-cut.

In the light of this information, perhaps the interest shown by one of the leaders of worldwide Masonry in my research can readily be understood. Whether it is true is not the point, the point is that it is claimed to be true; thus it means that mystical Masons would naturally take an interest in my findings. It is ironical that all of this was in print while I was writing my book and I knew nothing whatever about it. I still don't know that much about it, but I thought I at least ought to mention it.

Notes
1. Samson, Edward, *The Immortal Tooth*, John Lane The Bodley Head, London, 1939, pp.188–93. Samson points out that the rarity of cases of three sets of teeth is such that it is one of the great enigmas, and dentists are still trying to find a modern example in order to be able to study what it is that is really happening when this takes place. With regard to my forebear, I must stress that he grew a complete third set after the second fell out, and therefore the third set was not a survival of 'baby teeth' coming to the fore or instances of tumours or anything of that kind. I only wish he were alive today so that he could be x-rayed and properly studied!
2. Bailey, Alice A., *Initiation, Human and Solar*, Lucis Publishing Company, New York, and Lucis Press, England, no date given, pp 17–18.
3. Ibid., p.168.

Bibliography

Aitken, Robert G. *The Binary Stars*, Dover Publications, New York, 1964.

Allen, C. W. *Astrophysical Quantities*, 3rd edition, Athlone Press, London, 1973.

Allen, Herbert J., trans. and commentator, 'Ssuma Ch'ien's Historical Records', in *Journal of the Royal Asiatic Society*, London, April 1894–July 1895.

Allen, Richard Hinckley. *Star Names, Their Lore and Meaning* (formerly titled *Star-Names and Their Meanings*), Dover Publications, New York, 1963.

Anscombe, G. E. M., trans. See Proclus.

Apollonius of Rhodes (Apollonius Rhodius). *The Voyage of Argo* (*Argonautica*), Penguin Books, London, 1969, trans. by E. V. Rieu.

Apuleius (Lucius Apuleius of Madaura). *The Metamorphosis or Golden Ass and Philosophical Works*, trans. by Thomas Taylor, London, 1822. Contains 'The God of Socrates' and three essays on Plato.

The Works of Apuleius comprising the Metamorphoses, or Golden Ass, The God of Socrates, The Florida, and His Defence, or a Discourse on Magic, trans. apparently anonymous, Bohn's Classical Library, London, 1878.

Aratus (Aratos) of Soli. *Phaenomena*, trans. by G. R. Mair, in Vol. No. 129, *Callimachus Hymns and Epigrams, Lycophron, Aratus*, of Loeb Library series, Heinemann, London, and Harvard University Press, America, 1969.

Armstrong, A. H., ed. *The Cambridge History of Later Greek & Early Mediaeval Philosophy*, Cambridge University Press, 1970.

Asher, D. J. and Clube, S. V. M. 'An Extraterrestrial Influence during the Current Glacial-Interglacial', *Quarterly Journal of The Royal Astronomical Society*, Vol. 34, No. 4, December 1993.

Asimov, Isaac. *The Universe*, Allen Lane, the Penguin Press, London, 1967.

Asimov, Isaac, and Dole, Stephen H. *Planets for Man*, Methuen, London, 1964.

Aubrey, John. *Brief Lives*, ed. by Oliver Lawson Dick, Penguin, London, 1972.

Babbitt, Frank Cole, trans. See Plutarch.

Bailey, Alice A. *Initiation, Human and Solar*, Lucis Publishing Company, New York, and Lucis Press, England, no date given.

Baize, Dr P. *Le Compagnon de Sirius*, Bull. de la Société Astronomique France, 1931, 383–4.

Barbera, André. *The Euclidean Division of the Canon: Greek and Latin Sources*, University of Nebraska Press, USA, 1991.

Bauval, Robert, and Gilbert, Adrian. *The Orion Mystery*, Heinemann, London, 1994.

Beer, A., Ho Ping-Yü, Lu Gwei-Djen, Needham, J., Pulleyblank, E. G., and Thompson, G. I. 'An 8th-Century Meridian Line: I-Hsing's Chain of Gnomons and the Pre-History of the Metric System', *Vistas in Astronomy*, Pergamon Press, Oxford, etc., Vol. 4, 1964.

Benardete, Seth. *Herodotean Inquiries*, Martinus Nijhoff, The Hague, 1969.

Benest, Daniel and Duvent, J. L. 'Is Sirius a Triple Star?', *Astronomy and Astrophysics*, Vol. 299, 1995.

Berossus (Berossos, Berosus, etc.). *The Chaldaean History* (*The Babylonian History*), surviving fragments of which in Greek and English are in Cory's *Ancient Fragments*, for which see Cory; surviving fragments in English are published as Appendix III in this book.

Berry, Adrian. *The Next Ten Thousand Years*, Jonathan Cape, London, 1974.

Bibby, Geoffrey, *Looking for Dilmun*, Collins, London, 1970.

Bodde, Derk. 'Myths of Ancient China', in Samuel Noah Kramer, ed., *Mythologies of the Ancient World*, Anchor Books, New York, 1961.

Bonwick, James. *Pyramid Facts and Fancies*, Kegan Paul, London, 1877.

Booker, Christopher. *The Neophiliacs*, Fontana/Collins, London, 1970.

Bowra, C. M., trans. See Pindar.

Bracewell, Dr R. N. 'Radio Signals from Other Planets', 'Life in the Galaxy', 'Communications from Superior Galactic Communities'; in *Interstellar Communication*; see Cameron, Dr A. G. W.

Budge, see Wallis Budge.

Burney, Charles, and Lang, David Marshall. *The Peoples of the Hills, Ancient Ararat and Caucasus*, Weidenfeld & Nicolson, London, 1971.

Burkill, H. M. *The Useful Plants of West Tropical Africa*, Edition 2, Vol. 2, Royal Botanic Gardens, Kew, UK, 1994.

Burkill, I. H., *Dictionary of Economic Products of the Malay Peninsula*, 2 vols, London, 1935.

Burrow, Thomas, *The Sanskrit Language*, Faber and Faber, London, 1955.

Callimachus. *Hymns*, trans. by A. W. Mair, in *Callimachus Hymns and Epigrams, Lycophron, Aratus*, Vol. No. 129, Loeb Library series, Heinemann, London, Harvard University Press, America, 1969.

Calvin, Dr Melvin. 'Chemical Evolution', in *Interstellar Communication*; see Cameron, Dr A. G. W.

Cameron, Dr A. G. W., ed. and contrib. *Interstellar Communications*, W. A. Benjamin, New York, 1963. Contribs. to vol.: 'The History of Our Galaxy', 'The Origin of the Solar System', 'The Early Development of the Earth', 'Stellar Life Zones', 'Future Research on Interstellar Communication'.

Caton, Dr 'Delphi', 'Delos', in *Aegean Civilizations*; see Lunn, Sir Henry.

Chaldaean Oracles. See Mead, G. R. S.

   Also: *The Chaldaick Oracles of Zoroaster and His Followers* (with the expositions of Pletho and Psellus) by Thomas Stanley, London, 1661.

   Also: 'Chaldaean Oracles', etc., in *Collectanea* of Thomas Taylor, London, 1806.

Chang Ping-leung. 'A Study of the Flood Myth of the Yao People: a Comparative Approach', in *Essays in Commemoration of the Golden Jubilee of the Fung Ping Shan Library (1932–1982)*, Hong Kong, 1982.

Chatley, Herbert. 'The Sixty-Year and Other Cycles', *China Journal*, Vol. XX, No. 3, March 1934.

   'The True Era of the Chinese Sixty-Year Cycle', *T'oung Pao*, Leiden, Vol. XXXIV, Parts 1–2.

Clarke, Arthur C. *The Coming of the Space Age* (ed.), Gollancz, London, 1967.

   Profiles of the Future, Pan Books, London, 1962.

   The Promise of Space, Hodder and Stoughton, London, 1968.

   Report on Planet Three and Other Speculations, Corgi Books, London, 1973.

   Voices from the Sky, Previews of the Coming Space Age, Gollancz, London, 1966.

Condon, Dr Edward. *Scientific Study of Unidentified Flying Objects* (with introduction by Walter Sullivan), Bantam Books, New York, 1968.

Copernicus, Nicolaus. 'On the Revolutions of the Heavenly Spheres' trans. by C. G. Wallis, in *Ptolomy, Copernicus, Kepler*, Vol. 16 of *Great Books of the Western World* series, pub. by Encyclopaedia Britannica, Chicago, London, Toronto, 1952.

Cook, Arthur Bernard, *Zeus: A Study in Ancient Religion*, Cambridge University Press, 5 vols., 1914–1940.

Cory, I. P. *The Ancient Fragments*, London, 1828 (first edition). See also Berossus; see Appendix III; see Index. Two later editions were published in London, 1832 and 1876. Each of the three editions differs considerably from the others in the content of the volume.

Cramp, Leonard G. *A Piece for a Jigsaw*, Somerton Publishing Company, Ltd., Newport Road, Cowes, Isle of Wight, England, 1967.

Crocker, Dr Richard L., and Kilmer, Dr Anne. Letter to *The Times*, London, 15 April 1974. Article about their discoveries in *The Times*, 7 March 1974.

Crombie, A. C. *Augustine to Galileo*, 2 vols, Penguin Books, London, 1959.

Daily Telegraph, London: 3 July 1990: 'Legend Lives on as Surveys Find Dugong Is Flourishing'.
  28 January 1991: '"Mermaid" Beast Faces Extinction in Dead Sea of Oil'.
Däniken. See von Däniken
Daremberg, Charles Victor, and Saglio, Edmond, *Dictionnaire des Antiquitiés Grecques et Romaines*, Librairie Hachette, Paris, 9 vols, 1873–1919.
Dechend. See von Dechend.
Demarest, Kenneth. 'The Winged Power' in *Consciousness and Reality*; see Young, Arthur M.
Dieterlen, Germaine. See Griaule, Marcel.
Diodorus Siculus. *The Library of History*, Loeb Classical Library, Harvard University Press.
Diogenes Laertius. *Lives of Eminent Philosophers*, trans. by R. D. Hicks, 2 vols, Vols. Nos. 184, 185, of Loeb Library series, Heinemann, London, and Harvard University Press, 1966.
Dittrich, E. 'Woher das Epitheton "rot" fur Sirius stammt' ('Where the Epithet "Red" for Sirius Originated'), *Astronomische Nachrichten*, Number 5542, 1927.
Dodds, E. R., trans. See Proclus.
Drake, Dr Frank D. *Intelligent Life in Space*, Macmillan, New York, and London, 1962.
  'How Can We Detect Radio Transmissions from Distant Planetary Systems?' and 'Project Ozma' in *Interstellar Communication*; see Cameron, A. G. W.
Drar, Mohammed, and Täckholm, Vivi. 'Flora of Egypt', Vol. III, *Bulletin of the Faculty of Science*, No. 30, Cairo University Faculty of Science, Cairo University Press, 1954. Contains reference to Burkill, I.
Dudley, D. R., ed. See *Penguin Companion to Literature.*
Dufeu, A. *Découverte de l'Age et de la Véritable Destination des Quatre Pyramides de Gizeh, Principalement de la Grande Pyramide*, Paris, 1873.
Dyson, Verne. *Forgotten Tales of Ancient China*, Shanghai, 1927.

Eddington, Sir Arthur. *New Pathways in Science: Messenger Lectures 1934*, Cambridge University Press, 1935.
Edward, I. E. S. *The Pyramids of Egypt*, revised edition, Viking, London, 1986.
Emery, Dr Walter Bryan. *Archaic Egypt*, Penguin Books, London, 1972.
Encyclopaedia of Mythology; see Larousse.
Epic of Gilgamesh. trans. by Alexander Heidel, *The Gilgamesh Epic and Old Testament Parallels*, University of Chicago Press, 1970.

trans. By Kramer, S. N. (Sumerian fragments) and Speiser, E. A. (Akkadian/Babylonian main text) in *Ancient Near Eastern Texts* (1955); see Pritchard. Also trans. by Grayson, A. K., successor to the late Dr Speiser, in *Supplement* vol. (1969); see Pritchard.

The above are the only full-scale English translations of the *Epic of Gilgamesh* for scholarly use, but are hopelessly out of date.

See also Temple, Robert K. G. (My translation contains all the material to 1991, including the Elamite fragments.)

Epictetus. See Simplicius.

Eriugena, Iohannis Scottus. *Periphyseon (De Divisione Naturae)*, Book I, ed. and trans. by L. P. Sheldon-Williams, with Ludwig Beiler, The Dublin Institute for Advanced Studies, Dublin, 1968.

Eiselen, Frederick Carl. *Sidon: A Study in Oriental History*, Columbia University Press, New York, 1907. The entire book is about the history and culture of the city of Sidon, one of my proposed oracle centres.

Euclid. See Proclus.

Eunapius (of Sardis). *Lives of the Philosophers and Sophists*, trans. by Wright, Wilmer Cave. In Vol. No. 134, *Philostratus and Eunapius*, of the Loeb Library series, Heinemann, London, Harvard University Press, 1961.

Fage, J. D. *A History of West Africa, An Introductory Survey*, Cambridge University Press, 1969.

Fairservis, Walter A., Jr. *The Ancient Kingdoms of the Nile*, Mentor Books, New York, 1962.

Findlay, J. N. *Plato: the Written and Unwritten Doctrines*, Routledge and Kegan Paul, London, 1974.

Forde, Daryll, ed. *African Worlds*, Oxford University Press, 1954. (Contains chapter on Dogon with *arche* mistranslated 'arch' instead of 'ark'. Written by Griaule and Dieterlen.)

Frankfort, Henri. *Ancient Egyptian Religion*, Harper Torchbooks, New York, 1961.
Cylinder Seals, 1939.
Stratified Cylinder Seals from the Diyala Region, Volume 72, University of Chicago Oriental Institute Publications, 1955.

Galpin, Canon Francis W. *Music of the Sumerians, Babylonians, and Assyrians*, Cambridge University Press, 1937.
(See also *The Times*, London, 14 March 1974, letters column for letter from Canon Galpin's son Brian Galpin on same subject.)

Gardner, P. See Imhooff-Blumer.

Garstang, John. *The Syrian Goddess* trans. by Professor Herbert A. Strong of *De Dea Syria* of Lucian with a Life of Lucian, ed. with notes and introduction by Garstang, London, 1913.

Gaster, Theodor H. *Thespis; Ritual, Myth and Drama in the Ancient Near*

East, Harper & Row, New York, 1966 (Harper Torchbook).

Gilgamesh, Epic of. See *Epic of Gilgamesh*.

Goodwin, William W., trans. See Plutarch.

Gordon, Cyrus. 'Beltwrestling', *Journal of Near Eastern Studies*, Vol. 7.

    The Common Background of Greek and Hebrew Civilizations, (previous title *Before the Bible*), W. W. Norton & Company, New York, 1965.

    Forgotten Scripts, Penguin Books, London, 1971.

Gottschalk, H. B. *Heraclides of Pontus*, Oxford University Press, 1980.

Gow, The Rev. Dr J. 'Oracles' in *Aegean Civilizations*; see Lunn, Sir Henry.

Grant, Frederick C. *Hellenistic Religions*, Library of Liberal Arts, Bobbs-Merrill, New York, 1953. This important book is a compendium of source material in translation. It includes four hymns by Proclus, texts of oracles from Dodona, Egyptian material, etc.

Graves, Robert, *The Crane Bag and other Disputed Subjects*, Cassell, London, 1970.

    The Greek Myths, 2 vols, Penguin Books, London, 1969–71.

    The White Goddess, Vintage Books, New York, undated. Originally published 1948.

Grayson, A. K. See *Epic of Gilgamesh*.

Greenhill, Sir George. 'Astronomy and Navigation in the Odyssey' in *Aegean Civilizations*; see Lunn, Sir Henry.

Griaule, Marcel, and Dieterlen, Germaine. *Le Renard pâle* ('*The Pale Fox*'), Tome I, Fascicule 1; Institut d'Ethnologie, Musée de l'Homme, Palais de Chaillot, Place du Trocadero, Paris 16ᵉ (75016 Paris), 1965. 544 pp.

    'Le Harpe-Luth des Dogons', *Journal de la Société des Africainistes*, Tome 20, Fascicule 2, 1950, pp. 206–227.

    'Un Système Soudanais de Sirius', *Journal de la Société des Africainistes*. Tome XX, Fascicule 2, 1950, pp. 273-94. This article is published in translation in its entirety in Appendix I of this book, and accompanied with diagrams.

Griffith, F. *Stories of the High Priests of Memphis*, Oxford, 1900.

de Groot, J. J. M. *The Religious System of China*, Taipei reprint, 1976, Vol. V.

Gurney, O. R. *The Hittites*, Penguin Books, London, 1966.

Guthrie, W. K. C. *The Greeks and Their Gods*, Beacon Press, Boston, 1961.

Hallet, Jean-Pierre. *Pygmy Kitabu*, Random House, New York, 1973.

Hardie, Colin, trans. See Kepler.

Harrell, James M. 'The Spinx Controversy: another Look at the Geological Evidence', *KMT*, Vol. 5 No. 2, Summer, 1994.

Harris, Rendel. 'Apollo at the Back of the North Wind', *The Journal of Hellenic Studies*, London, Vol. XLV, 1925.

Hawkins, Gerald. *Beyond Stonehenge*, Harper & Row, New York, 1973. Particularly interesting is the account of the rare spider drawn on the Nazca sand: pp. 143–5.

Hébert-Stevens, François; Jahan, Raoul; and Rambach, Pierre. *Expedition Tortoise*, Thames and Hudson, London, 1957.

Heidel, Alexander. See *Epic of Gilgamesh.*
    The Babylonian Genesis, University of Chicago Press, 1965.

Henrard, J. *Monograph of the Genus Digitaria*, University of Leiden Press, Leiden, 1950.

Hermes. (*Hermetica. Hermetic Writings*, etc.) *Thrice-Greatest Hermes*, ed., trans., and comm. by G. R. S. Mead, 3 vols, John Watkins, London, 1964. Contains entire surviving *Hermetica* and fragments in English. In this work the term 'Trismegistic' is used to describe the writings.

Herodotus (Herodotos). *The Histories*, trans. by Aubrey de Sélincourt, Penguin Books, London, 1971.
    translated by A. D. Godley, Loeb Classical Library, Harvard University Press, 4 vols, 1960.

Hesiod. *Theogony* and *Works and Days*, trans. by Dorothea Wender, in *Hesiod and Theognis*, Penguin Books, London, 1973.
    The Theogony, translated by Hugh Evelyn-White, Loeb Classical Library, Harvard University Press.

Hicks, R. D. See Diogenes Laertius.

Higgins, Godfrey. *The Celtic Druids*, London, 1827.
    The Anacalypsis, 2 vols, Macy-Masius, New York, 1927.

Holmes, Captain David C. *The Search for Life on Other Worlds*, Bantam Books, New York, 1966.

Hopkins, L. C. 'Dragon and Alligator: Being Notes on Some Ancient Inscribed Bone Carvings', *Journal of the Royal Asiatic Society*, July 1913.
    'The Dragon Terrestrial and the Dragon Celestial. Part II: The Dragon Celestial', *Journal of the Royal Asiatic Society*, January 1932.

Horst. See van der Horst.

Homer. *The Iliad* and *The Odyssey*, many editions, take your pick.

Homeric Hymns, trans. by Andrew Lang, London, 1899.

Huang, Su-Shu. 'Occurrence of Life in the Universe', 'The Problem of Life in the Universe and the Mode of Star Formation', 'Life-Supporting Regions in the Vicinity of Binary Systems', 'The Sizes of Habitable Planets', 'Problem of Transmission in Interstellar Communication', all in *Interstellar Communication*; see Cameron, A. G. W.

Hume, David. *The History of England*, 5 vols, Porter and Coates, Philadelphia, undated (nineteenth century).

Hurry, Jamieson B. *Imhotep, The Vizier and Physician of King Zoser and Afterwards the Egyptian God of Medicine*, Oxford University Press, 1926.

Hutchinson, R. W. *Prehistoric Crete*, Penguin Books, London, 1968.

411

Helbig, Wolfgang. *Wandgemälde der vom Vesuv Verschütteten Städte* (Wall-Paintings of the Cities Buried by the Eruption of Vesuvius), Leipzig, 1868.

Ideler, Christian Ludwig. *Untersuchungen über den Ursprung und die Bedeutung der Sternnamen*, Berlin, 1809. This is the main critical compendium of information on stellar names, consisting of a translation of the Arab Al Khazwini's *Description of the Constellations* (thirteenth century) with Ideler's extensive additions. Ideler is the primary source in turn for Richard Hinckley Allen.

Imhooff-Blumer, Friedrich, and Gardner, P. *A Numismatic Commentary on Pausanius*, 1887.

Imhotep. See Hurry, J. B.

Jacobsen, Thorkild. *Toward the Image of Tammuz and Other Essays*, Harvard University Press, 1970.

Jahan, Raoul. See Hébert-Stevens, François.

Josephus (Flavius Josephus). *The Works of Flavius Josephus*, trans. by William Whiston, London, 1856.

Julian (Julian the Apostate, Julian the Emperor). Works in 3 vols, trans. by Wilmer Cave Wright, Vols. 13, 29, and 157 in Loeb Library series, Heinemann, London, Harvard University Press.

Jung, Carl Gustav. *Flying Saucers, A Modern Myth of Things Seen in the Skies*, Harcourt Brace, New York, 1959.

Kawerau, Georg, and Rehm, Albert. *Das Delphinion in Milet*, 1899. (Archaeological work on Miletus.)

Kepler, Johannes. *Kepler's Conversation with Galileo's Sidereal Messenger* trans. by Edward Rosen, No. 5 of Sources of Science Series, Johnson Reprint Corp., London and New York, 1965.

    Kepler's Dream (Somnium) trans. by John Lear and P. F. Kirkwood, University of California Press, Berkeley and Los Angeles, 1965.

    Epitome of Copernican Astronomy (Chapters 4 and 5 only) and *Harmonies of the World* (Chapter 5 only) trans. by C. G. Wallis in Vol. 16, *Ptolemy, Copernicus, Kepler*, of the 'Great Books of the Western World' series, pub. by Encyclopaedia Britannica Inc., Chicago, London, Toronto, 1952.

    Six-Cornered Snowflake, trans. by Colin Hardie and Lancelot Law Whyte, Oxford University Press, 1966.

    Kepler's Somnium, trans and comm., Edward Rosen, University of Wisconsin Press, 1967.

Kerenyi, Carl. *The Gods of the Greeks*, Penguin Books, London, 1958.

Khazwini, Al. (Arab astronomical writer of the thirteenth century). See Ideler.

Kilmer, Anne, Crocker, Richard, and Brown, Robert. *Sounds from*

Silence: Recent Discoveries in Ancient Near Eastern Music, Bit Enki Publications and Records, California (BTNK 101) *c.* 1976 (record album and booklet).
(see also Crocker, Dr Richard L.).
Kirkwood, P. F. See Kepler.
Klibansky, R. See Proclus.
Koestler, Arthur. *The Sleepwalkers*, Penguin Books, London, 1964.
Kramer, Samuel Noah. See Pritchard, James.
History Begins at Sumer, Doubleday Anchor Books, New York, 1959.
Mythologies of the Ancient World, ed. and contrib. 'Mythology of Sumer and Akkad', Doubleday Anchor Books, New York, 1961.
Sumerian Mythology, Harper Torchbooks, New York, 1961.
The Sumerians University of Chicago Press, 1963.

Labowsky, L. See Proclus.
Lang, Andrew, trans. See *Homeric Hymns*.
Lang, David Marshall. See Burney, Charles.
Lang, Kenneth R. *Astrophysical Data: Planets and Stars*, Springer-Verlag, New York et al., 1992.
Larousse Encyclopaedia of Mythology, Paul Hamlyn, London, 1965.
Laude, Jean. *African Art of the Dogon*, Brooklyn Museum and Viking Press, New York, 1973.
Lauterborn, Dr D. Participant in seminar held at Elsinore Castle, Denmark, and pub. as *Mass Loss and Evolution in Close Binaries*, Copenhagen University, 1970. See pp. 190–4.
Layard, Austen H. *Discoveries in the Ruins of Nineveh and Babylon* (Second Expedition), London, 1853.
Lear, John. See Kepler.
Legge, James. *The Yi King*, Oxford, 1882.
Lessing, Doris. *Shikasta*, Jonathan Cape, London, 1979.
The Sirian Experiments, Jonathan Cape, London, 1981.
Levi, Peter, S. J., trans. See Pausanius.
Lindenblad, Dr Irving. Account: *Sky and Telescope*, June 1973, p. 354.
'Relative Photographic Positions and Magnitude Difference of the Components of Sirius', *Astronomical Journal*, 75, No. 7 (September 1970), pp. 841–8.
'Multiplicity of the Sirius System', *Astronomical Journal*, 78, No. 2 (March 1973), pp. 205–7.
Lockyer, Sir Norman. *The Dawn of Astronomy*, London, 1894.
Lucian, *De Dea Syria*; see Garstang.
Lunn, Sir Henry. *Aegean Civilizations*, ed., London, 1928. Contains many brief contributions by an array of scholars.

McCrea, W. H. Query in *Quarterly Journal of the Royal Astronomical*

413

Society, 13, 506 (1972), p. 517. Letter to the Editor in *Journal of the British Astronomical Association*, 84, 1 (1973), p. 63.

MacGowan, Roger A. and Ordway, Frederick I., III. *Intelligence in the Universe*, Prentice-Hall Inc. New Jersey, 1966.

Macrobius. *Commentary on the Dream of Scipio*, trans. by William Harris Stahl, Columbia University Press, 1952.

    The Saturnalia, trans. by Percival Vaughan Davies, Columbia University Press, 1969.

    Macrobius, or Philosophy, Science and Letters in the Year 400, by Thomas Whittaker, Cambridge University Press, 1923.

    Macrobius and Numenius by Herman de Ley, Collection Latomus, Société d'Études Latines de Bruxelles, Brussels, 1972.

Marinus. *Life of Proclus*; see Proclus.

Marshack, Alexander. *The Roots of Civilization*. Weidenfeld and Nicolson, London, 1972.

Mathers, S. L. MacGregor. *Kabbala Denudata: The Kabbalah Unveiled, Containing the Following Books of the Zohar: 1. The Book of Concealed Mystery 2. The Greater Holy Assembly 3. The Lesser Holy Assembly*, Kegan Paul, London, 1926.

Matz, F. 'Minoan Civilization: Maturity and Zenith' in *Cambridge Ancient History*, Cambridge University Press, issued as fascicule, 1964.

Mau, August. *Pompeii, Its Life and Art*, trans. by F. W. Kelsey, 1899. Revised 1902.

Mead, G. R. S. See Hermes.

    The Chaldaean Oracles, Vol. VIII, *Echoes from the Gnosis* series, Theosophical Publishing Co., London and Benares, 1908.

    Did Jesus Live 100 BC?, London and Benares, 1903.

Meissner, O. 'Über die antiken Sternfarbenschatzungen' ('Concerning the Ancient Estimates of Star Colours'), *Astronomische Nachrichten*, Number 5542, 1927, pp. 392–6.

Meyrowitz, Eva. *The Sacred State of the Akan*, Faber, London, 1951.

    Akan Traditions of Origin, Faber, London, 1952.

    The Akan of Ghana, Their Ancient Beliefs (originally entitled *The Akan Cosmological Drama*), Faber, London, 1958.

    The Divine Kingship in Ghana and Ancient Egypt (originally entitled *The Akan of Ghana, the Akan Divine Kingship and Its Prototype in Ancient Egypt*), Faber, London, 1960.

Monier-Williams, Sir Monier. *A Sanskrit-English Dictionary*, Oxford University Press, 1951. (First edition 1899.)

Morrow, Dr Glenn. See Proclus.

Moscati, Sabatino. *Ancient Semitic Civilizations*, Elek Books, London, 1957.

Müller, Max. *Lectures on the Science of Language*, Second Series, London, 1864.

Muses, Dr Charles. See Young, Arthur M.

Needham, James. *Science and Civilisation in China*, Vol. I, 1954; Vol. II, 1956; Vol. III, 1959, all Cambridge.

Neugebauer, Otto. *The Exact Sciences in Antiquity*, Dover Publications, New York, 2nd edition, 1969.

and Parker, Richard. *Egyptian Astronomical Texts*, Brown University Press, 1960–7. (Issued at intervals, completed in 1967.)

Oliver, Dr B. M., 'Proximity of Galactic Civilizations', in *Icarus*, 25, 360–7, 1975. 'Arguments are presented for expecting intelligent life in certain multiple star systems . . .'

Olympiodorus (the Neoplatonist). *Scholia to Plato's Gorgias* trans. by Thomas Taylor, pub. as footnote to trans. of Apuleius's essay 'On the Natural Philosophy of Plato', p. 333 of Taylor's vol. of Apuleius (1822); see Apuleius.

Alternatively, trans. by Taylor of part of Olympiodorus's *Scholia* may be found on p. 82 of *Ocellus, Taurus, Firmicus and Select Theorems of Proclus*, trans. by Thomas Taylor, London, 1831.

O'Neill, W. See Proclus.

Ordway, Frederick I., III. See MacGowan, Roger A.

Osthoff, H. 'Zur Farbe des Sirius im Altertum' ('Concerning the Colour of Sirius in Antiquity') *Astronomische Nachrichten*, Number 5495, 1927, p. 444.

Parke, H. W. *Greek Oracles*, Hutchinson, London, 1967.

The Oracles of Zeus, Blackwell, Oxford, 1967.

Parker, Richard. See Neugebauer, Otto.

Pausanius. *Guide to Greece*, trans. by Peter Levi, S. J., 2 vols, Penguin Books, 1971. With extensive notes by Levi commenting on the state today of the sites described by Pausanius in his day. An excellent work of outstanding scholarship and dedication.

See also Imhooff-Blumer.

Penguin Companion to Literature, The, Volume 4: *Classical and Byzantine, Oriental and African*, ed. by D. R. Dudley and D. M. Lang, Penguin, London, 1969.

Philip, J. A. *Pythagoras and Early Pythagoreanism*, University of Toronto Press, 1966.

Pindar. *The Odes of Pindar* trans. by C. M. Bowra (Sir Maurice Bowra), Penguin Books, London, 1969.

Plato. *The Timaeus* trans. by B. Jowett, in *The Dialogues of Plato*, Vol. 2, Random House, New York, 1937.

The Cratylus, Phaedo, Parmenides and Timaeus with Notes on the Cratylus, trans. by Thomas Taylor with notes, London, 1793. (See particularly p. 388 of Taylor's introduction to *Timaeus*.) The Bodleian Library at Oxford has two copies of this book, one of which belonged to Percy Bysshe Shelley; in the Shelley Collection.

Plato the Man and His Work by A. E. Taylor, Meridian Books, New York, 1963.

Pliny the Elder. *Natural History*, trans. by various hands, 11 vols. of Loeb Library series, Heinemann, London, Harvard University Press.

Plutarch (of Chaeronea). 'Isis and Osiris', 'The E at Delphi', 'The Oracles at Delphi No Longer Given in Verse', and 'The Obsolescence of Oracles' all trans. by Frank Cole Babbitt in vol. 5 of Plutarch's *Moralia*, Vol. No. 306 in Loeb Library series, Heinemann, London, Harvard University Press, 1962.

'On the Face Appearing within the Orb of the Moon', 'Against Colotes, the Disciple and Favorite of Epicurus', 'Platonic Questions', and pseudo-Plutarch 'Of the Names of Rivers and Mountains, and of Such Things as Are to Be Found Therein', trans. by various and all pub. in Vol. V of *Plutarch's Morals* ed. by William W. Goodwin, Little, Brown, and Co., Boston, 1874.

Porphyry (the Neoplatonist). *Select Works of Porphyry*, trans. by Thomas Taylor, London, 1823.

Price, Derek de Solla, *Gears from the Greeks: The Antikythera Mechanism, A Calendar Computer from ca. 80 BC*, Science History Publications, Neale Watson Academic Publications Inc., New York, 1975. (Originally published in *Transactions of the American Philosophical Society*, Philadelphia, New Series, Vol. 64, Part 7, 1974.)

Prigogine, Ilya, and Nicolis, Gregoire. *Exploring Complexity*, W. H. Freeman, New York, 1989.

Pritchard, James B., ed. *Ancient Near Eastern Texts Relating to the Old Testament*, 2nd edition, Princeton University Press, 1955. The fundamental source of scholarly translations of Sumerian, Akkadian, Egyptian, Hittite, and other material, including all known portions (to 1954) of the *Epic of Gilgamesh*, the Babylonian creation epic, etc.

There is a supplementary volume of photographs *The Ancient Near East in Pictures*, 1969.

The Ancient Near East Supplementary Texts. Princeton University Press, 1969. A supplementary volume intended to bring the coverage up to date (to 1968), as every year new texts are either discovered or translated, with an enormous backlog due to the shortage of competent scholars to handle the material in this field. This later volume contains 274 pp., which represents less than 15 years' worth of accumulated additional material. A combined volume is available of the 1955 and 1969 volumes bound together. Supplementary volumes were meant to be issued at approximate fifteen-year intervals but did not appear. The only way to keep abreast of new material between volumes is through personal contact with some of the handful of relevant scholars, or through the scholarly journals in the field, which generally carry the new material in separate articles as it is prepared, though this procedure follows no predictable pattern. Much new material never appears in English, but only in German.

Proclus. *Commentary on the First Alcibiades of Plato*, trans. by W. O'Neill, The Hague, 1965.

Commentary on the First Book of Euclid's Elements, trans. by Professor Glenn Morrow, Princeton University Press, 1967.

Philosophical and Mathematical Commentaries of Proclus on the First Book of Euclid's Elements, trans. by Thomas Taylor, 2 vols, London, 1792. This work is bound with Marinus's *Life of Proclus*, trans. by Taylor, and other material. (Marinus was a pupil of Proclus and wrote from first hand.)

Commentary on the Parmenides of Plato, last book and *pars inedita* only, trans. by G. E. M. Anscombe and L. Labowsky, pub. in *Plato Latinus*, Vol. III, of *Corpus Platonicum Medii Aevi* series ed. by R. Klibansky, Warburg Institute, London, 1953. Obtainable as: Kraus Reprint, Nendeln, Liechtenstein, 1973.

Elements of Theology, ed. and trans. by E. R. Dodds, Oxford University Press, 1963.

Commentaries on the Parmenides of Plato and the First Alcibiades of Plato; substance of them given in notes by Thomas Taylor to his 5 vols *The Works of Plato*, London, 1804. The same is true of the *Commentaries on the Phaedo, Gorgias, and Philebus of Plato* by the Neoplatonist Olympiodorus; see Olympiodorus.

The Six Books of Proclus ... on the Theology of Plato, trans. by Thomas Taylor, London, 1816. 2 vols.

Commentaries of Proclus on the Timaeus of Plato, trans. by Thomas Taylor, 2 vols, London, 1820.

Lost Writings of Proclus, trans. by Thomas Taylor, London, 1825.

Two Treatises of Proclus ... of Ten Doubts concerning Providence ... and ... the Nature of Evil, trans. by Thomas Taylor, London, 1833.

The Philosophy of Proclus by L. J. Rosan, Cosmos Books, New York, 1949. This book also includes an English translation of Marinus's *Life of Proclus.*

Assorted passages from other works of Proclus are to be found scattered throughout the various publications of Thomas Taylor. There have been several translations done of *Elements of Theology*. There is an Elizabethan translation of Proclus's *Sphaera.*

(Pseudo-Plato). *The Epinomis*, trans. George Burges, in Vol. VI of *The Works of Plato*, George Bell and Sons/Bohn's Classical Library, London, 1891.

Ptolemy (Claudius Ptolemaeus). *The Almagest*, trans. by R. Catesby Taliaferro, pub. in *Ptolemy, Copernicus, Kepler*, Vol. 16 of *Great Books of the Western World* series, pub. by Encyclopaedia Britannica, Chicago, London, Toronto, 1952.

The Geography, trans. and ed. Edward Luther Stevenson, Dover, New York, 1991.

Tetrabiblos, trans. by J. M. Ashmand, London, undated (1920s).

Another translation is available in the Loeb Library series, Heinemann, London, Harvard University Press.

Quincey, J. H. 'The Beacon-Siter in the Agamemnon', *The Journal of Hellenic Studies*, London, Vol. LXXXIII, 1963.

Rambach, Pierre. See Hébert-Stevens, François.

Rehm, Albert. See Kawerau, Georg.

Rodenwaldt, Gerhart. *Griechische Porträts aus dem Ausgang der Antike*, Number 76 of 'Programm zum Winckelmannsfeste der Archaeologischen Gesellschaft zu Berlin', Berlin, 1919. Plate VI of this book shows both front and side views of a bust which has since been identified (Pauly-Wissowa under 'Proclus') as one of Proclus. This is reproduced in this book, its first publication as far as I know correctly identified, since Rodenwaldt does not identify it.

Rosan, L. J. See Proclus.

Roscher, Wilhelm Heinrich. *Die Zahl 50 in Mythus, Kultus, Epos und Taktik der Hellener und Anderer Volker Besonders der Semiten*, Vol. 33, No. 5 of the *Abhandlungen der Philologisch-Historischen Klasse der Koengl. Saechsischen Gesellschaft der Wissenschaften*, Leipzig, 1917.

Neue Omphalos Studien, Leipzig, 1915.

Omphalos: eine Philologisch-Archäologische-volkskundliche Abhandlung über die Vorstellungen der Griechen und Anderer Völker vom 'Nabel der Erde', Leipzig, 1913. (In: *Sächsische Akademie der Wissenschaften. Philologisch-historische Klasse.* Vol. 29, No. 9.)

Der Omphalosgedanke bei Verschiedenen Völkern, besonders den Semitischen, Leipzig, 1918. (In: *Sächsische Akademie der Wissenschaften. Philologisch-historische Klasse.* Vol. 70, No. 2

Rosen, Edward. See Kepler.

Roux, Georges. *Ancient Iraq*, Penguin Books, London, 1966.

Sagan, Carl, *The Cosmic Connection*, Doubleday, New York, 1973.
and Shklovskii, I. S. *Intelligent Life in the Universe*, Delta Books, New York, 1966.

Samson, Edward. *The Immortal Tooth*, London, 1939.

Santillana, Giorgio de. *The Origins of Scientific Thought*, London, 1961.
and von Dechend, Hertha. *Hamlet's Mill*, Macmillan, London, 1969.

Sarton, George. *A History of Science: Ancient Science through the Golden Age of Greece*, Harvard University Press, 1959.

A History of Science, Volume 2: *Hellenistic Science and Culture in the Last Three Centuries B.C.*, Norton, New York, 1970.

Schatzman, E. 'Les naines blanches', *L'Astronomie*, 1956, pp. 364–9.

Schwaller de Lubicz, R. A. *Sacred Science: the King of Pharaonic Theocracy*, trans. by Andre and Goldian Van den Broeck, Inner Traditions International, Rochester, Vermont, USA, 1982.

Scully, Vincent. *The Earth, The Temple, and the Gods*, Yale University Press, 1962.

See, T. J. J. 'Historical Researches Indicating a Change in the Color of Sirius, between the Epochs of Ptolemy, 138, and of Al Sufi, 980 AD', *Astronomische Nachrichten*, Vol. 229 (1926), pp. 245–72. Despite an appearance of erudition, this article is unreliable and contains fundamental errors of fact and translation. See maintains, for instance, that the Greek word *poikilos* means 'red', which it has never meant. *Poikilos* means 'variegated', etc., referring to the scintillation of the star. See also Dittrich, Meissner, Osthoff, and Stentzel.

Shinnie, Margaret. *Ancient African Kingdoms*, Edward Arnold, London, 1965.

Shklovskii, I. S. See Sagan, Carl.

'Is Communication Possible with Intelligent Beings on Other Planets?' in *Interstellar Communication*; see Cameron, A. G. W.

Siorvanes, Lucas. *Proclus: Neo-Platonic Philosophy and Science*, Edinburgh University Press, 1996.

Simplicius. (Neoplatonist) *Commentary on Aristotle's Treatise 'On the Soul'*: substance given in paraphrase in notes by Thomas Taylor to his trans. of 'On the Soul' in *The Treatises of Aristotle: On the Soul* etc., London, 1808. This vol. is not in either the British Museum or the Bodleian Library, Oxford. However, a copy was owned by a friend of mine and I have used the book. Simplicius's *Commentaries on the Physics of Aristotle, on the Categories of Aristotle, on the Heavens of Aristotle (De Caelo)* as well as Olympiodorus's *Scholia On Meteors of Aristotle* are all given in much the same way in other like volumes of Taylor's Aristotle pub. London between 1806 and 1812, in only fifty copies! However, I have been unable to find any of these volumes anywhere.

Commentary on the Enchiridion of Epictetus, trans. by George Stanhope, pub. as *Epictetus His Morals with Simplicius His Comment*, trans. George Stanhope, London, 1694.

Smart, W. M. *Some Famous Stars*, Longmans Green, London, New York, 1950. Chapter Three concerns 'The Companion of Sirius'.

Smith, R. C. 'The Book of Job, and Stellar Dynamics', *The Observatory*, Vol. 97, No. 1020, October 1977.

Sozomen (Salaminius Hermias Sozomen). *Ecclesiastical History*, Bohns Ecclesiastical and Theological Library, London, 18— (prior to 1878).

Speiser, E. A. See *Epic of Gilgamesh*.

Stahl, William Harris. See Macrobius.

'The Greek Heliocentric Theory and Its Abandonment', *Transactions of the American Philological Association*, lxxvi (1945), pp. 323–5.

Stanhope, George. See Simplicius.

Stanley, Thomas. *The Chaldaick Oracles*; see *Chaldaean Oracles*.

The History of the Chaldaick Philosophy, London, 1662.

The History of Philosophy, 3 vols, London, 1655–6 and 1660.

Stapf, O. 'Iburu and Fundi, Two Cereals of Upper Guinea', in *Bulletin of Miscellaneous Information*, Royal Botanic Gardens, Kew, London, No. 8, 1915.

Stecchini, Livio Catullo. Author of Appendix to *Secrets of the Great Pyramid* by Peter Tompkins, Harper & Row, New York, 1971.

Stentzel, A. 'Ägyptische Zeugnisse für die Farbe des Sirius im Altertum" ('Egyptian Traditions regarding the Colour of Sirius in Ancient Times') *Astronomische Nachrichten*, No. 5542 (1927), pp. 387–92.

Stephenson, D. G. 'Extraterrestrial Cultures within the Solar System', *Quarterly Journal of the Royal Astronomical Society*, Vol. 20, No. 4, December 1979.

Stirling, William. *The Canon*. Garnstone Press, London, 1974.

Stubbings, Frank H. 'The Rise of Mycenaean Civilization', 'The Expansion of Mycenaean Civilization', 'The Recession of Mycenaean Civilization' in the *Cambridge Ancient History* Cambridge University Press, issued as separate fascicules 1964 and 1965.

Strong, Professor Herbert A. See Garstang, John.

Sullivan, Walter. *We Are Not Alone*, Hodder and Stoughton, London, 1965.

Swedenborg, Emanuel, *Arcana Coelestia: or Heavenly Mysteries*, London, 1788. Vol. III, pp. 81–3, 86, contains possibly the earliest survey of the number 'fifty' as symbolic usage in the Old Testament.

Täckholm, Vivi. See Drar.

Tarn, W. W. *Hellenistic Civilization*, Meridian Books, New York, 1961.
    'The Political Standing of Delos', *Journal of Hellenic Studies*, London, Vol. XLIV, 1924.

Taylor, A. E. See Plato.

Taylor, Thomas. See Proclus, see Porphyry, see Apuleius.

Temple, Robert K. G. 'An Anatomical Verification of the Reading of a Term in Extispicy', *Journal of Cuneiform Studies*, Vol. 34, 1982.
    Conversations with Eternity: Ancient Man's Attempts to Know the Future, Rider, London, 1984.
    The Genius of China (also published as *China: Land of Discovery and Invention*), London and New York, 1986.
    Götter, Orakel und Visionen: Die Zukunftsschau Im Altertum und Heute [Gods, Oracles and Visions: Perception of the Future in Antiquity and Today], Umschau Verlag, Frankfurt, 1982. (This book was only published in German. The figure at the top left of p. 55 is printed upside down and the figure on p. 229 is misprinted very seriously, thereby destroying the demonstration of the entire basis of the central point of the culminating chapter and the book's main purpose.)
    He Who Saw Everything: A Verse Translation of the Epic of Gilgamesh, Rider, London, 1991.

'House of Lords Debate UFOs', *Second Look*, Vol. 1, No. 6, April 1979.

ed., *The Illustrated Golden Bough* by Sir James George Frazer, Batsford, London, and Simon and Schuster, New York, 1996. (A new abridgement; the Introduction by R. T. was substantially rewritten by an editor without R. T.'s knowledge or consent and largely ruined.)

Introduction to The Dream of Scipio (Somnium Scipionis), *Studies in Hermetic Tradition*, Vol. 5, The Aquarian Press, Wellingborough, UK, 1983.

'In Defense of the Sirius Mystery', *Fate*, issue for October, 1980.

letter, *Nature*, Vol. 283, 17 January 1980.

'No Easy Solution to the Sirius Mystery', *Ad Astra*, London, Issue 8, 1979.

'On the Sirius Mystery: An Open Letter to Carl Sagan', *Zetetic Scholar*, No. 8, July 1981.

Open to Suggestion, Aquarian Press, Wellingborough, UK, 1989.

'Response to Appeal from W. H. McCrea Concerning Sirius', *The Observatory*, April 1975, pp. 52–4, Royal Greenwich Observatory, England.

Strange Things, Sphere Books, London, 1983.

Theophrastus (of Eresos in Lesbos). *Enquiry into Plants*, trans. by A. F. Hort, 2 volumes, Loeb Library Series, Heinemann, London and Harvard University Press, 1916.

Thesiger, Wilfred. *The Marsh Arabs*, Penguin Books, London, 1967.

Thompson, D'Arcy Wentworth. *A Glossary of Greek Birds*, Oxford, 1896.

Tighe, Chris, 'Scientists Tune into Teeth of Dolphins', *Daily Telegraph*, London, 28 November 1989.

Times, The (London): 'Science Report; Zoology: The Age of a Dugong', 1 April 1976.

Tompkins, Peter. *Secrets of the Great Pyramid*, Harper & Row, New York, 1971. With Appendix by Livio Catullo Stecchini.

van der Horst, Pieter Willem. *Chaeremon*, E. J. Brill, Leiden, 1987.

von Däniken, Erich. *Chariots of the Gods?* Bantam Books, New York, 1970.

von Dechend, Hertha. See Santillana, Giorgio de.

Wallis, C. G.: See Copernicus; see Kepler.

Wallis Budge, Sir E. A., trans. *The Book of the Dead*, London, 1928.

A Hieroglyphic Vocabulary to the Theban Recension of the Book of the Dead, London, 1911.

Egyptian Language, London, 1951.

Egyptian Magic, Routledge & Kegan Paul, London, 1972.

The Gods of the Egyptians, 2 vols, London, 1904.

An Egyptian Hieroglyphic Dictionary, London, 1920.

Osiris and the Egyptian Resurrection, 2 vols, London, 1911.

Wellard, James. *Lost Worlds of Africa*, Hutchinson, London, 1967.

West, John Anthony. 'Metaphysics by Design: Harmony and Proportion in Ancient Egypt', *Second Look*, Vol. I, No. 8, June 1979.

   Serpent in the Sky: The High Wisdom of Ancient Egypt, Wildwood House, London, 1979.

de Wet, J. M. J. 'The Three Phases of Cereal Domestication', in Chapman, G. P. ed., *Grass Evolution and Domestication*, Cambridge University Press, UK, 1992.

Whittaker, Thomas. See Macrobius.

   The Neo-platonists, Cambridge University Press, 1918.

Whyte, Lancelot Law. See Kepler.

Willoughby-Meade, G. *Chinese Ghouls and Goblins*, London, 1928.

Wilson, Robert Anton, *Cosmic Trigger*, Pocket Books, New York, 1977. (This is a very fascinating book, which makes disturbing reading. The original edition, which I have not seen, was published by And/Or Press of Berkeley, California, 1977.

Xenocrates. *Life of Xenocrates* by Diogenes Laertius. See Diogenes Laertius.

Young, Arthur Middleton. *The Bell Notes: A Journey from Physics to Metaphysics*, Robert Briggs Associates, Mill Valley, California, 1979.

   The Geometry of Meaning, Delacorte Press and Robert Briggs Associates, San Francisco, 1976.

   The Reflexive Universe: Evolution of Consciousness, Delacorte Press and Robert Briggs Associates, San Francisco, 1976.

   and Muses, Dr Charles, eds. *Consciousness and Reality*, Outerbridge & Lazard, Inc., distributed by E. P. Dutton, New York, 1972.

Notes to the Plates

Plate 1: The scientific achievement represented by this extraordinary photograph is considerable. Until 1970, no photographic record of the small white dwarf star Sirius B existed, despite attempts over several decades to obtain one. With much ingenuity, Dr Irving W. Lindenblad of the US Naval Observatory in Washington, D.C., finally devised a technique which made this photograph possible. Lindenblad (1970; see Bibliography) says: '. . . simultaneous observation of Sirius A and B by conventional photography has always presented a problem due to the small separation and large magnitude difference between the components, and because of various emulsion effects.' Since Sirius A is enormously brighter than Sirius B, it is easily understood that it washes out the smaller star which orbits it. How, then, to photograph the smaller star at all?

Dr Paul Murdin, then of the Royal Greenwich Observatory, provided some explanatory notes on Lindenblad's photograph and gave his permission for me to quote them here:

> The six spikes on Sirius A are caused by the hexagon used on the front of the telescope. The point of making the photo in this way is that Sirius A is about 100 times as bright as Sirius B so that its light tends to spread out over Sirius B rendering it invisible. By using a hexagonal lens (actually a twenty-six inch circular lens with a hexagonal mask) in his telescope, Lindenblad was able to compress the star image in certain directions; he chose the orientation of the hexagon so that Sirius B's image fell in one of the compressed zones and was thus able to be seen . . . The wire grating referred to by Lindenblad makes the small images of Sirius A on either side of the bright one (there are small images of B too, but they are too small to be visible). The point of this is that the bright image of Sirius A (the 'zero order' image) is so big that Lindenblad couldn't measure the position of Sirius B with respect to A. He made first and second order images, measured B with respect to them and was able to *calculate* where B was with respect to the zero order image of A.

These calculations enabled Lindenblad to angle his hexagonal aperture so that Sirius B would 'hit' a depressed area of Sirius's light – a dip where the

423

light was teased inwards, and Sirius B could peek through. But it could only peek through if Lindenblad had first found it! The reader can by this point appreciate how clever Lindenblad had to be in order to achieve any results at all. However, these were not all of his problems. There was a serious emulsion contraction effect for the photograph, with such close images. Lindenblad said in 1970: 'The important correction to the separation of the components of Sirius due to emulsion contraction, or the Ross (1924) effect, depended, in van Albada's method, upon measurements of second-order [images] . . . However, this procedure could not be employed in the present work because the dispersion affecting the second-order images generally rendered them unmeasurable. Consequently, another technique for determining the emulsion contraction was devised.'

This is a perfect example of technological feats taking place constantly behind the scenes in order to produce results which the public then take for granted, with no appreciation of the difficulties involved. The story behind this photograph is part of the saga of the attempt to unravel the mysteries of Sirius. So loth has Sirius been to give up her secrets that she has denied us even this photograph until 1970. All the more reason to wonder at the Dogon, who, oblivious of our scientific labours, have always drawn pictures of Sirius in the sand, with its companion – nothing to it!

Plate 14: Top left: The beautiful omphalos stone found at Delphi in Greece, covered in the mesh thought to symbolize the latitudinal and longitudinal grid on the Earth. (For an exhaustive treatment of that theory, see *Secrets of the Great Pyramid* by Tompkins and Stecchini, particularly Appendix by Stecchini.)

Plate 15: The superb omphalos stone discovered at Delos, which incorporates the Delian palm design. (Reproduced in W. H. Roscher, *Neue Omphalosstudien*, Leipzig, 1915.)

Plate 16: Relief discovered at Miletus in Asia Minor. The figure of Apollo is resting on an omphalos stone (and an actual omphalos stone has also been discovered at Miletus) covered in mesh, while a second, smaller omphalos stone with a serpent is seen in foreground. The palm is prominent here again. Miletus is on the same parallel as Delos, and the palm is the 'tree-code' for that latitude in the oracle octaves schema. Delos is the western centre and Miletus is the eastern centre at 37°30'. The nearby site of Branchidae (also known as Didyma) to the south seems to have adopted the oracular functions presumably associated with Miletus itself originally. This relief appears as Figure 101 (the last in the volume), page 411, of *Das Delphinion in Milet* by Georg Kawerau and Albert Rehm, Berlin, 1914. Roscher also reproduced it. Kawerau and Rehm say with relation to it (page 410): 'We have already noted here in later periods the distinctive likeness of Pythian Apollo which is universally known, and there is nothing extraordinary in finding this cult image of the Delphinion, the omphalos-and-serpent . . .'

Plate 17: Two Babylonian altars to the god Anu which bear what appear to be omphali.

Plate 18: A bas relief in white marble of the Delos omphalos stone, excavated on the Island of Delos in a hall of a house adjacent to the so-called House of Dionysius. The oracular serpent is entwined around the omphalos stone, flanked by a palm tree on either side.

Plate 19: Another Egyptian omphalos marker reproduced from Tompkins and Stecchini (see Bibliography).

Plate 21: Top left: Votive relief of fifth century BC from Sparta; Apollo and Artemis, between them an omphalos flanked by two doves with their heads turned away in the customary manner for these scenes. (From Plate VII, No. 4, of W. H. Roscher, *Omphalos,* Leipzig, 1913.)

Top right: Votive relief from Aigina, showing omphalos with two doves, their heads turned away. (From Plate VIII, No. 3, of W. H. Roscher, *Omphalos,* Leipzig, 1913.)

Top coin: Coin from Delphi showing Apollo sitting on the omphalos stone and leaning on his lyre. He holds a laurel branch, which is the 'tree-code' for Delphi. Note the clear differentiation of trees in this compared with the earlier Delos and Miletus examples of Plates 15 and 16; at Delphi the laurel is appropriately shown, whereas Delos and Miletus display the palm. This coin is from Imhoof-Blumer's *A Numismatic Commentary on Pausanius.*

Below Apollo: Two further examples of omphali on ancient coins, with serpents and geodetic mesh visible; both in British Museum. One is from Delphi and the other from Pergamum.

Two bottom coins: Two coins from Delphi showing the entrance to the Temple of Apollo in ancient times. The letter 'E' hangs suspended in the entrance way; it is the second vowel, and Delphi is the second oracle centre in descending order (the ancient octave was taken as descending rather than as ascending – the ignorance of which fact has led many modern experts astray when trying to unravel the complexities of Pythagorean harmonic theory). These two coins may also be found reproduced in Imhoof-Blumer (above). The second of these coins is to be found in the Copenhagen Museum, while the first was in Dr Imhoof-Blumer's private collection in the last century, and its fate today is unknown to this author.

Plate 22: Painting from ancient vase in the Etruscan Museum, Rome. Jason apparently being vomited forth by the serpent/dragon, rests on the serpent's teeth. 'Serpent's tooth' is euphemism for Sirius (see Chapter Eight). Looking on is a female figure in serpent-headed robes, holding an oracular dove; she may be Medea or a goddess. In the background the golden fleece is seen suspended in the grove guarded by the serpent. Note that the breastplate of the female figure, on which is a fanged Gorgon's face, is composed of scales identical to those of the serpent/dragon. On her helmet is the Greek sphinx (a mythological being associated with Greek Thebes). Though the elements can here be identified in this way, the story implied by them cannot so easily be unravelled. The author has not been able to learn the mythological incidents referred to in this curious vase. The female figure most nearly resembles the goddess Athena, but what is the incident, why does she hold a dove, why is there a sphinx on her helmet, and why do serpents issue from the folds of her garment? The scene is very mysterious.

Plate 23: This is one of the most interesting cylinder seals to survive from the Babylonian culture. It is reproduced in Henri Frankfort, *Cylinder Seals*, Plate XX; and in *Sumerian Mythology*, Plate XII, by Samuel Noah Kramer, where Kramer says of it: '. . . two gods are guiding a plow, which is perhaps drawn by a lion and a wormlike dragon.' Frankfort says of it: 'Two gods plowing; one holding a plow, the other driving span (consisting of snakelike dragon and lion) with left hand, which either holds or is shaped like a scorpion; bird, eight-pointed star, and crescent in field.' It is Plate 62 in Frankfort's later book *Stratified Cylinder Seals*. It is Akkadian style, Late Agade period in date.

This cylinder seal is such an important item of evidence that it requires extended comment. The lion is the earth-lion well known as the earth goddess's symbol from the ancient Near East. (See, for instance, *The Syrian Goddess* by Strong and Garstang.) But note that directly beneath the symbol of a star, ploughing is taking place, and leading right down to the plough blade is the strange form of a serpentlike dragon. It looks almost as if the mouth of the serpent/dragon is being ploughed into the ground. And this, I suspect, is exactly what is intended. For what seems to be represented is the act of ploughing and sowing the serpent's teeth, which we know to be a hieroglyphic pun in Egyptian for 'the goddess Sirius'; we also know that the growing up from the ground of the 'serpent's teeth' is another pun for the rising over the horizon of the star for which 'serpent's tooth' is the other meaning, i.e. Sirius. Its once-yearly rising was the basis of the Egyptian calendar.

If we assume this to be the case, the figure whose hand has become a scorpion can be explained. Obviously, the constellation Scorpio is intended, which is approximately a third of the sky 'round' from Sirius. From the ancient Greek astronomical writer Aratus, we know that when Scorpio rises, it chases Sirius and Orion away below the horizon. He describes it as follows (*Phaenomena* 634–80):

> The winding River (the constellation Eridanus near Orion) will straightaway sink in fair flowing ocean at the coming of Scorpio, whose rising puts to flight even the mighty Orion . . . Wherefore, too, men say that at the rising of the Scorpion in the East Orion flees at the Western verge . . . what time all the rays of the mighty Dog (Sirius is in this constellation) are sinking and all of Orion setting, yea, all the Hare (the constellations Lepus), which the Dog pursues in an unending race.

The disappearance below the western horizon, then, of the 'serpent's tooth' (Sirius) which is going into the ground (to 'grow up' from it again in seventy days' time at its heliacal rising) seems to be indicated here, for the figure representing the sky has had his left hand (the east) become Scorpio, while his right hand (the west) is swallowing the 'serpent's tooth'. Over this proceeding of the setting of Sirius presides, as would be expected, the earth-lion itself which pulls the plough that makes the furrows (three of which are visible) into which will be swallowed that fast-disappearing star just above the plough-blade. The crescent may be taken as an indication of the waning of the light of the star, almost to vanishing point – not surprising, as the moon is a front man' for Sirius in many myths. (Kramer thought, because of the ploughing, that this scene involved 'gods of vegetation'.)

Plate 24: The ram is in the crucible, its fleece presumably being transmuted into gold in what we would call an alchemical sense. Was there such a thing as alchemy at this time in history? Perhaps the attempt to transmute base materials into gold is an ageless concept, and in antiquity it could have been less concerned with chemistry and more with symbolism, as I suspect is the intention here.

Plate 25: In the centre, the sun god Shamash, who has flames emanating from his arms and shoulders, is seen stepping over the horizon from between the two mountains-of-the-rising-sun called Mashu. The name Mashu has long been recognized as a non-Babylonian foreign word, and I have proposed that it is Egyptian, *ma Shu*, meaning 'Behold the Sun God!' (see my book *He Who Saw Everything: A Verse Translation of the Epic of Gilgamesh*). To either side of the Mashu peaks are the cosmic portals topped by rampant lions which have been opened by divine attendants; the lions top prominent door hinges, which were of esoteric cosmological importance. The sun god faces, to his right, the star Sirius, which has just risen. It is depicted on the end of an arrow placed in a bow, as Arrow Star or Bow Star, which were the Babylonian, Assyrian and Persian names for Sirius.

Plate 27: Zeus had become enamoured of Io, a Greek mythological figure derived from the Egyptian goddesses Isis and Hathor (who had become amalgamated in Greek eyes), but his wife Hera was jealous. Zeus transformed Io into a heifer (the Egyptian Hathor was symblised by a cow). But Hera set Argus to watch over her since he had so many eyes she could never escape his scrutiny. Hence Zeus wished Argus to be disposed of. Io was said to be the ancestress of Aegyptus (representing the Egyptians), who had fifty sons, and Danaus (of *Argos* in Greece), who had fifty daughters; the fifty boys married the fifty girls, thus reconstituting the number of one hundred, and matching the number of Argus's eyes. After Argus's death, his eyes were placed by Hera on the tail of the peacock. Of the 50 Egyptian boys, 49 were murdered on their wedding night, and the one remaining became the ancestor of the royal family of Argos.

Plate 31: The similarity between this and the Chinese bas relief depicted in Figure 50 is striking and suggests a common origin for the design motif. Reproduced from 'Monuments Relatif au Culte d'Isis à Cyzique' in the *Révue Archéologique*, Paris, Vol. 5, May 1879, Plate IX. These objects at that time were in the personal collection of M. A. Mordtmann, Jr., of Paris. Isis wears on her head the horns of a cow (symbolising the moon phases adopted from the goddess Hathor) and a disc surmounted by a lotus. Serapis wears on his head the *kalathos*, the sacred basket or bucket traditionally carried by the amphibians Oannes and Dagon.

Plates 40 and 41: The identification is found in the classical *Encyclopaedia* of Pauly-Wissowa under 'Proclus'. The bust is in the Athens Museum, and may be found reproduced (though unidentified) in Gerhart Rodenwaldt *Griechische Porträts*. Rodenwaldt also reproduces photographs of front and side view of a bust later identified as being that of the earlier Neo-platonist philosopher Iamblichus.

Index

429